STUDENT LIFE IN A CLASS SOCIETY

STUDENT LIFE IN A CLASS SOCIETY

BY

JOAN ABBOTT, M.A., Ph.D.

Director, Falk College Ecology Study,
Chatham College, Pittsburgh

PERGAMON PRESS

Oxford · New York · Toronto
Sydney · Braunschweig

Pergamon Press Ltd., Headington Hill Hall, Oxford
Pergamon Press Inc., Maxwell House, Fairview Park, Elmsford, New York 10523
Pergamon of Canada Ltd., 207 Queen's Quay West, Toronto 1
Pergamon Press (Aust.) Pty. Ltd., 19a Boundary Street, Rushcutters Bay,
N.S.W. 2011, Australia
Vieweg & Sohn GmbH, Burgplatz 1, Braunschweig

First edition 1971

Library of Congress Catalog Card No. 73-113397

Printed in Hungary

08 015654 1

To my mother, father and sister and they know why.

CONTENTS

PART IV

APPENDICES

LIST OF TABLES AND ILLUSTRATIONS

CHAPTER 1

CHAPTER 3

CHAPTER 4

CHAPTER 7

CHAPTER 9

CHAPTER 15

CHAPTER 16

PREFACE

THIS book began as an undergraduate study for a M.A. dissertation of the Honours Degree in Social Anthropology. This study was based on original research which took the form of a survey conducted among students of the University of Edinburgh between September 1962 and May 1963. By regulation, the research was carried out without assistance or supervision, and may therefore be regarded as a somewhat tentative preliminary exploration of the field which served to reveal areas worthy of further investigation. The aim of the original survey was "to examine the social class composition and influence in the student body of the University of Edinburgh in the light of post-war changes in British education". The approach of the investigation was primarily factual, and the findings tended to suggest rather than prove certain hypotheses. The one hypothesis proved was that social classes are meaningful cultural groups *within* the University and that their particular composition in the student body *does* have influence in student groups both formal and informal. The particular forms which this influence takes could only be suggested.

However, this preliminary research was never intended to be more than a primarily fact-finding survey, and in the dissertation itself the author stated that her aim "was to gain as much information as possible on as many aspects of the subject as possible. Rather than follow up one hypothesis I was intent on building up a reasonably comprehensive picture of the influence of social class in the student body from the viewpoint of both the objective observer and the students involved".[1]

Indeed, it is true that the unstructured nature of this preliminary survey allowed meaningful problems to present themselves which might otherwise have been obscured or overlooked. In a sense the material observed appeared to structure itself.

Findings which emerged from the first survey were of such interest that it seemed valuable to test them as hypotheses of a more general character in differing situations. It was therefore necessary to conduct

[1] Abbott, J., Unpublished M.A. dissertation, Social class composition of and influence on the student body of Edinburgh University, May 1963.

comparative surveys in two other universities of widely differing setting and organisation to see if any real conclusions could be drawn about factors in student social relations meaningful in similarly structured situations in different institutional contexts. Differences in residential organisation were particularly relevant since it appeared that spatial relations are a particularly important factor in the formation of student groups. Thus a residential and non-residential university were chosen in widely differing urban settings.

The comparative study which resulted is that presented in this book in which certain primary hypotheses have been proved and certain secondary hypotheses suggested. In a sense the book represents three stages in a development of ideas and of a progressive testing of hypotheses. For since the three surveys were carried out by the researcher over a span of 3 years, the problems which became formulated were in turn tested in the next stage of the inquiry. This presented a unique opportunity of narrowing down the perspective of the research—although the original framework and major areas of investigation remain the same.

However, although the research design encouraged the testing of certain hypotheses concerning social class as a factor in intergroup relations, it nevertheless inhibited the investigation of the problem at the interpersonal and small group level. Since much that was being investigated had to remain basically the same in each survey in order that findings could be directly comparable statistically, the level of analysis could not be taken beyond a certain point. Intra-university research rather than inter-university research would represent the next stage in such an analysis and would necessitate completely fresh research design and technique. This would take the form of analysis of similarly structured situations in the *same* context and *over time*—rather than synchronic studies in different contexts. This would represent the dynamic aspects of social relations taking place within the structural and contextual formations analysed here in terms largely of statistical models. It is hoped that the level of analysis reached where the book leaves off will be continued in further studies of student relations at small group level which the present study cannot, and did not, attempt to investigate.

However, what has been attempted has been the narrowing down of focus through a series of interlocking and overlying structures within the institutional context from the institutional context itself, through various levels of group activity both formal and informal to the interpersonal level of small group student relations—and in which social class is a meaningful factor. If there are various discrepancies, incongruities, and inconsistencies throughout the book, they reveal that "something real" is being studied; that the empirical evidence invites explanation rather than that a theoretical model is being furnished with empirical illustration.

The collection of the original empirical evidence was guided by questions which seemed pertinent to the author, at that time herself an undergraduate. Patterns of student participation and leadership and of formation of groups on social class lines were of interest as much to one participating as observing. The questions first asked on the Edinburgh questionnaire were therefore largely suggested by the material itself than by any preliminary reading of work already done in this field. Also at that time little had been written about British university students, although the volume of this material has been growing steadily ever since.

Thus in a sense the book represents a rather particular viewpoint of one who is herself a product of the system which she investigates and whose approach is structured accordingly. The questions asked are of immediate interest to those now passing through the universities, for they are questions which they are themselves asking. The usual time-lag which takes place between research and changes which have been effected is eliminated, for the changes are taking place now. It is for this very reason that the author undertook her comparative survey immediately after graduating—so that her "student" perspective should not be lost.

For the reasons stated the amount of literature directly related and useful to the survey was limited—although much that was "peripheral" was of great help and a stimulus to new approaches. However, at each successive revision of the manuscript since then new studies and research have been published. The author has tried to keep up to date with this material and to refer to it in the text, even though it was unavailable for consideration at the time the surveys were undertaken between 1962–5. This should serve to confirm the contemporaneity of the findings and discussion, and to show that certain questions answered in this volume still have not been asked elsewhere by the end of 1969. The present volume refers to works written up to the end of 1969 and represents a continuous process of rethinking and rewriting and, hopefully, of growth and development.

Since it is necessary, nevertheless, closely to define the areas under scrutiny, the author presents a short preview of topics discussed in the book with hypotheses proved and hypotheses suggested by the material presented.

The author submits that:

The findings discussed show:

(1) That the social class differentials manifest in the composition of the student bodies of the three universities have changed very little since the 1944 Education Act and that this may be a result of cultural differences inherent in the different social classes.

It would appear that the lower middle class rather than the working class is benefiting from the expansion of educational opportunity.

This has been noted by other writers.

(2) That social class patterns emerge with regard to:
  (a) family size of students;
  (b) education of students' siblings;
  (c) education of students' parents; first-generation university students occur in every social class—predominantly the lower middle class.
  (d) motives for coming to university;
  (e) reactions to certain aspects of university organisation, and especially (i) residence, and (ii) course of study;
  (f) school last attended;
  (g) participation and leadership in student organisations.

Most of these points have been noted by other writers.

(3) That the social classes in the student body, represented by the one-dimensional occupational status of father, constitute real groupings in terms of culture and value patterns within as outside the university, and that this reveals:
  (a) That the occupational status of father implies a whole configuration of social variables, and that such an index is a useful tool for the discovery of other dimensions of social class. The fact that it does not *always* imply meaningful configurations in the university context reveals difficulties of social class measurement at different times and in different places. The configurations themselves may be changing in composition.

Hence the drawbacks of comparing different studies of social class since it may not be the same thing which is being measured.
  (b) That working-class students may retain distinct social class characteristics within the predominantly middle-class student body,

i.e. they do not automatically become "bourgeoisified" upon entering or being selected by a middle-class university, nor are they so atypical of their social class of origin as to be already middle class.

Certain conditions are necessary for this to take place. General works on "social class", "bourgeoisification", and "social mobility" in other situations are of direct relevance but do not discuss this particular example.

(4) That social class is a factor in student social relations, in both formal and informal student groups, and that this is tacitly or explicitly accepted by students in terms of:

(a) organisation;
(b) inter-group relations;
(c) personal attitudes and relations.

This has not previously been investigated since it has been normally assumed that social class is *not* a significant factor in social relations at the student level—in keeping with the "melting pot" and "educated élite" visions of university. The reason why this kind of assumption of a social class m"ososis" at university has gone solong unquestioned may be partially a result of the research time-lag mentioned earlier. Perhaps the relevance of social class in student social relations suggests itself as a problem to be investigated less readily to the post-war generation of researchers who possibly attended university as mature ex-servicemen than to the products of today's universities.

(5) That social class as a factor in students' social relations is *not always* relevant, and that its relevance varies with situation, or perceived situations, and with the variety of other social factors involved and the *weighting* accorded to each factor in that particular situation.

The "situation" may be analysed at the institutional, inter-group, or interpersonal level, and the same basic factors apply. The "perceived" situation is a symptom of certain structural relationships governed by these factors.

(a) At the institutional level, inter-group relations of members of social classes are influenced by the statistical composition of the social classes in the student body by internal and overlapping divisions of the social classes and by the degree of contact which members of different social classes have with each other.

(b) At the *small-group* level, situations are patterned in terms of cultural and spatial divisions exhibited by the larger groups in the wider context. The special combinations of these factors operate in such a way that they determine which groups students identify with in the immediate situation and groups to which they refer in a wider context.

Much of what is discussed in terms of situational patterns may be inferred but not proved.

(6) That different social class distributions in residence, faculties, and student organisations influences the degree of contact with members of social classes in work, leisure, and living accommodation and therefore the degree of mutual adaptation.

In some cases the coincidence of social and spatial distance serves to accentuate existing social class divisions.

(7) That social space is on a continuum so that the influence on students' social relations of university siting, distribution of buildings, situation of room or work bench differs in degree but not kind and may be seen to operate on all the different contextual levels.

Geographical/regional divisons among students represent both cultural groupings sometimes confused with social class, and spatial/cultural reference groups and as such are a dominant factor in students' social relations.

(8) That where social/spatial groups and social class groups tend to have common boundaries, social class divisions become dominant and defined—where there is much cross-cutting of boundaries social class divisions become blurred and relevant in fewer situations.

It has not been possible within the present framework to study interpersonal space. This would be a topic for further study.

(9) That social class of students is largely attributional in the university context but that it becomes interactional in certain residential situations—or where there is distinct and enduring spatial concentration of social class members. This needs further investigation.

(10) That the mutual transmission of elements of social class culture depends upon the relation of the social classes within the university, i.e. certain conditions are necessary for this to happen or, for example, a working-class student to become bourgeoisified (see point 3b).

Students have shown that they acknowledge this to be so. This has implications for the process of social mobility and its relation to institutional socialisation.

(11) That social mobility and social motility should be differentiated in the study of student mobility.

Mobility is the structured property of movement undertaken; motility is possession of the characteristics of motion and need not necessarily imply mobility. Motility refers to the individual potentially mobile. Different combinations of mobility and motility may be used to describe and analyse different kinds of mobility experience among students. For students do not all experience social mobility at the same time or in the same degree. Patterns of mobility and attitudes to mobility are meaningful in terms of internal value systems of the social classes.

(12) That attitudes to expansion of university places are influenced by the degree of Contest or Sponsored mobility experienced by the student, along with the organisational constraints with which students interact.

The author submits also that: the findings suggest but do not prove:

(1) That there are certain *defined* social situations in which attributional social class is relevant in social relations, and that the situational patterning itself is probably regulated by the interaction of spatial/ cultural factors previously described.

These situations if discovered and analysed would give a clue as to how roles are changed in response to certain social stimuli.

(2) That in these defined situations certain *attributes* are seen as relevant or irrelevant, in terms of past, actual, or vicarious social experience, and those which are seen as relevant are differentially weighted—one of these being social class.

The process involved represents the dynamic aspect of role and role performance—or the constant movement between roles. Social class is seen as a variable rather than a constant attribute.

There has been no attempt systematically to discover and isolate a series of defined situations—so that what happens within them may only be inferred. It would be possible to formulate a hypothesis on the basis of findings at other levels of investigation which seem like "defined situations writ large", as in structured institutional contexts and inter-group as opposed to interpersonal relations.

The testing of such hypotheses would require a fresh research design for investigation at the micro-sociological level. The study of defined situations in which certain attributes are relevant is different in approach from that which analyses groups in possession of a particular attribute in order to discover the relevant situational patterns. It may be said that the present book approached the problem of students' social relations from the latter standpoint and attempts to open up some way of combining also the former approach.

In this way the book moves further and further away from its first orientations.

A chapter has been added on student "revolt" to demonstrate the relation between internal and external movements and constraints and in an attempt to relate in structural terms particular educational and social processes in society to the organisation of particular institutions.

ACKNOWLEDGEMENTS

THROUGHOUT the progress of the research and during the actual production of the book, a number of people have been involved in official and unofficial capacities in a variety of ways to ensure that the book eventually should appear in print. Whatever the task—be it encouragement, advice, card punching, typing, or negotiation of official support for the project— each represents a necessary and invaluable part of the whole enterprise. It is therefore impossible to single out particular individuals whom the author would like to thank above others—to all those involved she is extremely grateful and acknowledges her indebtedness for their particular contribution to the finished product.

The following people are those who have been centrally concerned with the research and the physical production of the thesis and later book and include mentors, learned colleagues, university authorities, secretarial and administrative staff, student leaders, and student respondents: The names are given alphabetically, with positions occupied at time of research:

Mrs. R. Balmer, Assistant Warden of Lodgings, Newcastle University.

Professor M. P. Banton, Department of Sociology, University of Bristol.

Miss J. Berry, MSC, Newcastle University.

E. Bettenson, Esq., Registrar, Newcastle University.

Dr. Joan Brothers, Institute of Education, London University.

D. Casson, Esq., Senior Man, Grey College, Durham University.

Miss M. Chapman, Durham University.

L. Crawford, Esq., Warden of Lodgings, Newcastle University.

Miss E. Croft, Secretary to the Warden of Lodgings, Newcastle University.

Erik Ekeid, Esq., President, SRC, Newcastle University.

Professor W. B. Fisher, Department of Geography, Durham University.

James Foley, Esq., President, SRC, Durham University.

George Foulkes, Esq., President, SRC, Edinburgh University.

Miss A. Graham, Fee Office, Edinburgh University.

Ian Graham, Esq., Registrar, Durham University.

Mrs. R. Harrison, York University.

Miss S. Harrison, Durham University.

Miss J. Hills, Durham University.

Mr. Howe, Chief Clerk, Registrar's Office, Newcastle University.

Miss Rita Hughes, New York.

Miss Lois Knoll, New York.

Professor K. L. Little, Department of Social Anthropology, University of Edinburgh.

Miss S. Macdonald, Social Sciences Research Centre, Edinburgh University.

Mrs. McIntosh, Fee Office, Edinburgh University.

Miss I. McKay, Fee Office, Edinburgh University.

Dr. H. Meinhard, Department of Anthropology, Newcastle University.

Mr. J. Munro, Fee Office, Edinburgh University.

Mrs. Paterson, Fee Office, Edinburgh University.

Miss E. Rose, Social Sciences Research Centre, Edinburgh University.

Miss V. Rumble, Durham University.

Charles H. Stewart, Secretary to the University of Edinburgh.

A. G. Watts, Careers Research and Advisory Centre, Cambridge.

Mrs. Lona Wong, New York.

The author thanks all those who have made comments and suggestions which have resulted in amendments to the original text, especially Prof. A. H. Richmond, but takes full responsibility for the finished book.

Despite the author's desire not to single out particular individuals, special mention must be made of the work of Miss Flora Mitchell, then Secretary of the Department of Social Anthropology in Edinburgh. Miss Mitchell typed most of the two drafts of the original thesis of 500 pages and then gallantly typed a further five chapters of the book manuscript, ending on a climactic note as a car crashed through the wall of the office where she sat working.

In this typing she went far beyond the call of duty—always working against the clock—and for her unflagging devotion to the cause deserves a special word of thanks.

PART I

CHAPTER 1

RESEARCH PROBLEMS IN EDUCATION

1. Some Contemporary Issues

The increasing differentiation of occupation and economic roles, which is associated with the growth of technological economies, gives rise to two broad conflicting pressures in the educational system—innovation and achievement versus conservation and ascription. The first pressure is related to the need for specialised manpower, selected from the society's most able individuals—coupled with the need to make the process of selection as effectively and efficiently as possible.[1] Through this process ideally individuals are not only selected for specialist training but are also allocated to those positions which they most adequately and appropriately fill, and for which in terms of talent, training, and inclination they are most fitted. Since education is the intergenerational transmission of all societal culture and values, it is not meaningful at one point in time to categorise learning entirely by its "usefulness", so that this will include social positions which on the face of it have no immediate economic or productive value. Nevertheless, it is important for the continuance of the culture system that these roles also be adequately performed. Thus it is necessary in moving to this desired goal to sort and sift individuals through the system according to a set of rational criteria in order that existing knowledge, skills, techniques, and human potential be fully utilised and developed. This goal is clearly difficult to attain in an imperfect world since there is in fact no invisible hand or consciously self-regulating, perfectly articulated system, and the processes which take place may be the result of complex series of actions and decisions, not consciously related.

However, such are the networks of social pressures and constraints that changes do come about in a particular way, adaptive to structural differen-

---

[1] For discussion see, for instance, Halsey, A. H., Floud, J., and Anderson, C. A. (eds.), *Education, Economy and Society*, Free Press, Glencoe, New York, 1961, especially parts I and II.

tiation. Preconditions and first-order consequences of these changes are rapid geographical and social mobility in an increasingly urban society and a system of meritocratic advancement which vies with the traditional ascriptive order.

The causes and effects of these social changes are seen most dramatically in economically underdeveloped areas which have recently felt the impact of industrialisation and modern market economy, and in which growth of institutions of formal education and mass media are necessary for social and economic development and emergence of national goals.[1] "Although factory production or commercialised agriculture may be introduced with an illiterate and largely unskilled labor force for manual operations, at least a minority must have higher education and technical skills. As industrial or agricultural operations become more complex rising levels of general education are needed."[2] In time "the uneducated are doomed to poorly paid and low-status jobs, whatever their potential talents".[3] The emerging occupational and educational differentiation poses a threat to the traditional status system which in a pre-industrial society is usually based on ownership of land, descent, and birthright.

> "When the gulf which divides rich and poor is as impassable as that of a backward nation, we cannot expect to find on the part of the favored classes an interest in change, in ferment, in "progress". The "anciens regimes" of the poor nations —many of which are still current regimes—find their natural self interest in the preservation of accepted ways, or at most in the most cautious introduction of new social outlooks and opportunities.[4]

It is only with difficulty, therefore, and against various kinds of opposition from those well placed in the existing ascriptive status hierarchy, that a system of universal education is ever set up.[5] Nor do the obstacles disappear with the advent of a so-called "advanced" technologically sophisticated, industrial societal organisation, although they may appear in a different guise.

For there is a constant counter-pressure working against these trends towards an achievement orientated system and yet which, in a sense, is

---

[1] Rogers, Everett M. (in association with Lynne Srenning), *Modernisation Among Peasants: The Impact of Communication*, Holt, Rinehart & Winston, 1969.

[2] Moore, W. E., *The Impact of Industry*, Prentice-Hall, 1965, p. 98.

[3] Heilbronner, R. L., *The Great Ascent: The Struggle for Economic Development in Our Time*, Harper Torchbooks, 1963, p. 51.

[4] *Ibid.*, p. 51.

[5] Witness the opposition, particularly of the landed aristocracy, to the British Education Act of 1870 which provided free, compulsory primary education.

intimately linked with them. Through the process of occupational and economic differentiation, individuals stand in different positions in relation to one another in the economic and occupational structure and, through differential status ranking, in the hierarchies which are created. This situation involves not only differential prestige and status ranking but ultimately a differential possession of power, through power to *command* resources including industrial property and capital and control of the governmental organs of society.[1] The power of both governing and non-governing élites is legitimated by the value orientations of society, by which they are sanctioned.

In the case of the "developing" nation the problem of achieving legitimation through consensus may involve some indoctrination and coercion, less likely in an established democratic political system. The "heirs" to Western industrialisation and technology in developing nations may comprise only an educated minority of the population who take certain "developed" nations as their reference group and formulate goals for the rest of society.

> Since the inheritance value system will almost inevitably conflict with the traditional culture and attitudes of the society concerned. The proportion of the population for whom the élite can authoritatively define the situation by imposing the inheritance value system naturally becomes an important factor in any judgement on the existence of consensus or cleavage within any particular society.[2]

Clearly the problem of "consensus" of "cleavage" of values in relation to educational and societal goals exists for every society. The recent worldwide outbreak of student movements and rebellions bears witness to the conflicts of another kind of "inheritance" situation in which the "juvenocracy" revolts against the situational definition of the "gerontocracy" in power in much the same way as peasants revolt against absentee landlords and workers against capitalist bosses. "A gerontocratic order is not a sufficient condition for the rise of a student movement. Among other factors, there must also be present a feeling that the older generation has failed. We may call this experience the process of the de-authoritization of the old."[3]

---

[1] Aron, R., Social structure and the ruling class: Part I, *BJS*, **1** (i), 1950, for discussion of the relation between social differentiation and political hierarchy.

[2] Nettl, J. P. and Robertson, R., *International Systems and the Modernisation of Societies: The Formulation of National Goals and Attitudes*, Basic Books, 1968, p. 89.

[3] Feuer, L. S., *The Conflict of Generations: The Character and Significance of Student Movements*, Basic Books, 1969, p. 12.

The process of de-authoritisation is not new—the drama is an old one but the groups of actors are different and have different characteristics. It seems inevitable that the results of an educational system set-up to provide new channels of achievement and selection in direct opposition to the ascriptive system of inheritance of status through age, sex, and seniority should eventually prove successful. Conflict arises in any system when the educational process inculcates new values and new aspirations in the "new heirs" to power, but does not bring with it a collapse of the old status system which allows the heirs to come into their inheritance. Power is rarely willingly relinquished by those who hold it and has to be seized forcibly. Black students in the United States are "new heirs" to a new social order which they have been promised but do not see materialising. In this situation they are in the process of de-authoritising the White power structure, particularly that which for them is closest at hand in terms of college presidents and administrators. Changes in educational structure do, and always have, brought about changes in the power structure, whether explicitly recognised or not; but when claims to power which education brings are not recognised conflict results. The Black Panther Party, first organised in 1966, appeals particularly to the young and stresses pride in being black, self-help, self-defence against White aggression, and striving for the right of self-determination, in which the party feels it has much in common with other "colonised" people throughout the world who are the "victims of imperialism".

> "Education is the theme: the Panthers hold classes for members and work with black high school groups. Detailing the styles of oppression, they also study liberation movements. They particularly stress the contradictions and fantasies throughout the United States history, especially the fiction of equal opportunity. Even at times of glittering prosperity, there has always been an economic depression for blacks."[1]

Not unnaturally the Panthers are regarded with fear and suspicion by the White power structure.

In all societies access to education is related to access to the power structure of society as well as to economic and social gain, and this is why it is such an area of contention and rivalry in all contemporary societies. Since education is a scarce resource and is differentially allocated, certain groups do continuously find themselves hampered in the competition. Where membership of any group is marked by visible characteristics such as skin

---

[1] Sayre, N. The Black Panthers are coming: America on the eve of race revolution, *New Statesman*, 2 May 1969, pp. 613–16.

colour, then, of course, it is possible for discriminatory constraints to be applied to their progress by those in power. A social class situation, or one of cultural differentiation, is consequently less rigid but does exhibit some similar trends in relation to development or non-development of educational and hence social opportunity.

Where any kind of social differentiation exists, through the process of intergenerational transmission of material and non-material culture and values, and their expression in life styles, involved in the family socialisation process, the differentially ranked hierarchy of occupational and economic roles is given permanent expression. Where there is intergenerational and intragenerational aggregation and concentration of persons occupying similar positions involved in this process, there are identifiable social classes—the classes varying in number and heterogeneity from society to society. In a situation defined by skin colour and segregation, of course, the structure is closer to "caste". Membership of élites, or of the "ruling classes", is restricted to those who are inducted into the élite culture—either by birth or selective recruitment. Education, or certain kinds of education or educational institutions, may be consciously geared to this end, and thus help to preserve social distance and social inequalities. For the resulting differential access to élite culture ensures that life chances in a competitive industrial society are also differentially distributed, and the systems of selection are prevented from working unhampered and efficiently—with certain groups being more or less favoured purely by accident of birth.

> Education has always stood necessarily in close relation to class, status and power. In the past half century it has become part of the economic foundations of an industrial society, a major avenue of social mobility, and one of the principle agencies of social distribution. An advanced industrial society is inconceivable without the means through which people are selected and trained for places in a highly diversified labour force. The educational system is accordingly used to establish claims and opportunities. If education is unavoidably an instrument for distributing life chances we can only argue profitably about what kind of distribution is both desirable and profitable.[1]

There is, then, the pressure for conservation of existing structure of positions, existing channels of mobility, existing culture and values—in the face of the pressures for innovation and change. These two conflicting pressures are reflected in the way in which educational systems, or certain aspects of educational systems, are geared either to preserve existing soci-

---

[1] Halsey, A. H., Education and equality, *New Society*, 17 June 1965, No. 142.

etal culture and values and transmit it from one generation to the next—
or geared to explore new frontiers of knowledge, which may necessitate
value change—even though in pushing out the frontier it may be possible
only to transmit the resulting discoveries to fewer and fewer individuals.
The first kind of pressure preserves relative homogeneity, both of what is
taught, and to whom it is taught. The latter kind of pressure results in heterogeneity of culture, and consequently of educational institutions and
their functions, and may lead to wider and wider gaps appearing between
those who manage to reach succeeding stages in the process. In an achievement system any gaps that there are become more a factor of ability and
less of birth. However, where "drop-out" is due almost entirely to lack of
ability, the process may have painful consequences for the unsuccessful
individual that cannot be blamed upon the system and which may have to
be institutionally mollified and deflected.[1]

Obviously the way in which the system is allowed to work itself out,
or consciously prevented from doing so, by those who frame educational
policies will depend on the value orientations of society and of the dominant élites and the goals to which education is seen to be directed.

In the discussion of these goals it must not be forgotten that in highly
militarised societies such as the United States, the military élite and
military institutions play an important part. Indeed, "it would be extremely difficult to disentangle the effects of economic development as
such and the effects of military requirements and policies".[2] In 1966
the United States spent $63 billion on military expenditure, 38·4 per cent
of the world total, or $317 *per capita*, while the United Kingdom spent
$7 billion, 4·2 per cent of the world total, or $126 *per capita*. "Certainly,
military spending is far from a totally negative factor in the world's
economies—but such military spending is far less productive than most
alternative spending."[3] Such "alternative spending" might be on educational facilities—on which at present is spent less than on defence
provisions.

Military influence is felt in many ways in education—for "not only
may military demands shape the development of technology, but also
military service may be a principal agency of technical education where
the schools have not produced persons with appropriate technical skills".

---

[1] Clark, B. R., The cooling out function in High Education, *AJS*, **65,** May 1960.

[2] Moore, *op. cit.*, p. 100.

[3] Soderlind, S. E., The outlook: current trends in business and finance, *The Wall Street Journal*, 5 May 1969, **173** (88).

In more sinister ways the University may become part of the military/industrial complex.[1]

In the United States much of student unrest has been caused by a desire to "demilitarise" education, particularly in the universities, by attempting to persuade authorities to relinquish government defence contracts, and to deny special facilities for ROTC on campus, for instance, and to refuse interviewing facilities to recruitment officers from companies which manufacture war materials such as Napalm. In addition, of course, the whole issue of compulsory military service in the unpopular Vietnam war is a rallying point for students, particularly those of the New Student Left of the Sixties.

The spring of 1965 saw the advent of the new political/academic institution—the "teach-in"—and with it a growing galvanisation of the academic community—both students and faculty. Soon

> a new political claim was advanced: that the national administration was under an obligation to be confronted by the academic community, that it was especially incumbent upon the administration to defend its policies before the academic community, and that this was an obligation especially mandatory for those administration officials who had an academic background.[2]

In 1969 new tactics are now being used in sit-ins, takeover of university buildings, demonstrations pacific or otherwise—the campuses are in uproar. The unrest has spread to Britain and there are many "sympathy" strikes and sit-ins on international issues in solidarity with American and other international student movements. Students have become increasingly political and vocal in national and international affairs. The "goals" of education are still being thrashed out, and are still unclear, for the "goals" of society are similarly ill-defined and by an increasingly disbelieved power minority.[3] The relation between the élites and the masses is as always still in the process of being hammered out. In this process the basis of selection for education is clearly of paramount importance.

---

[1] Kopkind, A., The military connection: the Pentagon shadow over U.S. universities, *New Statesman*, 12 Sept. 1969, pp 327–8.

[2] Feuer, *op. cit.*, p. 412.

[3] Hence the phrase, coined during the Johnson Administration, the "credibility gap".

It must be asked therefore whether education of certain kinds is to be exclusive, limited to a privileged few recruited for induction into the élite culture—or whether it is to be a more inclusive process designed to embrace all who show themselves desirous and capable of benefiting from it. The main area of ideological contention in industrialised societies has moved with the growth of technology from "level" to "level" of education, so that with the achievement of universal primary education the area of dilemma and debate moves on to secondary education and, latterly, to higher education—with consequent stress on expansion of provisions.[1] It is clear, therefore, that on the outcome of the interplay between these practical and ideological issues depends the answers to questions of who shall be educated, what they shall be taught, by whom, in what institutions, for how long and at what age, and with what desired outcome for the individual, wider group, and society of which he is a member.

The push-and-pull forces discussed are thus the central concerns of educational policy of economically developed and developing nations and of those underdeveloped nations who aspire to technological progress.[2] The ways in which the attendant structural dilemmas are solved and the social priorities decided will obviously vary somewhat in each case, while the fundamental structural problems remain the same.

We can see, for instance, in many parts of the world at the present time the very great and growing demand for education, and the pressures to expansion of places in schools, colleges, and universities in order to cope with this demand, in order to avoid "wastage" of well qualified and able persons. Figures produced by UNESCO surveys show that between 1950 and 1959 total world enrolment in education moved from 256,861,000 in 1950 to 413,885,000 in 1959—or an increase of 61 per cent. During the same time the increase of total population in the age group rose from 1,016,500,000 to 1,178,100,000—an increase of only 16 per cent. The percentage of the population age group enrolled in education rose from 25 per cent in 1950 to 35 per cent in 1959—a considerable increase.[3] This increase may be attributed to changes in the "forces of aspiration"

---

[1] Particularly in Britain since the Robbins Report, *Higher Education*, Cmnd. 2154, London, 1963.

[2] See, for instance, Ashby, Sir E., *African Universities and Western Tradition*, OUP, 1964.

[3] Bowles, F., *Access to Higher Education*, vol. 1, UNESCO and the International Association of Universities, Columbia Univ. Press, 1963, p. 96.

associated with increases in standard of living; industrial developments; explosion of scientific knowledge and to changes in the "forces of national planning" which reflect a growing interest of national governments in education; stimulation of activity by voluntary and international organisations; and increasing stress on the need to train teachers.[1]

The pressure to expansion of existing educational institutions, building of new ones, and recruitment and payment of teachers presents its own problems of public finance and resources in order to utilise societies' intellectual resources. There are costs and benefits both social and economic, both universal and specific, in trying to extend the possibility of higher education to a larger and larger proportion of those appropriately qualified in any particular generation. Indeed, it may be argued that the present student unrest is a singular attestation of the *success* of liberal, democratic education, and certainly not its failure.

Different educational systems, however, differ in their degree of "openness" of selection; of class orientation; of criteria for allocation of educational resources. The United States and Britain are cases in point— the former having moved steadily towards a "mass" educational system, the latter clinging still to an élitist system linked in past times with the ideology of education being a privilege to be extended to the few. In the United States about 37 per cent of the age group entered college or university in 1965[2] while in Britain the corresponding figure was only 4 per cent for university and 8 per cent for all full-time higher education.[3] Of course these figures must be related to different historical trends in higher education, and represent different orientations of the system towards the functions of selection. In turn there are also certain important consequences for industrial nations. "The vast and rapid economic growth of the United States has been both the cause and the result of the vast expansion of secondary and higher education during the twentieth century. At the same time the expansion of education and the economy has made possible a very large degree of upward mobility."[4] The different historical trends in the British and American systems of edu-

---

[1] *Ibid.*, pp. 98–99.
[2] Cf. Havighurst, R. J. and Neugarten, B. L., *Society and Education*, Allyn & Bacon, Boston, 1967, p. 98, table 4.1.
[3] Cf. *Higher Education, loc. cit.*, Appendix 1, p. 14.
[4] Havighurst and Neugarten, *op. cit.*, p. 111. See also New York College Entrance Examination Board *Annual Report 1965–66*. Over 50 per cent and in some states up to 70 per cent of high school graduates enter college.

cation will be discussed later in the chapter in relation to studies of expansion of educational opportunity.

In Britain the student expansion has been greater than that predicted by the Robbins Report, and on the basis of present projections it is estimated that new places in higher education must be up 40 per cent on the Robbins' projections. In 1968–9 there were 59,550 new full-time undergraduate entrants—or 7·7 per cent of the age group.[1] Latest figures for 1967–8 show that there were 200,121 full time students enrolled in British Universities. Estimates for 1969 were 220,000;[2] and in November 1967 there were an additional 180,882 students registered for advanced courses at other institutions of Higher and Further Education.[3] Advanced courses are those defined as leading to qualifications comparable with first degree level, such as Higher National Certificate, degrees awarded by the Council for National Academic Awards, Diploma in Art and Design and some professional qualifications, such as Architecture. Included in the figures are students in full-time, short period full-time, day release and sandwich courses, who are studying in National and Regional colleges and Colleges of Art, and particularly in the new Polytechnics, proposed in April 1967 as reorganisation of existing colleges of art, commerce and technology into about 30 corporate units. These figures do not include the 103,815 students in 1967–8 training to be teachers at the 211 training establishments, or Colleges of Education.[4] From 1960 the basic training of teachers was increased from two to three years, but as of 1967 only a minority of the colleges outside the universities were involved in the preparation of students for the new B.Ed. degrees. Taken together these figures represent a massive increase in the number of young people going into higher and further education. The increase is a consequence of a growing demand for places, and a growing number of qualified people able to take up those places. There was for instance a 52 percentage on 1962 figures by 1967 of boys and girls leaving school with two or more Advanced level G.C.E. passes.[5] It has been suggested that the "comprehensivisation" of education

[1] *Whitaker's Almanac*, 1970.

[2] *Statistics of Education 1967: Universities U.K*, Vol. 6, U.G.C., HMSO, 1969, p. viii and table I.

[3] *Statistics of Education 1967: Further Education*, Vol. 3, U.G.C., HMSO, 1969, table I, p. 2.

[4] *Statistics of Education 1967: Teachers*, Vol. 4, HMSO, 1969, table I, p. 1.

[5] Crampin, Alice (Higher Education Research Unit LSE), *Forecasting student numbers in Higher Education*, Paper delivered to the Society for Research into Higher Education, Annual Conference, Dec. 1969, table A.

will assist this growth by "netting" an increasing proportion of would-be secondary modern school leavers, and enabling them thus to at least attempt qualifications necessary for college entrance. The speed with which the changeover to comprehensive schools in Britain takes place will thus affect the proportion of any age group staying on at schools to any particular level.[1] If rapid comprehensivisation were to take place it is estimated that 34 per cent boys and 30 per cent girls in the year 1979–80 would obtain 5 or more Ordinary level passes in G.C.E., compared with 21 per cent and 20 per cent in 1967–8.[2] These compare with projections of the Department for Education and Science for 1979–80 of 29 per cent and 28 per cent.[3] The overall increase in opportunity which comprehensive education is likely to bring would represent a move from an élite system towards a mass system of education in Britain, with possible attendant changes in class proportions of students.

For attendant upon the expansion of educational provisions and places and often paradoxically requiring different kinds of policy decisions, is the expansion of educational opportunity among all classes and groups of the population so that differential access to education of differentially privileged groups may be overcome. The problems of inequality involved are universal although the attributes of the group may differ. The structural relations of these groups and degree of social distance between them will determine the ways in which democratisation is eventually achieved. For the structure and degree of distinctions or segregation of these subgroups bring different dimensions to the problems concerned and the way in which they are defined. This book is concerned with inequalities in educational opportunity between socioeconomic classes in class societies. Of course there are differently defined unequal groups or classes of persons in class societies one of which as has already been mentioned as the most clearly defined class of all—the racial minority. The findings of the book on class inequality in education may be extended to apply even more forcibly and explicitly to situations of racial inequality. Comparative studies in the United States show this. However, the general conclusions hopefully may be applied in similarly structured situations to any educationally disadvantaged group—be it an immigrant minority, rural community in industrial society, or ghetto poor White *and* Black. The criteria which are used to differentiate these groups,

[1] *Ibid.*
[2] *Ibid.*, table 2.
[3] *Statistics of Education 1967: School Leavers*, Vol. 2, HMSO, 1969, table 34.

socially, culturally, or racially, will also represent the different sets of "blocks" to educational opportunity. Whereas in the British class situation the class differentiation, and consequently the associated "blocks" to opportunity, are based on rather subtle cultural clues, in the United States the disadvantaged may suffer more serious financial and material set-backs despite the lack of a thoroughgoing hereditary class system. However, the difficulties faced in schools in Britain by many children of Commonwealth immigrants now approach those faced by Black Americans.[1]

Whilst overcoming cultural problems of differential education, access is in itself a major structural dilemma; once the process of democratisation is under way the new status groups which result in themselves create new structural dilemmas and changes. The expansion of educational opportunity increases social mobility rates[2] and ultimately leads to fragmentation of existing classes by creation of new élites, a movement characterising the development of industrial societies.[3] A possible next stage in this "circulation of élites"[4] is the creation of new social classes based upon new value criteria—with an interim period of status ambiguity or confusion. In addition, there emerges another status group if not élite, which is neither economic nor occupational—but which comprises those who are studying or training for roles which require most skill and are therefore highly ranked in the social order. "Student" becomes an identifiable and meaningful social category—which represents a "stage" in status change rather than a status group proper. This is because each particular cohort or *age set*[5] must pass through it as an age grade *en route* to other positions. To be a student is not an end in itself in terms of societal structure of positions although it may be so for the period of

[1] Rose, E. J. B. & Associates, *Colour and Citizenship: A Report on British Race Relations*, OUP, 1969; see ch. 18.

[2] Bendix, R. and Lipset, S. M., *Social Mobility in Industrial Society*, Heinemann, 1959.

[3] Mannheim, K., *Man in Society in an Age of Reconstruction*, Kegan Paul, 1940, part II.

[4] Bottomore, T., *Élites and Society*, Pelican Books, 1966 (developing Pareto's discussion on this), Chapter 3, and Pareto, Vilfredo, *Sociological Writings*, Selected and Introduced by Finer, S. E. (trans. by Mirfin Derick), Pall Mall Press, 1966, pp. 247–51.

[5] As used in classical anthropological studies, signifying a particular cohort of individuals of similar age who pass together through the crucial status changes (or age *grades*) of social life, as, for instance, between boyhood and manhood.

"tenure", implying, as it does, a way of life and a body of culture. This is the peculiar nature of the student "status".

However, initially the student identifies with and feels he belongs to his particular educational institution. It is only under certain conditions that students become aware of their common, universal "studentness" in the same way that Marx defines the ways in which a class "in itself" becomes a class "for itself".[1] These conditions are discussed later in the book, but are intimately connected with the process of democratisation of higher education. Where, for instance, higher education becomes increasingly the main, if not the only, means to occupational and economic mobility and advancement—a badge, as it were, qualifying the holder to the next and highest stage in the competition for status—the pressures to group solidarity are enormous. There emerges an ever-widening gulf in *educational* terms between the "haves" and "have nots". Membership of the student status group, so hardly won, both promotes a sense of "sharing" with fellow achievers, and separateness from those who fell behind at the last academic hurdle—and the whole of society encourages and prizes the distinction.

What is not often realised is that the changing class composition of the student body which results from expansion of educational opportunity may well change the whole nature and goals of the student body in any particular institution. Students do not enter universities as clean slates to be written upon—they are already shaped in many ways by the class culture from which they come. In a sense all the institution can hope to do is remodel the existing human material, but this will depend on certain structural features which encourage such changes. These and other aspects so far overlooked in their wider implications are the concern of the present analysis. Suffice it to say at this stage that students will increasingly be in touch with the grass roots of the social and political movements of society and of certain socioeconomic groups within it from which groups, indeed, many of them will increasingly be selected.

Kenniston and others have, however, pointed out that many young radicals and student leaders, although in touch with grass-roots movements, are not themselves sons and daughters of working-class families. Indeed, many come from affluent middle-class families where the liberal or left-wing parents inculcated values they themselves were not able to put into practice. The values of the young radicals are aligned with

[1] See Bottomore, T. B. and Rubel, M. (eds.), Karl Marx: *Selected Writings in Sociology and Social Philosophy*, Pelican, 1963.

those of their parents and are expressed in action. The young radicals are characterised by a "belief in a set of basic moral principles: justice, decency, equality, responsibility, non-violence, and fairness".[1] In other words not only do young radicals idealise an egalitarian society, like their parents, but they want to bring it about.

As larger and larger numbers of such sections of the population, and indeed of the whole population, although small in proportion, share the same educational experience, they become conscious of "belonging" to a particular status group. Following upon this is the desire to exert power—particularly for change. Whereas the students from the landed aristocracy and leisure classes in times past had latent power vested in family position which became actual through inheritance and family influence, today's students from families of dispossessed workers of an industrial society have latent power in their own skills and talents—marketable commodities with a high price. Their power becomes actual in utilisation of those skills and talents in specialised occupational and economic roles. As students are made more and more aware that their skills are needed for the continuance of the social order, in their hands is put the weapon which helps them to maximise their potential power position—the unstated threat of withdrawal of necessary services. The more organised and group conscious they become, the more power is gained from this structural and, as yet, only implicit threat—that a whole generation of students could opt out of an existing structure of positions, refusing to play the roles to which they were to be assigned. Nor is the threat only a vague possibility—students have always been in the forefront of revolutions. "Revolutionary intellectuals" are usually involved in formulating new goals in a changing order.[2]

This is not to be wondered at since coming at a time of young adulthood the experience of being a student has a galvanising effect, particularly in relation to youthful criticism of the established social order, which academic independence and scepticism, into which they are inducted, tends to encourage. Innovation and exploration are the stated goals of higher education and when coupled with democratisation, there will obviously be inevitable attendant social consequences for conservative ageing societies. Expansion of educational opportunity is a two-edged sword.

[1] Kenniston, K., *Young Radicals*, Harcourt, Brace & World, 1968, p. 28.
[2] Bottomore, *op. cit.*, 1966, p. 71.

The growth in number and strength of student protest and political movements all over the world at the present time in, for instance, the United States, Britain, France, Germany, Argentina, Spain, India, Indonesia, China, and Japan to select only a few areas[1] bears witness to the acceleration of the processes outlined above which in time gather their own momentum. (A few cases are selected for analysis in the book.) The forces of innovation, of which some student protest movements are the spearhead,[2] in turn, of course, lead to disruption of existing culture and values, to increasing and perhaps increasingly conflicting heterogeneity and fragmentation, and therefore to situational dilemmas which can only be solved by the individual "conscience" rather than by recourse to non-existent "societal" norms. This is the extreme case, but since the educational system fosters "individualism", it may not long remain so.

Within the student body itself these societal pressures have implications for the whole quality and purpose of student life and for the student's own conception of his role. The movement from the ideal of the "community of scholars" to the "multiversity"[3], with its multiple campuses, has long been underway, and with it has changed the idea of what a "student" or an "academic" should be. The situation is increasingly characterised by the need for efficiency and rationality[4]—often bureaucracy— and "productivity" is thought by some to be measurable on tables of input and output.[5] It is not surprising, therefore, that there are individual "casualties" who are not entirely happy to be "processed" by the system. Indeed, student movements are often triggered off as a reaction to the impersonality and lack of communication experienced on the campus.[6] Is higher education really a "knowledge industry"?[7] Is the academic

---

[1] See, for instance, Lipset, S. M., Special issue on student politics, *Comp. Educ. Rev.*, 1966, **10** (2), 129–31. This contains 15 articles on the problems of student political behaviour in various countries but with some stress on Latin America and India.

[2] Lipset, S. M. and Altbach, P., American student protest, *New Society*, 1966, **205**, 328–32.

[3] Coined by Dr. Clark Kerr, ex-President of the University of California.

[4] As used by Max Weber. See Gerth, H. H. and Mills, C. Wright, *From Max Weber*, Kegan Paul, 1964, chs. 8 and 13.

[5] See Woodhall, M. and Blaug, M., Productivity trends in British university education, *Minerva*, 1965, **3** (4), 483–98.

[6] Lipset, S. M. and Altbach, P., US campus alienation, *New Society*, 1966, **206**, 361–64.

[7] Dr. Clark Kerr, reported in Kopkind, A., Crisis in the knowledge industry—the Berkeley sacking, *New Statesman*, 3 February 1967, 139–40.

life a "marketplace for brains"?[1] How satisfying are the relationships
which develop in such a system? The blatant breakdown of staff/student
communication, of corporate responsibility, of institutional culture and
solidarity—as at Berkeley,[2] noted for the free speech (or, latterly, filthy
speech) movement, and at the LSE during student protest at the appointment as Principal of Dr. Walter Adams,[3] tell us more than is implied
by the actual events. They reveal structural discrepancies and an underlying malaise which the explicit causes for unrest bring to the surface.
Unfortunately the hard learned lessons of industrial relations and group
interaction in large-scale organisations have not so far been applied to
the running of universities where they are much needed. This may result
from basic misconceptions on the part of planners of the changing nature
of universities and of those who study in them.

Why is university thought somehow to be "special" in terms of organisational theories? Why are the social relations within the university
thought to be quantitatively and qualitatively different from those relations which individuals have outside the institution? Obviously there are
special characteristics of the highly selected personnel in terms of the
restricted range of age, intelligence, and educational achievement. But
how homogeneous does this make any university? Is there really mechanical solidarity[4] which persists under all conditions regardless of size of
the total student population and its particular characterisation? The
"melting pot" theories of higher education—so prevalent though only
implicit in so much of university planning—are based upon misinformed
ideas about the nature of social identity and the formation of groups,
and, as the author hopes to show at least in the present study, are challenged by the facts.

These, then, in brief are some of the major issues of interest in higher
education which spring from the whole pattern of changing structural
relationships and which cannot be properly understood outside this
context. It is within this context, therefore, that the research, which forms
the core of this book, is set. It is a study of the effects of expansion of

[1] Caplow, T. and McGee, R., *The Academic Marketplace*, Anchor Books, 1965.

[2] Lipset, S. M. and Wolin, S. S., *The Berkeley Student Revolt*, Doubleday Anchor
Books, 1965; and Gales, K. E., A campus revolution, *BJS*, 1966, **17** (1), 1–19; and,
Glazer, N., The multiversity goes to war, *New Society*, **133**, 26–27.

[3] Ex-Principal of the University College of Rhodesia.

[4] As used by Emile Durkheim. See Durkheim, E., *The Division of Labour in Society*,
Free Press, Glencoe, Ill. (trans. George Simpson), 1964, ch. 2.

educational opportunity in microcosm on the student bodies of three different institutions—on the internal and external relations. These institutions are not in any sense "typical" since no institution of higher education is like any other except in rather superficial ways; there is no such thing as a "typical" institution, but they illustrate the kind of structural features and processes discussed above (all except student protest, which may in itself be significant). The study is also concerned with the interrelation of the processes of overall expansion of educational places and the expansion of educational opportunity among all classes and groups. The first is a precondition of the second, but the second does not follow of necessity from the first. The relative rates at which these processes take place and the conflicting priorities they represent are seen to have ramifications in terms of institutional structure and internal organisation and upon individual experience of life within the university. Explanations are sought in terms of structural principles at work in particular situations in order that the conclusions may have a wider validity in other similarly structured situations. It is hoped that these will be widely applicable if, as Anderson suggests, under the two principal tendencies of expansion in size and progressive democratisation, universities in all lands develop similar features and problems.[1] It is not description of particular places and events which are necessary at the present time, but explanation that will have some predictive value for future occasions. Thus although the turn of events is such that with increasing rapidity educational changes themselves are almost out of date as soon as they are written about, yet it is hoped that general conclusions reached will not readily outdate and will provide a clue to the ways in which changes are taking place.

It is hoped, in addition, that a number of strands in current educational research will be taken up and woven together in a meaningful way. For, naturally, all those social processes mentioned above have been the concern of researchers at various levels of analysis, and in the last two or three years the body of research data has grown apparently according to the laws of geometric progression and shows no sign of a diminishing rate of increase. It is clearly impossible now to cover the whole field, and the brief review of material pertinent to this survey is not intended to be exhaustive but is selective of particular items of direct relevance and interest. Moreover, it is important to point out that much of the work

[1] Anderson, C. A., Common problems for universities, *Int. Rev. Educ.*, 1965, **11** (1), 3–19.

that is now available had not been published when the research was begun and a great deal did not appear until after the whole thing was written up. This will explain why certain questions were asked and not others, and why they were orientated in a particular way. Fortunately most of the work which has come out on certain points covered by the original thesis supports its conclusions. Where possible recent evidence is included in the text; more often it appears in footnotes. In this chapter it is hoped to take cognisance at least of the major contributions to the field. The bibliography has also been brought up to date—to the end of 1969.

From the discussion of tendencies for structural change inherent in developing educational systems it will be clear that there are various main areas of interest for the sociologist searching for structural explanations and their meaning for those acting within the situation. Each area is, of course, capable of being broken down into further areas of investigation, and the emphasis in any social context will be placed differently, depending on the culture-filter of the observer and his standpoint in relation to the policy decisions of controlling groups.

The main structural dilemmas or questions to be solved would seem to be:

(a) What is to be taught in order to equip future citizens with knowledge, skills, and techniques necessary for the continuance and development of the social order? This is the concern of educationists interested in the mechanics of teaching, content of curricula, form of institutions, and levels of specialisation.

(b) Who is to teach these different kinds of skills and levels of specialisation? Supply and training of teachers—education of the educators.

(c) How are individuals to be selected for different kinds and levels of education if "education", and especially "higher education", are scarce resources in any society? What are the social and academic criteria which qualify the individual for a "place" at any stage in the process, that is the way in which higher education as a "scare commodity" is "distributed according to relevant criteria".[1] How is competition to be encouraged or discouraged? How large a proportion of those suitably qualified in each age group will go on to each level of education?

---

[1] Halsey, *op. cit.*

(d) Once educated and trained how are the individuals at each stage in the process to be channelled off and allocated to those occupational and social roles where they can most usefully be employed? What mechanisms, if any, of information, distribution, and co-ordination are necessary?

(e) How are institutions and organisations concerned with education to be run? How are the positions within each organisation to be arranged? What will be the pattern of authority? To what body will they be responsible for their decisions? What kind of social system will each represent?

(f) What will be the social effects of having been through not only a course of education but also of having belonged to a particular educational institution? What will be the socialising role of the institution? What social as well as academic characteristics will be aimed for and/or achieved?

(g) What will be the economic costs and benefits to society of providing various educational facilities and varying degrees of efficiency and of modernising old and out-dated institutions? Who will pay, and how will they pay?

(h) What are the social costs and benefits to society of the educational facilities provided? Is individual opportunity improved or limited within any particular educational system? What is the prevailing ideology with regard to individual development of potential in relation to societal "needs"?

(i) What is the relation between the family and the educational process? How much choice should parents have in the education of their children? Will special choices be catered for? How much compulsion can the State use upon the family in the matter of education of children?

It is clear that these questions touch upon the economic, political, legal, religious, and welfare organisation with which education is intimately concerned, and that educational policies on the grand scale which embrace all these issues require formulations based on a series of philosophical and moral and ethical considerations. They reflect ideas not only about the nature of education, but also about the nature of society. And, indeed, the philosophy of education is less a separate area of thought than one which in terms of providing guide-lines for practical decisions is intimately interrelated with all other areas. However, such are the experiences of everyday life, the fragmentary and day-to-day basis on which many pragmatic decisions on educational policy perforce are made, that very rarely do educational systems reflect any overall plan or overall philosophy.

It is clear that the study of the *selection* and *allocation* functions of education is of more than purely academic interest—it is of practical interest to society and to those who seek to shape its future, and is central to the issue discussed above. And for this very reason it is one in which it is very easy to "take sides" and to become embroiled in heated arguments about the values guiding the formation of social policy—either in response to particular and present problems or with some long-term goal in view.

> But are we planning with some ultimate end in view, or are we engaged in a sparring match with each new economic, technological or social problem as it comes along, using education only as a means of satisfying immediate needs— the provision of nuclear scientists, for instance, or capable Russian linguists.[1]

Interminable debates about the "ultimate end" of education, if such there is, may sometimes obscure the researcher's real task of objective analysis. It is equally true that awareness of the problems of values inherent in his study may heighten his insight and sharpen his reasoning— though not always so. In general it is the sociologist's task explicitly to steer clear of debates on "social justice" and "ultimate ends", and one which in the study of education is most difficult to do.

In any study of education and of educational selection it is only too easy to confuse observations of what happens with what *ought* to happen. However, since ultimately all education is concerned with values and with the intergenerational transmission of values, it is necessary to be aware that the dividing line between studies which are concerned primarily with values embodied in the workings of the educational machinery and those which are not is indeed a thin one, and often almost imperceptibly crossed. The sociologist particularly is constantly aware that in a sense any investigation of higher education which is not totally divorced from practical realities implies some judgement or cultural interpretation of what is considered "just" or "efficient" or "profitable" or "beneficial", and that none of these interpretations should become a built-in assumption of any "scientific" analysis. This is especially true when one deals with concepts such as "expansion of educational opportunity"— which in themselves imply a whole wealth of social judgements.

[1] Castle, E. B., *Ancient Education and Today*, Penguin, 1962, p. 204.

While acknowledging that these arguments do exist and are of immediate interest, the author proposes not to consider them in this book. Debates about the aims and purposes of education in a way which can only hinder the progress of "sociological analysis" are better left to educational theorists and administrators, who may draw from empirical research which illustrations they choose.

> Ultimately the argument is one about values and their priorities. At this level we may never reach agreement; there is as Tawney said 'no argument with the choice of a soil'; but in practice we may never need to face each other with these passionate abstractions. Certainly we can start with the facts.[1]

However, what are the facts? Certainly as far as the pattern of decisions goes there seems no overall consistency, no unifying reference point which could give us the clue to the understanding of educational phenomena. Changes are made, for instance, in one area of the educational system only to be found to have affected willy-nilly other areas of the system which, in turn, demand further attention and adjustment. Thus rather than the whole mechanism receiving a complete overhaul in response to changing social conditions and changing societal values, there is a tendency to "tinker about" with the system and unwittingly to throw it out of gear.

One effect which is influencing students greatly is the lack of articulation between the educational system and the occupational structure, which results in problems of allocation of graduates in the job market. In the United States particularly it was estimated that the supply of college graduates after 1965 exceeded the demand for them.[2] Students, of course, are aware of their dimming social and occupational prospects and are led to ask "What are we being educated *for*?" So far no one has given a convincing answer—and, as every historian knows, nothing is more conducive to rebellion and revolution than a lot of free-floating, uncommitted, out-of-work academics.

2. Educational Changes and Educational Research in Britain and the United States

It is beyond the scope of this discussion to examine in detail the historical differences and developments in Britain and the United States which have resulted in the contemporary educational systems. It must suffice to

[1] Halsey, *op. cit.*, p. 13.
[2] Havighurst and Neugarten, *op. cit.*, p. 112.

make some remarks about some of the more important developments which are directly related to the expansion of educational opportunity. As has been already noted the English system particularly (excluding Scottish) has been traditionally élitist in its selection of individuals for higher education, whereas the "mass" orientations of the United States system found their origin in the large numbers of parochial and community colleges established during the seventeenth, eighteenth, and nineteenth centuries, during which time "American colleges were conceived and operated as pillars of the locally established church, political order, and social conventions".[1] American institutions of higher education have been founded to serve a broad base of the population, and were intended thus from their inception. By contrast, in England before the beginning of the nineteenth century there were only two universities—and those the prerogative of "gentlemen"—Oxford and Cambridge. Scotland, with a proportionately smaller population, had already four universities by the end of the sixteenth century—Glasgow, St. Andrews, Aberdeen, and Edinburgh—but did not acquire more until the twentieth century. The technologically orientated universities of the industrial north of England, which began to recruit students on a broader social base than the "ancient" universities, and which owed their establishment to the late-flowering of civic pride engendered by the Industrial Revolution, had to wait for their beginnings until the early twentieth century (and therefore named like their grimy, urban surroundings "Redbrick"). Meanwhile, in the United States, already by the nineteenth century, most of the religious and culture groups

> felt impelled to set up their own colleges, both to perpetuate their distinctive subculture and to give it legitimacy in the larger society. By 1900 there were special colleges for Baptists and Catholics, for men and women, for whites and blacks, for rich and not so rich, for North and South, for small town and big city, for adolescents and adults, for engineers and teachers.[2]

These colleges may be distinguished from certain eighteenth-century colleges which served, as in England, a relatively unified establishment, and were consequently more élitist. Examples of such latter colleges are the prestigious Harvard and Yale, founded in colonial times under the influence of a "mixture of sectarian and geographic considerations"[3]. Although

[1] Jencks, C. and Riesman, D., *The Academic Revolution*, Doubleday, New York, 1968, p. 1.
[2] *Ibid.*, p. 3.
[3] *Ibid.*, p. 156.

many local colleges such as Harvard and Yale have become national and even international in their outlook, "localism" and geographic isolation has always been a feature built into the American educational system in which "ever since colonial times states and cities have been unhappy about depending on colleges located beyond their physical and cultural boundaries".[2] One might say, therefore, that whereas the British educational system has been characterised by horizontal stratification, the American system has been characterised by vertical stratification—and that the blocks to mobility inherent therein are still being experienced.

Further features of the two systems should be briefly mentioned. In Britain although universities enjoy highest prestige there are, of course, teacher training colleges which grew out of a nineteenth-century demand for teachers to man the emerging elementary schools, while colleges of advanced technology are a product of the post-war period demand for technologists. "Their origins are to be found, however, in the extensive network of technical colleges which were established to meet the vocational training needs of an earlier period."[2] These institutions, along with art colleges, vocational and professional colleges which offer advanced courses, are the main sources of higher education whose structure has developed piecemeal.

> The universities, established by Royal Charter, retain the greatest measure of autonomy. They are independent of the Ministry of Education but receive public funds from the Treasury through the University Grants Committee. They are virtually free to determine their own admissions policies and to teach what they wish in a manner they think fit. Increases in the proportion of funds coming from public funds may, of course, affect traditional concepts of academic freedom.[3]

In the United States system one important distinction has been between the public and private institutions of higher education.

> Broadly speaking these differences could be attributed to differences in the sources of support of public and private institutions. Public institutions relied primarily on tax subsidies, and therefore had an interest in serving as many different kinds of students as possible and creating the broadest possible sympathy for their claims on the public purse. Private non-sectarian institutions which

---

[1] *Ibid.*, p. 153.

[2] Lauwerys, J. A., United Kingdom: England and Wales, in UNESCO *Access to Higher Education*, vol. 2, National Studies, UNESCO and International Assoc. of Univ., 1965, p. 505.

[3] *Ibid.*, p. 506.

relied heavily on individual gifts were concerned less with the number of their supporters than with their affluence.[1]

However, now that both public and private universities get substantial portions of their budgets from the federal government there has been a blurring of stylistic and programming differences while "the academic profession has been able to exercise far more control over federal funds than it ever did over state or private ones".[2] For the student one of the most important differences between public and private institutions is the cost to him of his education. Although fees for public higher education may be small or nominal, fees at many private colleges are prohibitive— and the trend is clearly upward. The situation with regard to scholarships will be discussed later, but in general the financial barriers to higher education are much higher in the United States than in Britain, where most students except the well-to-do are financed completely by their local education authority.

In the United States, therefore, institutions of higher education have traditionally covered a wide spectrum of local and national interests, social origins of students, selection procedures and fees while providing a large number of places for growing sections of the population. The system is characterised by its heterogeneity. In Britain, on the contrary, institutions have catered for a select social élite until the beginning of the twentieth century and have been relatively homogeneous in their structural characteristics and social origins of students, with limited places reserved for a favoured few. It is characteristic, therefore, that in Britain the first moves to educational expansion represented a lifting of some of the financial constraints which kept gifted sons of workers out of college, with expansion of places coming later.[3] In the United States expansion of places has been going on for decades while increase in financial aid to students and growth in number of scholarships is largely a feature of the last 20 years. The following diagram will illustrate the way in which underlying structural differences are expressed in the way in which barriers to opportunity are defined.

[1] Jencks, C. and Riesman, D., *op. cit.*, p. 267.

[2] *Ibid.*, p. 268.

[3] The most recent move in this direction is the setting up of the Open University of the Air which will start in Jan. 1971 with Dr. Walter Perry as its Vice-Chancellor. First courses will take up to 25,000 students and will hopefully attract working-class students who earlier missed their chance.

BRITAIN   *Contribution to expansion*   THE UNITED STATES
                 of opportunity.

Proportionately fewer   −   **+** Proportionately

University places for age group   University places for age group

                    +
Higher education largely free   Higher education largely expensive

This diagram shows two main positive and negative forces working out in the expansion of educational opportunity and which clearly affect which social groups are under- or overrepresented. Not surprisingly, although the American system is more "democratic", certain similarities of the English system in class bias do emerge which will be discussed later.

In the light of these remarks let us first look at some recent changes in British and American education which have had widespread impact on both the expansion of numbers and the expansion of places.

It was mentioned in the first section that many policy decisions about the different levels are made piecemeal in an attempt to tinker about with the system. We see this clearly in the British case, where, after a long period of socially segregated education at all levels,[1] the need was seen for changes in secondary education in 1944,[2] changes in higher education in 1963,[3] and this in turn in 1965 led to a need for changes in secondary education again,[4] and latterly, in 1967, for changes right back in primary education.[5] The "supply" of qualified personnel at each stage is clearly regulated by what happens at previous stages *some time before*—but this is not always realised in time to prevent gaps and stoppages appearing at certain points. Therefore what happens is not always related to what is sup-

[1] Peterson, A. D. C., *A Hundred Years of Education,* Gerald Duckworth and Co. Ltd., London, 1952, p. 122.

[2] 1944 Education Act, published in *Chitty's Annual Statutes,* J. Burke, vol. 38, 7 and 8 George VI, part I, no. 8.

[3] *Higher Education, loc. cit.*

[4] Newsom Report, Ministry of Education, *Half Our Future,* a report of the Central Advisory Council for Education (England), HMSO, 1963, SO 27–361.

[5] Plowden Report: Dept. of Education and Science, *Children and their Primary School,* a report of the Central Advisory Council for Education (England), HMSO, 1967, SO 27–401.

posed to happen or what is planned, and reflects a lack of predictive power among policy makers.

Nevertheless, it is important for the sociologist to compare the blueprint, as it were, with what actually happens in order to seek the underlying reasons for convergence to or divergence from what was intended. In the study of the expansion of educational opportunity in three British universities it is important first of all to consider the implications of the 1944 Education Act, which was the first step towards removing social inequalities in secondary and consequently higher education, and which now is "the statutory and legal basis of education in England and Wales".[1]

The provisions of the Act were based on educational theories and policies which had been formulated to meet some of the practical and longstanding problems of education between the wars, and of these the Hadow (1926), the Spens (1938), and the Norwood (1943) reports related most directly to post-primary education. Changes in secondary education had to wait upon changes in the social structure.[2]

The Act, which at last brought together into a coherent pattern the three stages of education—primary, secondary, and further—provided free compulsory education for everyone up to the age of 15 years, and in Holmes's words "superficially, at least, implied the most radical changes in every sphere of English education".[3] By making available to all those of sufficient ability, a high school or grammar school education, it theoretically threw open the universities to the most gifted members of every social class. The kind of education which until then had been the prerogative of the "privileged classes"[4] of title and wealth was, with the exception of that provided by the "independent" public and private fee-paying schools, to be enjoyed by all who should prove themselves academically to deserve it, irrespective of social origins or economic means.[5]

Local education authorities, from whose rates the new secondary schools, like the existing primary ones, were to be financed, were instructed by the Act:

[1] Lauwerys, *op. cit.*, p. 495.

[2] Banks, O., *Parity and Prestige in English Secondary Education*, Routledge and Kegan Paul, London, 1955.

[3] Holmes, B., *Problems in Education: A Comparative Approach*, Internat. Lib. of Sociol. and Soc. Reconst., Routledge and Kegan Paul, 1965, p. 226.

[4] Peterson, *op. cit.*, ch. 6.

[5] Of course those parents who wish to pay for their children's education may do so. In 1960 6·5 per cent of the pupils in school at the age of 14 were in the private sector; cf. Lauwerys, *op. cit.*, p. 500.

To secure provisions of primary and secondary schools sufficient in number, character and equipment to afford for all pupils opportunities for education offering such variety of instruction and training as may be desirable in view of their differing ages, abilities, and aptitudes, and of the different periods for which they may be expected to remain at school, including practical instruction and training appropriate to their respective needs.[1]

Ideally, education was in all cases to be suited to the recipient. This is a state of affairs which is difficult to achieve in practice. E. B. Castle says that "The Education Act of 1944 recognises the fundamental inequalities in children by making provision for the best kind of *appropriate* education for all, although, of course, we are far from achieving this. Nevertheless, in theory, at least, both fundamental equalities and fundamental inequalities are recognised."[2] It is the fundamental inequalities which have caused growing concern, particularly in terms of the far-reaching consequences of selection made at 11-plus for the tripartite secondary system, in which "half our future" is branded as failure. The tripartite system is now being slowly replaced by "comprehensive" education.[3] However it has been noted by some writers that comprehensive schools conceal rather than eliminate social selection.[4]

These "fundamental equalities and fundamental inequalities" are those which form the basis for so much research into higher education, and yet as Halsey and Floud say,

The emphasis in investigation has shifted in recent years from study of the material disabilities traditionally underlying these inequalities to attempts on the one hand to identify social factors impinging on the intellectual development of individuals, and on the other hand, to explore the social and cultural circumstances affecting their attainment or performance at a given level of ability.[5]

The 1944 Act applied only to England, Wales, and Monmouthshire since differences in the Scottish educational system made a uniform application of the Act impracticable. In 1945 the Education (Scotland) Act was passed and was put into operation in 1946. This Act was in many respects

[1] Education Act, 1944,
[2] Castle, *op. cit.*, p. 201.
[3] These changes signify an attempt to move from a multiple-track school system towards the kind of single-track system found in the United States where a majority of pupils follow the track that can lead to University. In Britain the majority still are shunted off to other tracks at preceding stages.
[4] Jackson, B., *Streaming*, Routledge, 1964; Pedley, R., *The Comprehensive School*, Penguin, Revised Edition, 1969; Ford, J., *Social Class and the Comprehensive School*, Routledge & Kegan Paul, 1969.
[5] Halsey *et al.*, *op. cit.*, *Education*, 1961, intro., p. 7.

a direct parallel of the English Act and was based like it on the principle of providing free secondary education for all. It differs, however, in various details of its application to the Scottish system as, for instance, in that provision is made for certain types of fee-paying schools which do not exist in the English educational system.

> In general the education provided in public schools and junior colleges was to be without payment of fees, but the customary proviso allowing the retention of a limited number of fee-paying primary and secondary schools by local authorities was continued under the control of the Department. This was in direct contrast to the policy in England where only direct-grant schools were permitted to continue charging fees and it seems to imply that Scottish democracy is less suspect where educational provision is concerned.[1]

It is inappropriate here to compare the English and Scottish educational systems, but it is important to note at this point that they are different and result from different historical processes, and this presumably affects what happens at university level. Differences now are slight compared with what they were, and, as Knox says: "It would appear that Scotland which had a national system of education when England was groping in the dark, has been marking time or even falling behind;"[2] yet it is clear that people who are products of different systems of education, even within the framework of a territorial unit such as the United Kingdom, must of necessity differ in certain cultural respects.

If seen as part of a developing process long underway the effects of the 1944 Education Act become more understandable. It is now 25 years since the 1944 Act, and those who have benefited from it have not long been passing through the universities. It is about now that the effects of the Act should be beginning to be felt both in education and in society at large, for the "service of the University activity to man is not restricted to the student who is to be taught but extends directly or indirectly to the whole people".[3] As researchers in all fields have pointed out, it is vital that we should know what these effects are.

The 1944 Act set up the machinery for providing equality of opportunity, and a body of research has been carried out by workers from every discipline to find out how far the ideal is being attained. Halsey has asked: "How far has the 1944 Act redistributed educational opportunity

[1] Knox, H. M., *Two Hundred and Fifty Years of Scottish Education*, Oliver & Boyd, Edinburgh, 1953, p. 230.

[2] *Ibid.*, p. 242.

[3] Peterson, *op. cit.*, p. 192, quotes *Report of German Commission on University Reform*, 1949.

between social strata?"[1] Jackson and Marsden say: "Everyone working in this field knows that since 1944 there has been a shift in middle class education, and no one has altogether defined it."[2] D. V. Glass says that, "So far as social stratification is concerned," the Act is probably the most important measure of the last half century. "However, no central provision was made to ascertain the social consequences of this great expansion of educational opportunity—its effects upon the existing middle classes for example and the formation of new élites."[3]

A further development in higher education which increased opportunity for the working class was the establishment of a system of grants by local education authorities after the Second World War. "Before the war it was accepted that only exceptionally gifted students should be educated at public expense," and competitive scholarships offered by the universities themselves, state scholarships, and teaching bursaries offered by the Ministry of Education were the main sources of finance for poor students.[4] Some local education authorities made awards on the promise to teach. After the war and the beginning of the impact of the 1944 Education Act, the local education authorities took over the major function of providing bursaries and scholarships for students who had won a place at a college. Local authorities may still, however, make their own conditions, and in an attempt to review the situation a national committee was set up—the Anderson Committee, which reported in 1960.

More recently in the United States the Higher Education Act of 1965 was designed to improve the situation of financial support for students, and "placed the federal government squarely in the position of the major resource for student support".[5] The federal government came into the student assistance field in 1959 with loans under the National Defense Education Act. The Economic Opportunity Act of 1964 established government finance for employment in a work-study programme or socially useful projects. The federal government had provided stipends or scholarships for certain categories of graduate students since about 1955.

[1] Halsey, A. H., Education and mobility. Talk on BBC Third Programme, 10 April 1963.

[2] Jackson, B. and Marsden, D., *Education and the Working Class* (Inst. of Community Studies), Routledge and Kegan Paul, 1962, p. 9.

[3] Glass, D. V. (ed.), *Social Mobility in Britain*, Routledge and Kegan Paul, London, 1954, p. 4.

[4] Lauwerys, *op. cit.*, p. 549.

[5] Havighurst and Neugarten, *op. cit.*, p. 116.

Once fully operative the new scholarship programme will aid about 140,000 students. If one takes into account *all* forms of financial assistance, the estimated percentage of full-time undergraduate students receiving aid was 24 per cent in 1963 and 30 per cent in 1966.[1] Congress anticipated that the new undergraduate scholarships would help students who would not otherwise attend college—intellectually able but financially poor; but the effects of this are not yet known. If the situation mirrors the impact of the British 1944 Act perhaps the scholarships will largely continue to assist middle-class youth.

Of course any change in social origins from which students are drawn, or lack of change, has to be seen within the whole context of overall expansion of places in higher education in the two countries. As has already been noted, there has been a tremendous boom in the field of higher education which has affected every aspect of its social, institutional, and organisational structure. There has been *overall* expansion of places but not *overall* expansion of opportunity. Indeed, in both Britain and the United States, expansion has hardly kept up with the increased demand created by changes in the birth rate and in proportion of students staying on and qualifying from high school. In Britain between 1950 and 1960 the number of high school students staying on until 17 years or over nearly doubled, for instance, while in 1961 there were an average nine applications for every place in universities.[2] In the United States, "if the proportion of young people in college is not reduced between 1965 and 1970 the colleges must expand at least 30 per cent".[3] New institutions are being set up all the time to cope with the insurge as well as by the expansion of existing institutions. Proof of the comparatively smaller size of British colleges lies in the fact that there are now approximately 800 institutions of higher and further education in Britain[4] compared with 2200 in the United States.

Given the nature of the educational systems—their relative selectivity, number of places, and financial provisions for students—there were until the mid-1950's certain assumptions underlying policy decisions in both countries which research evidence began to refute. In Britain in the

---

[1] Havighurst and Neugarten, *op. cit.*, p. 116.

[2] Lauwerys, *op. cit.*, p. 517.

[3] Havighurst and Neugarten, *op. cit.*, p. 115.

[4] Of these in 1969 there were 36 universities and university-type institutions in England, 5 federated colleges of the University of Wales, 7 Scottish universities and 2 in Northern Ireland. *Stats. of Educ.*, Vol. 6, *op. cit.*

early 1950's—after the effects of the 1944 Education Act were beginning to be felt and at the threshold of university expansion—it was assumed that equality of educational opportunity was virtually a reality. In the United States it was assumed it was already a reality, embedded in a democratic system. These assumptions resulted from the premiss that there is a direct relationship between provision of places and equality of opportunity. Evidence from research in both countries refutes this assumption, and reveals the intervention of a whole array of cultural and evironmental factors which intervene in the processes of application and selection to enhance or depress the chances of members of particular subgroups in the population—socioeconomic, racial, religious, and geographical—with, in addition, an inevitable sex bias.

Studies carried out in Britain since the 1950's, particularly in the field of grammar school education, have shown that the educational system "has been sluggish in its response to the Act, and that opportunity can no longer be narrowly defined in the pre-Act terms of provision of places. It became clear that although there was theoretically a random relation between grammar school places and the social class of those gaining places, in practice the proportions of places were definitely graded between the social classes." Indeed, with reference to university education, to quote Little and Westergaard, "the social class composition of the student body in the universities has remained roughly the same during the past three to five decades—this despite expansion, maintenance grants for students, and the changes which occurred in secondary school provision".[1]

This surprising fact has drawn the attention of researchers to reasons for "drop-out" at various stages and the *continuing* effects of social selection even at the higher levels. It had previously been tacitly assumed that at the higher levels of education, where competition of ability was paramount, the influence of social class and family environment mattered less and less. This was proved not to be so by, for instance, the studies of Glass[2] and Kellsall[3] in Britain, and more recently Sewell and Shah[4]

[1] Little, A. and Westergaard, The trend in class differentials in educational opportunity in England and Wales, *BJS*, December 1964, **15** (4).

[2] Glass, *op. cit.*

[3] Kelsall, R. K., *Report on an Enquiry into Applications for Admission to Universities*, Assoc. of Univs. of British Commonwealth, London, 1957.

[4] Sewell, W. H. and Shah, V. P., Socio-economic status, intelligence and the attainment of higher education, Paper presented to the Research Group on Sociology of Education at Sixth World Congress of the Internat. Sociological Assoc., Evian, France, September 1966.

in the United States. Studies in other countries, mentioned later, corroborate this evidence of class differentials at university level, and in turn shatter the myth of the relative homogeneity of the student body.

Estimates of the proportion of working-class students in British universities are (Kelsall) 25 per cent and (Glass) 26 per cent, and studies of particular institutions like those by Marris[1] and Zweig[2] put the proportion in certain civic universities at not much higher than 30 per cent. Since the 1961 census showed 65 per cent of adult males in Britain in manual occupations,[3] this shows a distinct imbalance in social class opportunity in education, and other evidence supports this. Kelsall showed that 1 in every 4 of the non-manual middle-class children who entered a grammar school type course at 11 eventually went on to a university but only 1 in 15 to 1 in 20 of the grammar school entrants from unskilled working-class homes did so. Disparities later on are mainly noticeable among girls, although inequalities in sex are not important until the sixth form. Then disparity between the social classes widens down the social scale, for the resources necessary for the working-class child to overcome obstacles on the way to a university place are rarely expended on a girl. An unskilled manual worker's daughter has a chance of 1 in 500–600 of entering a university and a 100 times lower than a girl of the professional class.[4]

Further data was given on this point by the Robbins Report (1963). The report uses some of the pre-war data for brief comparison of access to universities then and now for the last 30 years. The startling evidence shows that university entrance in 1960 compared with earlier years indicates no increase in the working-class share. The proportion of children from non-manual homes reaching courses of degree level is about eight times as high as the proportion for manual homes. Commenting on these facts, Little and Westergaard say: "It is likely that qualified working class sixth formers rather more often than those from middle class homes fail either to seek or to obtain entry to Universities and go instead to technical colleges, training colleges, or directly into the

---

[1] Marris, P., *The Experience of Higher Education*, Routledge and Kegan Paul, London, 1964.

[2] Zweig, F., *The Student in the Age of Anxiety—A Survey of Oxford and Manchester Students*, Heinemann, 1963.

[3] *Census 1961: Eng. & Wales. Occupational Tables*, HMSO, London, 1966, table 27, pp. 195–7.

[4] Little and Westergaard, *op. cit.*

labour market."[1] Since it has so often been shown that it is cultural differences rather than purely economic underprivilege which influences educational achievement, it is small wonder that a number of writers suggest that it is the lower middle-class children who are beginning to flood into the universities rather than children of the working class. Now that financial restraints are removed it is those who aspire to higher education and whose culture patterns are congruent with it who are able most to benefit from university expansion.

T. H. Marshall had made this same point 12 years earlier when after remarking of places in grammar school that "it may look at first as if the bourgeoisie had, as usual, filched what should have gone to the workers", he says: "And since the [middle-class] children were backed by a better educational tradition and stronger parental support because most of their families could afford to forgo earnings of the children because they came from more comfortable homes, where it was easier to work, and from smaller families, were certain to be more successful."[2]

Corroborative evidence from the United States derived from a number of studies shows that, for instance, in 1960 only 29 per cent of the working-class youth entered college compared with 50 per cent of the lower middle class and 80 per cent of the upper and upper middle class.[3]

Of course, we must always examine the particular institutions, for it is clear that any expansion that occurs will be felt quite differently by different institutions, and that as a result the social class composition of institutions of higher education will vary. For instance it is increasingly remarked that the aspirations of students of different social classes are expressed in terms of applications for different kinds of institutions of higher education. One study of Sandford, Couper, and Griffin[4] investigates student motivation to higher education in the light of home background. This survey of Bristol College of Science and Technology compared its social composition with that of Nottingham University and found 55 per cent of the total student population were children of the Registrar-General's class III, IV, and V compared with Nottingham's 34 per cent. The authors attribute differences in class composition to differing de-

---

[1] Little and Westergaard, *op. cit.*

[2] Marshall, T. H., Social selection in the welfare state, *Eugenics Review*, 1953, **45** (2).

[3] Havighurst and Neugarten, *op. cit.*, p. 98, table 4.1.

[4] Sandford, C. T., Couper, M. E., and Griffin, S., Class influences in higher education, *Brit. J. Educ. Psych.*, June 1965, **35** (2).

grees of support of parents for higher education and the lack of confidence of working-class sixth-formers in applying for university. The "working class parents emphasised the view of the importance of job training" and thought that life and work in a CAT or tech. was not so incompatible with working-class life. This is only one example of the enduring influence of social class *values* and their expression in educational and mobility patterns even in times of growth of educational opportunity and material affluence.

Indeed, it is studies like this which suggest that expansion of educational opportunity is taking place but that its effects are not being seen in the universities as yet. It is other institutions of higher education like CATs, technical colleges and teacher training colleges, which are netting those first-generation students of the working class that the universities have long been awaiting. In a sense the structure which emerges is reminiscent of the hierarchy of universities and colleges in the United States—from the Ivy League down to the smallest local college—which represent a wide variety of social and academic standards, but not necessarily corresponding exactly with the "image" or ranking on the scale of student aspirations. This kind of hierarchy of institutions, however based, is symptomatic of other ramifications of the move to expansion and democratisation, where grades appear *within* the system which was previously more homogeneous in its provisions. This in itself may give rise to inequalities in opportunity, particularly in certain areas of provision. Increased provision of places does not mean increased equality of educational opportunity, and this is being realised at length by the universities. Little and Westergaard point out that:

> The widening of the educational provisions does not by itself reduce social inequalities in educational opportunity; it does so only if the expanding facilities are made proportionately *more* accessible to those children previously least able to take advantage of them. To some extent this has happened. Conclusions concerning reductions in class differentials will thus be conditioned by the relative weight one attaches to the proportion achieving, as opposed to the proportion who fail to achieve, selective secondary school education. But even on the more favourable basis the reduction is neither very large nor a unique phenomenon of the 1944 Act.[1]

Two recent comparative studies of specific universities mentioned earlier add more information to the analysis of the social class composition

---

[1] Little and Westergaard, *op. cit.*

of universities. Both Zweig (1963)[1] and Marris (1964),[2] although discussing
student life and culture in general, give figures on social class background
of students interviewed. Although in Zweig's case the sample of Oxford
and Manchester could hardly be called representative, it is interesting to
compare them with Marris's figures from Cambridge, Leeds, and Southampton universities and Northampton College of Technology. In both
cases social class is based on parental occupation. The sizes of the sample
involved—102 (Oxford), 103 (Manchester), 112 (Cambridge), 86 (Leeds),
96 (Southampton), and 92 (Northampton)—are clearly rather too
small from which to draw conclusions about general trends. A table, in
which the author puts the various findings together, is presented as
Table 1.1.

TABLE 1.1. SOCIAL CLASS BASED ON PARENTAL OCCUPATION (per cent)[3]

Social class	C'bridge	Oxford	Leeds	M'chester	N'ton	S'ton
UMC[4] profes-sional	75	80	45	48	45	32
LMC white collar	15	13	25	21	25	36
WkC manual	8	9	30	33	30	30
Not known	2	—	—	—	—	2
TOTAL	100	102	100	102	100	100

Despite the size of samples some amazing similarities emerge between
certain of the universities. As one might expect, Oxford and Cambridge
appear as the most upper middle-class universities. Then follows the
redbrick northern universities of Leeds and Manchester, corresponding
in composition to Northampton CAT. Rather surprisingly, Southampton
University stands on its own. Given, then, that there is no real "national"
level of expansion of educational opportunity and that different regions
and institutions will exhibit quite different tendencies and class composition, one is left with the question as to why and how this should happen

[1] Zweig, *op. cit.*
[2] Marris, *op. cit.*
[3] Marris, *op. cit.*, p. 185, table 1, and Zweig, *op. cit.*, p. 11 and p. 93 (combined).
[4] The following abbreviations are used; WkC, working class; LMC, lower middle
class; MMC middle middle class; UMC upper middle class; UC, upper class.

and how the different social class composition affects differently the different institutions and student culture: this question neither author attempts to answer. It is a question which the present book investigates.

In that both books deal primarily with total student culture they will be discussed again later. Suffice to say at this stage that the general working-class share of university places standing at 30 per cent does not represent the great influx that was expected.

A study for an unpublished B.Ed. thesis by McDonald in Glasgow (1964) goes even further to show that "the general pattern of class representation as seen in the present samples has changed little in the fifty year period (1910–1960), certainly not sufficiently to be statistically significant".[1] McDonald took three samples from university records of matriculated students in 1910, 1934, and 1960 and classified them according to the Registrar-General's classification of occupations. Although he admits that he had difficulty in weighting samples and in allowing for the changing status of occupations, he comes up with the interesting finding that the size of the working class in the university had remained at around 30 per cent for 50 years. The only marked changes which had gone on were in the professional and white-collar classes—the former having shrunk slightly and the latter expanded to compensate—again a small sign of the advantage taken by the lower middle class.

If these figures can be relied upon they would seem to point to the fact that in the institutions mentioned at least, the 1944 Act has hardly begun to take effect yet, and that overall expansion has been felt equally by the classes, so that differentials remain: this despite the fact that Zweig, Marris, and McDonald all put the working-class percentage as higher than the 25 per cent estimated by Kelsall.

It is at this point that one asks whether the same thing is being measured in each case. In the British case the system has always tended to be élitist; in the United States, moving forward to a more universal experience of higher education, it has long been assumed that inequalities which do exist in educational opportunity are slight and will disappear in time, and that this is true particularly at the higher levels. "Consequently, studies of college plans and college attendance have noted the relatively great influence of socio-economic status, while those of college

[1] McDonald, I. J., Educational opportunity at University level in Scotland assessed in the light of a comparison of the social origins of a sample of students in the University of Glasgow in the years 1910, 1934 and 1960, unpublished B.Ed. thesis, Glasgow University, 1964, p. 56.

graduation have tended to emphasise the influence of ability."[1] This is the result of the fact, argue Sewell and Shah, that "the aspirations of many cross-pressured individuals (those who are low in status but high in ability or vice-versa) are encouraged by the ideology of equal opportunity and the great diversity of colleges and universities to fit the financial and intellectual capacities of most students."[2]

In discussing the American custom of drop-outs enrolling in another college and eventually graduating, as studied by Eckland,[3] Sewell and Shah make the point "that a student's persistence in his educational pursuit even in the face of academic failure plays an important part in the selective mechanism of the educational system", and that this factor may be influenced by social origins "because a determined student of modest ability but high status can ultimately find an institution where he will not be weeded out; or a student of low socioeconomic status but superior ability may find an institution in which he will be given adequate opportunities and motivation in higher studies".

This point reflects what was said about the hierarchy of institutions earlier except that in Britain a "drop-out" of one institution usually drops out of higher education for good.

At this point it is interesting to discuss a point made earlier about the way in which expansion of educational opportunity will be experienced differently by different institutions because of latent or explicit bias in both applications and selections. Again, one may draw comparisons between the British and American situation.

Let us look first of all at a taxonomy of college types suggested by Havighurst and Neugarten.[4] They outline five main types in relation to admissions policy, tuition fees, "campus life", and social origins of students. These are the Cosmopolitan University, State College, Opportunity College, Ivy College, and Warnell College. The characteristics of these college types are summarised as follows:

1. *Cosmopolitan University.* Large municipal, midwestern or western state; little tuition; liberal admissions but high academic standards; diverse social life, including fraternities and sororities.

---

[1] Sewell and Shah, *op. cit.*, p. 2.

[2] *Ibid.*, p. 2.

[3] Eckland, B. K., Social class and college graduation: some misconceptions corrected, *AJS*, July 1964, **70**, 36–50.

[4] Havighurst and Neugarten, *op. cit.*, pp. 104–7.

2. *State College.* Supported by state or local urban funds; situated diversely; little tuition; often developed liberal arts out of teacher training programme; social life centres on the dormitories and student's union.

3. *Opportunity College.* Several versions; low costs; easy admissions; mediocre academically; draws mobile sons and daughters of working class.

4. *Ivy College.* High status; traditional long-founded colleges; highly selective admissions; sometimes single sex; social life centres on dormitories, clubs, fraternities, and sororities; high academic standards.

5. *Warnell College.* Several hundred of these usually small-town liberal arts; often church related; often culturally homogeneous; some Negro Warnells in south; social life diverse—some fraternities but also variety of other clubs.

Now in order to carry out our comparisons we must also present a taxonomy of British universities and this the author proposes to do. The main types could be classified in a manner which relates to age and character—not an accidental matter in Britain, where the layers of different educational pasts seem to represent different stages in educational policy and philosophy. The suggested seven types are as follows: Oxbridge, Oxbridge Style, Historic Civic, Industrial Civic, Younger Civic, New New, New Old.

Some of the characteristics of these types are:

1. *Oxbridge.* Applies exclusively to Oxford and Cambridge—highest social and academic status; prestigious; élitist; residential; uni-sex colleges.

2. *Oxbridge Style.* Relatively small universities which have certain features of Oxbridge such as residential colleges, history, and traditions; social caché; prestigious but less academically and socially selective than Oxbridge—such as St. Andrews, Durham.

3. *Historic Civic.* This classification covers most of the historic Scottish universities; the various colleges of London University; older civic universities such as Bristol. These universities have both high social

and academic prestige—predominantly the latter, with high admissions standards and high standard of academic excellence. Large in size; mainly non-residential but with halls of residence; situated in large, often historic, cities—even if the university is not historic.

4. *Industrial Civic.* Large universities situated in the centre of industrial cities; usually founded around the turn of the twentieth century; academic reputation usually centred upon particular faculties and departments—often scientific and technological; largely non-residential with some halls of residence; fragmented social life; attract mobile lower middle- and working-class students. Examples are Birmingham, Liverpool, Manchester, Leeds.

5. *Younger Civic.* A variegated group of smallish universities in smallish towns which were either founded well into the twentieth century or were up-graded from university colleges. Exeter and Southampton are examples of this type. Often a high proportion of students in university residences because the town cannot provide sufficient accommodation. University usually dominates small town and has to provide internally all its own entertainment and social life. Social group from medium high to medium low.

6. *New New.* These small but growing universities have alternatively been called "Plasterboard" universities because the speed of building from scratch has necessitated much use of this material (as opposed to the redbrick of the Industrial Civic); or sometimes the "Shakespeare" universities—York, Warwick, Lancaster, Kent, Essex, for instance being names of characters in Shakespeare's plays. Also something of the "historic" flavour has been built into these universities in the manner of "instant tradition". Many are residential, even collegiate, adopting some features of the Oxbridge system both socially and academically; usually situated in the country near historic small market towns; self-contained social unit; attractive campus. Attracts students of high socioeconomic status as alternative to Oxbridge, Oxbridge Style, and Historic Civic. Young faculty; new ideas; reputation for academic innovation and experimentation. Date from beginning 1960's.

7. *New Old.* Very often CATs or colleges of older universities which have been upgraded to university status following the Robbins

Report recommendations. They are therefore instant universities usually with a long and reputable history of technical and liberal arts education; usually set in industrial centres with links with surrounding industry and commerce reflected in practical training for students; non-residential; often high proportion of "local" students who live at home; fragmented social life. Examples of New Old universities would be Strathclyde (RCAT Glasgow), Dundee (College of St. Andrews), Newcastle (King's College, Durham), Salford (CAT), and Bradford (CAT). Will eventually include the new Polytechnics.

This classification is merely a general outline: of course there are "corporate" types in that, for instance, Glasgow would be both Historic Civic and Industrial Civic. Such features we should expect to affect the social class composition of the student body. The reasons *why* members of particular social classes "end up" in particular institutions are a complex mixture of factors in both self-selection and selection by the university or college concerned. "Differential processes of application and selection operate in different institutions and produce a different composition in the student body."[1] These processes we shall discuss in detail later. However, "from the applicants point of view the complexities of the university admissions procedure and the outcome in terms of selection, may sometimes seem like a game of roulette in which chance seems largely to determine the numbers, or candidates, who come up".[2]

We shall discuss in Chapter 5 students' reasons for wanting to attend a particular university as it relates to the particular "image" which different universities project and the kind of reputation which they establish. The hierarchy of social and academic prestige which is developed by and for students may differ from that developed by and for faculty and administrators, but it clearly operates within the self-selection process. Indeed, the hierarchy of institutions may represent a ladder of aspirations which the student will attempt only to a particular rung depending on both his academic and social background. The process works a little differently in the United States where the hierarchy represents for students a financial as well as a social ladder of costs and benefits—an added deterrent to the poor. In Britain grants for the ablest students are nor-

---

[1] Abbott, J., Social effects of university selection, *J. Careers Research Advisory Centre*, Summer 1967, **2** (3), 79.

[2] *Ibid.*, p. 78.

mally tenable at any British university. However, there is, of course, a prevalence of students in the United States participating in the time-honoured custom of "working their way through college", which represents a very gruelling enterprise.

In Britain, selection by the candidate of six universities for his University Central Council of Admissions application form is often undertaken in a state of relative ignorance about the universities concerned. In this situation any "clue" becomes a crucial fact on which to hang one's aspirations—as the results of the present study clearly show. Such a clue is the nature of the town—whether it is historical or industrial, picturesque or grimy.

> Nor is this kind of influence limited to the choice of university—within these universities the choice of particular courses and particular kinds of residence is often undertaken—in the same haze of uncertainty about what these decisions imply. This is particularly true of certain social categories of students: the first generation student who comes from a family where higher education was previously unknown is obviously at a disadvantage with regard to knowing what to expect. His school, and his peers who have gone on to university before him, are his only sources of information on these points. Where these sources are inadequate, his choice in terms of applications will be guided by other than academic reasons.[1]

Yet if the candidate thinks they are good reasons, then they are so for him in the sense that they are meaningful within his frame of reference. Through them we can see the development and internalisation of a university "image" and the way in which this affects the future application patterns of candidates. Although a university "image" influences the application patterns of candidates and in turn the social composition of the student body it may not be based in objective fact. Yet—in that it guides the future action and interaction of those who are selected—it becomes "true" in the nature of a "self-fulfilling prophesy"[2].

Before we go on to mention briefly the ramifications in terms of social class composition in the student body (which is a major concern of the book), perhaps we should mention some work done on different types of student culture which might be expected to characterise the different types of institution.

Clark and Trow identify four main types of college sub-culture: the Academic, Nonconformist, Collegiate, and Vocational, which they

---

[1] *Ibid.*, p. 80.
[2] Merton, R. K., *Social Theory and Social Structure*, Free Press, Glencoe, Ill., 1957, pp. 421–36.

represent as particular combinations of the dimensions of involvement with ideas and identification with college.[1] Although these cultures vary in their emphasis in different institutions, all the forms can be recognised in varying degree. Clark and Trow represent these cultures in the following model:

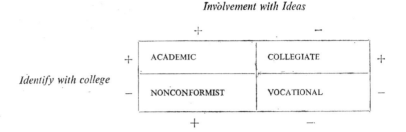

The collegiate subculture is one of sports, dates, fun, and college customs and competition. Extra-curricular activities are paramount, and in the United States are dominated by fraternity and sorority organisation. This subculture usually recruits its most active members from the upper and upper middle classes, for leisure activities are expensive. This subculture flourishes usually only on residential campuses, is compatible with strong college loyalty, but is resistant to involvement with ideas beyond what is necessary to "get through" the course. (The Harvard "Gentleman's C" and the Oxford Fourth Class degree.)

The vocational subculture is one in which students are preoccupied with preparation for jobs, so that "education" becomes instrumental to better paying employment. This subculture recruits most lower class students, particularly "commuter" students and those living at home. The culture is not really coherent, does not produce loyalty to the institution, and does not promote interest in extra-curricular activities (which are only "distractions" from the main goal in hand). Neither does it encourage commitment to academic values beyond what is necessary to pass the course.

The academic subculture is the way of life of the dedicated students who identify with academic concerns of the institution. These students centre their life upon their academic pursuits, spend most time in li-

---

[1] Clark, B. R. and Trow, M., The organisationed context, in Newcomb, T. M. and Wilson, E. K. (eds.), *College Peer Groups*, Chicago, Aldine Publishers, 1966.

braries, laboratories, and seminars, get best grades and talk about courses out of class. They may be regarded with resentment by their less academic fellows. Students in this culture come from every social class and cultural group, but proportionately more of them come from upper middle-class homes of well-educated parents. Such students usually plan to go on to do graduate work.

The nonconformist subculture has many subdivisions of nonconformity. The most prevalent is the nonconforming intellectual who is critical of the "establishment", hostile to the university administration, and some-what detached from the college. Such students are usually "concerned" with ideas raised in class, but even more with current issues in art, liter-ature, and political events. This subculture attracts members from all social backgrounds who strive for distinctiveness by adopting particular styles of dress and speech which may be regarded with disdain by other students—particularly of the "college" subculture.

These, then, are the four main "types" of college subculture which Clark and Trow identify, and which we may relate to our institutional types and status hierarchy previously discussed. We might, for instance, expect to find a preponderance of students belonging to one or two of these subcultures in different institutions depending on social class com-position, residential organisation, physical layout of the campus, history and traditions, and so on. Clark and Trow give us a starting point; but, of course, from that point we have to refine our classification since there are subtypes within each of the types they outline, and students belong to a variety of subcultures which overlap. However, the broad typology does outline for us some of the student concerns which operate to pro-duce student subcultures and institutional "images". These in turn affect applications and self-selection of future students in terms both of aca-demic ability and interests and social class of origin. This is true of higher education in both Britain and the United States.

Indeed, the author now proposes to relate the findings expressed in Table 1.1 above to estimated social class composition of students in various types of higher institutions as expressed by the Havighurst and Neugarten typology presented earlier. Havighurst and Neugarten present the "estimated proportions of young people from different social classes who make up the student bodies in these various types of colleges and universities". These estimates are based on various studies, which like the British studies represented in Table 1.1, were conducted in the early 1960's. The findings are therefore temporally comparable. Examples of the American studies are Clark, 1960;[1] Sanford, 1962;[2] Berdie *et al.*, 1962;[3] Astin, 1964.[4]

Havighurst and Neugarten present a composite picture of their findings utilising their five "types" of college.[5] Although the comparisons must of necessity be tentative, the author will present material from Table 1.1 under the heading of the British university types outlined above in order to give some idea of cross-cultural similarities and dissimilarities in the two educational systems.

The composite table is presented as Table 1.2. Ivy College is compared with Oxbridge; Warnell College is compared with Oxbridge Style universities and some younger civic universities (on which we have no British data here); Cosmopolitan University is compared with Historic Civic University (on which we have no British data here—but see Chapter 4); State College is compared with Industrial Civic; and Opportunity College is compared with British College of Advanced Technology.

One may take these comparisons too far, but the figures and estimates would suggest that in the élitist institutions—Ivy and Oxbridge—in both countries there is a very similar kind of social selection going on which results in similar class composition. The State University of the United

TABLE 1.2. (A) THREE INSTITUTIONAL TYPES COMPARED (per cent)

Social class	Ivy	Oxbridge	State	Indus Civic	Opp. Coll.	CAT
UC & UMC	75	78	20	46	5	45
LMC	20	14	50	23	40	25
WkC	5	8	30	31	55	30
TOTAL	100	100	100	100	100	100

[1] Clark, B. R., *The Open Door College: A Case Study*, McGraw-Hill Book Co., New York, 1960.

[2] Sanford, N. (ed.), *The American College: A Psychological and Social Interpretation of Higher Learning*, John Wiley, New York, 1962.

[3] Berdie, R. F., Layton, W. C., Hageniah, T., and Swanson, E. D., *Who Goes to College?* Minnesota Studies in Student Personnel Work, No. 12, Minneapolis, University of Minnesota Press, 1962.

[4] Astin, A. W., Some characteristics of student bodies entering higher educational institutions, *J. Educ. Psychol.*, 1964, **55**, 267–75.

[5] Havighurst and Neugarten, *op. cit.*, p. 107, table 4.2.

TABLE 1.2 (*cont.*)
(B) ADDITIONAL UNITED STATES INSTITUTIONAL TYPES (per cent)

Social class	Cosmopolitan University	Warnell College
UC & UMC	30	40
LMC	45	50
WkC	25	10
TOTAL	100	100

States and the Industrial Civic University of Britain are very similar in the proportion of working-class students (30 per cent vs. 31 per cent) but there are nearly twice as many lower middle-class students in the State University as in the Industrial Civic, suggesting an increase of opportunity in the United States situation. The difference is more marked at the level of Opportunity College and College of Advanced Technology—the latter being as biased in its social composition as the Industrial Civic. As has been pointed out before, however, the Opportunity College in the United States represents a real expansion of opportunity for children of the working and lower middle classes. Opportunity College obviously has no direct British equivalent. If we look at the figures in Table 1.2(B) in addition, we see that apart from Opportunity College nowhere does the working-class proportion reach more than 31 per cent of the student body—which in itself is remarkable allowing for the different orientations and structure of the two systems. If we can be allowed to make broad sweeping generalisations (always dangerous), we might say that in neither the United States nor Britain does the working-class proportion of any particular student body much exceed a third except in that particularly American Institution, the Opportunity College, for which there is no British equivalent[1] and which represents an expansion of opportunity because it represents a broadening of the scope and selectiveness of institutions of higher education. The British hierarchy of institutions of higher education is a ladder with fewer rungs. In addition we should say that the expansion of educational opportunity in the United States has been felt proportionately more in the lower middle class than the working

[1] Except perhaps in some of the colleges of technology and colleges of education. See Cantor, L. M. and Roberts, F. I., *Further Education in England and Wales*, Routledge and Kegan Paul, 1969.

class, and it is this section of the student population which has grown, while the upper middle class and upper class have shrunk.

These conclusions would suggest that there are factors operating in social selection of students—to some extent independent of cultural and structural differences—in the two systems of education, which have the effect of dampening the chances of members of the working class. This differential access to higher education has been the concern of a good number of studies since the early 1950's when it was first discovered that class and cultural disadvantages were not significantly being diminished.

If the educational system is to work efficiently in providing opportunity for individuals and qualified personnel for society, then the ablest young people should be selected at each stage up to and including college. It is true that abler youth do in general go further in the system, but a considerable proportion of able youth "drop out" at each stage, and many who would benefit by the experience do not enter college nor even complete high school. Although ability is a major factor in determining level of education, other factors do enter into the educational process to dampen or enhance the student's chances of reaching each successive stage. "Youth from upper middle-class families are likely to go to college even though they have only average ability, while youth from lower status families have less chance of entering college, even when they have high ability. It is clear that social class as well as intelligence determines who shall finish high school and who shall go to college."[1] Reasons for this in the American system lie partly in the inability of many working-class youth to pay for college education, but, as we have seen, this does not hold true in the British system with its availability of grants. Yet the proportions of working class, as we have seen, are comparably low in both systems.

Until recently it was widely assumed that there is an inborn intellectual inferiority in people of lower class origins and in people of non-white skin colour, and some of the early intelligence test studies seemed to confirm this belief by their uncritical use of culturally biased intelligence tests. On the other hand, studies like those done by Eells, for instance,[2] have shown this cultural bias in intelligence tests for what it is—a measurement of differences in experience with particular types of prob-

[1] Havighurst and Neugarten, *op. cit.*, p. 76.

[2] Eells, K., *et al.*, *Intelligence and Cultural Differences*, University of Chicago Press, Chicago, 1951. See also Deutsch, M., Katz, I., and Jensen, A. R. (eds.), *Social Class and Psychological Development*, Holt, Rinehart and Winston, 1968.

lems, differences in motivation, and differences in pre-school experience, and *not* necessarily of any innate differences in intellectual capacity.

More recent studies have shown that members of the working class are not congenitally less intelligent than members of other social classes, i.e. that the *range* of intelligence is much the same though environmental factors tend to depress the mean of measured intelligence, and that this in itself is not sufficient explanation of the working-class failure to take advantage of educational opportunities. Recent work on this by Farber (1965)[1] suggests that there may be different kinds of effects of social class on intelligence at the upper and lower IQ ranges. Conditions in an industrial society affect the interplay of environmental and genetic factors in intelligence in a complex *non-linear* manner. Explanations of differences in intelligence between social classes in the sense of a correlation coefficient or explained variance assume a linear relation which does not exist.

Certainly abler youth do go on to college, but there are discrepancies between ability and achievement at every level. Wolfle found this in his study in the early 1950's of the relationship between variables related to college attendance.[2] He distinguishes the relative influence of intelligence, academic record, money, desire to enter college, cultural background, sex, geographic factors, and ethnic differences. He says "of the brightest 5 per cent of an entire age group almost half finish college and slightly over half do not. Even at the 1-in-1,000 level of the top 0·1 per cent only 2 out of 3 graduate from college. Obviously there are factors other than those measured by intelligence tests which differentiate college graduates from non-graduates."[3]

In addition Wolfle notes the differences in intelligence range of students in different colleges.

> The diversity is sufficiently great that it is worth-while to emphasise that some colleges are so selective in admitting students that nearly all their graduates are above the average of all college graduates. On the other hand some colleges get a comparatively mediocre group. While most of the graduates of these schools are above the average of the entire population most of them are below the average of all college graduates.[4]

[1] Farber, B., Social class and intelligence, *Social Forces*, 1965, **44** (2), 215–25.
[2] Wolfle, D., Educational opportunity measured intelligence and social background, in Halsey *et al., op. cit.*, pp. 216–40. Reprinted from Dael Wolfle (ed.), *America's Resources of Specialised Talent*, Harper, New York, 1964.
[3] *Ibid.*, p. 223.
[4] *Ibid.*, p. 221.

These remarks can be related to our discussion of the hierarchy of institutions with its attendant hierarchy of opportunity, which reflects different sets of chances for children of the working class. These chances are clearly related to social and cultural factors operating in the home background and the school.

The Floud, Halsey, and Martin study[1] of 1956 was one of the earliest British studies of its kind and was to guide further research in this field. Their comparison of gross material factors in environment, measured ability, and entry to grammar schools in the two areas of south-west Hertfordshire and Middlesbrough, where there was a markedly different level of material culture in the home background of pupils, particularly at the lower social levels, showed that a pupil's success at the grammar school was influenced by his material background only up to a certain level of material prosperity, and that beyond this other social class factors came into play. Cultural and value patterns such as family size and the attitudes towards and preferences for education of their children by parents are examples of social factors operating in selection. At all levels the parents of successful children "were to a marked degree more interested in and ambitious for their educational future than were the parents of unsuccessful children."[2] The parents themselves were also better educated.

Floud, Halsey, and Martin conclude that "It has now been established beyond doubt that there is a process of social as well as academic selection at work in the schools".[3]

However, the problem they mention of the assimilation of working-class children into selective secondary schools with middle-class values and expectations has still not been satisfactorily investigated. Further evidence of class bias in selection was revealed by Floud and Halsey in 1957 in an article on "Intelligence tests, social class, and selection for secondary schools".[4] This was an analysis relating to the cohort of boys entering secondary schools in the educational division of south-west Hertfordshire in 1952, 1953, and 1954. Floud and Halsey set out to discover what was the social distribution before and after changes in selection procedure and whether there was equality of opportunity for

[1] Floud, J., Halsey, A. H., and Martin, F. M., *Social Class and Educational Opportunity*, Heinemann, 1956.

[2] *Ibid.*, p. 88.

[3] *Ibid.*, p. 114.

[4] Floud, J. and Halsey, A. H., in *BJS*, March 1957, **8**, 33–39.

children of equal ability irrespective of social origins. It was observed that the abolition of intelligence tests and the associated changes in procedure which depended more on a teacher's individual assessment appear to have resulted in a marked diminution in the opportunity of working-class children, and that in this sense their class chances had deteriorated.

The Early Leaving Report (1954)[1] and the Crowther Report (1959)[2] added to this picture of social selection at secondary level by showing that university entrance figures for the different social classes is out of proportion to the size of the classes in the country. The Early Leaving Report estimates that a third of the grammar school boys who are capable of reaching a standard of at least two passes at A-level in GCE leave school before doing so, and that the influence of home background is the major cause. The 15 per cent of all school children originating from the professional and managerial classes account for 25 per cent of grammar school population and contribute 43·7 per cent of those reaching the sixth form of the grammar school, whereas the 12 per cent from the homes of unskilled workers account for 5·6 per cent of grammar school pupils and contribute only 1·5 per cent of sixth-formers.

Say Floud and Halsey in their Reader, *Education, Economy and Society:* "Wastage from the Grammar Schools as the Central Advisory Council clearly recognised is a social class problem. The traditionally middle class schools are evidently failing to assimilate large numbers of the able working class children who win their way into them."[3]

The Crowther Report shows that in terms of educational opportunity the "pool" of talent is nowhere near exhausted, and even the idea of a "pool" itself is now discredited. Forty-two per cent of the one-tenth most able English boys leave school by 16 years, and boys from non-manual homes have a much higher expectation of long school life than boys from manual homes. Nine per cent of boys from unskilled manual homes stayed on at school beyond 17 years; 38 per cent of those from professional homes did so.

Comparable American data on the influence of socioeconomic class

[1] *Early Leaving*, Central Advisory Council for Education Report (England), HMSO, 1954.

[2] Central Advisory Council for Education, Crowther Report, **15–18**, HMSO, 1959.

[3] Halsey *et al.*, *op. cit.*, ch. 9; Floud and Halsey, English secondary schools and the supply of labour.

on academic attainment analysed by Glick (1954)[1] showed that while children of craftsmen and foremen comprised 22 per cent of all high school graduates, they represented in the 1950's only 4·5 per cent of college graduates. The drop in the share of children of operatives, service workers and labourers, farmers and farm labourers, was from 17·3 to 2·3 per cent, 9 to 2·1 per cent, and 8 to 2·4 per cent respectively. This is only the latest stage in a whole process of selection. By contrast the children of professionals—only 6 per cent of high school graduates comprised 55 per cent of the total of college graduates. Not only this, but as we have seen, the kind of college a student attends will differ in class composition.

Wolfle (1954) points out that socioeconomic class is related to educational achievement and that "high school graduates with fathers in professional and semi-professional fields are about four times as likely to become college graduates as are those whose fathers are farmers";[2] that there are sex inequalities in education, that there are geographic inequalities, and that there are special problems for students from minority groups.

Says Wolfle,

> the factors which determine whether or not a bright Negro boy or girl will get to college are not different in kind from those discussed in the preceding sections. But they are more acute. Fewer Negroes have the money to pay for a college education. Fewer live near a college which will accept them. Fewer grow up in families which place a high value of college attendance. Fewer attend elementary and secondary schools which provide good preparation for college work and encouragement to attend college. If the Negro student does graduate from college he has greater difficulties in securing a position in many of the specialised fields than does a white student. Perhaps because of the discrimination, a Negro youth is likely to be less highly motivated to continue his education than is a white student.[3]

Indeed, one of the most important factors in determining who will go to college is that of motivation—itself a product of a complex set of social and environmental factors. Studies of high school students in the United States have made this clear (for instance Barker and Wright,

---

[1] Glick, P. C., Educational attainment and occupational advancement, in *Transactions of the Second World Congress of Sociology, London*, Internat. Soc. Assn., 1954, vol. II, pp. 183–94, table 1.

[2] Wolfle, *op. cit.*, p. 231.

[3] *Ibid.*, p. 236.

1954; Stivers, 1958, 1959).[1] A study of Boston boys showed the influence of family social pressures on motivation for college (Kahl, 1953).[2] The boys in the study could be divided into two main groups—those who believed in "getting by" and those who wanted to "get ahead".

These attributes are related to degree and kind of parental encouragement. British studies have also shown that working-class children who succeed tend to have parents who had either some secondary schooling or at least have had aspirations themselves for educational achievement. The Crowther Report[3] notes a correspondence of better education among parents and greater success in school. Floud, Halsey, and Martin[4] showed that parental interest in education and encouragement was a critical factor above a certain level of material living standards. Jackson and Marsden also suggest further evidence of this in their study of eighty-eight working-class grammar school children.[5] Both parents of successful grammar school children proved in most cases to be very interested in the children's education and "Grammar School for their children was a new extension of living for themselves too"—though, of course, this did not hold true in every case. Nevertheless, this and other studies have shown that it is in homes where educational achievement is *valued* and where deferred goals are preferred to immediate satisfactions (as, for instance, in wage earning) that children will succeed.

Jackson and Marsden suggest that in working-class families it is the *mother* who often has the greatest influence on a child's education, and that if she herself had a grammar school education there is increased likelihood that her children will go.[6]

In his article on "The school class as a social system",[7] Talcott Parsons endorses the view that it is primarily the mother and her influence on the children which backs up the education process in terms of her part in the socialisation process. Parsons discusses the school class as a social

[1] Barker, R. G. and Wright, H. F., *Midwest and Its Children: The Psychological Ecology of an American Town*, Harper and Row, 1954. Stivers, E. H., Motivation for college in high school boys, *School Review*, 1958, **66**, 341–50; *id.*, Motivation for college in high school girls, *School Review*, 1959, **67**, 320–34.

[2] Kahl, J. A., Education and occupational aspirations of "common man" boys, *Harvard Educ. Rev.* **23**, 186–203, Summer 1953.

[3] Crowther Report, **15–18**.

[4] Halsey *et al., op. cit.*

[5] Jackson and Marsden, *op. cit.*

[6] *Ibid.*, pp. 112–22.

[7] Parsons, T., article in *Harvard Educ. Rev.*, Fall 1959, **29**, 297–318. Reprinted in Halsey *et al., op. cit.*

system and shows the relation of its structure to its primary functions in society as an agency of socialisation and allocation of roles. Individual personalities are made motivationally and technically adequate to the performance of adult roles and learn commitment to the values of the role within the structure.

In *Family Socialization and Internation Processes*,[1] Parsons goes more fully into the processes by which school emancipates the child from his primary emotional attachment to the family and helps him to internalise the values and norms of the society. Yet this is seen as part of a continuum begun in the home. An important development is the differentiation of the school class in terms of achievement and valuation of achievement, and the process of selection and allocation of society's human resources relative to the adult role system.

It emerges then that the working-class child who succeeds academically is usually atypical in family values and attitudes, and that there are obstacles to higher education in the working-class culture, so that reduced educability is rooted in working-class family life. However, it is important to distinguish between ability to reach a certain level of education and actual general performance at any given level. "Social class influences the level reached but (as measured by broad classifications of parental occupation) it appears to have no marked effect on performance at the upper level of secondary and in higher education."[2]

Although within the United States system there are additional barriers of financial cost of education, yet these have been found not to account sufficiently for marked class differences in school "drop-out" at any one stage. "A study of the Bureau of the Census in 1960 found, for example, that variations in parental income could explain less than 10 per cent of the variance in college enrollments among high school seniors."[3]

It is only popular mythology which explains inequalities in educational achievement among different racial, class, and culture groups in terms of either inherent inferiority of intelligence or inability to pay. The facts disprove such explanations of the inequalities which give rise to a situation

---

[1] Parsons, T., and Bales, R. F., *et al.*, *Family Socialization and Internation Processes*, Free Press, Glencoe, Ill., 1955 (see ch. IV).

[2] Little and Westergaard, *op. cit.* See also Newfield, J.G.H., The academic performance of British university students, *Sociol. Rev.*, Monograph No. 7, October 1963. (This shows that the proportion of students admitted in 1955 who obtained first or second class honours was virtually the same for students from manual and non-manual background.)

[3] Jencks and Riesman, *op. cit.*, p. 117, quoting Nam and Cowhig.

in which "Negroes get less education than Whites. Similarly Jews get more than Protestants, who get more than Catholics. Also urban boys are slightly more educated than rural boys."[1]

Factors which do emerge as important in determining whether members of a particular group will be advantaged or disadvantaged in the academic competition have emerged in relation to family structure, educational environmental, linguistic skills, attitudes, and values. (In addition one has to relate cultural background to the availability of educational resources in the schools attended. This we shall discuss later.)

Family size has emerged as an important factor in a number of studies. Its significance has been noted by Halsey, Floud, and Martin,[2] MacPherson,[3] Barger and Hall,[4] and Elder[5] for instance. The work of John Nisbet (1953) tests the hypothesis that family size has a direct effect on the environmental aspect of mental development. "This hypothesis derives from the view that language and words afford a system of symbols which greatly increase the efficiency of abstract thought."[6] Family environment means here the contact between the child and the adult and its relation to learning processes. The ability to manipulate verbal symbols, so necessary to educational achievement, seems to play an important part in thinking and in particular problem solving.

In the study the test scores of 2500 children at the stage of transfer from primary to secondary education in Aberdeen were correlated with various factors: (i) partial correlation of family size and verbal identity with intelligence held constant; (ii) correlation of family size and several tests with different verbal loadings; (iii) correlation of family size and intelligence at different ages. Nisbet comes to the conclusion that "it seems that part (though not all) of the negative correlation of family size and intelligence test scores may be attributed to an environmental

---

[1] Kahl, J. A., *The American Class Structure*, Holt, Rinehart & Winston, 1957, p. 281.

[2] Floud *et al., op. cit.*

[3] MacPherson, J. S., *Eleven Year Olds Grow Up*, Scottish Council for Research in Education, London, 1957. (Report of the 7 year follow-up of 1200 children from the 1947 Scottish Mental Health Survey.)

[4] Barger, B. and Hall, E., The interrelationships of family size and socioeconomic status for parents of college students, *J. Marr. Fam.*, 1966, **28** (2), 186–7.

[5] Elder, G. H., Jr., Family structure and educational achievement: A cross national analysis, *ASR*, 1965, **30** (1), 81–96.

[6] Nisbet, J. D., Family environment and intelligence, *Eugenics Rev.*, 1953, **45**, 31–42.

influence of the size of the family on verbal development and through it on general mental development".

Further work on family structure in relation to "drop-outs" by Cervantes draws attention to the differences not only in closeness of relationship (which may affect mental and linguistic development) but also differences in the kinds and quality of relationships which the family has with each other and also with family friends.[1]

Linguistic skill is another closely related factor in the socialising process which aids or prevents educational achievement. Bernstein drew attention to this fact in his paper of 1958,[2] where he stated his initial hypotheses which he is still redefining. Bernstein postulates that children from "extreme" social groups are exposed from an early age to separate and distinct patterns of learning before their formal education begins. "Speech marks out what is relevant—effectively, cognitively, and socially —and experience is transformed by that which is made relevant." Evidence suggests that level of linguistic skill may be independent of the potential IQ—certainly independent of measured non-verbal IQ.

Bernstein illustrates the difference between what he calls *public* and *formal* language—both of which are learned by the middle-class child, while the working-class child learns only public language. The middle-class child grows up in an ordered rational structure in which his total experience is organised from an early age and in which he is given more subtle cues for action than the working-class child. Public language encourages an immediacy of interaction and is the "linguistic form that maximises the means of producing *social* rather than individual symbols". In public language what is not said is as important or more important than what is said. A linguistic environment limited to a public language is likely to produce (from the point of view of formal education) deleterious effects, both cognitive and affective, which are difficult to modify.

Bernstein asserts that for the working-class child a situation is created of mechanical learning with its implication of forgetting when the original stimuli are removed, since new words have no cognitive framework to fit into. Where culture induces a low level of conceptualisation associational rather than "gestalt" learning in children is more efficient.

[1] Cervantes, L. F., Family background, primary relationships and the high school dropout, *J. Marr. Fam.*, 1965, **27** (2), 218–23. Also *id.*, The isolated nuclear family and dropout, *Social Quart.*, 1965, **6** (2), 103–18.

[2] Bernstein, B., Some sociological determinants of perception, *BJS*, June 1958, **9**, 159–74. See also Language and social class, *BJS*, 1960, **11**, 271–6.

Latest work[1] shows that working-class mothers relative to middle-class mothers studied emphasised the use of language in the "person area" while middle-class mothers emphasised more the use of language in acquisition of basic skills.

Further work in this field has been done by, among others, Deutsch,[2] who has noted that increasing age amplified differences in the quality of language usage between classes. Huffine[3] has come to the conclusion that in his study linguistic differences between socioeconomic classes did not emerge as statistically significant. He posits that common scholastic experience may help to reduce earlier linguistic differences. Also, since in using Bernstein's categories he found in some instances the opposite of what Bernstein suggested, he believes that it may be necessary to use different criteria for American culture.

However, it would seem that these findings and those of, for instance, Shatzman and Strauss[4] who distinguish also the poor skills of rural respondents, go some way to proving certain of Bernstein's assertions, but there is still much work to be done in this field.

Some of the factors involved are summarised by Floud and Halsey in *Education, Economy and Society:*

> Thus the working class child who secures a Grammar School place tends to come from a small family, his father is more likely to have received some form of further education, his mother to have received something more than elementary schooling, and, before marriage, to have followed an occupation 'superior' to that of his father. These factors are reflected in a complex of attitudes favourable to educational success and social mobility, and differences of this kind in home background presumably underline differences in motivation which in the absence of gross economic handicaps are the key to differences in performance in a substantial borderline range of ability.[5]

Since many of these studies in secondary education were conducted in the 1950's it may be thought that expansion of places and changing social conditions will have outdated the findings. However, this is not the case.

[1] Bernstein, B. and Henderson, D., Social class differences in the relevance of language to socialization, *Sociology*, 1969, **3** (1), 1–20.

[2] Deutsch, M., The role of social class in language development and cognition, *Am. J. Orthopsychol.*, 1965, **35** (1), 78–88.

[3] Huffine, C. L., Inter-socioeconomic class language differences: a research report, *Sociol. Soc. Res.*, 1966, **50** (3), 351–7.

[4] Shatzman, L. and Strauss, A., Social class and modes of communication, *AJS*, January 1955, 329–38.

[5] Halsey *et al.*, *op. cit.*, ch. 9, p. 87.

Of course, the influence of the home, school, and community operate in a complex process which may further affect the outcome in terms of individual attainment. There has been dispute as to the relative weighting of each. Kahl's study in the suburbs of Boston[1] shows the family to be almost twice as influential as the school, while Sewell's Wisconsin data[2] suggests the school to be almost three times as important as the family. Natalie Rogoff suggests that her nationwide sample "falls squarely between the two, with each of the sources playing about an equal role".

> From those at the top to those at the bottom of the social class hierarchy all students attending large suburban schools emerge from their educational experience relatively better equipped in academic skills, while youngsters who attend school in small villages or large industrial cities emerge from their educational environments less adequately prepared. Note how these trends account for some of the heterogeneity in scholastic aptitude *within* a given social class by the diversity in formal academic training received by the youngsters originating in that class.[3]

In situations where schools draw their pupils from the immediate neighbourhood then, community and school environment tend to coincide, and the "diversity in formal academic training is between social classes rather than within them". This situation obtains in those areas of towns where social class, ethnic, or racial groups[4] have settled and become segregated, and where the tendency has been for progressive homogeneity of culture to develop with successive movements in and out of the area.[5] The most extreme case is the immigrant ghettos in large towns which are beginning to develop in Britain in the manner of those in the United States. In these areas poor schools attract poor teachers in small numbers; poor material conditions, poor teaching, and overcrowding

[1] Kahl, *op. cit.*

[2] Sewell, W. H. *et al.*, Social status and educational and occupational aspiration, *ASR*, 1956, **21**, 203–11.

[3] Rogoff, N., Local social structure and educational selection, ch. 20 in Halsey *et al.*, *op. cit.*

[4] Bloom, R., Whiteman, M., and Deutsch, M., Race and social class as separate factors related to social environment, *AJS*, 1965, **70** (4), 471–6.

[5] Sewell, W. H. and Armer, J. M., Neighbourhood context and college plans, *ASR*, April 1966, **31**, 159–68. Sewell and Armer suggest, however, that past claims for the importance of neighbourhood context in development of educational aspirations may have been overstated, though it seems to be of more importance in some sub-populations than others.

result with consequent lack of academic success of the children.[1] A similar cycle may be observed in poor rural schools with similar though less dramatic results. In these cases the school environment and teaching does little or nothing to mitigate in cultural terms the deprived home environment. This is the contention of the Plowden Report[2] on primary schools, where the whole process of success or failure really begins.

Such influences of the residential environment have tremendous implications for local educational policy, particularly with relation to housing programmes and the allocation or non-allocation of certain kinds of housing to different social class or racial groups. For it has been found by MacPherson (1958)[3] that successful completion of secondary education, in this case by passing the 5 year Scottish Leaving Certificate, is more dependent upon *occupancy* (persons per room) than upon intelligence within the range IQ 120+. This relates also to the factor of family size.

Recently in Britain and America there has been growing concern about large-scale poverty which is seen to exist in affluent societies,[4] and the appalling conditions under which many families are condemned to exist. The present moves to do something positive to house the homeless will also ultimately affect the educational achievement of the children and the intellectual resources of the nation.

The problem of immigrant groups stands out particularly starkly both in housing and education. In Britain, where the number of immigrants now tops the million mark,[5] wide social issues are beginning to manifest themselves. Some local education authorities, like Birmingham, for instance, are faced with the situation of having some schools with over 50 per cent immigrant children, many of whom have language problems. Such a high concentration of immigrants makes teaching difficult and in turn affects academic standards. Again this results from residential segregation,[6] and can only be broken down where children are transported to schools outside their local area: this many local authorities are unwilling to do, as with Negro neighbourhood schools in the United States.

[1] Clark, K., *Dark Ghetto: Dilemmas of Social Power*, Harper Torch Books, 1965, ch. 6.

[2] Plowden Report, *loc. cit.*

[3] MacPherson, *op. cit.*

[4] See Harrington, M., *The Other America*, Macmillan, New York, 1962.

[5] This represents 2 per cent of the total population, compared with 11 per cent Black Americans in the United States.

[6] Rex, J. and Moore, R., *Race, Community and Conflict*, OUP (for Institute of Race Relations), 1967.

Clark, in his study of the ghetto, suggests that while "busing" seems to offer immediate desegregation, in many cases it would lead to bad education and, in the end, to even more segregation. "Whites would pull out of the public school system even more rapidly than they are presently doing. In Brooklyn, for example, if real integration were the goal, about 70,000 Negro and Puerto Rican children, under eleven, would have to be transported twice a day, some of them ten miles away."[1]

Neighbourhood concentration and White flight have resulted in a situation in the United States in which segregation in schools which is not sanctioned *de jure* is segregation *de facto*. Clark suggests that school segregation is in fact accelerating; and that meaningful desegregation of urban ghetto public schools can only occur when schools in the system are raised to the highest standards "so that the quality of education does not vary according to the income or social status of the neighbourhood".[2]

However, meaningful desegregation is a long way off, and in the meantime the effects of inferiority of segregated schooling are being felt by the children of the ghettos.

> The gross economic deprivation and social impoverishment in the lives of lower-class families generates what sociologists have repeatedly found as a syndrome of insecurity, pessimism, feelings of powerlessness and alienation. The disadvantaged, particularly Negroes, are estranged from the economy; they feel politically impotent and are mistrustful of politicians and the political systems; they are pessimistic and desperate over their own life chances.[3]

In this situation of pessimism, even self-rejection, the role of the school and of the teacher is very important. Studies have shown that teacher expectations operate as a self-fulfilling prophecy and that "when teachers expected that certain children would show greater intellectual development, those children did show greater intellectual development".[4] Unfortunately, many White middle-class teachers entering ghetto schools do not hold any high expectations for their pupils and may even discourage what they regard as unrealistic aspirations.[5] Small wonder that neighbourhoods

---

[1] Clark, K., *op. cit.*, p. 115.

[2] *Ibid.*, p. 117.

[3] Deutsch, S. E., Disadvantages of culturally deprived children, ch. 2 in Beggs, D. W. and Alexander, S. K., *Integration and Education*, Rand McNally & Co., 1969.

[4] Rosenthal, R. and Jacobson, L., Self-fulfilling prophecies in the classroom: Teachers expectations as unintended determinants of pupils' intellectual competance, ch. 6 in Deutsch, M., Katz, I., and Jensen, A. R., *Social Class, Race and Psychological Development*, Holt, Rinehart & Winston, New York, 1968.

[5] See *Autobiography of Malcolm X*, Grove Press, New York, 1966, pp. 35–37.

are clammering for decentralisation and community control of the local school board so that education may be made relevant and vital for its recipients. The New York teachers' strikes of 1968 and 1969, which kept one million school children out of school for months, was a result of the power struggle between the Teachers' Union and the community of Ocean-hill Brownsville district, for control of the school and its hiring and firing of teachers. The crisis represents a reaction to a situation of disadvantage which is worsening rather than getting better, and which seems to have no speedy solution.

> Opponents of plans for semi-autonomous neighbourhood school districts fear that local districts tend to freeze ghetto boundaries. Others are concerned that ward-type politicians or extremist groups might take over the schools. Still others recall that school district consolidation was a long time coming, and the recent proposals are a step backward. A long and probably bitter debate is inevitable; but as the Bundy Report in New York City stated, decentralisation is not a panacea. The need in the inner cities is so great that a "reconnection for learning" is imperative and this approach may cause school boards, professionals and the parents to stop blaming each other for failures and start working together for success.[1]

Not only are ghetto children hampered therefore by the "culture of poverty" but also by a school system which does not seem equipped to cope with their needs. Inevitably the result is low attainment and high drop-out.

A national sample survey conducted in the United States at the direction of the 1964 Civil Rights Act, for instance, showed that Negro students scored significantly below Whites. Since differences in scores hold for grade school and high school students, it appears that school experience does not enable Negro youth to overcome the deficiencies with which they begin school.[2] Clark, indeed, scorns the notion of "cultural deprivation" as an explanation, and says that quality of teaching may have a more important impact on a child's performance in school than the community environment from which he comes.[3]

Of course, not all Black Americans live in ghettos, neither are all those who suffer from the culture of poverty Black—but the correlation is

[1] Levenson, W. B., *The Spiral Pendulum: The Urban School in Transition*, Rand McNally & Co., Chicago, 1968, p. 242.

[2] Coleman, J. S., Campbell, E. Q., Hobson, C. J., McPartland, J., Mood, A. M., Weinfeld, F. D., and York, R. L., *Equality of Educational Opportunity*, Washington DC, 1966, pp. 550–68.

[3] Clark, K., *op. cit.*, p. 132. See also Rudman, H. C. and Featherstone, R. L. (eds.), *Urban Schooling*, Harcourt, Brace and World, 1968, pp. 177–95.

sufficiently high for it to affect statistics on Black education. Today there are between 40–50 million Americans, or one-quarter of the nation, living in poverty, and of these 22 per cent are Non-white (while Black Americans comprise 11 per cent of the population).[1]

Recent government statistics have highlighted the disparities in educational opportunity for White and Non-white. In 1966, 53 per cent Non-white males over 25 years had completed 4 years of high school or more, compared with 73 per cent White males. The figures for females was 49 per cent and 74 per cent. Such disparities occur all along the line. This is related, of course, to the fact that 41 per cent of Non-whites live in poverty and 14 per cent receive welfare compared with 12 per cent poor white, and 3 per cent Whites receiving welfare. Non-white includes Black, Orientals, and American Indians.[2]

The educational disadvantages, then, for the Non-white in both Britain and the United States are related to the same underlying factors of White racism which created the ghetto, and the social, economic, and cultural deprivation at home and school which maintain it. The problems for lower-class youth outside ghetto areas are less dramatic and less visible but stem from the same kind of social causes. Unfortunately these seem resistant to change over time.

A survey carried out in Britain by Douglas (1964)[3] showed that the position had not changed since previous surveys in the 1950's with regard to social class differentials in education and the influence of home environment on school performance. This large-scale national follow-up survey of children born in 1946 indicates marked social differentials in the chances of admission to grammar and technical schools as between children of similar measured ability. These children entered the secondary schools in 1958. Factors such as parental encouragement, family size, over-crowding and regional provision of grammar school places intervened in selection. Two years later Dale and Griffith[4] found social class factors associated with the deterioration in grammar school of thirty-nine movers from the A to the C stream, which were unrelated to IQ. Again, family size also emerged as relevant; 51 per cent of the deteriorators

---

[1] Deutsch, S. E., *op. cit.*, p. 22.

[2] *Social and Economic Conditions of Negroes in the United States*, US Government, 1967.

[3] Douglas, J. W. B., *The Home and The School*, McGibbon and Kee, 1964.

[4] Dale, R. R. and Griffith, S., Selected findings from a five year study of academic deteriorators in a grammar school, *Educ. Res.* **8** (2), 146–54.

were from families of four plus compared with 30 per cent of the control group; and 67 per cent of the improvers were first born compared with 48·7 per cent of the deteriorators—which implies factors of parental–child contact. Lacey[1] and Dockrell[2] have also very recently contributed to the understanding of class differentials in secondary education.

Finger and Schlesser,[3] and Pavalko and Bishop[4] have produced comparable findings in the United States and Canada which show that class factors are still at work and that a higher proportion of children from high status groups than from low status groups go on to college. There are obviously resistances to change in the culture groupings which do not encourage educational attainment, and these are very difficult to break down. As long as the differences in family structure and values and linguistic skills remain, the educational differentials remain. It is a circular process.

After criticising other studies made, because of inadequate samples, failure to take account of drop-outs and insufficient follow-up on eventual achievement, Sewell and Shah outline their study of a randomly selected cohort of Wisconsin high school seniors during the 7 years after their graduation from high school (1957–64), following them through to "diverse institutions of higher learning".

Among a number of other findings they show that of males in the low socioeconomic status category, 20·5 per cent attended college and 7·5 per cent graduated, while 73·4 per cent of the high socioeconomic status males attended and 42·1 per cent graduated. Comparative figures for females were 8·5 and 2·7 per cent (low status) and 62·6 and 35 per cent graduated. Females were found to be less likely than males to have planned on college or to have attended college or to have completed college. Both socioeconomic origins and intelligence were significantly associated not only with college plans but with progress through the system of higher education. The facts challenge Wolfle's[5] observation that while socioeconomic status plays an important part in who goes to college, once one has cleared the hurdle of college entrance, socioeconomic status

[1] Lacey, C., Some sociological concomitants of academic streaming in a grammar school, *BJS*, September 1966, **17** (3).

[2] Dockrell, W. B., Secondary education, social class and the development of abilities, *Br. J. Educ. Psych.*, 1966, **36** (1).

[3] Finger, J. A. and Schlesser, G. E., Non-intellective predictors of academic success in school and college, *School Review*, 1965, **73** (1), 14–29.

[4] Pavalko, R. M. and Bishop, D. R., Socio-economic status and college plans: a study of Canadian high school students, *Sociol. Educ.*, 1966, **39** (3), 288–98.

[5] Wolfle, D., *op. cit.*, p. 163.

sharply declines as a factor in college graduation, and intelligence becomes the determining factor. The stress is laid upon socioeconomic status as an "important factor in determining who shall be eliminated from the contest for higher education".[1]

The importance of these factors in the social background of students is confirmed by studies in a variety of different cultural settings and seem to prove the universal validity of the findings of the principles involved. Bourdieu,[2] Girard,[3] and Saint-Martin[4] have written on the influence of socioeconomic and cultural background in education in France; de Brie,[5] in writing of Belgian universities, notes not only the influence of social class but cultural differences as between French and Flemish-speaking groups. Gouveia[6] in Brazil shows the relation between ethnic groupings in São Paulo and choice for different kinds of school. Whyllie[7] discusses the expansion of educational opportunity in Ghana at university level of children of farmers and fishermen at the expense of the higher professional group, while the middle range craft and manual category is failing to gain ground. Reil[8] gives further evidence of the broadening social base from which Ghanaian students are drawn. Mangalam[9] notes rural–urban differences in academic performance of Pakistani college students. The role played by vertically or horizontally ordered cultural groupings in educational achievements is a recurrent theme in much of the present literature.

[1] Sewell and Shah, *op. cit.*, p. 29.

[2] Bourdieu, P. and Passeron, J. C., *Les Héritiers, les étudiants et la culture*, Centre de Sociologie Européenne, Paris, Éditions de Minuit, 1964. Bourdieu, P., La transmission de l'héritage culturel, in Darras, *La partage des bénéfices*, Paris, Éditions de Minuit, 1966. *Id.*, L'École conservatrice, les inégalites devant l'école et devant la culture, *Revue française de sociol.*, 1966, **7**, 325–47.

[3] Girard, A., Enquête nationale sur l'orientation et la selection des enfants d'age scholaire, *Population*, October-December 1951, pp. 597–634.

[4] Saint-Martin, M., *L'Engrénage; les étudiants en sciences originaires des classes populaires*, Centre de Sociologie Européenne, 1966.

[5] de Brie, P., Aspects socio-culturels des classes sociales ascendantes in Belgique, *Cahiers Int. de Soc.*, 1965, **39**, 19–109.

[6] Gouveia, A. J., Preference for different types of secondary school among various ethnic groups in Sao Paulo, Brazil, *Sociol. Educ.*, 1966, **39** (2), 155–66.

[7] Whyllie, R. W., Ghanaian university students – a research note, *BJS*, 1966, **17** (3), 306–11.

[8] Reil, M., Ghanaian students: the broadening base, *BJS*, 1965, **16** (1), 19–27.

[9] Mangalam, J. J., Rural–urban differences in academic performance of Pakistani college students, and their implications for change, Paper prepared for Research Group in Sociology of Education, VIth World Congress of Sociology, 1966.

To summarise points made by research into student selection and the democratisation of higher education, I quote Sewell and Shah:

> Many factors other than the ability of the student influence the educational experience he will undergo. These include differences in the level and quality of education available in the country, region, or community in which he lives; differential access to educational facilities according to his social class status, religious status, race and ethnic origins; differences in his motivations, values and attitudes; and differences in the willingness and ability of his parents and significant others to provide the financial and psychological supports necessary for the maximisation of his talent potentials.[1]

This statement made in 1966 is the summary of findings made by great numbers of people in the last 20 years or so, and pinpoints the interrelation of the many variables involved.

3. *Institutional Socialisation and Social Mobility*

The changes in education and the research which has surrounded them, discussed above, are predominantly involved in processes of *selection*, which take place at every educational level and which decide who shall go on to the next stage. Ideally, as was stated in the first part of this chapter, individuals are selected on the basis of intellectual merit—selection of some sort being made necessary by the scarcity of society's educational resources. However, despite changes brought about in the educational system, designed to reduce disadvantages of various kinds which are unequally distributed between groups in the population, social selection does take place at every stage. As a result members of particular socioeconomic, cultural, racial, and ethnic groups are under or overrepresented at each educational level and, given the workings and peculiarities of organisation of selection within a variety of different institutions this means that not only do we find certain social, as well as ability, distributions throughout the education process in general, but in addition we find different degrees of social, racial, and ethnic concentrations in different institutions. Clearly, then, the educational experience in social as well as in academic terms will be quite different for members of different social and racial groups and within different institutions. This is coupled with the fact that there is tremendous variety of organisational structures and authority patterns in institutions, particularly at the level of higher education (institutions, as we have seen, also being ranked in status).

[1] Sewell and Shah, *op. cit.*, p. I.

It has been generally agreed that universities and colleges *socialise* students, although the actual amount of non-academic socialisation varies between institutions. Exactly why this is so is not entirely agreed, nor why some institutions seem to encourage growth of particular student cultures whether or not intended by faculty. Certainly changes do take place particularly in values,[1] but it has always been a problem to decide how far the differences encountered in institutions is due to selection and how far to socialisation. Certainly one cannot keep distinct these two processes, as some researchers have done. The social input will always affect the changes which are effected in terms of social output. Thus the author hopes to demonstrate in the discussion of her study in three British universities. Social selection is taken as the starting point in the study—not its end point—as given in the situation which interacts with organisational structure and process to bring about certain outcomes for the individual and for society. In addition we cannot separate this part of the educational process from the process of *allocation* of individuals to specialist roles in the employment sector—another function of education. As we explained in the first section, in a class society the educational process operates both for and against socioeconomic inequalities, promoting mobility— even reordering existing social categories—but in turn creating new ones. The author's study is equally concerned with the effects of allocation as of selection along with the impact on student class changes and mobility patterns *within* as well as outside the institution. The social class composition of the institutions studied was merely a starting point for the investigation of institutional organisation and socialisation.

The processes at work may be said to interact in different ways in different institutional and organisational contexts to produce the character and quality of student life and culture but are never separate from it. Institutions of higher education are not, as this present study will show, classless oases in the class-ridden desert of society—places where different measures and different rules apply—but rather are they set squarely in the midst of society's social divisions, reflecting them, however distortedly, and working upon them in often unplanned ways.

Firstly, let us portray the processes which shall be our concern in diagrammatic form (Fig. 1.1).

---

[1] See, for instance, the report of the Bennington College study of changes in political attitudes in Newcomb, T., *Personality and Social Change*, Dryden, N.Y., 1943.

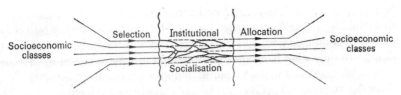

FIG. 1.1. Education in a class society.

Changes take place throughout the process—both in terms of individuals in positions in the social order and in terms of the nature of groups which make up the social order—since clearly one is contingent upon the other. The processes of selection and allocation decide who moves into what position in the educational, social, and economic order, but the process of socialisation decides who is best equipped to make the moves ahead and thus who is most likely to be selected for the best positions. One of the important questions asked by the survey is: "Do those who are advantaged at the beginning of the socialisation process remain advantaged at the end?" This, it appears, is a question previously overlooked in studies of student culture, which treat development of student culture as a feature of institutional structure rather than of student class input. This may have resulted from the fact that the three major processes of education—selection, socialisation, and allocation—have been largely treated by researchers as separate processes or separate at least for the purpose of the studies concerned. The present research treats these as intimately related and interwoven and makes an attempt to distinguish the organisational variables and the social class variables which combine to guide the outcome. Neither the nature of "social class" nor of organisation are taken as given. The study is in all areas exploratory and first of all, of course, in its investigation of the extent to which students themselves perceive the effects of social class and social selection on their university experience. For it would appear that within any institution the major role of socialisation is played by fellow students as being those organisational personnel with whom for the student there is generally most contact. The authority structure and organisational order may constrain or encourage relations between students as the study will show, but rarely supplants them in importance.

The social class structure of the student body then provides us with a structure and point of comparison and enables us to place our findings in a meaningful framework of some general validity. The processes at work are thus related by the linking thread of social class, which is a central factor in them all to a greater or lesser extent. Whether the nature of that "linking thread" is changed by the other variables with which it is variously combined is one of the central issues of the book and leads us to ask not only what is meant by "student" but what is meant by "social class". We must test many of our assumptions about what actually goes on in the university. This is central—particularly with reference to culture change and with reference also to the relation between student culture and adolescent[1] or youth culture in general of which in age terms all students are a part. For although much has been written about the process of educational selection and allocation and the cultural factors influencing class differentials, there is a notable lack of information about the supposed process of "assimilation" into the middle-class student body which it is assumed working-class students undergo. Nor is there any sociological evidence as yet of the effect on the *relations* of the social classes *within* the university of expansion in educational opportunity, and changes in the social class distribution, if such there be, in secondary and higher education. These are other unanswered questions which the present study attempts to answer.

Let us look now at some of the studies in the field of student culture and socialisation along with studies of social mobility which set the scene for the present study.

It is clear that in relation to societal inequalities in power, prestige, and material benefit, the university serves an important function as a means of mobility to the highest positions in society. For many, then, the university experience is seen as part of a complex *rite de passage*,[2] through which working-class and lower middle-class students must pass in order to be enculturated into the values of an élite. How this enculturation is effected, or indeed *how far* it is effected, has so far remained a mystery—and it is this the present survey seeks to unravel. How far, then, is the latent function of the university to be compared to that of the army replacement depot described by Merton and Rossi, which served "to loosen the soldier's previous army ties, thus making him more amenable to ready absorption into his combat outfit".[3] In addition, how far do different institutions prepare the students for entry into different

---

[1] Cf. Coleman, J. S., *The Adolescent Society*, Free Press, Glencoe, 1961.

[2] Van Gennep, A., *Rites of Passage*, London, Routledge and Kegan Paul, 1960.

[3] Merton, R. K. and Rossi, A. S., Contribution to the theory of reference group behavior, pp. 272–5 in Merton, R. K., *Social Theory and Social Structure*, Free Press, New York, 1957.

"outfits" or different élites? Since the value systems of secondary education, particularly in the grammar schools, tend to be essentially middle class, the successful working-class student is already in a sense in a situation of marginality[1] upon entry into university or college. He may find his own way of coping with that marginality in terms of values within disciplines he perceives as congruent to his own.[2]

Other ways of coping with marginality during this transitional period may involve moving away from home. This necessary movement has always been associated with social mobility, and is characteristic of induction into any élite;[3] it is also associated with what Talcott Parsons calls "compulsive alienation".[4]

As we shall see, the characteristics of the organisational structure may encourage or inhibit the process of induction into the élite. But herein lies the circularity of the process—through self-selection members of particular groups will tend to congregate where they feel most "at home", which may not be conducive to such a process. Indeed, it may lead to social and political bias. Rudd has pointed out that "if a university is noted for its revolutionary outlook it is likely to attract students holding revolutionary views".[5]

Such concentrations then tend to create a university "image" which further influences student applications and selection. In turn this must affect the development of particular kinds of student culture and university tradition and status.

In examining how social images of institutions develop, Clark has suggested that "(a) the characteristics of students entering a college are partly determined by (b) student self selection, that self selection stems from (c) public images, and that these images are in turn partly conditioned by (d) what the college has been and is like today".[6]

The process is obviously circular, and since students spend only a brief span within the institution it must necessarily be so—the culture changing at least to some degree with the personnel. Clark and Trow have suggested

---

[1] Cf. Stonquist, E. V., *The Marginal Man*, Charles Scribner, New York, 1937.

[2] Box, S. and Ford, J., Commitment to science: a solution to student marginality?, *Sociology*, 3 September 1967, 1.

[3] Musgrove, S., *The Migratory Elite*, Heinemann, London, 1963.

[4] Parsons, T., *The Social System*, Routledge & Kegan Paul, London, 1956, pp. 254–6.

[5] Rudd, E., The student conflict, *New Society*, 14 March 1968, no. 285.

[6] Clark, B. R., College image and student selection, in *Selection and Educational Differentiation*, Centre for Study of Higher Education, Berkeley, California, 1959, p. 156.

that the institution's "autonomy" from its environment is related to growth of a distinct student culture,[1] and this may be related to the concept of a "total institution",[2] discussed by Goffman. There have been attempts to investigate the nature of college "closedness" but no one yet has examined the structural variables involved. This the present study attempts to do. Certainly the ideal of the "community of scholars" is only one kind of closedness and one which is fast disappearing under the impact of expansion and bureaucratic growth. For Halsey the collegiate ideal is "a community of established older and aspiring younger scholars, living closely together and cooperating with leisurely confidence in the task of preserving and transmitting a cultured way of life".[3]

The idea of "community" is very fundamental to the concept of conscious university socialisation relating as it does to the era of education for the leisure classes. Our Ivy colleges and Oxbridges are most able to maintain this kind of "community" and are best equipped to act as socialising agents.

The concept of community has been associated very much with the idea of residential as well as academic concentration and influence. Residential organisation focuses the cultural influences of the college upon the student for the longest time span and with the greatest social intensity. Small wonder, then, that many studies have isolated out this factor of university residence for special scrutiny as it is seen to affect participation in student affairs, academic achievements, and values and goals. Such work, which will be discussed later, has been done in Britain by Marris,[4] Albrow,[5] Eden,[6] Thoday,[7] and Hatch[8], among others.

---

[1] Clark, B. R. and Trow, M., Determinants of college student subcultures, in Newcomb, T. M. and Wilson, E. K. (eds.), *The Study of College Peer Groups*, Aldine Publishers, Chicago, 1966.

[2] Goffman, E., *Asylums*, Anchor, New York, 1966.

[3] Halsey, A. H., University expansion and the collegiate ideal, *Universities Quart.*, December 1961, **16** (1), 55.

[4] Marris, *op. cit.*

[5] Albrow, M. C., The influence of accommodation upon 64 Reading university students, *BJS*, December 1966, **17**, 4.

[6] Eden, A., Social life in a provincial university, *BJS*, December 1959, **10**, 291–310.

[7] Thoday, D., Halls of residence, *Univ. Quart.*, 1957, **12**, 1.

[8] Hatch, S., *Student Residence: A Discussion of the Literature*, Soc. for Res. into Higher Educ., 1968, and Ackland, H. and Hatch, S., *Three Aspects of Student Residence—Recruitment, Participation and Academic Performace*, London, Institute of Education, 1968.

Other factors in expression of student values and goals were shown by Wallace[1] to be sex, high school rank, fraternity membership, faculty contacts, and "interpersonal environment". Fraternities and sororities within the American colleges do contribute to development of subcultures firstly, because of their relative social and cultural homogeneity;[2] secondly, because they provide a recognised "base", often residential, for informal and organised activities; thirdly they provide a basis for internal student rivalries, which are reflected in interpersonal relations, and what Waller has called the "rating, dating complex",[3] and, lastly, because they provide what Levine has called "goal consistency among institutional subgroups", which is supported by informal sanctions.[4] The role of fraternities and sororities in development of subgroup cultures is matched by that of some halls of residence in British universities. Such cultures are also related to the social class composition of the institution—fraternities and halls of residence being more prevalent in higher class colleges than others.

We have already discussed the contribution of Trow to our understanding of college subcultures and the prevalence of certain of his types in certain institutions, the academic subculture being most likely to develop in the Ivy College—the vocational subculture in the Cosmopolitan or Industrial Civic.

Recent British studies of student culture have noted differences in student custom and culture in different universities but have not altogether shown *why* they differ. This relates especially to a neglect of impact of class differences of students upon student culture and organisations. Indeed, because his respondents shied away from implications of social class membership in student life, it appears that Zweig (1963)[5] assumed social class to have little direct relevance in student social relations. Marris[6], too, (1964) whose particular findings about student residence, relations with staff, and so on, will be discussed in conjunction with findings of the thesis surveys, also seems to come to this conclusion. Indeed, Marris states that "the university by its autonomy and detachment enabled them to

[1] Wallace, W. L., *Student Culture*, NORC Monograph No. 9, Aldine, 1965.

[2] Segal, B. E., Fraternities, social distance and anti-semitism among Jewish and non-Jewish undergraduates, *Sociol. Educ.*, 1965, **38** (3) 251–64; Scott, J. F., The American college sorority—its role in class and ethnic endogamy, *ASR*, 1965, **30**, 514–27.

[3] Waller, W. The rating and dating complex, *ASR*, 1937, **2**, 727–34.

[4] Levine, The American college experience as a socialisation process, in Newcomb and Wilson, *op. cit.*

[5] Zweig, *op. cit.*, pp. 39–42, 113–16.

[6] Marris, *op. cit.*

postpone questions of class identity".[1] This statement is challenged by the findings of the present study.

Of course, since many studies of student socialisation are concerned with the student's eventual reintegration into "outside" society, there is a wealth of information on professionalisation among students particularly in the medical, and legal faculties.[2] Such studies are primarily concerned with the student's anticipatory socialisation into his professional role, the way he learns of the sets of expectations which surround his performance, and the way he learns to fulfil those expectations. Medical students and nurses particularly have to learn to cope with human crises such as death as part of their normal daily routine; through progressive stages they are detached from their previous culture and assume their professional role. This obviously is a special kind of socialisation which is distinct from intitutional socialisation *per se*, since it orientates the student very specifically to his post-college role. However, most students in non-professional or vocational faculties do not have a very clear idea of their post-college role, and must be prepared in general to take up any one of a number of professional roles.

Studies of professional socialisation are being undertaken in a number of countries, however, since professional faculties do in a sense exhibit best features of "closedness", and findings are cross-culturally comparable.[3]

As we discussed, some degree of institutional autonomy or closedness does seem to be related to growth of specifically student subcultures. However, since universities are constantly expanding and becoming more diffuse, this is a condition which is increasingly not being met. How far this is destroying student culture or making of student culture something else, for instance a politically active culture, is open for debate. Anderson sug-

[1] Marris, *op. cit.* p. 156.

[2] Cf. Hughes, E. C. and Strauss, A. C., *Boys in White*, Univ. Chicago Press, Chicago, 1961. Merton, R. K., Reader G. C., and Kendall, P. L. (eds.), *The Student Physician*, Harv. Univ. Press, Cambridge, 1957. Davis, F. and Olesen, V. E., Initiation into a women's profession, *Sociometry*, 1963, **26**, 89–101. Davis and Olesen, Baccalaureate students' images of nursing, *Nursing Research*, Winter 1964, **13**, 8–15. Olesen, V. and Whittaker, E. W., Some thoughts on images on man implicit in sociological studies of professional education, paper presented to VIth World Congress of Sociology, 1966. Eron, L. D. and Redmont, R. S., Effect of legal education on attitudes, *J. Legal Educ.* 1957, **9** (4). Olesen, V. and Whittaker, E., *The Silent Dialogue*, Jossey-Bass, 1968.

[3] Cf. Raynaud, J. D. and Touraine, A., Deux notes à propos d'une enquête sur les étudiants en Médecine, *Cahiers Int. de Soc.*, nouvelle série, 3ème année, 1956, **20**. Schaefer, H., Etudes médicales et réforme de l'enseignement en Allemagne, *Rev. Enseignment Superieur*, 1957, **3**.

gests that expansion brings common problems for diverse universities.[1] One of these is the impact of size on structure[2] and another is the growth of proportion of administration in relation to teaching faculty.[3] All these changes, in fact, change the role of the institution in society[4] and in relation to its students, for many of whom being a student becomes tantamount to an "occupation".[5]

Not only does this have an impact then on development of institutional culture and possibilities for socialisation, but also upon occupational aspirations and choice, which reflect those processes. As we have noted, the processes are intimately interlinked. Work in this field has, for instance, shown the relation between social class and occupational aspirations,[6] between academic ability and occupational mobility,[7] and between educational and faculty values and organisation and occupational choice.[8] Such studies lead to an examination of the mechanics of student mobility.

As to the study of student mobility, there is very little that is specifically a study of what goes on actually in the university—most work on mobility being concerned with occupational or institutional mobility. Yet this would seem a most fruitful area of study in order to discover and separate out the variables which are involved in moving from one social category to another. Societal *rates*, of course, must be considered in relation to this process as the framework within which mobility is taking place and which represents the relative stability which might be affected by an increase in democratisation of higher education. In Britain the stability in class differ-

[1] Anderson, C. A., Common problems for universities, *Int. Rev. Educ.*, 1965, **11** (1), 3–19.

[2] Beale, R. J., The organisational structure of large colleges of technology, *Tech. Educ.*, 1966, **8** (7), 310–12.

[3] Hawley, A. H., Boland, W., and Boland, M., Population size and administration in institutions of higher education, *ASR*, 1965, **30** (2), 252–5.

[4] Ducret, B. and Rafe-uz-Zaman, *The University Today: Its Role and Place in Society*, WUS, Geneva, 1960. Halsey, A. H., The changing functions of universities in advanced industrial societies, *Harv. Educ. Rev.*, Spring 1960, **30**, 119–27.

[5] Silver, H., Salaries for students?, *Univ. Quart.*, September 1965, **19** (4).

[6] Sewell, W. H., Haller, H. O., and Strauss, M. A., Social status and educational and occupational aspiration, *ASR*, 22 February 1957, pp. 67–73.

[7] Eckland, B. K., Academic ability, higher education and occupational mobility, *ASR*, 1965, **30** (5), 735–46. Gerstl, J. and Perrucci, R., Educational channels and elite mobility: a comparative analysis, *Sociol. Educ.*, 1965, **38** (3), 224–32. Nisbet, J. D. and Grant, W., Vocational intentions and decisions of Aberdeen Arts graduates, *Occup. Psych.*, 1965, **39** (3), 215–19.

[8] Werts, C. E., Social class and initial career choice of college Freshmen, *Sociol. Educ.*, 1966, **39** (1), 84–85.

entials over long periods of time might suggest some stability in inter-generational mobility rates when higher education is one of the main avenues to social advancement. Although general works on social mobility have contemplated this question they have little to tell us about the process of mobility going on *at the* university nor about how such mobility is achieved although the relation between educational and career mobility is clearly paramount.

Glass's study[1] in 1954 had speculated that the provisions associated with the 1944 Act might eventually increase the frequency of social mobility and that increased "educational" mobility may be counterbalanced by decreased "career mobility". The research reported was concerned with the processes of social selection and differentiation at work in Britain, the formation of social strata and the nature, composition and functions of those strata, in terms of a general investigation of social mobility. One particular investigation set out to examine the relationship between the social status of fathers and sons. This was supplemented by a study of self-recruitment in four professions—related particularly to university students. Glass and his associates stress that in fact the sample under study had passed through the system *before* the 1944 Education Act and were thus products of the 1870 and 1902 Acts. In the period before 1944, social origins and education tended to reinforce each other and thus acted cumulatively to produce a close association between social status of father and son. This was especially true for the higher levels of social status.

In the measure of association between social status of father's and son's occupations, the *norm* chosen postulates a random association between the occupations of fathers and sons. By the index of association used if parental and filial association were random, the index in both cases would be 1·0. Among men whose fathers were manual workers the index was 1·16. A comparable index for men whose fathers were professional was 13·16, showing a far higher degree of self-recruitment at upper levels of social prestige.[2]

D. V. Glass and J. R. Hall[3] say that the

> study has shown almost throughout an association in status between fathers and sons significantly higher than would be expected on the basis of "perfect

[1] Glass, *op. cit.*

[2] "The greatest opportunities for movement on the part of sons of manual workers are of necessity within the range of manual skills". Lockwood, D., Social mobility, in Welford, A. T. *et al.*, *Society: Problems and Methods of Study.* Routledge, 1962, p. 512.

[3] Glass, *op. cit.*, ch. 8, p. 126.

mobility" as well as highly significant differences between the degrees of association for the various strata into which the men covered by the inquiry were classified. The second main result is a negative one—the conclusion that, according to our data, there have been no major differences between successive generations in the overall intensity of the status association between fathers and sons.

Glass also concludes that the type and level of education attained by the subjects who co-operated in the investigation depended very heavily upon the social status (as measured in terms of occupation) of the subjects' fathers, but, as Hilde Himmelweit points out, "secondary education of the grammar school type provides the main avenue for upward social mobility for the children of the working class".[1]

However, in his study of social mobility in Sweden (1958), Gösta Carlsson says:

> It might be that the extension of the service of the educational system to larger groups makes education a more important criterion for future career and other things, including parents' status, less important that it removes most of the delayed effects. Whether this will be true or not seems hard to say. Perhaps society as a whole will become more "education conscious" or even "school ridden" and therefore apt to forget other grounds of distinction, including parents' status. It might, however, equally well be argued that the more general prevalence of higher education will make for instance employers more prone to take other things into consideration.[2]

These questions have yet to be further examined in the British context. Carlsson concludes in his study that in Sweden:

> To be sure schooling appears as an asset for those who have it, but hardly the decisive factor in the majority of cases where people have moved upwards on the social ladder. Neither does education appear to remove other influences of parental social status on the future status of the son. No-one has assumed that education (beyond the elementary level) is a sufficient and necessary prerequisite of social advancement, but perhaps it is a little further from being so than we have been aware of. The strong interest in the recruitment of certain elite groups, above all in the learned professions and related groups—the category sociologists themselves belong to—may have influenced our perspective too much.[3]

This challenge to the importance of education as a primary means of social mobility questions the nature of social inequality and its continuity in the social structure and suggests that education itself introduces new

---

[1] Glass, *op. cit.*, ch. 6, p. 141.
[2] Carlsson, G., *Social Mobility and Class Structure*, CWK, Gleerup, Lund, 1958, p. 126.
[3] *Ibid.*, p. 137.

division. Thus although education is at the same time a symbol of social position and a means by which higher position may be achieved "so that the amount of access to it is one of the keys to the amount of mobility possible in a society".[1] Bendix and Lipset in *Social Mobility in Industrial Society* interpret the evidence that "the overall pattern of social mobility appears to be much the same in industrial societies in various Western countries"[2] in terms of a "threshold" theory of more or less constant rates of mobility, beyond a certain stage of economic development.

This and other studies such as that by Miller[3] provide interesting national and international comparisons but one is left with questions about the impact of mobility experience within the social structure such as that raised by Hicks in *The Social Framework*:

> A less tangible question both because it has not been subject to investigation, so that present knowledge is limited and because the effect of reforms is necessarily very gradual—is the influence of Twentieth Century changes in education upon the skill of the working population.[4]

Certainly changes in education change values and aspirations.

For instance Jahoda[5] (1952) took a sample of adults in the urban areas and asked what occupation they would like their son to enter. More than one-fifth chose a profession, less than 8 per cent a clerical job and commonest choice, 36 per cent, was for a skilled trade. This latter represented an aspiration for security and mobility in terms with reality. Choices were made in terms of class values—therefore office work ranked low.

Kelsall[6] found that of university male entrants in 1953, 23 per cent had no classifiable occupation in mind; of the rest, 90 per cent contemplated a profession (including teaching, research, and the civil service); only 10 per cent envisaged industry or commercial occupations. What we know of the diverse but mainly middle-class composition would seem to show a shift of aspirations up the scale with higher status or higher education. A note on self-recruitment of professions is shown[7] in that medical under-

---

[1] Becker, H. S., Paper 10, Schools and systems of stratification, *ibid.*, p. 93.

[2] Bendix, R. and Lipset, S. M. (eds.), *Class, Status and Power—A Reader in Social Stratification*, Free Press, Glencoe, Ill., 1953, p. 13.

[3] Miller, S. M., Comparative social mobility, *Current Sociol.*, 1960, **9** (1).

[4] Hicks, J. R., *The Social Framework*, London, 1942, p. 192.

[5] Jahoda, G., Job attitude and job choice among secondary modern school leavers, *Occupational Psychol.*, April and October 1952.

[6] Kelsall, *op. cit.*, table 179.

[7] *Ibid.*, table 18(a).

graduates who were doctors' sons constituted 16·4 per cent of all men proposing to study medicine.

A recent article by Blau tells us more about certain features of the occupational structure in the "flow of occupational supply and recruitment".[1] The units of analysis are seventeen occupational groups into which the American labour force has been divided. Blau contributes something to the understanding of mobility structures by focusing attention on *relation among substructures*, which are characterised by the direction and flow of manpower between them. Horizontal as well as vertical mobility is related to class recruitment and change.

In showing how class change does or does not take place Lockwood and Goldthorpe have advanced a new approach to the study of "embourgeoisement". Although they analyse the process of *implied* changes in values, attitudes, and aspirations going hand in hand with the economic changes of the affluent worker, their postulations are equally applicable in the study of the embourgeoisement of students. They suggest that mobility is experienced in terms of the economic, normative, and relational aspects of class, and that therefore embourgeoisement must be discussed in these terms; that embourgeoisement—or change in value and culture patterns and acceptance by the group to which one aspires (i.e. assimilation)—is only the last in a process of progressive stages, and that in order to understand mobility one needs studies "of the individual's basic social imagery and the related normative predispositions".[2]

Since occupational and educational mobility implies movement away from the social class of origin and all that implies in terms of relationship with parents and peers, it is extremely important to ask also what kind of forces and personalities result in individual mobility—and what the effect is on the individual, the group which he has left and the group to which he aspires—in terms of a restructuring of relationships.

Elder[3] draws from evidence of five surveys conducted in the late 1950's and early 1960's and relevant research in monographs and articles to ex-

[1] Blau, P. M., The flow of occupational supply and recruitment, *ASR*, August 1965, **30** (4).

[2] Lockwood, D. and Goldthorpe, J. H., Affluence and the British class structure, *Sociol. Rev.*, 1963, **11**, 133.

[3] Elder, G. H., Jr., *Life Opportunity and Personality: Some Consequences of Stratified Secondary Education in Great Britain*, Inst. of Internat. Studies, Univ. California, Berkeley, California, Reprint No. 170, reprinted from *Sociol. of Educ.* **38** (3), Spring 1965.

plore the effect of allocation and "streaming" on opportunity and personality, which may have relevance for studies of individual mobility.

Elder draws the conclusion that "the primary effect of student allocation may be in the child's self image, both as a student and more generally as a person". Moreover, he says that "the restriction of a youth's opportunities, coupled with the punishment associated with failing, tends to engender a negative self image which in turn is apt to be associated with an *under-utilisation* of mental abilities".[1]

McLelland, Strodtbeck, and McKinlay[2] are among the writers who have drawn attention to the fact that certain personalities are more predisposed to mobility than others. The question of why some people should move socially and others not, given similar opportunities, is another question of absorbing interest in any study of social class, particularly in studies of student selection. Strodtbeck postulates that the consequence of a boy's upward mobility from lower status depends on the pattern of source of authority in family. Ascriptive role dissatisfaction and compensative achievement role activity shows the individual's alienation from or hostility to his father. (Other studies have shown that this is only true of the *highly* mobile individual.) His study showed that upwardly mobile sons came from families in which the father exercised less authority and the mothers somewhat more. McKinlay endorses this view and says that his findings point to the fact that individuals who are gaining status in the *achieved* roles (and therefore possibly experiencing inconsistency because their ascribed statuses are lagging behind) originate in families where the father is less powerful and the mother more powerful. This finding relates to that of Jackson and Marsden that the system selected not only individuals—it selected *families*. Jackson and Marsden[3], Lockwood[4] and others have pointed out "the stress and tension of striving under difficult conditions", with its implications for personality changes, but in Turner's words "a search for personality forming experiences specific to a sponsorship system

---

[1] Elder, *op. cit.*, p. 176.

[2] See McLelland, D. C., *et al.*, *Talent and Society*, D. Van Nostrand Co. Inc., Princeton, 1958, containing Strodtbeck, F. L., Family interaction values and achievement, pp. 135–194. McLelland, D. C., *et al.*, *New York, The Achievement Motive*, Appleton, Century Crofts Inc., 1953. McKinlay, D. G., *Social Class and Family Life*, Free Press, Glencoe, Ill., 1964, p. 191.

[3] Jackson and Marsden, *op. cit.*, p. 126.

[4] Lockwood, D., Can we cope with social change?, *New Society*, 28 November 1963.

has yet to be made".[1] This represents a study of *mode* rather then extent of mobility.

In his paper Turner suggests a framework for relating differences between the American and English systems of education to the prevailing norms of upward mobility. He suggests two ideal–typical normative patterns of upward mobility—Contest and Sponsored mobility. In the former system élite status is the prize of competition, whereas in the latter the élite recruits are chosen by the established élite or their agents so that what is "given" cannot be "taken". This patterning affects the school system since one of its functions, as has been already pointed out, is that of facilitating mobility. A sponsored system arises more readily in a society with a single élite with some monopoly of "credentials". When multiple élites compete amongst themselves the mobility process tends to take the contest patterns "since no group is able to control command of recruitment".[2]

Turner suggests that "English society has been described as the juxtaposition of the two systems of stratification—the urban, industrial class system and the surviving aristocratic system". Changes in stratification have, however, "taken place within the unchallenged organizing norms of sponsored mobility".[3] Different values characterise different systems.

> Under sponsored mobility schooling is valued for its cultivation of élite culture and those forms of schooling directed toward such cultivation are more highly valued than those who are not.[4] Under contest mobility there is not the same apparent homogeneity of moral, aesthetic and intellectual values to be emulated so that the conspicuous attribute of the elite is their superior level of material consumption.

Drop out rates are higher in the United States because higher education is run like a contest, while in the United Kingdom selection is *supposed* to have been relatively complete before entry to university. Mobility experience is thus shaped by the structure of competition, the structure of inequalities and the nature of constraints. The role of formal education in purveying an élite culture is mediated by the kind of recruitment or selection of those to be educated. The extent to which this role is performed

---

[1] Turner, R. H., Sponsored and contest mobility and the school system, *ASR*, 1960, **25** (5). Reprinted in Halsey *et al.*, *op. cit.*, ch. 12.

[2] *Ibid.*, p. 125.

[3] Halsey *et al.*, *op. cit.*, p. 125.

[4] *Ibid.*, pp. 130, 127.

is the extent to which values are changed. Changes in class education therefore centre upon differences in the value systems inherent in different class cultures. "From the point of view of the schools in a class society, class is culture; and education is a process of cultural assimilation through the reconstruction of personalities previously conditioned by class or race."[1]

This, then, is an outline of the central structural features and dilemmas involved in the democratisation of higher education and of the various cultural impediments to this goal which have been discovered by sociologists. It is clear that the research problems and work already done cannot be properly understood outside the structural framework outlined—and it is only within this framework that we are able to evaluate the contribution which each aspect makes to the whole.

For what is involved is clearly not only changes in education but changes in society—a world problem—and we cannot fail to see the importance of the repercussions which these changes may bring about or, alternatively the discontent and frustrations if no change occurs. The two pressures discussed at the beginning may mean stress and conflict—they certainly are attendant upon changes in values. The rate of change will determine whether there is a period of "*anomie*" and "transition" such as is appearing in Britain and the United States among the recipients of the previously élite culture. This in turn must affect the kind of status groups or social classes there are in society, and whether the existing structure is bolstered up or broken down—whether new people are put into old slots or whether the new people in themselves create new slots. The ramifications for social structure are endless. This is why the present analysis treats three universities as varying situations in which principles emerge applicable to similarly structured situations, and relevant in a series of interlocking structures as reference groups up to the level of the social classes themselves.

The author does not propose at this stage to examine at length her investigations of the *nature* of social classes, although this will be discussed in relation to survey findings. Stratification in any population exhibits various facets according to the contexts in which and the methods by which it is examined. The author has initially examined the socioeconomic classes of students in terms of occupation of parents. That this is only a rough guide and, in a sense, merely one dimension of a multidimensional phenomena is realised, and areas of analysis where it breaks down as a useful tool are clearly indicated.

[1] Halsey *et al.*, *op. cit.*, p. 8.

The author admits to the great difficulties facing those who study and attempt to define social class in agreeing with Littlejohn that:

> A social class is neither a mere category arbitrarily defined by myself on the basis of one or mere "characteristics" such as property ownership, nor is it a group in the strict sense of the term as implying clear-cut boundaries and a constitution laying down a limited set of relationships among its members. A class is rather for its members one of the major horizons of all social experience; an area within which most social experience is defined. Encompassing so much it is rarely conceptualized.[1]

Yet one of the aims of the survey has been to discover some of the limits of the *area* so defined in terms of social experience, and the situations in which attitude and action is regulated by other areas of social experience. An examination of students' conceptualisation of social class, as in Chapter 12, is a necessary introduction to such analysis and provides a bridge between the abstraction and reality. As T. H. Marshall says: "It is dangerous to start with the assumption that because the word 'class' is commonly used it must express a definable concept."[2]

This may, indeed, be a dangerous assumption, for one of the most difficult tasks of the book, and one which in terms of its wider relevance is by no means fully accomplished, has been to express "social class" as a "definable concept", meaningful both to observer and observed and in a sense not merely an abstraction from reality but an *operational* concept which may be used as a tool to gain further understanding of the nature of social relations in general.

The findings of research into aspects of education and social class have been discussed which set in context the findings of the present book. In comparing them one must, for convenience, take for granted that what is being measured as "social class" is a relatively constant and consistent phenomenon. However, this need not necessarily be so in "the real world", and even the single dimension of "occupational status" may be subject to change over time in different places and in different contexts studied. One of the unforeseen results of the survey is concerned with just that. Not only is social class revealed in its various dimensions by the findings, but it is shown to *vary in degree of relevance* as a factor in social relations with a complex set of conditions in any particular context. This will be seen to be

[1] Littlejohn, J., *Westrigg, The Sociology of a Cheviot Village,* Routledge and Kegan Paul, 1963, p. 111.
[2] Marshall, T. H., *Citizenship and Social Class,* CUP, 1950, pp. 86–113.

a development of the structure of the empirical evidence itself throughout the book, and the development will be traced accordingly.

Finally, one may ask what is the relevance of all this in the understanding of contemporary student unrest. The author would posit that it has everything to do with such issues, for the processes described have endless repercussions individual, institutional, and societal. Nothing can be overlooked. Yet it is hoped that by studying particular institutional and organisational variables we may better be able to understand why unrest occurs in some universities and not in others, why some are in constant revolution while others continue with their parochial concerns as though oblivious to events of great moment in the world political arena.

The study of unrest was not a first interest of the present survey, but a special chapter has been devoted to this topic (Chapter 15). If our theories about student social relations, student culture, and student organisation hold good, they should be able to incorporate the incidence of the kind of radical and abrupt changes which we are witnessing. If not, then sociology must always follow changes in society and never predict them.

CHAPTER 2

THE THREE UNIVERSITIES

IT WOULD be pleasant to be able to record that the three universities chosen for the comparative study were selected because they exhibited most clearly the kind of organisation and structure necessary for detailed comparative analysis. In fact this was not so, and, ultimately, the three decisive factors were cost, convenience, and chance. However, in retrospect, the author believes that whatever the processes which determined the choice of these three universities, they did, in fact, turn out to be excellent examples of the basic differences required and provided a sound basis for comparison. Moreover, since it is not intended to draw general conclusions about institutions but about structural *situations*, in a sense any contrasting three universities would equally well have served the purpose. As Robbins points out in fact, all institutions of higher education are different, with different history and structure.[1] One of the implications of the survey findings is that since all institutions are so different they may be expected to experience different effects of expansion of educational opportunity and in different degree.

The first survey was carried out in Edinburgh—quite by chance—since it was the university of the author's first degree. Since one might assume that the findings of the Edinburgh survey would have limited applicability primarily because Edinburgh is a Scottish university and for that reason alone in some ways atypical, it was first thought that any comparative study should embrace English universities, particularly of the south and Midlands. Before the nature of the research had been clearly formulated it was thought most profitable to do a large-scale "national" survey containing a varied selection of collegiate, civic, and "new" universities. If this had succeeded it is clear that a totally different thesis than the one presented would have emerged and would have represented a

[1] Robbins Report, *Higher Education*, Cmnd. 2154, London, 1963, ch. 2, para. 14, p. 4.

"broadening out" rather than a "narrowing down" of the sociological[1] scrutiny.

It soon became clear that a large-scale survey would be unpracticable because of lack of finance and time in which to carry out such a vast project. The number of universities to be compared with Edinburgh was narrowed to two. A three-sided comparison seemed more rounded than a merely two-sided one. Indeed, had not the third—in Newcastle—been undertaken, the significance of many results in the other two would have gone unnoticed and many explanations would have been misleading.

Findings in the Edinburgh survey had suggested that residential organisation is an important factor in student relationships, and, since Edinburgh is non-residential, a collegiate university clearly seemed to be necessary as a contrasting study. Fortunately, Durham University is within easy travelling distance and is collegiate—so it was chosen. The next most obvious choice was that of Newcastle University which until 2 years previous to the survey had been part of Durham University as King's College in Newcastle. In a sense this represented a "control" in that one could compare if one University were more regionally biased than the other in terms of its student population and why this situation arose. Newcastle, being at once an old and a "new" university, presented an interesting variation, and by virtue of its industrial setting contrasted sharply with the two other universities.

The three universities chosen differ in obvious respects of size, history, institutional structure, residential organisation, and urban setting, yet, since they are situated within a defined geographical area in the northeast of Britain, this, to some extent, eliminates the important variable of "region" or that based on any north south division. As 1 in every 16 persons in Edinburgh is English it would seem that in some ways Edinburgh may well have more in common with the English than the Scottish universities.[1] As the only Scottish university in the survey it introduces the additional variable of "nationality", and has a student population of both Scottish and English. It was noted in Chapter 1 that students of the two countries are products of different educational systems and traditions. In order to cope with this additional variable, the Scottish and English students have been largely treated as separate samples and in fact provide some interesting comparisons.

---

[1] Edinburgh University was at the time of the survey also the only Scottish university participating in the UCCA.

It is necessary at this point to compare the three universities in terms of size, history, structure, and residential organisation as an introduction to the survey findings.

1. Size

In 1962 the University of Edinburgh had 7509 students of whom 6266 were taking full-time courses. Of the full-time students 4258 were men and 2008 were women, although the proportion of men to women varied considerably between the different faculties of arts, law, divinity, medicine, dentistry, veterinary science, music, and science. These students come from many parts of the world, and the percentage of overseas students to British students is high compared with other universities. The students are divided by nationality into the following proportions (1961–2 figures):

Full-time only		All students (incl. part-time)	
Scottish	55%	Scottish	54%
England (and Wales and N. Ireland)	28%	England (and Wales and N. Ireland)	27%
Overseas	17%	Overseas	19%
No.	6266	No.	7509

In 1963 the university of Durham had 1916 full-time students and 13 part-time, of whom 1450 were men and 466 women—distributed throughout the faculties of arts, social studies, and pure science. Other faculties had been "lost" to Newcastle when it became a university in its own right. The proportion of overseas students in Durham is negligible—only approximately 3 per cent.

In 1964 the University of Newcastle had 4553 full-time students of whom 3384 were men and 1169 women. These took courses in the faculties of arts, economic and social studies, law, education, science, applied science, agriculture, medicine, and dental surgery. Of these students only 9 per cent were overseas students of which 4·3 per cent came from Commonwealth countries. All other students were almost exclusively English.

Basic differences in the three universities emerge as to size, nationality, and sex divisions.

2. History and Institutional Structure

Edinburgh University

While the fifteenth century was a period of intellectual stagnation in England, in Scotland it saw the dawn of higher education: between 1412 and 1495 three Universities were established. By mid sixteenth century a decay had set into the Catholic church—a decay in learning among other things, whose effect was felt in the Universities. The Catholic purge which accompanied the Reformation resulted in a desire to establish a new University of Protestant foundation. Edinburgh, the youngest of the four Scottish Universities, was founded in 1583 by the Town Council largely as a result of that purge.[1]

When "The Toun's College" first opened its doors to "students desirous of instruction", the teaching staff consisted of one man, Robert Rollock, a former professor at St. Andrews, and there was one class. In 1621 the "Act of Confirmation" ratified the college's privilege of conferring degrees, and granted it the rights, immunities, and privileges enjoyed by the other Scottish universities; these were renewed in the Treaty of Union and Act of Security in 1707.

In the early days there were no professors, their place being taken by "regents" or tutors. Professors, in fact, did not make an appearance until 1708, at which time the individual faculties were also beginning to appear, first divinity, then law, medicine, and the arts. Finally, in 1858 the University received a new and autonomous constitution—freeing it from the complete control of the civic authorities. The Universities (Scotland) Act of 1889 constituted the University as a body corporate to which all the property belonging to the University at that time was transferred with full powers of administration. In 1893 the academic organisation of the University was arranged into six faculties: arts, divinity, law, medicine, music, and science. The Faculty of Social Science began in 1963.

The University has always had close ties with the city, and the general awareness of this link is coupled with the fact that the dispersion of university buildings over a wide area brings students into constant everyday contact with city and citizens. The University is expanding rapidly in a numerical and physical sense, and this is something which every student experiences. It is already one of the largest universities in Britain (over 9000 students in 1966–7).

[1] Edinburgh University, *Student's Handbook 1964–65*, 69th edn., an SRC publication, p. 15,

At the head of the formal structure is the Chancellor, beneath him the Vice-Chancellor and Principal. The Students' Rector is a post filled by a person of national or international repute elected by the students every 3 years. This post is peculiar to the Scottish universities and the elections have been surrounded by controversy in recent years. The Rector is chief spokesman to the Senate and Court for the ordinary student and thus theoretically represents a direct link between the student and the governing body. Tasks of Rector in the ordinary running of the University are usually undertaken by a person nominated by him—called the Rector's Assessor. The Secretary is the principal administrator of the University. The main governing body is the University Court which is composed of the Chancellor, Vice-Chancellor, and Rector, certain of the Members of Senate, and a number of civic dignitaries. The Court is responsible for buildings and financial matters. The Senatus Academicus is composed of professors and certain elected members of the non-professorial staff and is responsible for academic matters within the University and also for the discipline of the student body ("A power which they wield lightly").[1]

Other bodies in the University constitution are the General Council of graduates and staff, and the Curators of Patronage who have the patronage of sixteen chairs.

The Students' Representative Council (SRC), instituted by the Universities (Scotland) Act of 1889 is one of the oldest in the country, being founded in 1884, and has developed quite a large bureaucratic machinery through recent years to deal with its various functions. These include finance; services to students; benevolent services; relations with university authorities; relations with Scottish Union of Students; and international questions.[2] As stated in the Constitution, these are as follows:

Para 2. The functions of the Council shall be:
(a) to represent the students in matters affecting their interests;
(b) to afford a recognised means of communication between the students and the University authorities;
(c) to promote social life and academic unity among the students;
(d) to provide for students such other services as seem necessary or desirable.[3]

---

[1] McDonald, A. H. (President, SRC 1962–3), in *Students' Diary 1962–3*, an SRC publication.

[2] Miller, W., Concerning student government (a study of the Students' Representative Council), unpublished M.A. dissertation of University of Edinburgh, June 1965, p. 25.

[3] Edinburgh University SRC, *Constitution and Standing Orders*, 1963, para. 2, ch. I, Laws.

The SRC is elected annually by the students on a faculty and year basis of seats, and is the formal machinery of communication between the Court, Senate, and student—particularly by means of the Senatus, SRC Liaison Committee, and the office of Rector.

Since most students exhibit great apathy concerning standing and voting in elections, the SRC is not a truly representative body and, like most informal organisations, depends largely for its successful working on a small number of individuals of personality and talent. However, in recent years, with the growth of numbers there has been increasing contesting of seats and a liveliness in elections.

The faculties have their own sub-committees on the SRC and their own means of communication with faculty heads. This kind of faculty organisation is representative of that running throughout the student body. Since the university unit is so large, students tend to identify increasingly with the faculty, and the proliferation of faculty scarves as opposed to university scarves (more marked than in either Durham or Newcastle) is merely one indication of a developing process. Much student organisation is run on faculty lines either consciously or unconsciously. There are over eighty societies, clubs, and associations, and they tend to be the centres of student social life. Since there are separate men's and women's unions with voluntary membership, there are no real centres of student activity in a physical sense.[1] The unions enrol only a proportion of students as members, and the Men's Union (known as the University Union) tends to be dominated by students in the medical faculty. Student societies are frequently dominated by members of a certain faculty, and this tends to perpetuate the existing structure. Some non-departmental "interest" societies and sports groups cut across these faculty ties as do groupings by years, between which there is an element of social distance.

The Medical Faculty is physically separate from the main student body—in the New Quad—and tends to remain a socially separate unit with its own special traditions and organisations. This is the oldest part of the University and, accordingly, the most well known outside Edinburgh.

Since buildings are separate and "digs" are scattered, the various student eating places tend to become the geographical bases upon which social groups are founded. Although from year to year the social group composition of students frequenting the Refectory and Common Room tends gradually to change, in any one year it is possible to locate a group

---

[1] This will change with the completion of the student Amenities Centre.

or society by its relations to a clearly defined social "space". This is tacitly accepted by all the students.

Many student groups have members in common, and one finds various societies with leaders in common. These linking bonds of individuals rather than institutions preserve unity within the student body as a whole. In fact, the personal element of unity in social organisation is very important as group leaders can draw together the student body and lack of them can mean a disintegration of corporate student life. Very rarely is the whole student body all together in one place at one time, exceptions being rectorial elections and charities' week processions. At formal occasions such as graduation, the student body is so large that at least two ceremonies have to be held. The relation of academic staff (of whom there were in 1963 some 1000 or so) to students is not institutionally defined outside the classroom. There is no Senior Common Room and Junior Common Room although the staff do have their own staff club whose facilities are strictly prohibited to students. The jurisdiction of staff over students is not, in general, thought to extend beyond academic matters, and the residential organisation of the University precludes any real kind of supervision. On the whole, the norms of staff–student relations are regulated by the individual, within certain limits, so that any mutual "avoidance" which exists is a personal phenomenon and is not institutionally prescribed. There is little social contact between staff and students, however, as one might expect. As the University gets larger, this becomes increasingly true, final honours students being those most likely to have some kind of informal contact.

Durham University

This University was founded in 1832 by an Act of Parliament and to some extent modelled on the then only two existing universities of Oxford and Cambridge: it established colleges with the aim of having as many people in residence as possible. The Act of 1832 made the Dean and Chapter of Durham Cathedral governors of the University and the Bishop Visitor, for the Act was to "enable the Dean and Chapter of Durham to appropriate part of the property of their church to the establishment of a University in connexion therewith for the advancement of learning".[1]

The first statutes were made by the Dean and Chapter in 1834, and the

---

[1] *Royal Commission on the University of Durham Report*, February 1935, Cmnd. 4815, HMSO, p. 8.

University was incorporated by Royal Charter in 1837 under the name of "The Warden, Masters and Scholars of the University of Durham". The University of Durham Act, 1908, and the Statutes of 1909 created a new Senate and modified the position and powers of the Dean and Chapter while retaining visitorial powers in the hands of the Bishop; they also created a Council of the Durham Colleges and constituted a Newcastle Division consisting of the College of Medicine and Armstrong College (Technical and Science College).

The first colleges to be set up not unnaturally established Durham as a centre of theological training although admission to the colleges was not confined to students of theology; the dominance of the cathedral is still felt to this day although present-day students try not to emphasise this image. However, the age and tradition of the cathedral and castle and the nature of their ancient links with the University are seen by students as part of its charm and a unique and attractive feature of Durham. Some of the students of University College do in fact have rooms in the castle (with its Norman keep for the most senior) which was given to the University by the Bishop of Durham in the 1830's, and this serves as a constant reminder of the age and tradition of the University.

The University has always been small, and in the early days drew its student population largely from the immediate neighbourhood. It was at one time known as the poor man's Oxford, and enabled the studious but poor miner's son, for example, to taste the benefits of higher education in a traditional setting. In 1932–3 there were only 475 students in the Durham division of the Durham colleges of which 457 lived in college.[1] Of the 333 at the Newcastle College of Medicine and the 822 at the Armstrong College, only 60 students were in residence, demonstrating early the differences between the two divisions.

About 1935 a crisis in the University's organisation and finances occurred and the "major defects in the Constitution of the University"[2] resulted in the Royal Commission on the University of Durham whose report was published in 1937. As a result the University was given a new Constitution by the Act of Parliament whose main articles established changes in the relationship with the Newcastle division and the government of both. The Commission said that one of the major defects of the Constitution was that the "comparative insignificance of the University, as distinguished from the units of which it is composed, and the limitations on

[1] Figures from Register of Admissions, Registrar's Office.
[2] *Royal Commission ... Report*, p. 13,

its resources and powers of initiative have tended to concentrate public support, interest and loyalty on the separate units to the disregard of the University as a corporate institution".[1]

The Commission recommended the limiting of the powers of Convocation and the extending of the powers of the Senate, along with the setting up of a whole-time headship of the Durham Division. The particular complexities which the Commission remarked in 1937 exist to some extent in limited form today, and it is worth quoting the original document on this:

> As a constituent unit of a University the Durham Division is unusual in its variety and complexity. It comprises no less than eight separately organised residential colleges, divided so far as their relation to the government of the Division is concerned into three dissimilar groups, it is specially concerned on behalf of the University with the students of two affiliated colleges and is also related to nineteen associated theological colleges; it has separately housed and organised science laboratories; and it has close relations with the Dean and Chapter of the Cathedral.[2]

To this day the University remains characteristic of both a collegiate and non-collegiate university—all teaching (with the exception of the two teacher training colleges) being done in the departments and faculties and organised on faculty lines, while colleges remain the major community division and are centres to which everyone at least in name only must belong.

The main officers of the University (1964) are the Visitor (Bishop of Durham); Chancellor; Vice-Chancellor and Warden; Pro-Vice Chancellor and Sub-Warden; and Registrar. They, together with certain appointed "heads of houses"—principals and masters of colleges—members appointed by the Senate, non-professorial staff, and members of the city and county council, constitute the University Council.

The Senate is composed of the chief officers of the university, the deans of faculties, all the heads of houses and professorial staff, along with other members appointed by the board of faculties.

The heads of houses wield great power in the organisation. They, to some extent, control entry to the University, and supervise the lives of the students within their care in accordance with the belief that they stand *in loco parentis*—which extends far beyond the limits of academic life. Within each college there is a hierarchy of Principal, resident staff, and

[1] *Ibid.*, ch. 1, para. 22.
[2] *Ibid.*, para. 51.

students, rigidly divided into Senior Common Room and Junior Common Room, High Table, and Low Table. Postgraduate students are in *statu pupillari* and so are definitely members of the Junior Common Room. Everyone is placed into one of these two categories—all status relationships are institutionalised—so that norms of behaviour are clear to everyone. This is reflected in terms of the rigid social distance between different years in the colleges. This social distance is expressed in terms of the arrangement of dining room tables for different years—first years being furthest from High Table.

There were in 1964 eleven colleges—four for female students and seven for male students. All are residential except the non-residential St. Cuthbert's Society. The students' organisations exhibit the same kinds of fragmentation as that of the staff and administration. Each college has a JCR committee and senior man or woman who controls student organisation within the college and acts as communication between the students and Principal and thus to the Senate. An informal meeting of senior men and women is held regularly by the Registrar for airing of grievances and formulation of policy. The SRC is elected from the general student body and, containing representative of colleges and organisations—by contrast with the senior men and women, has won the name of being a council of troublemakers, and although theoretically the chief negotiative body of the students is sometimes bypassed by staff and administration who go straight to the JCR committees and senior men and women. This has not unnaturally caused ill will and has resulted in a diminution of the powers of the SRC and its president.

Since the president is elected straight from the student body—unlike Edinburgh where he and the executive are elected from the Council itself after a hard apprenticeship—there is very little continuity, and the Council has the appearance of a familial organisation. The kind of bureaucratisation which marks all the Edinburgh student organisations is entirely lacking in Durham, partly because of shortage of personnel. A student likened the differences between Edinburgh and Durham to that between the supermarket and the corner shop.

There is a Students' Union which until recently was a debating society only and exclusively male. Since females were admitted in 1960 it has extended its range of social activities, but remains radically independent and often anti-SRC. Its officers—like those of the Edinburgh Men's Union—are assumed to be a cut above the rest because they dominate the last male stronghold in which still remain shreds of former days when universities were only for "young gentlemen". Even the excessive drinking is in accordance with this image ("drunk as a lord").

There are a variety of student societies, too, catering for most interests, but these sometimes suffer from shortage of people to run them, and there is cross-cutting of many other ties. In Durham, much more than in Edinburgh, there is duplication of personnel.

The most striking feature of Durham from the students' point of view is that it is so easy to get to know most of the people in the University in a very short time. This is a feature of a small university and a small town, and it results in an intimate and very personal atmosphere.

The colleges are the main centres of activity and communal life—despite all other cross-cutting ties—and most have their own societies and sports teams, it being more honour to represent one's college in certain circumstances than to represent one's university.

Newcastle University

This University, as we have seen, was known as the Newcastle Division of the Durham Colleges until the Universities of Durham and Newcastle upon Tyne Act established it as a university in its own right as from 1 August 1963. The College of Medicine, started in 1833, had become associated with the University of Durham in 1853, 20 years before the College of Physical Science—or Armstrong College as it later became known—was founded in 1871. The two colleges remained separate until the Royal Commission recommended that they unite as the Newcastle Division of Durham Colleges, later known as King's College. Although Armstrong College was the largest of the three units of the University in 1935—being a multi-faculty college with over 800 full-time students—the Medical College retained and still retains pre-eminence and complete autonomy of internal organisation. This extends to the organisation of the student body, for despite the setting up of the King's College SRC independently of the Durham SRC, the Medical Students' Council has maintained its authority as a duly elected body acting within the jurisdiction of the Medical School, and through the Medical Sub-Council of the SRC exerts considerable influence on the whole student body. No other faculty has this kind of organisation of influence. The Medical Sub-Council consists of "representatives elected by the medical students, including dental students, to the NUSRC together with any other members who may be elected by the medical and dental students to act with them, and together

94 *Student Life in a Class Society*

with the President of the NUSRC".[1] Thus it may be seen that the Medical Students' Council bears a rather special relationship to the SRC. As in Edinburgh, the President of the SRC is very often a medical student, and there is great group solidarity of "medics" at meetings so that the medical nominee may always be assured of a good block vote.

The Medical Students' Council was instituted in 1895 and is the representative body of medical and dental students in the University.

> Its objects are the provision and maintenance of means of social and academic intercourse and the management and protection of recognised means of negotiation between students and authorities of the University, and the Medical School and associated Hospitals, Institutions and Societies.
> The Council consists of annually elected members from the medical and dental student body, together with the representatives from the various sub-committees of Council, namely, Medical Society, Dental Society, B.M.S.A., Medical Gazette and the Medical Athletic Clubs Committee.[2]

The Newcastle and Durham divisions have always been separate to some extent, and according to some students the only time that Newcastle and Durham students met was at Durham regattas and Congregation (graduation). Thus the institution of King's College as a university in its own right was in many ways only acknowledging a division which was already there.

The principal officers of the University are the Visitor (the Lord Chancellor); the Chancellor; Vice-Chancellor; Pro-Vice Chancellor, Dean of Medicine; and Registrar. The Chancellor is the chairman of the University Court. The Court has fifty members drawn in roughly equal numbers from inside and outside the University, and includes members of local authorities; the Council, again equally composed of university and lay members, numbers about twenty-five and meets more frequently than the Court. These two bodies have power to take decisions about the property and finance of the University and "link the University with the life of its region".[3]

All established teachers in the University are members of the Academic Board, which meets at least twice a year, but the supreme academic authority within the University is the Senate, which is a relatively small

[1] University of Newcastle SRC, *Articles of Constitution and Bye-Laws*, 1st edn., 1963, ch. V, para. 1.
[2] University of Newcastle upon Tyne, *Students' Handbook, 1964–65*, p. 17.
[3] University of Newcastle upon Tyne, *General Information, 1963–64*, p. 16.

body of forty members. This body is advised by the boards of the faculties.

The Students' Representative Council is elected on a faculty and year basis from the student body and the executive committee are elected yearly by the Council. The SRC is responsible for all those student affairs not directly connected with the Union Society. The Council itself meets once a month during term when it hears reports from all the sub-committees and holds discussion on many burning topics. Unlike any other council, however, anyone may attend and speak. In Edinburgh non-members must have Council's permission to speak.

Theoretically, the SRC represents the chief negotiating body to the Senate and the means of communication with the student. In practice this relationship is greatly complicated by the existence of a strong committee governing the Union Society to which, technically, everyone belongs, and which controls *in toto* the magnificent union building with its variety of social amenities. The University has built and controls the debating hall, and the student-controlled rooms form a flying wing, at once—like the organisation—separate and conjoined. Thus in many respects the university authorities and the union officers form an avenue of communication and policy formation into which the SRC need not or cannot intrude. The issue is made more complex—and from the student point of view explosive—by the fact that the SRC officers are housed in half a corridor in the union building. This the SRC rents from the Union Society. The SRC also runs social activities only by courtesy of the Union.

"The Union Society is the central hub of student life in the University" claims the *Students' Handbook*,[1] but in fact only a part of the student body uses the union centre even though membership subscription is normally included in the university fees.

The Union President (1964–5), a medical student, compared the SRC and the Union to the House of Commons and the TUC, and one can see where the power conflict analogy is appropriate.

Like the unions of Durham and Edinburgh, it has its own independent management committee and originated in a purely male organisation—in this case an offshoot of the Durham University Union Society. The separate men's and women's unions were amalgamated in 1948.

There are nearly eighty student societies and these have centralised publicity through the Union and many hold their meetings on the premises. This kind of centralisation in terms of a physical base is entirely lack-

[1] University of Newcastle upon Tyne, *Students' Handbook, 1964–65*, p. 23.

ing in Edinburgh and Durham. Yet the Union is used mainly during the day since many students live at home and leave the campus at 5 p.m. every evening.

The main divisions of the University fall mainly along faculty and departmental lines and, since they are physically disparate—as is Edinburgh—spatial organisation emphasises organisational divisions.

3. Residence and Spatial Organisation of Buildings

The *residential* and *spatial* set up of the universities needs closer examination if we are to understand factors underlying student groups. As has already been mentioned, Edinburgh and Newcastle universities are both non-residential, with only a small proportion of students living in halls of residence and a substantial number of students living at home. If we put the figures for Edinburgh and Newcastle together on this, we have some idea of comparison. The Edinburgh figures, however, are for 1961–2; the Newcastle figures for 1963–4:

	Edinburgh (per cent)	Newcastle (per cent)
Home	32	23
Lodgings	54	51
Halls	14	26
TOTAL	100	100

There is nearly twice as high a proportion of students living in halls in Newcastle University than in Edinburgh University. However, in Newcastle 31 per cent of the students live within 30 miles of Newcastle, so that there are as many local students at the University although they are not living at home.

Durham University is collegiate with the express intention of allowing as high a proportion of students to "live in" as possible. Figures on university residence, however, show that in fact a considerable proportion of students are compelled by lack of places to live out even though they are "attached" to a college.

	Durham (per cent)
Home	2
Lodgings	27
Colleges or halls	71
TOTAL	100

In Durham only approximately 16 per cent are "local" students and live within a 30 mile radius of the city—half as many as in Newcastle, although the two universities are only about 20 miles apart and in a sense are drawing upon the same region.

The spatial relationship of the faculty buildings to one another are another interesting feature for comparison. In Edinburgh University the various departments are scattered, but there are marked concentrations which underlie the sciences–arts division which tends to split the University. While the arts departments used to be concentrated in and around the Old Quad, the traditional heart of the University, near the city centre, since 1921 science students have been situated in their own separate campus with their own individual facilities out at King's Buildings on the south side of the city. While the Medical Quad and the Divinity College are at least within easy walking distance of Old Quad in a visibly student quarter of the city near George Square, the science buildings are far enough away to necessitate use of public transport, therefore increasing the ecological and psychological distance. The fact that the science campus is situated on the fringes of suburbia, while the arts buildings are within walking distance of Edinburgh's historic Royal Mile, increases the disparity.

In the programme of expansion which the University is undergoing in a 25 year plan, provisions have been made which will attempt to centralise the arts, social sciences, and library facilities in and around George Square near the present concentration, and will try to bring at least some of the scientists into the same area in use of the first-year science block at one corner of the Square. So far the Law Faculty remains in the Old Quadrangle—somewhat alone. In time, the University, with the co-operation of the Town Council, will redevelop a 125 acre site involving not only the university buildings but also commercial and residential areas. Thus it should be possible to walk from one side of the site to the other, and so improve immediate face-to-face contacts of students which at the moment are regulated by spatial distance.

These changes will draw together work and leisure areas of various kinds into a coherent whole—but living accommodation will remain spatially separate and distinct. The halls of residence pulled down in George Square for new development have been rehoused some way out in the largely Victorian residential area of Morningside. Other residences for women are situated also some way out on the south side of the city in a similar kind of residential area. The new men's halls being built with an additional complex of tower blocks have one of the best positions in Edinburgh at the foot of Arthur's Seat, overlooking the Queen's Park, and within walking distance of Holyrood Palace. They are, however, some distance from the city centre and the George Square area. "Digs" and flat accommodation is to be had in all parts of the city from the historic and decrepit in and near the Royal Mile to the suburban terraces in Portobello, by the sea. There is an extremely wide variety of kinds and standard of accommodation providing for every taste, and since the University has grown so large the city's accommodation saturation point is being realised. However, the situation is better than in most towns because as an international festival city Edinburgh has a large number of boarding houses which take in festival visitors during the summer vacation when the students have all gone home. The city is geared to accommodating people in large numbers. This is not true of Newcastle, and even less true of Durham. Edinburgh has a built-in flexibility. This is true also of the kind of buildings there are in the centre where most people are used to living in flats rather than houses. Stone-built tenements are a common feature; separate dwellings are only to be seen on the city outskirts. The whole structure of buildings is more adaptable to student needs for flats and "digs" than are the English brick "semis". Probably a larger number of students live in flats unsupervised in Edinburgh than in most universities in the British Isles. Yet the system works well: outside the University as long as they do not break the law, students have a degree of freedom in the conduct of their own affairs. They are citizens of Edinburgh. Of course, not only does this increase independence and maturity but may accentuate loneliness, feeling of being "cut off", and of lacking support of student peers. Although there are certain student areas where student flats are concentrated, on the whole accommodation is very spread out in the city and initially the effect of distance from the social and physical student body could be terrifying for the first-year student.

In Newcastle University there is a much greater concentration of university buildings near the city centre, so that it is already possible to see the shape of a campus emerging. The older parts of the University including fine art, medical school, and administrative buildings, are being skilfully merged near the historic and administrative area with the new science blocks and extension to the union building which have sprung up since King's College became a university. Here again a vast programme of expansion is going on, and, as in Edinburgh, departments are being brought in and halls of residence remain towards the periphery. There is no conscious arts–science split, although science is very much in evidence everywhere in terms of faculty buildings and student numbers. It is the departments such as Town Planning and Agriculture which as yet remain in their converted accommodation somewhat spatially separate that feel the disadvantage of ecological distance. Yet the distances to be covered seem in no way as great as those in Edinburgh.

Indeed, in planning even in terms of residential placing, the University has been very conscious of the effect of distance or nearness of buildings on the student body. The aim is to bring together as far as possible the various disciplines in a recognisable complex of buildings which will enhance and be integrated with the planned civic centre of Newcastle and which will presumably, in physical form, express a closer link between city and University. The student social centres, particularly the new union building occupying a central and dominant position in the "higher education precinct" (as it is known by the planners). Thus in areas of work and leisure, by building on an already recognisable and recognised site, Newcastle University is able in a sense to achieve a more physical centrality than seems possible in Edinburgh. This is partly because land was available adjacent to the existing buildings in Newcastle, therefore allowing an almost fresh start, whereas in Edinburgh three of the sides of the lovely old Georgian square had to be destroyed in order for the University to expand anywhere near the centre. There was dreadful controversy over this, and half the city rose in protest, only to be defeated. However, the side of the square which contains a house once the home of Sir Walter Scott remains and is rather forlornly dwarfed by the huge point and slab blocks which now arise around it. Some say that the skyline of Edinburgh is ruined. No such opposition had to be met in Newcastle, particularly since the area round the precinct is not particularly historic. The area, however, is plentifully supplied with shops, cafés, cinemas, and clubs which keep the area alive at night. Conservative forces for preservation are at work in Edinburgh against the university expansion plans—in Newcastle the outlook is more radical. This cannot but affect the growth and shape of the universities concerned.

In terms of residential areas the plan in Newcastle has been to keep students as near to the centre as possible, and the Warden of Lodging's Office proudly sports a map with a huge blue circle within whose radius no student lives further than 20 minutes by bus from the University. Eighty per cent of students live within this area. The only major exception is the community of students in "digs" and flats in Whitley Bay—the far-flung seaside resort adjoining Newcastle. Such is the separateness of the Whitley Bay students that the author was not surprised to hear quite recently (February 1967) that students in Whitley Bay are trying to set up their own separate union. Although the accommodation situation will clearly worsen as the University increases in size and more students will be compelled to live further and further out, the residential areas do seem at the present time to be more compact than in Edinburgh, and, apart from Whitley Bay, more directly linked by main road routes.

In Durham the process of centralisation, which may seem no problem in such a comparatively small area, is just beginning with the planned expansion in student numbers for whom, in this case, places have to be built if the collegiate system is to remain unchanged.

Until recently there was a split between the colleges and departments based in "the Baileys" or on the Peninsula, as that bend in the river is called, and on the other side of the river the new science laboratories and newer colleges further up the hill. The River Wear, in fact, has been until recently a divisive factor in spatial organisation. The historical parts of the University, in keeping with the castle and cathedral with which they used to be so closely linked, are all centred on the Baileys and Palace Green (of the Bishop's Palace). Besides the colleges of University, Hatfield, St. Aidan's (now moved to the south side of the city), St. Chad's, St. Cuthbert's Society, and St. John's various arts departments and the administration building are to be found in this area. The Union Society is very central on Palace Green, and there the SRC also held its meetings until the building of Dunelm House on Old Elvet (after the completion of the study). The science laboratories are new and impressive and quite separate in Durham terms—on a hill on the outskirts across the river, although all within walking distance—and the arts–science split is thus preserved. It is as if, until recently, all that was known and tried, historic, and steeped in tradition, stood on one side of the river, and all that was new and untried and unsure stood on the other. The spatial separateness and the river (as of time, flowing under the bridge) accentuated the difference between the old and the new worlds and, indeed, one almost felt, having crossed Prebend's Bridge, a passenger in time. The stark, simple outlines of the science buildings and the new colleges high on the hill—grey St. Mary's, the new St. Aidan's designed by Sir Basil Spence, and now Van Mildert College, contrast in every possible way with the mellowing, slightly crumbling colleges on the Baileys with their dark, poky, slightly musty interiors. The river represents a real schism in the life of the University—a looking forward and a looking back—and the two must somehow be reconciled. With expansion is coming a shifting of the university centre from Palace Green as, due to lack of space, new colleges are built in the South Road area and the student population moves perforce from the peninsula.

Yet as the centre moves from Palace Green (PG as it is popularly called) it is uncertain as to where it will move if indeed there will be a physical centre at all.[1] In Durham all teaching is done in departments although there are resident "moral tutors" in college who are concerned with discipline, problems, and the issue of "exeats". As in both Newcastle and Edinburgh, the tutorial classes are accepted as a most effective way of teaching, but numbers are often too large for them to be frequent or effective. All that may be emphasised is that where students live and work and spend their leisure time may be quite separate centres of which the college itself as the residential and social unit forms only a part. Those concerned with planning expansion are extremely concerned about the effect which proliferation of colleges will have on the whole organisation. The building of Dunelm House on the river bank, a building which welds together in perfect harmony the new outlook in an ancient setting, is an attempt by the University to find some kind of a solution to the fragmentation of social groups.

This house contains refectory and debating chamber where the SRC at last has a permanent (and presumably now respected) home. There are also a number of social amenities including a bar, and the usual appurtenances of what civic universities call a union. How great a change in in-

---

[1] Since completion of research, Dunelm House has provided a new social centre, almost like a union building of provincial universities, and represents an interesting move to the strengthening of the SRC and centralisation of student authority.

ternal organisation the building of Dunelm House represents can only be understood by those who have experienced Durham's close-knit college life. This centre represents a drawing away to some extent of some of the social impetus from the colleges and, particularly for students living out, represents an alternative kind of meeting place for students at any college. The single-sex colleges, of course, in a sense inhibit real inter-student mixing by introducing an element of artificiality into social contacts with members of the opposite sex. This drawback Dunelm House overcomes— it is "neutral ground" where all kinds of institutional rivalries can be temporarily forgotten.

In all three universities, then, there are certain spatial unities and disunities which mirror or modify the social unities and disunities within the organisation. In all three the areas of work, residence, and leisure are to some extent separate and necessitating some form of travel several times daily between the separate areas—even if only on foot. The only exception is Durham where much of the social life goes on in colleges and where formal events are organised on college lines, thereby creating an overlap of leisure and residence spheres and cutting down on the mobility requirements. Durham is therefore more spatially and socially compact than either Newcastle or Edinburgh, of which Edinburgh seems to be most diffuse in spatial and social terms. In a sense it is only the long history and small beginnings of Edinburgh which ensure for it, in a sort of social memory, a myth and mystique of some invisible body corporate which is nevertheless nourished as a reality as much by the reverence of outsiders as by its student members. Were Edinburgh University much "newer" it could not maintain the amount of self-identification it has. Its corporateness is in spatial terms more imagined than real—in Newcastle, though newer, the spatial concentration of new buildings helps to create the impression of social solidarity and to establish new links which did not exist before. In a sense the social and spatial constraints are too great in Edinburgh and Durham for such new beginnings. The term "space" has been used as if it were some tangible property in social relations. In a sense it is, since it puts physical limits on social contact and determines areas of potential social groupings. Groups cannot be discussed as if they existed in a physical vacuum or independent of the physical environment. Space is as much a factor in the structure of groups as is mutual interest. However, we must not confuse real and objectively measurable or mathematical space and distance with the distances which the social actor perceives. The actor is conditioned by his social experience of a number of spatial distances to relative distance or nearness, and this will affect his reaction to mathematical space. Thus in Edinburgh, where the "norm" is a short bus journey to the significant focal points of daily life, a 10 minute walk is "next door"; in the centre of Durham a 2 minute walk might be "too far"; and for the outlying colleges a 20 minute walk to lectures is hardly noticed. This makes more understandable the fact that while it seems difficult, for instance, to consider any buildings in Durham as far apart if one compares the size of the city with Edinburgh or Newcastle, the fact of "distance" is extremely significant for Durham students. Transposing mathematical distances from one map to another can tell us nothing about what spatial relations mean to those in the situation. One's idea of nearness or farness is socially determined and intrinsically related to a particular situation. In a sense not only is there a social space continuum but it is a different *kind* of space in each social situation studied— just as the character of behaviour space is a product of the behaviour which goes on in it. An increase in mathematical space or distance, therefore, may not be directly mirrored by social distance, but will effect change only in so far as it affects a whole set of spatial relationships.

The way in which the three universities are changing in response to planning and new building throws interesting light not only upon existing spatial and social relationships, but on the way which these may be expected to change in time or be resistant to change. It also shows how far the authorities realise that spatial relationships of the university building are important influences in the development of groups and the community as a whole, and their manipulation a force for social change. It also affects imperceptibly the relation of the institution with its urban environment.

With the increase in size of the three universities, since the study was completed, have come interesting changes in organisation and atmosphere. Edinburgh—undergoing the most rapid rate of expansion—is becoming increasingly bureaucratised, rationalised, and diversified. The tendencies to faculty and departmental organisation and control, spatially expressed, are growing more strong, and segregation of various sub-units becomes more marked. Set this within the framework of towering, rather domineering buildings of many floors, containing long anonymous corridors with rows of green identical doors, and one has the first symptoms of the move to a "multiversity". At present the departmental groups as sub-units manage to maintain some social cohesion, but as student contacts become more work-centred and the work groups themselves become more large and impersonal, attendant social problems may appear. Many departments moved from cosy Georgian premises, where every room had a different kind of ceiling frieze, to large blocks of identical box rooms feel themselves begin to fall apart at the seams as warm familiarism gives way to clinical type organisation and control. Social contacts deteriorate as they take on some of the clinical aspects of the surroundings. All mystique which oils the wheels of social intercourse is brushed aside as men become part of the machine, and most people are upset by the change.

Nor are architects always sensitive to the little deceptions and myths without which social life becomes unbearable. Similar problems are faced in Newcastle and, for instance, a new fine art building has vast communal first-year studios with an overlooking balcony where presumably visiting dignitaries can come and watch the young people at work.

The problems of expansion will not be experienced in Durham on the same scale for some considerable time—and yet, again, it is a matter of relative values. For some people, as soon as the new first college was built, the character of Durham was spoilt and the past lost for ever. Some would argue that certainly Durham has felt the effect of expansion far more than Newcastle since in the latter case there was far less there already to change. This would show the influence of spatial relations and historical buildings since in terms of its history alone Newcastle is nearly as old as the parent University.

In terms of trends which expansion and development seem to show in the three universities, there is in each a more forward-looking awareness and a series of organisational changes of a greater or lesser extent which give the author no reason to change the views already expressed at the start of the survey.

4. The Urban Setting

The urban setting of the three universities supplies in each case a rather different environment in which students live and work. The "totemic"[1] aspects of this need further investigation, for, as we shall see, these aspects greatly influence the students' perception of situations and their behaviour in response. This will be discussed later in the book. The term "totem" is used to here signify those objects or aspects of the material environment which come to symbolise for members and for non-members of the insti-

[1] See Durkheim, E., *Elementary Forms of the Religious Life*, George Allen & Unwin Ltd., London, 5th impr., 1964: for example of discussion, pp. 113–27.

tution the corporate spirit, character, and life of the institution, which totem embodies as it were the nature of the institution itself. Durkheim speaks of the totem in relation to the social organisation of various preliterate peoples, but the principle is applicable here. He says: "The manner in which the name is acquired is more important for the organisation and recruiting of the clan than for religion."[1] And, again; "But the totem is not merely a name, it is an emblem, a veritable coat of arms, whose analogies with the arms of heraldry have often been remarked."[2]

As in the manner Durkheim describes, the process in universities is self-perpetuating: "In fact it is a very general rule that the members of each clan seek to give themselves the external aspect of their totem." As we shall see, the image is internalised and made real.

Edinburgh, which is so closely linked to the city, is also linked to its history, tradition, and castle—with all that implies. And being a capital city and the home of high-ranking professional people and retired businessmen and nobility it has an air of staid and genteel middle-classness. Durham, too, dominated by the river, cathedral, and castle, has the air of age-old tradition which people associate rightly or wrongly with sound merit, so that one forgets the mining village and blackened back-to-back houses on its outskirts which place it firmly in the north-east. Durham is considered small and picturesque, and has a population of 25,000. Edinburgh has half a million inhabitants of whom it is estimated every 1 in 16 is English. Newcastle also has nearly half a million inhabitants and is a lively northern town with all the signs which docks and grimy buildings and industry bring to a city. The "coaly Tyne" presents a rather different picture from the meandering River Wear in Durham. That these are evaluative and superficial assessments cannot be denied, but they are built up not merely by the author's impressions but from those of many of the students who live there and who confess that they were influenced, however erroneously, by their "images" of what life would be like there.

These, then, are the main basic points of comparison in terms of size, history, structure, residential and spatial set up, and urban setting, and they are points which must be noted in order to set the scene for findings about the social class composition of each student body and its influence on student groups.

To sum up, then, we have a large sized, medium, and small university.

[1] *Ibid.*, p. 106.
[2] *Ibid.*, p. 113.

Two of these (Edinburgh and Newcastle) are non-residential; one is collegiate. Two are historic universities set in historic towns (Durham and Edinburgh). The oldest part of Edinburgh and Newcastle is their Medical School. Both of these are set in large towns commanding a wide hinterland of activity, while Durham is set in a small, almost rural town. All are undergoing a period of vast expansion. A broad generalisation would be to say that at first glance Edinburgh appears to have more in common with both Durham and Newcastle than they seem to have with each other.

Although with regard to such variables as size, setting, and residential set up it is impossible in the "real world" to isolate completely each new variable in the university situation in the sense of a "clinically standardised" test, the three universities studied are at once alike enough and dissimilar enough to provide a sound basis for comparative analysis. In addition, since it is not clear which feature to take as constant in the analysis, it is better to leave the experimental situation unstructured.

CHAPTER 3

THE RESEARCH METHOD

IN MOST books of this kind the research method and methodology chapter is usually relegated to the Appendix. The author resisted the pressures to conform to this rule because of a firm belief that no research findings can be properly understood or appreciated except within the context of the way in which they were collected and selected. So deeply do the research techniques and methodological considerations and conceptualisation leave their imprint upon the final research analysis that the reader has only half the story before him if the former are omitted. Naturally the design of any survey, the reasons for undertaking any particular investigation or analysis, and the reasons for approaching such investigation in any particular way—indeed, the way in which the findings are limited and defined by the methods used—is inextricably bound up with the results obtained. Not only, therefore, is it essential for the reader to be aware of the methodological procedures and the strengths and weaknesses of the research design, but it is essential for him to understand them *before* he approaches the final, processed, rather cut-and-dried findings presented in the body of the text. The methodological chapter must come *first* to show the reader how the findings have come about, for what purpose, and how much reliance he can put upon them. The layman can appreciate looking at pictures of buildings and reading their description without technical expertise—he relies upon the expert knowledge of others—but the trained architect requires to see also the plans for the building and to know the purposes for which, and the conditions and constraints under which, it was built before he can make any informed judgement. So it is with the social scientist.

For this reason the author has attempted to be as honest and explicit as possible in describing her research methods and procedures, outlining the difficulties and drawbacks as well as the successes and achievements. It is hoped that, in addition, this may be of help to those undertaking a research project for the first time with as little background information as the author had at her disposal when she began. Thus they may be spared a little of the agonies of trial and error which fall to the lot of so many young researchers.

The survey was carried out in each of the three universities by means of postal questionnaires and intensive follow-up interview. This method was supplemented by long periods of participant observation preparatory to the collection of statistical data. Since the first survey in Edinburgh was carried out in the university of the researcher's first degree, the student organisation was already very familiar. However, in the case of the universities of Durham and Newcastle two terms were spent by the researcher in each place, living with the students as a student and participating in student activities.

Participant observation was invaluable in the interpretation and understanding of data, and provided many unexpected insights which might never have been gained by use of statistical methods only. What people said they did in questionnaires, or indeed thought they did, often proved to be different from what they actually did. Participant observation also helped to illumine the definition of certain social situations. For example, students in Durham may react to members of another college in terms of the social class image they have of that college. This may not correspond to statistical reality and would not be revealed by statistical analysis alone. For these reasons participant observation was not regarded as a means of discovering interesting sidelights but rather as an integral part of the survey methods.

The survey is thus at once quantitative and qualitative, and neither kind of data would be meaningful without the other.

Before the Edinburgh research was begun in September 1962, official permission of the Secretary to the University was granted for the survey to be undertaken among the students, and matriculation files were made available by him for the taking of a random sample. Without official sponsorship it is unlikely whether the surveys could have ever taken place, requiring as they did consultation of confidential records.

In both universities of Durham and Newcastle heads of departments corresponding to Social Anthropology in Edinburgh provided working space for the researcher and acted as physical and psychological bases in the University. The feeling of identity and confidence which this engendered was invaluable for the progress of research. The departments also stood as a point of reference for students and staff in each situation who needed somewhere to "place" the researcher.

The survey in Edinburgh was conducted between September 1962 and February 1963; that in Durham between January and June 1964; that in Newcastle between October 1964 and March 1965. These represent periods of actual fieldwork and do not include subsequent processing of data.

Although qualitative and quantitative methods in the three surveys were undertaken concurrently, in order to avoid confusion of detail it would be helpful to consider methods used under the two headings, whilst discussing concomitantly each of the three surveys.

1. Quantitative Methods

(a) Planning the Questionnaire

It is to be remembered that, as was stated in the Preface, when the researcher began the survey in Edinburgh University she was still an undergraduate. She was, therefore, in many ways ignorant both of research techniques and of their application, and thus the unavoidable inadequacies of the survey which thus resulted were such that they could only be overcome by research experience. It is clear that by the third survey better and clearer responses were obtained and a much higher response rate; but exactly how much was due to improved technique, how much to the researcher's increase in status (from undergraduate, postgraduate, to junior member of staff), and how much to the special circumstances of the research situation, would be impossible at this stage to ascertain. However, these changing factors must be borne in mind in consideration of formulation of the questionnaires and of their subsequent use.

In the formulation of the original questionnaire[1] the researcher was more interested in finding the answer to a number of separate questions than in any overall survey of the kind later contemplated. Questions raised by Jackson and Marsden[2] and Nisbet[3] prompted the questions on students' siblings. The researcher was interested in the relation of filial and parental educational level and the proportion of first-generation university students prompted by work such as that done by Floud, Hal-

---

[1] See Appendix III.

[2] Jackson, B. and Marsden, D., *Education and the Working Class* (Institute of Community Studies), Routledge and Kegan Paul, 1962, *op. cit.*

[3] Nisbet, J. D., Family environment and intelligence, *Eugenics Rev.*, 1953, **45**, 31–42.

sey, and Martin.[1] Questions on participation in student affairs and on class consciousness in the student body were formulated purely for personal interest as a result of personal observation. At that time the author had not read the work of Doris Thoday or Alice Eden and the books by Zweig and Marris had not yet been written. The report of the Robbins Committee[2] also had not yet been published. The social class composition of students was at that time of primary interest in any discussion of the social effects on the student body of the 1944 Act—still undetermined.

This kind of speculation gave added significance to the question of students' rating of parents' social class and their ideas on their own mobility.

These are the main topics first covered in the Edinburgh questionnaire and, in the words of the M.A. dissertation, "my aim was to gain as much information as possible on as many aspects of the subject as possible. Rather than follow up one hypothesis I was intent on building up a reasonably comprehensive picture of the influence of social class in the student body from the viewpoint of both the objective observer and the students involved."[3] The same topics were compared in each of the three universities despite minor changes in questionnaire or any shift in emphasis.

This kind of broad approach to the subject was initially in the nature of a pilot survey for subsequent research and helped to show what to look for and what was significant in the two following surveys. The whole 3-year programme of research has essentially been a continually developing process which is still going on, and hypotheses have been taken up and discarded all the way along the line so that it is difficult to remember the first point of reference. The researcher is only now beginning to be aware that this is how all research is carried on—but it has been exciting finding out.

The basic continuity of the research lies in the fact that the same questions are asked in each survey—some identically worded for direct comparison—so that there are some statistical facts on each university which are perfectly comparable. This forms the essential backbone of the thesis.

---

[1] Floud, J., Halsey, A. H., and Martin, F. M., *Social Class and Educational Opportunity*, Heinemann, 1956, *op. cit.*

[2] Robbins Report, *Higher Education*, Cmnd. 2154, London, 1963, *op. cit.*

[3] Abbott, J., Social class composition and influence in the student body of the university of Edinburgh, unpublished M.A. dissertation of University of Edinburgh, 1963, p. 19.

Minor variations occur on each questionnaire[1] for a variety of reasons. Firstly, because there are unique features in each university which warrant additional investigation—such as the "prestige ranking" of Durham colleges. These features do not directly compare with information from the other surveys but provide a more meaningful analysis of the university studied, which helps to illuminate certain *internal* problems of comparison. Thus the *whole* social system of the university is studied rather than a selection of abstracted features which compare directly with those in other universities. *Not* to have varied the questionnaire and areas of student life studied in each university would have negated the need for the kind of inter-university comparison envisaged by the researcher.

Another reason for changes in the questionnaire was that certain questions proved to be ambiguous and so had to be reworded, or they did not yield any fruitful information and were thus left out in the next questionnaire. Pruning was necessary not only for the sake of efficiency and clarity, but also because the progressive lengthening of the questionnaires suggested a possible problem of increased non-response.

Lastly, as has been explained, findings in each survey suggested areas of interest for further study in the next survey. For instance, in interview in Edinburgh, first-generation university students talked of their problems. Significant qualitative evidence emerged which needed to be tested statistically. Questions about the problems of first-generation university students were thereafter included on the questionnaires so that they could be quantified. This applies also to motives for coming to university, attitudes to work, and to place of residence.

The interviews and participant observation had much influence on the reshaping of questionnaires, and on the shifting of influence in the processing of data which they yielded. Through the analysis of qualitative data a continuous reappraisal of the statistical material was made which sometimes found expression in the quantitative method. Nevertheless, because it was necessary to make a structured statistical comparison, there is much basic repetition throughout the surveys and much of the narrowing down of focus which went on developed within this rather strictly prescribed framework. Any startling changes in the collection of quantitative data would have led to a total redefinition of the research problem and made meaningless the attempt at structural comparison. So the approach to and interpretation of facts developed within the confine of the research framework.

[1] See Appendix III.

As it happened, this method was particularly necessary in the light of the fact that right until the last moment it was never entirely clear what factors would emerge as most significant. The development of the questionnaires is rather representative of the development of the research as a whole, and the researcher feels that rather like Topsy, "it just growed" with a life of its own.

The questions on the Edinburgh questionnaire were basically ballot type, and, due to numbers involved and the difficulties of processing data, they have remained so in the succeeding two with slight modifications of ambiguous or unsuitable alternatives. Unfortunately, one only finds out ambiguity by trial and error, so that some answers have had to be scrapped rather than bias the survey.

In both Edinburgh and Durham surveys basic data on course, year of study, university and home residence, and so on was available in the files. This allowed for the shortening of the questionnaire, and these questions were only included in order to test the veracity of replies. However, it did mean that a code number had to be written on the form, and although naturally the names were only known to the researcher and afterwards destroyed, it to some extent destroyed its claim to be "anonymous and confidential" and no doubt raised doubts among the students. The effect on the response rate cannot, however, be measured. In Newcastle the researcher was not allowed to see the confidential files—only addresses—so that the forms were truly anonymous. Whether it was this which resulted in the extremely high response rate (81 per cent) or whether one must attribute it to the fact that the envelopes were franked in the Registrar's Office, again cannot be ascertained.

In Edinburgh the occupation of students' fathers is not known to the authorities (except in the Medical School) and does not appear on the entrance form. In Durham and Newcastle this is a usual part of the file of every student.

The different effects of the three *covering letters* must also be reckoned with since they represent a different approach to the student.[1] In the Edinburgh survey: "I felt that being an undergraduate was a definite drawback here, but the fact that the project was officially approved would tend to offset this."[2] The latter changes in the researcher's status have been earlier remarked upon.

[1] See Appendix II.
[2] Abbott, *op. cit.*, p. 13.

It will be seen that the Edinburgh covering letter is anonymous. The reason for this seemed very pertinent at the time. The researcher was fairly well known in student circles, having participated actively in the Students' Representative Council, Dramatic Society, and other organisations, and feared that if her identity became known it might bias replies or influence the response rate.

The wording of the Newcastle covering letter is changed completely, and there is, perhaps, an increasing note of authority in its wording. The change of format and content is so radical that one could not estimate the differing degrees of response elicited by the different letters. Therefore for this reason, along with all the others mentioned, the researcher does not propose to draw any conclusions from the different levels of response.

Since basically, as has been pointed out, the central theme of the inquiries and the factor with which all findings are correlated is the social class composition of the student body, the most difficult questions to formulate and those most painstakingly worked out were those on the social class of students and their parents.

The first point to decide was which social class categories to use in this survey. The researcher eventually carried out a small informal survey to find out which system of ranking is used in everyday student circles. This seemed appropriate since one of the aims of the survey was to look at social class as the student sees it. The Registrar-General's occupational classification of five classes was unsuitable, as students do not normally think in these terms, and do not usually identify with a *numbered* social class. The four social classes thus revealed were Upper Class (UC), Upper Middle Class (UMC), Lower Middle Class (LMC), and Working Class (WkC)— based mainly on an occupational model. These four social class categories are the ones subsequently provided for students' replies to the question asking them to rate their parents' social class. The omission of a "middle middle class" was intentional, for not only does it not feature very often in student discussion of social class, but also the existing four categories compelled respondents to make a genuine choice rather than take the easy way out and gravitate towards the middle of the scale. Of course one must not rule out the possibility that this made the respondents make a choice which they would not otherwise have made.

Since it was necessary to make a direct comparison of the students' social class ranking of their parents with social class ranking by objective indices (this being the social class composition), the same social class categories were used in each case. Thus the researcher had to devise a method of allotting a student to his social class of origin on the basis of questionnaire material. It was decided to use basically an index based on occupation of father and guided by the Registrar-General's classification of occupations.[1] However, in borderline cases in turn both father's education and mother's education and all other pertinent material obtainable from the form were to be taken into consideration. Thus, in a sense, the process of determining a student's social class of origin was in the nature of a multi-stage index primarily occupational.

In sections where the two rank orders have been compared the social class of origin of students as assessed by the student himself is termed the *professed* social class, that determined by indices is termed the *assigned* social class.

The *assigned* social classes represent as follows:

(1) *Upper Class*—based not on occupational status but on "titles of privilege" but seen to be a distinct category in the minds of students.
(2) *Upper Middle Class*—higher professional, managerial, and land-owner farmers.
(3) *Lower Middle Class*—lower professional, small entrepreneurs, white-collar workers, small farmers, and supervisory grades of manual (not foremen).
(4) *Working Class*—manual workers of all kinds, skilled, semi-skilled, and unskilled.

These represent primarily the one dimension of occupational status, which, as we shall see, implies and may be used to reveal some other dimensions of social class.

(b) *Planning the Sample*

It was imperative to draw as wide and as representative a sample of all full-time students as possible if any conclusions were to be drawn from the survey. However, initially hampered in the Edinburgh survey by lack of research experience, time, and finance, the task seemed almost impossible for one person to carry out, and of necessity the "coat was cut to the cloth". The question was not entirely what would be statistically significant, but also what would be humanly possible working at full stretch. This kind of consideration had to be borne in mind in all three surveys

---

[1] This relates to the classification used for the 1951 Census, before the revised classification of the 1961 Census was made.

since the original burdens of lack of facilities and money (mainly the latter) continued to hamper the researcher at every stage.

The researcher never aimed to produce a purely statistical analysis, and, moreover, is not qualified to do so, but has rather seen her task as one of utilising statistical evidence to serve a certain research purpose. For the aim of the research has been to study certain social phenomena in detail and in depth. Statistics have been used to show the *extent* of features of attitude and behaviour—they cannot in themselves show what those features are or what they *mean* in terms of the wider social structure. It is in this province of social research that qualitative methods are invaluable. Therefore the statistics are by no means of overriding importance in the research although there are so many of them, and must always be considered in conjunction with all other aspects of empirical evidence. Neither is the purely qualitative material meaningful in isolation from the attempt to *measure* what is shown. The statistics are regarded as evidence of certain social phenomena; they are not in themselves those phenomena. It is hoped that it will be possible at some future time to put the information into a computer for more sophisticated statistical analysis. In the meantime it is hoped that the use of statistical results will be judged according to the purpose for which they were intended.

The *sampling frame* in each university is the full-time student population of the current year at the time of investigation—as found in the university files of registered students. As has already been mentioned in Chapter 2, the full-time student population of Edinburgh University in 1962–3 was 6266; of Durham in 1963–4 it was 1916; and the full-time student population in Newcastle in 1964–5 was 4553.

These figures include all nationalities. The researcher decided to take a sample of *all* students whatever their nationality as being representative of the student body, and did not restrict the survey to British students. There were various reasons for this, the main one being that of avoiding any kind of bias at the outset which would be in turn reflected in sex, faculty, residence distributions, and so on.

The researcher explained this particular issue in the M.A. dissertation on the Edinburgh survey, to which this question is most relevant in view of the proportion of overseas students.

> I made no distinction between the British and overseas students in the phrasing of my questions. I did this purposefully as I wanted to have some kind of cross cultural comparison. I realise that this is a dangerous step to take when one is comparing two cultures, but when one is comparing many vastly differing cul-

tures as one does under the heading "overseas" it may seem at first sight truly fool-hardy. I also omitted any mention of "colour" class and did not attempt to divide the overseas students into racial groups, despite the diversity of these groups.

I have not been trying in any way to draw hard and fast conclusions from the results of my survey so I felt justified in trying to "see what would happen" if I followed the course I have outlined above, abstracting the factor of colour from the situation and subjecting each case equally to the criterion of social class.[1]

The overseas students are treated as a separate sample of the Edinburgh respondents—they form too small a group to be treated separately in the two other universities.

The size of the sample taken, as has been already shown, was chosen as a result of several factors including what would be representative and what would be physically manageable. In the Edinburgh survey the researcher ambitiously and optimistically decided to send out questionnaires to 20 per cent of the full-time students, or 1288. Fortuitously, as it now appears, the researcher was compelled to stop sending out questionnaires after the 710th after a report on the survey had appeared in a well-known daily newspaper. To continue would have meant running the risk of bias in the response, especially as the accounts were very highly coloured and were afterwards discovered to have been based upon the complaints of one student. The 710 questionnaires sent out represent a sample of 11 per cent.

In Durham the researcher was again limited by physical factors, but due to the size of the University was able to send out questionnaires to 485 students—a 25 per cent sample.

In Newcastle the researcher was assisted in addressing envelopes by the secretary of the Warden of Lodgings office, and this, plus a university grant towards cost of questionnaires and the use of the Registrar's franking machine, meant that in all 800 questionnaires were sent out—an 18 per cent sample.

Selection of sample was in each case a rather long and laborious task. Rather than run the hazards of taking a stratified sample in order to gain adequate representation of sex, faculty, residence, and age groups to name but a few, and thereafter of undertaking the complex and highly skilled task of weighting these, the researcher decided to avoid the many obvious pitfalls for which she was ill prepared and took a simple random sample. It was hoped that were the sample large enough and random enough the basic distributions of the student body would naturally emerge. This did in fact happen, as will later be shown.

[1] Abbott, *op. cit.*, p. 26.

In the Edinburgh survey access was granted to the matriculation lists in which names are, in fact, in random order as people matriculated. Therefore, since the original plan was to take a 20 per cent sample, every fifth name on the list was selected after starting at an odd number under ten. Questionnaires were distributed in batches at the same time as names were being extracted from the files. Thus when the process was so abruptly brought to an end there was doubt as to whether the sample would be biased in favour of early matriculaters who might represent a special section of the student body. This fear was put at rest by the discovery that two books and sometimes three were used concurrently at matriculation, the second one beginning at 2000. The sample taken therefore represented a cross-section of the whole student body matriculating early and late.

The task was rather more complex in Durham in that the only place in which there is a comprehensive list of full-time students is the published "residence lists" in which students names are placed alphabetically under the headings of colleges. In order to gain a random sample the researcher had to number all the names and then select the required number by means of a list of statistical random numbers. In terms of tests of representativeness this again seemed to work rather well.

The Registrar of Newcastle University declined to give access to student records so the sample was gained by means of statistical random numbers from the published "alphabetical" lists of all the students in the University. Since this included part-time students also, the task involved was beset with problems. These did not diminish when the time came to extract addresses from the files of the Warden of Lodgings, which were not confidential. These files are kept up-to-date only with the co-operation of the students themselves who are required to inform the Warden of changes of address. Despite a very efficient system, therefore, certain students could not be traced or had out-of-date addresses, and substitute names had to be found. Again, despite the rather hit-or-miss methods, the system worked well.

(c) *Responses Obtained and Representativeness of the Sample*

Three hundred and twenty-two completed questionnaires were received from the Edinburgh sample—representing a 46 per cent response, or 48 per cent if one includes incompletely filled-in questionnaires and letters only. This represents 5 per cent of the student body.

This is a low response rate, the reasons for which have already been partially discussed. The researcher's lack of experience in survey design may have something to do with it, as may lack of finance which prevented the enclosure of a stamped addressed envelope or the sending out of any follow-up questionnaires. The questionnaires were also sent out at a bad time from the students' point of view—at the time of the Christmas Term exams.

Fears that this low response might prejudice the representativeness of the sample, and so invalidate the results, were allayed after statistical tests were made comparing certain distributions of the sample with known distributions of the total student population. The results of these tests showed that, while not accurate in all respects, the survey sample may be taken as being reasonably representative of the student body as a whole. For example, faculty and university residence distribution are accurate and unbiased. There is a bias in the sex distribution towards the female students which is significant at the 5 per cent but not at the 1 per cent level; and the nationality distribution is biased in the underrepresentation of overseas students. On this last point, however, it seems unlikely that this bias will have prejudiced the conclusions since the survey was mainly concerned with British students, and in the analysis of results Scottish, English, and overseas have been treated as separate samples.

In the Durham survey 352 questionnaires were returned completed—representing 72 per cent overall, although the rate varied from college to college. This high rate of response was partly due to the help of the senior men and women of the colleges who organised collecting points in the colleges and personally supervised the return of questionnaires collected, notwithstanding the fact that the researcher had first to distribute the addressed questionnaires to the colleges in a suitcase.

The 352 questionnaires returned represent fairly accurately the distributions of the student body in terms of residence, faculty, and college, although, again, there is a slight tendency to overrepresentation of female students, though less marked than in Edinburgh. Considering the added complexities introduced by college divisions, the sample is surprisingly unbiased.

A very high response rate indeed was obtained in Newcastle. Six hundred and twenty-nine questionnaires were returned completed out of 800, and if one discounts twenty questionnaires which never reached their destination and were returned "unknown", then the response rate stands at 83 per cent.[1] This may have resulted from a combination of factors includ-

[1] Moser, C. A., *Survey Methods in Social Investigation*, Heinemann, London, 1958; see p. 179: "One of the highest response rates quoted in the survey literature [was] 81 per cent."

ing a more official-looking envelope and questionnaire, enclosed stamped addressed envelopes, and complete anonymity of the completed form. This sample is more nearly representative of the total student population, as may be expected.

A breakdown of the composition of respondents in terms of basic data of age, sex, faculty, year, and residence is given in Tables 3.1–3.5.

TABLE 3.1. AGE DISTRIBUTION OF THE THREE SAMPLES (per cent)

Age	Edinburgh (322)[a]	Durham (352)	Newcastle (629)
17 yrs.–20 yrs. 11 mths.	70	63	62
21 yrs.–24 yrs. 11 mths.	21	31	33
25 yrs.–28 yrs. 11 mths.	5	3	3
29 yrs.–32 yrs. 11 mths.	1	1	1
33 yrs. and over	2	1	1
Not known	1	1	—
TOTAL	100	100	100

[a] Figures in parentheses are the numbers of the completed sample questionnaire.

TABLE 3.2. SEX DISTRIBUTION OF THE THREE SAMPLES (per cent)

	Edinburgh (322)	Durham (352)	Newcastle (629)
Single males	54	67	66
Married males	4	4	5
Single females	40	29	29
Married females	2	—	0·5
TOTAL	100	100	100·5

(d) *Processing of Data*

The researcher devised her own coding and designed her own card layout, and learnt a great deal by trial and error. The sorted material was tabulated entirely by the researcher and, in the case of the Edinburgh data, all percentages were worked out by hand. However, this was found to be

Student Life in a Class Society

TABLE 3.3. FACULTY DISTRIBUTION OF THE THREE SAMPLES (per cent)

Faculty (alphabetical order)	Edinburgh (322)	Durham (352)	Newcastle (629)
Agriculture	—	—	5
Architecture	— (in Arts)	—	1
Arts	47	41	24
Dentistry	2	—	5
Divinity (Theology)	1	2	—
Education	— (in Arts)	10	2
Law	3	—	2
Medicine	12	—	11
Music	1	1	—
Science	29	36	28
Science (Applied N/D)	— (in Science)	—	18
Social Science (sub-fac.)	— (in Arts)	10	5
Veterinary Science	5	—	—
TOTAL	100	100	101

TABLE 3.4. YEAR DISTRIBUTION OF THE THREE SAMPLES (per cent[a])

	Edinburgh (322)	Durham (352)	Newcastle (629)
1st	36	21	32
2nd	25	41	27
3rd	25	28	25
4th	8	.6	9
5th	2	3	5
6th	4	1	2
TOTAL	100	100	100

[a] Edinburgh ordinary degrees take 3 years, honours 4 years. In Durham and Newcastle most first degrees take 3 years. The Edinburgh Medical degree is 6 years; in Newcastle 5 years.

such a laborious and soul-destroying task that results of the two later surveys were put into percentages by a member of the staff of the Social Sciences Research Centre working on a desk calculator. Of course there are many more tables than could be here presented.

TABLE 3.5. UNIVERSITY RESIDENCE DISTRIBUTION OF THE THREE SAMPLES (per cent)

	Edinburgh (322)	Durham (352)	Newcastle (629)
Lodgings and flats	54	23	54
Hostel, hall, college	14	74	27
Home	32	3	19
TOTAL	100	100	100

With regard to *tests of statistical significance* of the many thousands of results and correlations of the study, the exploratory nature of much of the research and its progressive development through a variety of phases prompted the author to lay more stress upon the sociological meaningfulness of many of the findings at the expense of determination of statistical significance. In fact it is not specific statistical differences which have been treated as the most significant bases for conclusions, but the *consistency* and *complementarity* with which a number of differences have supported and substantiated a particular hypothesis[1] and the *coherence* which these present within the whole framework of ideas. Thus slight differences have been interpreted in a more general way because of the weight of other findings by which they are supported. No one isolated finding is given any weight in interpretation of results. Of course in all this the actual participant observation was invaluable in bringing yet another dimension to the results, i.e. those phenomena which were *observed* directly in operation. Again this is supportive material which is often more illuminating than the measurement alone. The author has used statistical material to show the extensiveness of qualitative findings and analytical categories as tools rather than as ends in themselves, for this is not intended to be merely a statistical survey.

The application of tests of significance to survey research data is a controversial one and there are strong arguments both for and against their use.[2]

[1] Cf. Morrison, D. E. and Henkel, R. E., Significance tests reconsidered, *Am. Sociol.*, May 1969, 4 (2), 131–40. "At the risk of being too elementary we must point out that knowledge of *only* the level of significance of a simple statistic tells us *nothing* about the magnitude of the relationship of difference being studied nor does it provide any clues as to its theoretical or other interpretation" (p. 132).

[2] See, for example, Moser, *op. cit.*; Moroney, M. J., *Facts from Figures*, Penguin Books, London, 1962; Ilersic, A. R., *Statistics*, HFL (Publishers) Ltd., London, 1959. See also Bibliography.

The author feels justified in omitting extensive use of tests of significance at this particular stage in research, feeling it more appropriate to single out at a later date specific hypotheses from the many which are suggested by the material, for scrutiny, and testing in depth.[1] Since the present work is one of the first to try to draw together in a broad structural framework the complex strands of student social relations, it seemed more meaningful to use a broad canvas and a multi-dimensional approach. In this kind of study analytical categories initially seem somewhat crude, techniques unsophisticated, and measurements imprecise—yet in opening up new fields and new problem areas they pave the way for more precise investigations in areas which have thus already been defined. This is the hope of the author in exploring in breadth as well as depth the present area of research.

In support of these arguments it may be useful to quote here a passage from Walter Wallace's *Student Culture*, which takes much the same stance.

> The exploratory qualities of the study have also persuaded us to a technical omission which some readers will find disappointing: we have not subjected our findings to statistical tests of significance. We prefer to believe that a succession of observed differences between analytical categories can (even when each difference is in itself small and statistically not significant) contribute in critical ways to the formulation of hypotheses. In exploring a new problem, we hardly know what questions to ask, let alone the best way to ask them. A succession of small, statistically not significant differences can call our attention to more discerning questions to ask, and more precise ways to ask them, so that when these new questions are asked in a new study, statistically significant results will be forthcoming.[2]

With these arguments in mind it is hoped that the reader will understand why quite small differences are interpreted as sociologically meaningful—even significant within the whole body of fact presented—in addition to the generalisations made on the basis of many differences which are *manifestly* of a substantial nature.[3] What is being investigated, therefore, is often complex *relationships* between social facts, and as relationships these cannot be quantified. It is important to discover these relationships and the meaning of the analytical categories so related before sophisticated measurement and tests of statistical significance can be undertaken.

[1] Cf. Morrison and Henkel, *op. cit.*: "It is the social scientist's lack of theoretical development and theoretical concern that make significance tests attractive. It is only to the extent that a scientific hypothesis states a specific expectation under clearly specified conditions that the scientist can know what cases to select to test or *how* it is to be judged."

[2] Wallace, W. L., *Student Culture*, Norc. Aldine Publishing Co., Chicago, 1966.

[3] Each finding in itself is not treated as significant except in as far as it contributes to the meaningfulness and significance of the whole pattern of the results.

This is one of the main tasks of the present research. Winch and Campbell have recently argued that although significance tests are of "critical importance in weighing the plausibility that a relationship exists, we advocate its use in a perspective that demotes it to a relatively minor role in the valid interpretation of sociological comparisons".[1] This is the perspective of the present research.

2. Qualitative Methods

The main methods used were participant observation; informal and formal interviews; the keeping of a daily fieldwork diary; and study of all current documentation of the student body including student newspapers, handbooks, and minutes of meetings. Since each contributed largely to the interpretation of facts obtained by statistical methods, it is necessary to outline these methods here in greater detail.

As has already been mentioned, the researcher had spent three very active years as an undergraduate at Edinburgh University before undertaking the survey, and therefore further periods of fieldwork were not necessary. The author also had the advantage of being a student during the conduct of the survey and thus of "seeing things from the inside", while obtaining statistical evidence that would create an overall picture not limited by one vantage point. The author was determined to attempt to obtain the same kind of insights into the student body in Durham and Newcastle as she had in Edinburgh, and therefore to undertake the comparative surveys immediately while still in close touch with students and their opinions. The best way to do this was to live the life of a student in each university and if possible to remain undetected as an outsider.

There have been arguments, particularly in the United States, as to whether participant observation is ever really possible in that while one may be accepted into a group, if there is any suspicion of one's real role, the group will be affected in some way by the knowledge of being observed. Thus what one observes is a group under very special circumstances and affected by the introduction of a new element—the observer. One case of the effects of the observer may be seen in the "clinical conditions" of the Bank Wiring Observation Room described by Roethlisberger and Dickson.[2] In a sense this was an "unreal" work situation; by contrast

[1] Winch, R. F. and Campbell, D. T., Proof? No. Evidence? Yes. The significance of tests of significance, *Am. Sociol.*, May 1969, **4** (2), 140–3.

[2] Roethlisberger, F. J. and Dickson, W. J., *Management and the Worker*, Harvard University Press, Cambridge, Mass., 1939.

William Foote Whyte in his study of the Norton Street Gang[1] was highly successful in studying street corner society "from the inside" and becoming totally accepted.

Homans says of his methods that:

> Whyte studied Cornerville by becoming part of it. He learned to speak Italian; he spent the better part of three years living in the district; he hung out with the Nortons on their corner, won the confidence of the leader and the rest of the gang, and became one of the gang in its games, its political campaigns and other activities. Moreover, Whyte explained at least to the leader of the group what his purpose was in coming to Cornerville—he was making a sociological study. In fact, he enlisted the leader's help in the work.[2]

Whyte's is a classic example of the success of participant observation in a study which in a sense could not have been done any other way. Although the author hoped to use the same methods, her research problems were somewhat different. Firstly, she was not studying the interaction of a small group but the workings of a sizeable community in which over-identification with one small section of it could bias the findings. It was thought that statistical analysis would overcome this problem and put in perspective all personal observations, showing how, why, and where the researcher's observations fitted in to the wider social context. This is crucial to the resulting analysis.

Another problem of the study was the length of time at the author's disposal—everything had to be done quickly and the net of social contacts spread as widely as possible in the time available. As will be shown, the amount of integration achieved in Durham and Newcastle differed greatly in the same length of time—and the factors involved give some indication of the special social features of each community. This in itself was helpful in interpretation of data. Since the student body is unique as a community by virtue of its quick turnover of personnel, a lengthier study would have served no better purpose.

For comparative purposes we shall consider the Durham and Newcastle studies in chronological order and measure the comparative success of participant observation in each place.

The researcher had arranged the survey at Durham "from the top" through the Registrar and had received every offer of support and pledge

---

[1] Whyte, W. F., *Street Corner Society*, University Press, Chicago, 1943.
[2] Homans, G. C., *Human Groups* (International Library of Sociology and Social Reconstruction), Routledge and Kegan Paul, London, 1951, p. 157.

of secrecy. She was put in touch with the Principal of St. Mary's College who suggested that for the period of her stay the researcher should become "attached" to St. Mary's College in the normal way of registered postgraduate students. She would be treated as any member of the Junior Common Room throughout her stay. This would mean, of course, limited contact with the staff—no help unless called for; no special "sponsorship"; dining at Low Table; and, due to shortage of places, no room in college. The complete segregation from staff which this involved turned out to have been very necessary since such is the hierarchical organisation of Durham that if one were to be associated with the staff in any way one would be regarded by students as "different" and on the other side of the fence. No amount of being friendly, in-group, and jocular would overcome this first impression, and would merely be taken for condescension.

Students remarked in very scathing tones about a tutor who told them not to wear their gowns in her tutorials. "We immediately feel ill at ease when she says that, in an attempt to appear friendly. We are conscious all the time of *not* wearing our gowns. It's the same with tutors who ask you to use their first names."

This segregation resulted in some humorous situations. One member of staff at the college was known previously to the researcher as a graduate of Edinburgh, another had been introduced by the Registrar and was the same age as the researcher. Outside the Durham situation, the latter member of staff was friendly and informal and had invited the researcher to a conference in London. However, in the college these two members of staff were compelled either to ignore the research altogether or whisper subversively in corridors out of sight of the researcher's student companions. "I don't think you'd better be seen with us any more", said one, "when you come round for coffee, don't make it very obvious."

The situation was clarified for the more senior members of the college by the fact that as a postgraduate student the researcher was in fact clearly a member of the Junior Common Room despite her "visitor" status, and they would probably have been uncomfortable if the researcher had been allowed access to staff amenities. The Principal of the College, after a welcoming chat over coffee after dinner on the first day had no contact with the researcher whatever except for occasional greetings in corridors; from then on the researcher was on her own.

The researcher went to Durham just before the beginning of the Spring, or Epiphany, Term, and was fortunate enough to be given a room in St. Mary's College for a few days before most of the undergraduates came back. As luck would have it, a handful of final honours students came back early to do some work, and it was with these girls that the researcher made her initial contacts. Four of the girls became the researcher's firm friends over the months, and in them the researcher confided her real motives for being in Durham. To these girls the researcher owes a great debt, for in fact all the subsequent contacts made and insights gained were indirectly due to them. This nucleus of friends became the starting point and base from which all activities began, and these students gradually "enculturated" the researcher into the group norms and cultures. This latter point is very important since in a student society particularly, a stranger can be easily identified by ignorance of jargon, terms of reference used, meanings of abbreviations, university layout, and so on.

The researcher was greatly helped in all this by the fact that both University and city were small and easy to get to know, and the personal atmosphere of the collegiate set-up definitely did aid the setting up and spreading out of social networks. This is what must be discovered by "freshers" at first arrival. Strangeness soon wears off. The fact that the researcher had spent 4 years in a hall of residence in Edinburgh also meant that certain features of college life and organisation were familiar.

From the beginning of the survey the observer wrote up a daily detailed fieldwork diary so that spontaneous impressions and observations would be recorded before being overlain with further experiences.

At the same time, as contacts were being made at this level, participation was also progressing along another front. The Head of the Department of Geography had undertaken to treat the researcher as a full member of his department for the duration of her stay and had promised the use of a room for study purposes and to use as a base. This was essential in the establishment of a "role". As a postgraduate student it was quite feasible that the researcher had come from Edinburgh University to study in the Department of Geography (in which anthropology is a subsection). This provided a *raison d'être* for the researcher and somewhere to go when everyone else was at classes since a normal routine had to be followed. As the Geography Department was already overcrowded, the only work space that could be found for the researcher was in the Observatory, high on a hill overlooking Durham, and which could only be reached by a 20 minute tramp through fields—at that time covered in ice and snow. This tramp lengthened to half an hour when, at the beginning of term, the researcher had to move into a bed-sitter some distance away from the College. The whole thing lent authenticity to the researcher's "studentness" which no one questioned once they learnt that the researcher was working in the Observatory—observing they knew not what. There is a great stress in Durham on courtesy and acceptance of the *status quo*—so that once the researcher was ensconced in the College—coming in regularly for meals, having coffee with the final years, and being recognised by staff—no one dreamed of questioning why she was there beyond the limits of a few polite questions.

There is much to learn from this about perception of situations and of role performance. With the minimum of appropriate "attributes" the researcher was not seen as a stranger to the group but as a full member, and whatever she said and did could not destroy this perception of the situation. She learned towards the end of her two-term stay by the "college grapevine" that the younger girls had been speculating as to her identity since it was obvious that she knew the place and was well known although they had never seen her before nor heard of her name. Their eventual solution to this situational incongruity was that she must be one of those unfortunate girls who went away for a year or two to have a baby and then returned to complete their degree course. Thus was the available evidence fitted into the accepted perceptual pattern.

This happened in a college of 200 students who were used to postgraduates who lived out and occasionally came into meals; it is doubtful whether the researcher would have remained undetected in a much smaller college. As to the ethics of the situation, the researcher felt it her duty to tell the truth to those who openly asked her what she was doing there but not to tell anyone who did not ask. It was surprising how few people ever asked. This was in direct contrast to the Newcastle situation.

With St. Mary's College and the Geography Department as bases the researcher was able to wholeheartedly join in student activities and to enjoy joining in. She also made contact, through the official machinery, with heads of colleges and members of teaching staff who were very helpful in their comments and provided information which the researcher could never have gained at first hand. Other avenues of information were provided by the President of the SRC and senior men and women of the colleges. The researcher was assisted in her task by her feminine role and was able to join new groups more easily because she was a woman. Nevertheless, her knowledge of the men's colleges is more vague than her knowledge of the women's colleges.

The climax of her brief stay in Durham came when she was elected Chairman of the Bookshop Committee of the SRC though she was neither a registered student nor member of the SRC. The President of the SRC and the Senior Man of Grey College nominated the researcher with her permission—not merely as an experiment but also because they genuinely wanted her to take on the job. They both knew of her real purpose in being in Durham, and this did not deter them. At the SRC Council meeting no one opposed or questioned the nomination, so the researcher was unanimously elected. This in itself is rather a comment on the familial way in which the Durham SRC is run. After toying with the idea of actually running the Bookshop Committee and after being instructed in the workings of the Bookshop by the previous chairman, she was compelled regretfully to resign "through pressure of work" and sent a letter to the SRC to this effect.

This could never have happened in Newcastle or Edinburgh University due to the vast differences in organisations. The author in fact must record that the spheres into which she was accepted in Newcastle were very limited. Her sister had been a student at Newcastle for 2 years and she had already visited her several times and met her friends, so that this was to be her entrée into Newcastle student society. In effect this led to her being accepted only by the limited circle of her sister's friends who, being fine artists, tended to remain an isolated and enclosed group. Indeed, by being associated with fine artists the researcher found she could not be accepted by certain groups opposed to them on principle.

The Registrar, being slightly antagonistic towards the survey, did not put the researcher in touch with any members of staff, and the Department of Anthropology, although providing a base, was too small and too cut off to be the starting point for any social contacts. All official channels were therefore closed to the researcher, and the situation did not improve on this score until the researcher made contact with the Warden and Assistant Warden of Lodgings who were extremely co-operative, offered a room for interviewing, and gave some idea of what "life on the inside" is like. This was particularly useful since their supervision of accommodation gave them much information on students and their way of life. The bias one had to be aware of was that the wardens normally only saw the dissatisfied students.

The researcher shared a flat with her sister, and although it was in the student "bed-sitter belt" this immediately limited contacts to a selected few. She travelled in daily to the Department, or to the Registrar's Office or the Union, and got used to waiting and wasting time and seeing no one, and in fact led the rather miserable "cut-off" life that probably falls to the lot of quite a few students, undergraduate, and postgraduate, and which the researcher had not previously experienced. Although attending student meetings she never felt "in", and a visit to the SRC became a ceremonial surrounded by bureaucratic red tape and only sanctioned after a visit to the SRC President in his plush office. The President of the SRC and of the Union were very helpful in their comments, but their sponsorship went no further than inviting the researcher to visit further meetings of the SRC or MSC strictly as an observer. Visits were made, but the situations were unreal and "stagey". The researcher learnt far more from sitting round talking and drinking coffee in the Union than she ever did from these meetings.

Although she was accepted as "Wendy's sister" and a postgraduate student, the organisation was not geared to the perfect assimilation of new personnel, and the machinery was lacking which would have integrated her into one of the groups. More people questioned her reason for being there, and once known, the researcher was conscious of being "different" which made her seem more different to those around. It is a circular process. The progressive alienation set up mental reactions in the researcher which threatened to bias her findings, so the only solution was to stop attempting to participate; to carry out the survey, this time as officially as possible, and then leave. The experience in Newcastle, in which in a sense nothing happened, was as meaningful as the experience in Durham which was crammed with activity. It cannot be denied that the researcher's experiences as well as her observed information have helped to mould the findings of the surveys. Bias must be taken into account, but what must not be taken for bias is argument based on a general impression or consensus of opinion.

The researcher checked both her personal observations and some of the statistical evidence which needed clarifying by holding intensive one hour long *follow-up interviews.*

These were not meant to be a random sample but were chosen from students who had indicated their willingness to be interviewed to illumine certain points. Thirty-two interviews were held in Edinburgh. The researcher hoped to carry out 100 in Durham but was cut short after the fifty-fifth by acute appendicitis. The required 100 was achieved in Newcastle without mishap. These interviews were analysed in terms of the qualitative rather than the quantitative data they could supply and many interesting remarks were recorded verbatim. The interviewees were very co-operative on the whole and broadened the base of the qualitative material somewhat since they were a cross-section of students from every kind of faculty and background.

In contrast to the formal questionnaires the interviews were unstructured and the researcher encouraged students to talk about everything they thought pertinent to the inquiry while keeping within broad limits. In this way some points were raised which might otherwise have been overlooked. The researcher sat behind a table to establish her role and took notes throughout.

In some ways the questionnaire, interviews, and periods of participant observation represent different degrees of identification with the material studied, and each acts as a check upon the others.

In the interpretation of data which follows much of the process of identification, observation, analysis, cross-checking, and rethinking is naturally not seen, and by now the researcher has herself so internalised the whole process that she would be hard put to it to trace her stages of thought. Nevertheless, like the submerged nine-tenths of the iceberg, the basic groundwork supports all the material presented, and without it there would have been nothing to be seen.[1]

In the three chapters which follow, findings will be presented which show that there are meaningful social class groups within the university and that these exhibit different culture patterns with regard to the students' families, their own motivations for coming to university, and their participation and leadership in student affairs. These culture patterns are meaningful in terms of the index of occupational status of father discussed at the beginning of this chapter.

3. *Theoretical and Operational Definitions*

Finally, it is appropriate to give some indication of what is meant by some of the concepts used in the analysis of results. Many, it will appear, have been rather loosely defined—such as, for instance, social class itself—and although this may seem initially to be something of a drawback in fact it was one of the reasons why, with weight of evidence and consistency or inconsistency of certain results, it was possible for some

[1] In the many revisions of manuscript since the thesis was presented in November 1965 there are certain chapters which have hardly been rewritten—this chapter is one. I read it now almost as a stranger in December 1969 and think it a miracle that the research ever got done! But thus the reader has a "natural history of the research" and may be able to discover throughout the book the different strata of development in thought and approach as in an archaeological "dig".

of these concepts like class, status, and mobility to be *redefined*. In operation some of these concepts take on a slightly different character and show an increased number of dimensions than when we look at them in a social vacuum of theoretical discussion. The author was more interested in what social class *does* in terms of social relations—how it *acts* as a dynamic factor—than in what it *is*, believing that it would be revealed as a social reality through analysis of the various ways in which it is manifested in social life. Concepts are used as tools for the understanding of the complexity of social life, and yet in the process we learn whether the tools themselves are appropriate or inappropriate for the job, whether they are too blunt or too sharp, and what kind of pattern they make of our material. This process has happened throughout the prolonged period of the research.

Initially, though, social class is taken to be a quasi-group of persons and families of similar economic–occupational status who have some feeling of belonging and self-identification as well as objective categorisation by others—and who share similar life styles and a variety of sociocultural characteristics. Attributional social class, or that which takes the form of a social "label" rather than community membership, is distinguished from interactional social class, which is generated by cultural and residential concentration, and which circumscribes a wide range of social relations of those individuals who belong to it.

Students, as individuals abstracted from family and background, and all class clues which this implies, are seen as a status group in the context of the evaluations of the wider population, and one which is ranked on a special continuum of prestige. Thus the social class composition of the student body, as based on occupation of students' fathers, is referred to as "social class of origin"—or that social class to which students are perceived to belong by role affiliation when they are actually in residence with their family. As students they are still dependants, and have not yet forged for themselves an independent class membership.

What happens outside the institution obviously affects what happens within it, so that the "status" of a student, or his personal "standing" or prestige, and his "social class position" are often seen as different dimensions of the same phenomenon rather than as quite distinct and separate concepts. This may initially appear somewhat confusing, especially when the student's own viewpoint is taken into consideration, as with the comparison of *assigned* and *professed* classes—but it is hoped that the findings will throw explanatory light on the concepts themselves.

In this situation "social mobility" can only be considered after an examination of what the student is moving from and to and of what this involves in terms of status differentiation and crystallisation and of changes in prestige ranking by status equals as well as members of other status groups and social classes. Along with this must be taken into account the concomitant changes in personal social characteristics and the self-evaluation resulting from these various processes. Thus the consideration of mobility comes at the end of the book when a re-examination of these concepts and ideas has been attempted in the light of the findings. Each chapter attempts to advance our definition of concepts one step further in a progressive analysis. In this context it has been found necessary to separate out two separate factors in the process of social mobility—one the process of movement which the individual undergoes in institutional terms, or in terms of the categorisation by others—this being a structural phenomenon, the other the characteristics and processes congruent to the movement which are part of the individual himself. These are social rather than psychological attributes like ways of behaving, talking, dressing, and so on, and which do in fact imply a compliance of the individual to the requirements of mobility. The structural movement is called "social mobility", the personal attribute "social motility". Obviously this is only a first and rather crude attempt to rethink the social implications of mobility and the ways in which its study can be approached.

In all these analyses, and definitions, the issues have been complicated by the observation of the operation of the many facets of social class and social mobility as multi-dimensional phenomena. The limitations of approaching their study through the means of a uni-dimensional occupational index are discussed elsewhere though it is clearly impossible to approach the problem via every dimension at once. In conjunction with this problem the objective and subjective dimensions of social class are discussed and their relationship examined, but each are recognised as an indispensable aid to the understanding of the other and to the achieving of new insights into the complexity of the social reality. Therefore it has seemed reasonable at times to take into account the viewpoints of those being observed and to use their standpoints as springboards for analysis.

In this exploratory work the appropriateness of the tools can only be assessed after a preliminary examination of the material on which they are used: to some extent a circular process; it is hoped that the necessary rethinking and re-examination will have its own rewards.

PART II

CHAPTER 4

THE STUDENTS AND THEIR FAMILIES

As HAS been explained in the preface and Chapter 1, the author's first concern was to discover the social class composition of the three universities and to attempt to discover evidence of expansion of educational opportunity in response to the provisions of the 1944 Education Act. This sets the scene for the study of socialisation within the institution and the effect of those societal pressures discussed in Chapter 1 on the specified student populations. We must first establish the structure of some of the variables in the student populations themselves. It has been noted in Chapter 1 that cultural factors are at work in educational selection which prevent the working class from taking advantage of educational opportunity. This being so, the author has also set out to discover whether the social class groupings revealed by the occupational index reveal distinct cultural patterns *within* the university. If such cultural patterns or groupings emerge among students then it would seem that one may proceed to investigate social class as a factor in students' social relations as representing a meaningful social category within the university context. And if what we have called "social class of origin" is that which reveals these cultural patterns, one may use it also to discover other meaningful "social class" distributions in terms of attitude and behaviour.

We begin with an analysis of the students' social class of origin as determined basically by occupation of father, i.e. the student's *assigned* social class. Findings are shown in Table 4.1.

The most striking result here is the small proportion of working-class students in each university—smaller, in fact, than that which has previously been estimated.[1] In direct contrast to the paucity of working-class students are the large numbers of lower middle-class students.[2] It would

[1] For example, Glass, D. V. (ed.), *Social Mobility in Britain*, 1954, 26 per cent; Kelsall, R. K., *Report of an Inquiry into Applications for Admissions to Universities*, 1957, 25 per cent.
[2] For similar findings from Ireland and the Continent, see Nevin, M., A study of the background of students in University College Dublin, *J. Stat. Soc. Inq. Ireland*, 1967.

136   Student Life in a Class Society

TABLE 4.1. STUDENTS' SOCIAL CLASS OF ORIGIN IN EDINBURGH, DURHAM, AND NEWCASTLE

Social class of origin	Edinburgh		Durham		Newcastle	
	(per cent)	No.	(per cent)	No.	(per cent)	No.
UC	0·6	2	0	0	0	0
UMC	39	126	29	101	32	199
LMC	44	140	46	161	44	280
WkC	15	48	21	77	20	124
No occupation stated	2	6	4	13	4	26
TOTAL	100·6	322	100	352	100	629

seem that at least in these three universities, as has been suggested, it is the lower middle class and not the working class which is growing in relation to the upper middle class in the three universities—towards a reflection of its comparative size in the population.[1] Not unexpectedly, there were only two titled people in the survey—both at Edinburgh. Because they represent such a small minority they will be included in the upper middle-class category for statistical purposes. If we refer back to the comparison of social class composition in various types of institution in Britain and the United States made in Chapter 1, we see here an interesting addition to the table discussed (Table 1.2(a)). Let us use the Edinburgh sample as an example of Historic Civic, Durham as Oxbridge Style, and Newcastle as New Old. We then have a more complete comparison of the institutional differences and similarities as we see in Table 4.2.

This table draws attention to yet further similarities between the British and American class hierarchy of institutions.

Returning to Table 4.1, in the Edinburgh sample there is a higher proportion of upper middle-class students and a lower proportion of working-class students than in either of the other samples.[2] This result was checked

[1] Cole, G. D. H., *Studies in Class Structure* (Internat. Lib. of Sociol. and Soc. Reconstr.), London, 1955.
[2] Nevin's study of University College Dublin, which has certain features in common with Edinburgh, shows only 10 per cent children of manual workers, and 54 per cent professional, managerial and senior salaried employees. The disparity results partly from financial constraints and lack of scholarships. Percentage of manual workers' children in Queen's University, Belfast is on a level with Durham and Newcastle.

TABLE 4.2. CLASS COMPOSITION OF INSTITUTIONAL TYPES IN BRITAIN AND UNITED STATES (per cent)

Social class	Ivy	Oxbridge	Cosmopolitan	Hist. Civic	State	Ind. Civic	War-nell	Ox-bridge Style	Opp. Coll.	CAT
U & UM	75	78	30	41	20	46	40	29	5	45
LMC	20	14	45	44	50	23	50	46	40	25
WkC	5	8	25	15	30	31	10	21	55	30
TOTAL	100	100	100	100	100	100	100	96	100	100

and counter-checked in an effort to discover any underlying errors in classification or any bias in replies in terms of students' social class. No such bias or errors could be discovered,[1] so that since the sample has been shown in Chapter 3 to be representative of the student body as a whole, the social class composition must be taken as a true reflection of that which exists in the total student body. If working-class students were more reticent in returning the questionnaires it cannot have been in such large numbers as radically to effect the overall proportions. It has been speculated that the "unclassified" group in each university on certain evidence may be largely composed of working-class students (which would bring the proportions nearer to those of Kelsall and Glass), but it was decided not to collapse the unclassified into the working-class total on the basis of speculation.

There can be no suggestion that the selection machinery at the university entrance level is consciously biased in favour of any of the social classes since at Edinburgh the social class of the potential student, as indicated by parental occupation, is not known except in the Medical Faculty and no interviews are held. We must turn, therefore, for explanation to the "educability" mentioned by Halsey.

There are a variety of possible explanations for the exceedingly small proportion of working-class students in the Edinburgh sample. Firstly, it may be said that the long-standing tradition and high reputation of the Edinburgh Medical Faculty would tend to bias the social class composi-

---

[1] See Abbott, J., *Social Class. Composition and Influence in the Student Body of the University of Edinburgh*, 1963, pp. 34–38.

tion towards the upper middle class. In addition, it was discovered that a high proportion of students' fathers in faculties other than the Medical Faculty also are of the medical profession. Secondly, one might argue that the English students who come to a Scottish university may be expected to be largely of the upper middle class, since the English working-class student, assumed to be more parochial and eager to avoid extra travelling expenses, would tend to go to a university nearer home. This argument proves true for the majority in that those English working-class students who do come to Edinburgh, particularly from the north of England, choose it precisely because it is a long way from home and because as a "non-red-brick" university it represents a good choice for the socially ambitious. In this sense they are a special section of the working class. Since these and a variety of facts tend to underline to some extent the upper middle-class nature and atmosphere of the university, it appears more striking that in fact the results discussed show in some part the expansion of the *lower* middle class in the university at the expense of the upper middle class.

The breakdown of the Edinburgh sample into Overseas, English, and Scottish samples, alongside the Durham and Newcastle results, reinforces this viewpoint (Fig. 4.1).

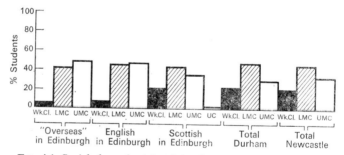

FIG. 4.1. Social class of origin of the three nationality groups at Edinburgh, Durham and Newcastle

From the figures on the three Edinburgh samples an interesting pattern emerges which looks roughly like some kind of cyclical expansion or con-traction of the social class proportions. In the Overseas sample, which we shall assume is biased in favour of the wealthier students gaining part of their education abroad, the working class is tiny and the lower middle class is slightly smaller than the upper middle class. In the English sample, which represents greater equality of opportunity, and yet, as explained earlier, exhibits a tendency to bias towards the upper middle class, the lower middle class and the upper middle class are almost equal and the working class has expanded slightly. In the Scottish sample the lower middle class is larger than the upper middle class and the working class is increasing in its wake. It is significant that the Scottish distribution approximates very closely to that of the other two universities and that these proportions are reasonably consistent.

It may be suggested that, in terms of a mechanistic model from which the element of time has been eliminated, the three Edinburgh samples represent something like three stages in the expansion of educational opportunity in which the lower middle class is the barometer of change and initiates movement. This represents a "seeping down" through the system of educational opportunity which will in time reach the working classes with increasing acceleration.

An increased proportion of *first*-year lower middle-class students was found which may be seen as a symptom of this developing process, which may also be represented in terms of "flows".

The researcher is only too aware of the weaknesses inherent in this theory of cyclical expansion of social classes as based upon the data here available. Much is speculation, much deduction, and such actions as the grouping together of overseas students bristles with flaws. Yet in this case the author feels justified in making a "leap in the dark". Although naturally each university will exhibit its own individual features of expansion of educational opportunity, the other findings in the universities here discussed would seem to justify that leap.

Side by side with the Edinburgh model the Durham distribution takes on the appearance of the next stage in the process with a declining proportion of upper middle-class students being replaced by an increasing proportion of lower middle-class students while the working class remains constant.

Before the Newcastle results were analysed, both students' and staffs' subjective interpretation of the prevailing atmosphere and mores of the University tempted the author to predict that the social class composition would fall yet further along this "line" of expansion with an increased proportion of working-class students approaching that of the lower middle class. These attempts at prediction were confounded by the discovery that the Newcastle social class composition does not differ significantly from that of Durham. Although initially this is surprising in the light of other findings, it becomes more understandable when one remembers that until 2 years ago Durham and Newcastle were one university and that many

students selected by King's College, Durham, are now members of Newcastle University. Thus it would have been even more surprising had the
social class composition of the two universities differed widely.

It was in attempting to discover why the expected and supposed social
class composition of Newcastle University differed from reality, and what
factors influenced these expectations, that the author came upon explanations central to the formation and structure of social groups which clarified certain problems to some extent and reorientated her analysis. This is
discussed fully later—and the author will attempt to lead the reader stage
by stage through her argument as she herself was led by the emergence of
new findings. Suffice to say here that the reasons why those within the
situation *perceive* the social class composition to be different are a complex
set of interacting factors crucial to a study of students' assimilation and
participation in the student body.

At this stage in the argument we must consider additional evidence of
the way in which the proportions of social classes may change within the
universities—in relation to the cyclical model of expansion discussed
above and of the part which the 1944 Act has played in such changes.
This additional evidence was gained by the author through an historical
analysis of the social class composition of a sample of students taken randomly from the Durham University admissions register at 3-year intervals
from 1937 when the University was reconstituted, until 1963, the academic
year of the survey.

The samples taken ranged from a 50 per cent sample in the late 1930's
when total numbers of admissions did not far exceed 100, to a 20 per cent
sample in 1963 of the 533 admissions of that year. The findings are in no
way meant to be conclusive since the numerical bases are too small for
this—yet in that they are representative of total admissions they may be
of some help in showing how in Durham University trends of social class
composition changes emerge. No provision has been made for changes in
status of occupations through the years although the time span is such
that such changes may not be radical; nor is account taken of *overall*
changes in the social class structure of the total British population. Naturally, these may bias the findings, but not sufficiently to make them completely without value. The "flow" diagram (Fig. 4.2) illustrates the way
in which the social class of admissions changed over the years.

Firstly, it may be seen that the process of educational expansion did in
fact take place in Durham in a manner somewhat like that already described in terms of a "mechanical" model. Nowhere is there a sudden influx of

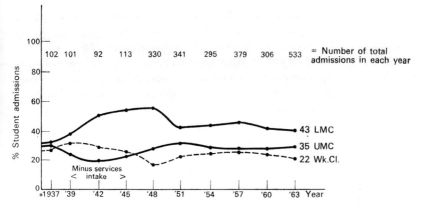

* 1937 reconstruction of the University of Durham.

FIG. 4.2. Changes in social class composition of Durham University, 1937–63. (N.B.; because of small numbers involved and changes in occupational status these figures are unreliable and only used to show general trends.)

working-class students—always the working-class proportion trails in the wake of the expanding lower middle class. Secondly, it is clear that such expansion as had taken place was already taking place *before* 1944—the effects of the 1944 Act were only part of a process already begun, as Little and Westergaard, among others, have surmised.[1]

A feature peculiar to this process in Durham is the sudden expanse of the upper middle class—between 1948 and 1951. While these figures were as yet unknown, one of the authorities of the University had stated in private communication to the author that the prestige of the University had begun to rise to its present height "around 1950". This rather special coincidence would seem to be indicative of certain features of university organisation which may have general validity with further implications for the argument of this book.

One may only speculate upon the causal relationship of these facts, and perhaps none are valid. Whether local miners' sons became supplanted at the "local" university by more middle-class students because of the attraction of a collegiate university with rising reputation or whether the increasing flow of Oxbridge "rejects"—in a growingly competitive field—into Durham University enhanced its reputation, one cannot know, but in each case the process becomes circular, and is in time reinforced as in a

[1] Little and Westergaard, *BJS*, December 1964, **15** (4).

"self-fulfilling prophecy". Thus there was a higher *proportion* of working-class students in Durham in 1938 than there is now. Of course, numbers themselves may be constant within an expanded student population, while only the middle class has grown relatively.

Many questions are raised by these findings and can only be answered by further research; but by raising questions the facts give the research its shape. One cannot escape the wider implications for the implicit status "hierarchy" of universities, which may significantly influence why certain students go to certain universities either in terms of choice or selection or both. From this stems the fact that the social class composition of every institution might be expected to be different and to undergo different processes of change in accordance with social as well as academic goals.

It may be suggested that, as has been speculated, in these three universities the working-class proportion has hardly increased in recent years and may even have remained static. Selective processes, therefore, which are at work at primary and secondary levels of education, would seem not to have lost all their potency at the stage of university entrance. This brings us again to a study of the cultural factors in the students' home life which encourage or discourage the taking of educational opportunities.

This would suggest also that the prevailing values of higher education are middle-class values and that, as Halsey says, the working-class child who succeeds academically is usually atypical in family attitudes and psychology.

To test the validity of this remark we must look at the characteristics of other members of the students' families. Firstly, we shall examine the comparative *family sizes* of the social classes in the three universities in order to discover if there is any distinctive class pattern of family size at this level that would in a sense compare with findings described earlier. The findings show firstly an *overall* preponderance of small families of one or two children among Durham and Newcastle students, but just over half in the Edinburgh sample.

Among the families of the students of the three universities there is a similarity of distribution between the members of the same social class. In each case the lower middle class emerges as the social class group with an overall proportion of smaller families. In Edinburgh *56 per cent* of the lower middle-class students come from small families compared with *72 per cent* in Durham and *69 per cent* in Newcastle. This would seem to be compatible with the fact that it is the lower middle class which is expanding in the universities—which could be assumed to be

TABLE 4.3. SIZE OF FAMILY FROM WHICH STUDENTS CAME. NUMBER OF SIBLINGS IN ADDITION TO STUDENT (per cent)

	UMC	LMC	WkC	Unclassified	Total
EDINBURGH					
	(128)	(140)	(48)	(6)	(322)
Only child	12 ⎫	18 ⎫	19 ⎫	17	16 ⎫
1 sibling	36 ⎭ 48	38 ⎭ 56	29 ⎭ 48	50	52 ⎰ 36
2 siblings	29 ⎫	22 ⎫	31 ⎫	17	25
3 siblings	14 ⎬ 52	13 ⎬ 44	15 ⎬ 52	—	14
4+ siblings	9 ⎭	9 ⎭	6 ⎭	16	9
	100	100	100	100	100
DURHAM					
	(101)	(161)	(77)	(13)	(352)
Only child	13 ⎫	22 ⎫	23 ⎫	38	21 ⎫
1 sibling	37 ⎭ 50	50 ⎭ 72	44 ⎭ 67	31	65 ⎰ 44
2 siblings	23 ⎫	19 ⎫	26 ⎫	8	21
3 siblings	19 ⎬ 50	6 ⎬ 28	4 ⎬ 33	15	9
4+ siblings	8 ⎭	3 ⎭	3 ⎭	8	5
	100	100	100	100	100
NEWCASTLE					
	(199)	(280)	(124)	(25)	(629)
Only child	11 ⎫	23 ⎫	19 ⎫	15	18 ⎫
1 sibling	43 ⎭ 54	46 ⎭ 69	48 ⎭ 67	27	63 ⎰ 45
2 siblings	26 ⎫	18 ⎫	16 ⎫	35	21
3 siblings	13 ⎬ 47	7 ⎬ 31	11 ⎬ 33	·4	9
4+ siblings	8 ⎭	6 ⎭	6 ⎭	19	7
	101	100	100	100	100

more aspiring in its aims and accordingly "geared" for success and likely to have limited the number of children. These findings are illuminated by those findings discussed which show that intelligence correlates with family size and educational success. (This also relates to economic factors.)

The working-class students on the whole also come from small families, and in Durham and Newcastle there is a larger proportion of these than in the upper middle class. If the configurations followed population trends the lower the social class the greater would be the proportion of larger families. So in this sense the working-class families of students are to some extent atypical of the rest of their social class. The fairly high proportion of small families in every social class shows that, despite the wide range of family sizes, the factors of selection operate in favour of members of smaller families and that this is to some extent irrespective of social class. Interesting institutional differences emerge in that while the Newcastle and Durham samples have very similar class distributions, in Edinburgh there is a marked difference at the level of lower middle class and working class with a larger proportion of larger families than in either of the other two samples measured as 2-plus siblings. There is also a larger proportion of 2-plus siblings, families in the total sample, suggesting an institutional or regional difference overlying social class differences.[1]

In consideration of the breakdown of the Edinburgh sample into "nationality" divisions, we may see other cultural factors brought into play. Fifty per cent of the Scottish sample were from families where the student was an only child or had one sibling compared with 56 per cent in the English sample and 26 per cent Overseas. These differences may partly be due to cultural differences in family size in the population. On the other hand, it could mean that the selection process in each case tends to pick out people from larger or smaller families.

If, as seems likely, the more stringent the selection, i.e. the fewer the working class who succeed in getting into university the greater the success of the able child from a small family, one would expect the working-class sample to have the smallest families. (In fact it may be observed that the opposite seems to obtain between universities—Edinburgh with the smallest overall proportion of working-class students, and therefore

---

[1] In the University College Dublin survey only 14·3 per cent of students came from families of 1 or 2 children and although religious influences may be seen to underlie the preponderance of large families, this group is under-represented—as small families constitute 25 per cent of the total population (Nevin, *op. cit.*).

one assumes more factors working *against* working-class selection, has the smallest proportion of *small* working-class families.) However, a detailed analysis of the child *order* of the successful student would throw light on this.[1] It may be that only *eldest* children come from small families, where there are not many other siblings to provide for, whereas in some working-class homes a son or daughter would be enabled to go to university by the presence of wage-earning elder siblings and would therefore be a *younger* member of a larger family. In this case, the sacrifice of the student as a wage-earner could be more easily overcome. If we consider figures on siblings' education level we have some small indication of child order, although the analysis was not designed to show this. However, some qualitative evidence in the investigation tends to back up this theory and show that, particularly among Scottish students, higher education is so prized that even a large family may be geared to getting at least one of its members into university. Here culture and family structure must be considered together. What does a particular family size or structure *mean* to those within it? Does it depress chances for education or make it possible, and for which *member*? This has been inadequately studied, and the present analysis may only suggest.

Table 4.4 shows the proportion of students' siblings of appropriate age who received or had received a university or college education. The figures for Edinburgh only show *university*-educated siblings since the question did not at that time ask about college—this was added later.

Firstly, if we consider the different proportions of families of each size in each university, it emerges that the Durham and Newcastle students' families have overall a smaller proportion of siblings who are of or over university entrance age than in Edinburgh, thus indicating a larger proportion of *younger* brothers and sisters. This is worth bearing in mind, for it is not fanciful to suppose that students from different social classes who come as the first of their family to university will be a different kind of sample from those who have elder brothers and sisters possibly also at university.

---

[1] Bayer' A. E., *J. Marr. Fam.*, 1966, **28** (4), 480–4, and Chapra, S. L., *J. Soc. Psychol.*, 1966, **70**, 133–7. A study of 50,000 high school seniors showed that in terms of intelligence test scores the first born had a slight superiority over last born with a tendency for intermediate to have scores between older and younger siblings. These differences are not large enough to account for differences in achievement between different ordinal positions noted by other studies. Burton, D., Birth order and intelligence, *J. Soc. Psychol.*, 1968, **76**, 199–206.

TABLE 4.4. SIBLINGS' EDUCATION—COLLEGE ENTRANCE AGE (per cent)

	UMC	LMC	WkC	Unclassi-fied	Total
EDINBURGH					
University	67	44	27	100	50
Others	33	56	73	—	50
TOTAL	100	100	100	100	100
No.	(107)	(148)	(52)	(3)	(310)
DURHAM					
University	36	38	19	—	33
College*	32	32	12	—	27
Neither	32	30	69	—	40
TOTAL	100	100	100	—	100
No.	(107)	(95)	(58)	—	(260)
NEWCASTLE					
University	23	30	15	—	24
College*	43	27	14	—	31
Neither	34	43	71	—	45
TOTAL	100	100	100	—	100
No.	(216)	(202)	(123)	—	(541)

* College as used in British sense.

The figures showing siblings' education reveal a marked difference between Edinburgh and the two other universities. A uniformly higher proportion of students' siblings in each social class are receiving or have received a university education. If figures relating to college education were available, no doubt the figures would be even more startling. The Edinburgh breakdown into "nationality" samples shows that the proportion of *English* siblings at university is generally lower than that of *Scottish* siblings, particularly in the middle classes. The goal of academic achievement seems more prevalent in Scottish middle-class families whatever their size.

Thus we may compare the overall academic achievement of students' families. As one might expect, there is in Edinburgh and Newcastle a definitely significant gradient of percentage of siblings at university from the upper middle class down to the working class though in Durham the break is between the middle class as a whole and the working class —a configuration mirrored by all the "college" siblings. This would seem to show that the chance of selection of students' *siblings* is not weighted in favour of certain family *size* (though child *order* may again be a factor)[1] since the lower middle class has the smallest families and except for Edinburgh the working class have a similar distribution of small families. Social class factors obviously come into play in the process of selection of "families" as well as individuals. The upper middle class is the class in which whole families of siblings have a better chance of obtaining a university education, even though the families are larger than in the lower middle class. It is lower down the scale that family size above a certain "threshold" operates as a factor in selection. In the working class it is obviously more a matter of *chance* getting a child into university and one not necessarily repeated in the success of other siblings. Where success is encouraged and *planned*, factors of chance alone are less important.

This would seem to modify Jackson and Marsden's claim that "the selective process in the schools picked out and held not just gifted individual children, it selected families".[2] If this were so, then working-class students' siblings of all family sizes would have increased likelihood of a university education. The only sample which would seem to confirm the argument is the English working class previously described as a small, highly selected, and ambitious group, who have 63 per cent siblings at university compared with the 21 per cent of the Scottish working-class sample. We may look for an explanation of this seemingly anomalous figure in the fact that the greater the degree of selection along social class lines, and therefore the *smaller* the working-class group, the more

[1] In Nevin's study in all "families the first child predominates" (Nevin, *op. cit.*, p. 16).

[2] Jackson, B. and Marsden, D., *Education and the Working Class*, 1962, p. 126.

will the system select families rather than individuals. This is reflected in the other distributions. It is to this which Jackson and Marsden are particularly referring in their study of working-class children. These families are atypical of the working class and therefore more likely to be selected in a system geared to the middle class. In this situation, since it is the family rather than the individual which is chosen by the system, it is likely that more than one member of it will benefit from a university education. This being true, the English working-class sample as an extremely stringently selected group may be expected to be unlike the other working-class samples in other ways too. This will be seen to be so in further analysis.

Twenty-one per cent of the Scottish working class had siblings at university compared with 12 per cent Durham and 14 per cent Newcastle. Since in each of these cases the working class represents about 20 per cent of the student body, the slightly higher Scottish percentage may represent some kind of cultural influence.

It may well be that there is a "threshold" of selection beyond which the Jackson and Marsden hypothesis does not hold good and in which situation an intrinsically different type of working-class child and family is selected. A specific project would have to be devised to show where that threshold is, i.e. where working-class candidates chosen remain more working class than middle class in their culture and values. This has many implications for future behaviour within the educational situation, and for the extent to which students may expect to be "socialised".

Halsey has suggested that working-class families selected are "atypical in family attitudes and aspiring in their aims". It well may be that there has been excessive concentration on the first half of this sentence and not enough on the latter half. The fact that these families are "aspiring" may well be more important than that they are atypical. This cannot be answered here. Only a suggestion is made.

It is not clear why there should be an overall higher proportion of students' siblings at university in Edinburgh than in the other two universities. One reason could be that there is conscious selection of students with other members of the family at university as a question is asked about this on the application form. This cannot be ascertained. Whatever the reasons it is clear that the proportion of siblings also at university is an important factor in a student's home background in any social class since the help and guidance of a contemporary at university is often of more help to the new student than that which could be provided by a parent's experience of university some time ago. Students asked about the problems of first-generation university students (i.e. students with neither parent having been at university) often point out this fact, i.e. that having had a parent at university may be an irrelevant factor in terms of the student's university experience.

Before we turn to an examination of the percentages of first-generation university students, a brief examination of further breakdowns of the Newcastle and Durham figures in terms of siblings' sex reveals an important indication of the way in which sex differentials at university level still largely exist (Table 4.5).

It is immediately apparent that students' *male* siblings have a far greater chance of obtaining a university place and that the sex differential

TABLE 4.5. EDUCATION OF STUDENTS' SIBLINGS OF COLLEGE ENTRANCE AGE—MALE AND FEMALE DISTRIBUTIONS (per cent)

	UMC		LMC		WkC		Total	No.
	Male	Fem.	Male	Fem.	Male	Fem.		
DURHAM								
University	36	28	36	28	16	7	27	(71)
College	23	50	31	45	16	22	33	(86)
Neither	41	22	33	28	68	71	40	(103)
TOTAL	100	100	100	101	100	100	100	(260)
	(107)		(95)		(58)			
NEWCASTLE								
University	55	31	34	20	22	7	31	(166)
College	18	28	30	30	15	14	24	(128)
Neither	27	41	36	50	63	79	45	(247)
TOTAL	100	100	100	100	100	100	100	(541)
No.	(216)		(202)		(123)			

increases down the social scale. Only 7 per cent of working-class students' *female* siblings obtained a university place compared with 36 per cent upper middle-class male siblings Durham and 55 per cent Newcastle. This is not entirely unexpected in the light of Douglas's writings and Early Leaving Report and Robbins Report findings.[1] A similar, though less-marked, differential emerges among college students as the sex and class distributions show, with proportion of female students decreasing down the social scale. (It is interesting to note that a higher proportion of female siblings gain *college* places and that class differentials at this level are not so marked—perhaps a sign of level of expectation and opportunity.) The social class and sex differentials combine to make it exceedingly difficult for the working-class girl to obtain a university place. Those who do, in Jackson's and Marsden's terms, are often of the "sunken middle class",[2] working class for a generation but with middle-class values and aspirations—often embodied in the mother.

This brings us back once more to a consideration of parental educational level which in turn influences family structure and attitudes. Mother's and father's educational levels are considered separately (Table 4.6).

In Table 4.6 one observes different distributions between classes and between universities. Firstly, as one might expect in all the samples, it appears that the lower the students' social class the larger the proportion of parents with low educational level, particularly primary, and that this is true for both parents. As one might assume on the basis of data on students' siblings, parents of Edinburgh students have an overall higher level of education than parents in either of the other two universities.[3] Only 18 per cent of both the mothers and fathers left school at 14 years or before—the equivalent of primary or elementary education—compared with 29 per cent and 30 per cent Newcastle and 28 per cent and 28 per cent Durham. There is no significant difference in these last two configurations, but there is a marked difference in overall parental educational level between Edinburgh and the other two universities. The level of Scottish middle-class parents in the Edinburgh sample emerged in other analyses as on the whole higher than that of English middle-class parents—this refers particularly to fathers. However, it is interesting to note

[1] Little and Westergaard, *op. cit.*: "A working class girl has a 1:600 chance of entering a University—100 times lower than in the professional class."
[2] Jackson and Marsden, *op. cit.*, pp. 53–56.
[3] Comparable figures for University College, Dublin are 27 per cent fathers graduates, 11 per cent mothers (Nevin, *op. cit.*, p. 1).

TABLE 4.6. EDUCATION OF PARENTS (per cent)

Left school	UMC		LMC		WkC		Unclassified		Total	
	Mo.	Fa.	Mo.	Fa.	Mo.	Fa.	Mo.	Fa.	Mo.	Fa.
EDINBURGH										
12, 13 or 14	3	2	22	23	50	50	17	17	18	18
15 yrs.	5	1	16	10	27	36	17	—	13	10
16 yrs.	19	6	22	16	6	2	17	17	18	10
17, 18 yrs.	17	7	17	26	11	6	33	—	16	15
College	19	8	13	12	2	—	17	17	15	8
University	29	71	4	4	2	2	—	50	15	32
Educated privately or finishing school	4	—	2	—	—	—	—	—	3	—
Night school/ Indus. exams.	—	3	—	6	—	—	—	—	—	3
Unknown	4	3	4	4	2	4	—	—	4	4
TOTAL	100	101	100	101	100	100	101	101	101	100
No.	(128)	(128)	(140)	(140)	(48)	(48)	(6)	(6)	(322)	(322)
DURHAM										
12, 13 or 14	8	3	28	30	61	66	23	38	29	30
15 yrs.	10	5	21	12	21	21	38	23	18	12
16 yrs.	15	7	21	22	9	9	8	15	16	15
17, 18 yrs.	23	6	14	19	4	1	23	8	15	11
College	24	12	11	9	3	—	—	8	13	7
University	15	63	1	1	—	—	—	—	4	19
Educated privately or finishing school	4	—	3	—	1	—	—	—	4	—
Night school/ Indus. exams.	—	2	—	4	—	3	—	—	—	4
Unknown	1	2	1	3	1	—	8	8	1	2
TOTAL	100	100	100	100	100	100	100	100	100	100
No.	(101)	(101)	(161)	(161)	(77)	(77)	(13)	(13)	(352)	(352)

TABLE 4.6 (*cont.*)

Left school	UMC Mo. Fa.		LMC Mo. Fa.		WkC Mo. Fa.		Unclassified Mo. Fa.		Total Mo. Fa.	
NEWCASTLE										
12, 13 or 14 yrs.	5	3	30	26	62	67	24	24	28	28
15 yrs.	14	2	23	22	23	13	20	17	21	13
16 yrs.	19	6	19	19	7	10	15	15	17	13
17, 18 yrs.	20	11	12	12	4	3	25	27	13	10
College	21	12	11	11	—	1	12	—	12	10
University	17	54	2	2	3	—	2	15	6	17
Educated privately or finishing school	1	—	1	—	—	—	—	—	1	—
Night school/ Indus. exams.	—	11	—	6	—	5	—	—	—	7
Unknown	3	1	2	2	1	1	2	2	2	2
TOTAL No.	100 (199)	100 (199)	100 (280)	100 (280)	100 (124)	100 (124)	100 (26)	100 (26)	100 (629)	100 (629)

that more of the English middle-class mothers, as well as the working-class mothers mentioned earlier have reached a higher level of education than the Scottish mothers. For example, 43 per cent of the Scottish upper middle class had a college or university education, while 53 per cent of English upper middle-class mothers reached this level. In the lower middle class comparable figures are 15 per cent and 24 per cent.

It would seem that the Edinburgh sample is special in the sense that it represents a greater proportion of families with a tradition of higher education, i.e. educational expansion to those families where higher education was previously unknown lags behind that of Durham and New-castle—which we might deduce from the actual social class composition.

Referring again to Table 4.6 we can see that the proportion of parents educated only to elementary level is very different between social classes

—ranging from 3 per cent mothers and 2 per cent fathers in the Edinburgh upper middle class to 62 per cent and 67 per cent in the Newcastle working class—a spectrum which reveals both class and institutional differentials. There are differences between the Durham and Newcastle samples but they are not marked enough at any level for us to draw any conclusions. However, the differences between Edinburgh and the other two universities are marked at each social class level, for instance, upper middle-class parents in each institution with university education are 29 per cent mothers, 71 per cent fathers in Edinburgh; 15 per cent mothers and 63 per cent fathers in Durham; and 17 per cent mothers and 54 per cent fathers in Newcastle. Figures for elementary schooling only in the working class are 50 per cent both mothers and fathers in Edinburgh; 61 per cent mothers and 66 per cent fathers in Durham; and 62 per cent and 67 per cent in Newcastle. Those who were educated to 15 years must have had at least some experience of secondary education, and there are appreciably more of these parents in Edinburgh than in Durham and Newcastle, and particularly in the working class.

This would seem to show what has been emerging in the study of students' siblings that different social class proportions, reflecting perhaps differential barriers to selection in either application or selection, may represent social classes of a slightly different kind—containing, perhaps, more or less aspiring, atypical, or "marginal" families. This may be true particularly with respect to certain attributes such as, in this case, family educational achievements of both parents and siblings. This will be demonstrated in examination of other attributes of class categories and of the meaning which they have within the whole complex of variables.

Interesting facts emerge when one compares mothers' with fathers' education. In the Edinburgh sample in the lower middle class and upper middle class, the father's education on the whole reaches a higher level than does the mother's, but the working class proves the exception with, for example, a greater proportion of mothers than fathers leaving school at the age of 16 years or over (21 per cent compared with 10 per cent). This seems to be illustrated by Jackson's and Marsden's suggestion that in working-class families it is the mother who often has the greatest influence on the child's education[1] and that if she herself has had a grammar school education there is increased likelihood that her children will go.

[1] Recent work on the achievement effects of the maternal relationship—Hiliard, T. and Roth, R. M., Maternal attitudes and the non achievement syndrome, *Personnel and Guidance Journal*, 1969, **47** (5), 424–8.

In such an event, an ambitious mother will encourage her child to think of going to university, and perhaps bring to fruition her unfulfilled ambitions for herself. In another sense, therefore, the family is atypical in attitude and aspiration.

This pattern is mirrored in the Durham and Newcastle samples although not perhaps so clearly. Perhaps these groups contain fewer *atypical* families. The sex distributions of the Newcastle sample (not shown here) seem to point to the fact that the conclusions just discussed hold true primarily for *male* working-class students—so that the sex differential emerges again. The fathers of working-class *female* students on the whole had a higher education than that of the mothers and higher too than the fathers' education of *male* students. This would seem to suggest that fathers who themselves have reached a higher level of education are more likely to see the value of educating a girl who will nevertheless get married. It would be interesting to see how many of the girls are eldest children who take to some extent the position of a son.

When one considers overall figures on parents who have been to university, one again finds a different configuration in the three universities. In Edinburgh, 15 per cent of mothers and 32 per cent of fathers have had a university education; in Durham the figures are 5 per cent and 19 per cent; in Newcastle 6 per cent and 17 per cent. Again we see that a greater proportion of Edinburgh students are from families with a tradition of higher education. If we include college education the discrepancy is not so marked and may bear out the contention in Chapter 1 that much expansion of educational opportunity may be felt at college level as part of a two or three generation process, before families experience university education. Those who jump the gap in one generation may be said to be atypical.[1]

This brings us to a discussion of the "first-generation university student", that is a student neither of whose parents had a university education. There has been increasing discussion of the position and problems of the first-generation student in recent years in terms which suggest that he may easily be identified within the student body by virtue of the fact that he is the first in his family to have the experience of higher education. As such he is often spoken of as though he were a member of a group

---

[1] A study in the U.S. of attitudes and behaviours of parents of successful students showed similar attitudes and "school reinforcement behaviours" of parents in lower working class and upper middle class. Coleman, A. B., Parents help their children succeed, *High School Journal*, 1969, **52** (6), 298–305.

which exhibits special characteristics, and which is subject to special problems and strains, not experienced by students whose parents went to university.

One must examine the truth of this assumption for it springs from the idea that within the university "educational" class and divisions are more significant for the student than social class of origin and all that that implies in terms of social class identity, i.e. whether a student is first generation or second generation is more meaningful than his social class and overrides such divisions.

We shall first examine this suggestion. As it happens, first-generation student has often been confused with working-class student since it has been assumed that first-generation students are almost exclusively working class as a result of expansion of educational opportunity. We must therefore discover whether the "labels" themselves are synonymous and interchangeable, and whether the concept of a first-generation student is in itself a useful classification. In discussing its limitations one may reveal when the concept *is* useful.

This will help to show how far first-generation university students are a group with certain social characteristics and how far they comprise other more meaningful categories. In this will be seen once more the influence of social class factors.

As many as 63 per cent of Edinburgh students and 80 per cent of both Durham and Newcastle students are first-generation students—so that they comprise a majority of the student body and not just a small group within it. Table 4.7 shows the percentage of first-generation students in each social class.

Table 4.7 and others (not shown) show the predominance which the *lower middle-class* students, and not the working class, have in the proportion of first-generation students in each university by sheer weight of numbers; 63 per cent of all first-generation students in Edinburgh; 57 per cent in Newcastle; and 56 per cent in Durham. If one accepts what was said at the beginning of the chapter that it is the lower middle class rather than the working class which is taking advantage of the expansion of educational opportunity and acts as the barometer of change, then this evidence would seem to support that view. It is the lower middle-class students from homes where higher education was formerly unknown who are flooding into the universities. However, the fact that there are first-generation students in every social class shows a general *overall* expansion in educational opportunity.

156 Student Life in a Class Society

TABLE 4.7. FIRST-GENERATION UNIVERSITY STUDENTS—CLASS DISTRIBUTIONS (per cent)

	UMC	LMC	WkC	Unclassified	Total
EDINBURGH					
Second generation	80	8	4	50	37
First generation	20	92	96	50	63
TOTAL	100	100	100	100	100
No.	(126)	(140)	(48)	(6)	(322)
DURHAM					
Second generation	68	2	—	—	20
First generation	32	98	100	100	80
TOTAL	100	100	100	100	100
No.	(101)	(161)	(77)	(13)	(352)
NEWCASTLE					
Second generation	60	4	3	17	20
First generation	40	96	97	83	80
TOTAL	100	100	100	100	100
No.	(199)	(280)	(124)	(26)	(629)

These figures, and particularly those which show a substantial proportion of *upper middle-class* first-generation students, point out that first-generation student is by no means synonymous with working-class student. Upper middle-class first-generation students are 20 per cent of the upper middle class in Edinburgh; 32 per cent in Durham; 40 per cent in Newcastle—again an example of differential expansion *within institutions*.

One next asks how far the social class distribution within this "group" is meaningful or whether it may be assumed that the similarities between first-generation students are greater than the social class differences. Interviewees in Edinburgh were quick to point out that first-generation students "are not all the same" and that they may be distinguished in other ways, particularly by social class. The Edinburgh interview evidence and that from informal remarks was all that was available to the author in the Edinburgh survey, but the evidence produced was so striking that it became necessary to ask questions about being a "first-generation student" on the succeeding questionnaires in order that views on this point could be quantified.

In interview firstly it emerged that upper middle-class students were to some extent put upon the defensive when asked about being a first-generation student. Presumably it smacked of being low on the social scale, at least educationally—so these students tended to stress socioeconomic features of their background which compensated, i.e. they weighted socioeconomic dimension of social class greater than the educational dimension of social class (because they already ranked high in the former).

Said one Edinburgh upper middle-class student: "All first-generation students are not alike. My parents did not go to university but they mix with professional people who did—so the idea is not new to me, and I have no particular problems."

The middle-class students, particularly the upper middle class, thus implied that in *their* case "first-generation student" was not a meaningful category and did not therefore influence their life at university in any particular way. On the other hand, upper middle-class students of the second generation claimed this did not give them an undue advantage since their parents' experience of university was too outdated to be of special help.

First-generation students were asked whether they had experienced any particular problems as a result of the fact that neither parent had a university education. No upper middle-class student admitted to having experienced difficulties either at home or at university; and in all their remarks was the implicit suggestion that the cultural background of their homes was thoroughly compatible with university "culture"—both being middle class, and this is true of both first- *and* second-generation students.

This was *not* true of all *lower* middle-class students, and here the social class divisions are sometimes less important than the fact of "being new" and not feeling assimilated into the new life. It was the students from the lower echelons of the lower middle class who experienced difficulties most, i.e. those socially nearest the working class. However, not all the working-class students said they had experienced difficulties as a result of being a first-generation student nor felt that this was in any way a "special" category. This resulted from the combination of a variety of factors.

Firstly, those whose elder *siblings* had been to university said that this had been a great help to them and had "eased" them into university life. This is true also of second-generation students. Since the help and information was contemporary, they argued that it was probably of greater assistance than having had a parent at university. This view was endorsed by some middle-class students who said that their parents' university education had been of little help to them as their experience and information was so *out-of-date*. They did not experience difficulties not because they were second-generation students but because they were *middle class*.

Thus we may see that the first-generation students are not a group with general characteristics and identity—they remain members of their social class and their experiences as students will be influenced more by their social class than by their parents lack of higher education. The social class differences still emerge in discussion of an "educational" category. Whether students experience difficulties as first-generation students depends on home background as expressed in socioeconomic as well as educational terms. These imply cultural differences not necessarily transmitted through the medium of university education. This would seem to show that there is little evidence of an *élite culture* preserved and transmitted through generations *only* by the university. One also has to consider the whole pattern of educational achievement within a family—not just the education of parents. It may be that "significant others" with experience of higher education are more likely to be siblings or even uncles and aunts. Of course, where the family is of higher socioeconomic status it is more likely that a *greater number* of significant others will have had higher education and therefore represent a cumulative fund of information and culture from which the student can benefit. In this sense we may have to separate out "information and culture" benefits and "encouragement" benefits which may not coincide. Certainly definition of first-generation student as based *only* on education level of parent may mean very little—concealing as it does not only socioeconomic differences but differences in family education structure.

This is also supported by the evidence that parental experience of higher education is not always relevant to the contemporary situation, and that a working-class student following a sibling at university feels as much at ease in the university situation as a middle-class student who follows a parent.

This needs further investigation, but the lesson to be learned seems quite clear that one must not take first-generation student to mean more than it does, and that within this category there are a wealth of cultural distinctions.

If we turn to an examination of the *kinds* of problems experienced by first-generation students, this point will become more clear.

In a sense the picture will appear to be lopsided because there is no *control group* of second-generation students who were asked what problems they experienced at university. This is, therefore, one of those unfortunate oversights hich cannot be remedied because there is no quantitative evidence on this. However, there is qualitative evidence from observation and interviews which suggests that the kind of problems experienced by first-generation students are by no means special to them and that they are indeed the sort of problems experienced by all students—whether first or second generation. This in a sense supports what was said earlier that in itself the first-generation division can tell us very little and that it is differences *within* this group which are interesting. We can examine, given the provisos already made, what these differences tell us about socioeconomic and educational differences in the student body, which may be extended to apply to a lesser extent to the second-generation group. The conclusions apply to a lesser extent because of the value of having had a parent at university, but the areas of problems in which this value manifests itself may be more open to doubt. Institutionally induced problems—problems of adaption to particular university circumstances—may be common to all students, and parental experience which is out of date may be no help. However, in terms of *general* educational culture, *home* atmosphere, and attitude, it may be that second-generation students will have fewer problems than first-generation students. One could even talk in terms of the *mesh* or compatibility of institutional and home culture determining a whole range of potential problem areas. This again is not merely a matter of educational divisions but socioeconomic status and material and cultural provisions in the home, i.e. books in the home, theatre-going, travel, etc. Although a high level of parental education and a home environment compatible with educational success may coincide, it is not necessarily so, whereas many homes where there is general cultural awareness, middle-class aspirations and reverence for learning, may have had no experience of higher education. Having been through the educational mill does not ensure a healthy respect for the process, as examination of the views of today's students will show. Therefore, in itself, having had a parent at university may not mean a great deal to the present-day student. It is, on the whole, likely to have more significance in the general rather than the specific sense, so that there is greater "fit" of his expectations in the main with the reality than is the case with the first-generation student. In terms of specific *information* about particular circumstances both kinds of student may be at a loss if their school and their contemporaries have not kept them in touch with up-to-date changes in universities.

In summary, then, it might be said that information problems are best dealt with by schools and contemporaries, so that students who suffer in this area are those who did not have either parental or school help or experience to assist them; general culture problems spring from degree of culture *mesh* and degree of encouragement in the home, and this is likely to depend at least to some extent on parental education level. This is the area most likely to distinguish the first-generation student, and the area in which he will experience most problems. Although for him a good school may decrease his information problems, it may increase his culture problems by increasing the disparity of home and school culture. There will be little mesh between home and school or university culture. This will emerge in discussion of particular problems suffered

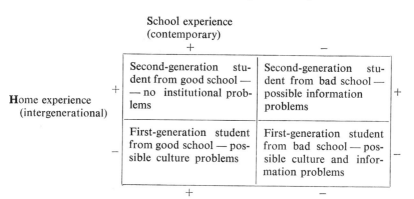

Fɪɢ. 4.3. Problems suffered by first-generation students.

by first-generation students—but perhaps a rather crude diagram (Fig. 4.3) will help to clarify this.

Of course it must be borne in mind that this represents extremes and that some individuals will fall in between these categories—also that socioeconomic factors will complicate the issue. However, it does outline the importance, which we shall encounter repeatedly of school culture in preparing the student for university and for his place in it. Now let us look specifically at first-generation problems.

In the Edinburgh interviews it emerged clearly that the disadvantages most often discussed were the practical ones of not knowing what university is like and of not being prepared for it; of not knowing enough about courses to be able to choose properly; of coming "completely in the dark about what to expect and what was expected of them". The kind of opinions expressed show that there is a distinct difference between this kind of problem and that experienced as a result of social class mobility or culture incompatibility—and the two should not be confused. Social mobility is discussed in Chapter 13. The views of students about the problems of first-generation university students were closely allied to opinions about the role of schools in helping to fill the gap in the knowledge of university and its ways which first-generation university students experience. Half of the students interviewed in Edinburgh in some way criticised their school or the university or both for not giving them any help to overcome their unavoidable ignorance in this field. Several students from the working class and lower middle class seemed to think they had got into the wrong course through sheer ignorance of what courses are available. A number in all three universities quoted examples of friends who had given up their courses because they had been so unhappy and unsuited for them. Ignorance about how to apply to university hostels, or to get good "digs", and such things which may seem very obvious and well known to all students, were a "closed book" to some of these first-generation students and their ignorance in many ways caused them misery. Some students fail examinations because they are continually changing their "digs", and others are prepared to "toil through their course just to get a degree at the end of it". For these students university is by no means an enriching experience.

In the Newcastle and Durham surveys some quantifiable evidence was gained from questionnaires about the problems which first-generation students face—and again the same opinions emerged, this time with the added weight of numbers behind them. Social class differences emerge—

Student Life in a Class Society

as expected—in the light of the Edinburgh survey, and the proportion of first-generation students who experience problems is small. Reasons given for this were those first described in the Edinburgh survey; effects of *lack of information* about university life resulting from parental lack of higher education is mitigated by having siblings at university or college, or through the help of school and teachers, or—in the case of middle-class children—because of their middle-class culture and values. Those who experience difficulties at university have a negative rating on any one or all of these points. Thus a working-class student from a "poor" grammar school who is the first of his family to have higher education is likely to suffer the most in terms of both lack of information and of attempt to reconcile differences in life at university and at home. Naturally, personality factors of both the student and his family may help to overcome these disadvantages.

Table 4.8 shows the analyses of problems of first-generation students in the Durham and Newcastle surveys in terms of social class of origin.

TABLE 4.8. PROBLEMS OF FIRST-GENERATION STUDENTS (per cent)

Difficulties experienced	UMC	LMC	WkC	Unclassi-fied	Total
DURHAM					
Yes	16	20	27	9	21
No	84	77	72	91	77
Don't know	—	3	1	—	2
TOTAL	100	100	100	100	100
No.	(101)	(161)	(77)	(13)	(352)
NEWCASTLE					
Yes	9	16	23	34	17
No	87	78	71	66	77
Don't know	4	6	6	—	6
TOTAL	100	100	100	100	100
No.	(199)	(280)	(124)	(26)	(629)

In Newcastle only 17 per cent of first-generation students overall said they experienced difficulties at university and 6 per cent did not know. In Durham 21 per cent said they had experienced difficulties and 2 per cent did not know. The slight rise in proportion in Durham may be attributable to the fact that, as we have seen, it is possible that there is a higher proportion of *eldest* children among the working class and lower middle class at this university than at the other two.

It will be noted that there are social class differences in proportion of students who experienced difficulties—as has been mentioned with reference to the Edinburgh figures. If one adds together those who said "Yes" with the "Don't Knows", a steady gradient emerges: in Durham 16 per cent upper middle class, 23 per cent lower middle class, and 28 per cent working class; in Newcastle 13 per cent, 22 per cent, and 29 per cent— an overall similar distribution. Thus among the working class of both universities nearly a third openly state that they have experienced difficulties. It is quite likely that a number of others felt too proud to do so. The problems which these students outlined are shown in Table 4.9.

TABLE 4.9. KINDS OF PROBLEMS EXPERIENCED BY FIRST-GENERATION STUDENTS (per cent)

	UMC		LMC		WkC		Total	
	D'ham	N'castle	D'ham	N'castle	D'ham	N'castle	D'ham	N'castle
Incompatible home culture	—	—	7	16	9	17	9	15
Lack of parental understanding or interest	80	56	59	48	34	31	55	40
Lack of information	20	31	17	12	32	43	19	29
Financial	—	—	8	9	3	3	5	7
Pressure to get on	—	6	9	3	6	—	9	2
Social class discrimination	—	7	—	12	16	6	3	7
TOTAL No.	100 (101)	100 (199)	100 (161)	100 (280)	100 (77)	100 (124)	100 (329)	100 (603)

Table 4.9 shows that incompatibility of home culture and lack of parental interest or understanding must be differentiated because al-

though they may be interrelated they represent different aspects of the same phenomenon. In the upper middle class there was no mention of incompatibility of home culture, but a large majority of first-generation students mentioned lack of parental interest in or understanding of their new life and the problems created. This was a problem of *attitudes*. In the lower middle class and working class not only does the importance of material culture begin to emerge (slightly more important in Newcastle than in Durham), but the importance of parental *attitude* begins to decrease relative to the other problems which emerge. Particularly in the working class the problem of *information* mentioned earlier takes on increasing importance—43 per cent of Newcastle working-class students mentioned this. It may be that parental attitudes were also a cause of friction, as emerged in interviews, but these pale in significance by the side of more immediate issues of lack of information. Only 20 per cent of the Durham upper middle class complained of lack of information. These figures do seem to confirm the diagram or model outlined earlier. There are slight differences between Newcastle and Durham which may relate to the differences in overall material environment.

The lower middle class in both universities experiences proportionately less lack of information, and more the influence of financial pressures and pressure "to get on"—17 per cent in Durham feel these pressures, 12 per cent in Newcastle. This is not unexpected if, as we assumed earlier, the lower middle class is largely an aspiring group but one previously financially constrained.

The only group in Durham who experienced problems of social class discrimination are the working class—no doubt because they feel the middle-class ethos of the colleges operates against their interests. In Newcastle a small proportion of each social class experienced discrimination with the lower middle class stating this problem most often; 12 per cent compared with Durham working class 16 per cent. This may well be because the ethos of Newcastle is in general working class although, as we have seen, it bears little relation to objective social class proportions. Thus one has to consider not only the operation and interrelation of home and educational factors, but the particular institutional context within which the student lives and interacts.

In interviews it became clear that the students had largely come to terms with problems inherent in being first-generation university students, but that lack of information of the most basic kind caused much unnecessary suffering. Indeed, it is likely that the percentage of first-generation students who said they experienced disadvantages would have doubled had they realised that the question embraced "practical" problems like lack of information. Students have said this. Many misunderstood and felt it was a discussion of their family. In interview they admitted to problems of a "practical" nature.

This relates particularly to course of study which is, after all, the *raison d'être* of being a student and the central part of his university existence. If he is unhappy in his course it will have ramifications in all spheres of his university life. Unhappiness results mostly from being unprepared for what university has to offer in both work and leisure—and it is the first duty of the schools to prepare potential students with the information which their parents may not be able to give.

> First-generation students are in a difficult position because they get no advice from their schools or their parents. It is very easy to get into the wrong course. I know at least eight working-class students who have failed their courses because of this, and one or two who have voluntarily given up theirs.

There seems to be some difference in approach to this problem by different types of school. The public, direct grant, and "better" grammar schools tend to be most organised in getting hold of and passing on all available brochures and leaflets often through the person of a careers master or mistress. Other schools assume knowledge in pupils which is lacking, and are disorganised in even basic essentials.

> I wanted to apply to London University [said one Newcastle student] and didn't know that you have to apply months in advance. We got no help at all with application forms and things; this was before the UCCA began. I went to my form master one day and told him I was going to apply. He said it was far too late to do anything about it—and by that time a lot of the other universities' closing dates had also passed.

Other students spoke of their ignorance of courses available and expressed a longing to study sociology or psychology or economics or town planning now that they knew they existed. Their school had channelled them into "safe" subjects in which they could "get by" academically but had little interest. Even with the advent of the UCCA forms, the business takes on the form of a sophisticated game of roulette with complicated permutations of subjects and universities representing better or worse chances of being selected.

A recent applicant for a sociology place at university, when asked why she had put Sheffield first, said that the previous year the school's only three university entrants had got places at Sheffield, and the teacher had therefore told the whole class to put Sheffield at the head of the list that year, whatever the subject. It is clear that many of the schools are as much in the dark about how to apply to universities as are the sixth-formers. There seems no logic in the system and in selection of people for places— so many schools obviously do not go about the process logically. However, there is a difference between inadequate information and positively misleading advice, and the first- and second-generation students alike are equally at the mercy of their school unless their parents are well informed and interested enough to intervene.

As we have seen in other ways, too, the student's school represents a cultural factor in his background which he brings with him to his university experience. For a number of reasons, hereafter developed, the school distribution of students represents a meaningful cultural division. Table 4.10 shows the distribution of the social classes in different types of schools which may illumine this problem yet further.[1] Unfortunately, no figures on school last attended are available for Edinburgh.

TABLE 4.10. SCHOOLS LAST ATTENDED BY STUDENTS (per cent)

	UMC		LMC		WkC		Unclassified		Total	
	D'ham	N'castle	D'ham	N'castle	D'ham	N'castle	D'ham	N'castle	D'ham	N'...
Public schools	32	31	11	8	2	—	13	19	17	
Direct grant	24	14	19	12	6	7	9	15	18	
State grammar	37	41	64	65	82	73	68	58	59	
Private or religious	3	4	2	3	—	3	4	—	2	
Secondary modern, comprehensive, or technical high	3	3	2	6	10	8	2	4	3	
Technical college	1	7	2	6	—	9	4	4	1	
TOTAL	100	100	100	100	100	100	100	100	100	1...
No.	(101)	(199)	(161)	(280)	(77)	(124)	(13)	(26)	(352)	(6...

[1] This table shows the over-representation of students from public schools in both universities compared with the proportion in the total school population.

Table 4.11 also shows the "school" composition of the colleges which
will be referred to in detail in Chapter 10.

In Newcastle, 14 per cent of students had attended some sort of public
school compared with 17 per cent in Durham. If we include direct grant
public schools, then figures rise to 25 per cent and 35 per cent—showing
an institutional difference. Thirteen per cent of Newcastle students had

TABLE 4.11. SCHOOL COMPOSITION OF THE DURHAM COLLEGES (per cent)

	Bede	Chad	Cuthbert	Grey	Hatf.	St. J.
Public	12	27	11	15	17	48
Direct grant	18	27	19	23	28	4
State grammar school	59	33	55	60	53	44
Private	—	—	6	—	2	—
Secondary modern	6	7	4	—	—	4
Technical high or college	6	7	4	3	—	—
TOTAL	101	101	99	101	100	100
No.	(17)	(15)	(47)	(62)	(47)	(25)

	Univ.	St. A	St. H	St. M	NC	Total	No.
Public	18	29	—	8	—	17	(59)
Direct grant	5	15	29	19	—	18	(64)
State grammar school	74	57	64	64	83	59	(206)
Private	—	—	—	4	—	2	(6)
Secondary modern	—	—	7	2	—	2	(7)
Technical high or college	3	—	—	3	17	2	(10)
TOTAL	100	101	100	100	100	100	(352)
No.	(39)	(28)	(14)	(52)	(6)	(352)	

attended a secondary modern, comprehensive, or technical high school or college; only 4 per cent had done so in Durham. Apart from these distributions having interest in the present discussion, they are a meaningful division of the student body in terms of cultural groups (as we shall see in Chapter 10) and operate as a factor in student social relations. It will be seen that "school" and class divisions to some extent coincide. This will be seen to be a meaningful indicator to students in their social class relations.

Not only does a gradation in type of school appear in relation to social class, but there appear to be meaningful differences between the two institutions. For instance, if we take public school and direct grant school together and compare with the state grammar school category, there appears to be a *steeper* gradient of differentials in the Durham case than in Newcastle. (It is possible to deduce from other evidence that were the material available Edinburgh would exhibit an even steeper gradient.) In Durham the public school direct grant proportions are 56 per cent in the upper middle class, 30 per cent in the lower middle class, and 8 per cent in the working class compared with 45 per cent, 20 per cent, and 7 per cent in Newcastle. The state grammar school category is 37 per cent, 64 per cent, and 82 per cent in Durham, and 41 per cent, 65 per cent, and 73 per cent in Newcastle. These figures perhaps suggest more school selection in Durham than in Newcastle—both in application and selection.

With regard to the present discussion it is clear that if the schools have much to do with the transmission of information, as well as culture and values, the class differentials which emerge in the school composition will be meaningful in the student body in terms of student experience. The college distributions in Durham in terms of school as well as social class add to the variety of cultural divisions in the student body.

Before we discuss the implications of this in relation to students' satisfaction with their course it may be useful briefly to consider yet more evidence of the nature of the social class differentials which emerge within the student body. In the Durham survey figures were available on the students' grants or awards which were collated and analysed in terms of social class. The results are presented in Table 4.12.

Ten per cent of the students have no grants compared with 8 per cent in Edinburgh, and the figure varies from class to class. As many as 20 per cent of the upper middle-class female students are supported privately, and female students as a whole have fewer grants than male students.

TABLE 4.12. STUDENT GRANTS AND AWARDS—DURHAM UNIVERSITY (per cent)

	UMC		LMC		WkC		Unclassified		Total	
	M	F	M	F	M	F	M	F	M	F
State schols	—	3	7	4	11	7	9	—	6	4
Other grants	85	76	88	84	84	93	73	100	85	83
No grants	15	21	5	12	5	—	18	—	8	13
TOTAL	100	100	100	100	100	100	100	100	99	100
No.	(72)	(29)	(106)	(55)	(63)	(14)	(11)	(2)	(252)	(100)

No female students of the working class are supported by parents, showing—as may be supposed—that working-class parents are less willing to finance a daughter through her education although as many as 5 per cent working-class male students are supported by parents.

If we turn to an examination of the proportion of state scholarships in each social class it is immediately clear that by far the highest proportion of state scholarships in any social class is found in the male working class—11 per cent. None of the upper middle-class male students had a state scholarship. The lower middle-class male student also had a high proportion—comprising 40 per cent of all state scholarships gained and 50 per cent of all male state scholarships.

The proportion of working-class girls having won state scholarships was twice that of the other two classes and as high as the proportion of lower middle-class male students.

These results are comments on the process of selection, as the proportion of state scholarships is some indication of the proportion of extremely gifted students in each social class admitted. It is clear that the process of selection picks out more highly gifted working-class students than middle class—or rather their giftedness compensates for social features which work against them. Similarly, working-class girls have a double barrier of selection against them on account of sex and class differentials so that among those who succeed is as great a proportion of gifted students as is found among the boys. There is a steady increase of state scholarships down the social scale, indicating the counterbalancing property of ability in the face of social class disadvantage.

This is yet another example of how social class of origin may constitute a meaningful category in the student body which implies a complex configuration of variables rather than purely a "label". The fact that these configurations are by no means sharply defined in relation merely to socioeconomic status is an indication of the fact that beyond a certain point in the process of educational selection there is blurring of social class divisions, and that other aspects of social class come into play— like educational tradition. Nevertheless, the blurring does not obscure the basic social class configurations which emerge in a number of cultural areas meaningful for the student. What this chapter has attempted to do is to investigate what the basic socioeconomic categories in the student body *do* mean in cultural terms and therefore what kind of student population we are dealing with in each case.

We have seen how problems of first-generation students tend to pattern on class lines in terms of lack of information about courses and residence and so on. In the Newcastle survey there was an attempt to quantify students who were dissatisfied with course of study or type of residence. The latter point on residence is considered in the next chapter in the light of student expectations of university life. Some facts on the former are presented here (Table 4.13), since it has a good deal of bearing also on school experience already discussed.

Eleven per cent of students were dissatisfied with their course and 12

TABLE 4.13. STUDENTS' SATISFACTION WITH COURSE (I.E. SUITED TO ABILITIES AND INCLINATIONS)—NEWCASTLE UNIVERSITY (per cent)

	UMC		LMC		WkC		Unclassified		Total	
	M	F	M	F	M	F	M	F	M	F
Yes	79	81	74	74	81	73	86	80	78	77
No	9	9	13	15	8	9	14	30	11	11
Don't know	12	10	13	11	11	18	—	—	11	12
TOTAL	100	100	100	100	100	100	100	100	100	100
No.	(142)	(57)	(189)	(91)	(91)	(33)	(21)	(5)	(443)	(186)

per cent were not sure. This leaves 77 per cent who were satisfied that the course was suited to their abilities and talents.[1] This would be less remarkable were it not that as we know the "assault course" to university is so difficult and bestrewn with hazards and obstacles that one would imagine only a real desire to study a particular subject would pull one through. There are obviously other reasons for sticking the course— and these are discussed in the next chapter. It is interesting to note the similarity of sex distributions. It is the lower middle class of both sexes who show the most dissatisfaction with their course—perhaps a sign of being pressurised willy-nilly into university whatever their individual preferences.

Most of the dissatisfied students in interview described a system of channelling which began almost before they were old enough to know what was happening and then when it was too late they found themselves at university unhappily reading the wrong subject. Even more depressed and depressing were those who were taking a *second* degree in subjects they did not like. Working class, aspiring, and yet on a band-wagon they could not get off, they represented a pathetic minority.

Once again one must phrase one's analysis in social class terms, for they are meaningful in the student situation. We have seen in this chapter how the social class distribution of family size is not in all respects clearly marked, although patterns emerge modified by other factors, and it is quite possible that in certain other material ways concomitant with family size the students' families would not show such marked class differentials as would appear in the total population, for example with regard to gross material prosperity. From this one might *superficially* assume a relative homogeneity in that because gross "clues" of rags and riches are missing the social classes are undifferentiated. However, in terms of educational level of parents and siblings, students' school background and social problems, distinct social class patterns do emerge when considered in interrelation which show that there is some cultural differentiation in the student body on social class lines, more meaningful than purely socio-economic categories. It is not accidental that education and values are so closely related, for it is in terms of social class internalised value systems and educo-cultural patterns that most significant divisions among students begin to emerge. These will be discussed at greater length throughout the book. These patterns emerge in distribution of first-gener-

[1] Nevin shows only 53 per cent satisfied with studies in University College, Dublin Nevin, *op. cit.*, p. 19).

ation university students and their problems at university and in student attitudes and motivations for coming to university, to be discussed in the next chapter.

Although the socioeconomic categories with which this chapter began reveal some kind of social class patterning—meaningful also to students themselves—it is not in fact in socioeconomic or gross material terms that these divisions are most meaningful. This apparent contradiction results from the fact that the socioeconomic dimension although *implying* others need not *always* be seen as the most significant and may be affected by other cultural factors discussed—as we shall be led to examine—and this applies particularly to the student context which represents a *new* cultural situation. We are in effect looking at a set of interdependent cultural factors associated closely with socioeconomic classes and which seem to retain their relevance even at university level.

Thus already we are led to question what the socioeconomic classes *mean* to students within the student body, particularly in terms of the *values* they most often stress or exhibit. We continue with our discussion of social class distribution within the student body in the next chapter in terms of motivations to and expectatinns of higher education expressive of these educo-cultural divisions defined in this chapter.

It is clear that we cannot understand the student attitude and behaviour patterns at university unless we first examine the variable cultural influences which students or categories of students have undergone and which must to some extent condition their future responses to the university environment and socialisation process. Depending on their cultural "filter" will depend the kind of social and academic stimuli which they perceive as meaningful or discriminate in certain ways, and ultimately what they put into and get out of the university experience will be determined by just these influences or barriers.

CHAPTER 5

STUDENTS' REASONS FOR COMING TO UNIVERSITY: A COMPARISON OF MOTIVATIONS, EXPECTATIONS, AND REALISATIONS

IN THE last chapter an analysis of the basic data about the students and their families was presented which went some way towards showing "who the students are" in terms of observable social class *identities* or cultural configurations relevant outside the institutional framework as characterising the family background from which students come. It will be our concern later to discover whether, indeed, the same points of reference are as meaningful to the students acting and interacting in defined social situations as to the objective observer of statistical social and cultural norms. Does, for instance, the role-affiliation of the student to his family continue to some degree even when he is physically separated from his family and social class "clues"? Culture patterns have emerged in terms of students' family background and social class of origin in addition to purely socioeconomic status patterns. How far they themselves recognise these patterns and consciously identify with a social class, and how far their identification affects attitudes and behaviour within the student body, will be discovered later. Suffice it to say that divisions in terms of statistically quantifiable constant and consistent culture patterns have emerged in terms of certain characteristics of the students' families as categorised by occupational status, and will be seen to emerge in an analysis of characteristics of the students themselves similarly categorised—particularly at the level of internalised value system. We can thus begin to see in what ways we can speak about "class" composition—and its relevance in a structural rather than a descriptive sense—for "in presenting our positional picture we do not perhaps freeze an ongoing course of events at some arbitrary point; but we do try to extract from it an orderliness assumed to be continuous and persistent, that is, to have a relatively timeless validity".[1]

Social class membership is taken as the point of reference in this analysis so as to ascertain conversely when and how membership of the "student" category becomes meaningful to the students themselves and to others. The previous findings, by showing that in a sense the socio-economic classes analysed are meaningful *cultural collectivities*, allow the validity of this point of view. One therefore approaches the complex network of student relations particularly through the unravelling of one particular strand, and although this may seem to give the one strand over-emphasis it nevertheless provides a meaningful framework within which to seek explanations of various kinds of student behaviour. This is particularly true since it provides us with a baseline for the comparison of institutions and structural principles at work and allows us to make generalities of wider validity. The statement of Little and Westergaard that "social classes constitute genuine groupings, not quasi-communities",[2] needs testing, for it presupposes not only a structure of statistical norms but a subjective identification of those within and outside the "groupings" which may only be ascertained first hand at the level of role performance.

It also involves a question of whether social class in the university is attributional and if and when it becomes interactional. These terms were discussed in Chapter 3. At this point in the argument we are speaking about social class as a "cultural collectivity" or as an *attribute* which implies possession of certain cultural characteristics. Whether those possessing this attribute stand in certain relationships with one another will be discussed in the following chapters. At this stage we seek to establish that social class is a meaningful attribute *within the student context*. For "needless to say, a class of people in the society sharing some attribute or series of attributes is not for that reason also a 'group', viz. sub-group it becomes one when 'class' equals 'role' (or quasi-role) and more important when being of a like kind goes with being 'held together' by relationships".[3] The findings of the book will show that within the student body these attributional social classes are in some ways groups in the sense spoken of by Nadel, but only in certain circumstances—particularly defined in terms of cultural and social space in social situations. In other

---

[1] Nadel, S. F., *The Theory of Social Structure* Cohen & West Ltd., London, 1957 p. 127.

[2] Little, A. and Westergaard, J., *BJS*, December 1964, **15** (4).

[3] Nadel, *op. cit.*, p. 89.

words, "social class" equals role only in certain situations, and situations in which "student" equals role are differently defined, particularly by the social "actors".

It is therefore necessary at this stage to show ways in which social class is a meaningful attribute, i.e. that it signifies certain objectively quantifiable characteristics. This is particularly true at the level of "non-material" culture. For it would seem that within the university context only a narrow band of differences in material culture exist. Not only is the student body largely middle class, but the working-class category is composed mainly of skilled workers' children and children of "foremen" and other artisans at the top level of the working class. Only a minimal percentage are sons and daughters of unskilled labourers.

The question now most pertinent is whether as products of the same process of selection, co-operating, and competing within a defined institutional framework, as individuals to some extent isolated from family status they are socially and culturally more alike than different. This involves analysis not only of social class "clues"—dress, speech, manner, and so on—but also the internalised value systems which are class-based and which culture and behaviour patterns express. One asks how far internalised value systems are maintained unchanged and how far overlain with new values? Can one speak with Floud and Halsey of the reconstruction of personalities previously conditioned by class or race?[1] Or must we try to find out whether social class differences and identities persist and for whom; and how far the student body exhibits its own specific social patterns, and how far its links with external kinship and social networks predominate?[2]

With these questions in mind we examine first the student's reasons for seeking a university education, and his particular expectations of it—in other words, the particular value patterns and achievement norms with which he came—and how far these correlate with social class identity. Naturally, as has been already postulated, the student's background influences his attitude to a university education and in consequence his subsequent actions and interactions within the student body are guided by the perceptual terms of reference with which he came. So we shall

---

[1] Floud *et al.*, *Education, Economy and Society*, 1961.
[2] Nadel, *op. cit.*, p. 15: "Pattern" is taken to mean "any orderly distribution of relationships exclusively on the grounds of their similarity and dissimilarity". "Network" on the other hand, means "the interlocking of relationships whereby the interactions implicit in one determine those occurring in others".

follow up with an examination of student behaviour patterns and formal and informal groups in succeeding chapters. Institutional constraints and socialisation obviously affect the patterns which emerge.

Conversely, as Wilson says rather more succinctly, "the clientele obviously affects an institution". He posits that "today there is an alien youth culture which plays on the University through young people who are not primarily committed to the ideal of education".[1] We leave aside the reference to the rather undefined "ideal of education" and observe that Wilson imputes "two characteristics of the clientele"—"the demand for a qualification and the demand for a good time"—which may be for some justifiable reasons for seeking a university education. But the influence of clientele on an institution is by no means a one-way process, or even merely two-way; it is a continuous spiral of change. "The relationship between group and environment is essentially a relationship of action and reaction; it is circular."[2]

The process is a spiral in that once change has been effected, the relationship never returns to the previous point in the process. What the author also hopes to show is that the action and reaction are prompted by the subjective interpretation of the actors in the situation, i.e. their *perception* of the situation—and that this may be in terms of an internalised "image" built-up in the process and not in fact corresponding to any statistically constructed action model.[3] Inquiries into students' reasons for coming to university uncover some of the elements which come into this process from the beginning. The student states what he thought were his reasons, and this memory may have changed over time. However, it is a convenient starting place for analysis and more practical than searching for unconscious goals of actors in the situation which, being unconscious to the student, cannot be discovered by the observer.

The relevance and significance of students' motivations and expectations had not been anticipated in the Edinburgh survey so that no questions on this were included in the questionnaire. However, it soon became clear in interview that these questions are central to any investigation of the structure of the student body in determining the student's definition of what a university education signifies, at least for him. In conse-

---

[1] Wilson, B., Threats to university values, *New Society*, 22 April 1965, No. 134, p. 7.

[2] Homans, G. C., *Human Groups*, 1951, p. 91.

[3] See Clark, B. R., College image and student selection, *Selection and Educational Differentiation*, Centre for the Study of Higher Education, Berkeley, California, 1959.

quence, questions were asked on the Durham questionnaire and were expanded in the Newcastle questionnaire, where distinction was made between seeking entry into *any* university and this particular university. This last differentiation is relevant to any analysis of perceived and real differences between universities, which brings us back to the "characteristics of the clientele".

Differences in reasons for coming to university had begun to pattern themselves in the course of the Edinburgh interviews, although due to smallness of numbers it was not always clear whether this was usually along social class lines. The English working class appeared almost unanimous in choosing Edinburgh as a non-redbrick university, a long way from home—geographical and social mobility being closely identified. Other "groupings" were more difficult to see, although by comparison the Scottish working-class students seemed to accept without question that they should go to the local university, and travel in daily, often for many miles, and this attitude tended to highlight by contrast the higher need for achievement of the English working class.

At that stage it seemed to be mainly the middle-class students who came to university "as a matter of course" because everyone else was doing it and it seemed just one more hurdle. First-generation working-class and lower middle-class students seemed most eager to learn, and put their learning to good use. The element of "service" was most prevalent in the replies of those who had struggled most. There was an overall impression, discussed in the last chapter, of a somewhat haphazard choice of courses, of students particularly of the working class falling by accident into certain courses as a result of school indifference or mismanagement and of suffering greatly in consequence. The unhappiness and disappointment experienced had widespread repercussions for the student on his whole university experience.

We shall look first, then, at some quantitative evidence which emerged in the Durham and Newcastle surveys about students' reasons for wanting to go to university, and for wanting to attend the particular university of which they were members. A word of clarification is necessary first of all with regard to particular organisational features which could be suspected to distort the figures in particular ways.

Firstly it will be realised that the introduction of the Universities' Central Council on Admissions and the Clearing House scheme for university applications in 1962 introduced a different method of applying to universities, and therefore a different way for students to express particular preferences.[1] Previously, applications were made by the student to the individual institutions concerned on a purely personal basis, although rank order of preferences usually had to be indicated on each form. These preferences did tend to be altered by students in the light of subsequent rejections and re-applications where closing dates for applications differed. Thus the indication by the student of having had a particular preference for his university may be partly a judgement on events as they resolved themselves. This must be taken into acount in considering the tables showing how often the particular university featured as "first choice", but is of less importance in tables listing "particular reasons" for wanting to attend the university. This is true because the student would have different reasons for choosing different universities—whatever their position on his list. This continues to be true for applicants under the UCCA scheme. Through this scheme the process of application was rationalised so that each candidate for university fills in a standardised UCCA form on which he is allowed six choices of university (at the time of the survey excluding Oxford, Cambridge, and all the Scottish universities except Edinburgh).[2] The duplicated forms are circulated to the universities concerned, who are all naturally made aware of the order in which they stand in the candidate's preference list. In this sense the candidate has less opportunity for manœuvre than the universities, who may choose to consider a candidate more or less favourably depending on their position on his list. This factor operated under the old methods, but, as has been explained, the candidate's preference ranking might be varied over time. The only way now that the candidate can vary his choices is by indicating in interview that he has changed his mind. However, one could say that a student admitted to university after the introduction of UCCA who states his preference order of universities is more definite and consistent over time than the student admitted before. Whether this makes his set of preferences qualitatively different is open to doubt—and certainly the candidate may have a variety of different reasons for putting a university at any point on the list. Under both systems the eventual outcome of where a candidate will find himself at university is the result of a complex interplay of self-selection by the student and selection by the university in competition with other universities. In each case there is the complicating factor of the conditional offers made by universities to the candidate about to sit

[1] University Central Council for Admissions, *First Report 1961–63*, London, 1964.
[2] In 1960 all British universities participated except Aberdeen, Dundee and Glasgow.

A-level GCE. Therefore where the candidate finds himself will also depend on how far he achieves the conditions which particular universities set him. His choice will therefore depend not only on what he sees as desirable but what he believes to be possible in terms of his own capabilities.[1] The only modification under the UCCA system is made by the rules of the game that only a certain number of offers may be held at any one time—which involves the candidate in a *continual* reassessment of his position as the offers arrive. This process in a sense makes the candidate's position with regard to preferences and reasons for choice as much subject to change as the pre-UCCA situation. As long as it is realised, therefore, that the expression of student preference or choice, and of particular reasons for wanting to attend a particular institution, is at least to some extent dependent upon the possibilities open to him over the total period of his application, it seems sociologically meaningful and logically correct to put under the same category those who applied to university before and after the UCCA scheme. In a sense, UCCA has rationalised the system of applications only from the universities' point of view although, of course, cutting down on the candidate's form filling. For since universities largely retain different standards and methods of selection as, for instance, in the matter of interviews or aptitude tests, the candidate may be as much in the dark as ever. The matter of differing university and course quotas—differing from place to place and over time—also confuses the issue and, as has been mentioned in the last chapter, makes the process seem to the candidate like a game of roulette in which it seems only a matter of chance as to which number will come up.

The logic of the operation of all the factors involved is not perceived by the individual candidate from his limited vantage point. Any successful permutations of universities and courses which schools may suggest can only be built up on the basis of past experience of successful candidates, so that the more successful a school and its candidates the better able is it to advise its students and therefore ensure a better chance of future success. The school which has few successful university candidates, unless it is in constant communication with better schools, will have little evidence to go on as to how the system has worked out in individual terms. The lack of evidence will result in less judicious use of the system. The process is circular. This being true, under the UCCA system and before, it has been the custom for schools to establish particular traditions

[1] Albrow, M. C., Ritual and reason in the selection of students, *Univs. Quarterly*, **21**, No. 2, March 1967.

of applications to particular universities and as it were to "play safe".
On the other hand, such traditions are to the advantage of universities
who have found that they can rely upon certain schools to recommend
satisfactory candidates of the kind they want. But these factors operate
against the free working of individual choice and represent a bias in the
system. And, of course, preference expressed for particular schools must
be at the expense of other schools, just as preference for certain universities must be at the expense, in terms of human material, of other universities. University admissions is by no means a system of "perfect
competition" (in the sense used by economists) and the operation of
supply and demand is controlled, boosted, or depressed in various areas
in various ways. Thus universities have a differential chance of being
selected by candidates or by candidates' schools for various reasons
—social and academic—and departments within universities also have
differentially weighted chances. This system of weightings is mirrored by
and meshes with the differential of selection of certain categories of
students for various reasons—again social as well as academic—by any
university; and, in addition, certain categories of student have differentially
weighted chances in relation to *certain* universities. All this is *implicit*
in the admissions procedure but not always recognised or accounted for.
However, given that few students pick universities with a pin, just as few
universities pick their students at little better than random, there must be
known reasons for preferences for students or universities and which
give rise to the eventual distribution of students in universities and to
the composition of the student body. It is therefore pertinent to study those
reasons as a key to our understanding of the student body. It is quite
credible that since cultural and social as well as academic factors enter into
the weighting of differential chances of selection, the categories of the
candidates who express preferences and who feature in university preferences may represent cultural and social configurations as well as groups of
similar academic ability or qualification. Therefore, an analysis of successful candidates' (i.e. students') preferences for and reasons for wanting to
attend particular universities may give a clue to the kind of "fit" of self-
selection and university selection which goes on in the process of admissions and the explanation of it. Of course, in order to complete the
process one should really look at *unsuccessful* candidates for each university and see if and how they quantitatively and qualitatively differ
from those who were successful. In this case, for a variety of reasons this
comparison with a control group was not possible.

This, then, is the context in which students' reasons for wanting to attend their particular university will be better understood.

An additionally complicating factor in this particular study is the fact that until 1963 the present Newcastle and Durham universities were one university and at least nominally all applications to either the King's College division or the Durham colleges went through the same central channels. In effect much of the real selection went on separately, perforce because of the different distribution of courses and faculties in each place. From the student side it could only have been a very small minority of candidates who were unaware that King's College, Durham, was actually in Newcastle, although some students did admit to this. Of course, here we must distinguish between what the applicant believes to be the case and what is the case in selection by the university, since the applicant's motives and reasons will depend upon what he believes to be the case rather than any objective reality. Objectively the candidate applied to Durham University, but he applied to one of the colleges of the Durham division which are residential and have at least partial control over admissions as they control their own college places; or he applied to the King's College division, in Newcastle, which is non-residential and which again had almost total control of its own admissions subject, of course, to the central machinery, which also co-ordinated the Durham colleges' admissions. In each case he would apply also to the department or faculty in which he hoped to pursue his particular course of study. In the King's College division, as a non-residential college the department or faculty therefore had most influence in the selection process. One can therefore describe the selection processes from the university point of view as being differentiated in various ways with regard to King's College or Durham College candidates, and that these usually followed from the candidate's stated preference. Since some courses were not available in the Durham colleges division which were available in Newcastle King's College—such as the much-coveted Medical School—this must have been clear to the students expressing their preferences. However, what these preferences *meant* to the student stating them, with regard, for instance, to the separateness of the two divisions, and the urban setting, can only be deduced from their stated reasons for those preferences. That candidates would realise that they were applying for *King's College*, Durham, is not in dispute, but whether they realised its true physical, spatial, and organisational relation to Durham University in each case may be in doubt and may be used as evidence of some confusion of preference patterns. The different *kinds* of reasons given by King's College and Newcastle admissions from those of Durham colleges and Durham University admissions would seem to show that the confusion was not very prevalent, and that those who truly expressed a preference realised they were applying for *different places*. Of course, in the UCCA system this point was made more clear for potential candidates. Forty-one per cent of the Newcastle University sample in fact registered as Durham students, and therefore applied originally for King's College, Durham—so that 41 per cent of the sample in giving reasons why they chose Newcastle, are really giving reasons why they wanted to go to King's College, Durham. Because, however, as has been explained, some candidates were confused as to the real relation of King's College to the Durham colleges in Durham, those who stated that they thought they were applying to Durham more than to King's, or those who did not realise that King's was in Newcastle, were purposefully excluded from the tables which are presented. Those then who were members of the Newcastle University sample and who appear in tables as having said they had a particular reason for wanting to attend this university are all those registering both before and after the split, who expressed a definite desire to be a member of King's College (as it then was) or Newcastle University (as it now is), which they knew to be *physically situated* in Newcastle, and of which by virtue of the organisation of their particular course makes—and made them then—a member.

One might argue that it would be logical to add to the Durham sample those who in applying to King's College thought they were applying to a unitary Durham University. However, since their ideas were erroneous and their recollections of them are likely to be biased by the fact that they did not find themselves where they had anticipated, it would seem to be a dubious procedure to place them alongside the Durham sample. This is particularly true since, as we have seen, the outcome of the choice involves selection by the university, and the Newcastle or King's College students are products of slightly different selection pressures.

Given all these provisos it may now seem somewhat more strange than it did in Chapter 4 that the social class distribution of Durham and Newcastle is so similar since in some ways the self-selection at least may appear to be different and will be shown to be differently perceived at least in terms of reasons given. Objective indicators like area of home residence, as containing cultural differences, too, will be shown later on to be closely associated with the different patterns of self-selection

Other indices will indicate the categories of persons already mentioned with differential selection and application chances which are to some extent independent of personal or idiosyncratic motives and which may be traced to social class affiliation.

This, then, is the total complex of factors—both general and specific—working in this particular situation in determining the outcome of university admissions, and it is here that we must examine the self-selection principles of those who have already been selected themselves by these particular institutions. (We must assume for the purposes of rounding off the argument and analysis that those who *are* students, i.e. who have been selected by the institution, are the kind of people it wants to be students—for varying reasons at which we can only guess.) For those students who did not want to come to their particular university we can only posit that the sorting-out procedure was a partial success, and that perfect fit of self-selection and university selection was not attained. Our analysis of the figures may give us clues to why this is, though they remain only clues.

First, let us look at reasons of Durham students for wanting to apply to Durham University. Table 5.1(a) shows what proportion of Durham students had any particular reason for wanting to apply to Durham or to one of the Durham colleges: Table 5.1(b) examines the reasons given by those so motivated.

Twenty-three per cent of the Durham students said that they had no particular reason for wanting to come to Durham University rather than any other, and this proportion varies with social class. As many as 34

TABLE 5.1. DURHAM STUDENTS' REASONS FOR APPLYING TO DURHAM UNIVERSITY

(a) Those with a particular reason for wanting to attend Durham University (per cent)

	UMC	LMC	WkC	Unclassified	Total
Yes	86	80	63	85	75
No	14	17	34	15	23
Don't know	—	3	3	—	2
TOTAL No.	100 (101)	100 (161)	100 (77)	100 (13)	100 (352)

TABLE 5.1. (*cont.*)
(b) Durham students' reasons for wanting to attend Durham University (per cent)

	UMC	LMC	WkC	Unclassi-fied	Total	No.
Collegiate or second Ox-bridge	24	28	30	30	28	(118)
Attractive town	15	15	16	—	15	(64)
Personal recom-mendation	11	9	7	12	9	(39)
Prestige department	5	11	7	17	9	(38)
Particular course or facil-ities	10	7	4	12	8	(33)
Distance from home	8	7	7	17	8	(32)
School tradition	4	8	11	6	7	(30)
Traditional university/ not redbrick	8	5	9	—	6	(26)
Prestige university	5	4	3	6	4	(18)
Size of univer-sity	5	2	5	—	4	(16)
Family tradition	2	1	—	—	1·5	(6)
Other	2	2	1	—	1·5	(7)
TOTAL	99	99	100	100	101	
No.	(128)	(209)	(73)	(17)	(427)	(427)

per cent of working-class students, compared with 14 per cent upper middle-class students, expressed this view. This result was clarified in interview when some working-class students said that they had not known when they applied to Durham that it was collegiate, nor indeed had known little else about it, but they had chosen quite randomly as with all their choices. This lack of information already mentioned operates against the working-class students. Some were profoundly unhappy in the traditional collegiate setting, particularly, as it was unexpected. Further evidence of ignorance of the collegiate organisation was given by principals of colleges quoting examples of men applying to women's colleges and vice versa. One student admitted that his choice of college had been in alphabetical order—fortunately, and accidently, all men's colleges. However, it must be pointed out that of those working-class students who did have a particular reason for wanting to come to Durham as high a proportion of working-class as middle-class students chose it specifically because it is collegiate. Nevertheless, it is clear that higher up the scale fewer students choose in absolute ignorance, and they more often have informed reasons for wanting to apply.

Given, however, that we might expect a rational and informed choice of any university to be made on the basis of some particular merit of the university, social or academic, the particular reasons given by students show that the "name" of a university means very different things to different applicants, and what may seem a sound basis for choice on their part may seem less rational and informed in terms of what the university is trying to offer. It appears, therefore, very often that what students are choosing positively or negatively is a place, i.e. the city of Durham or of Newcastle, in the absence of further information. It is very often a geographical choice rather than purely academic or even social,[1] since the information of the candidate may be limited or lacking on these points, particularly if he has no contemporary evidence to go on as provided by his school or his peers. The fact that we have excluded from the Newcastle sample all those registering for Durham who were not aware of the geographical situation of King's College in Newcastle, as well as its other differing organisational features, will help to highlight this later on. It would appear that few students make their selection on the basis of academic, social, and organisational features of which they have some specific knowledge.

Obviously this proportion will increase with relation to more well-known universities, about which more is known irrespective of the knowledge of the town in which they are set. Table 5.1(b) sets out the reasons which Durham students gave for having wanted to attend Durham University. Students were asked for their main reason, but since many students gave two or more reasons it was thought best to give each reason category a score for each time mentioned rather than equate the number of reasons with the number of students.

As may be imagined, the reasons given often proved difficult to code, and the twelve categories outlined are fairly broad, and, also as may be

---

[1] Similar influences were found by Cowley. See Cowley, W. H., The American higher education labyrinth, in *From High School to College: Readings for Counsellors*, New York College Entrance Examination Board, 1965.

seen, cover a wide variety of reasons. Despite, however, this wide variety, 28 per cent of all reasons given concentrated on the fact that Durham is collegiate. Thus this represents a positive and informed option for this particular kind of organisation which surprisingly enough shows little social class differentiation, the working class ranking this reason slightly more often than the middle class. In this category 5 per cent upper middle class, 3 per cent lower middle class, and 7 per cent working class stated specifically that for them Durham represents a "second Oxbridge" and therefore being in the status and social prestige element, which is no doubt implicit in many of the options for the collegiate university. The distribution of these reasons would seem to show that the working-class sample who specifically want to go to Durham are to some extent atypical and aspiring. The fact that 11 per cent of the working-class reasons stated "school tradition" as important as opposed to 4 per cent upper middle class and 8 per cent lower middle class seems to reinforce this view, and would seem to show that it is working-class students, encouraged by good schools who already have a tradition of entry to particular universities, who are likely to eventually end up there. They are otherwise less likely than their fellows to know about, for instance, the difference between a collegiate and a non-collegiate university. A further factor is that 9 per cent of working-class reasons, 8 per cent upper middle-class reasons, and 5 per cent lower middle-class reasons emphasise that Durham is an "old" university, it is traditional, and it is "not redbrick". All these reasons in a sense reinforce one another in their concern with social prestige and status as well as organisational factors of college life rather than academic prestige.

It is the lower middle-class reasons which give most weight to the academic prestige of the department—11 per cent of all lower middle-class reasons as opposed to 7 per cent working-class and 5 per cent upper middle-class. If we take "Prestige of the University" to include general academic and social prestige, this adds to the reasons already mentioned more specifically but represents only 5 per cent upper middle-class, 4 per cent lower middle-class, and 3 per cent working-class reasons. The fact that 10 per cent of all upper middle-class reasons mentioned availability of particular courses may in part be due to the prestige of the theology courses and the presence of largely theological colleges of St. Chad's and St. John's.

The second most mentioned reason for wanting to attend Durham is the attractiveness of the town—accounting for 15 per cent of all reasons given, with equal proportions of the classes making mention of it. The urban environment is in this case a positive draw for the potential applicant. It is interesting to speculate how often questions of "scenery" and urban setting are uppermost in the university applicant's mind. Are the environmental elements which go to make the university "totem"—the "spirit" and the "image"—initially more important than questions of academic prestige—so relative at the sixth-form level? Could it be that to the sixth-formers universities are relatively undifferentiated in terms of academic prestige since they are *all* so very difficult to get into? Differences within academic prestige only become visible once one is on the other side of the barrier and conscious of *internal* differences. Certainly they only have the words of others to go on, and *visible* differences are so much easier to grasp. These considerations could have great influence on the *kind* of clientele attracted by any one university—and thus in time the kind of university which in terms of its students it will become. The question of totemic aspects of universities is considered later in Chapter 7 and has been touched on in Chapter 2.

And, of course, in a sense the idea—the visibly graspable idea of "colleges"—adds more than anything else to the totem and the romance and the image of "dreaming spires". We know that 28 per cent of Durham students wanted to attend Durham because of the "colleges"—but that this fact meant different things to different applicants, and was for many quite outside the scope of their experience and expectations. The reason may *sound* the same, but for different categories of applicants, with different sets of reference groups, the reason may have completely different meaning, particularly as a guide for future action.

Nevertheless, in interview it clearly emerged that whatever was meant specifically in particular cases by reference to "tradition", "college", "attractive town", "Oxbridge", and so on, in general these key images meant a great deal to the applicant who implied that Durham *felt* like a historic, traditional, and academic community because it *looked* like one, and was a positive stimulus to which he could respond. If students' observations are to be accepted, the "dreaming spires" image with which it seems so many sixth-formers come up to university, undergoes less modification in Durham than in Newcastle. Whether students like the tradition and organisation when they experience it is another matter.

Before we go on to consider particular reasons of Newcastle students for wanting to attend Newcastle University—or King's College, Newcastle, as it used to be—let us look at the additional information on why Newcastle students had wanted a university education in general (Table 5.2).

In the Newcastle sample 12 per cent of the students had no particular

TABLE 5.2. NEWCASTLE STUDENTS' REASONS FOR WANTING TO GO TO ANY UNIVERSITY

(a) Those who had a particular reason (per cent)

	UMC		LMC		WkC		Unclassified		Total
	M	F	M	F	M	F	M	F	
Yes	89	84	89	85	93	76	95	100	88
No	7	11	7	12	4	21	5	—	8
Don't know	4	5	3	3	2	3	—	—	3
TOTAL No.	100 (142)	100 (57)	99 (189)	100 (91)	99 (91)	100 (33)	100 (21)	100 (5)	99 (629)

(b) Reasons given by Newcastle students for wanting to attend a university (per cent)

	UMC		LMC		WkC		Unclassified		Total
	M	F	M	F	M	F	M	F	
Want a degree	28	31	26	18	29	8	20	20	25
Specific professional training	29	25	21	21	20	16	20	20	23
Want to study	21	21	21	23	14	40	35	20	22
Interest in subject	6	8	15	16	16	8	15	—	12
Independence and challenge	7	12	10	15	11	20	5	20	10
Money—better than work	5	—	5	4	6	—	5	20	5
School pressure	2	—	2	2	1	4	—	—	2
Parental pressure	1	2	1	1	2	4	—	—	1
TOTAL No.	99 (127)	99 (48)	101 (169)	100 (77)	99 (85)	100 (25)	100 (20)	100 (5)	100 (556)

reason for wanting to go to *a* university, which is a rather sad comment on the present system of selection. In interview one student spoke dispiritedly of hurdles which one had been trained to jump and which one became so used to facing that at the end of school one just looked round for the next one. Certainly there was no pleasure in it—it was almost automatic. The female students in each social class provided the highest proportion of "uncommitted" candidates with a slight increase in the working class which is a little surprising in view of the extra effort involved for a girl. One can only speculate that this is related to specific job aspirations. The highest proportion of committed students was among the male working-class students.

Reasons given for wanting to come to university were varied and sometimes brutally honest—as for instance of 2 per cent of students who came for "money". Although a very small percentage, this was higher among middle-class than among working-class students. If we add to this proportion those who said university is "better than work" we find 5 per cent of students in this category. It is not clear what the monetary gain of being a student was seen to be—either in terms of grant or future earning power—but it would seem from the equal class proportions that it is not only working-class students who stress the purely material benefits of a university education. Strikingly, the only girls giving this reason were 4 per cent in the lower middle class.

The most-quoted reason was the desire for a degree, a qualification —which appeared in 25 per cent of the replies—and was least quoted among working-class girls. These working-class girls most often give reasons indicating genuine desire to study, to learn, and to learn more about their particular subject. These account for as much as 48 per cent of all reasons stated, which as one might expect, in view of all the social obstacles put in the way of this group, indicates a very high degree of academic interest and determination. The girls on the whole show more pure academic interest than the boys, and in both sexes less interest is shown by the upper middle class—where specific professional training (as with medical students) emerges as a major motivation. This, of course, in its turn implies an interest and willingness to study, so one cannot draw the conclusion that any one group, outside the working-class girls, is particularly academically orientated. Twenty per cent of working-class girls also saw university as a challenge to their abilities, and as an end to independence. The proportion of upper middle-class girls wanting only a degree was slightly larger, at 31 per cent, than that of

TABLE 5.3. REASONS OF NEWCASTLE STUDENTS FOR WANTING TO GO TO UNIVERSITY—
ANALYSED BY SCHOOL LAST ATTENDED (per cent)

	Public school	Grammar school	Secondary modern	Technical college	Total
Want a degree	19	18	23	18	22
Specific professional training	25	5	9	7	20
Want to study	19	24	20	27	19
Interest in subject	8	12	9	14	11
Independence and challenge	8	20	23	25	9
Money—better than work	6	3	3	5	3
School pressure	2·5	4	2·5	5	2
Parental pressure	2·5	1	2·5	—	1
No reason	11	14	9	—	12
TOTAL No.	101 (179)	101 (371)	101 (35)	101 (44)	99 (629)

working-class boys—a perhaps surprising and yet not entirely inexplicable finding.

At this point it may be advantageous to turn to Table 5.3 which analyses motives for coming to university in terms of schools last attended.

In Table 5.3 we see that 25 per cent of public school students were interested in professional training and 19 per cent in getting a degree. Among entrants from grammar schools, secondary modern, and technical colleges, the proportions are the other way round, with 5 per cent, 9 per cent, and 7 per cent interested in professional training, and 18 per cent, 23 per cent and 18 per cent interested in getting a degree. The technical college entrants are most motivated by the desire to study—27 per cent, with the grammar school next with 24 per cent—and technical college people express most often the desire for challenge and independence—25 per cent. Only 8 per cent of public school students gave this reason. The idea that university is better than working, coupled with monetary reward, is almost equally distributed among the groups with public school and technical college slightly higher at 6 per cent and 5 per cent. The group which felt most school pressure was, surprisingly enough, in the grammar school category—with 4 per cent giving this reason for applying to university.

As has been said before, school is an agency of culture, and in some respects its influence obviously overrides social class of family. This is seen in other correlations.

We must also bear in mind that we are dealing here with two types of technical college entrant, and perhaps social class is the counterbalancing feature. In fact, quite a few public school boys were discovered to have failed exams and worked their way through technical college in an attempt to get a university place. They differ in obvious respects from industrial entrants to technical colleges and colleges of advanced technology who then proceed to university entrance.[1]

Sixteen per cent working-class male students (15 per cent male lower middle-class students and 16 per cent lower middle-class female students) came to university because of particular interest in their subject compared with 6 per cent upper middle-class male students, and, indeed, both grammar schools and technical colleges provide a higher proportion of students with this motivation than the public schools. It would seem that the kind of built-in assumption of the influence of changing clientele on university "image" needs some qualifying.[2] The kind of patterning on class lines which emerges is not altogether what is normally supposed, and clearly factors such as schooling must enter into the analysis. Nevertheless, the findings do not suggest that "in their account of why they applied to University no differences of background seemed to influence their reasons strongly".[3] The influence of background is there but it cannot be entirely isolated from the other variables with which it is closely associated, such as "school" background. If one adds together students who came for interest in subject, because they wanted to study,

[1] See Sandford, C. T., Couper, M. E., and Griffin, S., *Brit. J. Educ. Psych.*, June 1963, **35** (2).

[2] Possibly in relation to social/academic dimensions.

[3] Marris, P., *The Experience of Higher Education*, London, 1964, p. 29.

TABLE 5.4. STUDENTS' REASONS FOR APPLYING TO NEWCASTLE UNIVERSITY

(a) Those with particular reason for wanting to attend Newcastle University (or King's College of Durham University for those Newcastle students registering before 1962) (per cent)

	UMC		LMC		WkC		Unclassified		Total
	M	F	M	F	M	F	M	F	
Yes	63	65	52	48	63	55	81	80	58
No	37	35	46	61	37	45	19	20	41
Don't know	—	—	2	1	—	—	—	—	1
TOTAL No.	100 (142)	100 (57)	100 (189)	100 (91)	100 (91)	100 (33)	100 (21)	100 (5)	100 (629)

(b) Newcastle students' reasons for wanting to attend Newcastle University or King's College, Newcastle) (per cent)

	UMC		LMC		WkC		Unclassified		Total
	M	F	M	F	M	F	M	F	
Prestige of department	46	30	38	30	33	33	18	—	36
Live at home	25	24	8	7	33	17	24	25	19
Specific course	8	22	17	21	21	22	17	—	15
Domestic reasons	6	5	6	9	4	6	17	25	7
Easy to get in—or nowhere else would have me	1	3	6	7	5	—	6	—	6
Wanted to know area	7	11	6	15	—	11	12	25	8

TABLE 5.4 (*cont.*)

	UMC		LMC		WkC		Unclassified		Total
	M	F	M	F	M	F	M	F	
Distance from home	3	3	6	5	—	6	6	—	4
Prestige university	1	3	7	5	2	6	—	—	3
School tradition	3	—	5	2	2	—	—	25	3
TOTAL No.	100 (90)	101 (37)	99 (98)	101 (44)	100 (57)	101 (18)	100 (17)	100 (4)	101 (365)

because they responded to a challenge to their capabilities or for specific vocational or professional training, then 62 per cent of students fall into this category, which seems a slightly more optimistic proportion than some writers would lead us to expect.

Let us now look at reasons why Newcastle students wanted to attend Newcastle University (Table 5.4).

In the light of previous discussion about the complicating factor of students applying to King's College as part of Durham before 1962, it is not perhaps surprising that as many as 41 per cent of the students had no reason at all for wanting to attend Newcastle as such. This proportion then comprises those students who did not particularly want to be in the Newcastle division of Durham University before the split, and also those students who did not rank Newcastle high on their preference list after it became independent. Of course, the fact that it would be an unknown quantity as a "new" university would also tend to depress students' preferences. However, so high is the proportion of uncommitted candidates that some reference to "totemic" aspects must be made again.

How little perception of the "image" is based on fact and how much on a conglomeration of hearsay is borne out by comments such as that of the upper middle-class student from Surrey who said:

> The first thing that surprised me about Newcastle was its yellow buses. They were quite unexpected as I had never thought that anywhere so black and dirty could have yellow buses. Before I came I had a terrible impression

of slag heaps and coal barges and dirt everywhere—my friends all commiserated with me when I knew I was coming here. Now I realise how misinformed I was. I quite like the city now.

This student was by no means alone in his views—and it is not accidental that he was from the south of England. Geographical divisions, representative as they are of cultural divisions, nevertheless increase misunderstandings and misapprehensions. Where students come from is significant in any analysis of their expectations, and this will be discussed later in the chapter.

As many as 3 per cent of students said openly "Nowhere else would have me" and 3 per cent said it was easy to get in with their qualifications. These answers are representative of an air of inferiority which pervaded a small minority of student groups—this despite Newcastle's new buildings and laboratories and major research grants. Is this another example of the difference between the perceived and real situation?

It is not surprising that over a third of the students who wanted to attend Newcastle did so because of the prestige of the department in which they applied to study.[1] In this there is little difference between classes and sexes except that 46 per cent of upper middle-class males stated this reason. If we couple with this the availability of particular courses, 51 per cent of students come into this category. Indeed, academic reasons of prestige or facilities feature far more frequently than in Durham, and there is a corresponding decrease or lack of reference to social organisation, social status, or prestige. This is not surprising in the light of what we know about the two universities and the images which they try to create.

No one mentioned the attractiveness of the town although 8 per cent did find the area interesting and wanted to get to know it better. The second most-quoted reason was the possibility of being able to live at home—which underlined Newcastle's place as a *local* university. Both upper middle class and working class put this reason forward in nearly a quarter of the cases, with 33 per cent working-class males giving this reason. This reason was, however, much less important for the lower middle-class students both male and female, and only 8 per cent and 7 per cent quoted it at all. Indeed, a slightly higher proportion of lower middle-class students than others chose Newcastle precisely because it was a long way from home.

---

[1] Marris, *op. cit.*, p. 18. Compare Marris's finding that "about *40 per cent* were influenced in their choice by the reputation of suitability of the course available".

The general prestige of the University features only to the same extent as in Durham—and by comparison with Durham there is less stress on family and school tradition and personal recommendation.

The figures as a whole go some way to conveying the local and regional atmosphere of Newcastle and the non-regional atmosphere of Durham. This brings us back to a consideration of *where* the students come from in terms of regional cultural variations. But before we do this it is useful to consider the universities of students' first choice as this is also related to the part played by geographical and regional distributions of candidates and, therefore, students. Geographical self-selection is all part of the process which decides who will end up where, and therefore which decides certain cultural distributions of the student body (Table 5.5).

Sixty-four per cent of Durham students claimed that the University was their first choice, compared with 49 per cent of Newcastle students having Newcastle as first choice.[1] This finding fits in with what has previously been discussed. In Durham the proportion of first choices was highest in the lower middle class compared with the upper middle class in Newcastle—particularly among male students. This latter result may seem unexpected in the light of previous findings, but may be accounted for partially by the public school boys from the Newcastle area who chose to go to the home university because of their many years away at school. The other highest proportion in the Newcastle samples is among male working-class students—mainly applying, one assumes, for science and applied science. These assumptions are confirmed by other data which shows that Newcastle was first choice most often among students from public schools and technical colleges.

In the Durham sample it was discovered that many students who had put Durham as being first choice admitted in interview that it was first "after Oxbridge", but they had assumed that it was so obvious to anyone that they had not bothered to mention it. This may confuse the issue somewhat. Perhaps the smaller proportion of upper middle-class than lower middle-class students who have Durham as their first choice originates in the fact that they are more open about their desire to get into Oxbridge first and foremost. Certainly, in Durham, it was generally realised that many students who failed to get a place at Oxford or Cam-

[1] Compare these figures with those for all universities. 50 per cent of all candidates admitted to universities through UCCA in 1963/64 were accepted by the university of their first choice, 42 per cent by another university choice and 8 per cent by a university not listed on their form. *UCCA Third Report*, 1964–5, London, 1966.

TABLE 5.5. UNIVERSITY OF FIRST CHOICE

(a) Whether present university was first choice (per cent)

	UMC		LMC		WkC		Unclassified		Total	
	D'ham	N'castle	D'ham	N'castle	D'ham	N'castle	D'ham	N'castle	D'ham	N'ca
Yes	59	51	66	42	61	46	85	55	64	48
No	40	48	33	52	38	48	7	42	35	47
Don't know	1	1	1	6	1	6	7	2	1	5
TOTAL	100	100	100	100	100	100	99	99	100	100
No.	(101)	(199)	(161)	(280)	(77)	(124)	(13)	(26)	(352)	(629)

(b) Other universities of first choice (per cent)

	UMC	LMC	WkC	Unclassified	Total
(i) *Durham students*					
Oxbridge	75	68	55	100	68
London	—	2	14	—	4
Birmingham	8	11	3	—	8
Bristol	5	11	24	—	12
Manchester	5	2	1	—	2
Other Redbrick	5	—	—	—	2
Irish, Welsh, Scots	1	—	—	—	1
New	2	6	3	—	4
TOTAL	101	100	100	100	101
No.	(41)	(55)	(30)	(2)	(128)

TABLE 5.5 (*cont.*)

	UMC	LMC	WkC	Unclassified	Total
Newcastle students					
bridge	8	5	4	—	6
ndon	23	27	17	36	27
ming-					
1am	7	5	4	—	5
stol	8	3	9	—	5
nches-					
er	6	7	14	—	9
1er					
Red-					
rick	34	45	42	47	40
h,					
Welsh,					
cots	10	5	6	16	7
w	4	2	3	—	2
TOTAL	100	100	99	99	101
No.	(96)	(148)	(64)	(11)	(319)

bridge came on to Durham. Said one student in interview: "There are so many Oxbridge rejects here that to have had an interview puts one up a notch." Countless student conversations confirmed that those who so nearly *failed* to get a place are regarded rather as an élite.

In Table 5.5(b), therefore, it is not surprising to see that of those who did not put Durham as first choice as many as 48 per cent had first chosen Oxford, although Cambridge comes a poor second with 20 per cent. Although 68 per cent seems a very high total, as one might expect, both Oxford and Cambridge were chosen most frequently by middle-class students: the proportions increase up the scale. Bristol was the third most popular first choice particularly with working-class students. Only 1 per cent upper middle-class students in this sample chose an Irish, Welsh, or Scottish University.

The categories "other redbrick" **account** for only 2 per cent of first choices, which is significantly small when one considers how many other "redbrick" provincial or large civic universities there are. This perhaps indicates the special nature of the Durham sample, who aspire to something better than what they consider to be "provincial redbrick". Large numbers of staff and students consciously stress the "differentness" of Durham by referring to it consciously as "non-redbrick" or "grey-brick" even. The fact that Durham is the third oldest university in England was the first thing that the author was told again and again soon after arrival. Indeed, there seems almost a fear of being classed with "the others"—a fate which everyone in the University is concerned to avoid. As has been mentioned in Chapter 2, even naming of customs, such as "Oak Up",[1] obtaining "exeats",[2] paying "battels",[3] pays deference to Oxford, and no one would dream of calling them anything less traditional.

By contrast, Newcastle students put "other provincial universities" first on their list of choices more often than any of the others mentioned, and these account for 40 per cent of all first choices—a startling contrast to Durham's 2 per cent. London came second with 27 per cent first choices, followed far behind with Manchester 9 per cent. Celtic universities with 7 per cent top Oxbridge—in part due to those applying to the Edinburgh Medical School and having Newcastle as second choice. These latter assured the interviewer that in fact they were sorry now that they had not put Newcastle first originally since they now think it is undoubtedly the best in the country. That Oxford and Cambridge did not hold pride of place for Newcastle students is shown by the fact that they received the same proportion of first choices as Leeds and Bristol. It is quite possible that many students thought them quite beyond their reach and neither tried for a place nor were encouraged to do so.

It is significant that over twice as many male upper middle-class as male lower middle-class students put Oxbridge as first choice and four times as many as the male working-class students, which bears out what has just been said. On the other hand, a higher proportion of aspiring lower middle-class and working-class girls than upper middle-class girls put Oxbridge as first choice. While most working-class girls opted for Bristol rather than "other redbrick", most middle-class girls opted for London, perhaps indicating a trend of aspirations.

In the light of these expressed university preferences, it is interesting to

---

[1] Exclusion of visitors to students' rooms, usually during working periods. Students thus "put up their oak" against the door.

[2] Obtaining official permission to leave campus.

[3] Paying college dues.

note the report of the UCCA[1] on proportions of entrants with three C's or one A plus one B, or better, Advanced level GCE passes, to the different universities. Durham was 19th out of 30 in arts, 15th out of 30 in pure science, and 23rd out of 23 in social studies. Corresponding figures for Newcastle were 26th out of 30 in arts, 25th out of 30 pure science, 12th out of 23 in social studies. The author was interviewing students at Newcastle at the time the UCCA report was published and discussed in the Press. Students said that it "did the reputation of Newcastle no good"; that "the figures are misleading"; and that they might "deter the better candidates from applying". It is to be remembered that the preferences discussed cover all years, not just those of 1964 admissions, including those before the establishment of the UCCA, so that no comparisons may be drawn. However, since Durham takes a comparatively high place in student preferences of those already at Durham yet is mid-range on its proportion of 1964 "good" admissions, one may conclude with the author that student choices were made often on other than academic grounds.

Of course, one does not know entirely on what kind of information these choices were originally made—whether on headmaster's advice or attraction of the prospectus—whether on social or academic prestige. Yet the reasons given for choice of Durham and Newcastle perhaps give some indication of what kind of things attract certain types of students to certain universities. This needs further investigation but it could have wide implications for planning in terms of student populations. "The pattern of higher education cannot be decided only by the aspirations of its institutions. It must also take account of the needs which students will recognise as *personally* relevant."[2]

What has emerged is the relative significance of *where* a student comes from and how this factor of geographical distance interacts with that of social distance in terms of social class to place the students in certain universities, and thus greatly to influence the total student composition of any one university. We shall see that it also influences social patterning *within* the university.

One might assume that the greater the attractiveness of a university to a student the further he will be willing to travel to study there. Attractiveness may be interpreted among other things in terms of social aspirations

[1] University Central Council on Admissions, *Second Report 1963-4*, UCCA, London, 1965, p. 11, table 14.
[2] Marris, *op. cit.*, p. 13.

TABLE 5.6. AREA OF BRITISH STUDENTS' HOME RESIDENCE

(a) Edinburgh (total percentages only)

Area	No.	(per cent)
Edinburgh	82	27
East Lothian, Midlothian, West Lothian, Clackmannan, Fife (W)	41	13
Aberdeen	1 ⎫	
Dundee	3 ⎬	23
Glasgow	4 ⎪	
Other parts of Scotland	62 ⎭	
	193	63
London	11	4
Surrey	4	1
Kent	11	4
Other South	22	8
Lancashire	9	3
Yorkshire	15	5
Cheshire	8	2
County Durham	3	1
Northumberland	8	2
Other North	10	4
Wales and Ireland	9	3
	110	37
TOTAL	303	100

(b) Durham and Newcastle (per cent)

Area or city	UMC		LMC		WkC		Total	
	D'ham	N'castle	D'ham	N'castle	D'ham	N'castle	D'ham	N'castle
London	8	2	7	4	5	—	7	2
Surrey	6	4	5	3	1	3	4	3
Kent	3	7	4	2	1	2	3	3
Other South	30	17	27	20	23	11	27	18

TABLE 5.6 (*cont.*)

Area or city	UMC		LMC		WkC		Total	
	D'ham	N'castle	D'ham	N'castle	D'ham	N'castle	D'ham	N'castle
ncashire	13	5	10	8	22	7	14	7
rkshire	9	10	15	12	18	18	14	13
eshire	8	2	1	4	3	2	4	3
unty Durham	10	15	11	16	9	20	10	16
rthumberland	1	26	4	9	8	18	4	17
her North	3	5	11	15	8	14	8	12
ules and Ireland ⎱		1		2		1	2	1
otland ⎰	3	1	3	—	1	1	—	1
erseas	7	6	2	5	—	2	3	5
TOTAL	101	101	100	100	99	100	100	100
No.	(101)	(178)	(161)	(274)	(77)	(124)	(339)	(567)

N.B. — Newcastle figures minus 52 unclassified. Durham figures minus 13 unclassified.

and strengthening or attenuation of parental and kinship ties. One must bear these facts in mind whens tudying Table 5.6, which shows the regional distributions of students in relation to social class. The Edinburgh figures were not correlated with class so must be treated as total percentages.

Of the British students in the Edinburgh sample, as one might expect, 63 per cent lived in Scotland and as many as 27 per cent came from Edinburgh itself. Thirteen per cent came from districts near Edinburgh and travelled in daily; only 23 per cent came from other parts of Scotland. One may see how parochial is the Scottish sample in Edinburgh, in keeping with the Scottish University tradition which in general assumes that one will go to the local university. Only eight students came from the university towns of Aberdeen, Dundee, and Glasgow. As high a proportion of English students came from the south as north, i.e. counties south of the Wash. Edinburgh's attractiveness to them may be measured by the distance they have to travel. The largest contingent from the north of England came from Yorkshire. This is witnessed by the thriving Yorkshire Society at Edinburgh University which is reputed to be the largest in the University, although members do not by any means all live in

Yorkshire. Although there is no social class breakdown, one may assume this group to be mainly those aspiring working-class northerners discussed in Chapter 4.

Durham University only draws 14 per cent of its students from the immediate area of Durham and Northumberland compared with 33 per cent in Newcastle.[1] We may see from the class breakdown the high proportion (41 per cent) of upper-middle class local students already discussed. Conversely, 7 per cent of all Durham students come from London and only 2 per cent of Newcastle students. The 4 per cent of Londoners at Edinburgh is quite high comparing the distance between the two cities. Forty-two per cent of Durham students come from London and the south combined, compared with 26 per cent in Newcastle. In Durham the southerners are largely middle class: in Newcastle the middle-class students, too, are largely northern.

These results establish Durham and Newcastle as, indeed, what they appear to be—the former a non-regional university drawing its students from all over Britain; the latter as a regional university with students mainly northern and local. This is a significant difference when one considers that these two universities are barely 20 miles apart and were, until 2 years ago, one university. One asks what factors are involved here, and whether the totemic aspects of the two universities are related to the regional status of the type of students they attract. Do the students as members of regional groups affect the character of the institution, or does the institution attract particular regional groups? This problem is solved to some extent if one accepts the idea of a hierarchy of counties in a prestige ranking of status—the "image" of a county which is self-perpetuating and labels its members socially. Certainly, this hierarchy is reflected in the acceptability of accents. A Somerset accent is more acceptable than a Lancashire one—although basically this seems fairly irrational. In the same way, Yorkshire and Lancashire with their "Coronation Street image", rank as low status counties—Surrey and Kent as high status counties. Some may claim this is a doubtful generalisation, but often it is implicit in what people say and do—most people act in accordance with these beliefs—no one has defined or explained them. Almost one feels that they are never made explicit

---

[1] Taylor notes that 32 per cent of students accepted by colleges of education lived within 30 miles of their home, compared with U.G.C. figures for universities of 19 per cent. See Taylor, W., Regional origins of students in colleges of education, *Educ. for Teaching*, No. 74, Autumn 1967.

because then they would be seen to conflict with the prevailing values of society. Yet they constitute real divisions and concrete cultural realities which may cut across other social and cultural groups. Indeed, there are differences in class distribution, educational facilities, and job opportunities in north and south and in particular counties in the north or south. If one accepts that these divisions and evaluations exist and persist, then one may inquire more closely how they mirror totemic factors at work in their institutional setting.

Perhaps it may help to analyse the expectations which students had when they first came to university and see whether they fit in with this "image building". We shall examine also the truth of Wilson's argument that:

> Students often arrive at University with two distinct and contradictory, indeed unrelated, sets of assumptions. In the first place they expect an elevated intellectual atmosphere and look forward to a mysterious experience which will result in intellectual transformation: they expect to emerge with new power. They are vague about how such transformation will be accomplished and temperamentally ill-disposed to the idea of its imperceptible gradualness. They have no idea of what might be entailed in the process, but there is a vague hope of increased articulateness and heightened understanding.[1]

The second assumption is that they will be part of the prevailing: "youth culture". This will be discussed later.

In interviews students of all three universities referred as much to the city in which each university is set as to the university itself and the actual working of the student body. Edinburgh and Durham students seemed to think that on the whole the two cities had lived up to expectations, although naturally they were not without criticisms. Southern students coming to Newcastle seemed to have almost nightmarish visions of what they were coming to—not only dirty and ugly, but barbaric and lacking in culture. It often seemed that a city's "cultural" life was assumed to be inversely proportionate to its distance in road miles from London. Many of these students admitted their early fears almost shamefacedly and agreed that they had radically changed their views. One student waxed lyrical in his praises. He was glad, he said, to have escaped from the "flaccid pig's belly of the south" to the "sinewy tough north" that while it (life) was harder there "the city was withall virile and bounding with energy". There are people who would agree with his description while not ignoring the smoke and industry which provide the energy.

---

[1] Wilson, *op. cit.*, p. 8.

TABLE 5.7. NEWCASTLE STUDENTS' EXPECTATIONS OF AND REACTIONS TO UNIVERSITY LIFE

(a) Those who think university life is as they expected (per cent)

	UMC		LMC		WkC		Unclassified		Total
	M	F	M	F	M	F	M	F	
Yes	69	72	53	41	41	46	62	80	55
No	28	26	44	56	57	52	38	20	42
Don't Know	3	2	3	3	2	3	—	—	3
TOTAL No.	100 (142)	100 (57)	100 (189)	100 (91)	100 (91)	101 (33)	100 (21)	100 (5)	100 (629)

(b) Reactions to university life of those who did not find it as they expected (per cent)

	UMC		LMC		WkC		Unclassified		Total
	M	F	M	F	M	F	M	F	
Favourable	57	55	73	72	71	47	88	100	68
Unfavourable	17	20	20	12	14	24	12	—	17
Neutral	26	25	7	16	15	29	—	—	15
TOTAL No.	100 (142)	100 (57)	100 (189)	100 (91)	100 (91)	100 (33)	100 (21)	100 (5)	100 (629)

In all three universities there was a sizeable proportion of students who had come up with a picture of dreaming spires firmly implanted in their brain, and were thus disappointed—Wilson would say "disenchanted"[1]— when they did not have intellectual discussions far into the night over mugs of coffee with brilliant and witty companions who compared in eloquence to Shelley or Keats. Said one student: "I came up expecting to feel dull in comparison with all these brilliant brains, but in fact I have

[1] *Ibid.*

found that nearly everyone is as thick as I am." The highest proportion of those who did find this kind of stimulation seemed to be in halls of residence, where naturally both conversation and companions are easier to find and sustain and one's choice of both is less limited than in dispiriting "digs". However, since out of 100 Newcastle interviewees for instance about 60 mentioned the same kind of expectation and disappointment, one wonders whether they did not make enough effort to find the components which make up the desired situation or whether in fact the institutional arrangement put barriers in their path of search for "an academic and intellectual excitement which they did not find".[1]

Table 5.7 shows results of answers from the Newcastle sample put to students only in the Newcastle and Durham survey. Only 55 per cent of students said that they felt they had a reasonable idea of what university would be like before they came. Ignorance of what to expect was most prevalent among working-class students (both male and female) and among lower middle-class females. Over 50 per cent of these students did not know what to expect—and we may assume that sources of information were less readily available to them than to other students. Of the 27 per cent upper middle-class students who did not find university life as they expected it, we may assume that for these students especially the image of Newcastle is not in accord with their expectations. In fact, in the light of what middle-class students said, it is possible to assume that much information about universities is given out at public schools, also grammar schools, by teachers who were themselves at Oxbridge, and whose memories in time have mellowed into only the most inspiring reminiscences.[2] It is very easy to imbue all universities with the same unreal atmosphere of ancient cloisters—so rudely shattered in the bustle of an industrial town. By contrast a number of northern working-class students felt that they knew what to expect, particularly because the university was *not* unreal and separate from daily existence.

However, although over a quarter of upper middle-class students did not know what to expect, as has been shown through discussion of interview material, the reactions of a large proportion of them to what they found was favourable. Only a small proportion (17 per cent male and 20 per cent female students) had "unfavourable" reactions, although

---

[1] Marris, *op. cit.*, p. 32.
[2] *Ibid.*, p. 32: "In the middle aged after-glow, all Universities have rivers and punts, and pretty girls decorating the worn plush cushions with the crisp folds of their summer frocks."

TABLE 5.8. DURHAM STUDENTS' EXPECTATIONS OF AND REACTIONS TO UNIVERSITY LIFE

(a) Those who think college life is as they expected (per cent)

	UMC	LMC	WkC	Unclassified	Total
Yes	59	60	46	46	56
No	39	40	52	54	43
Don't know	2	—	2	—	1
TOTAL No.	100 (101)	100 (161)	100 (77)	100 (13)	100 (352)

(b) Reactions to college life of those who did not find it as they expected (per cent)

	UMC	LMC	WkC	Unclassified	Total
Favourable	64	63	58	86	63
Unfavourable	15	18	18	—	17
Neutral	21	14	25	14	18
Don't know	—	5	—	—	2
TOTAL No.	100 (101)	100 (161)	101 (77)	100 (13)	100 (352)

these are sizeable enough proportions to be very significant in the light of the traditional and proper student loyalty which prompts the student to claim his own university as the "best" once he has got there. A large proportion of students have "neutral" reactions towards the University —26 per cent male upper middle class, 25 per cent female upper middle class, and 29 per cent the atypical female working class. This would seem to bode ill for participation in student affairs—a point to be discussed in the next chapter. It is a great pity that these questions were not put also in the Edinburgh survey.

However, it is useful to compare the Durham distribution on these questions (Table 5.8).

Students were asked about expectations, specifically of college life, and since all students are connected to colleges, the figures are directly comparable to those on Newcastle. There is an almost identical distribution of students who had some idea of what it would be like before they came: an overall proportion of 43 per cent had no idea. Individual social class proportions showed an increasing lack of previous expectation down the social scale, as in the Newcastle situation, but with a higher

TABLE 5.9. RESIDENTIAL DISTRIBUTION OF DURHAM STUDENTS' REACTIONS TO COLLEGE LIFE (per cent)

	Lodgings		College		Total
	M	F	M	F	
Favourable	60	38	68	62	63
Unfavourable	11	38	14	22	17
Neutral	26	12	17	16	18
Don't know	3	12	1	—	2
TOTAL	100	100	100	100	100
No.	(34)	(8)	(71)	(37)	(151)

proportion of upper middle-class students than in Newcastle knowing what to expect. There is a similar overall proportion of "neutral" reactions and of "favourable" reactions in the working-class sample in both Durham and Newcastle. Explicitly unfavourable reactions are almost equally represented in each social class, and the overall proportion (17 per cent) is identical with that in Newcastle. The upper middle class would appear to have, on the whole, more favourable reactions to Durham life than to Newcastle and to the collegiate situation than the working-class students. Indeed, it has been observed that the collegiate system by its very pressure to conformity tends to alienate working-class students with obvious class marks because they cannot easily be assimilated into the mainly middle-class student body. However, a different light is thrown on this issue in Table 5.9 where the replies are analysed in terms of both sex and type of residence within University.

Here it is found that those living in college are on the whole most satisfied—male students more than female students.[1] Female students living in lodgings emerge as the most dissatisfied section of the student body—only 38 per cent have favourable reactions to collegiate life. It must be remembered that these are reactions to collegiate life as *they* see it, i.e. mainly as an institutional fiction. Why female students more than male students living in lodgings should be so dissatisfied is not quite clear—or why a higher proportion of female students living in college than male students are dissatisfied with what they find of college life. This is yet another case among so many others already considered in which sex differentials are as important or more important a social and cultural factor as social class differentials. They demand further research, not possible in this survey, but certainly contribute to an understanding of certain features of the structure and organisation of the student body.

So many of such "divisions" have relevance within the student body that it begins to be necessary to ask under what conditions the "student body" can ever be or is believed to be by students a discrete entity, *or* a real community with its own generic collective representations. We have seen how reactions and future social behaviour are often guided by pre-conception and perception of the "institutional image" and that in a sense this is a cohesive factor in that it is a perception in which all participate and contribute. How far this engenders community sentiment and culture among students will be examined in later chapters. The kind of community envisaged is physically impossible above a certain size, as students realise, although their conception of the threshold limit varies from university to university—as we shall see in the discussion of attitudes to expansion in Chapter 14, and of student opinions on optimum sizes for colleges or universities.

Such fragmentation of the student body as exists in terms of cultural groupings reveals that patterning of attitudes and values along social class lines is made more complex and less clearly defined by the influence of additional variables such as "school" or "geographical region of home residence". In some ways these variables are intimately connected with social class and must be accounted for even if they cannot be isolated,

---

[1] Albrow found in his study of sixty-four Reading students that "lodgings students express dissatisfaction with the University as well as with their type of residence more frequently than hall students", and that this cannot be explained solely with reference to material conditions or loneliness as such. Albrow stresses the importance of the "ready made structure of hall" (Albrow, M. C., *BJS*, December 1966, 17 (4)).

so that what is often observed is a "cluster" of variables of different weightings in importance. The fact that social class divisions do not always emerge sharply defined has in no way shown that they may be discounted.

One may relate the findings of the last chapter to this argument, for we have already seen how "first-generation students" form a social category under certain conditions which may blur existing social class categories. Where these conditions do not obtain, social class divisions persist. Yet one must not forget that despite these distributions and divisions, total institutional "images" exist, and are perpetuated and students are enculturated into them from the first. "Freshers" conferences bear witness to the "initiation" rites that new students go through, and what they learn at this stage is crucial for the future organisation of the whole student body and for the cohesion of the different sub-groups which it comprises. Internalisation of student mores and year differences are important and will be considered later.

We therefore turn in the next chapter to an analysis of the ways in which social class patterns emerge within the total structure and organisation of the student body at the level of membership and leadership of student societies. We shall thus be examining the ways in which social class identity is expressed in *formal* relationships in the student body in both compulsory and voluntary groups (i.e. student government and "interest" associations).

In Chapter 7 we shall carry the analysis into the sphere of informal social relations in an attempt to discover what part is played by social class in the students' daily social interactions.

In this chapter it has been hoped to show the factors which operate as culture and value variables in the process of self-selection and application, and university selection—which interact in such a way as to decide who becomes a student at which institution. The composition of the student body in social class and cultural terms results from this process, and in turn affects the university "image", the complex of student relations, and the individual experience of higher education.

CHAPTER 6

SOCIAL CLASS AS A FACTOR IN PARTICIPATION IN AND LEADERSHIP OF STUDENT ORGANISATIONS

THE last two chapters have been concerned to show that cultural categories indicated by socioeconomic status of students' parents do exist within the student body and represent culture and behaviour patterns of the student and his family and imply a corresponding configuration of social and cultural attributes of the student himself. These are reflected in the self-selection of students applying for universities as well as the ways in which students are socially and academically selected by the institution or particular agencies of this, and we shall see that this applies also to the application and selection for different forms of residence, different faculties, or courses of study, and, in this chapter, different kinds of participation and leadership in student organisations and societies. The social as well as academic distribution of the student body in a variety of social spheres will be seen to be a result of these factors of self-selection and selection by significant others, whether institutionally or informally defined. We are, therefore, looking not only at self-selection and aspiration in a variety of fields of activity, but at acceptance patterns by others which alone make possible certain desired ends or goals of ego. It is a study of the meshing of values and value constraints within a whole cultural configuration of acting and interacting groups. It is also a study not only of aspects of selection by middle-class educational institutions which operate against the working-class student, but of ways in which working-class culture is or is not compatible with the culture of the selecting and accepting institution. The very resistance to change of working-class proportions in universities bears witness to the different dimensions of the problem involved and to the fact that removal of certain constraints or barriers, particularly economic, do not attack the problem of self-constructed barriers within the classes themselves. This is as true of distributions *within* the institution as of the initial distribution of students selected. Self-selection operates in such a way that barriers may be more imagined than real, but if they act as deterrents to action, as in applying for hall of residence, joining a student society, or taking a particular academic course, then they are "real in their consequences".

This study aims to look at *both* sides of the culture and value mesh in terms of the observed outcome in social behaviour and in terms of some of the stated intentions of individuals involved. It is obviously very diffi-cult to consider intentions and goals—and the last chapter has illustrated some of the shortcomings of looking back after the event. However, it does give us at least a rough perceptual guide to the kind of patterns of behaviour which emerge in different spheres.

Although the issues of self-selection, and of selection by significant others in social situations will emerge throughout the book, it is impor-tant to bear in mind that this is analysed with regard not to *ego* and *alter* but to a whole category of *ego* and *alter* who exhibit certain defined social and cultural attributes. It is not a study of role playing, but of group in-teraction and of physical and social distances between groups within the university which may have a number of implications for role playing.

These points are particularly pertinent in a study of student organisa-tion and student societies which may be taken as at least one aspect of student "culture". If we take student culture to be those value and be-haviour patterns generated or relevant solely or predominantly within the student context, and which are learned and internalised by students as part of a process of adult socialisation, then student self-government, authority, and organisational patterns and interest associations comprise some kind of "formal" framework within which student culture is estab-lished and develops. We are now looking at activities in which the non-student, or really the non-member of the particular institution, cannot participate, or participate only under defined circumstances. This chapter is concerned to discover whether the social class culture patterns already discovered affect and as it were carry over into participation in student organisation and societies and the taking of authority within this structure. This will tell us whether the social and cultural attributes already distin-guished as characteristic of particular social categories of students are pointers to social action and social interaction within the university. This would indicate that the same problems of culture "mesh" are pres-ent in the processes of interaction and socialisation as they are in the processes of initial selection at university entrance level. We might then begin to talk about social "classes" within the university, however constituted, and ascertain how meaningful these are to the persons involved.

It is for these reasons that we look now at participation and leadership in student organisation and societies both as aspects of student culture and organisation and also as an indicator of other processes at work in student interaction.

It is not easy to measure in any sophisticated way the degree of participation which students have within the student body or the extent to which they take over the running of student affairs. Although one may take as a measure the number of student societies joined—this may indicate nothing beyond nominal membership, and positions of "leadership" carry with them very differing amounts of power and authority. Thus one is to some extent moulding into a statistical model what cannot in all senses be expressed in this way. This is where participant observation and formal and informal interviews play their part in revealing the qualitative aspects of participation. Since we have already observed that the student body as such exhibits certain social class distributions, we may expect to find these running through both formal and informal student organisations, so that one is concerned also with intergroup relationships at each level and with assimilation of minority groups into the prevailing student mores; in this case one would assume this involves the bourgeoisification of the working class.

In this situation one asks how the members of the different social classes interact in the student body (a) in terms of formal student organisation, and (b) in terms of informal relationships and friendships. We shall be concerned with the first part in this chapter—as phenomena of cultural patterning in group participation and leadership and dependent to some extent on expectations of university life discussed in the last chapter. Only later shall we discuss the implications for students' perception of one another as students, or as members of social classes, in the situations and organisations described. Thus our study of participation and assimilation will not be complete until we have studied the intergroup relations which operate within defined social situations and which take place within the framework here discussed. Just how students define these situations will be discussed in Chapters 7 and 8, which will attempt to summarise the basic principles of inter-student and inter-group relationships which have emerged from the findings. Thus what has been treated as "student culture" by other writers—meaning virtually all that happens in the student context—is here differentiated in a variety of ways.

The formal organisational culture is differentiated from informal group-ings and interaction within the constraints posed by the formal organisa-tion. At each level, however, there will be internalisation of values and norms and the establishment of traditional ways of behaviour and social conventions appropriate within the particular institutional context. This, as we shall see, is related to (a) the kind of university image or ethos which is created and internalised, (b) the structural realities which underly this image and order relations in a variety of ways, for example, with regard to social distances of groups, and (c) the culture and value "mesh" of interacting social groups and the image as it is perceived. The outcome has both a subjective and an objective reality. How the process of meshing takes place, and how far socialisation therefore takes place, is discussed in Chapter 11 after consideration of the many cultural and social variables at work.

Therefore, at this stage, participation is taken to mean exactly what it says and where it implies socialisation into the student or institutional culture this will be explicitly stated. At the superficial level, participation means merely the act of "joining in" with whatever complex goal or set of goals in view—both expressive and instrumental. The goals are nevertheless implied by certain kinds of participation.

Although as has been pointed out the study of participation in student societies is not entirely satisfactory as an analysis either of (a) student participation or (b) student groups, it has certain advantages when used in conjunction with other qualitative methods. Firstly, it is capable of direct measurement in that one can analyse participation in terms of numbers of societies of which the students are members or leaders so that one can almost construct a scale of participation.

Secondly, since student societies are normally centres of student social activity and are voluntary associational groups based on interest—they are good means of testing to some extent a student's *willingness* to co-operate, i.e. involving the effort of joining. Where numerical membership of societies does not coincide with actual observed support of those societies, this in itself is meaningful. One may also observe in this way the difference between the formal and informal organisation and find out who are not members of societies and why.

Leadership of student organisations may be analysed in terms of what is already known of the formal structure so that undue weight is not given to positions which hold no responsibility and so that one may assess the kind of competition there is likely to be for certain positions.

Student Life in a Class Society

TABLE 6.1. MEMBERSHIP OF STUDENT SOCIETIES (BY SOCIAL CLASS AND NATIONALITY)
(a) Edinburgh   (per cent)

	SUMC	EUMC	OUMC	SLMC	ELMC	OLMC	SWkC	EWkC	OWkC	Total
Yes	90	88	56	72	100	88	54	100	100	81
No	10	12	44	28	—	12	46	—	—	19
TOTAL	100	100	100	100	100	100	100	100	100	100
No.	(68)	(51)	(9)	(82)	(50)	(8)	(38)	(8)	(1)	(316)

(b) Durham (i)

	UMC		LMC		WkC		Unclassified		Total	
	M	F	M	F	M	F	M	F		
Yes	94	97	99	98	94	100	91	100	9	7
No	6	3	1	2	6	—	9	—		3
TOTAL	100	100	100	100	100	100	100	100	100	
No.	(72)	(29)	(106)	(55)	(63)	(14)	(11)	(2)	(352)	

(b) Durham (ii) Exclusively university or college societies

	UMC		LMC		WkC		Unclassified		Total
	M	F	M	F	M	F	M	F	
Exclusive university	75	94	79	90	74	81	70	88	81
Exclusive college	25	6	21	10	26	19	30	12	19
TOTAL	100	100	100	100	100	100	100	100	100
No.	(68)	(28)	(105)	(54)	(59)	(14)	(10)	(2)	(340)

(c) Newcastle

	UMC	LMC	WkC	Total
Yes	94	96	89	94
No	6	4	11	6
TOTAL	100	100	100	100
No.	(199)	(280)	(124)	(603)

S = Scottish. E = English. O = Overseas.

The indications of what exactly to look for were found in the Edinburgh survey which was least structured to allow the unplanned responses to occur. For this reason there is more qualitative than quantitative data available on the Edinburgh sample; this omission was rectified in the two succeeding surveys.

First we shall examine the membership of student societies in the three universities in terms of social class distribution. Table 6.1 shows these results. These figures show those students who had been or were at the time of the survey a member of at least one student society—what may be taken as the "minimal" level of participation.

In the case of Durham the picture is complicated by the existence of exclusively college and exclusively university societies. These have been analysed together and separately in order to ascertain the general overall picture of society membership, and then the breakdown in terms of college and university attachment.

In the Edinburgh sample the figures have been broken down into "nationality" samples although this reduces the number of cases in each cell. The configurations for Overseas, Scottish, and English students are all different. In the Overseas sample the tendency is for those in the higher social classes to be less frequently members of societies, i.e. the percentage decreases up the social scale. In the Scottish sample the pattern is reversed so that there is a gradient of membership up from the working class to the upper class. In the Scottish sample the most striking results is that only 54 per cent of Scottish working-class students are or have been members of one or more student societies, which is not by any means a rigorous qualification. This points to a significant lack of "joining in" student affairs which may be associated with cultural factors of social class. Although numbers involved may here be too small to be significant, yet supportive evidence has been gained by observation. As we shall see later, other factors exacerbate the social distance of this group from the predominantly middle-class student body—expressed by these figures—although as we have seen in Chapter 4 this sample differs in various respects from the atypical English working class in Edinburgh. Some Scottish students blamed their school system for their reticence in joining in student societies. A Scottish female working-class student, speaking of her own experience and that of her friends, said:

> I think that the Scottish students should be left more on their own in the sixth form as in England. The English gain confidence in their abilities in their final year at school—and perhaps this is why they are more eager to participate in

student activities than are the Scottish. I think Scottish schools have a negative attitude to their pupils since they give them no responsibility in work or activities. I think this makes the Scottish students very retiring at first, and sets them back initially. I had no confidence and was very unhappy at first, but I am beginning to get over it. If you make an effort to meet people you find there are a lot of people in the same boat who are willing to be friendly.

This student was in her second term at university and lived at home about 30 miles away. She found having to worry about catching trains a hindrance to participation in student activities. From what one gathers her type of case is fairly common among the Scottish students—particularly working class.[1]

The Scottish lower middle-class figure of 72 per cent is also lower than the lower middle-class figure of either Overseas or English, so one may imagine that the arguments put forward may apply to them too.

Some of the upper middle-class English students tended to exaggerate the situation, and after extolling the virtues of the "prefectorial system in the English public school" said rather sweepingly: "The Scots are very young and behave as if they are still at school." Those who would make so broad a generalisation are few, but it does seem as if some of the differences in attitude between the Scots and the English are the direct results of different school systems. And, of course, the Scots are usually younger than the English on coming up to university. The normal age of entry is 17 years compared with the English 18 years—and this mirrors the difference between the Scottish "Highers" and the English A-level GCE.

The English sample has an overall higher rate of society membership, the working class and lower middle class all being members of societies. The proportion of the upper middle-class members in both Scottish and English samples is very similar, being 88 per cent English upper middle class and 89 per cent Scottish upper middle class.

The number in each social class group who are members of societies as a percentage of the total membership in tables not shown here shows that there is no numerical basis for thinking as so many of the students did that there is a preponderance of English in the societies. Yet students acted in the belief that there *was* such a preponderance. This is a perceptual problem discussed in the summary of Part II in Chapter 8. "National" identities may be confused in the same way that social class identities are confused and reflect the same kind of lack of culture "mesh".

[1] The problems of the "commuter" students in any university prevent participation and contribute to the growth of consumer/vocational culture discussed by Clark and Trow, *op. cit.*

The Newcastle and Durham distributions show that there is a higher overall proportion of membership (94 per cent and 97 per cent) than among the Edinburgh sample (81 per cent), but this is largely because the Newcastle working-class students take a much more active part in student affairs than do the Edinburgh *Scottish* working-class students. There is, therefore, a national as well as social class variable in the Edinburgh case. Eighty-nine per cent of the Newcastle working-class students are members of societies, but this is, nevertheless, a smaller proportion than in the middle classes. It would seem that there is less of a "cultural gap" separating the working class in Newcastle than the Scottish working class in Edinburgh from participating in the student body, and this may be partly attributable to the fact that the Scottish working class think that the English run all the societies although this is, in fact, not true. There is, as it were, a double set of distances involved. In addition, as we shall see in Part III, there are fewer factors making for *resistance* to participation and the accentuating of existing cultural differences.

Table 6.2 shows the proportion of membership of different *types* of societies as correlated with social class. It emerges that the overall proportions of students who are members of one, two, or more societies varies little between social classes, but the pattern in terms of *types* of society does vary with social class—again identifying certain cultural differences which pattern participation in various ways. Members of the working class were members of fewer departmental and sports societies than either middle class. Thirty-two per cent working-class students were not members of any departmental societies, and 48 per cent were not members of any sports societies. This latter figure could relate in some respects to school training. The upper middle-class students were members of more social and cultural societies than the other classes, and the lower middle-class students were members of more sports societies. The distribution of social and cultural society membership was similar in the lower middle class and working class.

Membership of political and religious societies was extremely low in all three social classes. There is a class differential in membership of religious societies which increases down the social scale—the highest proportion of members being in the working class. This may seem somewhat unexpected in the light of observations on working-class church-going. However, it was observed that the *nonconformist* church groups are most popular and active in Newcastle, and these tend to have

TABLE 6.2. TYPES OF STUDENT SOCIETIES OF WHICH NEWCASTLE STUDENTS WERE MEMBERS
(per cent)

Societies	Depart-mental	Social	Religious	Sports	Political	Other

(a) Upper middle-class students

Societies	Depart-mental	Social	Religious	Sports	Political	Other
None	21	56	86	42	91	80
1	68	31	14	39	9	19
2	10	11	0·5	14	0·5	1
3	1	2	—	4	—	—
4+	—	—	—	1	—	—
TOTAL	100	100	100·5	100	100·5	100
No.	(199)	(199)	(199)	(199)	(199)	(199)

(b) Lower middle-class students

Societies	Depart-mental	Social	Religious	Sports	Political	Other
None	20	64	80	36	92	79
1	65	26	19	42·5	8	19
2	14	8	1	14	—	2
3	1	2	—	5	—	—
4+	—	—	—	2·5	—	—
TOTAL	100	100	100	100	100	100
No.	(280)	(280)	(280)	(280)	(280)	(280)

(c) Working-class students

Societies	Depart-mental	Social	Religious	Sports	Political	Other
None	32	64	71	48	90	83
1	54	23	28	40	7	15
2	13	13	1	8	1	2
3	1	1	—	2	1	2
4+	—	—	—	2	1	—
TOTAL	100	101	100	100	100	100
No.	(124)	(124)	(124)	(124)	(124)	(124)

a proportionately high working-class membership. (This contrasts with the strength of the Anglican societies in Durham—a more middle-class phenomenon.) There may be some circularity here in that what is thought to be more in keeping with the university "image" may become more popular and supported, but this in turn strengthens the culture differences as value differences.

Membership of political societies was even lower than that of religious societies—in Newcastle only 1 in 10 of the students is a member of a political society. Of working-class members 3 per cent were members of two or more political societies—implying that for these students membership of political societies was an academic exercise rather than commitment to a political cause—at least if one assumes these different societies represent different political view points. The figures, and later those on Durham, seem to show that students are not on the whole interested in political and religious matters as such but in political matters as they touch student interests. It is only a few students who are in any sense politically active both inside and outside the university.[1]

Total membership of student societies in Durham, as has already been shown in Table 6.1 reveals not only class but sex differences in membership. When college and university societies are taken together, again we see the special case of the working-class female student who, one might assume, has been so highly selected that she is more middle class than the middle class. One hundred per cent of these girls are members of societies compared with 98 per cent lower middle class and 97 per cent upper middle class. One sees an increasing proportion up the social scale. On the whole the girls are more often members of societies than the men. When one analyses societies in terms of college and university there is a reversal of the class differential so that membership of females of exclusively university societies decreased down the scale. In a sense the college societies express a greater degree of integration or feeling of solidarity, since in them students are interacting with people they live with and whom they meet virtually every day. This would indicate the desire of the female working-class student to find integration into a social group rather than join societies merely for interest which could be fostered at the university level. The pattern is not so clear for the men although, as with membership of all societies, lower middle-class male students are more often members of exclusively university societies than

[1] This of course has implications for student unrest and seems to confirm the estimate of 10–15 per cent student activists made in ch. I.

TABLE 6.3. TYPES OF STUDENT SOCIETIES OF WHICH DURHAM STUDENTS WERE MEMBERS
(per cent)

Societies	Depart-mental	Social	Religious	Sport	Political	Other

(a) Upper middle-class students

None	24	20	57	35	77	85
1	55	42	38	37	18	13
2	20	28	5	17	5	1
3	—	6	—	8	—	—
4+	1	5	—	4	—	1
TOTAL	100	101	100	101	100	100
No.	(101)	(101)	(101)	(101)	(101)	(101)

(b) Lower middle-class students

None	17	30	60	44	81	85
1	61	32	33	34	15	12
2	19	22	6	12	3	3
3	1	12	1	7	1	—
4+	2	4	—	3	1	—
TOTAL	100	100	100	100	101	100
No.	(161)	(161)	(161)	(161)	(161)	(161)

(c) Working-class students

None	22	45	68	40	84	92
1	64	34	26	31	9	8
2	12	17	6	17	4	—
3	2	3	—	7	1	—
4+	—	1	—	5	1	—
TOTAL	100	100	100	100	99	100
No.	(77)	(77)	(77)	(77)	(77)	(77)

the other social classes.[1] That 19 per cent of the students are members only of exclusively college societies points to the duplication of activity which is carried on in Durham student organisation and which weakens to some extent the force and enthusiasm of the central organisations. This is a feature of the "federal" type of organisation involved in Durham.

Table 6.3 shows the distribution of Durham membersip in terms of the different *types* of societies involved. Again, a different social class pattern emerges which we may compare with Newcastle.

Upper middle-class students were members of more social or cultural societies than lower middle-class or working-class students although more markedly than in Newcastle, and there is a class differential which increases down the scale. Only 20 per cent of upper middle-class students were not members of any social societies compared with 30 per cent lower middle-class and 45 per cent working-class. One may speculate that this again indicates, as in the Edinburgh survey, a working-class reticence in joining in—a feeling of social disadvantage which persists in the university environment and in relation to a *particular* university environment or image which is seen as more or less sympathetic to or compatible with working-class culture. By contrast with Newcastle distributions, the working class had lowest membership of both religious and political associations, although both proportions of membership were higher than in Newcastle (68 per cent were not members of any religious societies, 84 per cent of any political societies). The author speculates that the former figure may reflect the tendency of the working-class student in Durham to equate religion with middle-classness, i.e. the Cathedral and Anglican high churches—which represent the "totemic" aspects already discussed and which does not "mesh" with their own expectations and values. The Labour Club in Durham has been described by Durham students as the "home of upper middle-class do-gooders who have no personal knowledge of the working class": if this is so it does not seem surprising that the working class themselves have comparative lack of enthusiasm for political organisations, particularly as the Conservative Club was in addition said to be composed mainly of upper middle-class students who saw no reason for "doing good to the poor". The higher *overall* participation however, indicates a different *institutional* level of participation. The upper middle class were more often members of sports societies than lower middle class or working class. Three per cent of those who were

[1] The high overall proportion of male members of college societies is explicable in terms of college sports.

TABLE 6.4. EDINBURGH STUDENTS WHO HAD HELD ONE OR MORE POSITIONS OF

	SUMC	EUMC	OUMC	SLMC	ELMC
Yes	38	22	40	22	26
No	62	78	60	78	74
TOTAL No.	100 (61)	100 (45)	100 (5)	100 (59)	100 (50)

members of sports societies were members of five societies which, it must be admitted, would be rather time-consuming.

Sports societies were often quoted by middle-class students as examples of how social classes could come together and co-operate and forget any previous barriers. Although the high membership rate of sports societies in every social class would seem to point to students hoping this to be true, working-class students sometimes expressed disappointment that co-operation and *camaraderie* did not always continue *off* the hockey field or tennis court. Perhaps to some extent this was due to their own lack of social initiative. One does not know. Certainly, in many cases, sport has provided an interest and bond which crossed all barriers—class, nationality, faculty, school, and so on, and had been the springboard for further social intercourse.

This has been a necessarily brief survey of some of the ways in which social class distributions in student societies may reflect "mesh" or lack of "mesh" in terms of goals and interests of the groups concerned. Obviously, the goals and interests of the student organisations or societies, the basis of membership, the constraints involved, must be considered in any analysis of why certain categories of persons are more or less likely to be members. It is clear that some societies are socially biased because of economic considerations involved in the provision by a member of his own equipment for instance. Ski-ing clubs, riding clubs, and sailing clubs are traditionally the particular provinces of the middle-class students, particularly the upper middle-class. In addition there may be cultural considerations in certain kinds of social and cultural society. This may be seen in terms of self-selection, of having no desire to join in certain activities because of not having been socialised to enjoy such pursuits, and also in terms of acceptance or rejection of the host society by persons "fitting in"

AUTHORITY IN STUDENT SOCIETIES (BY SOCIAL CLASS AND NATIONALITY) (per cent)

OLMC	SWkC	EWkC	OWkC	Total
14	19	25	—	26
86	81	75	100	74
100	100	100	100	100
(7)	(2)	(8)	(1)	(257)

or "not fitting in" by virtue of social or cultural attributes which they do or do not possess.

This latter point is, of course, true of religious, political, and sports societies too. Not only must the individual want to join but he must possess those characteristics which make him eligible to join. His possession of these characteristics may or may not be related to his social class background, and in certain directions very definitely is thus associated. The operation of these factors therefore determines the kind of social class differences in participation which we have just discussed. But, in addition, the prevailing institutional ethos which has certain social class connotations will modify these differences in different ways and thus make it more or less possible for instance for a working-class student to join in a traditionally middle-class activity.

Different cultural patterns emerge also in the analysis of positions of leadership in the student body. In the Edinburgh Table 6.4 we again present national distributions for interest, although numbers involved are too small for precise comparisons.

In the Overseas sample we see that 5 out of 9 upper middle-class students had joined societies, and 2 of these had taken on positions of responsibility in those societies. In general, overseas students tend to become leaders of "national"-based social societies, such as the Nigerian Union or Pakistani Students' Association. It is not often that they become leaders of the predominantly British social or academic societies. However, this group is very active and does have representatives on the SRC, Union Committee, and so on—and has the highest proportion of "leaders" among it. The Overseas lower middle-class provides the smallest *proportion* of leaders, though not the smallest number.

The increase in "leadership" with each "higher" social class is also seen in the Scottish sample. The Scottish upper middle class provides numerically the largest proportion of student leaders. It seems highly probable on evidence available that these are the anglicised Scots of public school education and English accent who often cannot be distinguished by working-class students from the English themselves. The percentage of Scottish upper middle class (38 per cent) who are leaders is far greater than the 22 per cent of the English upper middle class. Perhaps these are the "damned English who are running all the societies" that one so often hears criticised by Scots in Edinburgh. This springs from faulty perception of characteristics of "the others", however culturally defined.

There is hardly any difference between the proportion of working-class and lower middle-class Scots members of societies who become leaders —19 per cent : 22 per cent— showing perhaps that of those from both classes who are motivated to join societies there is little difference between their willingness or ability to take on positions of responsibility, i.e. once the Scottish working class overcome their initial disinclination to join societies they prove to be no less able and popular than the lower middle class. The same situation is mirrored in the English sample except that both working class and lower middle class have a higher proportion of leaders than the Scottish sample, and both English working class and lower middle class have a higher proportion than the English upper middle class. *Scottish* upper middle-class leaders of societies represent 32 per cent of all student leaders while the older and perhaps more aloof English upper middle class tend not to participate in student activities as much as the Scots.

The most interesting case is that of the English working class, 25 per cent of whom are leaders. Although in itself the figure involved is not statistically important, we have already seen how in various ways this group is anomalous as a working-class group. These figures on society leadership, although too small to draw very broad conclusions seem to confirm this finding. Holding a position in a student society or organisation indicates not only intention and motivation, but also a degree of acceptance by fellow students. The fact that the English working-class group has a slightly higher proportion of leaders than the English upper middle-class group seems to be a signal indication that members of this group have been completely accepted by middle-class students, perhaps so much so that in reality they are no longer considered as working-class students. In the same way the working-class female students in Durham (and Newcastle) exhibit middle-class characteristics. A remark of an English working-class student in Edinburgh illuminates this: "The working-class student can 'get on' in university if he has a character which is more sociable than most, without distinctive class marks", i.e. if he is not perceived to be working class. These features of assimilation and the significance of class marks are discussed in the next chapter although, naturally, they underlie most of the discussions in this chapter, and will underline their significance.

It would seem to be true also that the English working class are highly motivated to become accepted by the middle class. Such motivation and the factors which would appear to give rise to it will also be discussed. We look next at the Newcastle figures on student leadership in Table 6.5.

TABLE 6.5. NEWCASTLE STUDENTS WHO HAD HELD ONE OR MORE POSITIONS OF AUTHORITY IN STUDENT SOCIETIES (per cent)

	UMC	LMC	WkC	Total
Yes	24	24	15	22
No	76	76	85	78
TOTAL No.	100 (199)	100 (280)	100 (124)	100 (603)

In Newcastle University only 22 per cent of those who are members of societies actually take responsibility in them—which is a low overall total for a university of this size. The author observed, and it was often remarked, that most of the societies which flourish are basically non-participating societies, such as the Film Society where entertainment or lectures are provided and students need make no effort as members outside attending the meeting. Indeed, there seems a general antipathy to organising of any sort, and it seemed that, if anything, the SRC and Union Committee were more remote and subject to student criticism than in the other two universities. It is acknowledged that a handful of students forming a somewhat closed stratus "run things" and the others stand back and let them get on with it.

Both the middle classes provide the same proportion of leaders (24 per cent), and the working class a significantly smaller proportion of 15 per cent—this despite some similar patterns of membership. Numerically the working class provides only 14 per cent of all student leaders, which would seem in general to point to cultural differences in leadership.

TABLE 6.6. DURHAM STUDENTS WHO HAD HELD ONE OR MORE POSITIONS OF AUTHORITY IN STUDENT SOCIETIES (per cent)

	UMC		LMC		WkC		Total
	M	F	M	F	M	F	
Yes	49	52	46	47	48	29	47
No	51	48	54	53	52	71	53
TOTAL	100	100	100	100	100	100	100
No.	(72)	(29)	(106)	(55)	(63)	(14)	(339)

In Durham as many as 47 per cent of all students hold or have held a position of responsibility in either college or university. Thus by contrast a far larger proportion of people have a hand in the running of affairs, and it would seem that there is a greater circulation of jobs of responsibility in the student body. Obviously in Durham there are special factors contributing to this state of affairs—firstly, the very size of the university and the complexity of its organisation means that if certain tasks are to be carried out a higher proportion of students must assist in organising student affairs. The fact that there is some duplication of activity at college and university level means in some cases double the number of responsible positions. That certain people fill more than one position is true and, indeed, students in Durham sometimes complained that power was contained in too few hands. It may have seemed to be few in number, but in proportion it far exceeds that of the larger university. In other words, more people have the opportunity of being elected for position of authority and responsibility, and through the collegiate system are brought more into contact with the many possibilities presented.

The class distribution of leadership in Durham is interesting in that the only two groups which show any signs of class differentials are female upper middle class and female working class. The female upper middle class provides a higher proportion of leaders and the female working class a much lower proportion of leaders than the other social classes—male and female. Apart from these two samples, social class factors seem not to matter much in Durham in the selection of leaders, i.e. the general environment does not seem to work against any particular group holding leadership positions once joining has taken place.

The case of the female working class is an odd one since, as we have seen, this group had 100 per cent membership of societies—indicative of a group seeking integration. Perhaps it is a sign of failure to be assimilated completely rather than lack of motivation, which results in only 29 per cent—low by Durham standards—becoming leaders of societies. This point cannot be answered, but is worthy of more research.[1]

The *types* of positions held in the student body were arranged into a broad scale of prestige observed by the author to be accepted by the student body concerned. Distributions proved this scale to have been in accord with statistical evidence. In Newcastle the scale goes from President of Union or SRC; Member Committee SRC (representing student government); President University Society or Hall of Residence; Committee University Society to Committee Hall of Residence (representing largely organisation of "interest" groups). In Durham there is a slight difference in order indicative of certain features of organisation. The position of senior man or woman of a college, for instance, carries more authority and prestige than the Presidency of the SRC or University Union Society. Presidencies of university societies have similar prestige, and then comes Presidency of College Society, other positions in university societies, and other positions in college groups. It is significant that the position of President of SRC or Union carries less weight than in Edinburgh or Newcastle, and, indeed, the organisation of these bodies is far less bureaucratic and structured and is split by internal factions including right and left wings—indicating at least some political alignment (Table 6.8).

In Newcastle (Table 6.7) in terms of actual number of positions held, the lower middle class holds more positions of leadership than either of the other two social classes; however, this means little in that, as has been explained, there is a different weight attached to these positions by students, and, in any case, the numbers are too small for any significant differences to emerge. When one analyses the figures in terms of this weighting, the first thing which emerges is that the only student in the Newcastle survey who had held the positions of President or Vice President of the SRC or University Union (two positions) was of working-class origin. He was obviously a highly integrated young man and one assumes atypical of the working class as a whole. In the Durham survey 2 per cent of all working-class students who were student leaders were or had been a senior member of a college. However, the Durham results differ in

---

[1] This could be an illustration of the difference as in race relations between partial integration and assimilation.

TABLE 6.7. TYPES OF LEADERSHIP POSITIONS HELD BY NEWCASTLE STUDENTS (per cent)

Positions	President Union/SRC	Cmttee. Union/SRC	President Univ. Soc. or Hall of Residence	Cmttee. Univ. Soc.	Cmttee. Hall of Residence	Total
(a) Upper middle-class students						
1	—	83	61	83	71	76
2	—	17	31	14	29	20
3+	—	—	8	3	—	4
TOTAL	—	100	100	100	100	100
No.	(0)	(6)	(13)	(29)	(7)	(55)
(b) Lower middle-class students						
1	—	94	91	82	92	87
2	—	6	9	16	8	12
3+	—	—	—	2	—	1
TOTAL	—	100	100	100	100	100
No.	(0)	(16)	(11)	(45)	(12)	(84)
(c) Working-class students						
1	—	75	100	75	100	79
2	100	25	—	25	—	21
3+	—	—	—	—	—	—
TOTAL	100	100	100	100	100	100
No.	(1)	(4)	(6)	(12)	(1)	(24)

that 3 per cent lower middle class were also senior men or women. Again, no upper middle-class student had held this position. This is in direct contrast to the kind of patterning which obtains in Edinburgh—in which student government is largely the province of middle-class students.

In Newcastle, although fewer working-class than middle-class students were leaders of societies, of those that were a proportion held a position of great authority in the student body, yet comparatively few compared with the middle classes held more than one position.

Fewer working-class than middle-class students held positions in hall
—basically because, as we shall see, a smaller proportion of them have
places in hall. Upper middle-class students hold most of the positions
of authority in hall.

Upper middle-class students are more often leaders of *more* societies
than other groups—they seem to hold a monopoly of power in certain
circles, whereas working-class students tend to hold *one* position—particularly as Presidents of University "interest" societies which do not
necessarily involve participation in the ruling stratum of student government. One may conclude from the figures that upper middle-class students
tend to dominate student societies and interest groups—representing
perhaps specifically middle-class interests, while working-class students
tend to hold *more* positions per person on Union and SRC committees
and committees of "interest" societies which are run predominantly by
middle-class students. It would appear that key positions in "interest" societies held by middle-class students are concentrated in fewer hands than
found in the working class. For example, 31 per cent of upper middle-
class students held two positions as presidents of university societies,
while 8 per cent held three or more positions. On the other hand, it
would appear that of the highly motivated working-class students a significant proportion do take an active part in student government, and as
leaders of student organisations may be assumed to have been "assimilated".

These assumptions are borne out to some extent by the Durham results
(Table 6.8) which show lower middle-class students predominating as
senior men and women, while the upper middle class holds predominantly
presidencies of college societies and other positions in college and university. They hold more positions per person, but these carry less weight in
the student body in terms of spheres of influence.[1] It would seem that the
lower middle class on the whole wield most power in Durham student
organisations in terms of numbers of most responsible posts held per
person. Although a minority of working class hold the highest executive
positions of the student body, most of them hold one or two committee
positions—particularly in university rather than college societies. As has
been seen, it is often the college organisations, junior common rooms,
and so on that are recognised by the authorities as proper channels of

---

[1] See Miller, W., Concerning student government (unpublished M.A. dissertation),
for comparison of features of Edinburgh student government.

TABLE 6.8. TYPES OF LEADERSHIP POSITIONS HELD BY DURHAM STUDENTS (per cent)

Positions	Senior Student	Pres. SRC Union or Univ. Soc.	Pres. Coll. Soc.	Other position Univ.	Other position Coll.	Total
(a) Upper middle-class students						
1	—	89	67	72	64	70
2	—	11	20	17	29	21
3+	—	—	13	10	7	9
TOTAL	—	100	100	99	100	100
No.	(0)	(9)	(15)	(29)	(28)	(81)
(b) Lower middle-class students						
1	100	94	90	79	70	81
2	—	6	10	15	23	15
3	—	—	—	6	7	4
TOTAL	—	100	100	100	100	100
No.	(3)	(17)	(19)	(34)	(40)	(113)
(c) Working-class students						
1	100	86	75	55	87	72
2	—	14	25	25	13	20
3	—	—	—	20	—	8
TOTAL	100	100	100	100	100	100
No.	(1)	(7)	(8)	(20)	(15)	(51)

communications to the students—and these are those in which the working class does *not* predominate.

When the author was in Durham various debates flared up in the SRC about the waning powers of the SRC as a negotiating body with Senate and Administration. Time and time again the SRC felt that it was side-stepped in discussion of policy issues by the authorities, who conducted discussions directly through the senior men and women and the junior common rooms. The informal committee of senior students held by the Registrar, mentioned in Chapter 2, was a case in point which raised much antagonism. Thus voices were loudly raised over these issues and petitions made to the highest authorities which only succeeded in increasing the general wariness and hesitancy with which these authorities dealt with the SRC. I have heard the SRC described by certain university authorities as "rabble rousers" or the "rowdy elements of the colleges. They are the non-college minded members that the colleges get rid of".[1] It is an interesting indication of changes in university atmosphere that the SRC in Durham has managed to strengthen its position in some ways and seek further centralisation of student power. In a sense this has been assisted by the fragmentation brought about by university expansion and the increasing number of colleges. It has, however, become more "respectable" and conservative; this may reflect the pressures to conformity.

To be non-college minded in Durham is to be regarded as a most undesirable element, threatening the basis of the university organisation. Therefore, the above criticism was a very strong criticism indeed. And it is interesting to note that "rowdy" and "non-college minded" are terms denoting a real offence—it is a virtue in itself to be quiet and accept the system.

It may not be entirely coincidental, then, that it is the working class who tend to hold positions in the SRC and other *university* positions— the middle class who run the affairs of the colleges. One result is that the "difference" between the two "types" is marked by external characteristics such as the difference in accents of these groups. More thick northern even accentuated accents are in evidence among members of SRC than among senior men and women, and there are differences in dress and manner. These groups also represent to some extent the right and left elements. The working-class senior students may be regarded as a second, separate category of working-class students regarded as middle class by both staff and students. The author has heard a lower middle-class senior man being criticised by some working-class friends for being too conciliatory to the SRC and "for joining the establishment" since becoming senior man. Those who do not conform entirely to the accepted norms

[1] Personal communication.

on being elected are often transformed, or socialised, during their term of office. This may cause unrest in the ranks among those who voted for someone they thought progressive, even revolutionary.

For in Durham as the class composition changes—but not necessarily as a result of it—there is a growing body of students with built-in resistance to tradition of any sort. This is becoming an increasing problem for university and college authorities when students object to wearing gowns, coming to formal meals, observing rules of being in college before a certain hour, and so on. This kind of change in the Durham scene will be discussed in Chapter 14, along with effects of expansion on institutional organisation. However, it is useful to consider here whether these changes may have something to do with social class which is not recognised for what it is and is therefore not planned for.

It would seem from all the figures presented, then, that social class differences play their part in the running of student affairs and in the organisation of the student body, and it is important to note that students have shown that they realise this. One often hears of certain societies being run by a "certain set" of "public school people" dominating certain organisations—so that dominance of social class groups is recognised even if it is not explicitly referred to in terms of socioeconomic social class. One often hears of cliques with certain social characteristics dominating social activities of various sorts. This is an oblique reference to the effects of social distribution.

In Edinburgh, which the author knows best, there was better opportunity to see whether students consciously take social class into consideration in the running of student organisations and in the election of officials. It appeared that more often than not what appeared to be bias in *selection* of leaders was rather a bias in the proportion of any social class putting themselves forward for election in certain organisations. Thus it would appear that the SRC for instance in Edinburgh is a mainly middle-class, if not upper middle-class body, sometimes used as a debating ground for future members of parliament; and the University Union, too, in some ways embodies the atmosphere of a "gentleman's club" of a bygone era.

The author included questions on the influence of social class in elections of leaders of the student body on the Edinburgh questionnaire and the results are shown in Table 6.9. Attention is drawn most to overall totals and proportions as being significant in terms of numbers. Other remarks or subtotals are made for interest. Students were asked if they themselves were influenced by considerations of social class and if they considered others were.

Only 7 per cent said that they are consciously influenced by social class and family background although 15 per cent think they may be affected unconsciously. Together, these figures represent a significant proportion of 22 per cent and perhaps greater than one would expect in open declaration. The English working class was least affected by these considerations and 7 out of 8 said they were not influenced. The English lower middle class also had a high proportion (86 per cent said they were not influenced). However, 3 out of 8 English working class and 16 per cent English lower middle class thought that others were affected by these considerations, while 2 out of 8 English working class and 26 per cent English lower middle class thought others were influenced unconsciously by class. This seems to imply that these two groups experience the greatest "swing" of opinion or consideration of this point. The other groups admit influence more even in their own case.

There is indeed an overall change from Table 6.9(a) to Table 6.9(b). Only 7 per cent consider they themselves are influenced by social class, but 14 per cent consider that others are. The "possibly unconsciously" rather more "charitable" designation nearly trebles from 15 per cent to 41 per cent. If we add the first and third lines together we find that 22 per cent admitted that they themselves are affected by social class considerations—consciously or unconsciously—while 55 per cent think that others are so affected. This would seem to be an interesting case of students admitting that in some cases social class is taken into consideration, while putting the onus for this on to someone else.[1] It seems clear at least that social class is *seen* to be a real factor in student organisation at the former level, although it is not always clear in which way social class operates—either for or against. This would need to be studied further, but there are indications of *why* social class is sometimes taken into account in the findings of the next chapter showing the factors influencing formation of *informal* student groups, i.e. the influence of social class on students interaction with and perception of each other as members of the student body within the formal structure here outlined.

Predictably the Scottish working class seems most to suspect class discrimination in elections—74 per cent suggested some degree. As many as 89 per cent overseas upper middle class did so but in comment explained

---

[1] As with racial prejudice. See Banton's discussion of British landladies. Banton, M., *White and Coloured*, Jonathan Cape, London, 1959.

TABLE 6.9. (a) THOSE WHO THOUGHT THEY WERE

	SUMC	EUMC	OUMC	SLMC	ELMC
Yes	8	6	11	9	4
No	70	68	78	71	86
Possibly Uncon- sciously	18	20	—	13	8
Don't know	4	4	11	7	2
Unanswered	—	2	—	—	—
TOTAL	100	100	100	100	100
No.	(68)	(51)	(9)	(82)	(50)

(b) THOSE WHO THOUGHT OTHERS WERE INFLUENCED

	SUMC	EUMC	OUMC	SLMC	ELMC
Yes	15	10	11	13	16
No	33	37	11	41	44
Possibly Uncon- sciously	47	47	45	37	26
Don't know	—	—	11	1	8
Unanswered	5	4	11	6	2
Depends on organisa- tion	—	2	11	1	2
"All 3"	—	—	—	—	2
TOTAL	100	100	100	99	100
No.	(68)	(51)	(9)	(82)	(50)

this in racial rather than class terms. Other figures which show how many of the students who thought that considerations of social class background influence students in elections were actually themselves leaders of societies throw more light on this argument. The overall figures on society membership show that a smaller proportion of these students

INFLUENCED IN STUDENT ELECTIONS BY SOCIAL CLASS—EDINBURGH (per cent)

OLMC	SWkC	EWkC	OWkC	Uncl.	Total
—	5	—	—	17	7
63	64	88	100	83	72
25	18	12	—	—	15
12	10	—	—	—	6
—	3	—	—	—	0·6
100	100	100	100	100	100·6
(8)	(39)	(8)	(1)	(6)	(322)

IN STUDENT ELECTIONS BY SOCIAL CLASS—EDINBURGH (per cent)

OLMC	SWkC	EWkC	OWkC	Uncl.	Total
—	15	38	100	17	14
63	26	38	—	33	37
25	51	25	—	50	41
—	—	—	—	—	5
12	5	—	—	—	1·5
—	3	—	—	—	0·3
—	—	—	—	—	2
900	100	101	100	100	100·8
(8)	(39)	(8)	(1)	(6)	(322)

were members of societies than the proportion of the total sample, 76 per cent as opposed to 81 per cent, which seems to show that some of these people were merely hazarding a guess on incomplete knowledge. Of course, one cannot discount the fact that belief that this was so may have deterred them from joining societies.

The figure for leadership is also smaller than that of the total membership sample, 21 per cent compared with 26 per cent, intimating perhaps a number of disappointed candidates. This seems to be especially true of the upper middle class and working class. The lower middle class seems to have a more solid foundation for their views—a high proportion being both members and leaders in societies.

The overall impression that one obtains from the figures discussed and from actual experience of student organisations is that few students are consciously influenced by considerations of social class when electing fellow students to positions of responsibility. There may, however, be in certain *groups* and certain societies an unconscious preference for leaders from a certain social class. This depends largely upon the aims and activities of the society, as many students pointed out. It would also be true to say that any student who is obviously "different" from the majority of society members would have difficulties in being fully accepted by the group. The particular way in which "difference" is defined would be determined by the way in which the attributes of membership were defined by the group. Those who do not exhibit "differentness" in the terms defined by the group are then chosen in terms of personality and ability—the factors of social class do not come into play beyond a certain point because the overriding social class ethos has been internalised.

Thus it would seem to be true that social class acts as *a* factor, although there are obviously others such as sex, regional culture, and ability and personality in the organisation of the student body and thus in the formal relationship which students as members of social classes have with one another. For their participation and leadership in student government or interest societies prescribe the social areas in which they will interact, and the areas in which they will exert influence upon the actions of others, or have influence exerted upon them. Future directions of action will therefore be patterned on the basis of these structural relationships.[1]

The importance of this factor depends on the way the situation is defined by students and what for them seem to be the attributes relevant and necessary in the playing of the particular roles involved. Thus in certain situations certain factors come into play at the expense of the other factors. These situations are to some extent circumscribed by the formal organisation as it is perceived by the people in it. The next chapter will be concerned to discuss whether similar factors appear to have

[1] This may have implications for student unrest and its different expression at different universities.

relevance in informal organisation and situations, and if similar patterns emerge, at the level of informal interaction.

Certainly student behaviour patterns do not seem to be dependent merely upon institutional circumstances but upon the interaction of these with social class values and cultures of the students themselves. The interplay of institutional and social class values result in a set of social class configurations in participation and leadership, which represent the structural *distances* and relationships of social classes *within* the institution and which are related in various ways with the home background and external reference groups. Although one may look at student "culture" one may not abstract it from the home and school culture which has already shaped the students' values and behaviour.

We shall look later on at the influence of institutional and organisational factors, such as residence, upon student culture patterns—but it is clear that these factors are not the only ones at work. This would seem to be relevant to any study of student culture, or student socialisation within the institution. The outcome of these processes is not only dependent upon the social choices offered the student, or certain categories of student, but the way in which he perceives them through his particular culture filter and the way in which his previous socialisation has conditioned him to select and choose. These are crucial points, often previously ignored, in an understanding and explanation of particular aspects of student organisation and culture—both formal and informal.

CHAPTER 7

SOCIAL CLASS AS A FACTOR IN STUDENT SOCIAL RELATIONS

It is not intended in this chapter to discuss the broad spectrum of social and cultural factors in students' social relations—these will be considered in Part III. At this stage the aim is merely to continue sketching in the social *framework* within which "student" social relations are meaningful and therefore to look at those areas in which social relations are influenced by the students' social class of origin as previously examined. We saw in the last chapter the ways in which social class of origin operates as a factor in membership and leadership of student societies and therefore represents a real cultural influence in the working of the student body and its formal organisation. It emerged that the different patterns of participation of different social classes within student activities both reflect and in turn help to maintain the existing relationship of social and spatial distances which the social classes have with one another in certain spheres of student life. We can therefore say that cultural differences of the social classes or socioeconomic groups from which students come are reflected in and have at least some influence on what happens within the student body whether or not there is real consciousness among the students that this is so.

The next step then is to look not only at the influence of these cultural differences upon *informal* social groupings of students, upon their day-to-day social relations and the friendship and associational networks which they form, but also at the degree to which they are conscious of the cultural differences which exist and of their potential or real influence on their own social decisions. We have seen that cultural collectivities persist within the institutional framework and are reflected in organisations of the student body; we must now try to evaluate what this means in terms of the student's actual social experience—in his consciousness of kind and of difference and in the social choices which he makes in response to this consciousness. Does the student feel that he "belongs" to a social class as much as he "belongs" to the class of students or to a particular institution of higher education? Is social class of origin a membership group as well as a reference group for the student in the university? How far is identification of himself and others in terms of social class membership meaningful to the student, and how far does this identification influence, even regulate, areas and modes of interaction? Obviously all these questions cannot be answered within the confines of this chapter but require a more full and detailed analysis of the whole range of identities and social relations in which the student is involved. The analysis in the present chapter must therefore of necessity appear lopsided or thin because much of what we shall discuss later in terms of cultural and spatial factors at work in student social relations will modify and fill out the present framework in various ways. However, in order later to see where, how, and why social class is *not* a factor in student social relations because of other factors involved, we must here attempt to define the areas in which it is a factor. Not only this, but we here seek to establish that the students are conscious of the influence of social class, and therefore in terms of our original definition we may indeed speak of the "social classes" of students as meaningful groupings within the student body.

Although in this survey social classes as expressive of membership of socioeconomic status groups are the central concern, it is hoped that conclusions of wider validity may be drawn to cover any kind of culturally differentiated groups within the student body which experience in external society real and perceived inequalities of opportunity. This would cover a variety of status groups as, for instance, in the United States and Canada ranging over the ethnic, immigrant, religious, or rural groups mentioned in Chapter 1. It is likely that these groups, too, exhibit different culture patterns within the university or college, and that these culture patterns are reflected in differential participation and leadership in the student body. These patterns would probably emerge as the result of similar kinds of influences of self-selection and selection by others to those discussed in the last chapter. Certainly sororities and fraternities —so central a feature of organisation of American college campuses— have been seen to operate various kinds of social selection, membership being more or less exclusive depending on the status of the fraternity or sorority.[1] The social distribution of each sorority and fraternity is not random—just as its academic distribution is not random — and the partic-

[1] Segal, B. E., *Sociol. Educ.*, 1965, **38** (3), 251-64.

ular bias will depend on the goals and status of the sorority and fraternity and also of the total institution itself.

> For membership the cues may be: his secondary school training (prep. school
> or public school); his father's social status; where he lives; his high school or
> prep. school record; his interests; the way he dresses and talks and looks; his
> religious, national, or racial origins. If his father is an alumnus of the fraternity,
> or if he has been recommended by an *alum*, his chances of being chosen are
> improved.[1]

These factors, we shall see, operate in a number of spheres of association of students, and it will be shown in this chapter and those succeeding
that students are well aware of the kinds of discrimination that are
operating for and against particular social groups.

It may be wondered why sororities and fraternities were not considered
in the preceding chapter on student societies and organisation. The
omission was intentional because of the special nature of sororities and
fraternities as organisations with no direct parallel in the British system.
They will be considered later in relation to other cultural factors in
organisation and in relation to the influence of institutionally prescribed
social and academic divisions which interact with the kind we have
been discussing. Outside these "formal" organisations, which nevertheless represent the "hub of social life and the guiding principle of
community organisation on many American college campuses",[2] the
influence of social selection on social relations seems to have been ignored
by American researchers so that there is no material which was thought
to be directly comparable with the data in the present and preceding
chapter. The role of sororities and fraternities in "socialisation" of
students will also be considered later as a special aspect of student social
life. The ways in which institutional and subgroup norms are internalised
will be considered in relation to spatial and cultural factors in social
relations.

It will be seen that in order for the present chapter to be properly
meaningful the data which are discussed must be seen in their proper
context. This "context" of spatial and cultural factors will be discussed
in Part III.

It is hoped, however, that the present analysis will give some pointers
to the way in which students themselves perceive social class differences

[1] Goldsen, Rosenberg, Williams, and Suchman, *What College Students Think*, Van
Nostrand, 1960, p. 62.
[2] *Ibid.*, p. 60,

and divisions as factors meaningful in themselves and as structural principles at work in social relations. The presence of other attributes will help to explain some of the attitudes and conclusions expressed rather than appreciably to alter the analysis which is presented. Therefore when we look at the wider cultural and spatial context in which social class relations are set we shall have a deeper understanding of *why* the situation is as it is described in this chapter. The analysis must therefore at this stage of necessity seem incomplete in a number of respects.

The basic initially crude question asked in this chapter is whether the student, passing as he does continuously through a kaleidoscope of identities, thinks of himself and is thought of by other students primarily as a member of his social class or as a "student". We may consider this as a structural norm rather than at this stage a situational variant since the generalisation covers a very wide range of situations and configurations of social variables.

The answer to this question is most difficult to obtain and the resulting observations equally difficult to quantify and measure. For this basic information, apart from that gained by direct observation, must be obtained from the persons concerned in the form of an attitude or opinion survey. While the answers to such a survey may of necessity make explicit what is only implicit in social relations, the respondent's opinion of what he does may also not correspond to an objective appraisal of what in fact he does—so that results may not portray exactly an objective "social reality". Indeed, what the researcher may be left with is an analysis of what those acting within any given situation *perceive* to be socially meaningful. In itself this perception may not be central to an analysis of the situation—yet in that it is a symptom of certain structural relationships it may provide a key to the solution of problems presented by the analysis. In fact, where observed facts about a situation do not correspond with what is perceived of the situation by those within it, the "discrepancy" itself may be indicative of additional factors, not previously accounted for.

Thus the author observing first the situation as students themselves saw it was able then to compare with the statistical norms which emerged from the surveys. A summary of what this shows us about the structure of social relations will be summarised in the next chapter. For the present, we shall concentrate on the students' perception of situations in which social class is a factor in social relations. To be able to understand this completely, and therefore to set in context what will appear as signifificant discontinuities in patterns of social behaviour, the reader must to some extent disregard what has been shown about the statistical structure of the total context and step *inside* the student situation. For the student acting in any situation has only limited knowledge of the situation available to him and his vantage point at any one time is severely restricted.

Perhaps the best way to begin this investigation is to go straight to the heart of the matter and investigate how many students admit that they are influenced by considerations of social class and family background in making close friends of the same and the opposite sex respectively. Initially the question itself may seem too blunt to discover imperceptible degrees of influence of social class in social relations, but by making explicit and more defined what is possibly so rarely defined, we are enabled to construct a model of statistical norms in which actual behaviour is meaningful. The statistical model of opinions constructs, as it were, out of a generalisation of behaviour the implicit substructural guide lines on which over time the fragmented social behaviour is run. But in the actual statistics we see, as it were, a single compression of a variety of responses in a variety of situations at different points in time. The model is static; it cannot tell us what *actually* happens as we should see it at first hand.

Table 7.1 shows the different responses of male and female students in the Edinburgh sample, although, again, numbers in each cell are too small to admit of more than cursory comparisons. More attention is paid therefore to *overall* numbers and percentages..

Only 18 per cent male students and 16 per cent female students admit to being consciously influenced by considerations of social class in the choice of the same sex friends, although this may be regarded as significant when one remembers that open expressions of "class consciousness" are generally thought to be antithetical to the kind of community values which students reputedly hold. Why it is thought to be more improper to express class consciousness within the student body than in society at large is not always clear, but may result from thei deal of the "liberalising" effect of higher education. Similarly, racial consciousness is frowned upon, along with other expressions of prejudice. Learning is supposed to bring general enlightenment in every sphere of life. However, it may be that stated institutional goals, and stated goals of the academic "community" do not coincide with individual goals and attitudes as translated into action in real situations. This is likely to occur, as we shall see, where institutional organisation is not effective in "socialisa-

TABLE 7.1. INFLUENCE OF SOCIAL CLASS ON CHOICE OF CLOSE FRIENDS—EDINBURGH UNIVERSITY (per cent)

(a) Male students

	SUMC	EUMC	OUMC	SLMC	ELMC	OLMC	SWkC	EWkC	OWkC	Unclassified	Total
(i) Friends of same sex											
Yes	31	29	29	9	7	12	18	—	—	40	18
No	39	29	29	51	50	62	41	66	100	20	44
Possibly unconsciously	30	42	43	40	43	25	41	33	—	40	37
TOTAL	100	100	100	100	100	100	100	99	100	100	99
(ii) Friends of opposite sex											
Yes	85	83	57	74	100	88	60	100	100	100	81
No	15	17	43	26	—	12	40	—	—	—	18
Possibly unconsciously	—	—	—	—	—	—	—	—	—	—	—
TOTAL	100	100	100	100	100	100	100	100	100	100	99
No.	(39)	(24)	(7)	(47)	(28)	(8)	(22)	(6)	(1)	(5)	(187)

TABLE 7.1 (*cont.*)

(b) Female students

(i) Friends of same sex

	SUMC	EUMC	OUMC	SLMC	ELMC	OLMC	SWkC	EWkC	OWkC	Unclassified	Total
Yes	21	15	—	18	13	—	12	—	—	100	16
No	38	22	100	41	48	—	59	100	—	—	42
Possibly un-consciously	41	63	—	41	39	—	30	—	—	—	42
TOTAL	100	100	100	100	100	—	101	100	—	100	100

(ii) Friends of opposite sex

	SUMC	EUMC	OUMC	SLMC	ELMC	OLMC	SWkC	EWkC	OWkC	Unclassified	Total
Yes	97	93	50	71	96	—	47	100	—	—	81
No	3	7	50	30	4	—	53	—	—	100	19
Possibly un-consciously	—	—	—	—	—	—	—	—	—	—	—
TOTAL No.	100 (29)	100 (27)	100 (2)	101 (34)	100 (23)	—	100 (17)	100 (2)	—	100 (1)	100 (135)

tion" of students into its norms and values, and where "community" of interests exists only in name. In this situation the student may be aware of what he *ought* to think and believe as a scholar, and feel somewhat guilty because he does not conform to the ideal. There are various courses open to him. Either he can suppress what he thinks and admit it only when he is sure that others will agree, or he can belligerently compensate for what he believes to be minority views by overstating them. We possibly have evidence of both reactions in the figures. Upper middle-class students show themselves to be most influenced by considerations of social class—31 per cent of the Scottish upper middle-class male students and 21 per cent Scottish upper middle-class female students admitted to being influenced by social class compared, for instance, with only 7 per cent English lower middle-class males and 13 per cent English lower middle-class females. Social class proportions were more uniform than "nationality" proportions showing that in this case social class divisions override national divisions. One must, of course, regard the expression of being influenced by social class in choice of friends of the same sex as indicative of different things in different classes. This emerged clearly in interview. In the upper middle class being influenced by social class means seeking the company of people of similar interests—people of similar background; it is an indication of preservation of group or social class solidarity. At the other end of the scale, for the working-class student it may mean much the same—some students expressed the desire to be with people "with whom I feel at home", and who "don't make me feel uncomfortable". This feeling can work both ways. For an aspiring minority, however, to be influenced by social class means to associate with groups of which one is not a member but by whom one wants to be accepted. This is something to which few students would own up to. For the lower middle-class student being influenced by social class almost always means out and out "social climbing" standing as he does in the midway status position. Therefore proportionately fewer lower middle-class students admit to being influenced by class. The sex differences in response are not very marked, which is in some ways surprising as it is often postulated that women are more interested in matters of social class than are men, and in interview male students often referred to this. It would appear here, however, that there is a certain consensus of opinion between the sexes both regarding making friends of the same sex and of the opposite sex. Those students who said they were "possibly unconsciously" affected by considerations of social class showed that they were trying to express as honestly as possible that they are influenced by these considerations in social relations but neither in the manner nor the degree which the question seems baldly to suggest. Their qualifications added in interview will be discussed later.

In consideration of making friends of the "opposite sex" in the case of both male and female students, it appears that attitudes crystallise and for both sexes in the same way. Eighty-one per cent of both male and female students say that they are *consciously* influenced by considerations of social class in making friends of the opposite sex and, significantly, no one put themselves into the "possibly unconsciously" category. Again there are social class variations, and it would appear that fewer Scottish working-class and lower middle-class students are influenced by social class considerations than their English counterparts—a "national" variation. In each case fewer overseas upper middle-class students express themselves influenced than either their British or Overseas lower middle-class and working-class counterparts, perhaps because as Overseas students their choice of close friends of the opposite sex is basically limited by cultural or colour differences anyway. Excluding the overseas group the upper middle class as a whole and the English lower middle class emerge as most influenced by social class in choice of opposite sex friends which means a closing of ranks at the top.

Scottish working-class students, both male and female, are those who say they are least affected by social class background of friends. There are various explanations which could be put forward for this: either they are intrinsically less conscious of social class divisions or less influenced by them or less concerned with social climbing—more reprehensible in Scotland than in England. Or, on the other hand, because as we have seen they are to some extent separate socially and physically from the rest of the student body, they mix mainly in their own circle and therefore do not normally consider the background of friends. One must merely suggest these possibilities.

The most interesting conclusion one may draw from these findings is that social class is not *always* relevant in close friendships but that its relevance is seen to vary in relation to the other attributes taken into account, for example, in the particular relationship involved with members of the opposite sex. Students discussed the question in interview and explained that in any close friendship with the opposite sex there is always the possibility, however distant, of marriage, and that this requires similarity of tastes and attitudes usually moulded by social class and

family background. Male as well as female students were quite firm
about this. One student in Newcastle even went so far as to say that one
could tell at a glance the difference between the "steadies" and the
"one-nighters" in that in the former case the social class of the students
was closely matched, which was not so in the case of the latter, since it
did not matter. This suggests that with the degree of "closeness" of
the relationship the relevance of social class would vary. Zweig has
noted that a high proportion of the students he interviewed were of the
opinion that "it wouldn't work" to marry beneath their class,[1]
and this will be discussed in the next chapter. Studies of dating patterns
in American colleges also seem to point to a degree of social selection
in dating which may vary with the "seriousness" of the date. This is,
of course, related to the organisation of fraternities and sororities which
in reality express certain kinds of social bias, and represent social status
divisions within the student body.

> Members of fraternities and sororities are more likely than non-members to
> have active dating lives; fraternities are influential in determining dating patterns,
> for example, the fraternity system acts as an important framework for the choice
> of a dating partner, fraternities are informally "rated" on the campus; some girls
> restrict their dates to members of the higher status fraternities.[2]

Thus, what is expressed individually in the British university as a
factor in dating may become institutionalised within the American college
culture. The same factors of status and "suitability", however, play their
part in both situations, whether more or less explicitly.

"The status system on the campus provides the members of similar
status groups with access to suitable dates—suitable in the sense of
possible husbands and wives—and the fraternities are an intrinsic part of
this status system."[3] In both the British and American situation it is clear
that the "status system" of the student body, although uniquely student
in some ways, is still intimately connected with the status groupings of
external society and with the social class from which the students originate.

We shall look at college status hierarchies in some detail later on, and
it would seem that these are comparable with fraternities in some ways
particularly in relation to dating patterns between colleges of similar status.

Most students in answering the questionnaire seemed to have interpreted "close" as "very close" or "intimate", and in the case of such

[1] Zweig, F., *The Student in the Age of Anxiety—A survey of Oxford and Manchester
students*, Heinemann, 1963, p. 67.
[2] Goldsen *et al.*, *op. cit.*, p. 67, and Waller, W., *ASR*, 1937, **2**, 727–34.
[3] Goldsen *et al.*, *op. cit.*, p. 66, and Waller, *op. cit.*

relationships with the opposite sex the attitude of parents also had to be taken account of. The author was told of countless romances which flourished in the university environment but which broke up under the stress of the realities of different home backgrounds outside university or after graduation. Sometimes parental disapproval was involved in the break-up, but not always. In some cases the relationship broke up because of differences which appeared when the partners were on "home ground". Here again is evidence of different attributes becoming relevant in different situations. It *is* possible to disregard the class attribute in student circles, but in an external situation which continually brings to the fore class attachments, as in the family environment, it is no longer really possible. So that even personality seems to change in the new definition of the situation.

The question of "closeness" of friendship was also seen to define the relevance of social class in any relationship, too, with members of the same sex, so that knowledge of a fellow student's background and one's reaction to this would depend on the depth and length of the friendship. Indeed, as often repeated, students in the main do not know of one another's social class origins since it is generally considered bad mannered to ask about parents without being told. In this, only obvious class clues act as immediate indicators in superficial contacts. This will be discussed in detail later in the chapter.

One other reason that was put forward by male students, particularly in Newcastle, for the added relevance of family background in friendships with the opposite sex, was that whereas one can talk "to the chaps" about "women, drink, and football", one has to have "something in common" with a woman to be able to talk to her, and the relationship is on an altogether different level. Obviously the girls here considered differ radically from the "one-nighters" mentioned above. The English lower middle-class students in Edinburgh without exception said that they are influenced in friendships with the opposite sex by considerations of social class and family background. The female students of the English lower middle class had a high score in this respect too—96 per cent. With other evidence this seems to show a group with social class aspirations. However, the group has a large proportion of students of both sexes who say they are not influenced by social class in friendships of the same sex. Perhaps this has something to do with the large size of the lower middle class in which many friendships would be formed.

In the Newcastle sample shown in Table 7.2 a different distribution

TABLE 7.2. INFLUENCE OF SOCIAL CLASS ON CHOICE OF CLOSE FRIENDS—NEWCASTLE UNIVERSITY (per cent)

(a) Female students

	UMC	LMC	WkC	Unclassi-fied	Total
(i) Friends of same sex					
Yes	11	5	–	–	6
No	61	66	58	60	63
Possibly unconsciously	28	29	42	40	31
TOTAL	100	100	100	100	100
(ii) Friends of opposite sex					
Yes	14	13	3	–	11
No	47	51	61	60	52
Possibly unconsciously	39	36	36	40	37
TOTAL	100	100	100	100	100
No.	(57)	(91)	(33)	(5)	(186)

(b) Male students

	UMC	LMC	WkC	Unclassi-fied	Total
(i) Friends of same sex					
Yes	10	10	10	10	10
No	59	67	67	67	64
Possibly unconsciously	31	23	23	24	26
TOTAL	100	100	100	101	100

TABLE 7.2 (*cont.*)

(ii) Friends of opposite sex

Yes	23	19	17	14	19
No	38	50	61	48	48
Possibly unconsciously	37	31	21	38	31
Never made any	2	1	1	—	1·5
TOTAL	100	100	100	100	99·5
No.	(142)	(189)	(91)	(21)	(443)

appears, which in turn will be seen to relate to the external university situation.

It appears that 10 per cent of the male students as compared with 18 per cent in Edinburgh were influenced by considerations of social class in choice of friends. Comparable figures for female students are 6 per cent and 16 per cent. It is interesting that in each case the figure for males is higher—perhaps because more females put themselves in the "possibly unconsciously" category. None of the female working-class students said they were influenced compared with 10 per cent male working-class students. This relation is repeated in other findings in which male students are more *explicitly* influenced by social class than female students. However, if one adds together overall figures of those influenced both consciously or unconsciously by social class, the proportions are almost identical—37 per cent female and 35 per cent male (58 per cent and 55 per cent in Edinburgh), and this would probably be a closer approximation to the ways in which students have shown they are influenced by considerations of background, although they hesitate to express it as such. Social class factors are taboo in conversation in Newcastle student circles although they exist in certain forms later to be discussed. A Newcastle student would have to be very firm in his views to answer "yes" to this question—in Edinburgh social class is more openly discussed and thus an answer in the affirmative may mean not much more than a Newcastle "possibly unconsciously" answer. It was a Newcastle student who said: "Students say they are 'not bothered' by social class because they prefer not to talk about it. Of course they are aware of divisions and think that they *do* matter—but they try to put it out of their conscious mind and put it off until later. Just as some people here are anti-semitic—but they don't go around Jew-baiting." This may again reflect divergence of personal and institutional values.

In consideration of friendships with the opposite sex there is the same kind of trend as in the Edinburgh sample and an increase in the number of definite "yes's", but this is not so marked in relation to overall proportions. However, the proportion of students saying "yes" nearly doubles, as in the Edinburgh sample, so that the "differential" still appears and confirms what has already been said about the sexes although the whole effect of the swing is dampened down by approximately 50 per cent of students who say they are not at all influenced by social class.

Naturally it is quite possible that half the Newcastle student body do not consider such factors at all in informal student relationships, although this state of affairs would not seem to correspond exactly to the observed tendency of students to stress their "common man" attributes and to be suspicious and ill at ease in a situation of blatant middle classness. This does not apply to students in "professional" faculties who reputedly adopt middle-class attitudes even if they did not have them before.

As many as 23 per cent upper middle-class male students and 19 per cent lower middle-class male students said they were influenced in making friends of the opposite sex compared with 14 per cent and 13 per cent female. In each case, males are more often influenced than females and middle class more than working class. This may be a result of the fact that the total situational setting, engendering as it does a working-class ethos, is less geared to aspiration, as has been discussed, whereas Edinburgh is aspirationally geared. Thus, in Edinburgh, there is an "aspirational overlay" which tends to blanket out expected patterning. In Newcastle this overlay is missing and influence of social class represents a preference for those "with whom one would feel comfortable or at ease", i.e. students of one's own social class, as one perceives it. Preservation or improvement of one's status is not involved. Thus only those who are concerned with preservation of status will respond "yes", i.e. particularly certain middle-class students in what they consider a working-class situational setting and certain female students concerned to preserve or improve status—particularly on marriage.

In the Durham sample (Table 7.3) something of a similar picture emerges.

In the case of friends of the same sex, 5 per cent males and 6 per cent females express themselves influenced by social class, changing to 13 per cent and 18 per cent in the case of friends of the opposite sex. Again,

TABLE 7.3. INFLUENCE OF SOCIAL CLASS ON CHOICE OF CLOSE FRIENDS—DURHAM
UNIVERSITY (per cent)

(a) Male students

	UMC	LMC	WkC	Unclassified	Total
(i) Friends of same sex					
Yes	6	5	5	9	5
No	58	69	70	45·5	65
Possibly unconsciously	36	26	24	45·5	29
Don't know	—	—	1	—	0·5
TOTAL	100	100	100	100	99·5
(ii) Friends of opposite sex					
Yes	19	10	10	9	13
No	40	52	59	36	50
Possibly unconsciously	38	34	25	46	33
Don't know	3	4	6	9	4
TOTAL	100	100	100	100	100
No.	(72)	(106)	(63)	(11)	(252)

b) Female students

	UMC	LMC	WkC	Unclassified	Total
(i) Friends of same sex					
Yes	—	9	7	—	6
No	62	71	71	50	68
Possibly unconsciously	38	20	21	50	26
Don't know	—	—	—	—	—
TOTAL	100	100	99	100	100

TABLE 7.3 (*cont.*)

(ii) Friends of opposite sex

Yes	28	16	7	—	18
No	31	58	71	—	51
Possibly unconsciously	41	25	21	100	31
Don't know	—	—	—	—	—
TOTAL	100	99	99	100	100
No.	(29)	(55)	(14)	(2)	(100)

middle-class students show themselves to be more influenced by social class than working-class students. Female students are more often influenced than male students. This distribution appears more clearly in consideration of friendships with members of the opposite sex.

If one includes students who said they were "possibly unconsciously" influenced by social class, again one finds a substantial proportion of students express themselves to be influenced in *some way*. In what ways one may discern from interview material and observed behaviour.

The qualitative material can help our understanding of student perception of the influence of social class in social relations as a desirable or entirely undesirable state of affairs. This raises also the whole question of "social climbing" within the student context and the attitudes to higher education as a means of social mobility which will be discussed in Part IV.

It would seem from interview and observation that "social climbing" is heartily despised by most students. This would seem to be "unsuccessful" social climbing in that it is performed without much social skill and is therefore obvious to everyone. No one therefore wishes to be known as a social climber, and it is doubtful therefore if many students who admitted to being influenced by social class in choice of friends were willingly taking on this label. Indeed, many wrote in the margin of their questionnaire in order to make this point clear. Those who are in fact mobile and become assimilated into the group to which they aspire do so because they "fit in" and do not stand out as "social climbers". These students are not likely to say that they are influenced by social class in choice of friends. Indeed, they are most likely to be those who say that social class "does *not* matter", since for them it has not acted as a barrier to advancement. They are able to manipulate the social class "clues" and attributes primarily because they have certain social skills.[1]

[1] These skills relate to total modes of behaviour in differing situations. See for instance Argyle, M., *The Psychology of Interpersonal Relations*, Penguin, 1967.

These points may account for the fact that more people admitted in interview to being influenced by social class considerations than had stated this on their questionnaire. They reacted against any imputation of social climbing on the form, but in discussion admitted that they found they "got on better" with people like themselves with similar background. It is thought less offensive to choose to mix with people like oneself than to refuse to mix with those who are *not* like oneself. "Snobbishness" or discrimination *against* certain groups is to be criticised, while to associate with student sof similar background because one feels more at ease with them seems quite acceptable. Criteria for membership may be based on social status so long as distinctions are not too finely drawn and are not blatantly exclusive. There is for students a positive and negative side of class and their consciousness of "belonging".

The categories provided therefore for replies are too crude to give any subtle indication of students' appreciation of social class divisions. This criticism is also true of the questions on student attitudes to class consciousness in the university—when they were asked if they consider social class consciousness at university is maintained, fostered, diminished, or irrelevant. Naturally, "class consciousness" is very vague and has different interpretations and the qualifications "fostered", "maintained", etc., will obviously only have meaning in relation to class consciousness as the student has experienced it outside the university environment. Students' ideas of social classes outside the university are analysed in Chapter 3. Here we are concerned only with the university

TABLE 7.4. OPINIONS OF STUDENTS ON SOCIAL CLASS

	UC	SUMC	EUMC	OUMC	SLMC
Maintained	50	27	20	22	20
Fostered	—	2	10	—	4
Diminished	—	33	39	33	33
Don't know	—	2	—	11	—
Irrelevant	50	35	27	33	41
Depends on organisation	—	2	4	—	2
TOTAL	100	101	100	99	100
No.	(2)	(66)	(51)	(9)	(82)

situation, and although the analysis is in broad, even "coarse" categories, it enables us to move however slowly from the general to the particular.

Table 7.4 shows the distribution of students' opinions in the Edinburgh sample. Again, we show the subtotals for interest rather than for significance.

Five per cent of students thought social class consciousness is actually fostered in the University; 27 per cent thought it maintained; 31 per cent diminished; and 35 per cent irrelevant—one-third maintained or fostered to two-thirds diminution. The Scottish working class was the group with the largest proportion of students who felt that in university social class awareness is fostered—13 per cent. None of the English or Overseas working class expressed this view. This may be explained by earlier findings which show the Scottish working class as an isolated group while the English working class are largely assimilated into the middle-class student body. The Scottish working class tends to think that in university existing social class divisions are exacerbated because they themselves feel separate. They also tend to show the distinction which a university education draws between those who have been at university and those who have not—a distinction often drawn within their own families. For, as we have seen in the analysis of siblings' education, the proportion of siblings at university in this group is not high.

The figure of 35 per cent of students who say that social class is irrelevant in university seems not to correspond with figures already discussed showing influence of social class in choice of friends. However, apart

CONSCIOUSNESS IN UNIVERSITY—EDINBURGH (per cent)

ELMC	OLMC	SWkC	EWkC	OWkC	Total
28	50	31	38	100	27
2	—	13	—	—	5
28	25	20	38	—	31
2	—	—	—	—	0·6
38	25	36	25	—	35
2	—	—	—	—	2
100	100	100	101	100	100·6
(50)	(8)	(39)	(8)	(1)	(316)

from those students who have answered what they think the situation *ought* to be like rather than what it *is* like, it may appear that many of the students seem to have answered "diminished" or "irrelevant" in an unconscious and paradoxical effort to mitigate the effect of their earlier responses. And although this would initially seem to be a contradiction in terms, in fact it is very near the truth. For a single response covers a multitude of occasions and situations and the student may feel that on the whole in a majority of cases social class is irrelevant, and having only one response, although he may be able to think of exceptions, he will opt for the answer *generally* true. It may not be true in the case of close friends, or close friends of the opposite sex, but then one is not always interacting with close friends. Thus apparent contradictions are as meaningful as apparent conformities.

"Class consciousness", on the whole, has an unpleasant connotation for students. In interview they were often willing to admit that there are class differences and divisions and that most students are conscious of their existence and are influenced in *some cases* by them in their opinions and behaviour. They were ready to state that one has "more in common" with someone of similar background and is therefore more likely to make a close friend of such a person rather than one with whom, because of differences in attitude and way of life, one would not feel completely at ease—yet they were unwilling to recognise this as "class consciousness". I think they perhaps confused "class consciousness" with class conflict and were eager to show that conflict situations on class lines do not develop at university. This view would seem to be entirely justified. Although there is evidence of "class consciousness" in all three universities, there is very little real evidence of any class conflict in any field of interest.

I should, at this point, make it perfectly plain that by class consciousness I mean the awareness of being a member of a class rather than awareness of need to pursue any particular class interest. Social class identity and links with external divisions, and the existence of "group" sentiment are discussed later in an analysis of what students mean by social class. But here we are trying to examine the existence of a social attribute meaningful in student social relations called "social class". Having isolated it we can examine it in detail.

It may be seen in the Edinburgh findings that there are no startling differences in opinion between the various social classes. More of the working-class students than middle-class think that social class consciousness is maintained in the university. This could be because they are in the minority in the student body. It is difficult to see, though, why the Scottish working class has a greater proportion of students than the English working class who consider social class consciousness to be either maintained or fostered. An explanation of this could be that the English working class are so small in number that they are easily assimilated by the middle class and in fact do not think of themselves entirely as working class, which would account for 3 out of 8 of them saying that in university awareness of social class is diminished. The Scottish working class, on the other hand, are too large to be assimilated into the middle class and yet too small to feel more than a minority group—in which situation 20 per cent think that awareness of social class is diminished.

The fact that the Scottish lower middle class is the largest group numerically could explain the high percentage—41 per cent—who consider social class consciousness irrelevant, largely because they mix with each other. However, the Overseas lower middle class does not follow this pattern since it is as small as the English working class—yet 4 out of 8 of the students in this group think that social class awareness is maintained. It is difficult to see why a greater proportion of the English upper middle class think that social class consciousness is fostered, but, of course, the numbers are too small for conclusions to be drawn. A larger proportion claimed that social class consciousness is diminished than the other upper middle class groups. One questions whether there are two groups within the English upper middle class.

Some of the speculations involved may seem to show certain contradictions in student attitudes and behaviour. In interview students would often contradict themselves two or three times over in discussion of their attitudes to social class and then show at the end that they realised this. "Oh, dear", said one, "You must think that I don't know my own mind; I seem to contradict myself so often— but really it is so difficult to have any clear views on anything so complicated as social class." The researcher realises the problems involved in expressing attitudes on social class and describing behaviour, and recognises that the complexity is not only in the "expression" but in the "action". Human behaviour is rarely systematic—nor does it run along single lines of choice—rather is it, especially where social class is involved, an accumulation of post-choices, often arbitrary, each performing the next attitude or reaction, and changing therefore constantly in relation to past, actual, or vicarious experience. At any point in time, therefore, it is extremely difficult to "pin down" one's social class attitudes and behaviour.

Additional figures make it clear that students believe "students themselves" do play the most important part in the regulation of social class consciousness. The staff do not play a large part at all, being mentioned only by three students in any context. This seems to show a situation in which the student body is a community in itself, in many ways separate from the teaching staff, organising and regulating itself completely from within—in social rather than academic terms—with respect to formal and informal student organisation.

The whole system of education is thought to play a minor part except in so far as it diminishes and makes irrelevant the awareness of social class. No one considered that the system of education fostered social class consciousness, and only sixteen considered that it maintained such awareness. As the special frame of reference is the particular university surveyed the system of education is that found within it. By this token, most students seem satisfied that their university education is not class based or biased, and that, indeed, it helps to break down class prejudices.

What social class divisions represent and how they are maintained is discussed in relation to qualitative material from interview and observation later in the chapter. First, we turn to a comparison of the situation in Durham and Newcastle. The Newcastle distribution is found in Table 7.5.

Only 4 per cent of Newcastle students thought that social class divisions within the University are fostered compared with 5 per cent in Edinburgh, 12 per cent maintained (27 per cent Edinburgh), and the rest thought

TABLE 7.5. OPINIONS OF STUDENTS ON SOCIAL CLASS CONSCIOUSNESS IN UNIVERSITY—NEWCASTLE (per cent)

	UMC	LMC	WkC	Total
Maintained	13	13	10	12
Fostered	3	4	4	4
Diminished	36	30	35	33
Irrelevant	46	51	47	49
No reply	1	1	5	2
Race prejudice	2	—	—	1
TOTAL	101	99	101	101
No.	(199)	(280)	(124)	(603)

ocial class diminished or irrelevant in social relations apart from 2 per
ent non-respondents antagonised by the question. Although the topic
vas not comprehended by the question, 1 per cent of students (all coloured) said that they had experienced some race prejudice within the student body. This suggests that for these students colour equals class.[1] This
s sertion is a controversial one and not all sociologists would agree
vith this interpretation.

Sixteen per cent upper middle class and 17 per cent lower middle class
hought social class consciousness maintained or fostered compared with
4 per cent working class. The overall proportion is low and yet the slight
lifferential between the working-class and middle-class students would
uggest that all that has been observed about the prevailing ethos of the
tudent body has been justified, and that it is more often middle-class students who perceive divisions—perhaps feel at a disadvantage—than work-
ng-class students. In sheer weight of numbers it is the lower middle class
vho appreciate the class consciousness in the University most—they com-
orise 49 per cent of those who thought class consciousness maintained;
52 per cent of those who thought it fostered.

Table 7.6 shows the *means* of fostering or diminishing class consciousness in the University, outlined by students.

TABLE 7.6. STUDENT OPINIONS OF FACTORS INFLUENCING SOCIAL CLASS CONSCIOUSNESS IN THE UNIVERSITY—NEWCASTLE (per cent)

	Student	Staff	Educ. system	Combined	Total
Maintained	14	60	7	—	13
Fostered	5	—	2	—	4
Diminished	30	20	41	100	34
Irrelevant	50	20	50	—	49
Race prejudice	1	—	—	—	1
TOTAL	100	100	100	100	100
No.	(427)	(5)	(154)	(6)	(592)

[1] As suggested by Little, K., *Negroes in Britain: A Study of Race Relations in English Society*, Kegan Paul, Trench, Trubner & Co. Ltd., London, 1948, p. 232; and Banton, M. P., *White and Coloured: The Behaviour of the British People Towards the Coloured Immigrant*, Jonathan Cape, London, 1959, pp. 46–8, 101–2.

Staff were mentioned slightly more often than in Edinburgh, but agai
an insignificant proportion is involved. They were said most often t
"maintain" social class consciousness—yet this comprised only 4 per ce
of replies on this section.

Students are said to be responsible for fostering and diminishing cla
consciousness by 72 per cent compared with 26 per cent who held respo
sible the system of education. The latter was thought most often to mak
social class irrelevant in social relations, although 7 per cent of those wh
mentioned the system of education thought it "maintained" social clas
divisions and 2 per cent "fostered". The role of the "system of education
is on the whole held to "iron out" social class differences, although exact
how this is achieved is left rather vague. But by virtue of bringing studen
of different social classes together, students seemed to think that unive
sity education made the first step and after that the students themselve
take over.

In the Durham sample, shown in Table 7.7, a different pattern emerge
from that of either of the two previous samples.

TABLE 7.7. OPINIONS OF STUDENTS ON SOCIAL CLASS CONSCIOUSNESS IN THE UNIVERSITY-
DURHAM (per cent)

	UMC		LMC		WkC		Unclassified		Total
	M	F	M	F	M	F	M	F	
Maintained	18	28	21	22	25	29	27	50	23
Fostered	3	7	·5	2	3	7	18	—	4
Diminished	26	24	23	27	24	21	9	50	24
Irrelevant	39	38	45	46	41	43	45	—	42
Don't know	4	3	2	4	3	—	—	—	3
No reply	10	—	4	—	3	—	—	—	4
TOTAL	100	100	100	101	99	100	99	100	100
No.	(72)	(29)	(106)	(55)	(63)	(14)	(11)	(2)	(352)

Twenty-two per cent of Durham students thought social class main
tained at university and 4 per cent thought divisions fostered, while 3 pe
cent did not know. The rest again said that divisions are diminished o

relevant. There is a difference between those who said that social class "diminished" and those who said it is "irrelevant" within the University hich will be examined later. Nevertheless, it would appear that a greater proportion of students in Durham University than in Newcastle University ought that social class is maintained—nearly as high a proportion as in dinburgh, whose distribution it more nearly mirrors. Why this should be is one of the special problems posed which will be analysed in succeeding chapters, but first we turn to an analysis of these figures in terms of sex nd class.

Upper middle-class and working-class female students seem to be those ho feel most often that social class in the University is maintained, hile a higher proportion of the working class as a whole thinks social ass maintained or fostered. This would appear to be somewhat of reversal of the Newcastle University situation, and would seem to show at the working-class students in the generally middle-class atmosphere e more likely to feel that social class divisions are maintained than the iddle-class students themselves. However, since the atmosphere is largely *wer* middle class and broad regional accents abound, upper middle-class udents, too, are aware of social class differences. It does seem that the oup most likely to think social class divisions irrelevant is students who e at least *perceived* to be in the preponderance.

Table 7.8, showing by what means the students thought the situation is fected, reveals a surprising proportion of 15 per cent of students who

ABLE 7.8. STUDENTS' OPINIONS OF FACTORS INFLUENCING SOCIAL CLASS CONSCIOUSNESS IN THE UNIVERSITY—DURHAM (per cent)

	Students	Staff	College system	Whole educ. system	Combined	Don't know	Total
Maintained	27	100	18	18	37	2	22
Fostered	3	—	15	4	6	—	4
Diminished	28	—	36	40	26	—	24
Irrelevant	41	—	30	38	31	98	49
TOTAL	99	100	99	100	100	100	99
No.	(128)	(2)	(33)	(50)	(70)	(69)	(352)

thought that social class divisions are fostered "by the collegiate system
while 36 per cent thought that the collegiate system diminished social clas
consciousness. This must not be taken to mean the actual process of "liv
ing together in colleges" which as we shall see later was generally though
to have a beneficial effect in reducing class differences. What student
said they meant here is the effect of a specifically "college system" whic
introduces divisions in various ways. By its separate "ivory towerness" i
introduces a town–gown rift and gives students a "superior" attitude. It
status as an ancient institution and its emphasis on outdated traditions (i
students' eyes) stresses the separateness of the "young gentlemen" which i
at variance with modern living; and inter-collegiate rivalry which put
stress on "O.K." and "non-O.K." colleges increases awareness of socia
class features of college images. For example, University college men, i.e
"Castle men", are encouraged to think themselves upper-crust and supe
rior by both institutional reinforcement and traditional castle setting.

In Durham "students themselves" are thought to be less responsible fo
influencing social class divisions than institutional means—only 36 pe
cent mentioned them as the major factor and a large majority wer
thought to "maintain" class divisions. The only staff who were mentione
were thought to "maintain" social class consciousness.

The educational system was thought by 18 per cent of students t
"maintain" divisions and by 4 per cent to actually encourage them. Thi
refers once again to the "haves/have not" split of which Durham student
as they wander through the town in academic gowns, are particularly con
scious. A sizeable proportion of students, however (20 per cent), felt tha
the situation was too complex to be expressed in terms of any one facto
and of their own accord spoke of a "combination" of factors. In Durham
particularly, one can see that this is more nearly a representation of th
truth.

Since we have briefly discussed students' attitudes to the effect of th
collegiate system on class divisions it may be of help here to examine whic
factors students thought to affect the prestige of a college. Table 7.9 show
the results.

Sixty-eight per cent of students thought that colleges are ranked by stu
dents in terms of prestige. Seventy-seven per cent of female students livin
in colleges think that colleges are ranked—the highest proportion. Thi
may be accounted for by the fact that the men are normally thought of i
terms of their college, i.e. "He's a Castle man" (high prestige) or a "Cuths
man" (low prestige), and are commonly assessed in terms of college pres

TABLE 7.9. WHETHER STUDENTS THOUGHT THAT COLLEGES ARE RANKED IN PRESTIGE—
DURHAM (per cent)

	Male digs	Male college	Female digs	Female college	Total
Colleges ranked	66	66	50	77	68
Not ranked	16	16	11	9	14
Don't know	18	18	39	14	18
TOTAL	100	100	100	100	100
No.	(73)	(179)	(18)	(82)	(352)

tige in terms of "dating".[1] The personal deficiencies of a "Castle man" are outweighed by his social advantages—a "Cuthsman" will be assessed on personal merit alone. It is significant that of female students in digs who do not have to keep up dating prestige, or "dating rating" in the face of college mates, only 50 per cent think colleges ranked.

Those who thought colleges ranked by students in general—though not necessarily by themselves—were asked to state what reasons they would give for high prestige ranking of a college (Table 7.10).

Twenty-one per cent put "the abilities and talents" of its members —the highest single proportion, but by no means a majority; 10 per cent thought that college members' social class determined prestige—a reason most favoured by working-class female students. Seven per cent of this group also thought "wealth of members" to be the most important factor. Together with the 21 per cent who voted for "social adaptability" the distribution of replies in this group would seem to point to involvement of college prestige ranking with social class considerations. Lower middle-class female students mentioned most often "personality" and 'abilities and talents", which accounted for 39 per cent of all students' replies. Not one of the female working class mentioned "personality".

Again it is of interest to compare this status ranking of colleges with American fraternities and sororities. There is one major difference in organisation, however, and that is that it is a matter for competition to get into a sorority or fraternity at all, quite apart from the status "league table", whereas every student in a collegiate university must be a member

[1] Compare Scott, J. F., *ASR*, 1965, **30**, 514–27, in the American College Sorority.

TABLE 7.10. STUDENT OPINIONS OF BASIC CRITERION FOR RANKING COLLEGES—DURHAM
(per cent)

	UMC		LMC		WkC		Unclassified		Total
	M	F	M	F	M	F	M	F	
Academic achievement	3	—	11	7	6	14	9	—	7
Wealth	1	—	2	2	2	7	—	50	2
Family background	8	10	11	9	6	21	18	—	10
Abilities and talents	21	24	18	27	21	22	9	50	21
Social adaptability	17	17	7	4	8	21	18	—	10
Social conformity	7	4	7	9	8	—	18	—	7
Enthusiasm	11	17	6	9	8	7	9	—	9
Personality	13	17	24	20	19	—	9	—	18
Snobbery	—	—	—	—	3	—	—	—	1
No reply	20	10	15	13	19	7	9	—	15
TOTAL	101	99	101	100	100	99	99	100	100
No.	(72)	(29)	(106)	(55)	(63)	(14)	(11)	(2)	(352)

of a college even if only nominally. Therefore on the American campus there are two sets of status system—between fraternity and non-fraternity members and between members of different colleges. A comparison between fraternity and non-fraternity differences may be made between college members who "live in" and "live out" and is a vaguely approximate measure of participation in college activities. In selection, or self-selection, for fraternities there is the additional factor of *expenses* involved in being a member so that "there is a marked tendency for fraternities to recruit and to appeal to students who can better afford not only the fixed charges (fees, lodgings and so on) but also the *style of life*"[1] (author's italic).

Goldsen, Rosenberg, Williams, and Suchman admit that what has come to be known as the fraternity style of life may in fact be closely associated with economic and social status of the students involved—not only with having a preference for the fraternity style of life but the "bald fact of having the money to indulge it".[2] The "style of life" of the Durham colleges is certainly not so highly developed or differentiated as within the fraternities which the authors above discuss and is not quali-

[1] Goldsen *et al.*, *op. cit.*, p. 69.
[2] *Ibid.*, p. 70.

fied by necessity of *economic* advantage particularly. In this sense the fraternities may represent a more obvious and entrenched system of inequalities sanctioned by institutional acceptance. They at least represent a different kind of division from those exhibited in the British universities studied.

We have seen how external status systems find their expression in student life. It is important to consider how far the internal status system of the student body in turn mirrors and is based upon the indices of status systems prevalent generally in society or how far it is qualitatively a different kind of status system.

In the Edinburgh sample, students were asked what *in general* determined a student's status in the student body in an attempt to compare social divisions in the student body with those "outside" the institutional setting. This will only be mentioned here and will be discussed in greater detail along with students' ideas on social class in Chapter 12. "Family background" represents "social class" since students cannot be judged by indices such as occupation, income, etc. (Table 7.11).

Only 12 per cent of students think that a student's social standing is determined by his family background, although it is a proportion large enough to be significant. The greatest number of students choosing this criterion are the Scottish middle class. A high percentage of the Overseas lower middle class thought this too—25 per cent, as did one Overseas working-class student. Perhaps by "family background" the Overseas students meant also the factor of nationality feeling that "being foreign" affected their standing in the student body.

Only 3 per cent of students think that wealth determines a student's standing.

Said one Edinburgh lower middle-class student: "There is no keeping up with the Joneses in university like there is outside. As far as money goes we're all in the same boat." This contrasts with the American situation discussed.

An Edinburgh upper middle-class student said: "Some of the people with grants have much more money that I do—there is no one really poor at university."

Many students would strongly dispute that last sentence, but would agree that lack of money alone is no handicap to a student socially. Most of the students who thought "money" an important criterion were Scottish. By contrast Goldsen *et al.* report that 43 per cent of all students had to work in some job to help them pay their school expenses. Fifty-three per cent said they depend in whole or in part on their own earnings and savings to get through school.

The low figure of 7 per cent who think that academic prowess determines a student's social standing compares with the low Durham figures, and illustrates a point made earlier that it is the students who "stick out" in some way who do not "get on" socially in the student body. Someone who is extremely successful academically, or who is *seen* to be so, offends the norms of conformity, and is regarded as something of a deviant or a "ratebuster"[1] who makes other people feel uncomfortable. Academic prowess is not therefore regarded as a determinant of status.[2] It is interesting to note that more of the working-class and Overseas students as a whole chose this category, perhaps because they had needed a greater academic effort to get to university. Goldsen *et al.* note that the fraternity style of life to some extent "de-emphasises" the academic side of college life, and that "fraternity members are somewhat less likely than independents to obtain high grades probably because the tradition of the 'gentlemanly C' still prevails in many of the houses".[3] They say, further, that "the fraternity as a reference group, by and large, emphasises certain other forms of securing recognition and validating prowess over and

TABLE 7.11. CRITERIA DETERMINING A STUDENT'S SOCIAL

	SUC	SUMC	EUMC	OUMC	SLMC
Family background	—	14	8	11	12
Wealth	—	5	6	—	1
Academic prowess	—	5	6	33	7
Other abilities	50	45	33	33	53
Combination	—	11	18	—	4
Other	50	20	26	—	21
Don't know	—	1	4	22	—
TOTAL	100	101	101	99	98
No.	(2)	(66)	(51)	(9)	(82)

[1] As used in literature in the field of Industrial Sociology, for example Roethlisberger, F. J. and Dickson, W. J., *Management and the Worker*, 1939.

[2] This might have implications for the growth of what Clark and Trow call "academic" culture.

[3] Goldsen *et al.*, *op. cit.*, p. 73.

above grades".[1] Walter Wallace introduces other complicating factors to show that "fraternity membership was less negatively related to grades when admiration of faculty members was low, and indeed that relationship was strongly positive among high aptitude students who admired new faculty members".[2] No one factor can ever properly be isolated from the total social context.

By far the largest numbers of students said that "other abilities and talents" are most used to determine a student's status in the University —44 per cent—and of the 80 students who thought it was something else, 49 said "personality". It would seem from these figures that the majority of students feel that in the student body an individual is judged on his own merits, his status is achieved rather than ascribed, i.e. he is considered "primarily" by others as a "fellow student". It is important to remember that this is an impersonal judgement on impersonal "persons"—judgements in terms of immediate social relations may differ with *context*, making conscious perhaps something which is normally unconscious. One may here distinguish, too, the status hierarchy existing in the student body from the associational networks—the first is not thought to be influenced by social class background whereas the second is as a different aspect of

STANDING IN THE UNIVERSITY—EDINBURGH (per cent)

ELMC	OLMC	SWkC	EWkC	OWkC	Unclassified	Total
12	25	10	—	100	17	12
—	—	5	—	—	17	3
2	13	10	13	—	—	7
36	25	49	50	—	33	44
20	25	12	38	—	34	13
26	—	13	—	—	—	19
4	13	—	—	—	—	2
100	101	99	101	100	101	100
(50)	(8)	(39)	(8)	(1)	(6)	(322)

[1] *Ibid.*, p. 74.
[2] Wallace, *op. cit.*, p. 166.

social organisation. Status is a matter of what a student *does*, who he mixes with is a matter of who he is. It is clear that something of a paradox is involved here.

In trying to translate some of these statistical findings in their crude form into actual behaviour and experience of students, we may think of the attitudinal patterns which students present as something like the "thought of orders" described by Lévy-Strauss. He says: "These thought of orders cannot be checked against the experience to which they refer; since they are one and the same things as this experience".[1] And in the same way one can only quote students' experience in conjunction with the "thought of orders" rather than check it against, for they are one and the same thing.

Although in inverviews students expressed many prejudiced generalisations about members of other social classes, in practice it would seem to be true that social class divisions are not so clearly defined in the student body as they are in society at large. Indeed, the prejudiced generalisations expressed seemed often to be based on very little or no actual evidence and resulted from lack of contact experienced. In addition, a student's social class, as indicated by a complex set of indices, is very difficult to judge at university, as was constantly pointed out in interview. Most students are far away from home and must therefore be judged as individuals rather than as members of families. Thus social class is primarily a "label" or an "attribute" which refers to a cultural and interactional group *outside* the university, and its relevance in social situations will be perceived in terms of the student's past actual or vicarious experience of social class outside, as well as inside the university.[2] Social class "differences" which he perceives within the student body will be interpreted in the light of what he already knows of social class. This may partially account for different patterns of responses of social classes to some of the questions asked. Those who differentiate crude material categories will differ in their replies from those who lay stress on separate "values" and "interests"—and it would appear that the latter are in the majority.

As individuals at university, students are all in the same environment and are subject in a broad sense to the same influences; they are all

---

[1] Lévy-Strauss, C., Social structure, *Anthropology Today* (ed. Kroeber), University of Chicago Press, 1953, pp. 524–50.

[2] For discussion of continuum of interactional to attributional class see Plowman, D. E. G., Minchinton, W. E. and Stacey, M., Local status in England and Wales, *Soc. Rev.*, **10**, 161–202, July 1962.

within a certain range of age and intelligence, possibly also within a range of gross material prosperity. Said one student: "The top and bottom have been cut off the strata—so the picture one has is inaccurate."

It was repeated often in interviews that if students have got so far in their education they must to some extent be alike in outlook, attitude, and behaviour, i.e. the category "student" presupposes a certain degree of cultural uniformity. However, a small proportion of students suggested that by being students individuals are not any the less members of social classes—the one does not preclude the other. Social class may "not matter" in certain situations but it nevertheless exists as a meaningful social category with which students identify. The statistical findings at the beginning of this chapter would seem to show this conclusively. What they cannot show, by very virtue of their being statistical norms, expressing a *summation* of social behaviour, is the significant discontinuity and dissimilarities in response and interaction over time. These may only be discovered by an observation of "what people actually do"[1] in a variety of social situations. A short summary of observations on actual behaviour and interview material will be presented here, along with comments on how this compares with the statistical evidence. Reasons why "perceived" and "actual" situations and behaviour do not always coincide will be examined in Part III as well as an explanation of what happens when these two do coincide—with all the implications for structural analysis.

As far as students are concerned the principal way of ranking fellow students is to find out about family background and father's occupations as a socioeconomic indicator. In fact this is rarely done in student circles and it is thought bad mannered to ask "What does your father do?", or to boast of wealthy or successful parents. Therefore in the light of this students often began in interviews by denying that there is any "class consciousness" in the student body.

It would seem to be true of students' observed behaviour that they do not often discuss matters of family background with the intention of ranking one another in terms of social class. However, this is of limited significance in itself and as meaningless without qualification as the purely statistical results. Students do differentiate between members of different types of school for instance, and as we shall see in Chapter 10, this is a very significant "cultural" division; they are also aware of accents —and some either "iron out" or "broaden" their accents depending on

---

[1] Little, K., *Social Anthropology in Modern Life*, Inaugural Lecture delivered before the University of Edinburgh, 18 January 1965.

what they perceive to be appropriate in the particular context in which they find themselves. Although the basic "clues" of family and home residence are missing, there are present "personal" clues such as speech and manner which may be just as telling. However, the significant point here is that these "clues" are identifiable yet are not *rigidly* associated with socioeconomic status of parents—as in the person of a working-class boy who won his way to a public school and became "enculturated" into middle-class ways *before* coming to university. This kind of identification may thus tend to "blur" social class divisions in socioeconomic terms or rather tend to emphasise other dimensions of the existing social class.

Although students stressed lack of class consciousness among students, they nevertheless spoke of the "unconscious drift" together of people with similar backgrounds—and this was an inconsistency which they failed to reconcile—and were sometimes conscious of as an inconsistency.

The "unconscious drift" together of people with similar backgrounds was explained in terms of shared attitudes and interests. "One has more in common with people of similar background and feels more at home with them", said one middle-class Edinburgh student. The same idea was put in another way by a Newcastle working-class student who said that "The lads I go about with are ordinary chaps and like doing the same kind of things. I don't think anyone who wore a bow tie would fit in." The reference to "dress" as being symbolic of class membership is an example of the fact that such considerations are by no means absent in students' social class relations.

The stress on common interests shows the way that students *think* they distinguish between members of social classes in terms of non-material culture and internalised value systems, but, in fact, this distinction may be misleading and based on experience of "external" social classes. For instance, a middle-class student who says "Where I would go to a concert, a working-class student would go to a pub or a cinema" is making assumptions in terms of a social class stereotype which he possibly had *before* coming to university, and he allows impressions of the working class *in general* to cloud his appreciation of the working-class student's "studentness", i.e. that which they have in common. Said another middle-class student "You know I discovered that the father of one of my friends is a miner. But he is really quite intelligent."

Certain middle-class students, when asked whether it would be possible for a working-class student to have similar interests as a product of his

education rather than his family background, seemed to think it most unlikely that such a thing could happen. Thus for these students a hypothetical social class attribute precluded common "student" identity. Yet
because at the student level "interests" do not so rigidly follow social
class lines, their analysis is misleading and does not operate in practice.
However, where "interests" do diverge widely it is likely that such students would label these as social class differences and use them to reinforce assumptions already held.

As we have already seen, in analysis of choice of friends the extent to
which such factors operate, as it were, in ignorance and the extent to
which they are based on fact depends on the closeness of friendship—so
that students are not concerned with the social class of acquaintances
whom they meet casually in the university context while they gradually
find out about friends' backgrounds as they get to know them better.
Usually, they claimed, and quite by accident it often turned out to be a
similar background. Where it was not by that time in close friendships
it did not matter. Therefore closeness of relationship seems to be an important factor in analysis of the influence of social class and obviously,
in this, initial contact of social class members is a necessary prerequisite
to the development of such relationships. Where certain features of
structure—as we shall see in Part III—restrict such contact, there are
very obvious repercussions in terms of social class relations.

For a variety of reasons, therefore, social class divisions within the
university are "blurred". These may be summarised as follows:

(a) Students within the university are in general "cut free" from their
    family background so that many social class clues are missing.

(b) Students in fact represent only a restricted "band" of the population
    in terms of certain attributes including socioeconomic social class.

(c) Those attributes which they do exhibit are sometimes misleading
    as indicators of socioeconomic class.

(d) In any event the students do not in general discover the more ob-
    vious 'indicators' of socioeconomic classes in casual relations.

(e) Members of social classes do not always meet one another in the
    institutional context—so that the preceding points may for some
    never need to be taken into account.

As a result it is fairly common to hear students speak of the student
community as a little unreal; a community apart and that ordinary

social class distinctions become more personalised and based on feelings of "people like me" and "people who are different". Therefore it is those without distinctive class marks who are accepted into the group to which they aspire—and those who "stand out" in face of the prevailing norm who are not accepted and who experience particularly the "consciousness" of social class. This may apply equally to a public school boy in a "working-class" university or a working-class student in a "middle-class" college. And the fact that some students resent what they see as the "pressure to conform" results in "inverted snobbery", broadening of accents, coarsening of language and manners, in a conscious expression of "them and us" identity.

> Meeting people from a wide variety of backgrounds is one of the most worth-while experiences the University can offer, but this social diversity is also a source of conflict and anxiety. There is a risk that communal life in hall or college will make the divisions more obtrusive; cliques at table, secret societies, selective dining and wining clubs, define for the less privileged student the limits of his acceptability.[1]

The fact that students react in one way or the other to what they *perceive* to be the prevailing social class ethos or *mores* reveals not only that social class influences their attitude and behaviour, but also that its influence depends on the *perceived* situation—both at the institutional and small group level. A student who perceives Newcastle University to be working class when in fact in statistical proportions it is as middle class as Durham, or who perceives a fellow student to be middle class when in fact his father's occupation places him firmly in the working class, or as upper middle-class English when he is in fact Scottish, is influenced in his perception by the same set of cultural and spatial variables operating at different levels. These we shall be concerned to isolate and to examine in Part III. Therefore, because we separate out at this stage the social class attribute we must of necessity gain only an incomplete—even one-dimensional—picture of students' social relations, and its true significance as a factor in social relations will only be seen by comparison with the other factors with which it is variously combined. The ways in which these factors are combined will be seen to depend on the situation. For instance in one situation geographical affiliations will be as important as or more important than social class, i.e. social class will appear as more or less relevant. In order to test this hypothesis, actual situations would

[1] Marris, P., *The Experience of Higher Education*, London, 1964, p. 101.

have to be defined in order to ascertain the combination of social "attributes" perceived to be relevant in certain relationships and the differential weighting of each. In such analysis it would be seen that both "social class" and "student" are "umbrella" categories in that they cover a host of identities.

Where blurring of social class divisions and ambiguity of social class identity occur, it may appear that university is a little unreal—and its degree of unreality will, of course, depend on its relation as an institution with its external environment—as we shall see in Chapter 9. However, the fact that one might describe it as a "zone of transition" must be subject to qualification, and, as we shall see, results from a combination of a variety of prerequisite conditions. Similarly, it is only in a limited sense that university represents a "sort of limbo"[1] for the student. This "limbo" is not a social vacuum of "studentness" and cultural uniformity, for it seems clear that the "internalised value systems" of students are already well formed by the time they come to university, and that whatever life within the university does to change these "value systems" it cannot eradicate them and substitute new ones. "Student" as a social category is more meaningful to "outgroupers" and it is in contact with those outside that student solidarity is either reinforced or diminished in terms of the relations with the third party involved, and on occasions of common sentiment such as graduation. It is the fact of being a student which is emphasised by structural opposition of those who are *not* students. Among students themselves the identity is far less meaningful and does not in itself express "group" identity. This is more usually conveyed by subgroups such as "faculty", "college", or "fraternity".

It seems clear then that the relevance of social class in social relations depends on a variety of social variables, variously combined in different social situations. These are largely cultural and spatial and will be discussed in Part III in detail. The ways in which these are combined, by determining the degree of relevance of social class or the areas of social experience in which it is an appropriate attribute, will also regulate by implication the amount of "class consciousness" observable in any particular context. Thus will differences in degree of "class consciousness" in the social relations of the three universities be explained in terms of the variables operating in the overall situation. The fact that degree of "studentness" conversely is also regulated by the operations of the same factors may

[1] *Ibid.*, p. 129.

mean that student itself means different things in different university contexts. This has implications for the organisation of student political activity and for the ease or difficulty with which an awareness of common studentness and solidarity can be encouraged. This will later be discussed.

The following chapter will attempt to sum up the theories which may be abstracted from the empirical evidence and to suggest situations which may be "defined" in terms of the attributes discussed. It seems clear on the basis of available statistical and qualitative evidence that social class is a significant factor in students social relations and that students realise this, but that the relevance of social class depends on the way in which the institutional organisation and situations are defined. The definition of the situation will depend on the other factors with which it is combined. The variables which *define* the situational space and which determine *when* social class is relevant will be discussed in Part III.

This, of course, in turn will lead us to explanations of certain patterns of student behaviour—both within the institution in relations of students with each other and also outside the institutional framework in relations between students and non-students. This latter category, of course, comprehends peer group, family and intergenerational relations. It is clear that what goes on within and outside the institution of higher education cannot entirely be separated.

CHAPTER 8

THE RELEVANCE OF SOCIAL CLASS IN DEFINED SOCIAL SITUATIONS

THE last chapter has shown that social class is a significant factor in students' social relations. Yet the qualification which must be added, and which considerably redefines the nature of the problem investigated, is that social class is not *always* a factor in social relations nor is it seen so to be by actors in various situations. Sometimes social class is taken into account in role performance and sometimes it is not. The reason for this would seem to be because different social situations require cognisance of different attributes of the persons acting in them. The theoretical implications of this argument will be considered later in the chapter.

In the previous chapters we have examined the relations of persons with common attributes, i.e. social class as an attribute. If, however, one were to attempt to discover ways in which the particular attributes are meaningful at certain times, i.e. ways in which they become appropriate indicators of interactional response, then one would need to isolate certain defined situations and observe which attributes are taken into account in social behaviour and which are not.[1] In this way one would discover *how* the situation is defined in terms of the appropriate attributes. Such a study is beyond the limitations of the present, largely statistical, survey—yet some indications have been gained from analysis of variables in the wider context as to what factors may influence the definition of situations at the interpersonal level. These factors in the wider context will now be examined, for they would seem to suggest that within the institutional context configurations of variables occur and are defined as in the interpersonal situation writ large, with the same principles of organisation at work.

---

[1] Gross, N., Mason, N. S., and McEachern, A. W., *Explorations in Role Analysis*, John Wiley, 1958, p. 63. A role can be segmented into expectations for behaviours and expectations for attributes.

Indeed, we may begin to separate out some of the interdependent factors in operation at various contextual levels of a situation in order to understand the framework of constraints or what Talcott Parsons calls "conditions" within which certain situationally inevitable social dilemmas are posed and solved or left unsolved. Parsons speaks of the analysis of the situation into two elements: "those over which the actor has no control, that is which he cannot alter, or prevent from being altered, in conformity with his end, and those over which he has such control. The former may be termed the 'conditions' of action—the latter the 'means'."[1] In the study of conditions it is important to examine series of action or units of action and roles in orientation to other roles, as in the "relational specification of a position",[2] only as they relate to the social contexts themselves in which roles are structured, played, and changed. Such contextual conditions as have been outlined may be presented by the actual presence or absence of persons or groups with particular attributes within a defined institutional setting. We have seen some of the consequences of such conditions on the actual or putated behaviour of students as members of social classes in university. The areas of action over which the actor has control, his "means" are in fact defined to a large extent by those over which he has no control—the "conditions" (which in this case may be seen as various features of the composite groups in the student body). In effect there is an area of potential interaction in which every "situation" takes place—an area limited by constraints and predispositions of various kinds—which prestructures the area of choice and *contains* it. One may see for instance that spatial, cultural, and temporal factors delimit the boundary area by delimiting, though clearly *not determining*, the area or number of potential contacts and the relevant attributes of those social contacts. Physical areas of boundaries of interaction are especially important in that not only do all groups have a physical location which circumscribes their identity as well as their size, but space and distance put real constraints upon patterns of association. It therefore becomes necessary in discussing these factors in social relations to talk about *situational space*[3] or that social and physical space in which situations are structured and perceived. The relation of actors or groups of actors within situational space is the real or perceived physi-

[1] Parsons, Talcott, *The Structure of Social Action*, Free Press, Glencoe, Ill., 1949, p. 45.

[2] Gross *et al.*, *op. cit.*, p. 62.

[3] Author's terminology.

cal and social distance between persons in a situation, and between persons and their reference groups—these distances being expressed in their relationships.[1] Let us now consider some structural relations of the social classes in the survey which demonstrate the points made.

It would seem from an analysis of all available evidence of the surveys that the relations of the social classes within the university are regulated and defined by the size, "nature" (or complex of identities) and degree of contact of the social classes within the university. It is necessary to give examples before this point is developed further and to show the way in which these represent major "conditions" of inter-group situations.

With regard, firstly, to the size of the social classes within the university, it is clear that contact of members of social classes and consequent mutual adaptation and transmission of elements of social class culture is to some extent regulated by the number of *potential* contacts available in any one context. As a result, whether a minority group social class is assimilated into the predominant social class or whether it maintains a separate identity depends on its size *relative* to the other social classes. We have seen, for instance, how the English working class in Edinburgh University, besides being an aspiring group, is also *small* enough to be easily assimilated into the middle-class student body, whereas the Scottish working class is too big to be so assimilated and enculturated into middle-class norms. Other factors enter into this situation which will in turn be analysed.

Secondly, the "nature" of the social classes themselves to some extent defines the areas of social relations in which students as members of social classes interact. By "nature" is meant the particular dimension of social class as a multidimensional reality which predominates in any particular context—such as socioeconomic or educo-cultural class—and within this social class the kinds and number of cultural subdivisions which exist and are meaningful. These subdivisions refer to the cultural configurations discussed in Chapters 4, 5 and 6 in terms of, for instance, national and regional divisions, which are both cultural and spatial, family educational traditions and values, students own schooling, and so on. Where these subdivisions are closely overlaid so that their boundaries coincide with social class boundaries, then they serve to accentuate social class identities and dissimilarities. Where there is much cross-

---

[1] Ability to manipulate distance between roles differs for members of different social classes. See Ford, J., Young, D. and Box, S., Functional autonomy role distance and social class, *BJS*, **18** (4), Dec. 1967, pp. 370–81.

cutting of these subdivisions so that boundaries are blurred, social class becomes one of a whole "shatterbelt zone"[1] of identities and its influence in social relations in the total context is diminished or ambiguous. This is one of the reasons why social classes in Edinburgh University seem to be more easily identified and a more significant social division than they do in Newcastle University. In the former context, "school", "region", family educational tradition tend to coincide—as in the upper middle class—whereas in the latter they do not closely coincide, even in the upper middle class, and this leads to confusion of indices.

The third and perhaps most cogent influence on social class relations is the degree of contact which they have with one another within the institutional context. If there is no contact there can be no social relations. This may be expressed in both a cultural and spatial sense, primarily the latter. For example, the Scottish working-class students who live at home are cut off in a number of ways both culturally and spatially from the predominantly middle-class student body. As a result their social relations with other students are culturally restricted and confined to certain areas of contact in work and leisure, which again has spatial connotations. An indirect effect of this situation is that perception of "the others" is based on little evidence and gives way in some cases to unfounded and prejudiced generalisations. These in turn regulate future contacts and social relations. The "perception" itself is a symptom of the structural relationships which the members of these social classes have within the institutional context, and may influence interpersonal interaction.

The size, nature, and degree of contact of the social classes, therefore not only influences their relations within the student body but influences them through the effect which it has upon the student's perception of the situation in that he acts in terms of that perception. This is true of interaction within the wider context and at the small group level. For example, as has been observed, Newcastle University gives all the appearance of being a largely "working-class" university with respect to the predominating attitudes and mores of its members, this despite the fact that in terms of statistical proportions of social classes it is no less middle class than a middle-class university. One major reason why the situation

[1] Term used in urban ecology literature to describe certain functional sectors of towns undergoing change under encroachment of other sectors and resulting in functional diversity, cultural heterogeneity and breakdown of distinctive character. The term is given here a social meaning.

is different in Newcastle, where the upper middle-class public schoolboy "with a posh accent" may feel the odd man out in certain circles, may be that at least in residential terms the upper middle-class students have reduced influence on the total student body because so many of them live at home—38 per cent upper middle-class students live at home compared with 30 per cent lower middle-class and 24 per cent working-class students. If one considers the reduced contact which this represents, one can readily see that at certain times the university area will feel the impact of a predominantly working-class and lower middle-class student body. In addition, 16 per cent of the upper middle-class men and 11 per cent of the upper middle-class women are members of the Medical School which is largely separate from the rest of the student body, and in which working-class students comprise only 16 per cent of the total student population. This will tend to "remove" middle-class influence from the rest of the student body. This example shows the influence of *spatial* concentration on social relations in areas of "residence" and "work".

In this particular example it is the *spatial* factor which predominates over actual size of the group and its cultural features. Thus social relations are regulated by what is *perceived* to be the comparative sizes of the social class rather than their actual size.

Another example of the ways in which "perception" is influenced by factors of size, nature, and contact of groups, is the confusion among the working-class students—particularly Scottish—in Edinburgh University about the proportion of English students and their activities within the student body. It is often remarked by Scottish working-class students that "the damned English" run all the societies and no doubt this influences their social relations in certain spheres of university life. Yet in terms of *statistical* proportions it is seen to be the upper middle-class *Scottish* students who predominate in the running of student affairs. However, many of these students have anglicised accents and have been to public schools—often English. Because of these confusing cultural attributes, they are confused with English students—and the reduced contact which Scottish working-class students have with them in terms of student activities because they themselves live at home does not allow the misconception to be dispelled.

This instance, one of a number discussed, of confusion of expectations of behaviour on the basis of particular attributes, raises the important issue of *interstitial situations*. These situations are those in which persons or categories of persons come into a situation or a preliminary encounter with only inadequate prior knowledge of the other persons or categories of persons in the situation,[1] or with differing expectations of attributes involved. The particular type of interstitial situation with which we are here concerned is not that completely anomic and normless situation in which there is *no* structure of expectations, or in which "clues" and attributes are misread because of *lack* of knowledge or expectation—but that in which "clues" or "attributes" *mean* different things to different people so that their expectations do not *mesh*—or, indeed, may conflict. The clues are understood but understood in different ways because of both the membership groups and reference groups involved for different persons. Such a clue is "accent" which may be "read" as an indicator of nationality, region of home residence, social class or education, or combinations of these depending on syntax and vocabulary. A misreading, or a differing "reading" of the implications will determine responses of various kinds and may well lead to a breakdown of relations or a situation of unease and ambiguity in which exploratory or stylised behaviour takes place.[2] We see this in some of the social situations in which members of different social classes are involved. One may see, in fact, that for a number of students who come to university with only stereotypes of members of other cultural groups there are a variety of *interstitial situations* within the institution in which the real or perceived distances or spaces between relationships of such groups are adjusted in terms of situational space. How such situations become structured in terms of at least minimal consensus of expectations or at what point the situation "cracks" into avoidance, will affect future responses to the given "clues" or attributes.

Thus the spatial and cultural factors outlined combine in different ways within different social contexts to influence social relations of the social classes in terms of *how* they perceive the situation. And in that the situation is real for them, then it is in fact real. "If men define their situations as real they are real in their consequences."[3] The students act

---

[1] See Weinstein, E., The development of interpersonal competence, in Goslin, D. A. (ed.), *Handbook of Socialization Theory and Research*, Rand McNally, 1969.

[2] Garfinkel carried out demonstrations in which actors purposefully misread situations and thwarted the expectations of others—producing anxiety and anger. Garfinkel, H., Trust and stable actions, in Harvey, O. J., *Motivation and Social Interaction*, Rand McNally, 1963.

[3] Referred to by Merton as the "Thomas theorem" after its originator, W. I. Thomas. Merton, R. K., *Social Theory and Social Structure*, 1957, p. 421.

in terms of what they believe to be the situation and by their action and interaction constantly influence and redefine the situation. We have discussed the implications for social relations at the level of intergroup relations within the total institutional framework, but naturally this has repercussions through a series of interlocking contexts down to relations at small group and interpersonal level by ordering perception of meaningful attributes and the development of social class stereotypes.

> Men respond not only to the objective features of the situation, but also and at times primarily to the meaning this situation has for them. And once they have assigned some meaning to the situation their consequent behaviour and some of the consequences of that behaviour are determined by that ascribed meaning.[1]

It is the means in which persons interpret and respond to those situations that we must examine for, as Merton points out, the way in which people behave in terms of the perceived situation is in the nature of a "self-fulfilling prophecy".

> The mechanism of the self-fulfilling social belief in which confident error generates its own spurious confirmation bears a close theoretical connection with the concept of latent function. Both are types of unanticipated consequences of action or decision or belief, the one producing the very circumstances erroneously assumed to exist, the other producing results which were not intended at all.[2]

We have ample evidence of the self-fulfilling prophecy in the "image building" of the three universities which students internalise and promote and which influences behaviour as a perceived social situation witness— as we have just discussed—the working-class mores of Newcastle and the public school withdrawal or adaptation and the reverse situation in Durham where it is the working-class student who feels pressure to conform to middle-class ways—in each case a feature of perceived situation rather than statistical norms.

The factors of size, nature, and degree of contact of social classes which operate within the total context of the university in a manner which affects perception and regulates social relations in the nature of a self-fulfilling prophecy are the same which operate to different degrees in all contexts of social behaviour within the university. The size, nature, and degree of contact of social classes within a college or a hall of residence will affect social relations of students in the same way as they do within the total institution. As if on a continuum, these factors will differ in degree though not kind, as we shall see in Part III.

---

[1] Merton, R. K., *Social Theory and Social Structure*, 1957, pp. 128, 421.
[2] *Ibid.*, p. 128.

It may be said that the spatial and cultural concentrations defined by the interaction of the factors in social relations outlined above delimit the areas of interaction of members of social classes in both a social and physical sense. Within this social area or situational space the actors define the situation itself in terms of the attributes of the persons involved. For the situations are, in effect, structures of attributes.

The present analysis in terms of the evidence presented can suggest the factors which delimit the situational space and therefore the *range* of appropriate attributes—it cannot give any evidence of the mechanism by which attributes are actually selected as relevant in defined situations. This is the task of role analysis.

In order to discover something of the process of selection of appropriate attributes, one would need to select defined situations and examine which attributes are brought into play. This approaches the study of social relations from another direction, as it were, than that taken by role theory, where situations are constructed from the interactions of persons performing roles.[1] The analysis of situational patterns would give an indication of role *changes* and processes of role playing in terms of social class in both an attributional and interactional sense. This latter distinction will be discussed later. This would give some idea of the nature of social relations in general, and the way in which certain attributes are selected as meaningful by individuals—attributes of themselves and others. This analysis would show *what actually* happens in a dynamic sense within the general contexts examined and the delimited areas of situational space.

An attempt at analysis of situational patterning by Kohn and Williams[2] gives insights into the way that situations are structured by those within them. However, in that they controlled not only the "situation" but the "attribute" whose relevance they wanted to test, their experiment is only of restricted validity. Kohn and Williams make the point, spoken of earlier in terms of the empirical data, that *appropriate* behaviour changes in time in response to further interpretation of clues and build-up of experience.

In unpatterned situations there are *degrees* of appropriate conduct in a process of change where there is a growing uncertainty about what is

---

[1] For an overview see Biddle, B. J. and Thomas, E. J., *Role Theory Concepts and Research*, Wiley, New York, 1966.

[2] Kohn, I. and Williams, R., Situational patterning in intergroup relations, *ASR*, 1956, **21**, 164.

"appropriate" behaviour. Kohn and Williams conducted a study to discover the process by which "unpatterned" situations become *defined* by participants. They initiated forty-three situations in which they could observe, systematise, and analyse the components of the situation.

The actual situations focused on service establishments, particularly restaurants. Usual patterns of behaviour in serving customers, i.e. the normal customer–proprietor relationship was observed. Then Negro "stimulus participants" were introduced into the situation, and they and a White observer recorded events and impressions. The Negro represented an easily defined and perceived social component of the situation—in Talcott Parson's sense in that persons, objects and self are all social components of a goal-oriented situation.

In the situations presented it appeared that the participants attempted to achieve "cognitive clarity" by striving to assimilate the situation to their *past, actual, or vicarious experience* (author's italics), i.e. to categorise it as one of a *type* of situations with which they knew how to cope.

Confusion resulted from a wide range of possible degrees of inability to see any structure in the situation. (Here also we see the influence of personality and *use* made of past experience.) Clues were sought from (a) a leader, or (b) from anyone or everyone by degrees. The orientation of *confusion* was noted to differ from that of *contradiction*.

The interpretation of the situation depended on *prestige status*. The Negro was least secure and most sensitive to minimal clues (as a working-class student in a middle-class environment? or vice versa?). Conflict was resolved by (a) assigning priority to one *degree* of the situation more often than to others (the author would speak of attribute), or (b) a compromise solution in terms of norms of reference group, or (c) withdrawal or wavering.

A redefinition of the situation was not gained by conflict, which tended to reinforce a previous definition, but by a gradual process by which each new situation is viewed in the light of the previous situation. In time the participants change their reference. A new reference group and a new self-conception result, and with them a change in expectations and consequences.

The results of this study have much to show us in explaining the significance of situational patterning in which social class is the meaningful attribute corresponding to the "colour" or "race" attribute in the Kohn and Williams survey, although less visible. They show us particularly that within what the author calls "situational space" there is a defined area of *perception* of the actors of attributes of both persons and physical situation which result in a patterning or *defining* of the situation. Goffman calls this a "region" and says that: "A region may be defined as a place that is bounded to some degree by the barriers to perception. Regions vary, of course, in the degree to which they are bounded and according to the media of communication in which the barriers to perception occur."[1] Of the actor in the "region", he says: "The impression and understanding fostered by the performance will then tend, as it were, to saturate the region and time span, so that any individual located in this time-span manifold will be in a position to observe the definition of the situation which the performance fosters."[2]

For in defining a social situation, the individual perceives as relevant:

(i) certain of his own attributes;

(ii) the attributes of A (as opposed to B or C—the definition in terms of persons involved);

(iii) the *specific* attributes of A (as opposed to any other attributes of A which may be relevant in other social situations).

We must ask *what* is seen to be relevant and *why* it is relevant in this particular situation. What is seen to be relevant is determined for the individual (X) by X's perception of A as opposed to B and C, i.e. that they *are* different, and by X's perception of *why* and in *what way* A is different in this situation, and which of A's attributes are relevant in terms of the situation, in terms of X's previous actual or vicarious experience. In a sense this is a tautology, yet it emphasises the circular or spiral adaptivity of behaviour to situations and situations to behaviour.

The fact that identification of roles in terms of specific attributes is a problem to the actor in the situation as well as to the sociologist undertaking structural analysis is demonstrated by the importance of uniform,[3] for instance, and all other *visible* clues, and by the significant necessity of

---

[1] Goffman, E., *The Presentation of Self in Everyday Life*, University of Edinburgh, Social Sciences Research Centre Monograph No. 2, 1958, p. 66.

[2] Goffman, *op. cit.*

[3] Wood, S. N., Uniform—its significance as a factor in role-relationships, *Social Rev.*, July 1966, **14** (2). See also Banton, M. P., *Roles: An Introduction to the Study of Social Relations*, Tavistock Publications, London, 1965, p. 94; Wood: "Uniform may be seen then to contribute to the formation maintenance and alteration of the individual's conception of self, by making clear the announcement as individual makers of his role, and by enabling an explicit placement of that individual to be made."

rites of passage[1] to mark movement from one structural or ascribed role to another where it is of importace for the whole social system.

Yet again, a social situation does not exist except in terms of the persons within it. Persons in a certain relationship make up a social situation—rather a social situation is made up of persons relevant with attributes relevant to that particular social situation, which is already defined by the persons involved in terms of socially meaningful persons and attributes. Again tautological in that A perceives certain of B's attributes to be meaningful only in terms of their relationship which, in turn, is meaningful only with reference to and in terms of certain attributes of B and C.

The circle of this argument can only be broken—and then only partially—if we bring in the concept of a point of reference *beyond* the immediate situation which, as it were, acts as a lode star for the individual and orientates his attitudes and behaviour in a particular course at a particular time. In a sense it would be true to say that the circular argument still remains although it is widened in scope and comprehends a larger configuration of variables having basis in the wider social structure.

Of reference groups, Merton says that they

> are in principle almost innumerable: any of the groups of which one is a member, and these are comparatively few, as well as groups of which one is not a member, and these are, of course, legion, can become points of reference for shaping one's attitudes, evaluations and behaviour.[2] This, then, locates a further problem: if *multiple* groups or statuses, with their possibly divergent or even contradictory norms and standards are taken as a frame of reference by the individual how are these discrepancies to be resolved?

In the study of the student body one is dealing with *multiple* groups or statuses in which "student" is only one of many—which includes male, female, social class, school, and member of region. Thus in considering influence of social class in choice of friends, students differentiate between situations in which different *secondary* or contingent reference groups come into play.[3] The choice of close friends of opposite sex involves a situation of multiple reference groups *par excellence* and one in which, as Merton says, certain discrepancies have to be resolved. This may often cause individual unease, as seen in the Zweig observations.[4]

---

[1] See Van Gennep, A., *The Rites of Passage* (tr. Vizedom, N. B. and Caffee, C. L.), Routledge, London, 1960.

[2] Which relate to what Gouldner calls "latent social identities". Gouldner, A., Organisational analysis, in Merton, R. K., Broom, L. B. and Cottrell, L. S. (Jr.), *Sociology Today*, ch. 18, New York, Harper and Row, 1965.

[3] Merton, *op. cit.*, p. 233.

[4] Zweig, F., *The Student in the Age of Anxiety*, Heinemann, 1963.

Says Merton, "There is, however, the further fact that men frequently orientate themselves to groups *other than their own* in shaping their behaviour and evaluation and it is the problems centred about this fact of orientation to non-membership groups that constitute the distinctive concern of reference group theory."[1]

Banton deals with similar observations in an empirical study of "Social alignment and identity in a West African city"—again, an appropriate study in our analysis of student social relations. He speaks of identities where we have spoken of "attributes", but the principle is inherently the same. Speaking of the immigrant he says: "Is he able to modify the set of choices and forge an identity more acceptable to himself? If he does this then the pattern of *group alignments* will be affected."[2]

The same could be said of students who pass through a community at once alike and not alike and presented with a bewildering choice of identities—the more bewildering because there is more choice about the matter.

Banton says that the immigrant (like the student) is not absorbed into the urban system by a process of individual change in line with the melting-pot conception of assimilation, but through his membership in a local group of people drawn from his own tribe (i.e. school, locality, class, etc.), and that the definition of these groups and the things which symbolise them are determined by a pattern of *structural opposition*. Banton also says that "we have to look for the *sorts of incidents* that stimulate group alignment and how these incidents are generated".[3] What we have observed in operation among students is something rather in between Merton's "reference groups" and Banton's "group alignment" and yet owing much in formulation to both.

Merton acknowledges the difficulties in defining *how* and *why* reference groups as such become relevant to a given situation and says that

> Some simulants in status attributes between the individual and the reference group must be perceived or imagined. Once this minimal similarity obtains other similarities and differences pertinent to the situation will provide the context of shaping evaluations. Consequently, this focusses the attention of the theorist immediately upon the factors which produce the sense of pertinent similarity

[1] Merton, *op. cit.*, p. 233.

[2] Banton, M. P., Social alignment and identity in a West African city, paper prepared in advance for participants in Symposium No. 26, Wenner-Gren Foundation for Anthropological Research, 1964, p. 4.

[3] *Ibid.*, p. 28.

between statuses since this will help to determine which groups are called into play as comparative contexts. The underlying similarities of status among members of ingroups, singled out by Mead, as the social context, thus appear as only one special though obviously important basis for the selection of reference groups.[1]

In the student context we must ask what is meant by "minimal similarity" and whether this can be fully applied. For "pertinent similarity between statuses" does not comprehend in its rather one-dimensional frame of reference the multidimensional and multibonded character of both social class and student. In a sense these represent both membership and reference groups writ large in which smaller reference groups operate, and it is pertinent to ask if reference group theory can therefore be used as more than a partial explanation.

This would seem to be because we are dealing with clusters of statuses, and clusters of cultural variables when we analyse the categories "student" and "social class", and it is almost impossible to isolate any *one* of these variables because of their interdependent relation with one another—as we have already discussed.[2] It would seem in principle that certain variables are always related under these umbrella categories, but that the way in which they are related may change with the context or definition of the situation, and the weighting given to each in relation to the others may concomitantly change with perception and definition. Thus is the attribute itself not only meaningful in terms of a defined situation, but its relation to other attributes in fact *defines* the situation—they are inseparable components of social interaction.

In consequence, social class as it relates to the social person in the student body is an *attribute*, i.e. it is a quality which is present or absent. As it related to the situation, however, it is a variable and may be present to a greater or lesser extent—or perceived to be so.[3] As a result all such qualities are relative in some degree to the situation defined, so that not only may social class vary in relevance with situation, but its dimensions as such may vary in relevance. Therefore any analysis of social class in social

---

[1] Merton, *op. cit.*, pp. 242–3.

[2] See Merton, R. K., The role set: problems in sociological theory, *BJS*, **8**, 1957.

[3] Ossowski, S., *Class Structure in the Social Consciousness* (Int. Lib. of Sociol. and Soc. Reconstr.), Routledge and Kegan Paul, London, 1963 (trans. from the Polish by Sheila Patterson), p. 149, quotes Llewellyn Gross, The use of the class concept in social research, *AJS*, March 1949: "An *attribute* refers to a quality which has an all or none existence. A *variable* refers to quality which exists in varying degrees."

relations must take into account the other social factors present in the situation, for this will define the *areas* of validity of the conclusions.

For, indeed, in Shutz's terms there may be "multiple realities"[1] rather than one reality, or a "spread of truth",[2] which may seem ambivalent though not necessarily conctradictory.

Thus Oppenheim's observations on the influence of social class in clique formation in grammar schools,[3] and Jackson's and Marsden's apparently contradictory evidence[4] on the same subject may *both* be true and merely different aspects of the same phenomenon in *differently defined situations*.

Oppenheim failed to discover clique formation along lines of social class in a sociometric study of a number of grammar schools. Jackson and Marsden came to the conclusion that for the working-class children "their basic loyalties were local loyalties" and that in the "fuller social life" school was "hardly relevant".[5] In consequence the "rebels left", and even of those who did remain a large number "stand out uncompromisingly against the grammar school ethos", joined together by a "very tight mesh of friendship".[6]

At first sight these findings would appear to be contradictory, and yet we have to be sure of the *context* in which these relationships are set before wider conclusions can be drawn. As Halsey has said: "How a working class boy behaves in a working class grammar school differs from the way he behaves in a middle class grammar school",[7] i.e. the contexts are different, the situations are different, and the configurations of variables involved may well be different. So that it well may be that both findings are valid within the limitations set by their own contextual analysis and the parameters which they tacitly or explicitly accept.

This kind of analysis is relevant to the university situation where the factors of social class composition, strength of external divisions, and strength of locality ties operate in a complex configuration of variables which varies with external context. In the comparative analysis the attempt is made to compare contexts and internal situation in order to discover certain facets of the "multiple realities" of the student's social relations.

---

[1] Shutz, A., On multiple realities, in Nakanson, M. (ed.), *Collected Papers 1: The Problem of Social Reality*, Martinus Nijhoff, The Hague, 1962.

[2] Tropp, A., personal communication.

[3] Oppenheim, A. N., *BJS*, 1955, **6**, 288–45.

[4] Jackson, B. and Marsden, D., *Education and the Working Class*, 1962.

[5] *Ibid.*, p. 106.

[6] *Ibid.*, p. 103.

[7] Halsey, A. H., in discussion, BSA Exeter Summer School, 24 July 1965.

That this is extremely difficult is acknowledged, particularly since the one-dimensional tool of occupational status is being used to reveal the multidimensional phenomenon of social class, so that much has to be inferred. Indeed, what is often suggested is a series of logically possible relations some of which must still be proved to exist.

Thus it may be that Marris's findings on student attitudes to social class are true in certain defined situations in one context; Zweig's in another, and the findings of the present survey in yet another. Marris says of students that "The University by its autonomy and detachment enabled them to postpone questions of class identity".[1] Certainly, this question is not untrue—yet it is not *always* true and is *dependent* upon certain conditions. Analysis of those necessary conditions reveals that apparent contradictions, ambivalences, and compromises may be reconciled meaningfully within a social framework which comprehends dynamic aspects of behaviour. The dilemmas and inconsistencies inherent in the relations are at once symptoms of structure and aspects of change.

Zweig, for instance, quotes students as saying that they hate the idea of class distinctions, that they are generally reluctant to class themselves, and that classes are ceasing to be important.[2] Elsewhere he says that out of 81 students, 30 students "definitely declined any suggestion that they might marry beneath their class", in terms such as "It wouldn't work", "It would be difficult to get on", and so on. He concludes that this would show that "many students drew a distinction between views held on general grounds and their own personal attitudes".[3] Yet even this is too great a generalisation which he does not explain further. Neither set of views is incomprehensible in terms of the other if one considers them in terms of the structure in which they are expressed. As a property of the social structure the antagonism to social class is as meaningful as the tacit acceptance of it—especially as both would seem to imply behaviour appropriate in *different* contexts. Marriage implies a variety of special social contacts and situations not generally inherent in the vague "student" situation, and, as we have seen from the survey results, arouses a different response in students than considerations of student acquaintances. This is not only meaningful but crucial to any understanding of social class as a factor in social relations. Cohen suggests that it is not always easy to distinguish affects and modes of cognition which mingle to structure the perception

[1] Marris, P., *The Experience of Higher Education*, London, 1964, p. 156.
[2] Zweig, *op. cit.*, p. 40.
[3] *Ibid.*, p. 67.

of social situations and are in turn mobilised by the situation itself. "In some conditions the readiness to express an affective attitude may be influenced by the existence of categories, in other conditions the connection may be the reverse one. For most purposes the readiness both to 'cathect' and to categorise in certain ways is influenced by the qualities of the objects in situations as they are experienced by the actors."[1]

In this survey the author started by delimiting her social system in terms of "student" attribute with its subsystems of social classes and is now in the position to form hypotheses about the social situations, though not necessarily to prove them. A survey designed specially for this task would be necessary to fill in the gaps which now remain only too obvious.

Nevertheless, it would appear that the theoretical abstractions from the empirical data of the surveys could in principle be applied in a variety of social situations, and may have something to contribute to the delimiting of the situations at the level of interpersonal relations where similar kinds of social and cultural factors may apply. As has already been pointed out, the research design did not permit an investigation of interpersonal relations in the sense of actual role performance which could be defined and measured.[2] However, it may be possible that the findings on the interaction of cultural and spatial factors in the definition of the external situation may as principles of interaction be applied also to smaller groups in the internal, but related, situations. The analysis of the delimiting of the situational space in terms of cultural and spatial concentrations may have relevance here along with the finding that the degree of coincidence of cultural and spatial concentrations determines the degree of clarity with which the situational space is defined.

The preoccupation with social, physical, and ecological space will be explained in the light of empirical data in Chapter 9. Suffice it to say at this point that all these are crucial to any definition of the "situation". Again, it is not possible to discuss, as do Goffman[3] and Hall,[4] the *interpersonal* space—we may only infer from evidence of intergroup space.

[1] Cohen, P., *Modern Social Theory*, Basic Books, New York, 1968, p. 77.

[2] See Banton, M. P., *Roles: An Introduction to the Study of Social Relations*, Tavistock Publications, London, 1965, pp. 21–22, 25–29. The author would reiterate what Banton has said that: "Those [classifications] which concern us here are the classifications of roles in terms of the social structure and not those belonging on the level of cognitive or personality structure" (p. 29).

[3] Goffman, *op. cit.*

[4] Hall, E. T., *The Silent Language*, Fawcett Publications Inc., Greenwich, Conn. 1959.

Intergroup space seems to be associated closely with actual "places" in a sense of *physical* space—the concentration of interest, work, or residence group has a base which helps to define for it the situation, and also helps the definition by others. Findings have in fact shown that there are senses in which expectations regarding conduct come to be associated with particular places,[1] i.e. the place in itself becomes a variable attribute of the situation.

The cultural and social concentrations which combine to define situational space have been delimited for convenience to the areas of work, leisure, and university residence. These demonstrate the complexities of the realities studied because in themselves they are at different times (a) spatial, cultural concentrations; (b) situations; (c) external points of reference; (d) attributes of *other* situations.

These aspects will be dealt with later in the following chapters.

The degree of spatial and cultural concentration determines whether what we are considering is attributional or interactional social class, or indeed attributional or interactional studentness. In the main, we have discussed only "attributional" social class in the student body, but there are conditions under which this may become interactional.

Although it is clear that social classes as communities or quasi-communities can and do exist it is only in certain circumstances which must be clearly defined. Otherwise they constitute in Merton's terms a cultural or social category which are aggregates of social statuses the occupants of which are not in social interaction. These have *like* social characteristics, but are not necessarily orientated towards a distinctive and *common* body of norms. Thus social classes in general terms may be:

(a) *Groups:* "large numbers of people among the greatest part of whom there is no social interaction although they do share a body of social norms",[2] i.e., "quasi-communities"; or
(b) *Collectivities:* "people who have a sense of solidarity by virtue of sharing common values and who have acquired an attendant sense of moral obligation to fulfil role expectations", i.e. communities with collective representations; or
(c) *Social categories:* as just described.

---

[1] Wright, H. F. and Barker, R. G., *Methods in Psychological Ecology*, Ray's Printing Service, Topeka, Kansas, 1950.
[2] Merton, *op. cit.*, p. 299.

The student's past, actual, or vicarious experience of social class both inside and outside the university may be rooted in any one or combination of these types of social class and may influence his behaviour and attitudes accordingly.[1] (This is discussed in Chapter 13.) Thus social class experience *outside* as well as inside the university is an important indicator of patterns of social relations and may lead in some cases to *interstitial situations*. It is clear that reference group theory alone cannot comprehend the totality and variety of this experience which may operate synchronically and syncretically rather than in spatial and temporal sequence or opposition. Littlejohn says that class is "an area within which most experience is defined".[2] Among students one looks for the experience which is *not* defined by the area of social class and the experience *not* defined by the area student. "Area" perhaps conveys more than reference group in that it may comprehend reference groups within it. Therefore one looks also for situations in which reference group itself is relevant as an explanation.

It is clear that in the student context we are looking at instances of both attributional and interactional social classes which refer back to social class in any one of its many forms. Since occupational status is one-dimensional we may have distorted some aspects in the analysis which cannot be got at otherwise but by a one-dimensional tool. Since occupational status is linked so intimately to other statuses, it is a fruitful representation since it implies a meaningful cluster or configuration of variables.

Although we attempt to analyse the multidimensional nature of social class we do not assume it to be a quasi-community, i.e. an interactional class. For this to be true certain conditions are necessary. One of these is the *possibility* of members being *able* to form into a group.[3] This is most possible when the group is concentrated in geographical or spatial areas

---

[1] Particularly as it relates to normative prescriptions and accreditation which is given or withheld for certain performances. See Goffman, E., *Asylums*, Penguin Books, 1968.

[2] Littlejohn, J., *Westrigg: The Sociology of a Cheviot Village*, 1963, p. 111.

[3] Mayer, A. C., The significance of quasi-groups in the study of complex societies, in *The Social Anthropology of Complex Societies*, ed. Banton, M. P., ASA Monograph No. 4, Tavistock Publications Ltd., pp. 97–121. Mayer says of "quasi-groups" that the "classification may be made in terms of the common interest which lie beneath what could also be called a 'potential group' ". He quotes Ginsberg's (1934) definition as "entities without a recognisable structure, but whose members have certain interests or modes of behaviour in common which may at any time lead them to form themselves into definite groups".

In university, students are abstracted from their backgrounds in physical terms, and all clues which go with this, and are brought into association with others of the student community possibly from other backgrounds. Indeed, its very heterogeneity makes it a unique "situation" in which the influence of spatial factors emerges clearly. Thus student becomes the interactional category and social class a point of reference—or reference group—so that class is attributional—a one-dimensional label. However, it is possible for the "collective representations"[1] embodied in the individual to modify his perception of student representations and behaviour as a student.

When, in university context, students of a particular class are concentrated in a spatial or geographical area they become once again an *interactional* class or quasi-community. This obviously has implications for behaviour of students as members of social classes—behaviour both social and political.

An analysis of social class as a factor in student social relations concerns the factors which help the student to define the situations in interactional or attributional terms with regard to "student" and "social class" reference groups. These factors are spatial and residential structure, both of the immediate context, i.e. student residence, faculty organisation, etc., and of the context the student came from and which he refers to in terms of past, actual or vicarious experience as his reference group, i.e. region of home, locality, nation, and other cultural divisions. Other factors spring from socially and culturally spatial groups within the immediate and the wider membership groups, such as educational groups and the actual student groups of which the student is a member or leader. The latter group membership is in turn a feature of external cultural divisions and class value systems as, for instance, in "interest" groups discussed in Chapter 6.

The degree to which external reference groups are brought into consideration in social relations is in turn dependent upon the degree to which the institution isolates itself from external social divisions and is able to set up new and different inequalities. This will be considered in Chapter 11.

All this has implications for the development and internalising of specifically student culture and this will be considered in Chapter 12.

This concludes the summary of points raised by the empirical findings, some of which have been encountered in previous chapters; others are to be discussed in those which follow. It may seem presumptuous to con-

[1] As used by Emile Dunkheim, *Suicide*, Routledge and Kegan Paul (Int. Lib. of Soc. and Soc. Reconstr.), 1952, pp. 312–19.

dense into one short chapter what could form the basis of a whole researc
project, and yet the problems which are left unsolved may indicate th
next stage which research of this kind should take. Most of the problem
discussed in this chapter are not those which the research was designed t
solve, rather were they thrown into relief by the material itself, so tha
although they cannot be discussed in the depth which they otherwis
deserve, it is helpful to mention them here at the midway point.

This chapter links, as it were, two stages in the development of the ar
gument. The preceding chapters have shown that social class is a facto
in students' social relations; the following chapters discuss the spatia
and cultural factors which combine to define situational space in whic
social class is relevant in different degrees.

PART III

CHAPTER 9

SPATIAL FACTORS IN SOCIAL RELATIONS

IN THIS chapter we shall consider the part played by spatial organisation in students' social relations in the spheres of work, leisure, and residence, which represent *overlapping* spatial situations rather than contingent ones. Spatial factors will be seen to operate in social relations in such a way that they accentuate or diminish the relevance of the student's social class identity in varying contexts. The cultural factors with which they are associated will be discussed in Chapter 10. What we are considering cannot in the real world of course be divided into spatial and cultural factors, for it is not only the fact of *separation* which is important in the formation or non-formation of social relationships, but the general character of what is being separated. In this case it is groups of various kinds which are institutionally separated in terms of the very nature of spatial and social organisation of which they are a part. We shall consider these institutionally defined groups: work, leisure, and residence as representing the formal framework within which student social relations are set. In this chapter we shall consider the social and spatial distances between these groups as they contribute to the structure of social relations. If we take the institution as a structural "situation" with component groups in the same way that we have analysed in the last chapter the structure of *interpersonal* space, then one may say that we are trying to set the boundaries of the institutional situational space. Clearly, however, it is not only boundaries and distances which are involved in social relations of groups but the actual *content* of relations in a cultural and social sense. Indeed, the cultural content may well determine how rigidly the boundaries and distances are drawn, so that what we shall discuss in Chapter 10 is intimately associated with the present analysis. Nevertheless, for the purposes of understanding the structure of factors involved we shall concentrate in this chapter mainly on divisions and distances.

We first turn to consideration of the student's social relations in the sphere of *academic work*.

In Chapter 3 the proportions of students in the various faculties of the three universities was shown and some mention has been made of the way that the actual siting of the faculty and departmental buildings stimulates cohesion or division of groups along these lines. Influence of spatial organisation of buildings seems to be fairly obvious in that constant and continual contact with fellow students tends to build up feelings of group solidarity. This is particularly true in departments of science and in medical schools where lectures and laboratory work take up most of the day, so that contact with students of other departments is naturally at a minimum. This being so, students in such work situations often spend leisure hours together also. In this situation, as in the Medical Schools of Edinburgh and Newcastle, a specific student culture or ethos arises which it is possible to perpetuate despite the constant change in personnel. Since the change of personnel in medicine takes place at a much slower rate than in other faculties and after a greater number of years, it is possible for group mores and entrenched traditions to be maintained almost unchanged over time—witness the Medical Sub-Council of the Newcastle University with its own particular brand of student rule, quite different in conception and operation from that of the Newcastle SRC. Edinburgh Medical School also is generally known as the home of conservatism and tradition, and medical students take on the mantle of former glories with great pride.

In arts and social sciences faculties, where lectures are few and opportunities for drinking coffee numerous, the same *esprit de corps* cannot be maintained in quite the same way. In Edinburgh the Arts Faculty is a notable exception to the recent proliferation of faculty scarves which has overcome the University, and which obviously stand as badges of "belonging". The Arts Faculty students mainly wear the University scarf—this is their reference group, much larger and disparate and less easy to identify within the general range of day-to-day relations.

Thus often it seems that arts–science splits among many others are less features of cultural differences inherent in the two disciplines but more a symptom of cultural differences fostered by spatial and organisational divisions. That there are intrinsic differences of approach, language, and method cannot be denied, but it is debatable as to how deep the split need be under conditions favourable to mixing. Students of different disciplines do meet if only there is a common platform on which to do so. This has to be provided.

From faculty and departmental divisions grow certain "images" the like of which have already been discussed. Said one Newcastle undergraduate: "Here we acknowledge that Medics are snobs and Agrics are slobs—it's as simple as that."

But we must ask whether it is "as simple as that". Yet students use these labels in their dealings with each other, and the resulting stereotypes may have a prohibitive effect on the development of student culture and community life, and encourage the growth of faculty subcultures. The growth of specifically departmental "in-group" identity and culture seems closely related to its spatial relation to other university departments. Even inter-departmental antagonism may develop which finds its expression in certain institutionalised ways. In Edinburgh, for instance, at rectorial elections it has always been traditional for "Medics" and Arts Faculty to support rival factions of rectorial nominees. The fracas which ensue are the sign for much good-natured letting off of steam, and are an excuse for going wild with some sanction. Yet there have been some incidents in the past when rivalry has gone too far—people have been hurt and police called in. It is always the opposition of the same factions which gives rise to these fights. Definition of certain groups has become "built-in" to the whole student way of life. And since the particular way in which departmental and faculty groups combine or oppose seems to vary with the institutional context, it cannot merely be a feature of inherent disciplinary differences, but rather the particular way they are organised in spatial and social terms. This, of course, springs originally from certain historical accidents. One cannot help noticing, for instance, that there is less arts–science split in Newcastle where both faculties are more or less side by side than in Durham where they are situated on either side of the river.

In relations of departmental groups—or particular faculties—there seems always to be an indication of status or prestige ranking among students, just as they are conscious in an external context of ranking their own university. And however proud they may be of belonging they are well aware of how their particular department, faculty, or university stands in the ranking of others. (This structural opposition is reminiscent of the fission and fusion principle of non-literate political organisation.)[1]

---

[1] For instance, see Evans-Pritchard, E. E., *The Nuer: A Description of the Modes of Livelihood and Political Institutions of a Nilotic People*, Clarendon Press, Oxford, 1940; Gluckman, M., *Custom and Conflict in Africa*, Blackwell, 1955.

Student Life in a Class Society

Students speak disparagingly of applied science and engineering, while members of these faculties leap to their own defence before a critical word is spoken. And in the criticism by students of what would seem to be an aspect of student culture, there is always an underlying note of what is thought proper in certain social class situations. For example, medics are thought to be halfway or more to being doctors, especially after the clinical year,[1] and they are seen as conservative, middle class, neat in appearance—even over-neat—and well spoken, whereas agrics and engineers are the roughs and toughs, the hard-drinking common men of the university—particularly true in Newcastle where this was almost a matter of pride with some students. How close an approximation are these stereotypes to the actual students in these departments? Are students absorbed into the departmental culture and made into the type they are thought to be?

Firstly, in the Edinburgh survey the author asked students for a prestige ranking of faculties and then analysed the members of faculties in terms of social class of origin. Some interesting comparisons emerged.

TABLE 9.1. SOCIAL CLASS DISTRIBUTION IN THE FACULTIES OF EDINBURGH UNIVERSITY (per cent)

	UC	UMC	LMC	WkC	Unclassified	Total
Arts	—	51	42	56	50	47·5
Divinity	—	—	1·5	2	—	1
Law	50	4	1·5	—	—	2·5
Medicine	—	14	12	6	17	12
Dentistry	—	2	3	—	—	2
Veterinary science	—	2	5	6	17	4
Music	—	1	2	2	—	1·5
Science	50	26	33	27	17	29
TOTAL	100	100	100	99	101	100
No.	(2)	(126)	(140)	(48)	(6)	(322)

[1] This results from the role change involved in contact with "the patient" and his expectations—noted, for instance, by Hughes, E. *et al.*, *Boys in White*, Chicago, 1961.

TABLE 9.1 (*cont.*)

	UC	UMC	LMC	WkC	Unclassi-fied	Total	No.
Arts	—	42	39	18	2	101	153
Divinity	—	—	66	33	—	99	3
Law	13	62	25	—	—	100	8
Medicine	—	46	44	8	2	100	39
Dentistry	—	43	57	—	—	100	7
Veterinary science	—	22	50	22	7	101	14
Music	—	20	60	20	—	100	5
Science	1	34	50	14	1	100	93
TOTAL	·6	39	44	15	2	100·6	322

Table 9.1 shows Edinburgh students in the eight faculties and courses (Dentistry and Veterinary Science courses being taken in separate colleges). The distribution in the sample is unbiased and mirrors almost exactly the distribution in the University.

Firstly, one must note that there are no working-class students in law and dentistry and very few in medicine. It would seem that the professions are still regarded as the prerogatives of the middle class, particularly the upper middle class in the older professions of law and medicine, the lower middle class in the younger one of dentistry. In this particular sample, divinity is the exception with two students of the lower middle class and one working class, and with no upper middle-class divinity students. In this sample at least divinity as a profession seems to have moved down the social scale. This could have something to do with the democracy of the Church of Scotland.

In the newly emerging profession of veterinary science there is a higher proportion of working-class students. All this would seem to show what one might expect that the older a profession the higher the proportion of upper middle-class students training for it and the lower the proportion of working class—this may be a combination of both applications and selection.

The highest proportion of students in any class were in the Arts Faculty—working class 56 per cent—the highest proportion of any one class and the lower middle class the lowest proportion of 42 per cent.

The lower middle class had the highest proportion in the Science Faculty —33 per cent. If one accepts that this is the group with the highest proportion of first-generation university students and that this group seems also as a result to be an ambitious group, one might see this distribution as a reflection of practical aims anchored securely to a course which knows more than the arts "where it's going"—a fact which matters particularly to students lower down the social scale.[1]

If we compare, in the second half of the table, the proportions of the social classes in the total student population with their distribution in particular faculties, we can see what all this means in real terms. As discussed, the working class is significantly underrepresented in law, medicine, and dentistry; in science and arts it reflects closely the overall working-class proportion; and is overrepresented in varying degrees in veterinary science, music, and divinity. As we have seen, it is often *relative* size which is a more important factor than real numbers.

When one considers students actual ranking of faculties it is important to bear in mind that students are guided in their choice by both their own internalised value system, which is largely class based, and also on what they take to be prevailing societal values.

For example, it seems that courses which train people for a profession rank high, whereas the Arts Faculty, particularly the General Arts degree, ranks low because students "don't know where they are going", and tend to "drift into" arts courses without much forethought. The social value of medicine was stressed by many students, particularly those *not* studying medicine, and some thought that those studying science feel superior because "they probably feel unconsciously that they have more practical importance for the country at large" (than the arts).[2] The economic value of taking a science degree was also mentioned.

Those who ranked the Arts Faculty high stressed the breadth of knowledge gained and the independent thought that this encouraged. This contrasted with what they considered the "technical college" mind of the

---

[1] Sandford *et al.*, *Br. J. Educ. Psychol.*, June 1965, **35** (2), *op. cit.*, p. 190. "Working class parents emphasised the view of the importance of job training."

[2] The recent change in the situation in 1967, with the continued swing from science to arts and social science student applications, has been explained by Professor Drew, Professor of Psychology at University College, London, as "a feeling that technology and the physical sciences have outrun man's understanding of man and his capacity to make proper use of modern discoveries and inventions" (Royal Society Symposium on Scientific Manpower). See Crampin, A., *op. cit.*, table 4.

science student. In all cases, the phrase "technical college" was used as a criticism. If one takes a general consensus of views in the Edinburgh sample, one finds that law, dentistry, and medicine—particularly the latter—are ranked high by a majority of students. Science comes next, followed by arts, and finally by veterinary science. Divinity and music tend not to be ranked at all, in keeping with the isolation of these particular faculties. This is in itself an expression of the relation of spatial and social distance.

In the higher ranking courses the social aspects and background of students were stressed, i.e. what "kind" of people they were, although in medicine the fact that they were not regarded as very intelligent but were the hardest working was mentioned also. (This evaluation was also prevalent in Newcastle.) In the lower ranking science courses intelligence of students taking the course and practical application of knowledge was often stressed, whereas in the Arts Faculty and the Veterinary Science course, especially the former, the lack of practical intelligence of students was named as a factor of ranking. Arts students were generally thought to be "pseudo"—verging on "hippie"—who try to show they are "cultured patrons of the arts".

It is a pity that there was no Social Science Faculty at this time in Edinburgh—nor in Durham or Newcastle—since in universities where social science is strong a particular ethos has grown up about social science students which may not entirely be unfounded. Since social science is concerned with the sociological study of society and contemporary issues in society, it is thought that social science students, and lecturers alike, must be particularly socially committed individuals whose sights are set rather more on external social and political events than on the cloistered libraries and lecture halls of the campus. How far this is true is not yet established although it *seems* that social scientists participate more in the running of student affairs than other students and that staff in social science take on more committee work per head in community organisations than other members of staff. Their commitment to social investigation is often interpreted as being interlinked with the espousal of particular causes—usually of a reforming kind. Be that as it may, it is true that in a recent study of 1966 sociology and social anthropology graduates, about half said they had feelings of social commitment and 75 per cent indicated left wing political beliefs.[1] Less than 4 per cent

[1] Abbott, J., *Report on a Survey of Career Patterns of Sociology Graduates*, sponsored by the BSA Sociology Teachers' Section, 1969.

said they were Anarchist, Trotskyist, Marxist, or Communist—which probably compares favourably with other student groups.

The important role of social science students and social science orientated universities in student protest movements of various kinds will be discussed in Chapter 11. How far this situation is seen as a threat by university authorities will also be discussed.

A complex set of factors will be seen to be in operation in students' ranking of faculties:

   (i) the practical material pressures of society;
  (ii) the societal worth of an occupation;
 (iii) the imagined intelligence of those pursuing the course and/or their degree of hard work;
 (iv) the social background of students.

The rank order of students in Edinburgh of the various faculties will be seen to be inversely proportionate to the proportion of working-class students in each faculty—8 per cent, 14 per cent, 18 per cent, and 21 per cent. It is impossible to establish exactly the causal relationship, for again one comes up against the spiral of action and reaction which brings about what was assumed to be true. In such circumstances there are students who fit in and those who do not fit in to the prevailing social pattern. In Edinburgh the higher the faculty in the rank order and the lower the proportion of working-class students, the more frequently was mentioned the class consciousness of its members. For instance, it was often remarked that certain groups in the Medical Faculty were very class conscious, and one girl told of a society called NOCD or "Not Our Class Darling". Her husband had been able to join because he had been to public school, but she was frowned upon slightly, for although upper middle class she had not been to public school. The divisions created by "schools" will be discussed later as they represent further subgroups in the student body.

We shall now examine the social class distribution in the various faculties in Durham and Newcastle to see how these compare with Edinburgh, bearing in mind the general points made (Table 9.2).

One has to bear in mind that due to historical influences a smaller *overall* proportion of students read arts in Newcastle, 24 per cent as opposed to 45 per cent in Durham and 48 per cent in Edinburgh. In Newcastle the proportions have been further broken down by sex, so this throws additional light on the faculty distributions. As in Edin-

TABLE 9.2. SOCIAL CLASS DISTRIBUTION IN THE FACULTIES OF DURHAM AND NEWCASTLE
UNIVERSITIES (per cent)

(a) Durham

	UMC	LMC	WkC	Unclassified	Total
Arts	53	40	43	54	45
Divinity	6	4	4	8	5
Social Science (sub faculty)	13	3	10	—	7
Education	2	7	9	—	6
Science	23	42	34	39	35
Music	3	4	—	—	3
TOTAL	100	100	100	101	101
No.	(101)	(161)	(77)	(13)	(352)

(b) Newcastle

	UMC		LMC		WkC		Unclassified		Total
	M	F	M	F	M	F	M	F	
Arts (inc. Arch.)	13	42	16	44	18	49	34	40	26
Law	4	5	2	1	—	—	—	—	2
Medicine	16	11	11	9	9	6	—	20	11
Dentistry	7	5	5	—	3	3	10	—	5
Agriculture	4	4	8	4	4	3	10	—	5
Applied science	29	—	24	—	28	—	5	—	18
Pure science	23	21	28	31	34	33	33	20	28
Education	—	2	1	4	2	3	4	—	2
Economics and social studies	4	11	5	7	2	3	4	20	5
TOTAL	100	101	100	100	100	100	100	100	101
No.	(142)	(57)	(189)	(91)	(91)	(33)	(21)	(5)	(629)

burgh, a greater proportion of working-class and lower middle-class students in both Newcastle and Durham read Science than do upper middle-class students, who tend to concentrate in the professional faculties. What is perhaps surprising is that in Newcastle—the only sample of which we have sex distributions—as high a proportion of females as males read pure science, although, of course, they represent only a small proportion of the total sample of those reading pure science. The proportion of females reading arts in each social class is almost three times as large as the male proportion, and no females were reading *applied* science.

Working-class men represent only 16 per cent of those reading medicine at Newcastle (12 per cent working-class women), although this is higher than the combined 8 per cent in Edinburgh. There are no working-class students reading law at Newcastle, and they represent only 18 per cent of those reading divinity at Durham—which faculty is more middle-class biased than in Edinburgh.

In Durham 53 per cent of the upper middle-class students were reading arts subjects compared with 51 per cent in Edinburgh and only 27 per cent in Newcastle—this last proportion being comprised mainly of female students. On the whole a greater proportion of working-class students read for arts degrees than do middle-class students, although this is not entirely true in Durham where the upper middle-class students just tip the balance.

On the whole one can see the same pattern emerging that was first seen in Edinburgh—though not so clearly marked. There is a small proportion of working-class students in law, medicine, and dentistry in Newcastle and divinity in Durham, also surprisingly few in agriculture—or rather surprising in view of the remark previously quoted. They are mainly concentrated in science, pure and applied, and education in both Durham and Newcastle—and to some extent social studies in Durham. This latter remark does not apply to Newcastle where there is a preponderance of middle-class students taking economics and social studies. This is not entirely surprising in the light of the study of sociology graduates discussed earlier.

Although it is commonly assumed that sociologists must be marginal men in terms of social background, socially inadequate in some way, and perhaps aspiring, the figures on social class of sociology graduates do not bear out this hypothesis.[1] It was found that 18 per cent were

[1] Abbott, *op. cit.*

working class, 39 per cent lower middle class, 40 per cent upper middle class, and 0·2 upper class, with 3 per cent unclassified. The proportions varied in each institution and were closely related to what has been called the university league table and the structure of the degree course. Social anthropologists tended to be of higher social status than sociologists.

Thus it would appear that certain faculties and/or departments are predominantly middle class or working class in terms of students in them and few represent an unbiased cross-section of the student population. Indeed, if one were to take a sample of courses of study, this picture would change again, as Table 9.3 of Newcastle shows.

TABLE 9.3. SOCIAL CLASS DISTRIBUTION IN THE COURSES OF STUDY—NEWCASTLE UNIVERSITY (per cent)

	UMC		LMC		WkC		Unclassified		Total
	M	F	M	F	M	F	M	F	
Ordinary	4	16	7	18	7	36	33	20	11
Honours	85	79	85	74	79	55	19	20	78
Postgraduate diploma	4	2	3	8	4	3	48	60	6
M.A. or M.Sc.	1	—	1	—	—	3	—	—	1
Ph.D.	6	4	4	1	10	3	—	—	5
TOTAL	100	101	100	101	100	100	100	100	101
No.	(142)	(57)	(189)	(91)	(91)	(33)	(21)	(5)	(629)

In these tables it may be seen that a higher proportion of female students than male take ordinary degree courses and a lower proportion of them take postgraduate courses. A higher proportion of working-class students than middle class take both ordinary degree courses and post-graduate courses, which would seem to show a different kind of distribution curve from that of the middle class in terms of ability and/or inclination. For instance, 10 per cent of the male working-class sample were studying for Ph.D. degrees compared with 6 per cent upper middle class and 4 per cent lower middle class. In interview some of these students, mainly in the science faculties, confessed that they were not entirely happy in their subject and yet they had got into the way of achieving and passing exams so that once on the treadmill they could not get off and could not think of anything else to do. Research seemed the only possibility. This despite the fact that postgraduate grants are so paltry by comparison with salaries in industry.

This kind of approach was not found in arts and social science where research is less automatic and less supervised in terms of time-table and allotting of specific tasks. It would seem that only those who really *want* to go further in their particular subject embark upon a second degree in arts or social science rather than get a second degree as additional qualification. There seemed to be very few working-class postgraduates in arts and social science.

If one accepts that certain social classes are concentrated in certain faculties and levels of study, it is easy to see how the existing faculty divisions and organisation discussed at the beginning of the chapter may accentuate the existing cultural divisions in terms of social class patterns. Since class groups and faculty concentrations tend to coincide—if only vaguely—they may become confused with one another and result in further regrouping on class lines. In this way what is in reality a division based, as we have seen, on spatial and departmental organisation, in the presence of social class biases may become transformed into social class divisions or divisions in which class is relevant. Of course the spatial divisions do represent social and cultural divisions, as of faculty culture touched upon earlier, and this is internalised by the student. This will be discussed in Chapter 11. This involves detailed discussion of institutional socialisation.

The translation of class culture by students into faculty culture may be largely unconscious in that aspects of class culture may be *mistaken* for student culture or vice versa. This kind of analysis would be hardly meaningful if students were all of one social class with a common class culture. In such a situation it is unlikely that the traditional arts–science split would be nearly so significant or so deep. Nor would the distinction between professional faculties be so meaningful in terms of student cultures and it is in professional faculties that social class is most relevant. Yet the fact that this distinction is so meaningful to the students themselves is not merely because of intrinsic differences in curriculum, but rather because of the kind of students they see to be in a preponderance in those faculties. Thus members of a particular professional faculty may feel enabled to say, as did one medical student in Edinburgh: "People who don't fit in go to the gymnasium and meet people of similar interests." He was thinking primarily of working-class students. In turn, therefore, by a process of internal social control, members of a particular faculty are made to conform or are excluded from social life. This may count later in life when failure to be assimilated into the general professional culture may disadvantage professional occupational advancement.

Of course one has to take into account the whole nature of professional education which involves internalisation of culture, code, and ethics outside what can be taught in a lecture room or laboratory. Here assimilation into the prevailing class culture which is intimately bound up with professional culture may be crucial for the student. The very high selection and self-selection rate of doctors' children in the samples studied shows the attempt by the system to play safe in recruitment from the start. It is thought that those born to a particular professional way of life will in the end prove better practitioners of the profession in all respects than the gifted achiever who can never properly catch up what was learned by the children of professional parents from the cradle. However, a full discussion of the professions and professional training is not appropriate here, for this concerns socialisation *within* particular faculties, while we are at present discussing essentially relations *between* the faculties which make up the university. At this level it is convenient to discuss firstly their *spatial* relations as it affects social class divisions. The cultural aspect of faculties and the way in which they socialise students will be discussed in Chapter 11 in relation to other cultural divisions in internal organisation and in Chapter 13 in relation to job choice and social mobility. Suffice it to say at this juncture that the culture of certain faculties is compatible to a greater or lesser degree with the culture of working-class students, and that this is reflected not only in distribution of social classes within it but in the response of members of different social classes to this situation and which is exacerbated by the *spatial* separation of faculties.

Those working-class students who do fit in are the atypical working class, the high achievers with high motivation and aspiration without distinctive class marks. Since students are abstracted from their background it is on those distinctive class marks such as dress, manners, and accent that they are classified. Of course, what is seen as distinctive varies from context to context. The remark of an engineering student in Newcastle quoted earlier illustrates this: "The lads I go about with are ordinary chaps and like doing the same kind of things. I don't think anyone with a bow-tie would fit in."

For this student a bow-tie was a crucial indicator of class which implied a whole configuration of indices. These indices, like accent, particularly, mean even more in student society than they do outside, for they are all that students have to go on. That Medics are snobs is a simple and easy categorisation which implies a factor of student social organisation. They are "like us" or "not like us", and like tends almost imperceptibly to seek like.

This principle is based, as we have seen, in the minds of students on common interests which often seems to correlate for them with background and upbringing (and thus social class). In terms of university organisation and student groups it is necessary to consider whether interests as expressed in *student societies* cut across existing faculty and social class divisions. This represents to some limited extent degree of contact of social classes in leisure activities. Marris remarks that "the students recognised firstly that people cluster naturally about a common interest or meeting place".[1]

As we have discussed before, in fact, student societies tend to be dominated by faculty groups, thus perpetuating existing divisions in terms of student and class sub-cultures. This is true also of sports societies and teams. Medics, with their traditional *esprit de corps*, tend to form their own teams and take great pleasure in the group solidarity which playing sport engenders. This is rather a significant fact when it is remembered that it is often hoped university team games will engender group solidarity of a rather more comprehensive kind.

This remark applies also to the Durham colleges which often raise more enthusiastic teams than does the University as such.

We saw in Chapter 6, that there are distinct social class patterns in student participation in and leadership of societies which would tend to make for the assimilation of some groups and the exclusion of others. The English working class and the Scottish working class are contrasting examples of this, and the latter's lack of participation in student affairs is a real factor in reduced contact between the social classes. This lack of contact, as we have seen, leads to misconceptions of the attitudes and behaviour of members of other social classes.

Yet the reduced contact which certain students, e.g. the Scottish working class, have with the rest of the student body is rather more a symptom of a structural relationship than one in itself, and it is in the

[1] Marris, P., *The Experience of Higher Education*, 1964, p. 93.

main due to the residential organisation of the University in terms of its social class distribution—again in terms of spatial groups and degree of contact.

However, before we turn to the factor of residence it is important to note that only in a few societies in terms of certain general interests do the social classes meet in equal proportions. There is, for instance, the question of the purpose of the society. If it is a ski club or yachting club, its members will be limited to those who can provide their own equipment, often their own transport, and who can afford expensive holidays in which to indulge their sport. This would tend to restrict membership of certain social classes. Even in other "interest" societies, as we have seen in Chapter 6, there tends to be a middle-class bias, with working-class students attending mainly the departmental and academic societies in which social interaction is limited.[1] It is not true to say that class divisions and society groups coincide by any means, and such societies as dramatic and debating groups tend to bring together students of every social class. This could result perhaps from the fact that activity is orientated to a positive goal which all are interested in achieving, and for which the abilities of everyone are necessary.

Nevertheless, even societies such as these seem to have a geographical base—a specially defined area within the university precincts—often an eating or coffee house where members of the group may be sure of meeting without previous arrangements. Marris also has noted this point. He says that: "At Leeds the coffee lounge on the ground floor of the Union was thought to attract characteristically different patrons from the café in the basement."[2] Similarly, in the three universities "places" within the institution are defined in terms of the characteristics of the people who use them.

By very virtue of its geographical situation the group comes only into contact with those other groups which frequent the same social area. This may inhibit or accelerate the processes of assimilation. For instance, in Edinburgh, the Dramatic Society had a special corner of the Refectory which is held generally to be the most middle class and "upper crustish" of student eating places. It is frequented by law students, members of Ski Club, Boat Club, and so on. By very virtue of meeting in this middle-class atmosphere, the Dramatic Society members, however "beat" or working class, imbibe some of the surrounding middle-class

---

[1] This may have implications for development of "academic" or work centred culture.
[2] Marris, *op. cit.*, p. 94.

culture, and adopt the ways of middle-class students they meet there. In consequence the Dramatic Society gives the air of being middle class, but "arty", which is not entirely a faithful picture, as the presence of a sprinkling of working-class science students reveals on closer examination.

Societies, sports clubs, and "interest" groups in a sense represent student sub-cultures, and yet, as we have seen, these owe more than a little to social class sub-cultures. The student governing bodies of the universities—the unions and SRCs—are an interesting example of this. Those who run student affairs—particularly in the councils and committees of the SRC—do tend largely to be drawn from the middle classes, although whether this is due to inclination and ability or the students' choice of leaders is unclear.

Certainly in Newcastle and Edinburgh the SRC tended to be categorised as "socialites" (a student sneer implying a variety of upper middle-class traits) although, in fact, these people work extremely hard at the job of student government. This criticism was made less often in Durham, perhaps because it had less foundation, in that since student government has a broader social base and since the whole University is so small—this fact is seen to be so.

Groups do form along the lines of "interest" certainly, but again they tend to become confused in certain respects, although unconsciously, with social class.

We have now considered some of the main groupings in terms of work and leisure and we now turn to the important factor of residence referred to earlier in this chapter.

Residence Groups

Residence groups play an important part in the social organisation of the student body and particularly in halls of residence groups are formed which cut across faculty divisions. This is also true of the Durham colleges where bonds are formed across faculties, which permeate other aspects of Durham social life.

Groups in large digs may also form small communities, with common leisure activities. Sometimes digs groups, formed at the beginning of the university year, may stick together through succeeding years and even move out into flats together, with very little change in personnel. This is often true of groups which are formed by freshers in halls of residence. If one decides to move out the others will move rather than split the group.

Students often stressed (in all three universities) that groups are formed on "coming up" to university, and these usually form for them the nucleus, at least, of all other acquaintances or friends throughout the university life. This group may act as a springboard to other groups—it is rarely entirely left behind. Thus initial groups are often formed by accident, students find themselves put in digs together, even sharing a room with a stranger, or they make friends with others on the same stair in the college or hall of residence. Sometimes things "don't work out"—usually sheer habit of living together forges bonds of friendship. Where these distributions are purely random, they make for stimulating community life, binding together people of different disciplines and backgrounds. A truly student culture of that particular group is developed. (It is debatable as to whether there is such a thing as a "student" culture of a total institution, for, as we have seen, there is too much fragmentation of groups for this to emerge.)

However, such is university organisation that in fact the distributions are very rarely random. Helpful landladies, wardens of lodgings, heads of halls of residences, and principals of colleges seem to try to juxtapose students who they think will get on and fit in in terms of background and outlook, so that although there may be some randomisation of subjects studied there is rarely total randomisation of social class. Indeed, it is often admitted that conscious selection goes on. Mixing of students is therefore at a rather superficial level at which "learning from contemporaries" involves nothing more stimulating than students of basically similar outlook, background, and interests reaching some point of contact in terms of subjects studied.

> It would be far more stimulating and productive [said one Newcastle student living in a hall of residence] if people in the same faculty but of different backgrounds were thrown together rather than the other way round. Then they would have a common interest and something to talk about, but a different way of saying it. After all, we are here to *learn*, aren't we? Some of the conversations about work in Hall are so trivial they never get off the ground. But what can you expect when with glorious ideas of mixing you up, they put *one* physicist and *one* chemist in the midst of a whole load of linguists.

Despite certain drawbacks of this kind of distribution, at least the student living in large digs or hall of residence or college, particularly in his first year, is enabled to become part of a group and find his feet in the new environment. Those who initially are cut off in terms of residence either at home some distance away, or in isolated digs, may find that they have greater difficulty in joining a group—a problem which increases with time as groups "solidify". (Of course, "isolation" may also result *within* halls, etc., where there is spatial concentration of social class members in certain parts of the building—an isolation different in degree but not kind.)

One girl in Newcastle told how certain personal problems became magnified out of all proportion because she lived in cut off "digs" and had no one to talk to or go to for support and advice. This, coupled with the problems of a neurotic landlady, combined together to make her attempt suicide. She said that she thought that this would not have happened had she been in hall. Her case, though extreme, is by no means unique, and some students are unutterably lonely, especially in first year when everything and everyone is strange.

Table 9.4 shows whether students in Newcastle felt that residential places in the University should be increased.

TABLE 9.4. NEWCASTLE STUDENTS' ATTITUDES TO EXPANSION OF PROPORTION OF RESIDENTIAL PLACES (per cent)

	UMC		LMC		WkC		Unclassified		Total
	M	F	M	F	M	F	M	F	
Support increase	81	81	76	81	65	82	81	80	77
Do not support	1	—	4	1	4	18	5	20	4
Keep same proportion	14	19	19	17	28	—	14	—	17
Build student houses	4	—	2	2	3	—	—	—	2*
TOTAL No.	100 (142)	100 (57)	101 (189)	101 (91)	100 (91)	100 (33)	100 (21)	100 (5)	100 (629)

* Because this category was not provided on the questionnaire this figure does not give an indication of strength of support.

Seventy-seven per cent wanted an increased proportion of residential places, and in interview and in remarks on questionnaires explained that this did not necessarily mean in the form of traditional halls of residence. Some (2 per cent) mentioned specifically—adding their own response category—the kind of university houses or collection of bed-sitters which Newcastle has just started building and which Edinburgh has found very successful for the past four or five years. If this category had been included, no doubt many more would have ticked it. In these houses students are able to live to some extent independently, although a basic number of rules are observed and there is usually a resident member of staff or senior student.[1] Accommodation is modern, bright, and cheerful, and well equipped, and prices are not high. This contrasts pleasantly to the squalor in which some students are compelled to live by shortage of accommodation in the town. The author knows of some very poor standard accommodation in Edinburgh, but felt that Newcastle provided some examples of unequalled degradation, where fungus grew on kitchen and bathroom walls, plaster fell off ceilings, floorboards rotted, and lavatories refused to function. In such conditions how can students learn to be young professionals or internalise the values of a middle-class élite? It is as well that parents are often ignorant of the way in which their student sons and daughters live at university—or some of them would no doubt refuse to let them continue with their studies away from home. There are numberless student jokes and anecdotes about finding and living in certain types of accommodation, but often this is the only way to put up with an almost unbearable situation. Certainly the number of times which students change their accommodation testifies to the conditions which prompt them to move even in the middle of their studies. Of students interviewed in Newcastle, almost all had changed their place of residence at least once a year, some moved once a term. In all cases but one it was a matter of choice on the student's part because conditions were unsuitable. One girl had moved four times in her first term from one dismal place to another, and nearly had a breakdown as a result. Table 9.5 shows that 89 per cent of students were reasonably satisfied with their accommodation at the time of the survey, though they had probably gone through a series of moves to achieve this desired goal.[2]

In terms of social class, working-class men were most dissatisfied (17 per cent), and this may be accounted for later when we study class distributions in different forms of residence.

---

[1] The National Union of Students' Executive is moving away from the idea of traditional halls in its residential policy—partly because of the authority structure—and favours the increase of student houses.

[2] National concern about the shortage of student accommodation and the poor conditions in which many students live has prompted the NUS to prepare a survey of existing conditions.

TABLE 9.5. NEWCASTLE STUDENTS' SATISFACTION WITH RESIDENCE (per cent)

	UMC		LMC		WkC		Unclassified		Total
	M	F	M	F	M	F	M	F	
Satisfied	89	90	91	89	84	94	86	100	89
Dissatisfied	11	11	10	11	17	6	14	—	11
TOTAL	100	101	101	100	101	100	100	100	100
No.	(142)	(57)	(189)	(91)	(91)	(33)	(21)	(5)	(629)

When these figures are broken down by type of residence in which respondents lived at the time of the survey, people in digs (including flats) were most dissatisfied—14 per cent compared with 11 per cent in hall, although there is not much difference here. However, it must be made clear that the dissatisfaction is for entirely different reasons. Students in hall, particularly in later years, tend to resent what they believe to be curtailment of liberty, while students in digs and flats are more concerned with material discomforts and the practicabilities of cost. Thus there is quite a different *degree* of dissatisfaction in each case. Even students dissatisfied with hall life praised its merits in interview, and said that "particularly for first years" it was almost an essential of an integrated student life. Thus although college or hall of residence may be seen by some as a "retreat from the realities of life" or a "cushy existence" (Durham students), they do provide a basic minimum standard of living which promotes well being and allows for working in a suitable environment quite apart from providing some kind of community life in which everyone can (but need not) share.

Durham students were asked whether they had any previous idea of college life and whether their reactions to it were favourable or unfavourable. Table 5.9 (p. 207) has shown their replies to this question, but it is helpful to reconsider them here. Fifty-six per cent said they had an idea of college life before they came; 43 per cent had not. As one might expect, a higher proportion of working-class students than middle-class had no idea before they came. In the light of what has been discussed it is also understandable that a slightly smaller proportion of working-class than middle-class students had a positively favourable reaction to college

TABLE 9.6. REACTIONS OF DURHAM STUDENTS TO COLLEGE LIFE ANALYSED IN TERMS OF UNIVERSITY RESIDENCE (per cent)

	Digs and flats		College		Total
	M	F	M	F	
Favourable	60	38	68	62	63
Unfavourable	11	38	14	22	17
Neutral	26	12	17	16	18
Don't know	3	12	1	—	2
TOTAL	100	100	100	100	100

	Digs and flats		College		Total	No.
	M	F	M	F		
Favourable	22	3	51	24	100	95
Unfavourable	16	12	40	32	100	25
Neutral	32	4	43	21	100	28
Don't know	33	33	33	—	99	3
TOTAL	23	5	47	25	100	151
No.	(35)	(8)	(71)	(37)	(151)	

life. On the whole the proportion of students satisfied (including those with neutral reactions) with their accommodation is approximately the same as Newcastle. However, one has to take into account that not all students actually live in, so Table 9.6 gives a rather clearer picture by making a distinction between those who "live in" and those who live in digs.

A higher proportion of people living in digs or flats are actively dissatisfied with their accommodation than those living in college. Forty-nine per cent as compared with 65 per cent are satisfied; 25 per cent as compared with 17 per cent are dissatisfied. By far the highest proportion of dissatisfied students are girls living in digs—perhaps they are more conscious of standards of accommodation than are the men. It would seem from all the surveys that men tend to accept more readily the drawbacks and discomforts of unsuitable digs and flats than girls. Perhaps this is because men see it as a phase of life which will quickly pass, while girls need to make a temporary home for themselves which, in a sense, will reflect their tastes and status.

Said one male student in Edinburgh: "There is competition among women to share a flat with women who 'have arrived' in student social life, particularly around Bruntsfield. In that way they can get a foothold on the student social ladder and go out with somebody 'who is somebody' in the University."

This remark reveals what was constantly emerging that not only are places of residence centres of social groups and activity, but that they have a geographical base on a map. There are spatial groups within groups. This is true of the Jesmond area of Newcastle which is a most desirable area in student terms because students who "have arrived" live there, social groups have formed round them, therefore if one wants to be in the centre of student activity and able to entertain frequently, Jesmond is the place to go. In consequence, certain areas are ecologically central to the University, while others are cut off and devoid of activity. Sometimes students will accept flats and digs well below standard in order to be able to live *near* the centre of groups and social activity. It would seem that the *social* properties of certain types of residence often outweigh the factor of material comfort.

Thus students in halls of residence sited outside the city centre in Newcastle rarely commented on the physical convenience of hall life but often on the social inconvenience of living so far out. This is also true of students living at home who may be happy and comfortable and yet bewail the many disadvantages which living some distance away from the university always entails. Remarks such as these were common:

(1) "I live at home and so am not forced to mix inside the university very much. Many of my friends are outside the university."
(2) "People who live at home seem not to enjoy university as they should. Of course, it depends on their attitude—whether they have come for a degree or to widen their outlook. I lived at home last year and have benefited from moving away. I know many students who just sit at home and complain and don't join any societies. They have no enthusiasm for university."
(3) "I live at South Queensferry and feel that I have a different atti-

tude to university from the English who come a long way from home; they seem to be very active in societies and to mix a lot. I would have done better academically, too, if I had come away from home."

For students living at home there is not only the problem of distance but also the dichotomy of interests which living with family and friends brings. Many of these students said that living at home made them regard university as a continuation of school—a 9–5 job—which they left to return to clubs and friends at home. They often regretted this, however, feeling that they would like to join in more but not able to make the break with home ties. This was particularly true of Scottish working-class students in Edinburgh who appeared to feel reticent in joining in what seemed to them to be (and is) a predominantly middle-class student body. In this situation spatial distance is allied to social distance in a way that prevents the integration of this group of students. These findings and those on the influence of residence on participation in student affairs discussed later show different patterns of student activity from those found by Alice Eden in her Newcastle survey.[1]

Indeed, it is clear that in any study of the spatial divisions and groups of a university, the question of social distance cannot be excluded especially since, as was stated above, social distributions in the different forms of residence are rarely random. For instance, the new Principal of one of the women's colleges in Durham said that her predecessor had had very clear ideas abut the "type" of girls that she wanted in the college in terms of background and also religious convictions. Said the Principal with a sigh: "I fear it will be rather a shock for some of these girls when next year they find themselves next door to a lorry driver's daughter." This assumption was proved true when, after dinner, the senior woman said that her particular group in first year had had very mixed backgrounds and yet they had got on very well together. When asked the occupations of the fathers she said that one was a doctor, one a BBC announcer, another a senior civil servant, and another a naval officer. In fact, St. Aidan's College at the time of the survey had 43 per cent girls from public and direct grant schools and 36 per cent upper middle

---

[1] Eden, A., Social life in a provincial university, *BJS*, December 1959, **10** (4). Findings show that students active in home-centred affairs were likely to be active, too, at university. Marris, *op. cit.*, p. 114, shows that Northampton College students did not follow this trend but kept college and home strictly separate. These latter findings accord with those of the present survey.

TABLE 9.7. SOCIAL CLASS DISTRIBUTION IN UNIVERSITY

	UC	UMC			LMC		
	E	E	N	D	E	N	D
Lodgings	—	59	42	19	50	63	20
Hostels	—	14	31	79	17	27	76
Home	100	28	27	2	33	10	4
TOTAL	100	101	100	100	100	100	100
No.	(2)	(126)	(199)	(101)	(140)	(280)	(161)

E = Edinburgh. N = Newcastle. D = Durham.

class—proportions second only to the two theological colleges. Thus the community life which common residence is seen to generate is in fact generating a corporate spirit among the same kind of people who had much in common anyway. If we look at the social class distribution in different kinds of residence in different universities, this is seen to be true. It is less true of all the Durham colleges but more true of some than others.

Table 9.7 shows figures for the three universities.

What is immediately obvious in all three cases is that the proportion of working-class students living in halls of residence in Newcastle and Edinburgh and in colleges in Durham is significantly lower than the proportion of either of the middle classes. Evidence as to how far this is due to a bias in applications or selection is as yet incomplete, though it undoubtedly owes something to the latter. Nineteen per cent working-class students in Newcastle and 8 per cent in Edinburgh are in halls of residence, although Newcastle has far more hall places in absolute terms. In Edinburgh this figure compares with 14 per cent upper middle class and 17 per cent lower middle class, but with 31 per cent and 27 per cent in Newcastle, a similar differential between working class and lower middle class. In Newcastle a higher proportion of male working-class students than female live at home and a lower proportion in hall; this could account for the high degree of dissatisfaction with accommodation displayed by this section of the student population. The highest proportion of students in Newcastle living in hall is in the male upper middle

RESIDENCE OF THE THREE UNIVERSITIES (per cent)

WkC			Unclassified			Total		
E	N	D	E	N	D	E	N	D
50	63	34	66	54	31	54	55	23
8	19	65	—	19	62	14	27	74
42	18	1	33	27	7	32	19	3
100	100	100	99	100	100	100	101	100
(48)	(124)	(77)	(16)	(26)	(13)	(322)	(629)	(352)

class—35 per cent. The upper middle-class Scots students have this distinction in Edinburgh. In Edinburgh 32 per cent of students live at home, the largest proportion of which are working class. In Newcastle there is a significantly larger proportion of upper middle-class students living at home than working-class students. It was discovered that some of these are medical students whose fathers are local doctors; others were away at boarding school and wanted to return to their home university; an even more significant proportion are ex-public school who did not make the grade, attended a crash course at a technical college, and then got into the local university because it was a "safe bet". This kind of composition affects the dominant groupings of the student body.

Many students claimed that selection for halls of residence in Newcastle was biased—particularly in one hall, which it was claimed was "half full of public schoolboys". The analysis of respondents showed, in fact, not much less than 50 per cent—42 per cent public or direct grant school people in all male halls compared with 28 per cent in the total student body. The *social class* distribution in this particular hall is 52 per cent upper middle class, 45 per cent lower middle class, and 3·5 per cent working class, which seems to show indications of distinct bias in selection. This is not found to such an extent in the other male hall, or, indeed, any of the others, except one of the female halls—considered "the top" female hall. This had 57 per cent upper middle-class girls. Students claimed that they could pick out a "Henderson man" at a glance, and certainly constant interaction seemed to engender a group solidarity which

TABLE 9.8. DISTRIBUTION OF SOCIAL CLASSES AND

(a) Social class

	Bede	Chad	Cuthbert	Grey	Hatf.
UMC	18	53	28	29	28
LMC	35	27	30	44	51
WkC	47	20	32	19	19
Unclassified	—	—	10	8	2
TOTAL	100	100	100	100	100

(b) School

	Bede	Chad	Cuthbert	Grey	Hatf.
Public school	12	27	11	15	17
Direct grant	18	27	19	23	28
State grammar school	59	33	55	60	53
Private or religious	—	—	6	—	2
Secondary modern/technical high	6	14	8	—	—
Technical college	6	—	—	3	—
TOTAL	101	101	99	101	100
No.	(17)	(15)	(47)	(62)	(47)

found expression in attitude and behaviour. The relation between social class and school is discussed in the next chapter.

However, "images" of such groups are not always founded on statistical fact, which we may see if we consider the figures in Table 9.8 showing schools and class in the Durham colleges. Colleges, of course,

TUDENTS' SCHOOLS IN THE DURHAM COLLEGES (per cent)

distribution

St. J.	Univ.	St. A.	St. H.	St. M.	NC	Total
40	18	36	14	31	17	29
48	49	54	57	54	67	46
12	33	11	29	14	—	22
—	—	—	—	2	17	4
100	100	101	100	101	101	101

distribution

St. J.	Univ.	St. A.	St. H.	St. M.	NC	Total
48	18	29	10	8	—	17
4	5	15	18	19	—	18
44	74	57	64	64	83	59
—	—	—	—	4	—	2
4	—	—	7	4	17	3
—	3	—	—	2	—	1
100	100	101	99	101	100	100
(25)	(39)	(38)	(14)	(52)	(6)	(352)

and groups of colleges, as discussed in Chapter 2, represent real spatial and cultural divisions.

University College, as has been mentioned above, was always quoted as the "upper crust" College in which public schoolboys, Oxford rejects, and upper middle-class gentlemen lived a life in certain respects more genteel than that of the average Durham student. Just to be labelled a "Castle man" was entrée enough into all student circles, and Castlemen were in demand as partners at all social functions. "Castle day" was the social event of the year, and girls vied with each other to be invited. However, the statistical facts show a different picture. University College has approximately the same proportion of public school men as Hatfield—its nearest social rival, and although this proportion is slightly higher than that of the other men's colleges, excluding mainly theological colleges, it has by far the highest proportion of state grammar school people of any college, save Neville's Cross, the teacher-training college. St. Aidan's College and the two theological colleges have the highest proportions of students from public schools—as high as 48 per cent in St. John's although the figures involved here are very small. The theological colleges rarely figure in any "social" assessment at all.

The same pattern appears in terms of social class except that University College is further down the list with fewer upper middle class than and as many working class as St. Cuthbert's Society, which is reputed to be full of "drunken scruffs". This is, indeed, a case of image building which is founded on a perceived rather than an actual situation, and which is internalised and perpetuated. Of course, tradition and history have much to do with this, since University College was no doubt the home of sons of "gentlemen" in the past—yet this does not account totally for the firm belief which students in general hold today. The "totemic" aspects of the "castle" itself help to perpetuate the image—so that people living or dining within it live up to the standards they think it requires. This kind of enculturation is possible in a college where there is a pressure to conform to the prevailing ethos. As we can see, University College has a fair proportion of working-class students. It would appear that they are atypical and aspiring and are now perhaps more middle class even than the middle class themselves. Thus they are able in the nature of a "self-fulfilling" prophecy to live like the gentlemen they are thought to be. And who can say that they are not now such gentlemen?

St. Cuthbert's Society, which, on the other hand, is ranked socially low, differs in another way from the perceived "image" in that it is by no means a college of "working-class loafers" as is generally supposed. St. Cuthbert's is non-residential, so that its members are in a better position to hold wild parties in digs and stay out late and get drunk. This they do in order to live up to the college "name". Members also pride themselves on being "individuals", and are frequently good debaters.

and leaders of societies. Their nonconformism may in fact socially down-
grade them in a conforming society.

The two colleges with the highest concentration of working-class
students are St. Bede's and St. Hild's—both teacher-training colleges and
spatially quite distant from the other colleges. This distribution may be
linked to class bias in occupational choice.

As regards sex differences the women's colleges, apart from St. Hild's,
have a generally smaller proportion of working-class students than the
men's colleges (11 per cent St. Hild's, 14 per cent St. Mary's, and none
in the Neville Cross sample), suggesting that, as has been said before,
there is more social selection of female students than males. There is
concomitantly a much higher proportion of lower middle-class students
in women's colleges—54 per cent, 54 per cent, 57 per cent, and 67 per
cent. If, as discussed earlier, the expansion of the lower middle class is
an indication of expansion of class opportunity, then it would seem that
this is being experienced in the women's colleges.

In each case the social organisation encourages a certain kind of community life which, in turn, affects student attitudes and behaviour and,
indeed, the whole concept of participation in student affairs.

It may be appropriate to discuss again at this point the fraternity system on American campuses because it represents a structure of social
and spatial distances as well as a way of life and "rests ultimately on a
principle of exclusion".[1] Not only, as we have seen, does one have the
separation of different fraternities and sororities, but also the separation
between those who are members and those who are not—proportions
which vary from institution to institution. These distances are accentuated by the associated living and eating arrangements. The exclusive "eating clubs" of Yale and Harvard fulfil the same function. As we have
already seen that social selection for membership goes on, it can be assumed that fraternities and sororities represent the kind of basic organisational division which accentuate social class factors and distances in
student social relations, whether they are seen in these terms or not.
Since the prevailing ideology of American campuses is against social
inequalities and for personal achievement, it is likely that such divisions
will be given other names or not recognised for what they are.

Of course it is not only living accommodation which is important in
spatial organisation of day-to-day activities—eating places may be just

[1] Goldsen *et al.*, *What College Students Think*, p. 60.

as important. It is over food and coffee that much student interaction takes place, so that where dining rooms, refectories, and snack bars are situated will be influential in the way in which social relationships are formed.[1] Where eating arrangements are associated with faculties or work places, for example, the social bias which may characterise faculty organisation will be carried over into informal interaction over meals. Thus existing social and spatial relations are reinforced. Where eating places are designed to draw their clientele from a wide variety of work places there is more chance not only of meeting members of other faculties but also other social classes. Medical schools usually preserve their own social solidarity and cultural integrity by having slightly different hours from other faculties and by having their own dining arrangements. This sequestration, of course, assists the socialisation process and accentuates the division from other students.

The case of professional faculties may illustrate a somewhat conscious and necessary holding apart, but in many cases the university buildings and facilities have grown up and been expanded in rather a random way without proper realisation of the ways in which the built environment will help to decide the kind of groups that are formed. The new British universities have shown their awareness of the importance of physical as well as of social planning and are *using* the built environment to help create from scratch the kind of university which they want. In a sense this is a unique experiment—building a university very rapidly from nothing—and the outcome in terms of institutional growth and adaption will be watched with interest by architects and sociologists alike. It is no accident that great stress has been laid by all the new universities on residential as well as faculty structure, and whereas the latter has tended to innovation and experiment the former is in some respects conservative. Differing degrees of rigidity in *college* structure appear in the universities of Kent, Lancaster, and York (or the Shakespeare universities as they are known by students). This results from the express desire to build a community—almost with instant traditions—which will have none of the impersonality of the multiversity. However, much of the present cohesion and informality in the new universities is a feature of *size*, and one may expect that when the institutions grow in size and complexity much of the present "personal" atmosphere will inevitably be lost. For, as we have seen, institutional distances are relative as well as real dis-

[1] Sommer, R., Further studies of small group ecology, *Sociometry*, 1965, **28** (4), 337–48. Study of seating arrangements and influence on student activity.

tances, and even though a university may be concentrated on a compact
campus much will depend on the *internal* structure of distances in the
ordering of relations and their formality or informality.

However, we are not considering here only internal institutional distances but those involving the urban setting as, for instance, residential
organisation in the non-residential university.

Therefore if we look again at the figures on Newcastle residence in
Table 9.9 we can see further the actual *spatial* organisation of the student
body in terms of ecological distance within the town.

TABLE 9.9. SOCIAL CLASS DISTRIBUTION IN RESIDENCE IN DIFFERENT SPATIAL AREAS OF
NEWCASTLE (per cent)

	UMC	LMC	WkC	Unclassified	Total
University House	4	2	3	—	3
Jesmond	19	25	21	41	23
Easton Hall	3	1	1	—	2
Henderson Hall	11	7	1	—	7
Ethel Williams Hall	3	7	4	6	5
Eustace Percy Hall	13	9	12	6	11
Other Newcastle areas	31	30	27	41	30
Whitley Bay	6	8	13	—	8
Outside Newcastle	11	11	18	6	12
TOTAL	101	100	100	100	101
No.	(199)	(280)	(124)	(26)	(629)

The *class* distributions in different university halls are shown along
with distributions in Jesmond, already mentioned, and other areas including Whitley Bay. This last mentioned represents the most socially and
spatially distant and distinct area of university residence in which students band together to form a community of their own, separate from
the university community in the city centre.

In fact, as we see from Table 9.9, 13 per cent working-class students
live in digs or flats at Whitley Bay compared with 6 per cent upper middle
class and 8 per cent lower middle class. Another 18 per cent live outside
Newcastle, often at home, compared with 11 per cent of both upper mid-

dle-class and lower middle class-students. These students, 31 per cent of the working class, are both socially and geographically separated from the middle-class student body who would most benefit from being "brought in" to the university community. For, as we have seen, the influence of "propinquity" in overcoming latent social divisions cannot be discounted

After consideration of all the points so far raised one might frame the hypothesis that where and how students live will affect their *degree of integration* into student life, i.e. if they are centrally situated in a hall of residence where they immediately get to know many other students they will feel more of an integral part of the student body than someone who is living in isolated digs.[1] The formation of initial springboard groups is pertinent here.

If one takes as an indication of participation in student affairs member-ship of one or more societies, one obtains evidence to prove this hypoth-esis. In Edinburgh 85 per cent of students living in digs had been or were at the time of the survey members of one or more societies compared with 93 per cent in hostels and 70 per cent of students living at home.[2] The drop in proportion of students living at home who are now or have been member of one or more societies is an indication of the division of interests which living at home causes, mentioned earlier, and which pre-vents the student from entering fully into university life. Interviews in Newcastle and Durham confirmed this finding.

We have already seen in Chapter 6 the social class pattern of partici-pation in student affairs. When this is combined, as in the Edinburgh sample, with the residence distribution the patterns become more mean-ingful in the light of what has been said about the relation of spatial and social distance.

We have seen how more people in Edinburgh in hostels join societies than do students in digs or at home (and, indeed, the higher *overall* level of participation in the Durham colleges would seem to corroborate this), and how the Scottish upper middle class in Edinburgh are most active in societies. It is therefore not surprising that the group which takes the

---

[1] The influence of authority structure is considered in Chapter 11. Here it is contact of status equals largely which is discussed.

[2] This kind of distribution has been found before. For example, see Thoday, D., Residence and education in civic universities, *Int. J. of Soc. Psychiat.*, 1958, **4** (3). Findings that hall students in Birmingham University not only took a more active part in sports and societies but also more often read books outside their sub-ject and had friends in other departments and faculties, accord with those of Marris, *op. cit.*, on Leeds and Southampton universities.

most active part in societies is seen to be the Scottish upper middle class living in hall—100 per cent membership; 62·5 per cent leadership—an example of the way in which the "influence of hall" may be "masked by *other differences* between students"[1] (author's italic).

That one cannot attribute Scottish reticence too much to the school system is seen in the fact that a greater proportion of Scots working class living in digs who are members of societies hold positions in them than do the English working class. Thus it would appear that residential factors outweigh certain cultural disadvantages.

Another indication of the influence of residence on group formation, though only vague at this stage, is shown by Table 9.10.

It is perhaps not surprising in the light of what was said initially about mixing in the different types of residence that in Newcastle a higher proportion of students live at home than in hall or digs and have most of their friends in the same faculty—68 per cent. This is presumably since because they interact mainly with fellow students during working hours they know these particular students best. These need not necessarily be friends. Perhaps other students living at home would agree with the Newcastle student who said: "I wouldn't call the people I know at university friends—they're more acquaintances—people I work with—my real friends are at home."

Students with most friends outside their own faculty live in hall, which testifies to the mixing outside work which hall life promotes. This com-

TABLE 9.10. STUDENTS WHOSE FRIENDS ARE MAINLY IN THE SAME FACULTY AS THEMSELVES
(per cent)

(a) Newcastle

	Home	Hall	Digs	Total
Yes	68	33	53	50
No	32	67	47	50
TOTAL	100	100	100	100
No.	(117)	(168)	(344)	(629)

[1] Marris, *op. cit.*, p. 88. Marris poses a question—he does not attempt to examine what the differences might be.

TABLE 9.10. (*cont.*)

(b) Durham

(i) Friends of *same* sex mainly in own college

	Bede	Chad	Cuthbert	Grey	Hatf.	St. J.
Yes	53	87	70	89	87	80
No	47	13	30	11	13	20
TOTAL	100	100	100	100	100	100

	Univ.	St. A.	St. H.	St. M.	NC	Total
Yes	82	79	93	92	100	83
No	18	21	7	8	—	17
TOTAL	100	100	100	100	100	100

(ii) Friends of *opposite* sex mainly in own faculty

Yes	42	20	64	35	28	16
No	58	80	36	65	72	84
TOTAL	100	100	100	100	100	100
No.	(17)	(15)	(47)	(62)	(47)	(25)

Yes	28	21	50	33	50	35
No	72	79	50	67	50	65
TOTAL	100	100	100	100	100	100
No.	(39)	(28)	(14)	(52)	(6)	(352)

pares with Marris's findings that "students in lodgings at Cambridge did not differ from those in college—but at Leeds and Southampton residence in hall did encourage a wider choice of friends if not, perhaps, as much as expected".[1]

Not unexpectedly, 83 per cent of Durham students said that most of their friends of the *same* sex were in the same college, although this varied from college to college, and obviously with the size of the college. The mainly non-residential St. Cuthbert's Society and St. Bede's College had smaller proportions of students with most friends in their own college. The colleges with the highest proportions were those most spatially separate—Grey, St. Mary's, St. Hild's, and Neville's Cross—suggesting the influence of distance once again.

With regard to members of the *opposite* sex, quite a good "control" group in a way, 35 per cent only said that most of their friends were

TABLE 9.11. RESIDENTIAL DISTRIBUTION OF THOSE WHO ARE INFLUENCED BY SOCIAL CLASS IN MAKING FRIENDS—NEWCASTLE (per cent)

(a) Female students

	Digs	Hall	Home	Total
(i) When making friends of *same* sex				
Influenced	3	12	7	6
Not influenced	68	59	54	63
Possibly unconsciously	29	29	39	31
TOTAL	100	100	100	100
(ii) When making friends of *opposite* sex				
Influenced	8	16	14	11
Not influenced	58	47	39	52
Possibly unconsciously	34	37	46	37
TOTAL	100	100	99	100
No.	(109)	(49)	(28)	(186)

[1] Marris, *op. cit.*, p. 76.

TABLE 9.11 *(cont.)*

(b) Male students

	Digs	Hall	Home	Total
(i) When making friends of *same* sex				
Influenced	10	8	12	10
Not influenced	67	65	59	65
Possibly unconsciously	24	27	29	26
TOTAL	101	100	100	101
(ii) When making friends of *opposite* sex				
Influenced	20	13	24	19
Not influenced	50	54	37	49
Possibly unconsciously	30	33	39	32
TOTAL	100	100	100	100
No.	(234)	(119)	(90)	(443)

members of the same faculty. Here again there were differences between colleges, with the two theological colleges ranking lowest. The highest proportion of students with most of their friends of the opposite sex in the same faculty as themselves was St. Cuthbert's Society. This again shows clearly that where students are *less* likely to meet in spatial–social terms through residence (obviously applying to both sexes), they will turn increasingly to work contacts for friendship. This may account in other terms for the tendency of working-class students to seek "work" friends in their own faculty (Table 9.11).

It is possible to see the effect which residential grouping in Newcastle has on class divisions in terms of choice of friends. Of female students those living in hall are most influenced by class in choice of friends, though more students living at home admit to being "possibly unconsciously" influenced. The male distribution is slightly different; those living at home are most influenced (we must remember that a fair sprinkling of these are upper middle class), those living in hall least influenced, and it would appear that in this case spatial separation accentuates class consciousness as opposed to consciousness of being a student. It becomes apparent in this case, as with so many other findings, that social class distribution must be taken into account. Thus the more random the class distribution in this case the less class seems to matter.

We must ask also what the effect of residential distributions have upon the *experience* of the student both of "student" and social class divisions. Suggestions of this have been made throughout the preceding chapters—that where the university brings together members of different social classes—whether at work or particularly in residence—although it may bring to the surface unconscious differences, it also helps some people to get rid of the imagined differences in the face of real ones.

Examples of the effect which spatial closeness has had on those who are socially distant from the predominantly middle-class student body, especially in Edinburgh, are too numerous to mention here, but it seems clear that most of the working-class students living in halls of residence benefited greatly from the experience and were encouraged to "join in" fully in the social side of university life. This will be more fully discussed in Chapter 13 which deals with the assimilation and bourgeoisification of the working-class students.

However, "living together" is beneficial not only for working-class students but for all who hold prejudiced views about "the others" whom in effect they have never met. And, by its very nature, the university is in a unique way able to bring together students of every social background. It is the greatest pity that it does not always succeed *physically* in this aim. For it would seem that through its residential organisation, particularly, it is able to accentuate or diminish existing social class divisions and the resulting consequences for student experience of university life.

Propinquity has been acknowledged to be one of the principal factors in the formation of social relationships.[1] This would seem to operate not only between status equals but between members of different social classes. In other words, "propinquity" may help to overcome social distance while physical distance may widen the existing social gap. Examples of this are found among the working-class students living at home as compared with those living in hall; among working-class students who felt socially cut off as a result of living in digs far from the university; among lower middle-class first-generation university students who felt

[1] For instance see Erbe, W., Accessibility and informal social relationships among American graduate students, *Sociometry*, 1966, **29** (3), 250–64.

that even a limited experience of hostel life had helped them to overcome initial difficulties of assimilation into the student body.

In any situation of ambiguity about social class indices, propinquity is an influential factor in the process of mixing and will affect the mutual adaptation of social classes and the transmission of elements of social class culture. That certain students consciously or unconsciously realise this is seen in the fact that they often try to share a flat with the right kind of person who will introduce them into a desirable network of social relationships; for the same reason they choose a flat in a certain area; and certain groups have their own particular "meeting site" in the university precincts.

Yet the students who seem to realise least about the influence of propinquity and those who would most benefit from the knowledge, are the working-class students for whom social and spatial distance are often allied.

All the findings discussed therefore would seem to show that spatial organisation is an important factor in student social relations in work, leisure, and residence, yet it is seen to operate almost indivisibly with social class factors to produce the student groups which do form and change. One cannot understand student groups or sub-cultures without a full comprehension of both the spatial and social factors at work.

Thus in any study of student sub-cultures he overlooks the essential point that what often emerges is a *social class* sub-culture expressed no doubt in student terms, but owing its origins to the values and attitudes which students brought with them to the situation as well as those they learnt when they got there.

Half the story is missing if the social class distribution in the different types of residence is not studied in conjunction with this, yet none of the studies of residence mentioned take this into account. Home ties and locality ties become more meaningful and understandable if they are set within the social class environment and culture, so that relationship to parents and peers is seen in true perspective.

Then spatial divisions may be seen to be working *with* or *against* social divisions in the formation and structure of formal and informal social groups. Empirical observation combines with statistical analysis to suggest that these spatial divisions operate within each context of interaction on a continuum—from the siting of the university in the city; the spatial organisation of buildings within the university framework: the "corridors" or stairs in hall or college—the laboratory bench in the department, and so on in a series of interlocking space "cells" which help to define the social situations within them.

As has been stressed, attributional classes within the university are more likely to become interactional classes or quasi-communities within the university setting if they become concentrated in defined geographical areas or residential settings, and this process is a kind of self-perpetuating one and one which has repercussions on the whole university experience.

It is true that perception of social class or residential groups may differ from the statistical norm, but this usually occurs in the face of the operation of yet further factors in student social relations. These one may call the *cultural* in conjunction with the spatial factors, and these will be discussed in the next chapter, along with examples of how different combinations of cultural and spatial factors—in addition to social class—may affect students' perception of the situation at all levels of interaction.

CHAPTER 10

CULTURAL FACTORS IN SOCIAL RELATIONS

IN DISCUSSING socio-cultural factors which operate concomitantly with spatial factors in the formation of student groups, we have to differentiate clearly between those operating within the institutional frame of reference and those which owe the origins of their influence to aspects of external organisation. This would seem to make distinction between internal and external reference groups, and it is clear that the spheres in which they operate are delimited by the individual institutional framework. This last point will be discussed in the next chapter along with the way in which the relationship of the institutional framework to external societal influences determines greatly the relative significance of the internal and external reference groups here outlined.

In each case one may see the membership group within the student body as being basically attributional, but referring to interactional groups outside the institution. The main groups to be considered are those based on school, area of home residence (in geographical and cultural terms), and other cultural dimensions of social class not comprehended by the socioeconomic categories such as value systems based, for instance, on educo-cultural classes. One must also consider that sex differentials are a factor in these groupings where sex is a latent identity.

Under this heading also one may consider faculties, colleges, and student societies and organisation which combine spatial and cultural factors in social relations. Indeed, one is always conscious in any such analysis of the tremendous overlapping of groups and interrelation of factors—particularly the spatial and social—so that one is often dealing in reality with the dimension of social "space".

First, let us consider the factor of school membership in students' social relations—not only in terms of "type" of school, but also of particular schools. Some of the elements which schools contribute in student social relations have been mentioned already, but it is useful to summarise the various aspects all together.

The importance of school groups was something which first began to emerge in the Edinburgh survey, so we will consider this first. For it became apparent, quite by chance, that students often confused "class consciousness" with consciousness of being public or grammar school people, and confused class divisions with the same school differences. Thus it became important to inquire about school divisions in the later surveys as being very relevant factors in students' social relations. Perhaps this is because school membership is an attribute of the student himself—it is both a mark of "achievement" and of "ascription"[1]—it is an inalienable "mark" which he carries round with him. This contrasts with social class of origin in terms of parental occupation which is most comprehensible and relevant in the home environment. School membership represents an "independent" attribute which nevertheless carries with it complex marks of status. It is only one such attribute, of course, and the possession or non-possession of certain attributes may assist or militate against the acceptance into particular groups of particular persons. What will appear is that whether a student becomes accepted or a misfit is not entirely dependent upon personality. This is particularly true in the student situation as a way of life which encourages "other directedness". "The term 'other-directed' was used by David Riesman in *The Lonely Crowd*[2]] to describe the personality of someone who is motivated principally by the desire for social acceptance and approval who takes his cues for conduct mainly from the social group."[3] The rather artificial nature of student society makes this true, and the unnatural distribution in terms of age and intelligence which increases the importance and influence of the peer group. The consequences then for the misfit may be severe.

"The visitor to the American college campus is struck by this quality of other directedness; sociability and 'groupiness' seem to permeate the atmosphere. The lone student is the rare bird—usually the isolate, the misfit."[4]

[1] As used by Linton, R., *The Study of Man: An Introduction*, D. Appleton–Century Co., London, 1936, p. 115.

[2] Riesman, D., in collaboration with Denney, R. and Gleizer, N., *The Lonely Crowd*, Yale Univ. Press, New Haven, 1950.

[3] Goldsen *et al.*, *What College Students Think*, 1960, p. 16.

[4] *Ibid.*, p. 17.

Goldsen *et al.* do not investigate what makes a misfit a misfit outside, inferring that it is connected with wanting to be liked and to be a success. But it remains to be seen whether misfits are as likely to have certain social as well as personality characteristics in the American university as in the British, where class consciousness may help to define the problem.

In interview many students who considered that there is much class consciousness in the student body based their criticism on prejudices which they said exist between students from different schools, i.e. public and fee-paying schools and grammar and senior secondary schools (in the Scottish context). One of the Edinburgh students said: "I think there is a good bit of class consciousness, especially among students from the Edinburgh public schools. They tend to stick together in groups and this makes others stick together in groups."[1] Another said:

> From my own experience I think there is more class consciousness even than in society. Perhaps is it more obvious in student life because we are all roughly of the same age and intelligence, so it cuts across. I think the type of school one goes to is important—one tends to group together with others from the same school or type of school. This is true of Halls of Residence where the Warden accepts people from a certain school. There is some hostility to "public school types" which is quite widespread. I was the only Public School boy in my digs and I found it uncomfortable.

This latter quote shows that school divisions can operate both for the individual and against. It will be seen that the kind of social class consciousness and/or prejudice criticised by the two students differs from that criticised by students in Chapter 7—such as is exemplified by one Scottish working-class student. This student came from a small rural community where he said that: "The differences between people are created by their intrinsic worth and the skills which they acquire, so that a man may work himself up through the hierarchy." However, he said that at university the situation is very different.

"The criteria used are so artificial that it doesn't matter what you are like underneath. As long as you assume middle-class traits and keep up the pretence, with others who are also pretending, you can get on—but, of course, certain ways are blocked to certain people." At length he admitted "This life is pretty awful, but life in society at large is worse."

---

[1] Marris found that "the students chose most of their friends not only from the same faculty but also from the same academic year and school background as themselves". (Marris, P., *The Experience of Higher Education*, p. 77.)

It is important to note that the social class reference group which influenced this student's attitude differed in some ways from the majority in that it was based on *rural* status groups in a fairly closed community.[1] This brings us to the point, considered later, of the way in which the external point of reference influences the perception of the internal situation.

Nevertheless, it is useful to compare the attitude of this student with those made on school divisions. The working-class student criticised students who exhibit prejudice against students of different social class backgrounds, while the upper middle-class students criticised also divisions *within* the upper middle class. It will be seen that the school divisions cut across the social classes in some cases and in such cases obscure other differences in social class background.

With reference to the other two universities, it might be pertinent to consider whether the factor of school becomes increasingly relevant in situations of relative social class homogeneity (as in middle-class sections of Edinburgh) and less relevant in relatively heterogeneous social class situations where existing divisions are more significant. It will be seen, in fact, that school divisions are less important in Durham than in Edinburgh and slightly less important than either in Newcastle, although this varies with context.

Eight of the thirty-two students interviewed in Edinburgh said that there is a good deal of class consciousness in *certain groups*. In all eight cases the groups referred to were based on certain schools or types of school. Five of the students were upper middle class, two working class, and one lower middle class. Some of these groups were located in certain faculties. The Medical Faculty was mentioned most often.

Twelve students said that "there is not much class consciousness" in the student body and of these seven mentioned the different attitudes inbred in different schools. Of the nine students who said that there is no class consciousness at all, an upper middle-class student said that there might be certain school groups which proved the exception.

This shows that in 18 out of 32 interviews, schools were mentioned as a possible source of class consciousness. Even in other interviews they were mentioned at least as a factor in the formation of groups of some kind. This seems a high proportion, and along with further conversation and

[1] For discussion of rural–urban continuum moving from interactional to attributional social class see, Plowman, D. E. G., Minchinton, W. E., and Stacey, M., Local status in England and Wales, *Sociol. Rev.*, July 1962, **10**, 1961–202.

participant observation would seem to indicate the overall importance of this distinction in the student body. Of the 19 mentioned, 8 students were Scottish, 9 English, and 1 American; 11 were upper middle class, 5 lower middle class, and 2 working class. Perhaps the working-class students do not so often come into contact with "public school types", or perhaps for them the social class divisions are based on different criteria—for instance economic factors.

Naturally the type of school which students had attended was seen to be closely connected with their whole way of life and a number of easily recognisable characteristics. Like occupation in society at large, it stands as an indicator of a whole range of indices intimately connected. For example, those who had been to public school were thought to possess a certain accent, manner of dressing, a good deal of money, and certain tastes and attitudes. These marked them off from "grammar school types" who were also believed to be easily recognisable.

An English upper middle-class male student said: "Those who went to public school tend to group together because of the school, not their social class background—though, of course, it might be correlated with background. They have a genuine feeling of superiority born of the knowledge of the value of their education. They also have interests in common."

A Scottish female lower middle-class student said: "In the fee-paying schools people are encouraged to take part in a variety of school activities so that students coming from these schools are willing to accept responsibility more readily without reward than are grammar school people."

Another English upper middle-class male student said: "The difference between those who go to a fee-paying school and an ordinary school in England lies in the difference in broadness of outlook. At public school one is encouraged to do things outside one's work. One hears the phrase 'character building'—but this could have a basis in fact."

The differences which students felt to exist between students from different types of school were often developed almost into stereotypes.[1] This probably springs at least partly from the fact that the spatial organisation of the universities, discussed in the last chapter, tends to keep separate the different types of school groups, so that judgement is made

---

[1] Marris suggests that "students are sometimes afraid of each other and protect themselves by identifying stereotypes to avoid, or retreat into neutral topics" (Marris, *op. cit.*, p. 119).

without personal experience of the matter. A typical remark was, "Well you see I just wouldn't have anything in common with someone from a grammar school. Whereas we were encouraged to play sport, enter into school activities outside work, and take on responsibility, people from grammar schools seem not to be interested in these things. Where I would go to a concert a grammar school person would go to a pub or a cinema." The remark about the concert-going was quoted several times—not only in interview. It seems to be a stock example.

Students from grammar schools and ordinary Scottish senior secondary schools also voiced generalisations about public school types. "The public school types are all snobs. They sit together in the Refectory and talk loudly in 'U' accents, and think that they are lords of creation."

This question of accents as an important social class indicator will be raised later in the chapter.

Another quote which again illustrates the geographical bases of group is: "The public school types who go to the Refectory seem to think that people who go to the Common Room are absolute riff-raff."

In this case the "image" of the eating place is eventually fulfilled in terms of the "kind" of students using it.

The upper middle-class American interviewed remarked on the feeling of the importance of going to the right school which had struck him on coming to Scotland. He said a great deal of social prestige seemed to be attached to going to certain schools. He had been surprised when other parents had said to him of his small son: "Where are you going to send him to school?", as he had not thought it mattered much. He said that the matter of getting their children to the right schools is very worrying to a certain class of parents as far as he could see.

This throws interesting light from a different angle on the school divisions perceived by students. A further sidelight is added by a student studying for a postgraduate mental health diploma. She said that:

> There seems to be a stigma attached to not being of sufficient intelligence to get into certain schools. There is great parent participation in homework in order to help the children to pass their exams. Academic progress is a great mark of success. Sometimes the children cannot stand up to the pressures which are put upon them and are referred to the psychiatric unit. Often the parents cannot face the implications of what they are doing. Most of the parents I have come across are middle class. There is both academic and social advancement in getting into certain schools.

This respondent stressed that one must not draw conclusions from the few examples that she knew of since they naturally tended to be the excep-

Student Life in a Class Society

tions. However, it does add to the general picture which has been created by other data. These latter remarks are concerned with the Scottish school system rather than the English.

Indeed, it may well be that school divisions in Edinburgh are more relevant in student social relations partly because of the different school system in which there is a wider range of fee-paying schools than in the English setting. The situation may also owe something to the fact that academic excellence, so long a matter of pride and prestige among Scots, in terms of present processes of selection is easily translatable into a matter of social status.

It is important to note also that in the Scottish situation attendance at one particular university is far more often a matter of school tradition than in any of the English universities outside Oxbridge. In this way one may find large numbers of students from the same school coming up to university together and forming a primary group in consequence.

It was said by some students that they intended to stay with the people they had come up with from school all through university. This is no doubt why certain students stated that "one's circle of friends" or "friends you come up with determine your social standing in the student body". In the light of what has been discussed in the previous chapter of the way in which first groups formed on coming up are of crucial importance in a student's life, this attitude becomes more comprehensible.

Cliques from various schools are formed apparently among students from the ordinary senior secondary schools as well as among those from public schools. This may lead to Scottish working-class students, for example, never really meeting anyone outside the group from his old school. One Scottish working-class student said he had gone into hostel for that very reason because he wanted to meet more people and enjoy university social life.

This student unconsciously realised that the controls of the peer group from the same home background are as restricting within the university environment as they are when links are maintained with them in the home locality. They bring the peer group culture with them—representing resistance to the change which university can bring about.

Although most of what has been said about the Edinburgh University context applies also to the other two universities on this point, it is of a more limited relevance. Even in Edinburgh it was admitted that the operation of school factors was limited to certain sections of the student population. These factors are more apparent in halls of residence and professional faculties where there is spatial concentration of other cultural groups, and this would remain true in the other two universities. The absence of a Medical Faculty in Durham may account to some extent for decreased relevance of school divisions, particularly among the middle class. However, in the context of certain colleges it is seen to be a relevant factor in social relations.

This brings us once again to the observation that where spatial and cultural concentrations coincide—as in school and residence, for instance—an attribute becomes interactional in terms of a group with which students can positively identify, with the growth of collective representations which this implies.

We saw in the last chapter how public school students are definitely concentrated in certain forms of residence in all three universities, and in Newcastle in certain areas of the city, and even within particular halls of residence. Thus the school attribute comes to have interactional meaning where such a cultural group is either assimilated or its difference is stressed in these terms. That school is definitely correlated with social class is in no doubt (see Table 4.10 (p. 166)). In Newcastle, 71 per cent of all public school people were of the upper middle class and 31 per cent lower middle class. Perhaps where school and class more nearly coincide, the school division becomes more relevant in certain student circles, i.e. these attributes are differentially weighted in different contexts. The largest proportion of state grammar school people in each university were of the lower middle class—51 per cent Newcastle and 49 per cent Durham. However, if one takes public and direct grant schools together, a higher proportion of upper middle-class students in Durham fall into this category than in Newcastle—57 per cent as opposed to 45 per cent: quite a significant difference. And in itself this kind of difference may affect student groupings in that it represents a school–class culture which adds another dimension to the student social class composition. This overlapping and overlaying of different dimensions of social class will be referred to later in the chapter.

Differences emerge constantly between males and females in terms of class and school composition so that in a sense sex itself becomes yet another social factor in student social relations with important implications for the formation of student groups. Indeed, as we have seen, in consideration of influence of social class in choice of friends, sex is an attribute which is differentially weighted in different situations; its relevance varies with situation, and where it is combined with social class it influences the relevance of *that* attribute. This is particularly true because of the high degree of visibility of sex attribute. The implications of this analysis of the *cultural* and *status* dimensions of sex roles are not examined, but demand further study. In some situations it is quite possible that the student attribute outweighs that of sex—particularly in the context of academic work which is the most student activity of all student activities and also has its highly visible indicators. The examination of the relevance of sex in social relations would demand as much vigorous research as that devoted to social class, for it well may be that in some contexts sex differentials outweigh those of class. Unfortunately, there is not enough evidence at this point to discuss this further here.

The way in which students tend to confuse school and class indices may be seen in an analysis of the Newcastle distribution of schools in terms of where students live.

In the last chapter it was seen that a bias in terms of social class of origin existed in the male halls of residence. This was described by students in terms of them being "half full of public schoolboys". In fact, Table 10.1 shows that the halls are nowhere near half full of public schoolboys, and, indeed, that the proportion of public schoolboys is not much larger in Henderson than Eustace Percy—35 per cent public, direct grant, and private in Henderson; 30 per cent in Eustace Percy. However, we have seen how Eustace Percy Hall has more lower middle-class and working-class students, so it would seem that in some cases public school is synonymous for some students with upper middle class. Certainly divisions are blurred or erroneously applied in situations of ambiguity, although there is often more overlap than would at first appear.

We saw, for instance, in the last chapter how in Newcastle a higher proportion of working-class than middle-class students are found accommodation in Whitley Bay. This picture is even more clearly defined in terms of schools as Table 10.1 again shows: 26 per cent secondary modern and technical high; 13 per cent technical college, and 9 per cent state grammar live at Whitley Bay, compared with 1·4 per cent public school and 5 per cent direct grant—which does not correspond at all to the proportions in the total student body. If this, then, represents a grouping in spatial terms of culturally compatible students, then it would appear that school may be a more meaningful indicator of culture class than occupation of father.

TABLE 10.1. SCHOOL DISTRIBUTION IN AREAS OF UNIVERSITY RESIDENCE IN NEWCASTLE (per cent)

	Public	Direct grant	State grammar school	Private	Secondary modern and Technical High	Technical college	Total
Henderson	10	5	6	6	—	13	7
Eustace Percy	15	2	12	13	7	6	11
E.W.	1	7	6	6	—	—	5
Easton	3	—	2	6	—	—	2
University House	1	7	2	—	13	—	3
Whitley Bay	1	5	9	13	26	13	8
Jesmond	27	12	24	13	18	25	23
Outside Newcastle	14	21	11	6	11	9	12
Other Newcastle areas	27	42	28	38	25	34	30
TOTAL	99	101	100	101	100	100	101
No.	(102)	(59)	(370)	(19)	(35)	(44)	(629)

Table 10.2 shows the schools distribution in the various faculties and again shows interesting if at first unexpected concentrations.

As many as 25 per cent public school are concentrated in applied science. This bears out what was said in the last chapter about this local public school element who came to do practical subjects in a local university. Public school people with technical college education most often put Newcastle as first choice, perhaps because of courses offered. The other school groups with high proportions in applied science are, as one might expect, secondary modern, technical high, and technical college. Perhaps the fact that these different school groups cut across both arts and science accounts for some of the lack of arts–sciences split in Newcastle. Other cohesive factors override this division.

It may be seen in other faculties, too, that school distributions sometimes blur the social class concentrations in various faculties. This must make for greater cohesion of cross-cutting work groups and act towards the decreasing relevance of social class.

TABLE 10.2. SCHOOL DISTRIBUTION IN THE FACULTIES OF NEWCASTLE UNIVERSITY
(per cent)

	Public	Direct grant	State grammar school	Private	Secondary modern	Technical High	Technical college	Total
Arts (inc. arch.)	17	32	27	42	17	26	5	24
Law	5	7	1	—	—	—	—	2
Medicine	12	14	10	11	—	22	9	11
Dentistry	7	9	4	—	8	4	—	5
Agriculture	8	2	5	5	—	—	9	5
Applied Science	25	14	12	5	25	30	52	18
Pure Science	17	15	34	16	50	13	20	28
Education	—	3	2	5	—	—	2	2
Economics and social studies	10	5	4	16	—	4	2	5
TOTAL	101	101	99	100	100	99	99	100
No.	(102)	(59)	(370)	(19)	(12)	(23)	(44)	(629)

In fact, it would seem that by virtue of the "shatterbelt zone" of reference groups which exist in Newcastle no one factor is able to dominate to the exclusion or diminution of all others, i.e. the weighting of different factors tends to cancel each other out. This applies to social class. It is where other factors support and therefore reinforce existing social class divisions that choice of groups is limited for the students and social class is increasingly relevant. So that where different cultural groupings share common boundaries with social class they tend to accentuate the relevance of social class.

Before we go on to a discussion of other cultural factors in students' social relations, it is interesting to note what some students said in interview concerning the influence of school divisions in student groups in both Durham and Newcastle.

A Durham student said that although he personally favoured comprehensive schools, it was true that public schools "breed a different type of person. Public school people have confidence and can express themselves better than the average grammar school person. Perhaps it has something to do with giving responsibility through the prefectorial system. Of course, no doubt grammar school boys could also get these qualities."

This remark is typical of many Durham students' attitudes that types of school breed different types of person, but that this does not necessarily bring them into conflict. They tend to group together, but this is seen as natural and not a cause for concern. Nor are the divisions which schools create seen as rigid, and there is mixing between the groups.

The general attitude and behaviour differs from that found in Newcastle where the feelings of many are typified by the following remark: "Before I came here I would never have dreamed of talking to anyone from public school with a posh accent. The accent put my back up. But now I have got to know one or two, I realise it is just natural to them."

This student was anxious to show how student community life (he lived in hall) had dispelled many of his previous misconceptions regarding "the public school lot". Unfortunately, many students do not have the opportunity to have their misconceptions and prejudices dispelled by the experience brought by contact, and this applied to all groups. Here is another example of this from an Edinburgh student: "I thought grammar school boys were the scum of the earth until I met some this year." This particular student said that his public school had encouraged him in his prejudice, and it had been quite a shock to him to find out "what decent chaps some of the grammar school people are".

It will be seen in some of these remarks what was found to be generally true among students that accent is taken to be one of the main indicators of school and social class. Very few students in any of the three universities said that accent does not matter at all, and many said that it matters more among students than it does in the outside world. The reason for this is that students when abstracted from the home environment leave many class clues behind, so that attributes which indicate class membership are more personalised—like dress, manners, values, and particularly speech.[1] Basil Bernstein's[2] hypothesis is not without relevance in this context, for it was often made clear that accent alone is not a clear indicator of background but that speech forms and vocabulary and expression are. Students spoke of "educated language" and said that it mattered more to speak "like an educated person" than to speak with a

---

[1] Plowman *et al.*, *op. cit.*, p. 195: "*Migration* will necessitate a more attributional means of placing status since many newcomers can be placed at first only by *outward signs*" (author's italics).

[2] Bernstein, B., *op. cit.*, *BJS*, 1960, **11**, 271–6.

completely accentless voice. To some extent, this language is something which all students are in a position to adopt, but this is a sign of bourgeoisification which, as we shall see, by no means happens automatically. Those who do adopt an educated language can pass into the group by which they wish to be accepted as long as they also demonstrate certain other class clues, particularly in terms of interests already mentioned and certain aspects of behaviour.

Accent was mentioned most often as a class indicator in Edinburgh. This may be because the variety of English and Scottish accents makes discrimination in placing people more fine, although this varies across the national division, i.e. a Scottish student, particularly working class, will be able to discriminate only crudely between the variety of English accents. This applies also to English students with no ear for U and non-U Scottish accents, although in the English context Scottish accents are more acceptable than, for instance, a north of England accent. The matter is further complicated by the fact the upper middle-class Scots tend to adopt an "anglicised" accent as a sign of their class position, especially as many have been to public school, often to English public schools. Thus although accents may matter more, the situation is rather confused and as a result students may be wrongly placed in terms of social class by other students. We have already seen in Chapter 6 how the middle-class English who run all the societies, according to the working-class Scots, turn out to be upper middle-class Scots with English accents.

In Durham and Newcastle, accents are more easily placed, so that in a sense trying to change one's accent is less easy and convincing, and fewer people than in Edinburgh admitted to trying to lose their regional accent.

This brings us to the point where one can see that it is very easy to confuse, as do the students, regional accents with social class indices. Not only is there a feeling that the stronger the accent the lower the class, but also that the particular accent itself is in some way a mark of social position. Northern accents are, for instance, seen as lower in status than southern accents—so that there is ranking not only in terms of degree but of kind. Much may be seen as good-humoured north/south rivalry, and yet underlying this is something of a more serious note, and which is an important factor in the formation of student groups. One often hears of students from London being assumed to be upper middle class and those from the north being perceived as working class—in keeping with the Coronation Street image which goes with a northern accent. Students have shown, too, that regional differences may initially separate students and similarities may draw them together.

Thus accent is seen as a crucial indicator because it is seen to represent social class in a dual way, and to refer to two sets of multidimensional groupings located both spatially and socially on a status continuum. In different situations and contexts the social and spatial elements are differentially weighted. In Newcastle, for instance, the stress is predominantly on locality, i.e. the spatial rather than the social, so that these reference groups operate but are seen as different kinds of reference groups. Thus less social stigma is attached to a heavy regional accent. Durham represents the midway case where spatial and social reference groups are increasingly interchangeable. In Edinburgh the social dimension of this particular continuum is particularly stressed, so that in Edinburgh an accent is taken more than in Newcastle as an indication of position on a social rather than a spatial scale. In other words, the situational space is more clearly defined in Edinburgh by the coincidence of spatial and social concentrations, for students' social class composition tends to correspond closely to their geographical composition. In Newcastle a high proportion of locals are of high social class.

This observation has important relevance for social class as a factor in student social relations in that where it is obscured or overlaid by these various other factors and dimensions and where its indicators are not uniquely defined, there is a tendency for cultural operations of social class to be perceived as operations of other factors. Thus social class is seen to be, at least superficially, less relevant. This would seem to be true in its different applications to the three universities studied.

In that the reference group of locality is taken to be something distinct and real in terms of the students' experience, one must come to the conclusion that different cultural areas exist and have extensive influence in the student body. Students from the south have already been quoted as saying how they feared to go to university in the north, and how, despite having certain prejudices removed, they perceive it as totally different from the south. If we look again at the distribution of students' home residence, we can see how this kind of perceived and actual cultural difference may have different effects in different universities. As we have already seen, Newcastle is a more local university than Durham, and Edinburgh is in a sense more cosmopolitan than the other two. One may readily see how this kind of distinction has its influence on the total image of the university, i.e. the most northern and local university, in the light of what has been discussed, is seen as the most working class. This is compatible with all other findings.

As we have seen in Newcastle, the upper middle class is largely local, whereas in Durham and to some extent in Edinburgh, the upper middle class is drawn largely from the south, particularly London and the Home Counties. In Newcastle, 41 per cent of the upper middle class has home residence in County Durham and Northumberland, while 14 per cent are drawn from Lancashire and Yorkshire and 7 per cent from other northern counties. This compares with 30 per cent from all southern counties. In Durham, however, 48 per cent of upper middle-class students come from London and the south compared with 44 per cent from northern counties. Of those from the north only eleven students were from Northumberland and County Durham.

In Durham and Edinburgh the greater coincidence of boundaries of spatial and social status concentrations tends to underline the influence of social class, whereas in Newcastle social status redefined in spatial terms leads to a generally reduced influence. Students themselves realise the close relation of social class and spatial divisions. One clear example of this is the way in which the most socially aspiring students travel to university far away from home in order to express geographically a social move. This is particularly true of the atypical English working-class students in Edinburgh—to be discussed in Chapter 13 on social mobility.

It is easy to recognise differences in behaviour and attitude in different geographical areas and to understand how these form the basis of certain student reference groups, particularly in terms of common interests. Even school systems differ in different areas, and this must surely affect the student's cultural background. It is important to note that since they represent certain cultural areas it may be suggested that different geographical areas therefore exhibit not only differences in class composition, but also differences in kind of social class or stress on different dimensions. In other words, both factors of association and indicators of factors may differ in different geographical areas, and those may influence student groupings in terms of their particular external point of reference. This is worth further analysis. However, certain findings would seem to indicate that at least this is partially true, although research would have to be done to define each particular case.

An indication of the point made is that in terms of educo-cultural classes Newcastle seems to be undergoing a greater expansion of educational opportunity than either Durham or Edinburgh. Although 80 per cent of students in both Newcastle and Durham are first-generation university students compared with 63 per cent in Edinburgh, there is a higher proportion of students' parents in Newcastle who have not been educated beyond the age of 14 than in Durham. One could almost say that the socioeconomic classes of students' parents in Durham and Newcastle are intrinsically of a different type, and that what is being experienced in Newcastle is the impact of the "new" middle class—the northern self-made managerial and white-collar workers of comparatively low educational level—compared with the "professional" middle classes in which the socioeconomic and educo-cultural classes coincide. If we look at a further breakdown of the social class of the three universities in these terms, the differing degrees of "middle classness" emerge (Table 10.3).

TABLE 10.3. EDUCO-CULTURAL CLASSES OF STUDENTS' PARENTS (per cent)

	Edinburgh	Durham	Newcastle
Professional	31	21	16
Managerial and white collar	52	54	60*
Manual	15	21	20
Unclassified	2	4	4
TOTAL	100	100	100
No.	(322)	(352)	(629)

* The author would hypothesise that student activists are most likely to come from these "new" middle classes rather then the higher professional families, and may occupy an interstitial educational rather than socioeconomic status.

This kind of dimension has obvious relevance for student social class relations in that the social class reference group may vary with context. Educo-cultural factors and value systems alone may have more relevance in certain student situations, and obviously do, than socioeconomic factors—particularly since we have shown that students are largely abstracted from socioeconomic clues. Thus this kind of social class composition may have more relevance than that based on the dimension of occupational status. Only trial and error can discover this, along with comparisons of student's own class models and reference groups. These will be discussed in Chapter 13.

Suffice it to say at this point that social class is not only a multiple reference group but may comprehend within it a series of multiple reference groups; it is an attribute in a whole configuration of attributes. In an educational setting such as a university, "educational" class would seem to be very important. For instance, first-generation divisions tend to some extent to cut across socioeconomic classes and this may act as a cohesive factor, although, as we have seen, only under certain conditions.

Indeed, where in a "shatterbelt zone" of reference groups identities cross-cut, there is more cohesion of the larger contextual group than in one where a series of group identities tend to overlap and coincide and become interchangeable. We see examples of the two extremes in Edinburgh and Newcastle with Durham in the middle, but only again in terms of certain defined situations. Another feature of this interrelationship—which must not be forgotten—is the strength of links of internal and external reference groups which depends on the degree of separation of the institution from its external setting. This final factor in student social relations is discussed in the next chapter.

We have now discussed the main spatial and cultural factors in students' social relations and the way in which they define the situational space in which social class varies in relevance in different university contexts. It must be made clear, nevertheless, that the factors outlined set limits but do not determine the interaction of students and formation of student groups, as has been explained in Chapter 8. What happens at the interpersonal level in terms of definition of situation and attribute selection requires separate study.

One might summarise that the factors described operate in such a way that students' social relations are structured in terms of the size, "nature" (i.e. other overlapping dimensions), and degree of contact of the particular groups of which they are members or to which at any time they refer, and the way in which the groups and clustered variables are associated.[1]

Naturally, one cannot eliminate entirely social relations which are based on chance and interest—yet in a sense they are comprehended by the present definition and fall into the areas of spatial and social concentration and potential contact areas. Again, they are delimited, yet are not defined by these conditions. For people only group in terms of interest

---

[1] These principles of organisation apply not only to social class groups but also to racial groups and might be used to analyse racial relations in differing urban settings.

when their relation to one another is not legally defined.[1] In that all are students it would appear superficially that no association is defined. What the last two chapters have tried to show is that within the conditions set by certain factors, in fact relations are patterned and regulated by students themselves.

It will be clear that the student membership group, to a student, comprehends a multiplicity of roles and reference groups within it, of which a major factor is social class.

Indeed, it is clear that the student category is not in itself a membership group with a defined culture and way of life, but that there are comprehended within this category a number of membership groups. We have already outlined the most basic of these in the last chapter and the social distances between them. The broad spheres of work, leisure, and residence were used to define their relationship, although this kind of division is obviously artificial. However, it does serve to emphasise that as the student passes from one sphere of action to another different membership groups at different times become reference groups and vice versa—he is never a member of one group or community *all* of the time, and he changes identity with group membership.[2] This is meant to refer not only to informal groups, where it is obviously true, but to institutionally defined and organised groups within which status is at least to some extent ascribed. All students must take some courses in the university or they are not institutionally defined as students, and they must live somewhere at least in the vicinity of the institution. They may not have any particular leisure patterns and are not required to do so, but it is likely that interests of some kind will help to dictate membership of off-duty groups. Within these broad limits there is obviously a great deal of choice, but there are limits and there are institutionally prescribed sanctions and rules of membership.

The kind of culture groups we have discussed earlier in the chapter— such as school, area of home residence, and education history of family— do, as we have seen, affect student relations, but they are "givens" in the situation. They stand as attributes as well as reference groups and the student cannot change them. He has very little area of manœuvre

---

[1] Bendix, R., in discussion at conference on "Social Change and the Industrial Revolution", Edinburgh University, 20 March 1965.

[2] The degree of "time lap" between movement of the actor from reference group to membership group and vice versa will affect the stability of the actor's thought-of-order and his perception of his role.

compared with his choice of interaction in institutional terms. He may or may not choose to associate with others with similar school or residential background, but he cannot change the fact that he went to a certain school or lived in a certain area. He may feel the need to pretend in order to associate with a particular group, and the nature of student society makes this possible. Often students indulge in play acting because they know that it is probably their first and last chance to kick free the traces of their cultural heritage. But the influence of these ascribed statuses is either way inescapable. Contrasted with this, the institutional organisation offers the student a whole array of groups of which he may become a member, each presenting a new set of identities—academic, residential and interest group. It is at this point that most researchers begin—where the student chooses to join certain groups; is institutionally compelled into others and becomes a part of the prevailing group culture. However, we have seen that not only will those inescapable attributes and reference groups influence his own choice in certain directions, but will mark him out as belonging or not belonging to particular groups—even before he chooses. The situation is analogous to that in a very exclusive north country golf club where "the only qualification for new members (apart from being able to pay the subscription) is that they should 'fit in'. The Club captain had never known a Jew be turned down because none had ever applied."[1]

We shall look briefly, therefore, at the membership groups as socialising agents, bearing in mind that members may not represent a random social cross-section of students and that they have already been shaped by other membership groups to which they now refer. Although the institutional membership groups may overlay existing culture patterns with new ones—as in halls of residence—this greatly depends on the randomisation of social classes, schools, areas of home residence, and other cultural identities within them. Under these conditions there is more likelihood of mutual transmission of culture patterns and values. What has been discussed as principles of association at the institutional level are equally appropriate at the level of student sub-groups.

Residence groups—whether in halls, colleges, fraternities, digs, student houses, flats, or parental home—obviously represent fundamental student sub-groups. Residence provides a spatial as well as social iden-

[1] Article entitled "Britain's poshest village" in *The Observer Colour Supplement*, 9 April 1967, and taken from Turner, G., *The North Country*, Eyre and Spottiswoode, June 1967.

tity—it enables the individual to place himself, relative to others—it is
territory and home. Where the territory is shared with others, the common ground becomes community of interest and values related to the
act of living in that place.[1] A way of life grows up in certain kinds of residence and in particular residences. Hall life is not like digs life—the whole
ecological, group, authority and discipline structure is different. This
goes for all kinds of residence. On the other hand, no two halls of residence are alike either. One therefore has to take into account the character of the warden or principal, the character of the student inhabitants,
the degree of student responsibility for running the hall, hall traditions,
and relations with other halls. These contribute to the hall way of life
or culture, to its personality. In interaction with other students the hall
members will refer not to hall but to *his* hall. Albrow,[2] in his study of
sixty-four Reading students, shows that one may speak about hall culture,
and that the values of the particular hall he studied were in accord with
the general values of the university. This kind of identification of hall
values and culture with university value and culture results from the fact
that the university "ideal" of a community of scholars can only be achieved
where territory and work coincide. Therefore halls of residence and
colleges most nearly approach this image. As we have seen also from this
survey, and those of Albrow and Marris,[3] "living in" stimulates not
only community within residence but greater participation in other activities *outside* the hall. Having a secure home base and satisfying human
relations, the student is encouraged to strike out into new fields and join
in a variety of groups. The student who has few reassuring contacts with
his fellows in day-to-day living may lack confidence to branch out further. As we have seen, where social and spatial distance coincide, the opportunities for culture contact are remote. What happens *within* a particular residence group in terms of transmission of culture and growth of
group identity is the exact opposite of what happens between groups
prevented by institutional distance from interaction. In the first instance
one has a positive reaction, in the latter a negative—whatever the social
context. Where the institution is able to stimulate a positive reaction
between disparate social groups it creates new identities from old ones
and new distinctly student culture from existing class culture. This is true

[1] The basis of tribalism. See Morris, D., *The Naked Ape*, Corgi Books, 1968,
pp. 160–3.
[2] Albrow, M. C., *BJS*, December 1966, **17** (4).
[3] Marris, *op. cit.*

of all student groups in every sphere. What we have seen though is tha association is often promoted between those who already have muc in common outside the institution, so that reference groups become im ported into membership groups and make them somewhat less tha truly student.

Of course the situation varies always with the group, and residenc groups in particular may help to break down existing social divisions We have seen how colleges in Durham are ranked in prestige by student —each with its own image and particular culture. This ranking owe something to external social divisions, but it also incorporates much tha is particularly student—or rather that is meaningful to students in Dur ham. The social context qualifies and makes meaningful the categor "student", because in Durham particular responses are appropriate t particular situations which are not appropriate or meaningful elsewhere This is true of all student sub-cultures. The division of the students int colleges presents not only a significant ordering of membership groups but also provides all students with an institutional "reference group" i which all can share and which therefore provides some common ground— even if only in the form of rivalry. Newcomb's work on college pee groups underlines the peculiar nature of this internal organisation an status system, particularly with reference to provision of access to suit able dates by fraternities.[1] The "rating and dating complex"[2] is fa more characteristic of the American campus than the British univer sity, however, and other functions of the organisation seem more sig nificant.

It is interesting at this point to refer again to the fraternities and frater nity culture. We have already noted that fraternity membership implie a certain style of life—as in the British colleges. This may in certain way work either towards or against the institutional goals and values. Wallac shows how inter-fraternity rivalry may improve grades and therefor assist internalisation of "academic" culture, while Harp and Taretz show that there is a level of cheating associated with certain structura relations. Goldsen *et al.* found that "thirty seven per cent of all the stu dents who answered the question admitted they had done some cheatin some time during the course of their college careers".[4] The reasons fo

[1] Newcomb, T. M., *College Peer Groups*, 1969.
[2] Waller, W., *ASR*, 1937, **2**, 727–34.
[3] Harp, J. and Taietz, P., *Soc. Prob.* 1966, **13** (4), 365–73.
[4] Goldsen *et al.*, *op. cit.*, p. 75.

hese very high figures is associated with three important "value clus-
ers", state Goldsen *et al.*: "The first is the formal and informal nature
f the social controls." These are related to the size of the institution and
he group, and beyond a certain size social control begins to break
own. "The second cluster which links up with cheating has to do with
. tendency to conform to what is perceived as the current practices of
ne's peer group. Finally, cheating is likened to a general deprecation of
he academic experience as such: a certain disenchantment with, or per-
aps a jaded approach to, one's school work."[1]

It is, therefore, social pressures within and outside the institution which
esult in cheating.

This principle is true of other student membership groups, partic-
larly those associated with work and leisure. The great difference between
hese groups is that once having made his choice, of course the student
sually remains within it to the end of his degree, whereas membership
f interest groups is entirely voluntary and will be changed as the inter-
sts change. Membership of student societies fluctuates—they are start-
d and disappear—while departments and faculties are essential intitutional components. Therefore the quality of membership is different
nd more or less compulsive on the individual, and the student culture
iffers in quality and permanence. It is only certain kinds of society which
an withstand rapid turnover in personnel and, in fact, become something
f a community. These are the time-consuming, full-time occupation
ay of life societies like dramatic societies and debating societies. Those
vho are recruited must display certain skills necessary for continuance
f the group, and they are required to contribute their skills and their
ime to the common endeavour. This, in turn, breeds great *esprit de corps*,
nd is entranced by the fact that such societies, by the nature of their
oals, usually have a physical base or home where they work together
n their project—such as the theatre and debating chamber. The fact
hat they present themselves periodically before those who are not mem-
ers and display their skills of course increases internal cohesion and
ontrol of recruitment. It is such societies which are accused of being
liquey and keeping people out, yet it is really only such societies which
an be said to have an identifiable culture and may well again be associat-
d with "territory". It is only in an atmosphere of some permanence of
xpectations that group interaction can go on and members can be so-
ialised. Societies in which members listen or watch others, rather than

[1] *Ibid.*, p. 76.

interact, and which meet in a different lecture theatre each time, cannot be seen to develop a specific culture or personality. It is the "participation" societies only which have the opportunity of culture transmission—unfortunately many of them frighten away the working-class student.

We have seen that fitting-in faculty and work-group culture, too, is important, particularly in the professional faculties. In the latter case this is related to specific job training as well as being a student and a continual moving towards the day when the student will become a full member of the profession.[1] Indeed, it is only where there are conditions of continual interaction and reinforcement of group goals and values that a faculty culture as such can grow up. As in the total student situation the relative size, nature, and degree of contact of component groups will help to determine this—with the additional reinforcement of structural opposition of other groups. On the large impersonal campus the faculty or department group is not a group at all and can be said to have no culture other than that related to attending lectures and passing examinations. Therefore one must again consider this question of sub-cultures in their overall context.

Much has been written about socialisation within the professional faculty, and it is noted that of course this involves not only faculty culture but professional culture and a way of life which will be expected of the student as a future professional practitioner. Therefore here again we cannot ignore outside influences on student culture, nor, indeed, the occupational and social class implications. Nor, as we have seen, can we ignore the students' social class of origin whose culture may or may not be compatible with that of the future profession and which must therefore be modified in various ways. For this "modification" or socialisation to take place there must be as has already been stated various conditions—one of which is "sequestration"—"either formally as in the convent, or informally as in the music conservatory or residential medical or nursing school".[2] The degree of sequestration allows for the degree of social control—both by superiors and peers. It is a multidimensional process.

"Viewed as a set of interactions that implicate the student in his or her various roles, as student, as new professional and as young adult, with

---

[1] Merton *et al.*, *Sociology Today*, 1959. Hughes *et al.*, *Boys in White*, 1961.

[2] Olsen, V. and Whittaker, E., Some thoughts of man implicit in sociological studies of professional education, paper presented to the Sixth World Congress of Sociology 1967, p. 30.

multiple others it activates role sets that are outside the institution, as well as located within the formal structure."[1]

This is true of course of all student membership groups in which the student in transition is both backward looking and forward looking. But the kind of group and the kind of institution will interact to produce a different kind and quality of "membership" and a different range of influence. Student culture, therefore, is a complex multidimensional configuration of different cultures; and different kinds of socialisation are going on within the institution both concurrently and consecutively, and the student experiences them all. The process is composite rather than coherent. Obviously there are stages in the process—perhaps in terms of clearly demarcated status difference of different years. This again depends on the institution and will be discussed in the next chapter. These internal divisions are in turn related to the degree to which the institution is cut off from external, perhaps conflicting divisions. "Student group" and "student culture" therefore is only meaningful when we study the relation of the institution to its external environment, and to the promulgation of group solidarity among students by interaction and activity in which the outside populace cannot share. The opportunity for this kind of activity varies with the institution so that different degrees of "studentness" are generated in different institutional contexts. These are discussed in the following chapter.

[1] *Ibid.*, p. 40.

CHAPTER 11

STRUCTURAL DISTANCES AND INSTITUTIONAL SOCIALISATION

IN THE previous two chapters, spatial and cultural factors have been discussed which operate in students' social relations with each other, i.e. in the context in which student *per se* is not a meaningful social category to students themselves. In this context it is the membership of sub-groups and sub-cultures within the institution which serves to identify student roles—in combination with social class membership and reference groups. We now turn to an examination of the structure of student social relations within the total institutional context in its relation to external structure and culture. We shall see that internal social relations vary in their structure with the relationship which the student body as a whole has with those who are not students. The category of non-students will be seen to comprehend those who are not students within the institutional framework, e.g. academic and administrative staff of the university and those who are not students outside the university. These groups, and the others to be discussed, represent different degrees of studentness or non-studentness which regulate the degree of corporateness in student interaction. We could describe this in Banton's terms as a situation of "structural opposition"[1] in which those groups which are structurally opposed are conscious of their own special identity. This in turn will be related to institutional and sub-group socialisation and the way in which this is influenced by structural distances between groups both vertical and horizontal. Since socialisation or induction into a group involves some *sharing of experiences*, the structural distances may enhance the sharedness of certain activities and identities by emphasising the operational reality of "them" and "us". The students' social class of origin becomes another dimension of these structural realities, just as previously we observed structural constraints as a dimension of social class. This involves us in a new look at what we mean by institutional socialisation.

[1] Banton, *Roles*, p. 27.

Olesen and Whittaker have done much important work on adult social-isation in the field of medical education,[1] and their ideas will provide points for discussion in this chapter.[2] However, it is the aim to broaden in scope the examination from the analysis of induction into occupational and professional roles to socialisation within the total institution with its many component sub-groups and its complex configuration of social roles. Discussion in previous chapters may have given some idea of the complex configuration of identities, membership groups, and reference groups which interplay in the structure of the student role-set. Since much of our analysis has centred upon real and perceived distances be-tween these role-sets, as they are ranked in status, it becomes pertinent to speak of the structure of the student status-set. This status-set, as we have seen, is made up not only of identities, positions, and reference groups, but is made up in such a way that different parts of the status-set are differentially weighted in differently defined situations. This, as we have seen, in turn depends on the informal and formal structure of the institution. All these factors complicate our investigation of "social-isation", since the processes of unlearning or relearning undergone will not affect all parts of the status-set concurrently nor with the same de-gree of effectiveness. The particular structure and weighting of the status-set will determine the form, the speed, and the consequences of the pro-cess of socialisation undergone, so that within each institution processes of socialisation will not only be different but will be different for different groups and will have different social consequences within the constraints posed by the educational process itself.

The process of socialisation emerges as of central importance to the study of social class factors in student relations since, as we have seen, the process of acculturation[3] of social classes, or lack of it, is intimately connected with the structural interrelation of these groups. Not only are we concerned with what may be conflicting forces of socialisation in the home and the university, and with the anticipatory socialisation of the socially mobile student, but with the institutional conditions which aid or prevent the socialisation of students by each other. The importance of

[1] Olesen, V. and Whittaker, E. W., Some thoughts on images of man implicit in sociological studies of professional education, paper read at VIth World Congress of Sociology, 1966. See also Olesen, V. and Whittaker, E. W., *The Silent Dialogue*, Jossey-Bass Inc., California, 1968.

[2] Olesen and Whittaker, *op. cit.*

[3] As used by Banton in discussion of race relations. See Banton, M. P., *Race Relations*, Basic Books, N.Y., 1967, pp. 70, 74, 77–100.

peer group culture in a reciprocal, mutually adaptive process, as opposed to the imposed culture of those in authority, in a rather more one-way process, will again vary with the institutional structure and its particular authority pattern. These are the kind of issues we shall discuss. It is hoped to build some kind of model, although this can only be tentative at this stage.

Certainly one may argue, as do Olesen and Whittaker,[1] that many models of socialisation have in the past been based upon three prominent traditions: "one largely psychological, stemming from the studies of childhood maturation and socialisation; a second derived from the sociological studies of institutions; and the third, emerging from the cross and intra-cultural work of anthropologists."[2] Olesen and Whittaker show the inapplicability of these previous approaches to what has become known, since the late 1950's, as "adult socialisation", and relate this to the neglect of the concept of social role in the analyses of the process—only now being remedied in a number of works—particularly in studies of the professions.[3] Olesen and Whittaker posit, however, that sociologists have inherited the conceptual frameworks of these earlier traditions as a kind of cognitive lag and that these conceptual frameworks hinder rather than help the analysis of the complex processes at work in adult socialisation.[4] They criticise the "images of man" implicit in these concepts. For instance the analogy of the student professional as a child who is shaped by his faculty, as surrogate parents, who competes with his peers and who assimilates the professional values and culture crudely overemphasises the influence of faculty on the student at the expense of recognition of peer group influences in learning. The image also fails to recognise that the "student professional, unlike the child is partially developed *as a professional* by the time he or she starts professional schooling" or in other words some *anticipatory* socialisation has already taken place. We have already seen this will in fact influence self-selection of student for faculty or profession in the first instance Olesen and Whittaker do not specifically make mention of social class when they discuss "behavioural rehearsal of roles"—but this is of ut

[1] Olesen and Whittaker, *op. cit.*

[2] *Ibid.*, p. 6.

[3] Hughes, E. C., The study of occupations, in Merton, Broom and Cottrell (eds.) *Sociology To-day*, Basic Books, New York, 1959.

[4] Olesen and Whittaker, *op. cit.*, p. 14a.

[5] Merton, R. K., *Social Theory and Social Structure*, 1957. also Brim, O. G. and Wheeler, S., *Socialisation after Childhood*, Wiley, New York, 1966, pp. 265–8.

most importance to the present discussion. For some students "behavioural rehearsal" of certain roles is out of the question because it is completely out of their sphere of experience.[1] This must affect differential kinds of socialisation experience among students, particularly in professional faculties. Olesen and Whittaker refer to this obliquely by saying that students

> May or may not have the chance to develop conceptualisations of the professional role by observing relatives, as for example young lawyers, many of whom have relatives who are in law. The result of these various degrees of private rehearsal, behavioural experience and role acquaintance, among other factors, is that student movement through the professional school can differ drastically among and between students, defying any easy conceptualisation of developmental stages that parallel those of childhood.[2]

Olesen and Whittaker criticise also the image of the student professional as a stimulus response element who receives programmed learning from powerful transmitting agents in such a way that he responds with "proper role behaviours and value outlooks". This approach makes socialisation appear a smooth curve along whose trajectory he proceeds at a uniform rate. Rather is there a need, they point out, to study "role regression" and "reverses in role acquisition and views of self."[3] The same kind of drawbacks emerge in the study of student professional as "message receptor", of institutional and professional ideology which is supposed to alter role behaviour and self-definitions. Such studies look for changes in attitudes or behaviours which may be in response to institutional stimuli, or, on the other hand, the attributes necessary for successful assimilation of these stimuli.[4]

This assumes a willing student audience in a sequestered setting and implies an extreme communication model somewhat similar to brainwashing. Olesen and Whittaker point out that even in favourable settings of sequestration, the communication process cannot be assumed to sway students completely, and that "previous social position, psychological endowments and, very importantly, responses to others undergoing the

---

[1] "With respect to changes during the life cycle the emphasis in socialization moves away from motivation to ability and knowledge, and from a concern with values to a concern with behaviour", Brim, *op. cit.*, p. 25.

[2] Olesen and Whittaker, *op. cit.*, p. 14a.

[3] *Ibid.*, p. 16.

[4] See, for example, Eron, L. D. and Redmount, R. S., *J. Legal Educ.*, 1957, **9** (4), and Robinson, J. B. and Bellows R. M., Characteristics of successful dental students, *J. Am. Ass. Coll. Regs.*, January 1941.

same socialisation importantly filter the messages from those in authority, even in presumably perfect communication situations".[1]

It is the "responses to others undergoing the same socialisation"—particularly to the social *categories* of others—with which we are concerned in this book. Indeed, we are concerned to examine all those culture and communication filters which "are even more effective in diluting messages in other, less tightly structured situations".[1]

In this study of communication filters of institutional socialisation it is important to consider "student culture", say Olesen and Whittaker. From our present survey findings we would relate this very closely to class culture and the ways in which this acts as a particular communication filter, and would perhaps treat with some reservation the Olesen and Whittaker suggestion that student culture is "a highly innovative process".[2]

We should agree, however, that the student can in no way be considered as an "empty vessel"[3] into which good things are poured, since the argument of the whole book is that what processes of socialisation go on in the home and at school before university are influential on what happens within the institution, so that only under certain conditions do "students become more homogeneous with respect to role behaviours and values".[4] The student is very much a product of his cultural heritage and his past experience, and his social choices are mediated by these influences and will change over time. Similarly, not only must one consider the institutional culture within which the choices are made,[5] but also the cultural setting of which the institution is a part. Olesen and Whittaker posit that there is a vacuum in such descriptions despite warnings that "the social environment of such schools, presumably a part of the culture, is a critical and neglected variable".[6]

In addition to the models discussed there are those suggested by studies of institutions such as the prison and mental hospital. Olesen and Whittaker describe these models of treating the individual as one re-born, divested of previous attributes upon entry. These studies overlook influ-

---

[1] Olesen and Whittaker, *op. cit.*, p. 19.

[2] *Ibid.*, p. 20.

[3] *Ibid.*, p. 21.

[4] *Ibid.*, p. 22.

[5] Becker and Greer, *op. cit.*, ch. 4.

[6] Merton, R. K., Reader, G. C., and Kendall P. L. (eds.), *The Student Physician*, 1957, in Olesen and Whittaker, *op. cit.*, p. 24.

ences of differential recruitment (as in student selection and self-selection), "prior student socialisation, differential background and the configuration of roles undergoing socialisation".[1] They retain crucial influence even where the phase of socialisation is time bracketed and tightly structured and carries definite expectations for change within that time span— for changes are not only confined to the "professional" or "student" role as narrowly conceived in relation to performance of specific tasks.

Not only do Olesen and Whittaker note the influence of social class and other roles, but of sex roles in particular at a time in the life cycle "when young men and women are groping for maturity in sex roles, adult roles and identities as persons".[2] This may "point the sociologist to the hitherto neglected matter of tangential role socialisation in many life roles as well as the sex role". The crucial factor in the process of socialisation is the degree to which the student professional is sequestered —formally or informally—and this will determine the degree to which other life roles are socialised and are relevant. We shall extend this argument to cover the structure of relative distances between groups in the latter half of this chapter.

It is important to make the point here that has been made before that not "all events and persons within the institution are significant for the student",[3] nor are the messages at all homogeneous. In this book we relate this to the structure of groups and the differential relevance of structural attributes, also to the perception, of students of these structures which may be faulty in particular ways. It is important also to agree that the socialised student cannot be regarded as a finished product,[4] and it is hoped that the chapter on social mobility and bourgeoisification will underline this point. Olesen and Whittaker state, as Chapter 13 will state with regard to this survey, that students themselves (or in this case certain categories of students) recognise that they are not finished products.

This relates closely to what the student interprets as the social influences upon him which pose him with social dilemmas in a variety of ways and which change "the phenomenological attributes that constitute his *inner* world".[5] Therefore a study *only* of structure in terms of objective,

---

[1] Olesen and Whittaker, *op. cit.*, p. 26.

[2] *Ibid.*, p. 27.

[3] *Ibid.*, p. 31. See also Becker, H. S. and Greer, B., Latent culture: a note on the theory of latent social roles, *Admin. Sc. Quart.*, 1960. 5.

[4] Olesen and Whittaker, *op. cit.*, p. 34.

[5] *Ibid.*, p. 37.

external factors is not enough for an understanding of how socialisation occurs. Self-awareness and identification with a professional (or student) role are essential foci for study.[1] There is need for integration of the "subjective and objective aspects of professional socialisation".[2]

In summarising points of criticism of traditional models of professional socialisation, Olesen and Whittaker suggest some new approaches to this phenomenon. They suggest, firstly, that socialisation must be regarded as a multidimensional phenomenon which incorporates role acquisition in a number of other factors of life and which involves shifts in the student conception of self. "Viewed as a set of interactions that implicate the student in his or her various roles, as student, as new professional and as young adult, with multiple others, it activates role-sets that are outside the institution, as well as located within the formal structure."[3]

It is this set of interactions which we are considering broadly in this book.

Secondly, Olesen and Whittaker posit that socialisation is variegated in relation to the numerous groups involved and their communications designed to change "attitudes role definitions and behaviours" in a set of students who are themselves "far from being homogeneous in origin, outlook or expectation".[3] Thirdly, the process is continually problematic, and is "characterised by differential pacing within and among students along the way, and by differential realisation of role and identity at institutional conclusion".[4]

In their outline of "a model which will accommodate the structural, psychological and processional facets of professional socialisation",[4] Olesen and Whittaker stress the importance of the above considerations. They take up the stance of "soft determinism" with an image of man experiencing degrees of freedom and constraint. This would correspond with what the author has described as social choices within the constraints of situational conditions as posed by situational space.

Olesen and Whittaker express the position thus:

> As he or she confronts situations, the interplay of person and encounter lead to new definitions of role and self, new perspectives that then become replaced as further encounters occur. More specifically, our assumption is that man is a continually emergent creature, whose qualities are not solely self-generated as some

---

[1] Olesen, A. and Whittaker, E., Baccalaureate students' images of nursing, *Nursing Research*, Winter 1964, **13**, 8–15.

[2] *Ibid.*, pp. 8–19.

[3] Olesen and Whittaker, Some thoughts..., p. 40.

[4] *Ibid.*, p. 41.

critics have argued, but whose emergent qualities of self and role are a continual result of the confrontation between the person and the situation.[1]

This interplay of person and situation results in a state of existence and becoming in "three ways simultaneously, within the inner world, within the world of social relationships and within the world of the environment".[2] The student exists and becomes simultaneously in these three modes. These three modes therefore constitute elements in a model of socialisation. This model corresponds closely to that in the present book, especially in relation to the environment.

"The environment, for example, may be assumed to include the physical setting in which students encounter others, particularly the physical and structural arrangements of the institution and the official institutional calendar."[3]

The physical environment and the distances it presents is of major concern in the study of student relations.

"The relational world of the students, like that of all men, is made up of "multiple realities" (as used by Schutz) or phrased alternately the different worlds of the person. Multiple realities and the relationships involved are not bounded by the environment, that is, by the institution; they extend beyond it."

These multiple realities, as they influence student relations and perception of role, have been considered throughout and are specially discussed in Chapter 8. Thus we can ask not only questions about actors and situations but what the social world means for the observed actor and what he means by acting in it.[4] This relates, as we have seen, to the Thomas Theorem of men's definition of the situation,[5] so that "inter subjectivity as well as role structure is accommodated, a merger of self–other and role theories".[6] Thus the definition of conformity or deviance very much depends on the self–other or role perspective of the definer. Such recognition also gives weight to the phenomenon of "student discount, namely student

[1] Olesen, V. and Whittaker, E., *op. cit.*, p. 43.

[2] *Ibid.*, p. 43.

[3] *Ibid.*, p. 44.

[4] Schutz, A., Common sense and scientific interpretation of human action, in Natanson, *op. cit.*, p. 7.

[5] Thomas, W. I., *Social Behaviour and Personality*, Social Science Research Council, New York, 1951.

[6] Olesen and Whittaker, *op. cit.*, p. 46, in reference to Brim, O. G., *Sociology and the Field of Education*, New York, 1958.

evaluation of institutional practices and, more importantly, shaping their own socialisation".[1]

Olesen and Whittaker take cognisance of the fact that not only is the institution helping to shape the student, but the student is in fact transforming the system—usually in minute ways—but perhaps changing continually the meaning of the role itself. The recent student demonstrations and political movements have demonstrated both an unconscious and a conscious attempt to change the role of student—outside as well as within the institution.

It will have been realised how close the ideas of Olesen and Whittaker are in this paper to many of those in this book. The research and writing of the two took place, however, completely independently and bear witness if anything, not only to the simultaneous generation of similar ideas in different places but also to the general validity of conclusions drawn from such widely differing material. Also it must be remembered that the Olesen and Whittaker paper was available only in the later stages of revision of this book. The author acknowledges, however, that the Olesen–Whittaker paper was of great help in focusing some of the ideas which would otherwise have remained only implicit in the material.

Let us consider at this point some of these ideas in relation to the model of institutional socialisation of social classes as it relates to the structural relations in the three modes posited by Olesen and Whittaker of inner world, social relationships, and environment. The Olesen–Whittaker model in this case must be modified by the fact that student roles, as we have seen, comprehend within them faculty or student professional roles among multiple others, whereas for the student professional the student role as such may be only tangential. We are looking at a different role-set— a different configuration of attributes. Although both are multidimensional processes they involve different dimensions, differently related.

Certainly we must consider the process of socialisation as a complex response not only to institutional and faculty pressures but to others undergoing the same process. However, in this case institutional and faculty pressures must be differentiated and their relation must be examined. This broadens in scope and makes more complex the set of structural relations and distances. In turn, and at the other end of the spectrum, we are looking at a culturally and socially differentiated student body both in terms of membership and reference groups. Indeed, the areas of sharing which this suggests have to be examined—as sharing of heritage (to which refer-

---

[1] Olesen and Whittaker, *op. cit.*, p. 37.

ence is made) or sharing of experience (in terms of common group membership). If socialisation is effected by sharing of experiences of various kinds, then these different influences on shared experience have to be accounted for and act as complex communication filters. Expanding the Olesen–Whittaker model a little we might say that the structural interrelation and distances of groups will influence the ways in which certain communication filters operate both between peers and between students and agents of institutional culture (such as staff). The interrelation and distances will in turn regulate the degree to which certain persons are able to share the same institutional experiences and therefore to depend less upon shared reference groups alone.[1]

The degree of distance between groups will be seen to be related directly to the degree of sequestration which is possible, and the degree of internal group solidarity. Lack of structural distance between groups—even group overlap—leads to ambiguity of identity, lack of sequestration, and of group solidarity. In the sequestered group, internal divisions are imposed as they relate to the character of what has to be transmitted, i.e. professional or academic roles; where the process is lengthy and implies learning by stages, the movement from stage to stage will be given ritual significance—as in the change from pre-clinical to clinical year in medicine. The membership groups and learning situation are given more importance than the reference groups of those recruited. In the non-sequestered group, internal divisions reflect the quality of those in the environment, whether within the institution or outside. This gives more importance to reference groups in the structuring and response to situations as, for instance, we have seen the importance of social class in structuring certain situations in the urban university. Thus socialisation in terms of shared experience is less possible.

Naturally the scale of structural distances is on a continuum, but for the sake of our model we shall discuss the institution which is able to separate itself from its external environment and the institution which is not isolated from its external environment as though they were two ideal type cases at each end of the continuum. This in turn will be related to student problems of cultural adaption. The degree of sequestration or distance in each social context will also be seen to be related to what we shall call horizontal and vertical group transparency or opaqueness. This refers to groupings socially and spatially distributed which allow or do not allow

---

[1] In this case students become part of a more *generalised* value system which universities are concerned to synthesise. Williams, R. M. (Jr.), Individual and group values, *Annals of Am. Ac. of Pol. and Soc. Sc.*, May 1967, **371**, 20–37.

other groups of different social dimensions to be "seen through" or to predominate beyond the group as structurally defined.

We shall refine this concept later in the discussion as it relates to what we have earlier called "structural opposition". The model itself will be seen to be based upon the three universities studied, and we shall use illustrations from these universities although, as ideal type models, certain characteristics will be exaggerated. It is hoped to show how these institutional settings help to define the student role in society or student role-set and status-set and how, in turn, this may help to decide what action in society students feel able and desire to take. This may have bearing on the analysis of student corporate action—protest movements and revolts.

First let us look at the degree to which the institution as a whole is able to maintain itself separately from its external social setting and the influence which this has upon internal organisation and divisions. It is clear that the institution is able to separate itself from external environment and external divisions only in so far as its members are socially and/or spatially concentrated. Either its members must be culturally homogeneous and socially distinguishable from the surrounding populace, or where recruitment takes place from a number of culturally different groups—as social classes—there must be lateral solidarity or concentration. This lateral solidarity is best achieved through spatial concentration in residence which accentuates also a high degree of temporal concentration. Work concentration is less effective because it covers only partial interaction. Where social and spatial concentration, i.e. vertical and horizontal divisions coincide, of course the sequestration is almost complete. Coupled with temporal concentration, the institution is totally isolated from its external environment. One has this kind of sequestration in residential mental hospitals where the similarity of characteristics in terms of patients' mental disorders overrides the differences in other characteristics, and where the outside world is excluded.[1] In this situation the institution *can* be regarded as an isolated social system. Membership is total, and is usually marked by visible symbols. Nuns in convents are an example of this kind of membership. No university would normally come into this category, for, however spatially concentrated, recruitment is usually from heterogeneous groups with only academic ability in common. There is not even uniform desire to be a member of the institution. The vocational aspect of learning in times past at least presumed certain characteristics of motivation in common which cannot now be assumed.

[1] Goffman, E., *Asylums*, Anchor Books, New York, 1961.

The degree of lateral or spatial concentration (coupled with temporal concentration) is most likely in the modern university, therefore, to determine social and spatial separateness of the institution and what we have called "group opaqueness". One must, however, relate this also to the authority structure of the institution and the degree of institutional supervision exerted over each individual part to bring it within the overall sphere of influence. This is not, therefore, merely a matter of exchange relationships but also of power relationships. Where there is this institutional lateral and vertical group opaqueness there is a distancing from the environment, which means also a distancing from external reference groups. This enhances, as it were, the value of institutional membership and attenuates the connection of members with those groups outside of which they are or were members. In the case of students this means those family and neighbourhood groups from which they came.

In this situation the institution is able to impose its own conditions of membership and to exert its own forms of social control. There is growth of solidarity and identity from interaction in the institutional setting, and this depends greatly upon the relative size of the institution. The larger the institution the more difficult to exert strict forms of social control. The largest sub-groups will tend to be lateral—as in colleges—and therefore to accentuate cohesion by institutionalising the principle of structural opposition. Institutionally sanctioned rivalries of college membership exemplify this.

In this way the institution is able to overlay external social and cultural divisions with new ones, and to impose its own status ranking based on criteria special to the institution. In the case of academic institutions the criteria posed are academic. Therefore there is hierarchical ordering of those who have passed through the various academic stages of life. There is social distance between staff and students and usually between junior and senior members of staff. This increases the likelihood of social class acculturation because in each academic stratum individuals are presumed equal within the institution although unequal in their relations with other strata.[1] There is a possibility of particular institutional sub-cultures developing because of the possibility of shared experiences of members of the same stratum. This increases the sense of group identity and the separation between those who belong to the institution and those who do not. The separation is marked by symbols such as gowns.

---

[1] Student demands for equal representation in the running of the university therefore, as an unintended consequence, may make more difficult the processes of social and academic acculturation.

Since membership of the institution therefore presumes induction into a particular culture with its own marks of status, the stages through which the novitiate proceeds are clearly demarcated and surrounded by ceremony. Not only are there structural distances between institutional strata, but between years, or seniorities, within strata. Becoming a "fresher" is surrounded by what are the equivalent of initiation rites to mark entry proper into the group.

Relations of students with those who are not students within the institution are regulated by the distances between them. Staff–student relations are constrained by the hierarchical ordering of positions, and expectations of behaviour are institutionally circumscribed. The role of academic staff is very much that of bearer of an élite culture into which the young must be inducted, and the staff are able to promote a particular social class ethos. The confusion of residential and work divisions, particularly where teaching takes place in colleges, and the duplication of staff personnel works to the disadvantage of faculty departmental or work-based divisions. These work divisions are seen as only partial associations in a community of total associations, so that where residential and organisational groups are "opaque", faculty groups do not emerge as of prime importance.

In terms of authority structure—in return for the rewards of belonging to the group—members must submit to a more pervasive supervision than they would in other institutions. Colleges are empowered to act *in loco parentis* and to influence a spectrum of student role-sets. The paternalism of institutions is only possible under these conditions.

Where the situation is highly structured, the student may have problems of culture conflict between his university and home environment to which he returns in vacation (and this is where the pressures of the total institution break down).[1] He may, alternatively, suffer from over-socialisation if he succumbs to institutional pressures to such an extent that he submerges himself in the needs of the group. It is quite likely, whatever his background, that he will undergo an intense period of reorientation to institutional values and culture—and change may be painful for certain groups.

These social problem areas have implications for student social action particularly in its relation to social class for, as we have seen, stu-

[1] It is a factor related to the groups from which the student seeks approval as a reward for conforming. See Bredemeir, H. C. and Stephensen, R. H., *The Analysis of Social Systems*, Holt, Rinehart and Winston Inc., 1965, p. 93.

dents are not divested of past experience on entering the institution. This experience is just overlaid with new ones. Where there is lack of culture mesh in such a structured situation, the reaction may be to rebel against the supervisory forces of the institution and to attempt to restructure the power situation. The need for student responsibility over their own affairs will be expressed in attempts at lateral centralisation of student organisation as an expression of challenge to the policy of "divide and rule". The student leaders are most likely to be those who have to make the greatest social adaption to the institution, i.e. working-class or first-generation students, often of the "new" middle class.

Since institutional separation is necessary for organisation and identity, a gap will emerge between what happens within the institution and what happens afterwards, i.e. between the student role and the occupational role in a technological society. Final year students find it difficult to leave the cloisters of the ivory tower for the bustle of industrial life. The process of socialisation which goes on in the institution influences the value change and social mobility of its members, so that distancing from reference groups and class of origin may be expressed in movement up the social scale. The degree to which social classes are randomised in the institution will determine the sharedness of experience and the degree of socialisation. Where there is lateral or social concentration in any part of the system of particular social groups, the socialisation process will be impaired.

Now let us look, by contrast, at the university which is not spatially separate from its urban environment, particularly the large civic university which is spread disparately through the town. There is almost total lack of sequestration except in purely work groups which represent only limited temporal groupings. There is little institutional solidarity or feeling of identity, since it is only in work tasks that the outside populace cannot share, and work alone which defines the real conditions of membership. The lateral groups are diffuse and transparent, revealing the emergence of institutional sub-groups in provision of identity and culture such as residential groups of sections only of the student population for whom lateral and social groups coincide within an extended though not total temporal span. The sub-groups that there are in terms of work, residence, and leisure tend to be socially biased in composition, and these social divisions show through the transparency of the institutional group. The lack of sequestration means that the institution is less able to impose its own conditions of membership outside the sphere of work, and its social control is consequently limited to specific areas of life and only certain aspects of the student's role-set.

The social and social class divisions, therefore, of the external environment, which students meet daily, intrude into the institutional context, and the distance between membership groups of students and their reference groups is foreshortened rather than lengthened. Indeed, where they live at home their membership and reference groups will become interchangeable. The distances between groups within the institution may therefore be as great as those between internal groups and external groups. Membership of the institution as such, therefore, has little meaning, and it is membership of institutional sub-groups which is the real link between the individual and the university. The university as such hardly exists for the individual as a meaningful entity, particularly beyond a certain size and complexity.[1]

The largest sub-groups with which students tend to identify will be vertical, such as faculties and departments within faculties. There may be no clear laterality of divisions outside residence. In addition, since work contacts are the main enduring contacts in the institution, work groups emerge as the main meaningful centres of membership. Faculties may take on the role of non-residential colleges, combining certain kinds of spatial and social concentration with only limited temporal concentration. Where, however, faculty groups themselves are diffuse and transparent, they will reveal internal divisions of departments and particular social class groups or cliques within departments. Where there is group opaqueness in a faculty, as in the spatially sequestered professional faculties, the same principles of socialisation will apply which apply to the sequestered total institution. The professional faculty which controls recruitmen, is spatially separate, largely socially homogeneous, and hierarchically structured, will impose its own control and conditions on members and supervise their training and induction in exchange for benefits of membership faculty socialisation or culture, may therefore emerge as meaningful where institutional socialisation does not. Where there are social class overtones, the process may accentuate distances already existing between faculties. Many faculties, of course, are unable to socialise students because of the transparency and diffuseness of their organisation, so that external social divisions emerge as important in organisation, and the institution is unable to overlay them with its own

---

[1] It is this kind of situation which gives rise to the growth of "non-conformist" culture from which student dissidents are drawn.

membership groups. The lack of shared experience of certain groups in turn leads to an exacerbation of existing social distances. The general structure lacks definition, and attributes of membership may be ambiguous or misleading.

Since membership of the institution does not involve induction into a total group culture there is less stress upon the stages of student acculturation, although there may be hierarchical ordering of academic staff and administration. It is often as if staff and students constituted two groups side by side and quite separate—only meeting in the lecture theatre. Certainly year differences are less important as they do not mark advances in status and experience to the extent that they do in the sequestered university. At least year differences are not institutionally defined in terms of where, for instance, different year groups sit at dinner. Initiation rites are less important for freshers, and freshmen soon lose this particular label well before the end of their first year.

Sub-groups may, however, develop their own culture and membership rules as halls of residence,[1] fraternities, and sororities. In this case, lateral and social concentration accentuates membership, and group solidarity is encouraged by marks of status by separation of years and by often arduous initiation rites which increase the sense of belonging. Thus by distancing themselves from other groups within the institution—and concomitantly from those outside—these sub-groups are able to socialise their members more easily.

The authority structure of the university, as has been briefly suggested, cannot be as paternalistic as in the sequestered university nor supervise as many spheres of student life. Outside the confines of academic regulations students are more likely to be treated as young citizens subject to the law of the land. Attempts by universities, therefore, to impose outmoded disciplinary measures as if they still existed as meaningful communities seem to students to be anachronistic, and they demand what they consider to be their rights as citizens rather than as students. The days of the scholar living in monastic seclusion are long over, but in some universities the disciplinary procedure has not yet taken cognisance of this fact.

With the breaking down of the old modes in staff–student relations and co-operation, new ones are not always established, and the situation remains ill defined. The academic is less a bearer of culture than a specialist

[1] Taylor, W., Student culture and residence, *Univ. Quart.*, September 1965; also Acland, H. and Hatch, S., *Three Aspects of Student Residence—Recruitment, Participation and Academic Performance*, London, Institute of Education, 1968.

expert who is training the student in particular skills, and outside this context there may be little scope for contact. The response to this generally unstructured situation is often avoidance, and outside the classroom the student may never meet his teachers. In this way even the institutionally provided means of communication may eventually break down, so that contact will depend largely on the personality of the individuals involved. The structural supports are lacking for certain types of action and interaction.

In this situation it is not surprising that the student identifies much less with the institution and those figures of authority whom he hardly ever sees—and much more with the student body—particularly in times of crisis when he sees his interests as in some way being threatened. It is in this situation that he looks outside the institution for the support of those who have also suffered from the same disorientating experiences— students of other universities. And those with whom he shares reference groups of background will be those with whom he feels greatest solidarity. Where faculty socialisation is most dominant, this also may act at certain times as a cross-institutional reference point.

In the institution which lacks rigid structure and identity there is a strong likelihood that, firstly, external social divisions and movements will intrude upon the institutional organisation and, secondly, that the students will attempt to seek their own identity and certainty by structuring the situation for themselves in their own terms.[1] This must be related to their external reference groups which, as we have seen, are closely related to their membership groups, but they will also be related to their membership work groups in the institution. It has been thought that leaders of student protest movements must be members of particular social groups, i.e. particularly working class, but this has been found not to be true—even in very left wing groups.[2] It is here where faculty culture may be important and may override social origins. Some faculties, particularly the social sciences,[3] are particularly left wing in orientation because of the healthily sceptical training given to students and the concern for social reform. Therefore it is often social science students who, although not

[1] For influence upon educational values see Gamson, Z. F., Utilitarian and normative orientations towards education, *Sociol. Educ.*, Winter 1966.

[2] Westby, D. L. and Braungart, R. G., Class and politics in the family backgrounds of student political activists, *ASR*, 1966, **31** (5), 690–2.

[3] Lazarsfeld, P. F. and Thielans, W., *The Academic Mind*, Free Press, Glencoe, 1958.

working class yet identifying with the causes of the underprivileged, who lead civil rights, protest, and other movements. In universities, where the social sciences are particularly strong, i.e. their lateral and vertical groupings are opaque and solidary, there is often more likelihood of student political activity than where they are weak—witness Berkeley and the London School of Economics. Of course the characteristics of the staff may have much to do with it—whether they condone or oppose student activity of various kinds and whether they are institutionally or professionally committed (i.e. locals or cosmopolitans).

The question of academic staffs' previous institutional experience and socialisation is relevant here. Obviously the experience which members of staff have of other institutions in which they have trained and taught will influence their expectations of the present institution and also their attempts to structure it in particular ways. Their ideas of authority patterns will similarly be influential.[1] Students do not have this previous institutional experience—in this sense they are more malleable. In any institution where there is a concentration of staff with previous experience of particular institutions, then there is a strong likelihood that they will act—in such a way as to try to emulate what happened in the previous institution—or to react against it if their experience was unhappy. Either way, their past institutional background will play an important role in structuring of relations, particularly staff–student relations.

In the unstructured university the problems faced by the student are likely to be isolation (where social and spatial distance coincide to prevent participation) and under-socialisation or only partial socialisation within the institution or particular sub-institutional groups.[2] Where conditions for group culture do not obtain, whatever the social class of the individual, he will not benefit from shared experiences within that culture. Following on from this, and hinted at in earlier discussions, is the problem of normlessness or anomie which results from the lack of structure in the students' role and in the particular institutional situations in which

---

[1] Vreeland, R. S. and Bidwell, C., Classifying university departments: an approach to the analysis of their effects upon undergraduates' values and attitudes, *Sociol. Educ.*, 1966, **39** (3), 237–54.

[2] "One also correctly calls unsocialised a person with deviant values and bizarre behaviour, even when the primary drive system itself has been well socialized." Brim, O. G. (Jr.), Socialisation in later life, pp. 238–47 in Borgatta, E. F., *Social Psychology—Readings and Perspectives*, Rand McNally, 1969.

he finds himself. It is in this situation that he will cling to experience of former social groups for guide lines of action in his present predicament.

The importance of social class divisions and lack of socialisation and sequestration makes movement into a job a far less awesome business and a slotting back into the social structure which the student never really left.[1] This affects the process of mobility and the degree to which class values are changed or are resistant to change.

Some brief mention must be made of the relation between student culture and youth culture at this point. This relationship is dependent upon the degree of sequestration from external influences, and it is more likely that student culture will more closely reflect youth culture in the urban university than in the sequestered university. However, as we have seen that student culture itself is largely non-existent, the youth culture of the universities will be largely class biased by whatever the prevailing ethos is thought to be. There is, of course, also the generational gap which is widening in the age of experimentation and commercialised pop and youth culture. The norms and values of society are changing rapidly, and students seem always to be in the vanguard of the changes—perhaps by virtue of the fact that they are involved in pushing back the frontiers of knowledge, in testing the accepted ways of thought, and in being trained for innovation. There have been many stories recently of students involved in drug rings and in vice of all kinds. Actually, although some cases have been confirmed, a number of cases involving students are misleading. Those who want an excuse for doing nothing for a few years, for "bumming round the world", and for flouting the established conventions of society may call themselves students for convenience—particularly as they have no intention of working—although they may not have ever been registered at an institution of higher education.[2] Therefore there is danger of the misuse of the concept of student culture to cover such pseudo-student categories. The involvement of students in youth culture and in political movements will be discussed in Chapter 15. Suffice it to say at this point that youth culture is in itself by no means homogeneous and that social class and regional variations emerge which interact with student culture at various points and in various ways. These blanket terms do not advance our understanding of these social phenomena but rather cloud

[1] See Chapter on "Career choice" in Goldsen *et al.*, *What College Students Think*, 1960.
[2] Feuer draws attention to the role of non-students in the Berkeley disturbances and in student movements from the nineteenth century. Feuer, *Conflict of Generations, op. cit.*, pp. 438–45.

over those disimilarities and discontinuities which should be the proper focus of our study. These may be explained in structural terms.

This, then, brings us to an end of the discussion of the socialisation models in terms of extreme cases of institutional distance structures. In order to see them in perspective let us consider some of the points of comparison of the three universities studied, so that empirical realities can be measured against certain aspects of the model. The comparisons are not complete, but they give some indication of the way the analysis can be taken.

We have already seen how Edinburgh and Newcastle universities are set in the very heart of the city and that because the university buildings are scattered and few people "live in", students constantly mix unavoidably with ordinary townspeople. Not only do they meet them to and from work on public transport and in the street, but by virtue of actually living amongst them in scattered groups in digs and flats, students of necessity participate in the life of the actual community in which they are placed. In their daily visits to shops and places of entertainment and so on they are citizens as well as students, and in many ways indistinguishable from other young people of their age group. This is especially true in that they are not required to wear any identification in terms of badge or dress.[1] In Edinburgh, a few years ago, undergraduates tried to revive the custom of wearing the traditional undergraduate red gown to lectures and through the streets of Edinburgh. The revival collapsed after a short time as many students refused to wear the gown. Reasons given were those of impracticability in laboratories, on bikes, or on public transport; but the deeper reason, it would seem, was that the red gown clearly indicated and thus appeared to foster a structural opposition of groups which outside the university precincts students did not want or feel able to encourage. Studentness as expressed by a red gown was not meaningful to them. In the light of what we know about the fragmentation of Edinburgh student life and groups, this is understandable.

In Newcastle, too, a recent referendum on gown wearing decided in favour of the *status quo*. The present position is that gowns are worn on ceremonial occasions in certain traditional departments and on certain councils, e.g. the MSC. Otherwise undergraduates do not wear gowns.

A different case is that of scarves, for students in general seem to welcome

[1] In recent years, however, the tattered jeans and long sweaters of even affluent students have become another kind of uniform and even symbol.

the scarf as a badge of "belonging" both inside and outside the institution. Perhaps it is a welcome substitute for the gown in that it is a less blatant indicator and its true significance is often only known to the initiated. To the ignorant it might be just another scarf. But to members of another faculty, college, university, and so on, it is an easily recognisable clue. It is at once unobtrusive enough and yet noticeable enough to be noted by only those who should note it. A scarf also usually identifies one with a smaller unit than the university—such as a college or a faculty—so that it symbolises a group with which the student is able consciously to identify, i.e. which is meaningful to him. And in a sense in terms of structural opposition it is meaningful in a wider range of relationships than is a gown. For a red undergraduate's gown in Scotland or a black in England is symbolic only of being a student, in the sense of being a scholar in a community of scholars, and since this is not meaningful in the large civic university and no longer implies uniformity of life style and life chances,[1] it is a symbol with which it is increasingly difficult to identify.

It is usually the custom for first-year students eagerly to buy a scarf upon coming up and to discontinue wearing it in their later years. This may be due to a number of changing circumstances. Firstly, the student internalises his group identity so that he needs no clues to show others; also he feels that he should know others of the student group without being shown. As disillusionment with student life progresses and the student looks forward to life after university, he resents being always regarded as a student and welcomes taking on the more defined role of citizen. He may therefore get rid of as many student clues as possible. This process begins at different times for different students. In fact, some dislike being thought of as students almost from coming to university.

We have described Edinburgh and Newcastle as being closely related to the external setting. However, Newcastle manages to preserve the student category in a sense more often than Edinburgh in that whereas Edinburgh is spatially and socially fragmented in terms of residence and work, Newcastle gives the impression of some kind of campus life during the day.[2] This centrality has not long been in existence, so its operations in terms of

---

[1] Gerth, H. H. and Mills, C. Wright (eds.), *From Max Weber—Essays in Sociology* (Internat. Lib. of Sociol. and Soc. Reconstr.), Routledge and Kegan Paul, London, 5th edn., 1964, p. 300.

[2] The developments around George Square should recentralise Edinburgh student life to some extent, although in 1969 at weekends and after class these areas were pretty deserted.

social relations have not truly taken effect. However, during working hours the structural opposition of student and non-student is more evident during the day in Newcastle than in Edinburgh. The degree of intensity of this relationship does not necessarily imply good relationships, for it is often the case that great animosity exists between town and gown in Newcastle—worse than the author had ever experienced elsewhere. Although this may be somewhat subjectively biased, it was corroborated by students. This may result from the fact that student is a meaningful category to townspeople and that the associations are not always pleasant, especially in terms of residence experience. There were constant debates in the press on this issue at the time of the survey. This applies particularly to areas of spatial concentration as in Jesmond. This being so, the student label implies a multidimensional social group. This is less true in Edinburgh where the student body is so amorphous that the main way of categorising a student is one "who is studying". As the Scots are very education conscious, to be a student to them confers status and prestige, so that relations between town and gown on the whole are particularly cordial. Of course, tradition and ancient prestige have much to do with this, and Newcastle is still seeking to establish itself.

It is worth noting that one of the few ways in which structural opposition of student–non-student is expressed in Edinburgh and Newcastle— particularly the former—is actually in the performance of academic work. For in the lecture hall, tutorial room, or laboratory the student is as much aware of being a student as at any other time, possibly more so than in most other situations. Thus the place where the student interacts with others, as a student, in activity in which those outside the university cannot share, becomes associated for him with a special pattern of identities. This gives rise to growth of a departmental or faculty culture or collective representations, which marks it off for the student who belongs from the other sections of the university, and gives to the category student its own peculiar significance.[1]

Durham is unlike both Edinburgh and Newcastle in that its residential set-up, and also its distribution of buildings, keeps it largely separate as an institution from the town itself. Most of the students eat, live, and work within the institution itself, and since entertainment in Durham is limited, their leisure time is separate too. Thus in many ways students are cut off

---

[1] The "academic" culture in Edinburgh as a whole town alike is linked with prestige and tradition and makes conscious for the student in daily as well as ceremonial contacts his role in the world of learning.

from ordinary contact with townspeople, and in consequence the townsfolk show a remarkable lack of knowledge about the various colleges and their doings. This is in direct contrast to Edinburgh, where local shopkeepers and places of entertainment have been known to keep their calendar by university terms and know exactly when graduations, rectorials, and rags take place.

The separation is conscious in Durham, as it is thought that the development of student *esprit de corps* is good for work and discipline. In consequence of this defined structural opposition, students in Durham are very conscious when in the town of being students, and they are pleased to demonstrate their studentness in various ways. All Durham students wear black undergraduate gowns to lectures and formal meals in college, and in the street they either wear them or casually sling them over their shoulders. However casually they are worn they are still an obvious and inalienable sign of being a student. Scarves, too, tend to proliferate.

"Scarves are not worn as one might suppose merely to keep the neck warm", said one Durham student somewhat haughtily.

Relations between town and gown are therefore defined and somewhat distant. But for the townspeople the category student is obviously meaningful in a variety of different ways.

Naturally more specific information about town and gown relationships in the three university cities is needed before some of the generalisations can be fully substantiated. The qualitative evidence observed and gathered from students is used here to illustrate certain structural relationships.

The way in which student as a structurally defined category is meaningful both to those inside and outside the institution depends not only on informal interaction such as that circumscribed by the exigencies of everyday life, but also by those formal or totemic occasions on which the students can demonstrate both to themselves and to others their group solidarity. These occasions take the form of rag or charities weeks, rectorial elections, graduations, freshers' conferences, or any institutional occasion on which students and non-students meet. Shows for the public, boating regattas, and so on are also included in this category.

A topical example of the effect of these academic occasions upon the members of the university itself is provided by the recent academic protest in the United States about aspects of United States foreign policy which resulted in the series of teach-ins. Little makes a point of this in his discussion of the phenomenon.

However, ideology aside, teach-ins are a co-operative enterprise which breaks through the traditional structure. This, probably, is the appeal. Students at Michigan, for example, worked unstintingly in an effort to assure success, and claimed afterwards that it was the most meaningful educational experience they had ever had. For the first time they realised what a University might be. They felt a real affinity with members of the staff. Moreover, contacts among the latter are eased too.... They sense an artificiality about their academic position and would like to establish what is more truly a community of scholars.[1]

Student–staff relations will be discussed later in the chapter.

The three universities studied had a variety of occasions which could be said to stimulate and demonstrate group solidarity, though the extent of these varied between them.

As we have said, Edinburgh student life is very fragmented so that the occasions on which students as a body meet together are almost non-existent. For even the practical difficulty of assembling about 10,000 students together at any one time precludes the idea of vast rallies in which the student category is truly meaningful. The rectorial election may be said to represent a totemic occasion, yet, in that it really represents a war of rival factions, the existing divisions within the student body exclude consciousness of a wider structural opposition. When the Rector gives his inaugural speech, ideally to the whole university, he speaks in reality to a selected few in that the hall in which he speaks is too small to hold more than a third of the student body so that tickets must be queued for in advance. At graduation, three or even four graduation ceremonials are held for the same practical reasons, and, again, the groupings are along faculty lines. It might be true to say that a student's faculty in Edinburgh is in reality the largest single unit with which he can identify.

This begins early in that even at the freshers' conference, "faculty tea parties" encourage in the student group solidarity of a special kind which will remain all through his university career.

Thus the solidarity generating occasions which would stimulate student identity are, on the whole, lacking in Edinburgh. The only occasion which would seem to cross the faculty barriers is charities week, particularly Charities Saturday when students collecting in the streets or parading on a float are probably more conscious of being students than they will ever be again. Charities is usually a tremendous success for the students, and is enjoyed by the townspeople.

In the case of Edinburgh it would seem that lack of student identity

---

[1] Little, K., Academic protest in the United States, *The Listener*, 12 August 1965.

leads to accentuate other structural oppositions within the student body —often in terms of social class.

In Newcastle, although the social life of students is also fragmental, there would seem on the face of it to be more occasions when the category student is more meaningful than in Edinburgh. The very size of the university makes it a more practical proposition to have general ceremonials for the whole student body. In physical terms, too, their students' union stands as an expression of student oneness, though in reality it is already growing too small for the total student population.

As has been pointed out, students have felt that relations between town and gown have not been too cordial in recent years,[1] and this element of conflict only reinforces the students' studentness on certain occasions. Rag week is a case in point. Because of certain incidents in the town, the Vice-Chancellor shortened rag week to three days in which all collections and all social events were to be held. This made students even more belligerent and conscious of their group solidarity.

In Durham there are an abundance of occasions for generating student solidarity, and since all are rooted in tradition the institutional sentiment is also fostered. Congregations (graduation), freshers' conferences, rag week, regatta, "Castle" day—even the inter-college "raft race"—all play their part in stimulating the consciousness of being a student.

In fact Durham shows clearly that the more separate an institution and the more visible its totemic representations, the more will it give rise to particularly student culture manifested in various forms. The raft race is a case in point where a particularly in-group affair between the colleges is also watched with great interest and amusement by local townspeople. And the ridiculous and amusing proceedings and paraphernalia are seen as "typically student".

In the other two universities nothing quite comparable to a total student culture exists, and this is seen to be a feature of the institution's relation to the external environment.

Not only does corporate unity and student culture depend for growth upon this relationship, but also the kind of unity which will create its own internal distinctions and divisions.

In a discussion of student occasions, which tend to emphasise the meaningfulness of the student category, it is necessary also to consider those student occasions which divide rather than unite the student body,

[1] This expresses a view of members of the SRC and other student officials.

because they epitomise an élite culture in which all cannot or do not desire to participate. Such examples are furnished by lavish social occasions, usually of a formal and institutional nature. College formal balls, university sherry parties, college "days", and so on stress the values and mores of an élite, and often bring to the fore social class differences among students for this reason. Those of working-class origin, for instance, who feel unsure of themselves on these grand occasions, who do not have the appropriate dress, who are not enculturated into the correct behaviour required in certain situations, will stay away from such functions.[1] Thus the clientele on these occasions will be those who fit in and who themselves epitomise the élite culture such occasions tend to perpetuate. Those students who lack the appropriate class marks and yet attend are made to feel different, so that social class divisions within the student body are emphasised.

It is for these reasons that partners for formal balls are chosen with such great care, and these are occasions on which the social class of friends of the opposite sex would come into consideration. Some students show up well in these situations and some do not. Those who do not do not get asked.

Therefore it is quite possible that some student or university occasions designed to demonstrate a unity and common culture do, in fact, demonstrate the opposite.[2] This would be less true were all students enculturated into the prevailing middle-class mores. The previous chapters have shown that this is only possible in certain conditions. Where those conditions do not obtain, external divisions persist.

In Edinburgh and Newcastle, students come into contact more readily than in Durham with external divisions and reference groups such as those met with in the home environment. Thus there is no real separation and aggregation in the sense of the *rite de passage* described by Van Gennep.[3] Thus in Edinburgh and Newcastle the same divisions and inequalities are applied inside the student body as outside—there is a kind

[1] Those students who disapprove of such events (whether working class or middle class)—and there seem to be a growing number—may stay away primarily because such events epitomise traditional and élite culture. These are another kind of nonconformist.

[2] So that "college" culture as identified by Clark and Trow may be said to be largely an upper middle-class phenomenon—even an upper-classphenomenon.

[3] Van Gennep, A., *The Rites of Passage*, translated by Monika B. Vizedom and Gabrielle L. Caffee, Routledge and Kegan Paul, London, 1960, p. 11. See also Marris, P., *The Experience of Higher Education*, 1964, p. 126.

of continuum. In that Edinburgh is a middle-class town and Newcastle working class, this is the context in which the institutional groups are set, and it has its influence upon them. Thus in Newcastle students who interact daily with local folk are more likely to be influenced by common-man attitudes than Edinburgh students, who will be influenced in turn by the professional people with whom they come into contact. This class context embraces the institutional divisions—it does not dictate them. The local links of Newcastle and the cosmopolitan[1] air of the city of Edinburgh also have their influence on internal divisions.

In Durham, however, by virtue of having cut itself off from external society spatially and socially, the University is able to manufacture its own inequalities, using and imposing its own criteria. Since it is an academic institution it employs academic criteria to differentiate and distinguish staff, students, and administrative hierarchy. The relationship of staff to students is institutionally defined so that there is a structural opposition between the two categories which heightens awareness of group identity. Such is the definition that relations between the two categories are prescribed and proscribed in all situations. Thus student is a meaningful social category both inside and outside the institution in terms of this structural opposition.

Staff in Durham, as we have seen, eat separately at High Table; they have separate flats in colleges, separate common rooms, separate facilities in the faculty buildings—there is almost total segregation, and the system is hedged about with all sorts of social sanctions. The student internalises the inherent value system and learns to accept it: this applies also to postgraduate students who are *in statu pupillari*—so that should a member of staff attempt to cross the barrier in any way he is immediately under suspicion.[2]

One of the girls of St. Mary's College was quite upset one day because the Principal had said "Hello" to her in the corridor after she had said "Good morning". She then did not know whether to say "Hello" back or not, but thought that this would not be proper. There had been for her a moment of real unease.

A young geography lecturer—new from a redbrick university—said he had tried to get friendly with his students and had invited them round to coffee. One by one they had made rather transparent excuses, and he

[1] Gouldner, A. W., Cosmopolitans and locals, *Admin. Sci. Quart.*, **2**, 1957–8.
[2] Marris attributes "reluctance to approach the staff" to a "fundamental ambiguity in staff/student relations" (Marris, *op. cit.*, p. 62).

became painfully aware that he had done the wrong thing. It is not always true that students "do want to know the staff better".[1] It is almost as if outside the hierarchically structured context there is no common reference point or discernible basis for interaction.

In Edinburgh and Newcastle there is no institutionally defined relationship of staff to students—it is all very much an individual affair so that no structural opposition as such exists. Thus, outside the purely academic context, the staff–student dichotomy is hardly meaningful. Staff and students do not mix very much socially, but since there is no institutionally prescribed relationship this fact is not remarkable.[2] In Durham, students mentioned staff–student relationships time after time—complaining of lack of contact, of lack of staff interest, and so on. Although there is equally little social contact in the other two universities, staff–student relationships were barely a matter for concern—student divisions were of far greater import.

Thus does the degree of institutional inequalities influence the perception and operation of other social factors.

We can turn for explanation of this to writings on caste systems and other forms of structural stratification. Dumont, in his paper "Caste, racism and stratification", makes some theoretical points which are relevant here. He says that

> Equality and hierarchy are not, in fact, opposed to each other in the mechanical way which the exclusive consideration of values might lead one to suppose: the pole of the opposition which is not valorised is none the less present, each implies the other and is supported by it. Talcott Parsons draws attention, at the very beginning of his study, to the fact that the distinction of statuses carries with it and supposes equality within each status. Conversely, where equality is affirmed, it is within a group which is hierarchized in relation to others.[3]

Thus where the student body is "hierarchised" as a group in a distinction of statuses as in Durham, the organisation presupposes an equality within the student status. This tends to make external inequalities less relevant, i.e. students are less conscious of social class divisions as we have seen than, for instance, in Edinburgh.

---

[1] *Ibid.*, p. 121.

[2] *Ibid.*, p. 80: "In some ways the departmental organisation of the civic universities can provide more natural opportunities for staff and students to meet informally [than in colleges]."

[3] Dumont, L., Caste, racism and stratification—reflections of a social anthropologist, *Contributions to Indian Sociology*, October 1961, No. 5, p. 41.

An example of the way in which students themselves introduce their own distinctions and inequalities is the prestige ranking of colleges discussed in Chapter 7, and the development of college images and stereotypes.

The Edinburgh and Newcastle case is different, as we have seen, in that all members of the institution are structurally undifferentiated so that external inequalities apply.

> It is this structural relation that the equalitarian ideal tends to destroy, the result of its action being which is most often studied under the name of social stratification. In the first place the relation is inverted: equality contains inequalities instead of being contained in a hierarchy. In the second place a whole series of transformations happen which can perhaps be summarised by saying that hierarchy is repressed and made non-conscious: it is replaced by a manifold network of inequalities, matters of fact instead of right; of quantity and gradualness instead of quality and discontinuity. Hence for a part the well-known difficulty of defining social classes.[1]

It is the "manifold network of inequalities" which operates within the student body that we have been considering in these three chapters; and in that none of the three universities is completely separate from external setting, all exhibit the operations of this network to some degree. We have seen that it operates less in Durham, where the institution has to some extent substituted its own inequalities. (If one speaks in Merton's terms of reference groups as having similarity of status, one may take this to mean internal reference groups and external reference groups.

This being so, one might assume that in the Durham student body social class is less relevant as a factor in social relations than in either Newcastle or Edinburgh, and that in Edinburgh, because it is most fragmented, social class is most relevant. This in general could be said to be so, although in Durham students are conscious of social class divisions because of the operations of higher education as a means of selection and allocation. That is to say that the place of the university in society is associated with the cultivation of an élite so that the very stressing of its differentness seems to introduce social class divisions, although of a different kind.[2] However, students are aware of their existence and confuse them with other social class points of reference.

[1] *Ibid.*, p. 42.

[2] Marris, *op. cit.*, p. 156. In this particular context under the specified conditions and in certain situations "they [the students] were gradually forced to realise that the classlessness of student society was misleading since the bonds which override conventional class barriers also forged an educated élite."

The particular image of an institution may again be seen as a symptom of a structural relationship—this time of the institution with the environment. Edinburgh is seen as middle class because of its contact with the town which is middle class; Newcastle is seen as working class for the same reason. Durham has a middle-class image by very virtue of it being separate and hierarchically ordered.

This, then, ends the survey of factors operating in social relations among students—of which it would appear that social class is one of the most significant. Its relevance in different contexts and situations depends on the external and internal structural relations of groups and the way in which they are combined.

We shall now examine the external point of reference in social class by attempting to discover students' own social class models.

PART IV

CHAPTER 12

THE ASSIGNED AND PROFESSED
SOCIAL CLASSES

IN PREVIOUS chapters we have considered social class as a factor in student relations within the student body, and in Chapter 11 the institutional organisation and structural distances were discussed which affect those relations in various ways. In order to complete the analysis of factors in social relations among students as members of social classes, one must take into account what the students themselves understand by social class in the light of their past actual or vicarious experience. Obviously it is not possible at this stage to undertake a thoroughgoing investigation of students' social class "models"—yet the material described will go some way to outlining what it is to which students refer outside the institutional framework when they act in terms of social class. As we have already remarked, students do not come to university as a clean slate on which new experiences will be written, and all their student experiences and activity will be interpreted and acted out in the light of their existing culture and value patterns.

> "For the most part men visualise the class structure of their society from the vantage points of their own particular milieux, and their perceptions of the larger society will vary according to their experiences of social inequality in the smaller societies in which they live out their daily lives."[1]

Therefore if we are to examine the effect which the university has upon the students within it, especially in terms of social mobility and transmission of elements of social class culture, we must first understand what social class membership means for the student himself and what a change of class implies. This involves an examination of the student's own system of status ranking, and the position in this scale to which he ascribes his parents and, by implication, himself. So shall we take cognisance of the

[1] Lockwood, D., Sources of variation in working class images of society, *Sociol. Rev.*, November 1966, **14** (3), 249.

way in which factors external to the university context—as well as those within it—operate in students' social relations. In this way we are able to look at some of the components of the student's status-set as it relates to both internal and external membership and reference groups.

Students in the three universities were asked on the questionnaire what factor they believe to be the most important in society at large in determining an individual's social status and class position. Later in interview they were also asked what they understood by social class and what kind of person they would put into each social class. What was discovered in this way of students' social class models makes meaningful their ranking of their parents in social class terms, for this will obviously be guided by the indices which they see as important. The student's ranking of his parents' social class will be termed the *professed* social class as opposed to the *assigned* social class accorded by the researcher.

A comparison of assigned and professed social class undertaken in this chapter serves to explain certain features of social mobility, discussed in the next, which are central to "mobility experience" mentioned by Turner.[1] It becomes possible to see what the student thinks he is moving from and to, and at what particular times in his life mobility is likely to occur. For it is no use, for example, plotting social mobility at crucial stages in an individual's life—such as university—if that particular point is not crucial within his own experience. Examination of externally imposed stages may show nothing that is meaningful. Comparison of both mobility experience and crude mechanics of mobility may yield important clues to the structural relationships and changes involved.

We turn first of all to some statistics on the factors which students feel most significant in determining the individual's social class. Table 12.1 shows the distributions in terms of social class.

In Edinburgh 16 per cent of students thought that "family background" determined a person's social status compared with 20 per cent in Durham and 20 per cent in Newcastle. Since this applies to life outside the university it well may be that students of Durham and Newcastle are more conscious of the divisions of "ascribed" status[2] than are students in Edinburgh. This is no more than speculation based in a sense of confusion of regional and social divisions, and in any case the difference is not large enough to be statistically significant. What is interesting is that nearly a fifth of all the students thought that family background determines a person's social

[1] Turner, R. H., *ASR*, 1960, **25** (5).
[2] Linton, R., *The Study of Man: An Introduction*, 1936, p. 115.

TABLE 12.1. INDICES WHICH STUDENTS THOUGHT MOST IMPORTANT IN DETERMINING IN SOCIETY AT LARGE AN INDIVIDUAL'S SOCIAL STATUS AND CLASS POSITION (per cent)

	UMC			LMC			WkC		
	E	D	N	E	D	N	E	D	N
Occupation	42	21	32	46	30	36	25	35	29
Family background	16	18	25	17	20	17	14	18	21
Education	15	22	19	16	19	21	25	15	19
Income	6	5	8	6	9	11	14	7	19
Personality	—	7	9	—	9	6	—	3	6
Other	20	27	—	15	14	—	22	22	—
Don't know or non-respond	1	—	8	1	—	9	—	—	7
TOTAL	100	100	101	101	101	100	100	100	101
No.	(128)	(101)	(199)	(140)	(161)	(280)	(48)	(77)	(124)

	Unclassified new figures			Total			Per cent	No.
	E	D	N	E	D	N		
Occupation	—	31	39	38	27	33	33	(428)
Family background	20	18	19	16	20	20	19	(250)
Education	60	17	15	18	17	20	18	(238)
Income	—	14	12	7	9	12	10	(127)
Personality	20	—	11	—	8	7	5	(70)
Other		20	—	21	18	—	11	(138)
Don't know or non-respond	—	—	4	1	—	8	4	(52)
TOTAL	100	100	100	101	99	100	100	
No.	(6)	(13)	(26)	(322)	(352)	(629)		(1303)

status. In interview they explained that they were thinking of themselves, i.e. students of their own age group who have as yet no occupation. These people still gain their status and role from their family; they are not yet judged as independent people. This is a most important point which must be remembered later on in the discussion of mobility and of the place of university education in the mobility process.

A third chose "occupation" as the most important social class index 38 per cent in Edinburgh, 27 per cent in Durham, and 33 per cent in New castle. Again, a number of those in interview explained that by "occupa tion" in the case of students they mean parental occupation until they should be fully independent. This fact—coupled with the discovery tha many students believed "family background" status to be based largely or parental occupation—served to indicate the value of the use of occupa tional status as the main social class index of the survey. It would appea that what the researcher saw as the main status dimension of social class i that of a majority of the students also, although perceived from a differen angle. This means that to a large extent the social class structure analyse is meaningful also to the people in the situation. What is interesting is th way that students see the individual status-set as made up of a complex o achieved and ascribed statuses.

The fact that "family background" is interchangeable for many wit "parental occupation" and individual status with both these indices show the intimate interconnection of the indices and the element of intergenera tional continuity and affiliation.

The proportion of Durham students who think that social class is deter mined by education is surprisingly low (17 per cent) in the light of wha was said in the last chapter about the inequalities and distinctions fostere between students and non-students by the collegiate system. The percer tages in this category in Edinburgh and Newcastle are 18 per cent and 2 per cent respectively—an interesting though small increase but one whic in interview was seen to be attributable to different factors from those i the Durham situation.[1]

If we look at the breakdown into social class categories we see other i teresting differences. In Durham the largest proportion (22 per cent) students in this category are of the upper middle class—for the reasor outlined above. In Newcastle the largest proportion is in the lower midd class, at 21 per cent. This may result from the fact that in Newcastle tl lower middle class has expanded as we have seen in vast numbers in tl University not only in terms of a socioeconomic group, but as members

[1] Since only 18 per cent of students think that education determines social status or might expect only approximately this proportion to think they had changed class sin becoming a student.

overlapping educational classes. These students are conscious of the benefits of education gained even in the middle class. In Edinburgh it is the working class which contributes most to the percentage choosing this option. Twenty-five per cent of all working-class students chose "education" as the primary index of social class. This could be because, aware of breaking into a middle-class stronghold, they hope that education is the main factor in determining social class. This reinforces their position and mobility aspirations. The anomalous English working class in fact contributes 16 per cent to the total in this category, despite its minute size—only 7 per cent of the student body.

Other distributions are surprisingly similar in the three universities in terms of overall proportions. Only a few students have a completely economic model of social class. Those who thought income determined social class were 7 per cent Edinburgh, 9 per cent Durham, and 12 per cent Newcastle (only 10 per cent overall).

An interesting distribution is seen in terms of social class responses in this category. In Newcastle and Edinburgh universities the proportion of students stating "income" increased down the social scale, and as many as 19 per cent Newcastle working-class students were in this category.[1] There is a marked difference between the Newcastle and Durham proportions— in the latter only 7 per cent working-class students thought "income" the most important criterion. This difference would seem to correspond with other observations we have made about the two universities, and it is quite possible that the working-class students are intrinsically of a different type. "Income" as expressive of crude material factors was mentioned more often in Newcastle than in either of the other two universities. On the other hand, 5 per cent of Durham working-class students stated that push determines social status—which may be a comment on their own experiences.

About 7 per cent in each university thought personality determines social class or social standing—but in interview it appeared that this was more an expression of what ought to happen than what students think really does happen.

---

[1] There is, however, no overall preponderance of income models in the working class —contrary to expectations—and even this generalisation must be modified by institutional considerations. See Mayntz, R., *Soziale Schichtung und sozialer Wandel in einer Industriegemeinde*, Stuttgart, 1958. Dr. Mayntz notes a tendency contrary to that found by Lockwood—for income models to increase the lower the income of the respondent. See Lockwood, D., Sources of variation in working class images of society, *Soc. Rev.*, **14,** No. 3, Nov. 1966.

It is interesting to note that 3 per cent of Durham respondents felt moved to insert the category "manners"—which they may well have learned to accept in the hierarchical context. This was most stressed by upper middle-class female students followed by the working-class males. No lower middle-class or working-class females mentioned this factor.

In Durham University 15 per cent said the combination of indices is so complex that one single one cannot be separated out—compared with 9 per cent in Edinburgh. In Newcastle 8 per cent refused to answer this question—more it appeared because of sensitive feelings than any lack of understanding or ability to answer.

If one adds together the percentage of students who named "occupation" and "income" as the most significant factors determining social class, these may be taken as students with a socioeconomic "model" of social class. In Edinburgh this represents 45 per cent, in Durham 36 per cent, and Newcastle 45 per cent. Taken with those students who chose "family background" as signifying parental occupation, and an additional number who voted for "combination" of factors, it would appear that a majority of students, though not an overwhelmingly large majority, have a socioeconomic model of social class, so that when one compares professed with assigned social class one would expect some measure of agreement in ranking of social class of origin of students. This will be found to be so.

A brief discussion of points raised in interview will help to clarify students' ideas of social class and its relation to their own experience.

It appeared that although most students saw social class in terms of "occupational" categories, very few of them were able to express this fact in terms of a rational conceptualisation of social class. They were able to express social class categories usually in terms emotively as well as cognitively meaningful to them, i.e. social class categorisation which they personally had experienced. This tended to vary with the social class of the respondent, so that middle-class students were more able cognitively to conceptualise about social class, so that what they expressed were rational rather than emotive categories. They were also most likely to avoid "cognitive dissonance"[1] with what they believed to be the general "educated" view. Working-class students tended to evaluate social class in terms of emotive experience and association—often sociocentrically biased. This is by no means a universally applicable generalisation. However, it was

---

[1] Homans, G. C., *Social Behaviour: Its Elementary Forms* (Internat. Lib. of Sociol. and Soc. Reconstruction), Routledge and Kegan Paul, London, 1961, p. 104 and Festinger, L. A., *A Theory of Cognitive Dissonance*, New York, 1967.

rather surprising that, despite education and training, students were often unable to discuss social class outside the most unsophisticated terms. And, indeed, it seemed true that "encompassing so much it is rarely conceptualised".[1] It is perhaps significant that some of the more unsophisticated evaluations of social class came from Newcastle students. Examples of these remarks are: "The working class is all the people who work in boiler suits." "The working class is people who work at Fords." "People in the upper class have top, well-paid jobs, big cars and posh accents."

Although unsophisticated[2] these comments incorporate an assessment of crucial class clues—crucial at least to these particular students—these are work, money, material possessions, and accent.

A comment of a middle-class student of Newcastle University tends to reinforce the impression, as it were, from the other side. This student said: "I think the classes are coming together now because as jobs have got cleaner so have the working classes."

This stress on the way that gross material factors which at one time separated the social classes led some students to come to the conclusion that "class doesn't matter any more". "Only our parents' generation is very much concerned about social class—after all they lived through the depression—it mattered then", said one lower middle-class Durham student.

A lower middle-class student in Edinburgh said what was echoed by a few middle-class students in the other universities (significantly this category did not include any working-class students) when he stated: "To my mind there is no such thing as a middle class. Anyone who works hard is working class, surely". In this case his assessment seemed to be closely related to his views about his own course in the University—engineering—which he felt was of "low status in the University. Everyone imagines engineers as being non-academic and tinkering around with cars". In the case of this student the downgrading of everyone who works to the same level of working class seemed to be a form of protection against the opinions and possibly initial assessment of himself by other people. How far the other students who expressed this view were also reacting to a situation of their own insecurity, it is impossible at this stage to assess.

Nevertheless, the concentration of some students on the purely material features of social class tended to obscure for them more subtle differences

---

[1] Littlejohn, J., *Westrigg*, 1963, p. III.
[2] "The dominant model of society held by the proletarian traditionalist is most likely to be a dichotomous or two-valued power model" (Lockwood, *op. cit.*, p. 251).

in terms of values and culture. These they recognised and differentiated but did not call social class. Usually the terms used were "people with interests in common", "who like doing the same things", "who feel at ease together". Concepts expressed were embracing social class yet not giving it that name.

Some students—perhaps 50 per cent—however, stated that values and education in a way are more important than occupation or income because these influence more than anything "the way people live". Said one Durham student: "After all it's not how you earn your money that is important or even beyond certain extremes how much you earn; what is more important is how you spend it." This student was trying to discriminate between differences in life-style of social classes, which are largely determined by internalised value and culture patterns.[1]

Students whose model was phrased in these terms had a completely different appreciation of social class from those who saw social class divisions in crude terms of money and possessions, and, as one may see, this coloured their whole attitude to social class inside and outside the university and their own mobility experience. The economic and value models of social class seemed to be closely related to position on a scale of objective ranking, i.e. the lower down the *assigned* social scale students were the more they tended to speak of social classes in crude economic terms; and the higher up the scale the more attitudes, values, and interests seemed to matter.[2] Thus while working-class students attempt to show that in their terms social class differentials are narrowing, middle-class students are able to claim that they will never be eradicated by virtue of the middle-class monopoly of the élite values which are not easily learned in one generation. This distinction is important since it is likely that families of students at university on the whole do not exhibit such gross material differences as are apparent in the total population. Here the Floud, Halsey, and Martin[3] conclusion is relevant as an explanation of middle-class categorisation—that the fewer the gross material differences the more impor-

---

[1] Goldthorpe points out that social class divisions still widely exist "between working class and middle class even in cases where immediate material differences have disappeared." Goldthorpe, J. H., Social stratification in industrial society, *Soc. Rev. Monograph 8*, Keele, 1964, p. 1.

[2] Although this may seem to conflict with statistical material discussed earlier, the paradox is explained in terms of the instrumental role of the indices outlined earlier, i.e. Education may be a means to more money. The indices themselves therefore may mean different things to different groups.

[3] Floud *et al.*, *Social Class and Educational Opportunity*, 1956.

tant become social class value systems in differential achievement and mobility.

It is clear that the way in which students evaluate social class divisions in society will order the extent to which they see social class divisions within the university among the student body. If they use only crude material indices they will say—even believe—there are no social classes in the university, or that social class is not an important factor in student social relations. Yet prejudice against posh accents or public or grammar school students will belie the fact.

However, it would be true to say that, although ostensibly a sizeable proportion, students who evaluate social class categories in material terms are distinctly in the minority. This is true of all social classes, which would seem to show that the educational experiences of this specially selected group biases its life experiences in a particular way.

The difficulty with so many of these social class models and categories is that in a sense they blanket a variety of responses which are more meaningful, though more apparently inconsistent if they are analysed in separate configurations.[1] For students were quick to point out what has been discovered about social class in the university, that in any matter of social class "it depends on the situation". Said one Newcastle student: "I might drink with some of the local working men down at the pub, and get on with them very well, but, on the other hand, I should hate to meet them at a university social function." Said another from Edinburgh; "Of course social class in terms of school and accent for instance, may not matter on a variety of social occasions, but if one were going for an interview for a job it might matter very much."

Students could think of occasions when social class matters and when it does not matter, and they felt that they were being inconsistent in saying so. In fact, of course, such inconsistencies are central to our analysis of the relevance of social class in social relations. So, too, are the apparent inconsistencies in the actual social class categorisation. For just as different situations determine the relevance of social class, so do they determine the relevance of one particular dimension of social class rather than another. Occupational status may at times be more important than amount of income, at other times material possessions, at others life style, and, at

---

[1] "It is the participant who must react to the others and not the observer and at one level at least the intentions of others in their interactions may be more accessible to the participants." See Borgatta, E. F. and Crowther, B., *A Workbook for the Study of Social Interaction*, Rand McNally, Chicago, 1965.

yet others, value patterns. And it is true that these dimensions are combined in different ways at different points of the scale.

It is no wonder that students found it difficult to express themselves on the subject or often contradicted themselves: "Oh dear", said one female Edinburgh student, "I seem to have contradicted myself hundreds of times and I'm really more confused now than I was at the beginning." Perhaps many other students would agree with her. Indeed, it is clear that the whole concept of social class must be subjected to extensive and intensive empirical research before all the complexities and inconsistencies can be reconciled into a meaningful whole.

This kind of analysis is important for the discussion of the relevance of social class as a factor in social relations within the university, since the point of reference which the student has for his own perception of social class will affect and even order his immediate attitudes and behaviour in terms of social class. Whether he has experienced rural or urban stratification patterns, for example, may well influence his appreciation of social class divisions among students. All the dimensions and distributions of class must be accounted for.

In Chapter 7 the influence of social class on students' attitudes and behaviour in terms of informal groups has already been studied, but it is pertinent here to consider again whether social class divisions in the student body are of the same kind as those in external society—though perhaps differing in degree.

Findings of the Edinburgh survey show how criteria determining social standing within the university differ from those outside. This gives some indication of whether divisions continue on some kind of continuum as in society at large. In this case, family background would be the principal criterion, since indices such as occupation and income cannot yet be used for students.

In fact only 12 per cent of students thought that an individual student's standing is determined by family background. The greatest number of these are Scottish middle-class students. A high percentage of Overseas lower middle class thought this too (25 per cent) as did one working-class Overseas. Perhaps by family background these students meant also the factor of nationality feeling that being foreign affected their standing in the student body.

Only 3 per cent of students think that wealth determines a student's social standing.

By far the largest number of students said that other "abilities and talents" are important in determining a student's status among his fellows—44 per cent. Of 80 students who said "other", 49 thought it was "personality". Four per cent thought that a combination of academic prowess and other abilities and talents together determined a student's social status. Taking into account the various other categories which students invented, it seems that the majority of students feel that in the student body an individual is judged on his own merits.

This would seem to be true in a variety of contexts, and yet by speaking of "student's social standing" another ranking system is introduced —almost a red herring—which is indigenous to the student body and which does not operate instead of but rather in conjunction with the social classes of external society. And the two systems touch at many points where the same indices of status are used.

In the Durham context, as we have seen, an added complication to the overall analysis is introduced by the fact that colleges are ranked in prestige by students. It has been shown that 68 per cent of students thought colleges ranked in prestige and 18 per cent were not sure. The group which most often thought colleges "ranked" was female students living in college. This may well have something to do with the dating structure in which it is reputable to go out with someone from a high-ranking college whatever his individual merits or de-merits. This corresponds in some respects to the rating and dating complex of American fraternities and sororities noted by certain writers.[1]

It would appear that the colleges fall into two systems of ranking by sex. At the head of the male colleges are University, Hatfield, and Grey followed by the theological colleges St. John's and St. Chad's, with Bede College and St. Cuthbert's Society at the bottom of the scale. The women's colleges are ranked by the majority in the order of St. Mary's, St. Aidan's, St. Hild's, and Neville's Cross. It is interesting to see what criteria are thought to determine this ranking.

As one might expect, stress is laid in different colleges on different ranking criteria. This varies as for individuals on the position of the college of the respondent on the scale. On the male college scale, for instance, 15 per cent of St. Cuthbert's say that prestige is due to social conformity of college members. This is presumably in the nature of a criticism of University College, which ranks high, and a vindication of

---

[1] E.g. Waller, W., *ASR*, 1937, **2**, 727–34, and Scott, J. F., The American college sorority: its role in class and ethnic endogamy, *ASR*, 1965, **30**, 514–27.

St. Cuthbert's, which is bottom. An additional 26 per cent in St. Cuthbert's refused to answer this question.

Twenty-eight per cent of University College say that prestige is based on "personality" of college members and 23 per cent on other "abilities and talents". Fifteen per cent say it is also due to "social adaptability", which may be taken as a virtue since, as we have seen, so many of the members of this college have, indeed, been socially adaptable to the prevailing image.

Grey College and St. John's rate "enthusiasm" higher than the other colleges, and University ranks lowest on this.

In the case of both male and female ranking the two teacher-training colleges mention family background most often as determining prestige of colleges—18 per cent in Bede and 33 per cent in Neville's Cross. This may have something to do with the fact that each college contains both certificate and graduate trainees, which is not always socially satisfactory. "Snobbery" was mentioned only by University and Hatfield students— 3 per cent and 2 per cent, which suggests a dissatisfied element within them rebelling against the criteria they feel to be applied.

Among the women's colleges "abilities and talents" are stressed more than "personality"; and those in St. Aidan's College particularly stress the importance of "social conformity" and "social adaptability".

Although the pattern of indices varies from college to college there is some consensus of opinion which points again to a student system of ranking based mainly upon individual traits and talents.

The fact that students from different colleges are to some extent categorised again bears witness to the fact that in any hierarchical organisation each level is presupposed equal. In Merton's terms, each college as a group of status equals, in terms of college ranking, forms a reference group. In time, through the internalising of college values and the erroneous expectations of members of other colleges, the prophesy of group categorisation is fulfilled.

This system of ranking forms new kinds of unities and dis-unities in the student body which operate in the institutional framework in a peculiarly student way but which, as we have seen throughout, do not replace the external social class divisions. However, it would be true to say in the light of other findings that where cross-cutting unities occur, as in Durham, there is a great tendency for class lines to become relatively blurred.

Having examined how students rank each other, we now turn to students' assessment of parental social class. Most students made an attempt to classify their parents—about 97 per cent in all—although one or two wrote angry comments and said that they "did not believe in class". A comparison of assigned with the professed social class would seem to show that a large proportion of students are well aware of class indices and of where they would put their parents (and by implication themselves) on the social scale. In a sense, what was tested was the amount of overlap of the social class identification of the individual in terms of

TABLE 12.2. ASSIGNED AND PROFESSED SOCIAL CLASS OF STUDENTS (per cent)

Assigned / Professed	UMC			LMC			WkC			Total		
	E	D	N	E	D	N	E	D	N	E	D	N
UC	2	4	4	1	—	—	2	—	—	1·5	1	1
UMC	84	77	75	32	25	30	4	—	2	47	34	39
MMC	6	4	5	7	5	5	—	—	—	—	5	4
LMC	7	13	13	49	61	49	23	20	24	28	35	32
WkC	—	—	—	8	5	11	69	71	69	14	21	19
No class	—	1	1	—	2	1	—	4	2	—	2	1
Don't know	2	1	—	4	2	1	2	5	—	2·5	2	1
Not stated	—	—	3	—	—	3	—	—	3	—	—	3
TOTAL	101	100	101	101	100	100	100	100	100	100	99	100
N.	(126)	(101)	(199)	(140)	(161)	(280)	(48)	(77)	(124)	(322)	(352)	(629)

"interest"[1] and/or "aspiration" compared with that of identity accorded by others—in this case represented by an objective index. In fact there turned out to be a surprising amount of overlap, and students were in these terms extremely realistic.

Table 12.2 shows the distributions of assigned and professed social classes in the three universities.

As one might expect, the upper middle-class students in each university had the most realistic view of their parents' social class. In Edinburgh, 84 per cent of the assigned upper middle class were of the professed upper middle class, 77 per cent in Durham, and 75 per cent in Newcastle. In

[1] As used by Centers, R., *Psychology of the Social Classes: A Study of Class Consciousness*, Stud. in Public Opinion, Princeton, N. J., 1949.

each case 5 per cent invented the category "middle middle class" and the rest, with the exception of 2–3 per cent, professed upper class, were of the professed lower middle class. Students felt that in some ways the division between upper middle class and lower middle class was the hardest distinction to make. This is most evident in the Newcastle sample, which is what one expects in the light of findings already discussed. Not one of the assigned upper middle-class students was of the professed working class.

In consideration of the other figures one discerns an "aspirational overlay" in Edinburgh with a higher proportion of "upgraders" than either Durham or Newcastle (and a wider spread of aspiration) and only 8 per cent lower middle-class downgraders and 13 per cent upper middle-class downgraders. The aspirational overlay is most clear for all the universities in the lower middle class.

Of the assigned working class 69 per cent in Edinburgh were of the professed working class, in Durham 71 per cent, and in Newcastle 69 per cent. Twenty-nine per cent were "upgraders" in Edinburgh, 20 per cent in Durham, and 26 per cent in Newcastle. The greater overall agreement of professed with assigned classes in Durham would seem to indicate either a clearer idea of social class divisions or a greater acceptance of them. Despite the aspirational overlay the overall proportion of the professed classes are in many respects similar to those of the assigned classes. Only about 3 or 4 per cent in each university consciously opted out by putting "no class" or "don't know"—the rest implied by the very fact of answering that this kind of judgement is not something with which they are entirely unfamiliar.

Nevertheless, some students gave the impression that they dislike putting their parents in a social class category as it made them feel vaguely disloyal. This attitude also coloured their responses to questions on their own social mobility, which is discussed in the next chapter. Yet "attitudes" are extremely difficult to reveal and analyse, so that it is acknowledged that some reference is involved in terms of implicit motivation. This is why the author discussed initially the cultural patterns and statistical regularities which in terms of their clustering may be termed "social classes". Where these coincide with students' professed social class it would appear that these represent something real in terms of student identity and experience. The fact that something real is analysed makes it possible to speak of movement between these social classes in a way which is meaningful to those undergoing mobility experience. This will be discussed in the next chapter. However, it will be seen that not enough is known of the students' external status-set to make entirely meaningful their social class models and self evaluations.

In a sense the author has approached the problem of analysing social classes from two angles in a manner similar to those described by Ossowski.

> The formulae given here can be regarded in two ways; either as some kind of sociological laws concerning the sharpness of class stratification in the social consciousness, arrived at by observation of collective life and conclusions drawn from very psychological assumptions, or else as a partial definition of what is meant by the relative sharpness of class stratification. In the latter case we would interpret the degree of sharpness of the class stratification statistically as a certain set of characteristics of a status system. In the former case the sharpness of the stratification must be described in another way—by reference to psychological attitudes or to the behaviour of members of the collectivity in social interaction.[1]

Both approaches are necessary to an understanding of social class and of movement between social classes. For "movement" in itself is meaningless unless one may ascertain in what direction the movement takes place—from what and to what—and thus *how* it is achieved. If one analyses social classes in terms of a concept of structured gradation of defined levels, mobility is seen as a movement up or down the social scale. This kind of analysis is that most widely used at the present time, and tends to emphasise the structural importance of "barriers to upward mobility" and obvious gaps at certain intervals in the scale. As Ossowski points out, "a dichotomic scheme is the most suitable one for bringing out the sharpness of class divisions", and an increase in classes blurs the sharpness of class divisions.[2]

A scheme of structured gradation, as we have seen throughout, is not an entirely fruitful means of analysing social class within a range of educationally status equals. Nevertheless, the structured gradation scheme cannot be dispensed with, for it serves to describe in some respects the situation from which the students came and to which they refer in terms of past experience. And since by "social mobility" is meant that movement between social classes which individual students undergo in the total structure of societal social classes, a scheme of gradation is used in analyses of social mobility. Although the upward and downward typology of mobility seems a crude way of describing this complex phe-

---

[1] Ossowski, *Class Structure in the Social Consciousness*, 1963, p. 95.
[2] *Ibid.*, pp. 94–95.

nomenon, as yet no other satisfactory scheme has been put in its place. So we are at the point where we try to conceptualise social classes in a new way and yet have not the methodological equipment to test these concepts empirically nor fit them into a broader structural scheme.

Nevertheless, awareness of such inadequacy makes one accept traditional typology and terminology now only with reservations.

CHAPTER 13

STUDENTS' SOCIAL MOBILITY
AND SOCIAL MOTILITY

FOR the purposes of this chapter we will ignore the limitations of concepts of social class described in the last and preceding chapters and assume certain facts about social class which we must not otherwise assume. Unless we do this our feet are on shifting sand: we cannot take any further empirical steps.

We shall assume, therefore, that the social classes are identifiable social and cultural collectivities ranked in a system of gradation upon a social status continuum and relatively permanent. In other words, we shall be concerned only with "class boundaries conceived as barriers to the mobility of individuals on the social status scale" and not with the "sharpness with which the dividing line is drawn between classes".[1] In keeping with this social class model we shall speak of upward and downward mobility. Although these terms are used for convenience it is only with an awareness of their limitation, for a rethinking of concepts of social class should involve concomitant rethinking of concepts of mobility. This, however, would require the writing of an entirely different book—and space permits only one chapter. However, suffice it to say that the model of mobility so postulated is a crude simplification of the processes involved, for movement between multidimensional classes in a sense requires multidimensional movement. While recognising the difficulties we must unfortunately ignore them at this point.

In this chapter what is primarily discussed is what Turner has called "mobility experience"[2] rather than any structural analysis of mobility rates.[3] Indeed, mobility rates could not at this point be ascertained. The reason for this is because mobility rates are ascertained after people have

---

[1] Ossowski, S., *Class Structure in the Social Consciousness*, 1963, p. 93.
[2] Turner, R. H., *ASR*, 1960, **25** (5).
[3] As, for instance, undertaken by Glass, D. V. (ed.), *Social Mobility in Britain*, 1954.

moved, not when they are moving or are in a temporary zone of transition. In terms of external social class divisions, students may be thought to be in a transition zone, and some students have shown that they think of university in this way. However, to describe the process of being a student as passing through a complex *rite de passage* of separation, transition, and incorporation[1] would imply enculturation into the values of the élite which, as we shall see, is by no means automatic.

Students were asked if they consider that since coming to university they have changed their social class from that of their parents, in order to ascertain the importance of higher education as one of the main avenues (if not *the* main avenue) for upward social mobility for the children of the working class. Naturally, what is being investigated is the attitude of the student himself to the process of mobility and not the categorisation by others which he might undergo. In this sense the picture is one-sided. Yet it may provide insights into how mobility is achieved and by whom and what part higher education plays in the process.

At this stage it is necessary to make the distinction between what the author will call "motility" and what is usually called "mobility". What will largely be discussed will be the motile student, and his social motility rather than what is called mobility. This stems from the fact that since students are in a transition zone as far as the external structure is concerned, all that can be analysed is their capability of motion rather than the fact that they have moved, are moving, or will move. Therefore the concept of mobility is not adequate as a description of what happens within the university. In a sense all students are mobile in that they have undergone a certain amount of movement in an institutionalised system of mobility.[2] Thus the concept of mobility does not differentiate between them nor give us any understanding of their differential capacity to move further. Social motility may fill this gap in conceptualisation. Nor does a discussion of mobility aspiration comprehend those who aspire to move and yet are not capable of it, i.e. who are non-motile but aspiring. Therefore, mobility aspiration is not synonymous with motility.

There is a distinct difference between mobility and motility in that the

---

[1] Van Gennep, A., *The Rites of Passage*, 1960, p. 11.

[2] Lockwood, D., Can we cope with social change?, *New Society*, 28 November 1963, **61**, 13: "The fact that mobility has become increasingly *institutionalised* via the educational system means that while there may be increased chances of inter-generational mobility through education, the chances of intra-generational mobility through work are declining" (author's italic).

former is a structural property; the latter is a property of individuals relative to that structure. When movement of individuals occurs, the two are combined in various ways which are expressed in terms of mobility experience. Analysis of mobility rates shows only who has moved or what proportion of people has moved relative to everyone else, in terms of social structure: it cannot tell us much about the process of mobility itself. Thus the concept of motility separates out a special feature of what has normally been called mobility, for until now motility has been comprehended within this concept. To separate out this variable in the mobility situation may help in the understanding of mobility experience.[1]

The socially mobile person is one who is on the move, or who has moved in terms of structural position; the socially motile person is one "capable of motion" or with the in-built characteristics of motion. The fact that motility may not always be followed by mobility may lead to severe frustration, as when certain avenues are blocked. Conversely, when mobility is accomplished without motility—as in the case, for instance, of some institutionalised mobility—there may be much resulting anxiety.

In the latter case the person who is moving socially may not have within him characteristics congruent to the situation which enable him to cope with changing social positions. This is likely to happen in situations of institutionalised or of sponsored mobility rather than contest mobility[2]— where the latter implies a combination of mobility and motility. As one may imagine, this combination of mobility and motility leads to speedier and fiercer movement on the part of a few. In mobility situations in which individual motility is lacking, there may be slower and more restrained movement.

Motility refers to possession of social rather than psychological characteristics congruent with mobility—such as accent, dress, manner, schooling, and other attributes gained through social experience. The social characteristics may have been acquired by accident or by design, and in the latter case do imply a degree of aspiration—a motivation to acquisition of particular social characteristics or indices of particular social groups. Aspiration alone is not enough—possession of the requisite social characteristics alone ensures acceptance into the receiving group. Therefore there are more likely to be motile persons in a situation which

[1] Abbott, J., The concept of motility, *Sociol. Rev.*, July 1966, **14** (2).
[2] As used by Turner, *op. cit.*

allows for inter-cultural transmission, for emulation, sharing of experiences, and thus social class socialisation.

Mobility is movement between structured positions which are a summation of the individual's statuses in a number of spheres. Motility enables us to look at the structure of role-sets and role changes within this overall structural movement.

The relation of the individual and the structural property may well be expressed in terms of a simple two by two contingency diagram (Fig. 13.1).

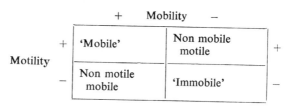

FIG. 13.1 Mobility and motility.

The properties and their combinations summarised may apply to mobility experience of individuals or groups, but particularly the former. It will be seen that what has previously been described as mobility is in fact a configuration of variables—which must be separated out if the nature of mobility is to be understood. Motility is one of those variables.

Social motility and "mobility experience" will be considered in their various aspects by:

(1) An analysis of students who thought that since coming to university their social class had changed from that of their parents. What they moved from and to in terms of social class.

(2) An analysis of those who thought they had not changed their social class. Why it had not changed. Other avenues of mobility involved.

(3) Examination of aspects of mobility experience in terms of (a) relations with fellow students and mutual transmission of elements of social class culture; (b) relation with parents and peers.

These points will be seen to cover the subjects for study outlined by Turner and described in Chapter 1.

We turn first to an examination of students' social motility, approached first through social class distribution of students who thought they had

15

TABLE 13.1. WHETHER EDINBURGH STUDENTS CONSIDERED THAT THEIR SOCIAL CLASS HAD CHANGED FROM THAT OF THEIR PARENTS SINCE COMING TO UNIVERSITY (ASSIGNED SOCIAL CLASS) (per cent)

	UC	UMC	LMC	WkC	Unclassified	Total	No.
Changed	—	8	12	40	—	14	(45)
Not changed	100	87	80	54	—	76	(250)
Don't know	—	5	8	6	100	9	(27)
TOTAL	100	100	100	100	100	99	(322)
No.	(2)	(126)	(140)	(48)	(6)	(322)	

changed their social class. Table 13.1 shows the proportion of students in Edinburgh University in each assigned social class who considered that their social class had changed from that of their parents since coming to university.

It is important to note here that it is the fact of attending a university in itself which is being treated as a means to social mobility, and not the matter of gaining a degree, since very few respondents had in fact gained a first degree. In their study of eleven universities in the United States, Goldsen and his colleagues discuss student evaluations of educational goals of universities, which is relevant to the present examination. They differentiate the academic, instrumental, and interpersonal "educational outlooks" of students as they relate to what students expect to get out of their university education. "The majority of students stress either a 'basic general education and appreciation of ideas', or 'vocational skills and techniques directly applicable to your career'—35 per cent and 36 per cent, respectively, select these as 'the single most important, aim of an ideal university'."[1]

The figures quoted compare with the figures of the present survey in Chapter 5, on students' reasons for wanting to attend university[2]—and clearly reasons for wanting to be a student must be related to what are perceived to be the educational goals of the institution. What Goldsen and his colleagues call "instrumental" outlook towards educational aims

[1] Goldsen *et al.*, *What College Students Think*, 1960, p. 6.
[2] Comparable figures are Newcastle 34 per cent and 48 per cent.

or goals must be related to perception of a university education as a means of getting on either occupationally, financially, or socially, and one might expect Edinburgh, Durham, and Newcastle students to reflect their previous expectations in their attitudes to mobility. This, as we shall see, is not entirely the case, and suggests some of the results of lack of socialisation and bourgeoisification discussed in Chapter 11. Socialisation must take place for bourgeoisification and mobility to be accomplished—and this as we have seen only takes place under certain structural conditions.

Goldsen and his colleagues very briefly relate social origins of students to their educational outlooks—but unfortunately do not continue with this analysis throughout the book, so that we can only deduce the effect of social origins in other areas of student life. However, incidentally they do make comment, although implicitly, on the kind of university "league table" discussed in Chapter 5 which results from self-selection and university selection, and from the perception of educational goals discussed. Individual motivations and structural conditions are always closely linked. Goldsen and his colleagues make comment in terms of the general response of students at particular universities.

> We have reason to suspect that they may be class-linked, since the point of view at Ivy League campuses and at the small Eastern men's colleges, which *recruit students from higher class levels* [author's italics], favored a general basic education. It is mainly at the state Universities and at Fisk (where proportionately more students identify themselves as "working class" in origin) that the vocational approach to education was distinctly prevalent.[1]

It is exactly those things which Goldsen and his colleagues take for granted in this analysis that we are here concerned to investigate. How and why is the social distribution of students related to the university status league and to the stated and perceived aims of education? The answer, as we have seen, lies in the structure of social relationships in each particular institution and in the image and reputation which it creates. In turn this is related to the perception of education as a means to mobility as a socialising and allocative process.

Goldsen and his colleagues point out that "a disproportionate number of students who emphasise the practical, instrumental value of higher education cluster in the group who say their origins are working class. It is to them, particularly, that college education tends to be appealing as

[1] Goldsen *et al.*, *op. cit.*, p. 14.

a means to an end rather than as a cultural end in itself."[1] This, we have seen, does not portray exactly the case of the British students where a number of other factors are at work and, as in the last chapter, even class models are not as clear-cut as might have been predicted. Even allowing for difficulties in cross-cultural comparisons, one wonders whether, within the American situation, there may not be similar factors at work which redefine the generalisation made.

The tendency to underestimate the importance of social origins in student attitudes and behaviour is borne out by the fact that in contra-distinction to their earlier remarks, Goldsen and his colleagues state that students are not necessarily "motivated to adopt or abandon their educational values by deliberately estimating how well they fit in with a particular class outlook"[2]—and they later relate this to the quality of "other directedness" which is one of the "values which students imply are important to them when they tell us something about their broad, general orientations to life".[2] In terms of the findings of this survey one might say that these remarks hide more than they reveal, and that the fact of "fitting in with a particular class outlook" may well be a clue to many kinds of student behaviour, whether characterised by "other-directedness" or not. The same is true of the approach to socialisation, bourgeoisification, and student mobility which are not closely examined, because it is assumed that:

> On the contrary, it is more likely that college students who come from working class families have *already begun* [author's italics] to accept certain general orientations characteristic of social classes higher than theirs on the status scale of American society and their college experience reinforces and accelerates these middle or upper class orientations.[2]

The findings of this book challenge the validity of these findings in the British context, and since their implications have never properly been faced in the United States, they may have some relevance there also.

In the light of what has been said already it is perhaps not too surprising that only 14 per cent of the students in this sample considered that they had changed their social class since coming to university, i.e. that they felt socialised into the middle-class ethos. However, there is a sizeable proportion of "don't knows" (9 per cent), which suggests an element of

[1] *Ibid.*, p. 15.
[2] *Ibid.*, p. 16.

uncertainty in some student quarters. When we consider the different class totals we see that, as one might expect, the highest percentage of students who feel their social class to have changed is in the working class— 40 per cent. However, this means that 54 per cent of the working-class students at university still consider themselves to be of the same class. This seems to point to the fact that for many students a university education *per se* is not a means to social mobility. Indeed, it implies, as we shall see later on, a lack of motility among working-class students in particular. Motility among students must not be assumed. It will be seen to be relative to networks of social relations and in particular to locality ties. (This is the same kind of social–spatial syndrome which affects the social class relations of students within the university.) It is also related to the degree of institutional socialisation examined in the last chapter.

Table 13.2 shows this motility in terms of the professed social classes examined in the last chapter. A clearer indication of students' views is gained from this table since it shows movement in the students' own terms of reference.

TABLE 13.2. EDINBURGH STUDENTS' OPINIONS OF SOCIAL CLASS CHANGE ANALYSED IN TERMS OF PROFESSED SOCIAL CLASSES (per cent)

	UC	UMC	MMC	LMC	WkC	Unclassified	Total	No.
Changed	40	7	6	16	38	—	14	(45)
Not changed	40	90	82	73	57	12	77	(244)
Don't know	20	3	12	11	5	88	9	(27)
TOTAL	100	100	100	100	100	100	100	
No.	(5)	(153)	(17)	(89)	(44)	(8)	(316)	(316)

The proportion of professed working-class students who still consider themselves working class rises to 57 per cent while the professed lower middle class falls from 80 per cent to 73 per cent. It would seem that students genuinely believed their parents belonged to the professed social class which they stated, since the figures seem more consistent with the professed rather than the assigned social class.

There is additional information which modifies the impression which

TABLE 13.3. WHETHER DURHAM AND NEWCASTLE STUDENTS CONSIDERED THAT THEIR SOCIAL CLASS HAD CHANGED FROM THAT OF THEIR PARENTS SINCE COMING TO UNIVERSITY (per cent)

	UMC		LMC		WkC		Unclassified		Total	
	D	N	D	N	D	N	D	N	D	N
Changed	7	6	6	15	25	28	—	39	12	16
Not changed	89	87	81	75	61	56	66	58	77	74
Don't know	4	6	12	8	11	11	25	4	9	8
Later	—	—	1	—	2	2	5	—	1	1
Earlier	—	—	—	—	1	—	5	—	1	—
Non-responds	—	2	—	2	—	4	—	—	—	2
TOTAL No.	100	101	100	100	100	101	101	101	100	101
	(101)	(199)	(161)	(280)	(77)	(124)	(13)	(26)	(352)	(629)

is at first given by these figures, gained from interviews and informal conversations. Before this is discussed, we turn to Table 13.3 which shows comparable material from the Newcastle and Durham surveys.

In Durham 12 per cent of students thought they had changed their social class of origin since coming to university. Of this proportion the largest section was the male working class. Thirty-seven per cent of them thought they had changed compared with only 14 per cent female working class, and these comprised 68 per cent of all who thought they had changed. It is rather surprising to see that, like the 7 per cent upper middle class in Edinburgh, 7 per cent of Durham upper middle-class students think they have changed their social class since coming to university. In Durham a greater proportion of female than male upper middle-class students felt they had changed. Although there were no such categories on the form, 2 per cent working-class students said that they had changed "earlier" and 5 per cent said they would change "later". These will be considered later on.

In the Newcastle sample, 16 per cent said that their social class had changed. Twenty-eight per cent of the working class said that their social

class had changed, 2 per cent "later", and 4 per cent did not reply. In both
Durham and Newcastle a sizeable proportion of working-class student
said that they "did not know". Only 5 per cent were "don't knows" in
Edinburgh compared with 11 per cent in Newcastle and Durham. In
Newcastle, 6 per cent of the upper middle class said that their social class
had changed since coming to university, which shows a significantly
similar proportion of mobile upper middle class in each university.

The proportion of working-class students in each university who say
that they have not changed their social class since coming to university is
57 per cent Edinburgh, 60 per cent Durham, and 56 per cent Newcastle
These proportions are remarkably similar when one considers the variety
of social factors operating on the individual motility and mobility patterns in different university contexts, and they are higher than may be
expected in the light of assumptions of status equals. However, the finding
is not unexpected in the light of the findings of this survey. As we have
seen, the university is not a melting pot in which all social classes benefit
from the mutual transmission of elements of social class culture. Certain
conditions are necessary for this to happen. Where these conditions do
not obtain, social classes may pass through the university as discrete entities whose members never have an opportunity to mentally rub shoulders
with each other. This fact has important implications for the process of
bourgeoisification later to be discussed. The fact of attending a university
alone does not make a student motile—membership must mean more than
having his name on the register if an indelible imprint is to be left upon
him.

First we turn to the social classes to which students believed that they
had moved. Table 13.4 shows the social classes to which students had
moved from both assigned and professed social class, showing movement
from the social classes with which students themselves identified. Table
13.5 shows the comparable Durham data and Table 13.6 data from
Newcastle.

In the Edinburgh sample 9 per cent of students fell into the "later"
category already shown in the other samples, and 7 per cent added the
category "academic class" and 2 per cent "no class". This compares with
the Durham 21 per cent "academic class" or "no class" and the Newcastle
14 per cent in this category. These students were consciously opting out of
the class structure as they saw it, and felt that by virtue of having been to
university they now formed a class of their own based on academic criteria. Most of the students in this category are working class in Edinburgh

Students' Social Mobility and Social Motility 419

TABLE 13.4. SOCIAL CLASSES TO WHICH EDINBURGH STUDENTS CONSIDERED THEY HAD MOVED (IN TERMS OF PROFESSED SOCIAL CLASS) (per cent)

	UC	UMC	MMC	LMC	WkC	Total	No.
UC	—	18	—	—	—	4	(2)
UMC	100	—	100	21	12	18	(8)
MMC	—	9	—	—	—	2	(1)
LMC	—	36	—	—	30	20	(9)
WkC	—	—	—	—	—	—	—
No class	—	9	—	—	—	2	(1)
Academic	—	—	—	7	12	7	(3)
Not yet	—	9	—	21	—	9	(4)
Don't know	—	18	—	50	47	38	(17)
TOTAL	100	99	100	99	101	100	
No.	(2)	(13)	(1)	(14)	(17)	(45)	(45)

TABLE 13.5. SOCIAL CLASSES TO WHICH DURHAM STUDENTS CONSIDERED THEY HAD MOVED (IN TERMS OF ASSIGNED SOCIAL CLASS) (per cent)

	UMC		LMC		WkC		Unclassified		Total	No.
	M	F	M	F	M	F	M	F		
UC	—	—	—	—	—	—	—	—	—	—
UMC	—	—	25	33	9	—	—	—	12	(5)
MMC	—	—	—	—	—	—	—	—	—	—
LMC	33	33	—	33	35	100	—	—	31	(13)
WkC	—	—	—	—	—	—	—	—	—	—
Don't know	67	33	50	33	30	—	—	—	36	(15)
No class	—	33	25	—	26	—	—	—	21	(9)
TOTAL	100	99	100	99	100	100	—	—	100	
No.	(3)	(3)	(8)	(3)	(23)	(2)	—	—		(42)

and Durham and lower middle class in Newcastle. They have been cut adrift in a sense from their old social class ties and yet do not feel that they have yet formed new ones. It is difficult to say whether these students do or will constitute a "floating population" in social class terms—root-

TABLE 13.6. SOCIAL CLASSES TO WHICH NEWCASTLE STUDENTS CONSIDERED THEY HAD MOVED (IN TERMS OF PROFESSED SOCIAL CLASS) (per cent)

	UC	UMC	MMC	LMC	WkC	Total	No.
UC	—	6	—	2	2	3	(3)
UMC	100	16	—	56	7	26	(32)
MMC	—	28	—	13	40	26	(29)
LMC	—	22	—	9	40	23	(26)
WkC	—	11	—	5	—	4	(4)
No class	—	17	100	13	9	14	(15)
Don't know	—	—	—	2	2	2	(2)
TOTAL	100	100	100	100	100	100	
No.	(1)	(18)	(2)	(45)	(45)	(111)	(111)

less at least in class values. There is also a large proportion of "don't knows"—38 per cent in Edinburgh (mainly working class), 36 per cent in Durham (again mainly working class), and only 2 per cent in Newcastle (both working class and lower middle class). These replies represent the students with uncertainties (sometimes anxieties) about their future social position. They feel that they are different from their families—often working class—but do not yet know quite what this means in social class terms.

It must be remembered that these percentages represent only small numbers in the student body since we are discussing now the 14 per cent of students who feel they have changed their social class in some way.

Apart from this body of students in Edinburgh, 30 per cent of professed working class thought they had moved to lower middle class and 12 per cent to upper middle class. In Durham the figures were 68 per cent lower middle class and 9 per cent upper middle class, and in Newcastle 40 per cent lower middle class, 40 per cent middle middle class, 7 per cent upper middle class, and 2 per cent upper class. It would appear that the more middle class the prevailing ethos the less far the working-class students, by contrast, feel they have moved. There is less uncertainty, too, in the Durham sample. Since the steps of gradation in Newcastle seem to be scaled down, it would appear to working-class students that they are easier to climb, particularly if the middle-class value systems are less apparent than in the other two universities.

The same upgrading appears in the lower middle-class sample in Newcastle in which 56 per cent of those who changed say that they have moved to the upper middle class. Again, a proportion invented the category middle middle class (13 per cent), which would appear to be a scaling down of aspirations to modest proportions. This compares with 21 per cent of lower middle-class "upgraders" in Edinburgh moved to the upper middle class. The rest of the lower middle-class motiles put themselves in "no class" categories. In Durham, 29 per cent lower middle-class upgraded themselves to upper middle class—the rest to "no class" categories. This would seem to show, on the whole, a more modest kind of upgrading in Durham and Edinburgh than in Newcastle.

In Edinburgh, 18 per cent upper middle-class motiles upgraded themselves to upper class, although half were assigned lower middle class. In actuality this represents only two students, so the numbers are too small to be significant. In Durham there were no upper middle-class "upgraders" and in Newcastle 6 per cent. Nevertheless, on the whole, this would point to the finding that upper class is usually thought of by students as one of rank and title—ascribed—not achieved.

The important finding to which we now turn is the proportion of middle-class "downgraders" who think that since coming to university they have moved down the social scale. The question was phrased in order to discover the significance of university as an avenue of upward mobility. It was a shock to find, therefore, in the Edinburgh survey that 45 per cent of professed upper middle-class students who had changed their social class thought that they had moved down the social scale to the middle middle class and lower middle class. These figures were small enough to be accidental. However, they repeated themselves in the following two surveys in a significant way and demand some explanation. In Durham, 33 per cent of the upper middle-class motiles thought that they had moved down to the lower middle class. In Newcastle the figures increased to 61 per cent upper middle-class "downgraders" and even 4 per cent lower middle-class "downgraders".

In Newcastle as many as 11 per cent upper middle-class motiles and 5 per cent lower middle-class motiles thought that they had moved down as far as the working class.

Again, the comparative length of shift may be seen in terms of the prevailing social class ethos. Some middle-class students in each university feel that their social class has been downgraded, and the proportion and the shift are increased in a more working-class university. This despite the fact that, as we have seen, in terms of statistical proportions, Newcastle is no more working class than Durham. Just as working-class students may feel themselves bourgeoisified, so may middle-class students feel themselves proletarianised (unfortunately both ugly words). These processes depend on the same complex set of conditions which influence all student relations. For only by constant social contact can there be any transmission of elements of social class culture.

In the Newcastle survey, students were asked if they thought that there is any prestige attached by others to being a student. The results, shown in Table 13.7, support the conclusions just made.

TABLE 13.7. WHETHER NEWCASTLE STUDENTS THOUGHT THAT PRESTIGE IS ATTACHED BY OTHERS TO BEING A STUDENT (per cent)

	UMC	LMC	WkC	Unclassi-fied	Total	No.
Yes	69	72	75	85	72	(453)
No	31	27	25	12	27	(171)
Non-responds	—	1	—	3	1	(5)
TOTAL No.	100 (199)	100 (280)	100 (124)	100 (26)	100 (629)	(629)

Over a quarter of the students think that there is no prestige attached to being a student, and some even added the comment: "just the opposite!" on their questionnaire. For these students, at least, the consciousness of being an élite is rather dim. This may in turn be associated with the fact that students increasingly are seen to epitomise the vanguard of youth culture as discussed briefly in Chapter 11. This may also result from the fact that, as one student remarked: "Anyone these days who wants to bum around the world calls himself a student—it covers a multitude of sins." Indeed, the low repute of students often results from misbehaviour of those who are posturing as students—who use this role label as an excuse for irresponsibility. Thus the real meaning of the student role is stretched and loses some of its currency value. This obviously has implications for student status in society.

On the other hand, being a student is often thought of as the time of experiment, of trying on roles and personalities in a somewhat unreal world. And since the time of youth is a time of preoccupation with style and fashion—with form rather than merely content—the student is able to immerse himself in the fashions of his peers virtually without restraint. Indeed, he is more free to experiment than his peers who are out at work and less bound by social restraints. He can spend more time in " 'dressing up' for the role, remodelling the face, the facial expression, the posture of the body, the mannerisms of gesture and speech, and deliberately cultivating a repertoire of styles".[1] In the eyes of the public the student is more likely to do everything in excess. This is particularly true of the much publicised cases of students involved in drug taking and trafficking, particularly at the newer *avant-garde* universities.

The proportion of students who think there is no prestige attached to being a student increases up the social scale, so that as many as 31 per cent of upper middle-class students fall into this category. This would seem to corroborate what has already been said about the working-class ethos of Newcastle and the attitude of those upper middle-class students who feel they have moved down the social scale since coming to university.

In Edinburgh a Scottish upper middle-class student in his third year said that he considered that he had moved from the upper middle class to the lower middle class since coming to university because "people don't usually put students into a social class, but if they had to it would be the lower middle class". "No student will afterwards be in the working class, but it depends on what one does afterwards whether one goes into the upper middle class or not. I haven't yet gone into the upper middle class." He thought that if he entered a profession like his father he would then move back into the upper middle class thus experiencing what Westergaard has called "shuttle mobility".[2] This echoes the views of many upper middle-class students. Nor was it only upper middle-class students who said that "students do not have a high standing in society"; working-class students also reiterated this point. It was noticeable, however, that the kind of remark stated above was most often made by first-generation stu-

---

[1] Hall, S., Leisure, entertainment and mass communications, paper presented to the BSA Conference, London, April 1967.

[2] Westergaard, J., lecture to the BSA Exeter Summer School, 26 July 1965. The fact that men shift occupational status during their careers is taken account of by, for example, Lipset, S. M. and Bendix, R., Social mobility and occupational career patterns, *AJS*, January and March 1952, **57**, 366–74 and 494–504.

dents of the upper middle class who felt they had more in common with first-generation students of other social classes. These students were less reluctant than their second-generation upper middle-class counterparts to say that they had moved down the social scale.

We now turn to the question of why more working-class and lower middle-class students had not said that they had moved and what were the reasons for upward non-motility. This should help to show us what particular social conditions differentiate the upwardly motile from the up wardly immotile.

In interview it appeared that many assigned working-class and lower middle-class students in each university did not think that they had changed their social class from that of parents since coming to university primarily because this point in their social career was not thought to be that kind of crucial stage. University *per se* was not for them the most important avenue to social mobility.

Some working-class students said that they had changed their social class already perhaps some years before university, for instance upon gaining scholarships to grammar schools and public schools. This depended on the home background and the cultural values of the parents, i.e. whether they were atypical or not in terms of educo-social aspirations. The more atypical of the working class the parents were and the more encouragement they gave their child to continue education, the more they were able to move with the child in his upward social mobility, thereby giving him the impression that he had not moved.[1] This represents a motile family. In the non-motile family the child feels early that he is making some social break with his family as soon as the process of social selection begins and he moves into a middle-class public or grammar school. He leaves his parents behind socially at an early point, and his university career is a continuation of something already begun.

An example of this kind of process was an assigned working-class third-year male student at Edinburgh and originally from Lancashire but now married and settled in Edinburgh. He said that he considered his social class to have changed a long time before coming to university. He had won a scholarship to a church-run boarding school which he attended from the age of 10 years, and during this time had gradually grown apart from his parents. He considered that his class had changed

---

[1] This relates to reference groups as "social mechanisms by which individual achievement is ultimately fostered". Kemper, T. D., Reference groups, socialization and achievement, *ASR*, **33** (1), Feb. 1968, p. 32.

at school, and he found that he could now hardly communicate with his parents. He was continually aware of social class consciousness in others. His wife's parents, who were upper middle class, had practically disowned her upon marrying him, and in consequence he and his wife had become a separate and rather isolated unit. He said that they had few friends and social activities, and he felt pressure upon him to work all the time to get a "first" in order to justify himself to his wife's parents.

The two main points which emerge in this and other case histories is the stress upon values and communication, and the expression of social distance in spatial terms which may widen any existing "generation gap". We have already seen how some English working-class students in Edinburgh, and working-class students in the other two universities also (particularly Durham), go to a university a long way from home because they are mobile and are expressing in physical–spatial terms a movement away from parents socially which has already occurred or is occurring. This may create problems and tensions within the home, or, on the other hand, it may be something for which parents are prepared and with which they can cope. This depends on their own motility and adaptability.

Those students by contrast who do not move socially from either working class or lower middle class—either before or whilst at university—are those with strong locality and family links, often strengthened by home residence. This home residence and spatial nearness to parents and peers puts brakes, as it were, on the student's mobility. This in addition to the fact that, as we have seen, home residence reduces the contact with other social classes within the university. The home residence and locality links, however, are not only a cause of non-mobility; they are a feature of the non-motile student who clings to his home links. Those few motile students who by reason of strong home ties are made socially immobile, become socially frustrated—often "inverted snobs", sometimes rebels.

Locality ties are often represented by groups of friends of long standing who have not gone to university and with whom the student still has social activities. There is a widespread refusal to drop these friends upon coming to university even though maintaining social links with them becomes increasingly difficult. Local activities associated with the home community take up the leisure time of the non-motile student, thereby preventing him from joining in extracurricular university activities through which he could get to know fellow students out of class. Such activities as youth clubs, church clubs, scout clubs, and local sports societies were mentioned in this connection by students.

Although these students try to keep up two sets of activities and friends —at university and at home—the outcome is not always satisfactory. Sometimes the local friends put strains upon the relationship by making the student feel different. Said one student sadly, "People don't understand about going to university and assume one must be a snob."[1]

These non-motile students have deep attachment to family and, particularly among the Scottish working class, would have regarded it as a deep disloyalty to their parents to say that they had grown away from them and moved up the social scale merely by their becoming just "one of them students". This is particularly true among those who feel that students have no particular prestige in society. And, as we have seen from the Newcastle survey, 27 per cent said that students have no prestige in society—often the opposite—and those who felt this most often and most deeply were upper middle-class students, 31 per cent of whom registered "no prestige".

In such a situation, if being a student does not seem to confer any particular status, it is felt by many working-class students to be nonsensical that they should have changed their social class on coming to university. This being so, it is not surprising that so few first generation university students of the working class and lower middle class experience difficulties in family relationships after coming to university, for the break or attenuation in relationships brought about by changes not only in life style but in values has not yet begun to take place. This brings us to a consideration of bourgeoisifications, for this implies not merely external categorisation but an enculturation into middle-class values and norms.[2]

If one accepts this definition, then there is a section of working-class students in all three universities who through the operation of certain social factors are resistant to bourgeoisification. If one discounts those who felt they moved before university, along with those who moved upon coming to university and those who have doubts about the matter, then about 50 per cent of the working-class students at university are non-motile although this is not to say they are not mobile. Sixty per cent

---

[1] Ellis and Clayton-Lane, Structural supports for upward mobility, *ASR*, October 1963: "Generally lower class youth find themselves confronted by an environment in which going to college is the exception not the rule, and in which strong counterpressures may be mounted against those who seek to deviate from the prevailing cultural norms."

[2] See Lockwood, D., and Goldthorpe, J. H., *Sociol. Rev.*, 1963, **11**, 133, for discussion of the economic, normative, and relational aspects of embourgeoisement.

of lower middle-class students are non-motile—this refers particularly to first-generation university students in this social class.

We have seen how the non-motile students do not feel that they have changed their social class from that of their parents either before, at, or during their university career. Yet this does not signify that they believe that they will never move. Indeed, a large majority of these 50 per cent say that they will move after they leave university. For a very few this is the result of the fact that a degree in itself conveys social prestige —for the majority social mobility comes upon "getting a good job". It was often stressed that social movement would almost come without their individual volition since it is "not what you think yourself—but the category that other people put you into that counts". "I suppose when I get a good job with good money my social class will change", said one working-class science student. "I mean it will almost automatically won't it? If I get a nice house and big car people will put me in the middle class. However, I doubt whether my own views will ever change. To myself I shall always be working class."

This student stated what was repeated by so many others—that their social mobility would be the result of their being moved rather than consciously desiring movement. Although looking forward to acquiring the material advantages of higher social status they want very little of the cultural and value systems, i.e. they are mobile but not motile. They look forward to experiencing what Lockwood has called an "institutional" mobility,[1] which will "jack them up a place"—they are not bourgeoisified—in their own minds they never will be, although that is too far ahead to judge.

For these students mobility is a structural property and not an individual experience, although in time their life-style may change their values will remain deeply rooted in their social class of origin. These students exhibit some of the characteristics of what Lockwood and Goldthorpe have called the "privatised" workers in an affluent society, cut off from their "traditional" working-class way of life and yet not inducted into the values and culture of the group to which they aspire. They are in some senses marginal and cut adrift.[2] "This again would tend to suggest that the factor of mobility by itself is by no means the

[1] Lockwood, *op. cit.* (1963) p. 13.
[2] Goldthorpe, J. H., Lockwood, D., Beckhofer, F. and Platt, J., The affluent worker and the thesis of embourgeoisement. Some preliminary research findings, *Sociology*, **1** (1), 1967, p. 11.

solely, or even saliently, operative factor."[1] The working-class students particularly interpreted social mobility purely in terms of "job and money", i.e. in terms of an achievement pattern conditioned by their socio-cultural background and which their parents would understand, for which they were prepared, and which implicitly they approved in the first place. As Kahl notes about a similar group of lower middle-class American students, "in this pragmatic approach toward schooling, the boys reflected the views of their parents (and of most of their teachers)".[2]

Links with family and friends need never be changed, attenuated, or broken, particularly if there is no geographical break, since mobility is expressed in terms of the working-class value pattern. Whether the students will in time become bourgeoisified on entering an occupation or profession which carries with it its own style of life and social as well as occupational obligations, remains to be seen. In this situation the experience of the student as worker might become more directly comparable with the experience of the economically affluent "privatised" worker discussed.

This finding reflects what was discovered in the last chapter about students' views on the factors which determine an individual's social status. It may help to look again at Table 12.1.

In Edinburgh 38 per cent of English working-class students mentioned income–occupational factors in social status compared with 33 per cent of Scottish working class; in Durham 41 per cent of working-class students fell into this category; in Newcastle 48 per cent. This differential between the universities tends to correspond to the increasing proportions of working-class students who are mobile and not motile, i.e. who are not bourgeoisified. It also corresponds to proportions of those who came to university to "get a degree" or "for money"—whose motivation in the terms of one young man was "so that I can sell my B.Sc. to the world for a living wage". It is easy to see how a degree may thus become a necessary, if not the necessary means to attainment of occupational status, and university merely an impersonal degree-giving machine. Yet not all working-class students and lower middle-class first-generation students by any means regard university only as a means to an end —as we saw in Chapter 5—and it is often among the hard-working lower middle-class first-generation students in particular that one finds

---

[1] Lockwood, *op. cit.*, p. 12.
[2] Kahl, J. A., *The American Class Structure*, 1962, p. 285.

students who want "to be educated", "to learn", to "to use learning to help others".

One must not forget also those students who are motile and yet who did not change their social class before or upon coming to university because of the comparative mobility of their families with whom they retain strong links. However, many of these students begin to feel at university the cultural differences which begin to separate them from their parents, i.e. the influence of bourgeoisification which comes from mixing and being influenced by middle-class students. These students were often in professional faculties such as a medical faculty—and became aware of the gradual effect upon them of the enculturation into a professional ethos. They tended also to be found in halls of residence and colleges, i.e. living in conditions which, as we have seen, are conducive to close intergroup relations and the mutual transmission of elements of social class culture.

Said one such lower middle-class student:

> I feel so strange now in my own home that I feel almost like a lodger. Yet even though there are tensions between us I still feel loyal to my parents and would like to help them financially some day. I came to Edinburgh because it is a long way from home. My school advised it. It depends on the personality of the parents whether they can adapt or not to the situation.

The fact that lower middle-class students as well as working-class students experienced tensions at home as a result of coming to university shows again that, in terms of values, it is the impact upon the educocultural classes rather than the socioeconomic classes which is important. Most working-class students who experienced difficulties—like the one above—were first-generation university students whose parents perhaps did not always appreciate the values of higher education and so did not wholeheartedly enter into the experience. The higher the parents' own education the more encouragement they tended to give to their student sons and daughters.

Very few parents of those interviewed actively opposed the idea of higher education, and, as one might expect, it was usually girls who found themselves in this situation. Said one female working-class student in Edinburgh: "My parents definitely did not want me to come to University. But I can get over the tensions and difficulties by 'being normal' and showing them that I do not feel superior."

Even in such cases of real antagonism there seemed to be mutual adaptation to the student's new role and status on both sides. In some

cases the parents were only too eager to see their children "get on"
—and some students spoke of their parents treating them like a status
symbol. This is true of overtly motile families. The majority, however,
said that their parents were proud and pleased for them to come but had
not forced them on in any way. If tensions arose it was usually something
which neither side could either avoid or fully understand, but both tried
to adapt and adjust. Said one working-class student:

> There has been some kind of break between myself and my parents even though
> I know they are proud of me. The fact that they are pleased for me helps them to
> adapt—as does the fact that they know parents of my friends who are in the same
> position. My parents help me in material ways because they can't help me academi-
> cally. My mother especially is very good to me.

Other students spoke of their parents' financial help as being a concrete
expression of their love and support, and the stress on the particular
role of the mother was often repeated by working-class students. It is
clear that difficulties and tensions with family and friends do not automatically result from the move to university, but that these are features of
certain structural relationships brought about by aspects of mobility.
These will be summarised later. Whether these problems are accentuated
or lessened depends largely on personality factors and on the quality of
the parent–child relationship before the move. Some family relationships
can withstand the effects of movement better than others, and in cases
which could lead to a break some are only attenuated. The mollifying
features of family love and loyalty have often been neglected in discussions
of the structural upheavals of mobility.

The following remark of a working-class girl is only typical of many:
"My parents are very understanding and I feel very loyal to them.
The strength of our family ties helps us to discuss the problems and
differences of opinion that arise."

Such students were well aware how much they owed their parents
and regretted the drawing away which they felt and could not avoid.
"I can't help feeling different from my parents, but I feel guilty about it
because after all I got my ability from them. I am aware of the problem
all the time. I think there should be a greater stress in education on the
value of family ties and the value of working-class intelligence."

These are some of the problems which beset working-class and lower
middle-class students, particularly those who are first-generation university students who undergo social movement and change while at

university. As we have seen, certain conditions are necessary for this to happen, so that in fact only about 30 per cent of working-class students do become bourgeoisified while at university. One must assume that this lack of contact leads to comparative social deprivation also in other social classes.

Although one may conclude that psychological factors enter into the process in terms of personality and motivation, it is clear that the explanation is rather more sociological. Motility in itself implies not only desire for movement,[1] but also "having the properties of movement" or those characteristics which will help movement. This is particularly true of the possession of "motile value systems" or those which in the working class are thought to be more typical of the middle classes and educational élites.

In the three universities surveyed the socially motile person seemed in most cases to be a product of a family environment in which the mother had a higher education level than the father and was aspiring in her aims for her son or daughter.[2] Repeatedly, the same relationships appeared during lengthy discussion of home background in interview, in which it appeared that a cold or indifferent father with little interest in his son's or daughter's education was counterbalanced by a warmly encouraging mother who "did everything possible and made every sacrifice" to get her son or daughter to university. This typical mother often encouraged her child to go away from home and thus facilitated the process of bourgeoisification which she not only did not resent but often welcomed— seeing in it a fulfilment of her thwarted ambitions for herself.[3]

Although the father in each case appeared as a background figure it did not appear that he was consciously opposed to the education of his child. Indeed, it is the undemonstrative father who often makes the venture possible by his provision of financial support. The findings did not go so far as to suggest as did Warner's and Abegglin's that the fathers were uniformly inadequate as male role models.

[1] As in McLelland's term "the need for achievement". See McLelland, D. C., *The Achievement Motive*, New York, 1953. The researchers demonstrate that the achievement motive is measurable and related to cultural values.

[2] This finding accords with those of Floud *et al.*, *Social Class and Educational Opportunity*, 1956; Jackson, B. and Marsden, D., *Education, and the Working Class*, 1962; McKinley, D. G., *Social Class and Family Life*, 1964; Strodtbeck, in McLelland, *Talent and Society*, pp. 135-94, discussed in Chapter 1.

[3] For similar findings on big business leaders in America see Warner, W. L. and Abegglin, J. C., *Big Business Leaders in America*, Harper, New York, 1955.

A further finding was that among the working class it is the eldes female child in a family who may benefit from this kind of relationship particularly if she has no brothers—representative for her family, as i were, "a female son". Such female working-class students have alread been shown to be atypical of the working class in certain ways; likewis they may be atypical of the female population in certain attitudes. This i speculation and demands further investigation.

Indeed, much of what has been said in these latter remarks of th socially motile working-class student has been based rather more or qualitative rather than quantitative evidence, and so no percentages hav been expressed or attempted. Yet the author is certain that there is enougl evidence of the intensive, qualitative kind to suggest certain meaningfu trends which are in accord with other findings in this field. Furthe investigation is necessary in order to qualify the trends reported. Never theless, since the qualitative findings are in themselves consistent, anc since they are compatible within the body of structural material, the author feels justified in outlining them at this stage.

In discussions of motility and mobility one is on much firmer empirica ground since the relation of these two properties is an expression of a structural phenomenon observable in many operations of the process of mobility and is in itself a concept. It has been clear throughout that, ir a sense, motility and mobility are variables which may be present ir situations in lesser or greater degree, just as social class itself may be relevant to a lesser or greater degree, and this depends on a combination of other factors. Therefore not only does the particular combination determine whether an individual will actually move and when he will move, but the combination itself is seen as a structural feature which varies with context. It is in itself a cluster of variables.

> The greatly enlarged need for highly skilled workers and the correlated down- ward trend in the demand for the unskilled represents a significant lever for un- blocking the life opportunities of youth from the lower classes. Rising educa- tion aspirations among parents and children, bolstered by an increase in the num- ber of places in institutions of higher education and by the requirements of mod- ern technology will also be instrumental towards this end.[1]

Thus we have the motile and the non-motile student at university. We have been speaking primarily of upward motility, although the

[1] Elder, G. H. (Jr.), Life opportunity and personality: Some consequences of stratified secondary education in Great Britain, Institute of Internat. Studies, Uni- versity of California, Berkeley, Calif. Reprint 170 (*Sociol. of Educ.* **38** (3), Spring 1965, p. 201).

concept also comprehends downward motility and could be applied to the upper middle-class students who feel they have experienced downward movement. The motile student, whose motility may be encouraged by certain family relations, may experience motility before university at some previous stage in the process of educational selection. He may experience it upon coming to university as a point at which his separation from his parents socially is expressed in terms of a physical break. He may experience it during university in terms of completion of the process of bourgeoisification, i.e. assimilation into the working class. He may experience it afterwards upon gaining a degree or attaining occupational or professional status. These will in each case merely mark a stage in a process long underway.

Certain structural conditions in the home and university environment are necessary for both motility and consequent mobility, and these are concerned with the spatial and social relations of the student with his parents and peers. Weak ties with local peers, and geographical separation from home environment, characterise socially motile students and assist mobility.

For the motile student mobility is achieved in terms of culture and values, i.e. he is the student most likely to be bourgeoisified. The motile student who cannot become bourgeoisified through lack of contact with middle-class peers becomes aggressively working class in compensation and may accentuate local features such as regional accent and behaviour. He is also the kind of student likely to lead student movements of various kinds and so to exercise his need for status in channels other than those which are institutionally sanctioned.[1]

The non-motile student with motile parents will feel anxiety through being "pushed on" against his will—and tensions will result. The non-motile student with non-motile parents will experience far more tensions in his relations with university peers than he does at home—and will seek refuge at home. He will therefore resist social movement and, in terms of institutionalised movement, will postpone movement for as long as possible.

This is a summary of the configuration of variables involved in the mobility of students and in the process of bourgeoisification, which quite obviously need not go hand in hand.

[1] This applies also to students from mobile non-motile families—or the "new" middle class—occupationally middle class, educationally and *emotionally* working class.

Certain conditions are necessary for the mutual transmission of elements of social class culture—where those conditions do not obtain social classes may pass through the University as discrete entities, whose members never have an opportunity mentally to 'rub shoulders' with each other. Working class students have been seen to be concentrated in certain Faculties, in certain forms of residence, in certain student societies. Members of each social class rarely meet one another and suffer accordingly. For these students bourgeoisification or alternatively the knocking-off of too highly polished corners does not take place in the long run.

Superficial contact of social classes within the University cannot have more than a superficial and temporary effect.

Student comments on this included:

'University is an artificial society, without much contact with other people who haven't a University education or people of another social class, so one doesn't find out what makes them tick.'

'University doesn't break down class barriers; once one gets mixed up with the population one gets back into the same structure of social classes.'

The point brought home forcibly by the surveys in Edinburgh, Durham and Newcastle is one that is already beginning to be generally realised—that the ideal of a full community life in which students leave the University not only with a degree but with an education gained in some measure from each other, is not something which happens naturally and quite by accident. It is something which has to be planned.

What is *not* generally realised is that positive steps must be taken to prohibit the accentuation of existing social class divisions in terms of University structure and organisation—since such divisions threaten the establishment of a community life of challenging possibilities.[1]

As we have seen in previous chapters, the structure of class divisions and social distances influences student behaviour in a variety of ways—both inside the institution and increasingly outside the institution in terms of the role of the student in society as a social and a political person.

This situation becomes increasingly accentuated when full expansion programmes are underway. This is especially true if expansion results in an increased proportion of students coming from homes where higher education was previously unknown. The structure of student social relations itself may change. The student and staff attitudes to change are examined in the next chapter, along with the social consequences of rapid institutional expansion.

[1] Abbott, J., Students' social class in three northern universities, *BJS*, September 1965, **16** (3).

CHAPTER 14

STUDENT ATTITUDES TO UNIVERSITY EXPANSION

IN DISCUSSION of the structure of student social relations and of the
distances between groups which make up the organisation, it has been
hoped to indicate ways in which change may occur under certain conditions. It has been hoped also to show ways in which processes of change
will in turn be constrained by certain aspects of structure. The structural
principles outlined are, of course, factors within a dynamic situation
and can only be fully understood within a dynamic frame of reference.
This is particularly true of present-day universities which are experiencing
and planning large scale expansion in provision of places and facilities.
Naturally such expansion as there is must take place within a whole
range of constraints institutionally defined as, for example, in relation
to existing resources and provisions and the capacity of the institution
to expand at a certain rate and in any particular way. Thus the rate and
kind of expansion will in turn determine not only the size of the institution
but adaptions in complexity of organisation and administration, number
and structure of component groups, and adjustment of intergroup
distances, and communication. This must inevitably lead to changes in
the quality of interpersonal relations in the institution. The role of the
university in providing education for more and more students must be
seen in relation to the way in which it is able to provide for those who are
selected.

"The University is being called upon to educate previously unimagined
numbers of students—to respond to the expanding claims of national
service; to merge its activities with industry as never before; to adapt to
and rechannel new intellectual currents."[1]

These claims which are being made upon the universities by the growth

---

[1] Kerr, C., *The Uses of the University*, Harvard Univ. Press, Cambridge, 1963. Quoted
in Lipset, S. M., and Wolin, S. S., *The Berkeley Student Revolt*, 1965, p. 47.

of what Clark Kerr calls the "knowledge industry" change the kind of institution which they are able to be, and the conflict with traditional aims of the "community of scholars" may be very disruptive. Where higher education is a scarce resource in terms of economic and social provision, too fast a rate of expansion may put serious strains upon an overloaded system and increase the structural distances involved to the disadvantage of particular *groups* of students.

The way in which the institution consciously or unconsciously socialises its students, or allows them to socialise each other, is related to the operation of two major factors. The first is the need to expand in terms of actual numbers of places (with all the resulting pressures on material resources) and the second the need to overcome the effects of class differentials and divisions within and between institutions through the encouraging of social relations of members of different social classes and the mutual transmission of social class culture. It is unfortunate that, paradoxical though it may seem, the operations of these factors often take opposite and even opposed directions. The role of the student in society is largely defined by the interrelation and operation of these factors in any particular institutional setting, and the extent to which there is expansion of places without corresponding overall expansion of social class opportunity is the related extent to which the whole conception of the student's role will change. This is true of student attitudes to their role—whether as an élite either occupational or educational—as mobile or non-mobile members of social classes, as performers of a particular job for which society is pleased to pay them, and the rewards for which are occupational advancement and good money, or as scholars in a community of scholars.

The institutional structure and pressures that there are result from the conflicting aims of higher education outlined at the beginning and the associated needs through which they are expressed. On the one hand the need to provide increased places, and increase these as quickly as possible, dictates the form of the university—its size, its internal organisation and complexity, and the kind or degree of material and social provisions which it makes for its students. On the other hand, the need to leave upon the student an institutional imprint, to socialise as well as educate, places certain constraints upon the ways in which expansion takes place. And underlying the way that the university settles these priorities there is also the interplay of the changing social class composition which mirrors to a greater or lesser extent the overall expansion of places.

We have seen how, under certain conditions, social class divisions remain and how social class culture finds its expression under such conditions in student organisation and social relations. Conversely, student culture develops where institutional considerations and pressures override these social class divisions and assist interaction on a predominantly student basis. Traditionally student occasions like rags, graduations, and now protest meetings, accentuate this common studentness. Thus where pressure to expand places, for instance, leads to growth of a large impersonal system, with work and leisure centres spread disparately through the urban environment—as in most civic institutions—the mixing of classes is prevented and socialisation is only vaguely effective. If, in addition, a pressure on residential places results in fewer students being able to live in hall—in use of more and worse city flats and an increase of students living at home—the process will be exacerbated and almost always to the detriment of the working class. Thus the system designed to establish equality of opportunity for the working class in its operation sometimes militates against their enjoying any increase in opportunity as it was meant to be enjoyed.

Conversely, where the needs of socialisation are paramount this restricts speedy institutional expansion. In collegiate universities for instance, like Durham, where places have to be physically built, expansion is exceedingly slow, so that in terms of overall numbers of working-class students expansion of opportunity is depressed—fewer enjoy a university education—but the ones who do are more readily assimilated into the system.

It is not proper to make any value judgements on the issues raised, and, indeed, they are too complex for any such judgements to be made. However, we can next look at the effects in terms of the student role.

Firstly, in the situation of an institution which values increased socialisation the student is able to internalise institutional norms and culture through participation in the activities of community life and so to become conscious of the meaning of student role as a member of an academic élite and so to internalise student culture. In Durham the wearing of gowns in the city accentuates this division. Therefore a new set of divisions is set up on the basis of educational as opposed to social class criteria. This continues the internal hierarchical ordering of relations. The role which the student has in the academic community is thus reflected in the relations which he has outside the university. He is *in statu pupillari*, his university or college is *in loco parentis*, he submits with varying degrees of willingness to its pastoral as well as academic care and to the varying institutional patterns of authority imposed upon him in exchange for the rewards of "belonging" in full to the community of scholars in which the students and staff go to make up an organic whole. The student is thus abstracted from the popular or youth culture which helps to define the place in society of other young people of his age—it places him in a stage of transition, a limbo, a prolonged period of a *rite de passage*—the institution acts for him like a chrysallis from which he will emerge at the end of three years a butterfly—perhaps estranged from family and friends—but a butterfly who has moved up a fairly well demarcated ladder. Of course, this situation represents one end of a continuum along which each institution falls and depends to some extent upon its overall size and comparative social class proportions as well as its organisational and residential structure. A change in one factor will affect the others.

At the other end of the continuum we have the university expanding too quickly for its existing provisions and compelled to resort to makeshift lecture theatres and inferior quality accommodation. As a result one has the suffering caused by poor material conditions with, for instance, aspiring working-class students compelled to live in conditions far worse than those at home and hardly conducive to the growth of élitist feelings. One also has the growing impersonality of social relations and the attenuation of any student identity with increasingly unfavourable staff–student ratios, and accentuation of social class groupings by the distances created in all spheres of social life. Community feelings exist only in terms of residential and faculty sub-groups, which make up the total, and, since these are often class biased, class culture remains. Indeed, since socialisation is minimal, since institutional pressures are minimal, the student is not abstracted from the divisions of the urban environment; he meets them in everyday interaction with city folk. It is his identity as a social class member rather than a student which is reinforced and which the institution must recognise and allow for. He is part of the youth culture of a class society, his commitments and attitudes are therefore not much different from other young people of his age except that he is in an artificial environment and abstracted from family and neighbourhood with little new identity to take its place.

Small wonder then that the ills of the mass university are social as well as academic ills—so strongly expressed in Berkeley[1] and now at the London

[1] Lipset and Wolin, *op. cit.*

School of Economics. The ostensible causes of student unrest and protest only express a far more deep-seated malaise at the root of so many other student problems. In the mass university the student is searching for a role, for an identity—he is not offered one in institutional terms. His reaction to anomie may then be in rebellion.[1] To be a student is increasingly akin to "having to job" with corresponding demands on time but not necessarily on commitment or values.

The student's identity, therefore, often is that of any young person who happens to be studying, so he increasingly resents in this situation any attempts at supervision; he wants to live a life of his own; to live in a flat not a hall of residence; to get married if he pleases; and live in sin if he prefers it. He is less a member of an academic community and more a product of the social class culture from which he came. The system is self-perpetuating in that he demands more say in student government, in the ordering of his own affairs, and, in turn, his demands for independence are conceded by the institution of which he is so often only nominally a member.

In this situation it is not surprising that students see themselves as social reformers and political agitators. What is also not surprising is that the speed of change has widened the generational gap between students and their teachers and led to many misunderstandings on both sides. In a sense we could speak of an interstitial situation where the staff and student expectations of a university education do not mesh. This leads to conflict or avoidance, and where the size of the institution and the speed of its expansion leads to breakdown of formal communication channels, the discrepancies in perception and response may not be able to be adjusted.

A newspaper article[2] on the LSE incidents in 1967 reports that some of the student placards read "Beware the pedagogic gerontocracy" —which emphasises the significance of the generational gap and the unsatisfactory nature of remote control.

Many academics recognise the limits of student self-government. Students come,

---

[1] Various episodes of unrest and even rebellion in the college of Durham during the research were afterwards discovered to have been in part instigated by a handful of students with decidedly left-wing sympathies. This may be seen not as a spontaneous reaction against the pressure to conform but as an attempt to structure in a particular way a rather ambiguous and ambivalent situation.

[2] Silver, E. and Shearer, A., LSE protest runs to the California pattern, *The Guardian*, 15 March 1967.

students go, but LSE goes on for ever. But none the less they believe that the school's administration has become too remote and paternalistic.

It is said that something of the same kind has happened in the teaching of students. One of the complaints we heard from almost all other pickets, some of them surprisingly awake after a night of sleepless protest, was the lack of contact with their tutors.

The writers of the article, in unison with others, relate student unrest in general to the evils of expansion and to emulation of student revolt in the United States. They argue, however, that the reasons why the "organised defiance" erupted particularly in LSE and (so far) nowhere else, lay in the particular character of the student body. This will be seen to emphasise general points made previously.

Although the new president of the students' union is a conservative, there was no attempt to camouflage the left-wing flavour of the demonstrations. Where the students differed from their elders was in seeing nothing sinister in this and in repudiating conspiracy theories.

The student body, they said, tended to be left-wing and iconoclastic for a variety of reasons. It was predominantly grammar and comprehensive school, first generation at University with no hereditary preconceptions about how one should behave there. Because the LSE was a social science college, its students tended to respond in political and legalistic ways. Since there is only one small hall of residence, student activity is concentrated in the union (a haven in the Big City), encouraging organisation and intensifying the introspection familiar in most universities.[1]

This extract notes the interrelation of student social groups and university structure which we have been discussing, and which complicates the issue of growth in size. The pressure to expansion is not in itself a bad thing—it is the way in which it takes place which may have a deleterious effect on students and which may encourage them in the thought that the aims of education are becoming subservient to the needs of technology. This has been true for a long time in the United States—it has become true in Britain. "The big universities have changed in precisely the ways Mr. Kerr has described. They have become corporations for producing, transmitting and marketing knowledge—and in the process have lost their intellectual and moral identity."[2]

In an age of mass production and conformity students see themselves as reintroducing the critical role and moral identity which their universities seem to them to have lost.

[1] Silver and Shearer, *op. cit.*
[2] Taylor, H., The academic industry, in Lipset and Wolin, *op. cit.*, p. 62.

When students talk about these political issues, they soon put a question that goes to the heart of college expansion and its purposes. This is: "Are we being educated or merely trained?" Their own experience is that they are not being given a chance to "broaden themselves" or to "develop as full men"—such phrases, once applied to a favoured few, now have a hollow ring—but are working long hours and getting little fun for three years to provide the nation with a profitable investment. Each new scheme for cutting the costs and increasing the productivity of the system strengthens the impression, as does the language of ministerial circulars about "better utilisation of plant".[1]

Expansion of places without changes in organisation which encourage expansion of opportunity and interaction results in a situation of structural stress and interpersonal anomie. The greater the expansion (and in the University of California campuses there were 107,000 students in 1969) the greater the conscious reorganisation which is necessary. The traditional pattern can only be stretched so far; similarly, attenuation of existing relationships between persons and groups beyond a certain point must lead to breakdown in communication. One must also remember that coming up to the university for the first time for the seventeen and eighteen year old fresh from home and school can be an unnerving and lonely experience in the midst of so many thousands of (apparently uncaring) strangers. Such an experience can lead to retreatism or rebellion.

Of course, the role of the academic and administrative staff is important in the conscious structuring of relations since they represent a more permanent personnel than the student body. It is they who can give directives for action and help to formulate the goals and aims of the institution in a direct and personal way. This is extremely important where structural supports for action have broken down. The influence of expectations grounded in the member of staff's experience of other institutions is pertinent here and will help or hinder in the adjustment to new and changing circumstances. The generational gap which appears to be widening may be important among staff and influence their alignments in disputes about student discipline and self-government. Staff who are young and recent products of the educational system themselves, may feel that they have more in common with the oldest generation of students than with the oldest generation of staff and will align their support accordingly. This is particularly true in universities where no very wide status gap exists between staff and students.

[1] Jones, M., What's worrying the students?, *New Statesman*, 17 February 1967, p. 214.

The university authorities—presidents, vice-chancellors, and principals—may have the crucial role of giving the lead to their academic and administrative staff in the formulation of attitudes to expansion and to change. This in turn will be related to the existing size and structure of the university as extracts from newspaper reports show. These extracts are from the annual reports of the vice-chancellors of Edinburgh and Durham and reveal the concern which is felt about the prospects of expansion—or expansion without adaption.

Sir Edward Appleton said in January 1965:

> Speaking in terms of the Scottish educational system, the Robbins Committee did not declare that a University place could be claimed, as a right, by anyone possessing the minimal qualification for University entry, which means the possession of an Attestation of Fitness. The Committee, in fact, supported the principle of admitting, over the next ten years, only the same proportion of young people with the minimal qualifications as were admitted when their Report was drafted. In other words, University expansion today is an expression of the numerical increase in the pool from which University entrants are drawn and not of a lowering of entrance standards.
>
> However, on one matter I disagree with Lord Robbins. He said that, in large Universities, he sees the danger—I use his own words— "of the emergence of a penumbra of mediocrity over the proceedings as a whole". Frankly, I see no such danger if, as I have indicated is the case, we maintain our entrance standards. Rather do I see virtues in size. In a large University, we can increase the intellectual contacts between really first-class people—in the case of both staff and students; and the way to encourage the development of real talent is to mix like with like. Education should not be an egalitarian process.[1]

Dr. D. G. Christopherson had special comments to make on staffing problems:

> Universities are likely to experience difficulty, particularly during the next few years, in recruiting staff to carry out their expansion programmes without reducing the standard of teaching, Dr. D. G. Christopherson, Vice-Chancellor and Warden of Durham University, says in his annual report.
>
> Dr. Christopherson says that in some subjects, especially mathematics and some of the social sciences, there has been for some years a shortage of university teachers of the quality which most universities think is essential if standards are not to fall. These shortages will clearly become worse, and others will appear in other faculties if the rate of university expansion is increased. . . .
>
> Durham has told the University Grants Committee that it is prepared to increase its rate of expansion by approximately 50 per cent over the next three or four years,

---

[1] Appleton, Sir E., Principal's Annual Address to the General Council delivered 29 January 1965, printed in *University of Edinburgh Bulletin.*

to meet the demands of the Robbins Report, provided that the necessary finance is forthcoming.

Dr. Christopherson holds some hope that the fear that "more means worse" need not be justified. Those who hold this opinion seem to look at the matter from the point of view of the senior members, he says; they argue that the average standard of students will fall, making teaching more laborious and research less possible.

What matters more in the long run is how the matter appears to our junior members. Can we maintain, without depreciation, the quality of the experience offered to our students?

Our circumstances in Durham have in the past enabled us to provide a pattern of student life which has been in some ways unique among British universities. We shall do everything possible to maintain in full what we think are our special advantages and at the same time to overcome the handicaps which the small size of Durham as a university centre has in the past imposed.[1]

These remarks must be seen within the context of the university structures to which they refer. Consideration of aspects of expansion in the three universities surveyed, and particularly of student attitudes to the effects of expansion, may make more specific the points already made about changes in higher education attendant upon increase in places.

It has been mentioned already in Chapter 2 that the three universities in the survey are undergoing a period of tremendous expansion which involves vast building programmes and expansion of existing departments. The situation in Durham is most delicate in that places for students have to be built if the present rate of "residence in" is to be maintained. It was claimed by members of the University that the rate of expansion laid down by Robbins did not take sufficient account of this fact, and there was much discussion among staff and administration as to whether the character of the University could be preserved if the Robbins estimates were striven for. Certainly among staff there seemed to be a general hesitancy to accept the need for vast expansion at least at so quick a rate, and a tendency to stress the rather more disquieting possibilities of expansion. The attitude of "more means worse" was fairly prevalent among certain sections of the academic—particularly resident—staff.

Attitudes to expansion among staff were not ascertained at the other two universities,[2] but since these are both non-residential there are fewer institutional restrictions on the form expansion may take. It appears that

---

[1] University standards threatened, report in *The Guardian*, 11 November 1964.

[2] Trow and Halsey note in their study of British academics "a form of élitism in relation to the university system, and to the appointments structure of university departments". Trow, M. and Halsey, A. H., British academics and the professorship, *Sociology*, **3** (3), Sept. 1969, 321–41.

in Newcastle and Edinburgh expansion is greater and more rapid because increasing numbers are fitted into existing buildings until new ones are built, and this, of course, applies only to work space. Accommodation problems grow as the threshold of student saturation of city accommodation is reached, but the situation is more flexible than in a collegiate university. Nevertheless, it may lead to a greater number of cases of individual discomfort and strain than in the small residential university where expansion is tempered to individual rather than institutional needs.

In the larger universities, therefore, there seems to be greater acceptance of the necessity to expand among students, staff, and administration; this is especially true after a certain threshold of size, cost, and administrative complexity has been reached. Once a university has grown beyond a certain point a few thousand students here or there makes little difference to the running of the university—it becomes geared to expansion. Durham has not yet reached this position and Newcastle has possibly only just passed it since it became an independent new university with increased means at its own disposal. Problems which seem almost insurmountable at the beginning of the process, as in Durham, begin to have their own built-in solutions by the time the University reaches the size of Edinburgh. It would seem that there is an intrinsic institutional resistance to change and expansion which follows a curve of diminishing effect once the process of change itself is under way. This is thought of in organisational and institutional terms, but it well may apply to the proportion of individuals within the institution who are themselves resistant to change.

The official aspects of expansion are more aptly dealt with in documents and reports than within the limits of the present chapter. The kind of investigation to be described has not so far been undertaken in any systematic way. This is an examination of the attitudes to expansion of the students themselves—those who are actually undergoing the institutional changes which expansion necessitates.[1]

Since expansion is meant to comprehend institutional changes of various sorts, the attitudes of students to the separation of Durham and Newcastle universities will first be discussed, particularly as this may help to throw more light upon the differences between them. It may also

---

[1] It must be remembered that the surveys were undertaken before expansion was really under way and before the deleterious effects of such expansion had received international coverage and publicity.

throw light upon the individual's knowledge or ignorance of what is going on in institutional organisation and the way in which it affects him personally.

Students were asked whether they thought that the changing of New-castle from a college of Durham to a university in its own right had in any way affected the lives or attitudes of ordinary students. If they answered "yes" they were asked to say in what way. This was left open-ended and answers were afterwards coded.

Table 14.1 shows the results of this survey.

TABLE 14.1. WHETHER NEWCASTLE STUDENTS THOUGHT THAT THE CHANGE OF KING'S COLLEGE TO UNIVERSITY STATUS HAD AFFECTED THE ORDINARY STUDENT (per cent)

	UMC		LMC		WkC		Unclassified		Total	No.
	M	F	M	F	M	F	M	F		
Yes	15	23	15	20	14	9	14	20	16	(100)
No	50	47	50	35	53	30	67	20	47	(297)
Don't know	35	30	35	45	33	61	19	60	37	(232)
TOTAL	100	100	100	100	100	100	100	100	100	
No.	(142)	(57)	(189)	(91)	(91)	(33)	(21)	(5)	(629)	(629)

Only 16 per cent of students said that students had been affected in some way. One must remember that many students in fact never knew Newcastle as a college of Durham, i.e. first- and second-year students, so could not possibly know what difference had been effected. If one abstracts these students (a little over 50 per cent), then it would appear that about half of the students who saw the change felt the change personally in some way—even if they were unsure of its particular effects. The figure also includes some first-years who were not involved personally but who heard other students talking about "what things used to be like", and shows the persistence of internalised divisions.

However, it is true that many students felt that the break only acknowledged explicitly a situation which had existed for some time.

"The only way I knew that we were part of Durham", said one male student, "was when we took examinations which were headed 'University of Durham, King's College'. And of course one had to graduate from Durham. That's all the effect it had on me."

Said another: "Occasionally we went through for sporting fixtures, or we had a joint regatta with them. Otherwise we were separate in every way. It didn't feel like one university." This student stressed that it had been bad for Newcastle sporting morale to play for a Durham team and, in fact, most of the good Durham sportsmen were, in effect, from King's. He thought that becoming separate would increase group solidarity and pride in the University.

There is a consistent percentage of male students from every social class (14 per cent) who feel that students have been affected by the institutional change in status. Among the female students, however, there is some difference between the social classes in which the proportion of students who experienced effects of change decreases with social class. Only 9 per cent working-class students thought that students had been affected in some way. Perhaps because of the fact that due to sex and class this group is probably least likely to participate in institutional activities such as team games. On the other hand, this group had 61 per cent "don't knows"—the highest in any sex or social class category.

On the whole, the "don't knows" tend to figure nearly as largely as the "no's", which tends to demonstrate, perhaps, the students' limited institutional perspective on this point.

Students' particular interpretations of the effects of the change tend to some extent to fall into social class patterns, although not markedly so. The largest proportion of replies in any category came under the heading that the change would stimulate "pride in our university". Thirty-six per cent of students held this opinion, which augurs well for the new university if these represent the small but enthusiastic proportion who leaven the dough. Two-thirds of working-class females came into this category, but of the total students in this category, upper middle-class and lower middle-class men formed 50 per cent. This could have some relation to participation in sport noted in Chapter 6.

Lower middle-class male students formed the largest proportion of those who spoke of a "loss of tradition" and proved to be those in interview who had hankered after the ties with a "collegiate" university and who preferred to say there were "at Durham" than "at Newcastle".

This group also spoke most often (38 per cent) of the degree having "less snob appeal", often quite wistfully. This is particularly true of members of the Medical Faculty who feel that a Newcastle medical degree is not yet established enough to be accepted in the medical profession even although the place of teaching is the same. It was often said by Medics that they supposed that the completely new medical course which had been started to coincide with the new university was an attempt to make a completely new name with a new tradition.

Students who registered in Durham still had the option of taking a Durham degree, and apparently those taking medical degrees nearly always opted for Durham. This is the opposite of subjects in the Science Faculty which has always had a reputation in its own right as a Newcastle section of Durham. The bulk of students in science usually opted for a Newcastle degree.

Feelings among medical students tended to be more heated on the subject of independence than those of students in other faculties, and one felt that much of this had percolated down from the top.

Strangely enough, 23 per cent of male working-class students thought that the change would involve loss of status for the University. On the other hand, 19 per cent of students felt that independence had led to healthy competition with Durham "to prove that we are as good as they are", and these students tended to be mainly middle class. No working-class girls came into this category.

The only students who spoke of "better facilities" were 4 per cent of the male lower middle class. Material aspects of the change in status were not otherwise mentioned.

If one adds together the "beneficial" and "disadvantageous" effects of the change in status upon students it would seem that for 65 per cent the change appears beneficial and for 33 per cent it appears disadvantageous. The weight of opinion of those who felt the effects of the change seem to be in favour of change.

If we turn immediately to a discussion of whether students favoured expansion of the University, a different kind of pattern emerges. Table 14.2 shows the Newcastle reactions to this question. Firstly, students were asked if they thought that expansion would have any effect upon the character of the University. If these figures are to be believed, it would appear that expansion touches students more closely than an institutional change in status, and that they believe it to have a greater effect upon the character of the University and the life of the individual student.

Forty-eight per cent of students thought that expansion would affect the character of the University and 23 per cent said they did not know.

448 Student Life in a Class Society

TABLE 14.2. WHETHER NEWCASTLE STUDENTS THOUGHT THAT EXPANSION WOULD AFFECT THE CHARACTER OF THE UNIVERSITY AND THE LIFE OF THE STUDENTS (per cent)

	UMC		LMC		WkC		Unclassified		Total	No.
	M	F	M	F	M	F	M	F		
Yes	47	56	44	54	44	55	57	60	48	(304)
No	24	23	33	23	29	21	19	—	27	(168)
Don't know	29	18	21	20	25	21	19	—	23	(143)
Happened already	—	3	2	3	2	3	5	40	2	(14)
TOTAL No.	100 (142)	100 (57)	100 (189)	100 (91)	100 (91)	100 (33)	100 (21)	100 (5)	100 (629)	(629)

In replies to this question the sex differential is more significant than the social class differential, which in effect hardly exists. A higher proportion of female students than male students in each social class think that expansion has certain effects on the student body, and the inter-class proportions are remarkably consistent. The female proportion is consistently up 10 per cent on the male proportion.

The proportion of "don't knows" again varies with sex and not with class. Even the pattern of replies specifying areas of change shown in Table 14.3 shows little in the way of a distinct class pattern. However, upon reflection, this is not entirely unexpected in that this question is directed to the respondent in his capacity as student as opposed to non-student. It is interesting to note that this area of student interest in which in a sense a "threat situation" exists invokes student rather than social class responses.

The largest proportion of replies (35 per cent) fell into the category of fears that the University would become like an "impersonal machine" instead of a student community. In interview some students said that the process is beginning already and spoke nostalgically of the "old bun room" in the old union building (now rebuilt and expanded) where one could be sure of meeting everyone who was anyone in the University. "Now all that is changed; instead we have the huge, brash buildings of the new Union, already too small and very overcrowded. And all the friendly intimate atmosphere is quite lost."

TABLE 14.3. PARTICULAR EFFECTS ON UNIVERSITY OF EXPANSION AS RATED BY NEWCAS-
TLE STUDENTS (per cent)

	UMC		LMC		WkC		Unclassified		Total	No.
	M	F	M	F	M	F	M	F		
Impersonal machine	31	57	36	43	15	44	23	—	35	(115)
Less staff–student contact	17	16	17	13	23	17	23	50	18	(57)
Drop in standards	14	8	22	9	30	6	31	—	17	(54)
Decentralisation	14	5	6	13	7	11	—	25	9	(30)
Overcrowding	11	5	11	7	3	—	—	—	8	(25)
Decline in social life	6	3	3	11	12	17	8	25	7	(24)
Less rat race	6	5	3	4	7	6	7	—	5	(16)
Better facilities	1	—	1	—	3	—	7	—	1	(4)
TOTAL	100	99	99	100	100	101	99	100	100	
No.	(142)	(57)	(189)	(91)	(91)	(33)	(21)	(5)	(629)	(629)

Even young first-years had this image of the old "King's" passed on to them in the way of myth and folklore and the "old bun room" became a mystical symbol of all that had passed and was worth preserving. In the time of its existence it is unsure whether it ever enjoyed such glory.

However, the fact that townspeople and students still speak of "King's" and the university buildings are situated in "King's Road", and so on, still tends to nurture the myth of "glory that is gone". Those were the days when the University really had character—when it was a close-knit community with its own distinctions. With change in status, and particularly name, and with expansion in numbers, this is passing away. Further expansion can only lead to a greater and more destructive impersonalisation. This is the students' view, and it is given encouragement by the physical expressions of expansion which are seen every day in terms of new buildings—particularly science blocks. This is important in itself for science blocks always tend to look more impersonal than cosy backstreet arts departments. Students believe the name Newcastle University to be expressive of this kind of scientific expansion, and the arts and medicals among them resent it. In a student referendum on choice of name before the new university status, apparently students voted overwhelmingly for "King's University"—a blend of the old and the new—but it was turned down by the authorities. Students wanted to keep at least the nominal link with the past.

Lower middle-class men are those who numerically comprise the largest proportion of those fearing impersonalisation—29 per cent of all replies in this category. However, in terms of class categories, female upper middle-class students lead with 57 per cent in this category of response.

The second effect most frequently quoted was that staff–student contact would become less frequent and more impersonal; this applies particularly to the work situation, provision of tutorials, etc. Eighteen per cent of students fell into this category, which was most favoured—perhaps surprisingly—by working-class male students. Eight per cent of these working-class male students felt that there would be "less of a rat race"—an interesting comment on their own struggles.

Nine per cent of students felt that there would be increased decentralisation and increased social activities within the faculties themselves rather than maintenance of some identity with the total student body. Evidence would seem to show that identity with the whole student body is weakened at some point where the university is larger than 4000 students.

As many as 30 per cent of these working-class students say that expansion will mean lower standards—both that a degree has less value and that the standard of students applying will fall. This pessimistic and reactionary view of the effects of expansion may be related to their own experience of sponsored mobility. This category in fact shows an increase down the scale.

Table 14.4 covers the total Newcastle sample and its response to the question of whether expansion has desirable, undesirable, or neutral effects, although the figures already shown suggest that only 6 per cent stated advantages in expansion. Only 1 per cent think that expansion will mean better facilities.

As many as 56 per cent of students say that there are undesirable effects and 24 per cent say neutral. This would seem to point to a student population which is largely unenthusiastic at the prospect of expansion—this despite the fact that the covering letter of the questionnaire spoke of the

TABLE 14.4. NEWCASTLE STUDENTS' ESTIMATION OF THE DESIRABILITY OF UNIVERSITY EXPANSION (per cent)

	UMC		LMC		WkC		Unclassified		Total	No.
	M	F	M	F	M	F	M	F		
Desirable	22	16	22	14	27	12	12	25	20	(86)
Undesirable	51	61	58	62	44	64	65	75	56	(243)
Neutral	27	23	21	24	29	24	24	—	24	(105)
TOTAL No.	100	100	101	100	100	100	101	100	100	
	(142)	(57)	(189)	(91)	(91)	(33)	(21)	(5)	(434)	(434)

fact that "an increasingly large proportion of students from families where higher education was previously unknown will have the opportunity of a University education".

One amusing comment on the covering letter was written on the questionnaire by a female student who said: "I cannot see how we shall ever achieve 'the full community life traditionally associated with Universities' mentioned in your letter. Already University is not so much a way of life but more a programme" (this referred to a popular television programme of the time).

It is surprising that so many working-class students—themselves sponsored by the system—should not want to extend the benefits of higher education to other members of the working class. In this the female working class were most critical of all; 65 per cent of these thought that the effects of expansion are undesirable. The male working class had the lowest proportion of any class in this category with 44 per cent—still rather high.

We may look for explanation of this fact to the operations of sponsored and contest mobility. We shall discuss this further in conjunction with results from the Durham survey.

Firstly, Durham students were asked to name "the ideal size for a college" in order to ascertain some kind of idea of the size of social unit with which students most easily identify and beyond which size feelings of group solidarity tend to weaken and disintegrate. This was especially pertinent since the largest men's college—Grey—now with 350 students

TABLE 14.5. DURHAM STUDENTS' OPINIONS

	Bede	Chad	Cuthbert	Grey	Hat.
Under 100	6	53	—	5	—
101–150	—	7	6	14	—
151–200	6	13	4	27	13
201–250	12	7	6	10	17
251–300	35	—	36	31	43
301–350	12	—	2	2	9
351–400	6	—	13	2	6
Over 400	—	—	4	3	6
Don't know	23	20	28	6	6
TOTAL	100	100	99	100	100
No.	(17)	(15)	(47)	(62)	(47)

and only 5 years old—had been experiencing various periods of student unrest which could have been caused in some respect by loss of group identity. The Student Committee found that they could not command the respect and obedience of the College as a whole and that splinter groups of rebels had formed.

The table of ideal sizes is shown in Table 14.5 along with colleges of students making each choice. There would seem to be two main camps of opinion in that choices cluster around two main alternatives. These are to some extent divided along sex lines.

Twenty-three per cent of students favour 151–200 and 24 per cent favour 251–300 as the ideal or optimum size of a college. Ten per cent fall between these two choices, so that in all 58 per cent—or a majority of students—fall within the range of 150–300—into which range, of course, fall most of the Durham colleges. However, it will be seen that beyond this size the percentage of choices tails off, even in Grey College. The majority of students would seem to agree that a college of over 300 students becomes too large in terms of community life. "A college should be large enough to offer a wide variety of people to mix with and small enough to know them all at least by sight", said one student.[1]

It is clear that students' ideas of the optimum size of a college are to some extent guided by the size of their own college, though they are by no

[1] The reader must remember that these are federated *residential* colleges.

ON THE IDEAL SIZE FOR A COLLEGE (per cent)

St. J.	Univ.	St. A.	St. H.	St. M.	NC	Total
12	—	—	—	6	—	5
52	3	36	14	27	—	15
28	13	46	57	33	66	23
8	13	4	14	9	17	10
—	41	4	7	9	17	25
—	8	—	—	2	—	3
—	8	—	—	2	—	4
—	5	—	—	4	—	3
—	10	10	7	8	—	11
100	101	100	99	100	100	99
(25)	(39)	(28)	(14)	(52)	(6)	(352)

means determined by it. This is witnessed, for instance, by responses from St. Chad's with a student population of 63. Twenty-seven per cent of these students put the optimum size at between 100 and 250. This would seem to imply that for a significant proportion St. Chad's is too small.

A difference between male and female choices emerges, guided at least to some extent by size of college. The highest proportion of choices in each female college fell into the 150–200 range, while the highest proportion in each male college, with the exception of the two smallest (theological) colleges, fell into the 250–300 range. These choices are obviously guided by sizes of individual colleges but by no means mirror them exactly. Perhaps it is useful to consider the student population of each college in 1963–4 so that figures may be compared (Table 14.6).

The figures for the teacher training colleges St. Bede's, St. Hild's, and Neville's Cross give a biased picture in that figures for university students only are given.

Naturally, the student's experience of community life will influence his impression of the optimum size for a college—he will measure size against his own sense of identity, how many people he knows in his own college, and so on. It is significant, then, that optimum sizes on the whole tend to be the same or smaller than the sizes of the present colleges.[1]

[1] Expansion in various colleges and universities up to a certain threshold represents for students a *relative* deprivation.

TABLE 14.6. SIZE OF THE DURHAM COLLEGES

Male colleges	Nos.	Female colleges	Nos.
St. Bede's	76*	St. Aidan's	121
St. Chad's	63	St. Hild's	51*
St. Cuthbert's Society	310	St. Mary's	249
Grey	300	Neville's Cross	45*
Hatfield	274		
St. John's	157		
University	270		

* Plus certificate students.

This being so, it is interesting now to turn to attitudes of Durham stu
dents towards expansion of the University. This is meant in genera
terms to comprehend all forms of expansion. However, in interviev
students made it clear that whereas they did not favour expansion o
existing colleges an expansion in the number of colleges might be accept
able. This latter is in fact the form that expansion will generally take ir
Durham. On the other hand, they pointed out an increase in the number
of colleges could have differently unfortunate effects in terms of decentralisation.

It is interesting to note that whereas Newcastle students were concerned with the impact of expansion upon the faculties, it is the impact
on colleges which is discussed largely in Durham. This emphasises the
centrality of these features in the institutional organisation.

Table 14.7 shows the distribution of students' replies.

As one might expect in the light of all that has been said of Durham
students and the institutional structure, there is a much higher proportion
of students in Durham than in Newcastle who feel that expansion will
affect the character of the University. (May this represent the initially
steep gradient of the resistance to change curve?) Eighty-five per cent
think that change will have widespread effects—only 6 per cent do not.
When the Registrar of Durham University saw the questionnaire originally he said he did not expect anyone to answer "No" to this question.
"They'll be mad if they say that expansion will not affect this University",
he said.[1] As may be expected, 10 per cent of working-class students fall

[1] Personal communication.

TABLE 14.7. WHETHER DURHAM STUDENTS THOUGHT THAT EXPANSION WOULD AFFECT THE CHARACTER OF THE UNIVERSITY AND THE LIFE OF THE STUDENTS (per cent)

	UMC	LMC	WkC	Unclassi-fied	Total	No.
Yes	87	88	79	69	85	(299)
No	2	5	10	15	6	(20)
Don't know	11	7	11	15	9	(33)
TOTAL No.	100 (101)	100 (161)	100 (77)	99 (13)	100 (352)	(352)

into this category. It would seem that for the working-class student the traditional character of Durham is less defined, or less worth preserving.[1]

Table 14.8 shows whether students thought the changes brought about would be desirable or not.

TABLE 14.8. DURHAM STUDENTS' ESTIMATION OF THE DESIRABILITY OF UNIVERSITY EXPANSION (per cent)

	UMC	LMC	WkC	Unclassi-fied	Total	No.
Desirable	15	12	27	8	16	(56)
Undesirable	55	58	36	46	52	(182)
Both	9	10	9	23	10	(35)
Don't know	5	5	3	—	4	(15)
Unavoid-able	17	16	25	23	18	(64)
TOTAL No.	101 (101)	101 (161)	100 (77)	100 (13)	100 (352)	(352)

A smaller proportion of students than in Newcastle thought effects of expansion desirable—only 16 per cent. A proportion of students (18 per cent) said that it was neither desirable nor undesirable—merely

---

[1] And as we have seen, the working-class students tend to be "outgroupers" anyway.

unavoidable. The working-class students were markedly less antagonistic to expansion than in Newcastle—only 36 per cent thought that expansion is undesirable. As a whole, however, students in Durham were less opposed to expansion and more resigned to it than in Newcastle— this may be a result of the fact that the problem of expansion had had much publicity in both student and staff circles and it was generally acknowledged as being inevitable.

TABLE 14.9. PARTICULAR EFFECTS ON UNIVERSITY OF EXPANSION AS RATED BY DURHAM STUDENTS (per cent)

	UMC	LMC	WkC	Unclassified	Total
Impersonality	54	60	41	100	55
Staff–student rift	10	6	12	—	9
More vitality–less apathy	13	10	20	—	12
Deterioration of social life	10	9	6	—	9
Loss of college spirit	4	6	6	—	5
More amenities	4	4	10	—	5
Loss of cliques	4	5	4	—	4
TOTAL	99	100	99	—	99
No.	(101)	(161)	(77)	(13)	(352)

Table 14·9 shows the form that students thought the effects of expansion would take. Although students were asked to name the most important of these, most students named two or three so that primary and secondary effects had to be analysed. Among primary effects outlined the most often mentioned—as in Newcastle—is impersonality and "loss of community" which naturally means a great deal in a university the size of Durham which has a very personal atmosphere. This effect is mentioned less frequently by working-class than middle-class students, perhaps because they participate less in community life.

The working-class students tend to mention the beneficial effects of expansion more often than the middle class, such as "more vitality" in social life 20 per cent, and "more amenities" 10 per cent.

Decreasing of staff–student contact is mentioned less frequently than in Newcastle and most often by the working class—12 per cent. However, it appeared in interview that some working-class students resent the hierarchical organisation of staff–student relations and feel that the social gap already exists which would widen even further with expansion. The recognition of a rift already existing may account for this being mentioned less frequently than in Newcastle.

Among secondary effects of expansion the fact of increasing impersonalisation is stressed by 21 per cent of students in a table not reproduced here. Fifteen per cent of students think that student affairs will become decentralised, leading to a greater fragmentation of groups than already exists.

A significant proportion of working-class students—18 per cent—think that Durham will become "more redbrick", although whether this is thought to be desirable or undesirable one cannot ascertain.

Twelve per cent of students think there will be a lowering of standards —most of them middle-class students. This differs from the Newcastle pattern. Three per cent of upper middle-class students think there will be less religious domination.

As in Newcastle, a higher proportion of working-class students than middle-class students tend to stress the beneficial aspects of expansion. Fourteen per cent of working-class students thought Durham would become more go ahead, for instance, compared with 7 per cent lower middle class and 8 per cent upper middle class.

In Durham it was thought that it would be interesting to compare the reaction to expansion of student leaders with those of the other students. This may give an indication of the relative positions of leaders and others and show which way any lead in opinion would go.

Table 14.10 shows that in fact the student leaders if anything were more conservative in Durham than the other students.

Fifty-six per cent of the leaders think the effects of expansion "undesirable" compared with 52 per cent of other students. But a slightly higher proportion think effects desirable.

The lower middle-class leaders tend to be the most conservative of all —60 per cent of these did not favour expansion. This discovery only serves to reinforce other findings about lower middle-class students, particularly male lower middle-class students. These students appear to be the most conservative in the student population despite the fact that this section is that which has most benefited from university expansion and the expansion of educational opportunity.

TABLE 14.10. ATTITUDES OF DURHAM STUDENT LEADERS TO THE EFFECTS OF UNIVERSITY EXPANSION (per cent)

	UMC	LMC	WkC	Total	No.
Desirable	20	13	27	19	(29)
Undesirable	58	60	41	56	(88)
Mixed	6	9	15	7	(15)
Don't know	4	8	3	6	(9)
Unavoidable	12	9	15	11	(18)
TOTAL	100	99	101	99	(159)
No.	(50)	(75)	(34)	(159)	

There would appear to be no statistically significant difference between leaders and others that cannot be explained by class differences which distinguish the students in general. Therefore as a result of class bias the leaders as a whole would seem to be those who support the establishment and the *status quo* which is perhaps a feature of a hierarchically organised structure. One would have to conduct further studies in order to find out. Of course one may relate these findings to the particular university structure, to the selection of student leaders, and to the pressures to conform. Certainly at this point in time in this University there seems to be little evidence of radical attitudes to university expansion.

The overwhelming weight of student opinion in Durham is in favour of maintaining the *status quo* since the effects of expansion are seen as largely if not wholly undesirable.

"I think expansion would be the very worst thing for Durham", said one student, "the new buildings would entirely spoil the scenery." This student was very serious and very committed on this particular point.

It would seem that the student attitudes to expansion arise because of the particular system of sponsored mobility through which present students are passing or have passed. When these students have passed a certain point in which they are sponsored into the educational élite, contest mobility is finished to some extent and the student enjoys the feeling of having mounted a barrier and come to a well-deserved reward. Therefore rather than wishing to extend his own opportunities to a greater number of his peers he wishes either to maintain the *status quo* or restrict selection even further—thereby limiting the area of contest mobility and the number of potential competitors.

Thus students in the two samples who felt the effects of expansion undesirable were, in terms of this analysis, expressing unconsciously fears about their own status position. For if achievement of educational status, i.e. becoming a university student, is widespread, there is little prestige in having won it, and there is increased need for competition in terms of personal merit. As we have seen, there is a real threat too to the meaningfulness of the student role in terms of increasing impersonality and bureaucratisation.

One would therefore expect working-class students to be most reactionary since they have themselves been most stringently selected. Indeed, one found that the small number of female working-class students did fit into this pattern. However, signs that the situation is changing, i.e. that me effects of expansion in terms of contest mobility are already being felt, thay be seen in the reactions of male working-class students. This latter group proved to be less conservative in their views toward expansion than students of the middle classes. If this is a sign of a developing process it is probable that both contest and sponsored mobility will increasingly have an effect upon the student population in terms of both attitude and behaviour. There well may be a special cut-off point in expansion, however, where the effects of expansion are seen in purely negative terms.

This discussion of expansion brings us back full circle, as it were, to the point where the argument began, for it is in relation to the expansion of educational opportunity that interest has been aroused in the changing social class proportions in the university and in the social relations of the members of social classes within the institutional context.

It has been supposed that in time the effects of expansion on the universities will bring in their wake wider effects on societal structure in terms of social class relations and social mobility rates in a spiral of action and reaction of individual and structural environment. This will only take place if expansion of places leads to a change in the relative proportions of the social classes within the universities, i.e. a diminution of the social class differentials. If the proportions remain the same no amount of expansion of places will bring about the looked for changes in social mobility rates and social class structure.

The pressures to expansion must be matched by structural adaption which will improve the quality of institutional relationships and a re-adjustment of the distances between them. The structure must be so designed that concomitant with overall growth in size will emerge a relative stability and closeness in the structure of intergroup distances and consequent definition of identity. As we have seen, students cannot make these adjustments for themselves—they must be helped by the pattern of institutional constraints. No amount of psychological reorientation will make up for gaps in the social fabric. Where gaps appear students may attempt consciously to build their own bridging mechanisms—with or without the support of the university.

In the next chapter we shall look at some current student reactions to changes in higher education as they relate to these structural factors, and to our conclusions about social class and expansion.

CHAPTER 15

STUDENTS IN ACTION—CONTROL
AND REBELLION

UNIVERSITIES all over the world have erupted into unrest, even into outright and sometimes bloody violence since the mid 1960's—and the question is being asked why now? Of course, as Schachner points out,[1] there were student riots and anti-student protests even within the medieval universities; one riot in Oxford in 1354 resulted in slaughter and wreckage, and there were many others, often likewise involving townspeople and political leaders. There is nothing new about student revolts; what is new is their extensiveness and their promotion by the mass and news media in a way which allows for imitation and synchronisation of movements on a scale hithertofore unimagined. The impact of instant information on student happenings around the world cannot be underestimated. Without the use of technology, which they purport so much to despise, today's students could not mobilise their fellows on any large scale.

Indeed, the extensiveness of student unrest has sometimes blurred not only differences in action and outcome at different institutions and in different countries, but also the variety of underlying causes. Just as there are many forms and expressions of activities classed by society as deviant or delinquent, so are there forms of student unrest. Similarly, just as delinquent acts of apparently similar form may stem from completely different underlying causes (so that explaining differences in action does not explain differences in cause), so with student revolt. Sociologists have always found it more difficult to explain deviancy and revolt—the breakdown of social control—than they have the strength and maintenance of social control. Similarly, successful socialisation and internalisation of society's norms is so much easier to comprehend than lack of internal controls, particularly when, as Dennis Wrong (1961) points out, sociologists assume

---

[1] Schachner, N., *The Medieval Universities*, Allen & Unwin Ltd., London, 1938, Barnes & Noble, New York, 1962, pp. 203–6, 340.

a direct relation between internalisation and conformity and further assume conformity to be normal, and therefore, in many senses, stress-free. As Wrong points out, it is often the man with the strongest superego, as Freud suggests, who is most wracked by guilt and conflict. Wrong asks for a return to the conception of man as an animal with animal drives and needs—a social animal, of course—but not necessarily and entirely socialised animal.

> His very social nature is the source of conflicts and antagonisms that create resistance to socialisation by the norms of any of the societies which have existed in human history. "Socialisation" may mean two quite distinct things: when they are confused an oversocialised view of many may result. On the one hand socialisation means the "transmission of culture," the particular culture of the society an individual enters at birth; on the other hand the term is used to mean the "process of becoming human" of acquiring uniquely human attributes from interaction with others. All men are socialised in the latter sense, but this does not mean that they have been completely molded by their culture.[1]

If we follow Wrong's lead we should suggest that varieties of student revolt should not be lumped together as a deviant phenomena which in part at least would therefore suggest the under-socialisation of a whole generation; but rather that there are certain kinds of satisfaction which students gain from their clashes with and questioning of institutional and societal authority which they do not gain from other forms of activity. To brand student revolt as deviant is, in a sense, to close discussion; to regard it as a source of student satisfaction is to ask "What do they get out of it?" or "What do they think they are getting out of it?", which is perhaps to open up discussion. The problem of explanation lies in the fact that the task of explaining has been taken up by those who did not revolt when they were young and are now wondering why they did not. There are two main outcomes of such looking back by the older generation. One is motivated by feelings of guilt and/or envy towards the young who seem to be accomplishing change previously discussed but never fought for, and results in over-idealisation of the youth struggles. The idealisation is extended to cover all youth struggles, since it is assumed that all spring from similar root causes which have flowered in a chosen generation. The other reaction is motivated by complete mystification, which gives rise to panic and fear of the unknown. The rationale is "if we were happy to obey why aren't they?" Repressive measures are urged to restore the *status quo*—

[1] Wrong, D. H., The oversocialised conception of Man. *ASR*, April 1961, **26** (2), 183–93. As we have seen, a large proportion of students are certainly almost untouched by *their* university culture.

such a *status quo* being that experienced by the last generation. Both reactions are equally extreme and in a sense equally unrealistic. Clearly not all students who rebel against authority are motivated by the highest humanitarian and egalitarian ideals; possibly, as in most social movements, only a very small proportion are so motivated, the remainder enjoying sharing in the ongoing social enterprise. This is neither to praise nor condemn—merely to make a comment on man's social nature. Certainly youth is the most idealistic period of life, but this in itself is not saying too much. It merely means that when today's idealistic youth grow old they will tend to become more disillusioned with the world and more conservative. How far today's youth are more idealistic than past generations is difficult, if not impossible, to measure.

In addition one must make the comment that idealism does not always result in better social conditions nor an increase in human happiness (witness, for instance, the affects of the increasingly fascistic element in the idealistic left).[1] Nor, of course, can we say that those who tag along in the wake of social revolutions for rather selfish and pedestrian motives never achieve humanitarian goals. Indeed, often the opposite—for such people may shore up the ruins left by the juggernaut of change.

Overreaction either way by the older generation and those in positions of political power in particular can only enhance the feelings already entertained by the young of their uniqueness in history, when, of course, each new generation is unique and has always been so.

What is special, however, at this time is the particular configuration of events, structures, values, and technology which has led to the rapid spread of both ideas and actions among the young, and which has resulted in the present dramatic outbursts. Very briefly, to draw together various findings and theories, we can suggest the following. Firstly, we have the rapid increase in student numbers and in the proportion of any age group entering college. The rate of increase is as important as the absolute increase since it represents a shock to the educational system and society, which are thrown out of gear. Secondly, we have the impact on existing educational facilities of these large numbers to the extent that for many higher education becomes a negative though necessary experience. In addition,

---

[1] "Those who want to go beyond liberalism always run the risk of retiring to a previous stage. Men born at the beginning of this century have learned this lesson by bitter experience; will they succeed in transmitting it to a generation which is in danger of repeating history because they do not know it?" Aron, R., Student rebellion: vision of the future or echo from the past?, *Pol. Sci. Quart.*, June 1969.

faculty lose touch with students and communication and social control breaks down. Thirdly, the students who are flooding into the universities are still largely middle class, and most come from relatively affluent homes. Since they take material benefits for granted they may seek for "alternative sources of satisfaction".[1] They are a post-war generation who knew neither the depression nor the deprivations of war—but their parents did. The students can theorise about material deprivation—their parents may have suffered it.

Consequently the parents may have spent so much time working to provide in material terms for their children what they themselves could not have that they omitted to transmit certain values of social responsibility. On the other hand, it has been suggested that young radicals tend to come from homes where liberal parents inculcated humane and egalitarian ideals but did not live them out.[2] Young adulthood brings disillusionment with the parents but not with the values. This leads to "deauthoritisation" of the older generation[3] of at least an attempt on the part of the "juvenocracy" to seize authority, since they believe the older generation has failed. This is in some senses related to the weakly defined role model provided by the "absentee father"—characteristic of the middle class and a product of a mobile employment system.[4] The position of youth is also defined by the break-up of the extended family under the impact of industrialisation and urbanisation, the consequent emotional strains and loss of control of the parents in the nuclear family, and the growth of influence of the youth peer group. The exploitation of youth by industrial markets and advertising has further encouraged the development of specifically youth culture, increasingly incomprehensible to the parental generation. This enhances youthful autonomy of values. In addition, the increasing sophistication of technology has placed in the hands of youth valuable tools of communication necessary for large-scale organisation. Finally, the almost hysterical pursuit of progress for its own sake in industrialised nations has led to a worship of energy, vitality, creativity, bodily strength, and beauty, since those with these qualities are best equipped to carry out the tasks of progress. Rather than

---

[1] Cf. Rostow, W. W., *The Stages of Economic Growth*, Cambridge University Press, New York, 1960, p. 11.

[2] Kenniston, K., *Young Radicals*, 1968.

[3] Feuer, L. S., *The Conflict of Generations*, 1969.

[4] Parsons, T., Youth in the context of American society, Erik H. Erikson (ed.), *The Challenge of Youth*. Basic Books, New York, 1963, pp. 110–41.

age and seniority being revered, as bringing wisdom through experience, they are regarded as signs of decaying power. Ageing brings shame instead of pride, and is disguised by whatever means. Death is obscene and is kept hidden. Consequently the young epitomise all that is valued for progress and are regarded with something of awe by those who have passed their prime. Rather than the parental generation being accorded credit for their past contributions to the building of society, they are criticised by the young for their failure to carry out ideals, and at the same time themselves feel guilty and inadequate. The very success and arrogance of the young is a threat to the mature instead of a tribute.

The situation is ripe for youthful revolt against authority of the older generation. However, of course, it has been ripe for some time. These conditions have existed most obviously since the late 1940's onward, when this generation of students was born. Why did revolt not happen before? Even as late as the late 1950's and early 1960's students were in a state of quiescence—relatively uncommitted politically and often concerned only with what now seem like trivial internal institutional matters.[1] At this point one has to bring in the impact on youth of world political events, which have had the effect of galvanising youth into action—both inside and outside the universities. Firstly, John F. Kennedy's presidency captured the imagination of youth; he appealed to youth consciously and thought to put their idealism into action. He was one of the first truly charismatic political leaders for decades who gave youthfulness a positive quality.[2] This was true for youth all over the world—not only in the United States. Then the Civil Rights Movement and the Vietnam War are the major political issues in which youth have voiced opinions, and on which they have taken action of every kind. The two are closely related because both issues appeal to the sense of justice of youth—the underprivileged Black and the war-tormented Vietnamese peasant are ever present figures in the mass media, and they call forth all the compassion and righteous anger of youth. Indeed of course it is not only youth who experience such feelings—but it is they who have least invested in the *status quo* and in a sense they dare most to dissent. Not only this, but students particularly exist in a transition zone, which is the last haven of individualism, before adult responsibilities and the economic

[1] Cf. Kenniston, K., *The Uncommitted*, Harcourt, Brace and World, New York, 1965; also Newfield, J., *A Prophetic Minority*, New York, 1966.

[2] Other charismatic leaders like Mao Tse-Tung, Fidel Castro and Che Guevara have helped to romanticise for the young the role of revolutionary.

machine swallow them up. Students know that if they do not dissent or at least question as students they may never do so again. Hence the final frenetic fling before mediocrity and compromise take their toll. But it is too early yet to assume that today's radical youth will be tomorrow's compromising adults. The changes effected may be lasting.

However, let us not assume, as do many, that a whole generation is in uproar.[1] It is not. Firstly it is really only students who are in uproar—youthful drop-outs, manual and clerical workers, and those burdened with family responsibility or materially deprived do not normally revolt at the present time; they have neither time nor leisure to debate the ills of society—they are victims of them. (Similarly, students who have never tasted physical violence are the first to promote the merits of revolution.) Secondly, of students only 10–15 per cent could really be classed as politically active or active in social concerns. The rest are still very concerned about grades, graduating as soon as possible in order to move into employment and the fully fledged adult world; or "healthy" student pursuits such as "ugliest man of the campus" competitions and panty raids in girls' dorms.[2] It is all too easy to forget that the majority of students are relatively unmoved by struggles for power inside and outside the institution and, like many faculty, remain on the side-lines as passive bystanders.[3] (Of course, sometimes bystanders get knocked over in the scrummage.) Change in any group or society is only ever really brought about by the few—so just to say that a minority of students are involved is not to lessen the power implications. Then, of course, one must consider that the proportion of socially concerned and radical students varies from university to university considerably, and we must take this into account. Some institutions are predisposed to radicalism, others to conservatism; some flare up into revolt; others remain quiescent. We must ask why. Similarly, some issues stir students on one campus which would

---

[1] If one assumes thus it is easy to put forward such theories as the expungement of war-guilt theory, which suggests that the generations born to parents who fought wars are equipped by their parents with unrealistically high values and ambitions for society as parental compensation and vicarious "cleansing"; consider, for instance, the idealism and radicalism of the 1930's, twenty years after World War I.

[2] Adults look upon return to typical student pranks with relief—as representing "letting off steam" in a way which is relatively undisrupting and easily controlled by university authorities.

[3] However it seems dangerous to assume that silence means health and dissent emotional unhealth. See Westley, W. A. and Epstein, N. B., *Silent Majority*, Jossey-Bass, California, 1969.

not in any way touch students elsewhere. We must again ask why—recalling the remarks at the beginning about the differences in cause and effect in student disturbances. We should note also that there is a very wide spectrum of activities which could be classed as "unrest" or "disturbances"—many entirely parochial and completely unnewsworthy but nevertheless important to those in the situation.

If we relate our investigation of disturbances to the structure of the institution we can also see the differences in tolerance capacity of institutions for different kinds of disturbances or threat, i.e. structural flexibility under strain. It should be pointed out here that in most cases even the extreme forms of student violence are directed against property and not persons, and that this is a very middle-class way of expressing frustration and aggression.

In analysis of student unrest one should first outline what seem to be some of the main differences in underlying issues or origins. These may be denoted as follows:

1. Internal matters of discipline and students' rights within the existing structure of the institution.
2. Internal matters concerned with changes desired by students and/or faculty in the existing structure of power or relationships within the institution.
3. Internal matters concerned with a desired restructuring of the relationship of the institution with outside agencies or communities.
4. External matters concerned with general political issues and movements as policy matters for existing power groups.
5. External matters concerned with a desired restructuring of groups or power sources in society as a whole.
6. Imitation of other student movements as an expression of solidarity (like trade unionism).
7. Imitation of other student movements as experimentation, or for kicks.
8. Imitation of other student movements as a youthful test of authority.
9. Imitation of other student movements for glory (as encouraged by publicity given by mass media).
10. Imitation of other student movements as a demonstration of status or social awareness (where high status colleges give the lead).

11. Influence of outside infiltration by whatever group, for whatever purpose.
12. Accidental development of a situation beyond the intentions of its originators.

One can see that these are not discrete and are not mutually exclusive —they may overlap. However, they may promote further thinking on this matter. In addition one may add that where unrest is a result of unsettled grievances the grievances may be (a) real, (b) imagined, or (c) prefabricated.

Further, unrest may be expressed through legitimate channels or illegitimate channels, and may represent (a) action, (b) reaction, or (c) imitation.

Thus to try to sort out the justifiable from the unjustifiable protests is a gargantuan task which depends for its solution on one's position in the structure.

Clearly all student revolt which eschews means of protest provided by the institution represents a threat to social control and authority. That internal and external issues in this are difficult to separate is certain —they have a habit of rebounding on one another. Student attempts to change the institutional structure very often become bound up with demands for changes in the society of which they must all too soon become members; and societal political movements usually enter the arena of institutional politics. In this the university represents a very special cyclone or low-pressure area which encourages dissidence and creates limited hurricane areas.

What we have to investigate, therefore, is the relationship between social changes, institutional changes, and human input, which operate in a complex kaleidoscope of ways to produce certain outcomes. Discussion of characteristics of a whole generation of students in relation to a whole generation of parents and to a whole generation of administrative officials is too simplistic, as is discussion of the role of the university in society. The evidence shows the variety of institutional structures, generational values, and decision-making machinery. Yet we search for some patterns in the kaleidoscope to repeat themselves—something which will give us a clue to what will happen next. Were this chapter to be devoted to discussion of the variety of student revolts which have happened throughout the world in the last 5 years it would develop into a book—and a book devoted to description of past events; a history of student unrest which might bring us no nearer to a predictive analysis. For we are so near the events in time that the cultural variety blinds us to the structural similarities.

A non-sociologist was asked recently "Are sociologists, do you think, behind all the recent campus revolutions?" "Yes," he replied, "always. They come along ten years after everything has happened and try to offer an explanation." This criticism is made as a result of the fact that studies of historical events which attempt to project into the future can only do so if it is assumed that "patterns of the future will be as they are at present, only more so".[1] Problems of analysis of student unrest are not so much centred on explanation of unrest *per se*, but on explanation of a vast panorama of changes in society in which student unrest is set.[2] If we see the issues as those of organisational crises or rapid organisational change, we are in a better position to judge possible outcomes since we equip ourselves with an organisational frame of reference. The author would suggest, therefore, that the kind of explanations discussed at the beginning of the chapter suggest necessary though not sufficient conditions for the development of widespread student disturbances—there are some missing links. The author does not suggest that she has found them; however, she hopes to show ways in which one might begin the search. That search in a sense is for predictive rather than descriptive explanatory power of analyses.

The student disturbances discussed therefore will be used as illustrative material for theories and not as a *source* of explanation alone. The examples are not in any way an exhaustive inventory—that is not the purpose of the analysis. It is assumed that logically possible sequences may give us clues to what will happen in addition to sequences which have happened in past historical time. Therefore this will enable us to suggest events which have not happened in time but are organisationally possible. The approach hopefully will not be outdated therefore by new events since events will fit into the existing framework (if it holds good). This would seem to be a sociological rather than pseudo-historical approach. It is not, however, fully worked out at the present time, and may not hang together with perfect fit at the seams. However, it is a beginning.

---

[1] Abbott, J. and Oromaner, M., A curvilinear model of social change in changing societies, unpublished manuscript.

[2] "If the function of adolescence is self-definition one would expect it to be very difficult in a society which suffers from a dearth of individuality and in which alienation is a critical problem." Friedenberg, E. Z., *The Vanishing Adolescent*, Delta, 1968, p. 15.

Since we are taking here a largely organisational approach to student unrest, we are first faced in our analysis with the nature of university organisations or the university as a particular kind of organisation in a changing society. In this we must be concerned with the mechanisms of internal controls as they respond (or fail to respond) to changing external social conditions. Here follow, therefore, some remarks on the internal controls of universities and the definition of the problem of student discipline or control by the institution or its acknowledged authorities of student behaviour. This, as we shall see, may or may not be related to wider political issues outside the institution.

Naturally, university authorities are always concerned with maintenance of internal order as it relates to the pursuit of goals set for itself by the university and with the internalisation of norms of university life. These norms may not be those which coincide with general societal norms or laws, but are usually constraints imposed by membership specifically of the university community. The medieval image of the university as traditionally a self-regulating community with its own internal rules and restrictions has hung on until, as we have seen, the universities are not communities any more. The normative structure and the corresponding "disciplinary" or informal judicial procedures laid down for dealing with infringements, increasingly are seen as anachronistic in the modern world. As we have seen, the student body is becoming more and more heterogeneous—and in the process of democratisation of higher education therefore membership, culture and values themselves become more heterogeneous. The body of received opinion on any subject is shrinking, and increasingly a matter for intense debate. For not only the values of the taught, but also the teachers themselves are heterogeneous and fragmented—there is no one imprint of socialisation that the institution can make on any of its members—no one cultural message which it transmits and which is dutifully received.

The multiple goals of universities become less defined in certain areas—as in fulfilment of the personality and development of the whole man—and these areas become the prerogative of intensely individualistic interpretation. On the other hand, certain goals become more defined in relation to material, economic, and technological gain and advancement—and are a matter of collective responsibility in the utilisation of resources. The expressive as opposed to the instrumental aims of the university and its inmates are often left in the background because they are so ill defined and fragmented. And with the decline of the expressive content in social relations at university comes a decline in membership satisfaction. Not only has this important consequences for the social experience of members but it inevitably involves structural ramifications in terms of the agencies of social control. It is a complete overhaul of the normative structure of universities which we are witnessing and a redefinition of the mechanisms of social control. What has been labelled a matter of student discipline is, in fact, a redistribution of power of control, of which changes in student discipline are only a part.

Burton Clark has pointed to the fact that strict selection of personnel is in itself a measure of social control[1]—the more stringently selected the members of the community the more homogeneous their attributes and the more uniform their goals. A relaxation of selection and the introduction of the principle of voluntary attendance, or the power of the student to opt out, leads to a relaxation of control of the institution over its members. There is an increased need to "cool them out" to come into line with institutional objectives, i.e. to inculcate some synthetic uniformity of purpose and goals in the face of heterogeneity of values. The power to inculcate institutional norms and values rests with the authorities. There is inequality of exchange—unlike the reciprocal exchange and reinforcement of the interpersonal contact of like with like.

In the days when the leisure class sent their sons to the universities to learn to be young gentlemen there was a good deal of consensus about the objectives of a university education and close identification with those objectives as they related to the maintenance of the existing societal culture and power structure. The student group was a privileged, largely homogeneous minority with power in society through family connections. In the university community of social equals, the matter of social control could be deferred for a few years for those who would inevitably become the leaders of men. The student community reflected the mores of a particular social group, and its internal cohesion reflected an interpersonal social control—to some extent independent of any "imposed" discipline. The close contact between staff and students to some extent reflected their equality of social status—as men of learning. The class cohesion of university men—whether teachers or taught—exerted its own kind of control. This resulted not only in the acceptance of special rules of membership but also of special ways of dealing with infringements. The need of the élite to preserve a unified front in the face of the masses

[1] Clark, B., *The Open Door College*, New York, McGraw-Hill, 1960.

was reflected in the need to deal internally with infringements of institutional rules—to settle matters without loss of face and without having to bring in external authorities. The community which was self-regulating protected its identity and the interdependence of its members.

Universities are no longer small, close-knit socially homogeneous communities—and the old methods of social control, and of dealing with delicts, do not work in the new setting.[1]

Social control of an informal, interpersonal kind is a property of a certain kind of social relation. In the small, close-knit homogeneous group there is great role density and role overlap, and there is restricted possibility of escaping the censure or praise of others who can be personally identified. Then the structure of constraints which ensure that individuals conform in their behaviour to the expectations of others emanate from the quality of the relationships themselves, i.e. the threat of disapproval of esteemed persons or groups may act as effective control without need of special penal sanctions. Indeed, penal sanctions administered by certain authorities with a monopoly of coercion (particularly physical) will be reserved for extreme cases, and particular cases may be dealt with entirely at the discretion of those in power (i.e. principals, heads of colleges, professors, or whatever) without "due process of law". The extreme punishment is, of course, complete withdrawal of rights of membership—expulsion. Even students guilty of law breaking in protest often request amnesty in relation to rights of institutional membership.

Where the group grows in size, heterogeneity and consequent impersonality, it is less possible to belong to or to identify with more than a mere minority of subgroups within the total group. Face-to-face contacts take place among only a small proportion of members, and it is possible to move from group to group in order to avoid censure or to gain praise. There is increased segregation and specialisation of roles—and consequently of expectations of role behaviour.[2] The interpersonal controls break down, so that there arises a need to make norms—previously

---

[1] In a study of 104 colleges in the U.S.A. between 1964/65 Scott and El-Assal found that large, complex, high quality schools had a much higher rate of demonstrations than small, simple, low quality schools. However, size alone was not a determining factor. Scott, J. W. and El-Assal Mohammed, Multiversity, university size, university quality, and student protest, *ASR*, Oct. 1969, **34** (5).

[2] This finds its expression for instance in the much discussed faculty conflict of teaching versus research which produces role strains in teachers and which students feel damaging to their interests. See Caplow, T. and McGee, R. J., *op. cit.*

implicit—completely explicit and indeed to promulgate a code of expected behaviour in certain spheres. Lack of socialisation means lack of internalised control. Between the individual and the organisational structure is the intermediate co-ordinating structure for the enactment and enforcement of organisational rules. As the rules themselves are made explicit, the bases of power for dealing with infringements themselves must become more explicit and formalised. Indeed, certain statuses within the organisation which have a monopoly of authority must become involved in universally recognised judicial procedures. However, within the heterogeneous bureaucratic organisation which many universities now represent, there are many sources of power which find expression in different kinds of legitimated authority within the university. This makes procedures for dealing with grievances cumbersome—often strangled by red tape. In the changeover from community to bureaucracy certain individual rights are overlooked.

In the American university, in addition, there is very often an invisible power élite of the university as in the Board of Trustees. Since this power is difficult for students to locate it is difficult to deal with, although university presidents may be pressured by the invisible élite in their decisions.

The students have institutionally recognised power to control certain of their own affairs through student organisations. If this power is neglected in the institutional regulation of members' conduct, conflict of interests must of necessity arise. A large-scale organisation run on bureaucratic lines must have a correspondingly rationalised and explicit structure of rules and procedures or the essentially irrational elements of power and control will produce strains and tensions which threaten to overthrow the system. This tendency we are seeing in the modern university where internal, irrational systems of control cannot fulfil the tasks with which they are faced.

In the paternalistic system of control which some universities still retain, there is a reliance on interpersonal controls where relations no longer exist of the kind which make such control possible. Firstly, there is the lack of homogeneous cohesion in which such control and appeal to common sentiment is meaningful. This is true of all members—both staff and student and administration. Indeed, staff of a university are increasingly less characterised by a vocation than by characteristics of bureaucratic employees with correspondnig lack of institutional commitment. They are sometimes pushed into this position, however, by the bureaucratic pressures to which modern universities are subjected.

A move by the British University Grants Committee to rationalise university teaching by suggesting pruning departments or courses was strongly resisted by the Association of University Teachers. One main reason is because it raises the possibility of dismissals of staff made redundant by the changes.

> The A.U.T. is not claiming that University teachers have an indisputable right to hold their posts for ever, but it is concerned to point out that dismissal in the past has only been for "good cause" and after a proper investigation of the facts "good cause" is a term precisely defined in the statutes of universities, and redundancy is not included and—says the A.U.T.—should not be included in the definition.[1]

It is clear that rights and obligations of everyone in the system—not only students—are being redefined and rationalised.[2]

The control of students by staff also has traditionally depended on some equivalence of values and goals and external status which governed expectations. These no longer exist—and nor do the close social relations which made such personal control meaningful. The personal lines of communication between staff and students, between authorities and members, have broken down, and there often are no more formal lines of communication to take their place. The myth of community has lingered on and has got in the way of a less emotive and more formal way of regulating social behaviour. The students recognise the need to repair the gaps in the social fabric which have appeared with the growth of large impersonal systems; they want to see a clearer definition of what is expected of them,[3] and in turn they naturally want to outline what they expect of the other sections of the institution. Social control is reciprocal— as are all rights and obligations.

The construction of formal agencies and channels of social control, of course, is needed to regulate not only student behaviour with regard to institutional expectations but student–student behaviour, student–staff behaviour, and staff–staff behaviour. All relationships in the institution have become attenuated—synthetic organisational bridges must be con-

---

[1] Gourlay, D., University teachers call for talks on redundancy, *The Guardian*, 22 May 1967.

[2] In 1970 the part played by universities in higher education, their economic structure and expenditure will be discussed by the Minister of State for Education and Science, the University Grants Committee and the Committee of Vice-Chancellors and Principals, and should have far-reaching effects.

[3] Students also need to know that there are those in the institution who *are concerned* about their academic and social wellbeing as *individuals*.

tructed to link the whole range of institutional relationships. It is to everyone's benefit to have their rights and obligations defined, and student discipline is only one aspect of this definition. Indeed, it is more often because individuals are ignorant of, or misunderstand, their rights and obligations—rather than that they reject the institutional definition—that conflict in universities arises. This may, of course, also cover the eventuality that in understanding a particular right or its restriction, its significance is misunderstood within the whole context of rights. This might be applied in varying degrees to both Berkeley and the London School of Economics—as we shall see. Certainly the demand for more student involvement in the running of university affairs is only part of the need to look again at the whole structure of social relations. Indeed, many of what seem to be excessive demands of students for power in university government are often only the results of frustration in being unable to locate and confer with existing power sources. Such is the nature of bureaucracy and what Weber calls the power of secrecy.[1]

The question of student discipline is related not only to conduct within the institution in relation to institutional norms, but also to conduct outside the institution, i.e. by all citizens. Students are not only subject to institutional controls but to the laws of the land. Institutional membership has in times past acted as some protection against societal legal sanctions—the university making out its own punishments according to its own laws. This is increasingly regarded as anachronistic and irrational, and in keeping with the changes in the definition of the student role there is an increasing demand by students and non-students for equal treatment under the law. Prosecutions of students are currently increasing for crimes associated with drug taking and drug peddling—a matter of contemporary societal concern. "It is generally known that in recent years the number of heroin addicts has rapidly increased while their age has decreased."[2]

The university therefore exerts less autonomous control over its members—it presents a less uniform face to society; there is a demand by students for its rules of membership to be known and strictly defined.

The general public, long subjected to student excesses which seem to be treated more leniently by the processes of justice than are anti-social activities of non-students, supports this plea for equal treatment. Many

[1] Gerth, H. H. and Mils, C. Wright, *From Max Weber*, p. 233.

[2] Kaldegg, A., Heroin addiction, *New Society*, 2 February 1967. See also Carey, James, *The College Drug Scene*, Prentice-Hall, NJ,

would agree with Sanford Garelik, Chief Inspector of New York' Police under Mayor Lindsay, when he said: "Universities should not b allowed to be sanctuaries for lawlessness."[1]

However, when the argument reaches this point, student radical and revolutionaries do an about-face, and seem to plead the cause o a dramatic paradox. While asking to be treated as citizens under th law in relation to the rights of membership of universities they stil claim certain exemptions from obligations of citizenship, i.e. when the break society's laws they wish to be treated as a special minority by virtu of their membership of the university sanctuary. This inconsistency put them in a dubious position. To be consistent, students who wish to breal societal rules should ask to be treated as ordinary citizens with regard t rights under the law, and also with regard to obligation to take punish ments (such as imprisonment).[2] If they feel laws are unjust they shoul demonstrate this fact by continued and extensive law-breaking—an suffer the consequences. There is a limit to the number of prisoners an society's prisons can hold. A law which is disobeyed more than it i obeyed cannot be maintained, and even the punishment system itsel becomes unworkable. Eventually the power élite must take note of th veto of the majority—if such a veto there is. If not enough students ar prepared to face society's punishments they clearly demonstrate that th price of change is too high and the change desired therefore not wortl the effort. By demanding amnesty for acts of trespass and violence stu dents merely demonstrate that they are playing the part of revolutiona ries without wishing to risk the consequences of their actions. This woul seem to suggest a lack of belief in what they are doing and a lack of grou solidarity.

If, on the other hand, students wish to return to the structure o community—with special rights of membership—they must face th fact that they may also be asked to conform to special internal rules anc obligations of that membership. There is a good deal of confusion amon students as to what they want from the institution, mainly because right always seem to dominate obligations. In addition there is confusion o

[1] Lecture on New York Crime, St. Thomas' Church, NY, 22 May 1969.

[2] This is compatible with Mahatma Gandhi's concept of *satygraha* (truth force) "When we do not like certain laws we do not break the heads of the lawgivers, we suffe and do not submit to the laws". "If this kind of force is used in a cause that is unjus only the person using it suffers. He does not make others suffer for his mistake" Gandhi, M. K., *Indian Home Rule*, Navajivan Trust, Ahmedabad, 1946.

oth faculty and students of the kind of internal relationships desired
nd the kind of controls possible.

There is certainly now less mystique surrounding the conduct of uni-
ersity affairs. The recent request by the British Government that the
niversities should submit their accounts to the Comptroller and Auditor-
jeneral was met by furore among university staff because it was thought
hat it would increase government control and infringe academic free-
om. It is academic freedom which has in the past justified much of the
losed-shop mystique of the universities.

In looking at the questions raised by the recommendation to Parliament
f the Public Accounts Committee that Parliament should be allowed to
nquire into how the universities spend public money, Mr. Charles
'arter, Vice-Chancellor of the new University of Lancaster, asks:
Are universities so different from industry or from other organisations
vhich draw aid from the State that the privilege of restricted accounta-
ility should be continued?" Mr. Carter outlines the concern which has
een felt by some university authorities, who fear "a system of detailed
ontrol of every aspect of university expenditure, imposed by people
vho have an imperfect understanding of what a modern university is
bout, and who will consequently damage the delicate structure of self-
overnment within which intellectual inquiry flourishes". He dismisses
he fears as unfounded and adds that "Academic freedom does not,
owever, include within its proper limits an unrestricted access to the
ublic purse, nor the freedom from public argument about the validity
f academic decisions."[1]

Faculty themselves may be a prey to confusion, therefore of rights
nd obligations within the structure and in relation to external controls.
Iow can faculty who act out their professional role in society, as an
'expert" or business associate, assume that societal constraints will not
ventually enter into their institutional role-playing?

The new openness and outward-lookingness of universities is a new
nvolvement in public affairs, and reveals an awareness of the importance
f societal forces as well as internal decisions. The walls of the sanctuaries
f learning are crumbling and with them the light of day is thrown rather
arshly upon the activities of the members. Students' movements and
nvolvement in social and political affairs as individuals and as students

[1] Carter, C. F., Do MPs threaten academic freedom?, *The Observer*, 29 January
967.

are, of course, helping to tear down those walls and therefore to threaten the *status quo*. A healthy outcome is that no longer can tradition alone be used to justify customs or statuses—now there must be demonstrated workability and competence.[1]

Student movements are therefore both an internal and an external political and social threat and, as such, pose their own complex problems of control and discipline. Whose responsibility is the control of certain kinds of student action inside and outside the institution? The students argue that they themselves should share more of this responsibility, but realise that the creation of a new kind of academic community is necessary before this can happen. (In effect the students are attempting to change the institution away from the monocratic bureaucracy, which universities are becoming, towards the collegial structure which they once were. The movement would represent a structural reversal, using Weber's polar ideal types, rather than a new structure. This will be discussed later.) Among other things there must be new links created between students in different sectors of the impersonal university and between students and their elected leaders if there is to be any chance of internal cohesion and control. At the moment it is merely a handful of charismatic and politically active leaders who are galvanising the mass of students into action.

This kind of personalised organisation is necessary in crisis, but there must be some "routinisation" of charisma, some permanency of statuses, some kind of bureaucratic organisation which expresses the changed relationships, in order for original initiatives to become organisational principles. Outmoded controls in a situation of change are ineffective—even disregarded—but in order for new controls to become operative there must be a change in the structure of relationships through which control is exercised.

It is often argued that younger and more junior faculty are only too keen to encourage students to change institutional relationships since it is junior faculty rather than students who stand to gain most from the change.[3] Since real power is located in the persons of departmental heads and top rank administrators who control the purse strings, it is argued

---

[1] The mass media, of course, assist in the build-up of charisma—see for instance, the exploits of Mark Rudd and Daniel Cohn-Bendit.

[2] In the autumn of 1969 British academics were asked to fill in forms, on time spent in various activities, and were understandably annoyed and affronted.

[3] On 31 Dec. 1967, 52 per cent lecturers and 95 per cent asst. lecturers in British universities were under 34 years old. *Stats. of Educ.*, Vol. 6, *op. cit.*, table 59, p. 106

that junior faculty are almost as far from the decision-making centres as students and their position in the power structure almost as tenuous. Indeed, in that in the student thrust for power they have been largely forgotten they are in many senses even more marginal. Students as members of a "lower caste" looking in from outside have assumed a monolithic structure of shared power among faculty, particularly with reference to existing faculty and departmental committees. Students therefore fight to become represented on such committees because they believe they will also then share in the power of decision-making. When the students gain representation they show up the committees for what they often are—a sham of collegiality. They discover the committees can only "recommend" and that decisions are taken elsewhere—"backstage". Indubitably student representatives then start asking awkward questions about the functioning of such committees, which raise issues of power distribution long dormant. This may have a variety of effects. Firstly, it may act to revitalise moribund committees and bring real power of decision-making back into the hands of faculty and students alike. Alternatively, it may serve to "window dress" committees as store-front exhibits without giving them any further power (which represents an attempt to keep the students happy without changing anything). Meanwhile the real decision-making machinery recedes further and further into the "backstage regions", as Goffman has termed it, and it becomes even more possible to develop a long-distance tyranny.

Kenniston and others have pointed out that the younger teaching assistants have an important role to play as leaders of the student masses as they are the most marginal in identity and power being, in many cases, both graduate students and junior faculty and yet enjoying full membership of neither group.[1] This borrows something from the Marxist analogy of the leadership of the proletarian masses by the *petit-bourgeoisie* or unaffiliated revolutionary intellectuals. The big difference, however, is that students are engaged in the "revolt of the privileged".[2]

Much is talked about student revolt, but we must be clear whether it is revolt or rebellion which certain activities epitomise. If we take Gluckman's definition[3] as our guide, then student activities which are concerned

[1] Kenniston, *op. cit.*

[2] Burns, Tom, Revolt of the privileged, **Paper** delivered at Conference on University Revolt, Univ. of Sussex, August 1968, published in Social Science Research Council News Letter No. 4, November 1968.

[3] Gluckman, M., *Custom and Conflict in Africa*, Blackwell, 1955.

to challenge or to change the existing decision-making machinery, and hence the pattern and bases of control, may be defined as either revolt or rebellion, depending on the means used to achieve this end. If action is taken through existing channels, or if changes desired are seen as modifications of the existing structure, student activities directed against the existing order may be seen as rebellion. If, on the other hand, completely unrecognised and illegitimate means are used to bring about changes —which may be seen as an attempt to overthrow rather than to amend the existing normative structure—then this is revolution and an attempt to establish a completely new social order. If one examines student means of protest one can find that rarely is there anything approaching real revolt. The students in the main accept their position as students and as occupying a subordinate status within the total institution. They do not usually suggest, for instance, that they should teach their professors or control the university finances, though they may increasingly want to share these functions. They do, however, want to be involved in various ways in the decisions which are made on matters affecting them—or at least they want to have the right to know what decisions are being made.

Structural changes are necessary in terms of the setting up of new committees—as staff–student committees—or in terms of changes in student representation on existing committees and bodies. These changes do not constitute a completely new order, and they are achieved through the accepted means available within the institution. Often, as we have seen, the changes only operate to accord to students the basic freedoms that are available for the citizens of the State (i.e. they rescind restrictions which are no longer seen as justified). Such changes should not therefore be greeted with fear and panic and counter-repressive measures since repression may push student reformists into the extremist camp from where they will push for truly revolutionary measures. On the other hand, everyone in the university has much to gain from orderly, even though rapid, change, which re-establishes the life lines of democracy.

A case which has since come to be known as the "Glasgow Student Affair" brought the issues of internal control and discipline to the fore in Britain. Six Glasgow students were suspended in July 1965 by the Principal and Dean's Committee, the sub-committee of the Glasgow University Senate which is concerned with discipline. They were suspended after investigation of a vendetta—in the form of abusive letters, telephone calls, and embarrassing advertisements in newspapers against a clerk who for 12 years worked for the Students' Representative Council. The Council's

President and Secretary were among those suspended. "One student admitted his part in the affair; the remaining five appealed to the University Court—the senior body that administers university affairs. On 5th January 1966 the Court pronounced, quashing many of the charges, altering sentences."[1]

After this decision a campaign of protest was begun by the students about the procedures followed in dealing with the matter, and raising the whole question of a need to overhaul the mechanisms of student discipline. The cry of protest was taken up by the press and questions were asked in Parliament which resulted in "an assurance from Judith Hart, joint Under-Secretary of State for Scotland, that the Privy Council is looking into the question of students' rights in disciplinary matters."[2]

Why so much interest and unease created by this particular case?

> If the secrecy in the case is one cause of alarm, the suspicion that it was conducted in disregard of the natural laws of justice is another. The first move in the affair came from the Principal and Dean's Committee, the sub-committee of the Senate that is concerned with discipline. The accused students believed that the investigating committee was concerned only with preliminary inquiries. But on July 1st they were called before the Principal and Dean's Committee and sentenced. The students were convicted on 19 charges, but they are reported as claiming that they were not told the charges nor invited to plead.
>
> Five of the students then appealed to the University Court, which under the Universities (Scotland) Act 1858, has the power to review Senate decisions if a member of the university is affected by its appeals. The SRC Secretary based his appeal principally on the fact that the charges could have been refuted had they been known and had an opportunity been given to answer them.[2]

In a number of ways, therefore, not only was the procedure inadequate but differed considerably from that of a normal court of law. After the rehearing of the court, nine of the charges were found "not to have been established" and nine others were found to have been established only in part or modified form. Only the charge relating to the Secretary was entirely upheld, although in a modified form. He was found guilty of not taking sufficient steps to investigate and to stop the campaign, and his sentence of one year's suspension was substituted with a severe reprimand. However, the SRC secretary and the SRC had informed the authorities and the police of the vendetta as early as March 1965. Also it could be claimed that the official conduct of the SRC officers can be thought to be the responsibility of the Students' Council that appointed them.

[1] Bugler, J., The Glasgow student affair, *New Society*, 10 February 1966.
[2] *Ibid.*, p. 6.

There followed a campaign to clear the secretary's name and to rational ise the disciplinary procedure of the University. During this period this student had to abandon his honours course, and his father is said to have spent £600 on legal representation for his son. Eventually, in February 1966, the University Court issued a statement which rescinded the repri mand on the SRC secretary and acquitted him on the technicality that there may be doubt "whether the court was technically correct in taking a more serious view than the special committee (the appeals committee) had originally done of the responsibility of one of the appellants".

The case ended in jubilation for the students of Glasgow, but it had created a new climate of critical appraisal of university discipline in gener al and one which is not likely to be reduced by recent happenings at the London School of Economics, for instance.

> The disciplinary machinery of a university is under no obligation to be akin to a normal court of law. At Glasgow the student signs on his matriculation form that he is willing to be tied to decisions of the Senate. And by and large the Senate has the right to frame whatever regulations it deems necessary for the maintenance of discipline.[1]

Nor is the situation confined only to certain universities—but is fairly general in Britain.

> The point then is not that the "ancient Scottish Universities" are especially archaic in their procedure. It is rather that university procedure generally is archaic. The just solution is a simple one: allow the disciplinary powers of a University court in criminal matters to be exercised only after proceedings in the ordinary courts. The University could retain authority over academic and domestic matters.[1]

The dispute is concerned with how far university discipline and judicial procedures should conform to those accepted generally in society, and in this case is concerned with "criminal" proceedings. But how far is it al ways possible to separate "academic and domestic" issues from those which affect in some way relations between members and those outside. Many cases of student "deviation", internal in origin, inevitably involve recourse to the existence of external norms and it seems less and less feasible for a university to maintain its own legal structure and penal codes in a number of spheres. In the Glasgow case the issues were clear cut—others which involve similar principles are not so, particularly be cause of the difficulty of defining "internal" and "external" issues. The in

[1] Bugler, *op. cit.*

terrelation of "internal" discipline disputes and "external" student political moves will be seen as one instance of this. In this case, however, certain points emerge clearly which have general validity. Firstly, where university disciplinary procedures are largely anachronistic, they are not realised to be so either by those who operate them, or by the students subject
to them, until a particular case of infringement raises specific legal issues.
That is, if the rights of a student as a citizen are endangered or restricted
this is seen as a threat to the whole body corporate of like citizens and is a
proper matter for investigation.

Secondly, a certain amount of the power of the authorities lies in keeping students in ignorance of judicial procedures to be followed in particular cases. This relates to the point made earlier about the implicit controls
of behaviour. Where there is ignorance there is consequent inability to
alter the existing situation.

Thirdly, much of the breakdown in proper communication between
the students and disciplinary committees, and of the disregard shown
by the authorities of student concern about disciplinary procedures, has
been attributed to a general lack of contact between staff and students.
This highlights the state of "disrepair" which may exist between certain
attenuated institutional relationships.

These three points emerged in the incidents at the London School of
Economics at the end of 1966 and beginning of 1967 which resulted in the
suspension of six students after disturbances on 31 January 1967 in which
a porter died. These circumstances will be dicussed later, but at this point
it may be useful to consider a few issues raised by the suspensions. In this
case the charges were raised against the students under the regulation
which required members not to do anything that would damage the
school's welfare or bring its character into disrepute. (Previously an issue
which had been fought out between the authorities and the Union president
was the prohibition against students writing to newspapers as members of
the School.) These regulations control the relation of the institution with
outside bodies and influences, and again it is infringements which raise
external issues which caused investigation of internal procedures.

As in the Glasgow case there was widespread ignorance of procedures
to be followed. A *Guardian* report of the time said that: "Because this is
only the second board hearing within the last 15 years opinion at the school
yesterday was somewhat hazy about the procedures being followed; it
was not known for instance whether the board may cross-examine witnesses, though it was believed that this was not taking place yesterday."

This ignorance, representing as it does lack of control within the existing structure, of necessity leads to militant action of some kind—in this case organised demonstrations, marches, and sit-ins at the school.

Thirdly, as has been noted in the last chapter, staff–student relations in the LSE have been for some time growing more distant and impersonal.

However, it would be wrong to say that student rebellion over matters of internal discipline occur only where staff–student relations are characteristically bad. There is, of course, the factor of imitation—which means that students may be led critically to examine the situation in their own university by the example of specific cases in other universities. The new universities in Britain, for instance, have shown a lively concern for matters of student discipline. These universities are small and united by a common pioneering spirit. Their staff–student relations in general are co-operative and friendly and might be thought to exert the kind of interpersonal control traditionally associated with the university community. However, as in York, this threshold of community living seems quickly to be passed, and the need for explicit statement of students' rights is seen as of prior importance to students. It is a matter of *relative* deprivation, ever within a consciously close-knit community. This may be related to certain features of the student bodies which seem to be politically active, social science biased, and closely involved in national student politics. The new universities, for instance, have been most active in the Radical Students Alliance— the group of dissidents within the National Union of Students —a movement to be discussed later.

There has been opportunity therefore for emulation, by the new universities, of events in older universities, and the lack of entrenched tradition made it possible for them to hope that change could be affected.

It may be wondered why new universities did not have explicit disciplinary procedures embodied in their original charters, but in new universities perhaps even more than in old the binding spirit of the academic community is planned for as an attainable reality. Therefore in York it was hoped that rules would just grow with the structure, and that community members would in time define for themselves what was acceptable or not acceptable behaviour. As in the other cases quoted, the fabric of the structure was strained under conditions which introduced external norms and judicial procedures. A student was suspended by the Vice-Chancellor after damaging sculptures in an outside exhibition at the university and after being fined in a court of law. At this point the general ignorance of students of disciplinary procedures was discovered, and the discretionary

nd summary powers of the Vice-Chancellor were questioned by the Stu-
ents' Representative Council. In turn these external issues again intro-
uced an examination of the internal structure of control.

An open meeting between the students and the Vice-Chancellor result-
d in some heated exchanges which revealed a breakdown of the infor-
nal institutional controls—even within such a small and cohesive univer-
ity (there were about 1400 students). In a report of the meeting in the
tudent newspaper the writer says:

> That the arbitrary, closed-door system can only be defended by, apparently, the
> assertion that if it goes compassion goes too. How does clarity of procedure reduce
> the chances of exercised compassion and arbitrary procedure promote them?...
> The Vice-Chancellor has claimed that as things stand, the student knows that con-
> fidentiality is preserved. Another way of putting that is to say that the student
> knows that he doesn't know what's going on.[1]

The plea of the student that he wants to know what is going on in mat-
ers affecting his interests is common to new and old universities alike,
nd it raises the question of whether particular university communities
an retain enough insularity to be able to put into practice the old world
alues and controls which the large civic universities have lost. The York
tudents have gained the disciplinary changes they sought, so that in the
vent of the Vice-Chancellor wishing to suspend a student he calls an
d hoc committee consisting of the Registrar, the Provost of the student's
ollege, the Deputy Vice-Chancellor, and the student's supervisor and
lso a friend of the student who can take an active part in the proceedings,
nd the President of the SRC who would attend at the direction of the
ffected student. The Vice-Chancellor reserves the right to suspend the
tudent, however, without such prior consultation—which seems a rather
asic limitation. Other requests to be represented on university boards
ave resulted in a staff–student committee being set up as a sub-committee
f the general academic board. The concessions gained after much negoti-
tion are therefore quite modest in their implications. In this case, as in a
number of others, there has perhaps been undue fear that the "students
ill take over". The ultimate control of staff over academic matters and
ver the awarding of degrees is sufficient sanction to ensure that overall
owers cannot be usurped.

This remains true even in universities where the students already appear
o have a measure of academic control. The "student revolt" in the Free

[1] Gray, M., Lord James' little talk, *Nouse*, 2 March 1967.

University of West Berlin which has been going on for some time ha‹ some of the appearances of an out-and-out war on the university author‹ itics.

> Student power is a reality already. The University authorities can only with dif‹ ficulty hold a senate meeting on the campus and would meet elsewhere if they di‹ not fear a fatal loss of face. In April, a Senate session was besieged by a massiv‹ sit-in which had been expressly prohibited, and had to send for the police to clea‹ the building (they failed to do so). A ban on the publishing of a review of a semi‹ nar in the student magazine was simply disregarded. The professors are divided‹ and, in many cases, demoralised.[1]

The main points of discipline at issue seem to be being lost sight of ir the midst of general chaos. "The ASTA is demanding more rights, join‹ student–teacher bodies to run each faculty including appointments research and finance, more co-ordination between faculties, more in dependence for the university as a whole, and the destruction of the 'pa triarchal power of the professional chair'."[1] These claims are being dam aged by the unruly conduct of the students. In other words, the natur‹ of the deviance threatens the whole structure and may therefore be sai‹ to verge on revolt rather than rebellion. It is no doubt that there are polit ical considerations which play their part and complicate the issue, an‹ also the special part played by the students themselves in founding th‹ university makes the Free University in some ways a peculiar case.

> From its foundation in 1948 the Free University has proclaimed itself to be a‹ educational establishment with a commitment to the cause of democracy. A few‹ years after the war the atmosphere at the old Berlin University in East Berlin, nov‹ known as the Humboldt University, became quite intolerable as the communist‹ gained control. It was then that a number of students set about founding a fre‹ University in Dahlem, in West Berlin with allied—especially American—assistance‹ From the outset both the academic staff and the students regarded it as their dut‹ to keep a critical eye on the development of democracy in Germany.[2]

The political implications of the student mores will be examined later but at the present this background serves as the context in which th‹ struggle of social control takes place—with characteristics not dissimila‹ to those already quoted.

> The origins of the university had created a state of affairs whereby the students a‹ the Free University possessed far more rights of consultation and self-governmen‹

---

[1] Ascherson, N., Students declare war on professors, *The Observer*, 7 May 1967.
[2] Rexin, M., The Berlin university crisis, *New Society*, 11 May 1967.

than their counterparts in West Germany Universities. For years the "Berlin model" had been regarded as the last word in University constitutions. People now began to question its practicability however, because staff and students have lost all faith in one another.[1]

In order for social control to be maintained, "faith in one another" of staff and students has to have some real foundation. When this faith breaks down, the orderly conduct of the normal business of the university is not always possible, as during student protests—which may be termed revolts where they use methods of protest unsanctioned by the existing order. The much-documented Berkeley students' revolt of 1964 comes under this heading as does the Columbia revolt and French revolts of 1968, and the LSE revolts of 1967, 1968, and 1969. The widespread disruption of university life which results from student action, as in the Berlin case, has clouded over the student claims for disciplinary reforms and consequent internal as well as external adjustments. The political issues and their ramifications are inextricably bound up with the questions of discipline of course. However, as in all the cases quoted it was the raising of external issues and norms, and consequent clashes with external influences, which affected the relation of the institution with external bodies. This led to a need for internal redefinition. And, as in all other cases, student ignorance was a measure of their lack of control over matters of discipline.

> Generally speaking student efforts to get an education befitting free men rather than slaves can succeed only with strong faculty backing, for the students are transient, they do not definitely know what they want, they do not know the score behind the scenes and thus they can be abashed by administrative double talk. On the other hand, given the supine history of American faculties in our sectarian and trustee-ridden colleges and given the present extra-mural careerism of the important professors, the students must lead if there is to be any change.[2]

In other words where there is ignorance and ambiguity and poor staff–student relations, a disillusioned student body will attempt to structure the situation in its own terms. However, it becomes obvious that structural consequences of student action cannot be divorced from the political motives which underlie the action itself. Here political is taken to cover all activities concerned with decision making and the structure of decision-making statuses and hence with the regulation of power. Internal

---

[1] *Ibid.*, p. 697.

[2] Goodman, P., Thoughts on Berkeley, in Lipset, S. M., and Wolin, S. S., *The Berkeley Student Revolt*, 1965, p. 317.

student politics are hardly a matter of general interest, but where these become inextricably bound up with the societal political structures the consequences may be forced upon the attention of the populace. In the case, therefore, of both the legal and political strucure of universities —interlinked as they are in all societies—where external pressures and interest come into play, there is forced into the open a re-examination of the university's role in today's society.

If we were to go back to our earlier point about the difference between rebellion and revolt and relate this to the means used by students to achieve their ends, we should be faced with an examination of political activity rather than of deviance in any strict sense of the word. Indeed, if we look at means used by students to attract attention to their grievances, to influence public and university opinion and to try to exert their own sanctions on what they consider to be institutional deviance from the ideal situation, we see that in a majority of cases this activity is conducted within the limits of the law. All citizens are allowed free speech and freedom of expression in newspapers and other mass media; all are allowed to organise orderly demonstrations and marches so long as they do not interfere with the rights of others. This kind of activity may seem to some unusual—it is not unlawful. Therefore much of what is put under the heading of "student revolt" is not so—waving a few banners and placards and heckling public meetings does not constitute an overthrow of university government. However, any attempt to obstruct or interfere with the orderly running of university affairs, or with the affairs or interests of the general populace, does constitute a threat to law and order and established university government. At the passive end of the scale sit-ins within university and public property, and at the active end of the scale physical coercion or violence of any kind, represent illegal actions. These actions usually take place when all accepted means of persuasion or negotiation have failed and represent a complete break in communication and therefore in social control. Were the workings of a university to be seen to be manifestly unjust it is conceivable that such deviant behaviour would be seen as justified within the wider society and a greater degree of tolerance extended. This situation is just possible because of the previous autonomous nature of most universities, and illustrates the problems introduced by the peculiar relation between institutional and societal norms. No other institutions spring to mind as having such influence and such autonomy. One might argue that universities have traditionally occupied an interstitial position with regard to societal legal controls—only because society condones or even encourages this situation. It is in the general interest to have a neutral zone in the midst of society's complexities of pressure group control in the same way that it is in the interests of all protagonists in war to allow certain countries to remain neutral. Such enclaves do not continue to exist because they represent a power source in themselves—they draw any survival power they have from the interest of surrounding groups. This being so one might ask, Why does society, however implicitly, condone the existence of these special sanctuaries? One's answer might relate to some kind of safety-valve theory, in that if highly able and intelligent youth did not have some specially sanctioned institutions in which to vent their critical energies, society itself would need to fear. What is now concentrated in highly specific areas would become dffuised throughout society and might well lead to a challenge to the normative and institutional structure of society itself. As long as students are concerned with matters of internal institutional structure, however violently, political leaders can sleep easily in their beds. But it is when some of these limited objectives are achieved that students look outwards for new fields to conquer. Alternatively, when university authorities call in the police on to university property to break up demonstrations and sit-ins and thereby destroy the sanctuary, they increase the area of conflagration and send resistance underground. Student dissidents who work unseen through societal institutions are far more dangerous to the existing societal order than student protestors who quite openly announce their opposition to university authorities. That this is not recognised is demonstrated by the fear and panic which has motivated the mishandling of many student protests.

When one considers these points one begins to ask not Why do students in universities revolt?, but Where else can revolt take place within the existing framework of society?[1]

In an explosive political situation, if students were not to show unrest establishmentarians might truly worry about the state of repair of their foundations.

The ramifications of what may begin as a largely internal matter may be endless and unanticipated because of the interrelation of internal and external controls. Indeed, the actors in the situation may precipitate events—as we shall see—without deliberate intention. This may result

[1] This is being recognised explicitly in Finland where the Finnish Parliament will be considering a Bill in 1970 to reform higher education and to strengthen the role of universities in the reform of society.

from a lack of "mesh" of expectations of university authorities and student leaders; firstly, of what are the university's goals and objectives
and priorities in provision, and, secondly, of what part is played by students, staff, and—increasingly—administration in the attainment of
goals and the allocation of provisions. This lack of mesh of expectations
will result in complete misunderstanding and misreading of situations
which arise and hence an interstitial situation will result. This reiterates
the point made towards the beginning of the chapter that conflict may
arise through misunderstandings about rights and obligations and
their significance for particular groups rather than merely through a
rejection of the *status quo*. In interstitial situations there may be no real
points of contact on matters of university discipline and reciprocal
rights and obligations of staff and students. Where such a situation exists
or develops it is sometimes possible to discern a spiralling effect within
the situation—as, with each new adjustment of the parties involved to
what they consider the opponent's position, the tension of the situation is
actually increased. This unintended worsening of relations if pushed too
far may result in a breakdown of relations and of established means of
social exchange. We shall look for this spiralling effect in the cases of
student political activity examined.

It will be seen, again in relation to internal and external controls, that
a spiralling situation is more likely to get out of hand where the university
is less self-contained and where external reference groups increasingly help
to define (wrongly) what is going on in the university.

If we look again firstly at the LSE situation in 1966 and 1967 it will
help to clarify some of these points. Firstly, the LSE incidents were
originally explicitly political in origin—both in an internal and external
sense. The initial student demonstrations—in the form of marches,
speeches, and other accepted means of protest—took place from June
1966 after the announcement of the appointment of Dr. Walter Adams,
previously principal of University College of Rhodesia, as the new Director.
The appointment itself did not attract much student criticism until the
Socialist Society Magazine, *Agitator*, issued a pamphlet on the Dr.
Adams appointment as a special number, using official reports on events
in Rhodesia since UDI and on Dr. Adams's role in these events. "The
charges it levelled against Adams were as much of bureaucratic inefficiency
as of effectively compromising the University with the Smith regime."[1] The

---

[1] Brewster, B. and Cockburn, A., Revolt at the LSE, *New Left Review*, May–June
1967 (issue on Student Power).

appointment and the demonstrations were widely discussed in the press and caused some embarrassment to the university authorities. The students' dissatisfaction at the appointment was based on the belief that Dr. Adams had not done all he could to prevent the implementation in the college of the racialist policies of the illegal Smith regime. "The wisdom of his conduct in Rhodesia is open, I suppose, to interpretations that may reasonably differ and no student has yet asked his views on the hardly unimportant question of the future of the School. They react as if they were making a last-ditch fight against apartheid."[1]

The protest was an attempt to make political comment of a recognisably left-wing nature. It was of general interest at a time when the British Government's relations with Rhodesia were a particularly burning issue and public sentiment unstable. However, not only was it a political movement in the sense of external social involvement, it could be seen as an attempt—however hopeless—to influence an important university appointment. It was a matter of internal politics therefore, too, that students exercised what they considered to be the right to comment on official school policy, and the way in which this "right" was exercised was found distasteful by the school's authorities and by external sections of the population.

The appointment of Dr. Adams was seen by many to be a "catalyst in the present dispute"[2] based on "long-term grievances"[3], and it was thought that the appointment provided a convenient political flag to be nailed to the masthead of "students' rights". Of Dr. Adams it was said that "there he had been under British Government pressure to keep the University going at almost any cost. He had been prudent rather than revolutionary and, most unfairly, the student leaders equated him with the Smith regime"[4].

Whatever the truth or falsity of student accusations, they served their purpose of rallying a body of student opinion and gave expression for the need for a corporate cause.

On the first day of the Michaelmas term, 17 October 1966, 750 copies of the *Agitator* pamphlet on Dr. Adams's appointment were sold and a further 500 two days later. It was sent to Dr. Adams, to all members

---

[1] Crick, B., Student politics and violence, *The Observer*, 5 February 1967.

[2] Donovan, P., Rebellion at the school for rebels, *The Observer*, 19 March 1967.

[3] Silver, E. and Shearer, A., LSE runs to California pattern, *The Guardian*, 15 March 1967.

[4] Donovan, *op. cit.*

of staff, and the Board of Governors. A motion was passed by the Union Council on 21 October seriously questioning the appointment and requesting Dr. Adams to furnish a reply to the charges levelled against him. By 24 October Dr. Adams answered that he had not seen the pamphlet; the Union sent him a copy, but on the advice of the Standing Committee of the Court of Governors Dr. Adams did not reply.

A letter from Lord Bridges, Chairman of the Court of Governors, appeared in *The Times* on 25 October deploring the campaign. A reply by the Union Council was submitted to the Director, as school regulations demanded, for permission to send it to *The Times*. Permission was refused since the letter was in the name of the Union and not of an individual student. Two days later the Union passed three motions asserting the right to take part in the appointment of a new Director, deploring Lord Bridge's letter, and instructing David Adelstein (the President) to send their reply despite the Director's ban. This Adelstein did, and was afterwards summoned to appear before the Board of Discipline where on 7th November the charges were conveyed to him.

At this point political issues became a matter for internal examination of disciplinary procedures. Adelstein claimed right to legal representation, cross-examination of witnesses in his defence, a record of the hearing, and a request that the Director, as an interested party, should stand down from the Board.

The Union organised a boycott of lectures during the hearing and felt that all Adelstein's demands had been met, and that although the final verdict was that he was guilty as he was adjudged to have acted in good faith, there would be no penalty.

Whether in order to play down the strength of political feeling, or with a true appreciation of the underlying tensions in LSE student life, many press reports stressed the other causes of student unrest.

> The students there are in ferment, I believe, because basically the undergraduates are beginning to feel the squeeze, in terms of overspecialised teaching, and some relative neglect, of its becoming more and more post graduate and vocational minded.[1]
>
> Students complained that they were left far too much to their own devices, given book lists rather than instruction by teachers preoccupied with research and outside activities (politics, Royal Commissions, work for newspapers and television.)[2]

---

[1] Crick, *op. cit.*
[2] Silver and Shearer, *op. cit.*

It is housed in a cramped site with inadequate facilities. It is part of an essentially commuter university, with students coming from lodgings all over London. It attracts a great many politically conscious and experienced militants from all over the world. In expanding it has put at risk the students' sense of belonging to a tightly knit academic community.[1]

The disadvantages of the multiversity, previously seen at Berkeley, are clear for all to see. The points made also illustrate the fact that internal structure and external movements cannot be dissociated. The presence of various kinds of activists of course is necessary for the effective organisation of protest. The activists at LSE were said to be left-wingers and Americans.

There are a number of highly active American post-graduate students here. They have brought the spirit of Berkeley in California to Houghton Street. They have brought an American conception of national justice to bear on University discipline.[2]

Why then has organised defiance erupted at LSE and nowhere else? One answer offered by Sir Sidney Caine and two of his senior colleagues yesterday is that dissent has been provoked and nurtured by a tiny minority with leanings towards the anarchistic left. Events, in his view, have been influenced by the student revolt in the United States—and in some cases by American students (of whom there are 300 at the School).[3]

It is not unlikely that imitation—discussed earlier—or the diffusion of ideas did indeed play a part in *galvanising* discontents which already existed. But Sir Sidney Caine's dealings with what he considered the anarchistic left may have been a misreading of the situation. On the other hand, it would be true to say that certain left-wing activists of the Socialist Society and producers of the *Agitator* pamphlets attemped to reduce the struggle to one of Marxist intensity between the capitalist and bourgeois administrators and the oppressed student group—and in so doing pushed the student leaders into increasingly extreme positions. Here, again, internal and external structure are used to pursue particular sectional goals which may have unforeseen consequences for the whole body of students. However, if students believe themselves to be oppressed it is important to ask why and to relate it to the institutional situation as well as to the political climate. "Students are an oppressed group—oppressed

[1] Students in revolt, Editorial Leader, *The Observer*, 19 March 1967.
[2] Donovan, *op. cit.*
[3] Silver and Shearer, *op. cit.*

economically by the state and their parents, oppressed intellectually by the suffocating weight of dead and conformist departments."[1]

The first week of the Lent term was quiet, and then two issues most dominating Union politics were the Government's decision to raise the fees of overseas students and the Union attitude to the newly formed Radical Student Alliance—both to be discussed later. Since protest about the appointment of Dr. Adams had died down, those who still considered the issue serious decided to raise support for the campaign by calling a discussion meeting with outside speakers. The meeting was approved by the Graduate Students' Association and the Union Council and was booked in the name of the GSA for Tuesday, 31 January. At this stage no one imagined that the meeting would attract many people, nor that the turning point of the affair would come at that meeting with the death of a university porter "when a demonstration at the London School of Economics turned into an ugly and violent scrimmage".[2] The porter, Mr. Ted Poole, aged 65, died from a heart attack when the students tried to force their way into the School's old theatre where a demonstration meeting had been planned. What was to have been an orderly meeting was turned by a series of accidents and unfortunate decisions into a tragedy of unintended consequences. At this point we begin to see the spiralling of the situation.

The student meeting, again to discuss Dr. Adams's appointment, had been arranged for 4 p.m. and outside speakers had been invited. At the last minute, supposedly fearing a threat of "direct action mentioned in a student leaflet", the Director informed Marshall Bloom, the GSA President, of a ban on the meeting.

Marshall Bloom, in a letter to *The Guardian*, said: "The Director told me that no meeting on the subject of Dr. Walter Adams could be held on that day. The notices which were posted stated that the Director was 'not prepared to provide facilities for the purposes for which this meeting fixed for 4 p.m. in the Old Theatre today was intended'."

At the time students assembled in front of the Old Theatre, in response to a request of the Union Council, they believed the discussion itself had been banned. It was considerably later, almost simultaneous with the tragic end of the day's events, that the Director gave the students permission to use the Students' Union pub for the meeting.

[1] Stedman Jones, G., Barnett, A., and Wengraff, T., Student power: what is to be done? *New Left Review*, No. 43, May–June 1967.

[2] Report in *The Guardian*, front page, 1 February 1967.

Of course the students saw this banning of the meeting as a restriction of free speech and were motivated to take more action than they would otherwise have done. "In spite of the ban, the 300 students gathered outside the theatre, shouting and pushing their way forward demanding to be let in. After about ten minutes of uproar Sir Sidney arrived and appealed to the students to obey his ruling which he said he had been forced to impose because he claimed the meeting was organised violence."[1]

Bloom asserts that there was never any intention of violence, and as proof of this he asks why Sir Sidney Caine should have finally agreed "that the banned meeting could be held in the bar at LSE? I submit that it was after he was satisfied with the assembled students' explanation that ' "direct action" entails the normal processes of peaceful protest.' If this is the case what is the justification for deciding to ban any future discussion of this issue from the school's meeting places?"

The students were incensed because they were using only legitimate means of airing grievances and also because they thought they were being treated like children and resented what they considered the autocratic handling of the situation by the Director. On the other hand, we must assume that the Director thought he was dealing with a set of violent hooligans. The misreading of the situation by both parties, in fact, lead to open conflict. The self-fulfilling prophecy of violence unfortunately became a reality. It could not have been more tragic for everyone when Mr. Poole collapsed as the doors of the Old Theatre were broken open by the irate and jostling students.

> When it was announced that someone had been badly hurt the demonstration collapsed into a shocked silence—to be superseded by heated recriminations when Mr. Poole, who had been at the LSE for many years and was approaching retirement, was taken to hospital. He was dead on arrival. Sir Sidney who remained near the doors of the theatre throughout, said afterwards that Mr. Poole had been known to be in poor health and that he had therefore not been asked to guard the doors, but he had decided to join his colleagues.[1]

The tragedy was that the death and the unruly behaviour surrounding it were unnecessary and resulted from a build-up of misunderstandings. The incident was, of course, seized upon, and there were newspaper headlines screaming of "murder". The emotional shock created a feeling of near hysteria which was largely synthetic. The situation, however, had, as it were, "cracked" and got out of control.

[1] *Ibid,*

The Board of Inquiry's report made no recommendations for disciplinary action, but the School's secretary, Mr. Henry Kidd,[1] decided that several students had broken Rule L which forbids students to bring the school into disrepute. Charges were made against six students involved in the events of 31 January. Bloom argued that "These students are not accused of entering the Old Theatre illegally or of participating in physical violence or obstruction. Rather, they have been accused of playing important roles in the discussion outside the Old Theatre and at the Union Councils discussion of the ban."[1]

The six students disciplined included Mr. Adelstein and Mr. Bloom. Of course things were made difficult by the fact that deliberations were conducted in a blaze of publicity. 124 of the staff, many normally regarded as well to the left of centre, publicly condemned the attacks made upon the Director-designate by some students of the school, and the violence to which they had led, as entirely contrary to the spirit in which the affairs of the school should be conducted, and a potential threat to academic freedom. The staff began to take their positions against or behind the students.

When the Disciplinary Board first met on Monday, 27 February, students stood outside with placards saying "Victimisation". At this stage students used legal means of protest—the accused were defended by Professor Griffith, Mr. Zander, and Mr. Downey—and Mr. Kidd, the Prosecutor, was also legally represented. Six students observers were allowed to sit-in on the proceedings.

A period of days elapsed while the Disciplinary Board heard the students' defence against charges of disobeying instructions of the Director. The Students' Union passed resolutions deploring what it considered to be unreasonable delay in the issuing of a verdict on the students, who were said to be being subjected to "considerable personal strain". The Board announced that it would rule whether the students were guilty or not, but that they would sit again that day and the following day to hear mitigating circumstances if the students were found guilty. Some of the students regarded this as a manoeuvre to defer the final announcement until practically the last day of term so there could be no demonstrations.

On Monday, 13 March 1967, Sir Sidney Caine announced the suspension of the two student leaders until the end of the following term. The

---

[1] Bloom, M., letter to *The Guardian*. Mr. Kidd has since written his account of the "first major demonstration of student power in Britain". Kidd, H., *The Trouble at L.S.E. 1966–67*, London, 1969.

four other students involved had been acquitted on 9 March. Between 400 and 500 students heard the verdict and rejected an invitation from Sir Sidney to send a deputation to discuss the suspensions, and threatened to boycott the classes for the remaining week of term. After waiting for 3 hours, a hard core of about 100 voted to stay in the school all night although the building is normally closed at 10.30 p.m. This signifies the beginning of "revolt" proper where illegal means are used by the students in a form of civil disobedience.

From this point the situation gradually worsened, with a state of war between the students and the authorities being exemplified by the mass sit-in in the school building. The staff began to take sides, with younger staff tending to support the students.

> In this deadlock the students picketed lectures and sat on the floor of the main entrance with the sort of enthusiasm that comes with a day out of school. At noon, a deputation met Sir Sidney and said they would block the main entrance of the school for a token couple of hours unless he lifted the suspensions immediately. He said this was not in his power and the main entrance was blocked, which caused some annoyance as people had to get where they were going the long way round.[1]

At a press conference Sir Sidney continued to blame the troubles on a fanatical minority, and particularly dissatisfied Americans. These he "accused of holding up the school's moves towards reform. Student representation was being discussed."[1] "About a third of the LSE students are from abroad so it is not surprising that foreign student participation was important. Adelstein is South African and Bloom American."[2]

Mr. Adelstein countered the suggestion that everything was due to a small body of agitators by saying that union meetings on big issues consistently attracted 800 or so students of no one political persuasion. "Had not the current sit-in been suggested by an ex-chairman of the Conservative Club? It was too easy, Mr. Adelstein said, to blame unrest on activists and gloss over real student discontent."[1]

The situation developed daily with, for instance, 102 students being removed by police from an administrative building on 15 March and subsequently being suspended. Meantime the factions of academic staff continued to harden. The normal life of the School was seriously threatened when at the end of the third day, on 16 March, Sir Sidney offered some concessions that representations of suspended students would be considered, and that appeals against suspensions of the two leaders

[1] LSE students continue night blockade, *The Guardian*, 15 March 1967.
[2] Brewster and Cockburn, *op. cit.*

would be considered without delay if the students would return to their studies. When the School returned to normal the Court of Governors was prepared to resume discussions with students' representatives on the School's affairs. The suspensions of the 102 students was commuted to a fine of £5 to be given to charity. However, the demonstration continued, and a protest march and an open-air meeting on the morning of Friday, 17 March, was joined by about 2000 supporters from a dozen other universities and colleges. Disaffection was rapidly spreading. A message from the Director, delivered by the President-Elect of the Students' Union, Mr. Peter Watherston, struck a conciliatory note by expressing the need to see established a more efficient system of consultation with student representatives and by accepting that the student body should be represented in the workings of the School's disciplinary procedures.

MPs addressed the meeting and complimented the students on their orderly behaviour.

Late on Friday night (17 March) the Governor's Standing Committee affirmed the findings of the Board of Discipline that Adelstein and Bloom were guilty of disobeying the Director, though the charge of encouraging disobedience was not proved beyond reasonable doubt. The sentence was slightly modified in that as from 1 April Adelstein and Bloom were to be allowed *de facto* use of the School's premises. While the sit-ins and demonstrations continued, the authorities issued a statement on the Saturday that there would be no discussion under duress and that changes in disciplinary procedure could not be considered until the School was back to normal.

A marathon meeting of the Union ensued, lasting 13 hours, and the students prepared to continue their protests into the vacation by setting up a "Free University" to which members of the academic staff would be invited to lecture to all-comers. This was an attempt to keep high the solidarity and tension which had just been built up in the previous week. This tension had been kept high by, for instance, a hunger strike by thirteen students from Tuesday to Saturday.

> If the LSE authorities had shown half the skill in dealing with the protestors as the student activists showed in organising the sit-in, the whole thing might have died an early and obscure death. As it was, they made the worst of every possible world. They gave the militants what all protest movements thrive on—martyrs and publicity. And then by offering concessions (which might have prevented much of the trouble in the first place) they appeared to justify the tactics of the protestors.[1]

---

[1] Students in revolt, Editorial leader, *The Observer*, 19 March 1967.

However, despite the misunderstanding and mismanagement, and despite the successful student vacation university, the situation was running down. "Elsewhere in the school the council of the Students' Union was holding its second 'pre-negotiations' with the Director. Hopes began to rise that the position of the two sides were at last beginning to move closer together."[1]

Behind the scenes the sides *were* moving closer together, and when, on Tuesday, 21 March, the staff members of the joint committee on regulations accepted most of the disciplinary reforms demanded by the dissident students, there was little left to fight for and the sit-in was ended. The "Free University" continued into the vacation—but in essence the struggle was over. The new machinery proposed removed nearly all the grievances provoked by the suspension of Adelstein and Bloom, and had the blessing of the Director.

> Under the new structure the Board of Discipline would have six members: two from the Court of Governors who are not members of its standing committees; two members of the academic staff nominated by the academic board; and two students nominated by the council of their union. In cases where it was divided three-three charges would be dismissed. Appeals from its decisions would be heard by an independent body. The Governor's Standing Committee would have powers to mitigate sentences, but not to increase them.
>
> Summary powers of the Director and other officers of the school are restricted by these proposals to small fines and short suspensions (up to a week). Stiffer sentences would be subject to appeal to the disciplinary board, which alone could impose suspensions of more than three months and fines of more than £25.[2]

The major aims in terms of changes of disciplinary procedure were achieved, while the original explicit cause for demonstration—the appointment of Dr. Adams—remained unchanged. Whatever the criticisms of student demonstrations, it is quite possible that they brought to a head matters of long-standing grievance and speeded up reform. "One of the staff members of the joint committee acknowledged, however, that changes would not have come so quickly or in this precise form but for the demonstrations of the past nine days."[3] Although there had been losses, much had been gained, and there is no doubt that the students felt that their efforts had been worthwhile. "The sit-in finished on the

---

[1] Report—*The Guardian*, 22 March 1967.

[2] Silver, E., LSE staff accepts demands for disciplinary reform, *The Guardian*, 22 March 1967.

[3] Silver, *op. cit.*

strokc of five with a ritual singing of 'We Shall Overcome'—and two minutes silence. A fitting end to a very English revolution."[1]

The student leaders were allowed to go back to their courses and reinstated in a general amnesty and upon signing letters of good conduct—regarded by left-wing activists as a capitulation and betrayal.

Of course we have not seen the end of the LSE affair or, indeed, of similar student activities in other universities.[2] "The LSE's troubles, however, may only be a rehearsal for other dramas elsewhere."[3]

There had already, at the beginning of 1967, been a general student show of strength in Britain over the matter of overseas students' fees, which we shall briefly examine; the incidents that have already occurred suggest that it is possible that there will be other dramas elsewhere. Indeed, the issue of student loans seems likely to be one of the next matters for student action. Certainly we begin to see in Britain the politicisation which has taken place in the United States and France though as yet only in an embryonic state.

The rather impressionistic account of the LSE incidents, gained from contemporary newspaper accounts, perhaps conveys the structure and flavour of the student actions involved which, as we have seen, are characterised by recurrent social features and close interrelation between external political movements and involvements and between internal disciplinary changes and reforms.

After the events were all over in 1967, the LSE Socialist Society wrote a pamphlet "LSE—what it is and how we fought it",[4] and presented the viewpoint of some of the students involved in the sit-in. It is interesting to compare their perspective. They state in their introduction that: "On April 14th, 1967, after four acrimonious meetings in nine days, the Court of Governors of London School of Economics announced that it had lifted the three month suspensions imposed on two student representatives on March 13th. This was undoubtedly the victory students had fought for in nine historic days of direct action."

---

[1] Silver, *op. cit.*

[2] Actually the movement runs through the whole of higher education. During 1968 for instance there was a six-week sit-in at Hornsey College of Art and a long summer sit-in at Guildford School of Art, aimed at a complete rethinking and restructuring of Art education.

[3] Students in revolt, *The Observer*, 19 May 1967.

[4] Open Committee, LSE Socialist Society, *LSE, What it is and how we fought it*, Agitator publication, Pirate Press, London, 1967.

The events had been described by *The Times* as "unprecedented in British University history"—and certainly the occurrences were really the first of their kind to take place among what until that point had been regarded as generally parochial-minded and quiescent students. But if student revolt had to happen anywhere in Britain, everyone agrees it had to happen first at LSE. "If the English Revolution were to be ignited by students, the London School of Economics would be an admirable base."[1] The reasons why are familiar enough in the analysis of student unrest, and emerge from both faculty and student accounts—lack of contact between student, faculty and administration; generally overcrowded conditions coupled with soul-destroying impersonality; lack of any kind of institutional solidarity; strong left-wing groups; highly motivated, strong leaders. The strong social science orientation has also been quoted as influential in promoting unrest in the LSE[2] and elsewhere because social scientists tend to be social reformers and critical of "the establishment". Indeed, a study of sociology graduates has shown a tendency to left-wing political views but little evidence of the extremely radical leanings that are often attributed.[3]

In addition, of course, the LSE, in the heart of London, is in a sense on the pulse of social and political happenings, and is, at the same time, a barometer of student activity with a long history of political involvement. If LSE students failed to react to political events who would then lead? Some of the new universities see themselves as heir to the LSE mantle, but the LSE has not yet let it drop.

The socialist students justified their objections to Dr. Adams's appointment by saying that they did not object to Dr. Adams's own politics but to the fact that at various times "he had given in to external pressures and sided with the racialist government. He had chosen to co-operate with Smith, the price for keeping the college open, even though this meant giving up any pretence of academic freedom. Adding to this Adams' reported disdain for students, the resulting militant opposition of LSE students to this appointment is no surprise."[4]

The student account of events thereafter shows that they felt they were dismissed out of hand without their grievances being answered. They refer to the matter of Adelstein's letter to *The Times* as the "first real confron-

[1] Beloff, M., The LSE Story, *Encounter*, May 1969, pp. 66–77.
[2] National Opinion Poll conducted 10 and 12 February reported in the *Daily Mail*.
[3] Abbott, J., *Career Patterns of British Sociology Graduates*, BSA, 1969,
[4] Agitator pamphlet, p. 2.

tation between the student and the authorities", and say that the ruling on Adelstein was a "direct denial of freedom of expression". This is reminiscent of the Freedom of Speech movement which inflamed Berkeley 3 years earlier.

The later meeting of 31 January which was banned was also seen by the students as a rallying point for a fight for "free speech". In a sense the objections to Dr. Adams became secondary to the student concern for open expression of their views, of which they felt there was little understanding among the authorities. Say the students, "the Director's equation of direct action with violence served only to impress upon people the high standards of knowledge required by those chosen to rule over academic institutions". The desperate bid to enter the Old Theatre and hold the meeting was inflamed, said the students, by the Director's denial of their right to do so. It became a symbolic act for the students in the struggle for power. "Inside, students felt they had been completely successful—the administration was now powerless. In the candlelit Theatre, Caine, who only an hour before had stated categorically that the meeting could not take place, now had to beg students to leave and hold the meeting elsewhere—anywhere but in the Old Theatre. His pleading had no effect, the Director of LSE was just one individual with whom others disagreed."[1]

At the death of the porter, "students, without exception, were stunned. Many of them felt in a quite irrational way that they were to blame".[2] The socialist students suggest that despite the fact that the Director had said that "no one should hold themselves responsible", many individuals and groups with grudges against the left began a campaignst again the Union Council and Graduate Student Association Committee, which was exacerbated by the hysterical reaction among the staff who included many nominal leftists. The students felt betrayed even by those from whom they had hoped to gain support.

This feeling of betrayal continued during the subsequent sit-in even though "the situation was not completely clear to the students". "The sharpness of the clash between their illusions—a more or less unreflective acceptance of liberal rhetoric—and the oppressive reality of one of the structures that continued to propagate them, was, however, beginning to teach them a great deal."[3]

This theme of disillusionment with the "theoretical liberal" appears

[1] Agitator pamphlet, p. 4.
[2] *Ibid.*, p. 5.
[3] *Ibid.*, p. 6.

continuously throughout student meetings and protests. In both the civil rights and anti-war movements the designation "liberal" has become a dirty word meaning an individual full of empty rhetoric and do-gooding ideas who does nothing. With the growth of active radicalism, the middle-of-the-road liberal is being swept aside as an anachronism. If, indeed, as has been suggested, many youth rebel against what they see as the inadequacy of their parents to live out ideals, it is not surprising that when they are faced with authority (father?) figures who appear to them to be doing the same thing they should feel doubly cheated and thwarted, and express twice the necessary amount of resentment.

At the LSE accusation by the authorities, said the students, against "provos, anarchists, trotskyites and Americans showed students their absolute ignorance and dishonesty".[1] During the sit-in students "were experiencing for the first time a real collective attempt to change their life situation. There was a general feeling of elation. Something seemed to be happening that was far more important than lectures or examinations."[2] Actually this is just a very sad comment on the state of affairs before the sit-in.

Public condemnation had one happy result. It fortified the students' consciousness of their corporate identity. The LSE affair began as a traditional issue of liberal morality, similar to the type of consciousness aroused by CND and Suez.

But "in the course of the struggle the issues became transformed into a controversy that concerns all students, as students, i.e. (1) students' power, (2) the status of the union, and (3) the *loco parentis* system of discipline".[3]

The students saw the mass suspensions of students, after the invasion of Connaught House, as a panic means by authorities which had the opposite effect of that intended, and instead of intimidating students only swelled their movement. The subsequent influx of supporters from all over England affirmed "student solidarity" in a unique way. This solidarity once experienced was to be appealed to thereafter on various occasions the first important one being in May 1968 when the students staged a one-night sit-in the school's entrance hall to show "solidarity" with their Parisian counterparts, who were already at the barricades.

In October 1968 there were further demonstrations and a week-end sit-in over the period of the large-scale Vietnam demonstration. "In December before the Oration by Professor Trevor-Roper the Socialist Society in-

---

[1] *Ibid.*, p. 6.
[2] *Ibid.*, p. 7.
[3] Stedman *et al.*, *op. cit.*

vaded the seats reserved for the visiting dignitaries, and festooned the platform while the guest speaker delivered himself of a brilliant lecture including remarks on the dangers of a new fascism."[1]

The reference to the "new fascism" relates to the monopoly on the truth claimed by some extremely left wing idealists, and is coupled with the natural arrogance of youth and the feelings of uniqueness of this particular generation of under 30. (Age is imputed automatically to bring hypocrisy, ignorance, intolerance, and dishonesty.)

Further disturbances at the LSE in the following terms culminated in the removal by students of the internal gates which had been set up in the wake of the October 1968 occupation. This event took place on 24 January 1969, after which the school was closed until 19 February. At this point militants at the LSE began to see themselves as "tinder to the proletarian fuel", and the "crackdown of authorities as a part of a general crackdown on militant students and workers throughout the country during the present crisis of British capitalism".[1]

Outside commentators saw the militancy as an attempt to "acquire some martyrs" and to "provoke a response from the authorities".

> Hence the militants found themselves able to exercise one of their well publicised ploys: to provoke resistance and then to complain that the authorities have used violence against them. It comes straight out of the revolutionary text book. In this way, the militant can show that authority however liberal or well-intended it may be, is at heart authoritarian, a prop for a reactionary bourgeois society. Then at the next stage, it is easier to win the support of a much wider band of liberals who are by nature suspicious of authority.[2]

Thus we have another view of the moves and countermoves in the game of protest. It is argued that "the hierarchy of the LSE happens to be the nearest target at hand, but they do not disguise that their main objective is society itself, the system, which they say, must be overthrown."

It is difficult, as we have seen, to discuss internal institutional controls without bringing in these outside political goals and interests with which they sometimes interact.

An editorial in *The Guardian* weekly of the time seemed to imply that this time the LSE militants had overstepped the mark in "trying to make academic life impossible" and in trying to "spread disruption to other academic communities". The main outcomes were suggested as an infringe-

[1] Beloff, M., *op. cit.*, p. 69.
[2] On the barricades at LSE, *Guardian Weekly*, Tuesday, 30 January 1969, p. 12.

ment of rights of students who want to study (a great majority probably, though ill organised) and antagonising of public opinion against students as a whole which might affect government or local authority funding of education and a discrediting of the student movement as such. The editorial says that "much unrest in the past few years has been justified, by the conservative bureaucratic tendencies of the Universities", and that the students "have done well to win from the Vice-Chancellors (as they have already done) a recognition that active student participation is necessary in a healthy academic community", but that more will not be achieved if it is "confused with academic exercises in revolution".[1]

The use of the phrase "academic communities" shows an unrealistic appraisal of what universities are and so, in a sense, what students are doing. However, the comment about revolution as an academic exercise is not without its points—students do have licence to posture as revolutionaries without necessarily bringing down the system. They are in an interstitial zone of control discussed earlier in which they are regarded tolerantly as doing and saying openly what others long to do and say, but cannot. Students are in a peculiarly favourable position, therefore, to criticise society—its hypocrisies and shams. And let us make no mistake—there are those in power who listen. Student militants are like the court jester who may get kicked for his remarks but is at the same time feared and respected for his biting honesty. Others would get hung.

Thus although student methods may have lost them sympathy in "engineering confrontation" with authority, their ideals and goals may still strike a sympathetic chord. However, the fascism of left-wing tactics in shouting down political opponents who are "subjected to abuse and even to personal violence" and in taking over property, it is argued, may tend "to feed the forces of right-wing authoritarianism".[2] The freedom of speech for which they fought and for which students in Czechoslovakia and Spain are struggling too, is sometimes denied as a right for others by the militants who are "autocratic, arrogant, and bullying". "To those who remember their history this looks all too like the road to authoritarianism".[2] The "rightness" of the cause may so overcome concern for rights of others that we may find "the idealistic spirit has done violence to itself and others, and has been transmitted into a destructive force in human history".[3] This despite the fact that "of all social movements those composed of

[1] *Ibid.*
[2] Student reform or revolution?, *Guardian Weekly*, 6 February 1969.
[3] Feuer, L. S., *The Conflict of Generations*, p. 3.

students have been characterised by the highest degree of selflessness, generosity, compassion, and readiness for self-sacrifice".[1]

> Students are not alone in being disenchanted with our society. The established order neither fulfils people's aspirations nor is sensitive to their grievances. The political parties are unpopular; government is seen to be slow, clumsy and secretive; and Parliament itself has come to be distrusted. In that light it is a mistake to belittle student unrest, even though the unrest comes from a minority. Here, however, the minority has been trying to take matters into its own hands by force. Are these students justified in doing so? May they not defeat their own ends?
>
> Much of what the revolutionary students claim to stand for deserves sympathy. In rejecting the materialist values of the consumer society (whether capitalist or Communist), in resisting bureaucracy (capitalist or Communist), in condemning the hypocrisy of the social structure (capitalist or Communist), they speak with idealism, indeed with moral fervour. Their appeal ostensibly is to total freedom. One London student slogan last week read: "It is forbidden to forbid. Everything is permitted." Of course that is naive, utopian, romantic, but it is also inspiring.[2]

(One must remark at this point on the general level of tolerance with which most British newspapers have greeted student disturbances.)

As we shall discuss later, the actual course of events of student disturbance is very much related to the handling by the authorities and the way they act out their role of "authority", as we have seen already from discussion of the examples. In relation to actual issues seen as important by students, it is interesting that a national opinion poll study found that "students from better-off families at the LSE were concerned with extreme political action, whereas sons of skilled craftsmen and manual workers were concerned with trade union issues like greater student-participation in university affairs".[3]

However, it is argued "that the whole extremist movement at LSE has only been loosely concerned with the purposes and functions of a university as at present conceived. Events have fallen into the now familiar pattern: political demonstration or activity carried out by methods unacceptable to the existing university authorities, then a wider demonstration against the attempted exercise by those authorities of their existing powers".[4] It is supposed that the "pacemakers among the student militants actually prefer conflict to co-operation"—so that "for the militants, representation is inadequate; for the moderates (still a majority) it is pre-

---

[1] Feuer, L. S., *The Conflict of Generations*, p. 3.
[2] Student reform or revolution?, *Guardian Weekly*, 6 February 1969.
[3] Reported in Beloff, M., *op. cit.*, p. 68.
[4] *Ibid.*, p. 72.

umably uninteresting".[1] This is the double bind that universities are in oday, with the authorities two steps behind the student demands—those emands having changed by the time they are granted.

The growing acceptance of violence by students as legitimate means at ne LSE and elsewhere seems to overcloud the stated idealism, as do the ttacks not only on groups but on specific individuals, by grave distor-ions of the spoken and written word. At the LSE Beloff suggests that the ower of the militant minority, which he estimates at around 500–600 tudents within the 3000 student body, has stemmed largely from their nanipulation of the Students' Union, and that "politicisation of the Union n Summer 1966 was a precondition for the subsequent outburst".[2] What as been achieved may be minimal, however. Beloff states: "Capitalism as not been overthrown. The School has not been improved", while vorking-class students and those from developing countries have suffered most from the activities of middle-class colleagues".[3]

Student intervention in political matters has not previously been a sual occurrence in Britain, and, as the first expression of unified and or-anised student sentiment and action, the boycott on 22 February 1967 gainst the raising of fees charged to Overseas students was a unique vent. It is not likely to remain unique for long now that students have orporately flexed their political muscles. The campaign of protest was led y the National Union of Students against the Government's decision o save £5 million by raising fees charged to Overseas students in Britain.

Mr. Crosland, then Minister of Education, put the case that subsidis-ng overseas students' fees cost Britain £18 million in 1966, and that in ome cases students could get a university education more cheaply in ritain than at home. The students replied that the decision—which put niversity fees up from about £70 to £250 a year and at other colleges o £150—would hurt those least able to pay—students from under-eveloped countries. There are 71,000 Overseas students in Britain. Almost 0,000 are training to be nurses or are in industry, and are not affected.)f the rest, 16,000 are in universities—12,000 at technical colleges and

---

[1] *Ibid.*, p. 71.

[2] *Ibid.*, p. 74.

[3] *Ibid.*, p. 76. Despite Beloff's appraisal of the situation it would seem that certain ains have been made. In the Autumn of 1969 new regulations for LSE students were romulgated. A committee consisting of the Director, six academics and five students ould interpret rules and decide whether a sit-in were legal or not. An Appeals Com-aittee was also to be set up. Students were also offered representation on the academic oard's general purposes committee and thus an increasing sphere of influence.

4000 working for the GCE. Roughly 70 per cent of those affected com
from developing countries and, according to the NUS Overseas Studen
Research Unit, about two-thirds were financed either by their famili
or by their own work here. It is these students who would be penalise
by the increase, and the NUS claimed that the trifling sum of £5 millic
should be raised in a more equitable way instead of singling out an alreac
under-privileged group.

The students had the benefit of having a number of academics and MF
on their side and a good deal of favourable public opinion. Public mee
ings were held and the student leaders of NUS and SUS discussed the sit
ation with Mr. Crosland, Secretary of State for Education, at the begin
ning of February 1967. The movement started out as an exemplary politic
action carried out through official channels with the full co-operation of tl
authorities. Indeed, the more left-wing elements of student opinion thoug
the conduct of protest too respectable and criticised the student leaders fe
not pressing hard enough and for being "lackeys of Transport House".

It was some of these left-wing elements who formed the splinter grou
of the NUS—the Radical Students' Alliance, which represents a schis
in student organisation. Its founding convention was held at the end e
January 1967, and there it openly pledged itself to a brand of stude
political involvement which the NUS has always studiously avoide
The initial line-up of the RSA sympathisers took place much earlier
the NUS National Council in Margate in November 1965, when stude
protest centred on three main issues—Vietnam, Rhodesia, and Immigr
tion—and a telegram was sent to President Johnson protesting about tl
course of the war in Vietnam. At this meeting the decision was take
to break with the pro-West International Student Conference, but th
decision was reversed in Exeter in April 1966. "Since then the RSA has
strengthened its position that it can present itself as a popular front fe
militant student action."[1]

Geoffrey Martin, the then President of the NUS, has heard hims
denounced as a fascist by militant extremists. "But then Martin hims
can't be said to deal very diplomatically with his opponents. He thin
RSA consists of some 'very questionable people indeed', negative in the
attitudes, unconstructive in their criticism. He talks of 'clandestine mee
ings' and firmly believes the communist influence in RSA is strong ar
dangerous."[2]

[1] Gourlay, D., The shape of student politics, *The Guardian*, 4 February 1967.
[2] Nightingale, B., The student schism, *New Society*, 16 February 1967.

The NUS "Reds under the Bed" scare is perhaps understandable when e remembers how respectable in recent years NUS has become as ief negotiating student body.

In recent years the NUS has increasingly been recognised by the Department of Education, Education Associations and Government Commissions as the responsible vehicle of informed student opinion. Its views have been sought by the Albemarle, Newsom, Robbins and Plowden committees. It has grown from a membership of 150,000 (representing 250 universities and colleges in 1962) to its present strength of 366,000 (representing approximately 700 in England and Wales and Northern Ireland).[1]

Scotland has its own separate national union, which works closely ith NUS under the then presidency of Mr. George Foulkes.

The RSA made no secret of its strong communist element—reckoned 25 per cent, but there were also Young Liberals, members of CND d idealists with no party affiliation. However, the issues raised cannot e polarised simply along Communist/non-Communist lines. In February 967 the RSA had a mailing list of 1500 with chapters at Newcastle, York, irmingham, Essex, and strong support at Keele, Hull, Leeds, Liverpool, alford, and Manchester. It is interesting that it is the large civic and ew universities which form the strongholds of RSA.

On 26 January, at Hull, delegates from sixty student unions passed resolution of no confidence, 208 to 42, in the philosophy of NUS. delstein of the NUS was one of the proposers. On 1 February came e mass lobbying of MP's on the issue of Overseas fees. The NUS anted 200 selected students to take part. RSA saw to it that over 4000 rned up. But despite its organising ability it regarded its council— hich included Terry Lacey of the Young Liberals and David Adelstein— ore as a co-ordinating body than a top echelon of law makers. The aim as to break away from the traditional pattern of student organisation.

When petitions and marches and speeches in Parliament seemed to ave no effect on the Government with regard to Overseas fees—and his included the joint efforts of university staff and Vice-Chancellors— e RSA was instrumental in organising the "day of protest" on 22 February. This was to be a day of concerted national student action—an vent never achieved before. The major activity was a boycott of lectures, ut opinions as to the efficacy of this method were divided as it made it ppear that activities were directed against university staff, when this as not the intention. The student strike was mostly supported by univer-

[1] Gourlay. *op.cit.*

sities where there was strong RSA membership. In the event, in fact a majority of students took part in the strike and demonstrations although the organisation was not as effective as it might have been. The activities varied from university to university and included silent vigils, marches and public meetings. The demonstrations achieved no overall change in government policy, but students were elated by the fact that they had shown a largely united front.

However, some government rethinking of the problem was revealed when Mr. Crosland announced in the Commons the establishment of a hardship fund of £500,000 to help towards the increased fees of Overseas students in case of proved need. This would operate by recompensing universities, colleges, and local education authorities to the extent that they remitted the increase in fees for Overseas students within the scope of the fund. Earlier, in the Commons debate on the government decision to raise fees, Mr. Crosland had said that much of the criticism had been unrealistic and even bordering on the hysterical. This accusation may have been the result of surprise at the warmth of feeling and strength of reaction shown by the staff and students alike in their concerted attack on what they considered to be a serious government error in principle. The issue of higher fees for Overseas students triggered off not only demonstrations but a new feeling of militancy among students.

The fact of belonging to the student category rather than to a particular university or college was borne in on them in a particularly forceful way—and it is a feeling which will not be forgotten. A number of student leaders admitted that the activities had largely been an exercise or rehearsal for occasions that might arise again and for which students ought to be prepared. The battle which they feel to be most imminent is the battle about the introduction of student loans. Many student leaders think that the Government will try to introduce a scheme to supply partial or full-scale repayable loans—this in effect means the withdrawal of free higher education.[1]

One must see present student disturbances in Britain within the context of developments in left-wing social movements in general. "The British

[1] This threat of 1967 seemed so much nearer in Sept. 1969. "A radical proposal that when students should only receive grants if they agree to be 'directed' into specific jobs they graduate is being considered by the government as one of the ways to reduce university costs in the 1970's." Among other suggestions "for economies" are "student loans instead of grants". Report by Peter Scott, *The Times Educ. Supplement*, Dec. 5, 1969 In Nov. 1969, NUS National Conference called for the Government to raise grants

New Left Movement, as it existed between 1957 and 1962 had its origins in the political events of 1956 and grew in the atmosphere created by the campaign for Nuclear Disarmament in the years after 1958."[1] The relation of the movement to the Labour Party has given it its special quality, adding impetus, for instance, to youthful contribution to the campaign of the general elections of 1963 and 1966. When the Labour Government failed to provide radical leadership, the student left became directionless and disillusioned, and ultimately set about changing policies in their own way. The NUS, with its 366,000 members, has concomitantly developed its range of activities.

"RSA and NUS agree upon broad aims, but the former is concerned more with the 'grass roots' and the mobilization of mass student support, with demonstrations and petitions."[2] Within the national scene may be set the particular political cultures shared by students in different institutions and the organisational links between them.

Many of the features of British student unrest discussed have broader implications, and we shall just briefly touch upon some comparable student revolts elsewhere in order, finally, to draw out some underlying trends.

In the case of Berkeley—which the LSE is supposed to mirror in some ways—the explicit causes of student rebellion were framed by the nature of political freedom and its place on the university campus, although there were clearly numerous ramifications within and outside the University of the principles involved. The Berkeley revolt is not discussed here in detail because it is already very well documented.[3]

Structural points at issue have already been noted briefly. However, because so many of the British movements have their original inspiration in the Berkeley revolt it is worth mentioning one or two points which tie in with what has already been said.

The Berkeley campus of the University of California was in a state of uproar and demonstration between September 1964 and January 1965 which virtually brought the University to a standstill.

Until 1960 the student body of Berkeley had not been a radical one,

---

[1] Halsey, A. H. and Marks, S., British student politics, *Daedalus*, Winter 1968, pp. 116–37.

[2] *Ibid.*, p. 130.

[3] Cf. Lipset and Wolin, The Berkeley student's revolt, 1965, Draper, Hal, *Berkeley: The New Student Revolt*, New York, Grove Press, 1965; Miller, M. V. and Gillmore, S. (eds.), *Revolution at Berkeley*, New York, Dell, 1965.

but between 1960 and 1964 there was a growing dissatisfaction and growing politicisation which centred upon the civil rights movement and gained its impetus from reaction to the murder of three civil rights volunteers in Mississippi in the summer of 1964. Feuer says that "The University of California at Berkeley was probably the freest campus in the country. The organisations of the New Left flourished at Berkeley meetings as they did on no other campus in the United States. Yet it was precisely here that the activists raised the cry that they were being persecuted and deprived of freedom."[1] Many of the escalations of the conflict can in fact be traced to the same kind of lack of "mesh" of expectations and resulting misunderstandings between the university authorities and the students.

The immediate cause was an announcement by campus officials that a 26 foot strip of land at the entrance of the campus, previously thought by most students and faculty to belong to the City of Berkeley, was the property of the University and subject, therefore, to existing university regulations dealing with political activity. This particular strip happened to be the place where students traditionally conducted political-action groups without interference. A student protest movement was rapidly organised—the Free Speech Movement (FSM)—and it advanced demands for the drastic reform of university rules and regulations affecting students' political activity on campus. "A running battle, which lasted almost the entire semester, developed between the administration and the FSM. Before the dispute had run its course, the faculty was drawn in and the effects of the controversy were registered throughout the entire state."[2] During the running battle, "one of the world's largest and most famous centers of learning was brought to the edge of collapse".

Through this dispute students were able to express dissatisfaction not only about restrictions of free speech but about the whole structure of academic and social relations within the institution. The emergence of sophomore Mario Savio as the charismatic leader of the protestors helped to swell the ranks. "Savio not only articulated latent sources of student unrest, he partially created them by the emotional fervour of his moral indignation."[3] The progress of the Berkeley student movement was marked by violence, protest in sexual behaviour, obsession with confrontation, and destruction. Finally, there was what Feuer calls a "psychological capitulation of a large section of the Berkeley faculty" brought about

[1] Feuer, *op. cit.*, p. 438.
[2] Lipset and Wolin, *op. cit.*, p. xi.
[3] Feuer, *op. cit.*, p. 443.

for "many by the desire vicariously to participate in the making of history". Subsequent events at Berkeley showed, however, that the matter did not end with reform of disciplinary procedures and settling of student grievances. In fact these events demonstrate in reverse the interrelation of internal and external political influences.

A *Guardian* report of 2 February, 1967 states the sequence of events somewhat baldly:

> Student campaigns are apt to be explosive sometimes, and self-defeating. At the University of California campus at Berkeley what began as a mixture of beatnick rowdyism and genuine political protest over civil rights and the Goldwater campaign, grew over two years into a series of riots and sitdown strikes. The culmination has been a cut in the University budget and the dismissal of its liberal president.[1]

Actually, the editorial was written as a warning to LSE students who had just embarked upon their programme of protest after the fateful Old Theatre meeting. At the same time, students in other parts of Britain were protesting about the government decision to increase fees of Overseas students. But the political climate was somewhat different from that in California, where the national political climate is influential in the conduct of university affairs.

In November 1966 Ronald Reagan, right-wing former movie and television actor, was elected as Governor of the State of California and was "thought to have raised a fat harvest of votes from the so-called Berkeley 'backlash' ".[2] "To the voters in last November's election the name of Berkeley resounded from Marin County in the north to San Diego County in the south as a symbol of student rebellion, a herald of the New left, a reminder of weakness in University government, or simply as a dirty word."[2]

The political ramifications of student activity were widespread. The new Governor made clear from the first that he intended to impose a new, tougher regime over the university and its student rebels, and by various means to bring them to heel. He began by proposing to cut the university budget by 10 per cent and by proposing "the alarming novelty of fees for all students in State-supported colleges".[2] Dr. Clark Kerr, the University President, opposed the changes as detrimental to the interests of the University (which they have since proved to be—many faculty members moving elsewhere). He retaliated against the Governor's plans by freezing all student admissions until the University should get

---

[1] "When protest becomes obsession", Editorial, *The Guardian*, 2 February 1967.
[2] Cooke, A., Berkeley victory for extremism, *The Guardian*, 30 January 1967.

a sizeable increase in its budget. On this and other matters there was open conflict between Dr. Kerr and the Governor, and the outcome was the dismissal of the University President by the University of California's Board of Regents on 20 January, 1967. Many student activists rejoiced in this "Symbolic Parricide".[1]

> The vague terrors produced by the accession of Ronald Reagan to the governorship have been realised: the threat from the Right is real and present.
> That at least is the widely held perception. Kerr's own account of his firing feed and supports it. As he explained it, the turmoil of student protests and the deepening of left radicalism at Berkeley (only one of the nine campuses of the university have "triggered an intense reaction among the right wing radicals in California" The result was the injection of "the Berkeley issue" into the governorship campaign last year, and the unfortunate entanglement of politics with education. Kerr was caught in the classic squeeze.[2]

However, it has been inferred that political pressures were such that "Kerr's reign was tottering before the first student riots. Clark Kerr is a liberal, which means that he is an anathema to the financial and social establishments of Southern California, a widespread middle class establishment that populates Los Angeles County where 46 per cent of the State's voters live and assert themselves."[3]

It may be, therefore, that the student riots helped to topple Kerr from his position.

> The University could not conceivably be divorced from politics. Governors appoint regents for political reasons. Legislatures appropriate operating funds for their own purposes and Californians agree to keep the system going because it meets their most urgent need: it is the up escalator in the most mobile society in the world.[4]

The political battle was waged on a number of fronts, with demonstrations of thousands of teachers and students being held against the proposed college and university budget cuts. At one meeting the Governor was booed and his voice drowned by catcalls as he attempted to address demonstrators on the Capitol steps in Sacramento.

In March 1967 the regents of the University of California voted by a one-vote margin to defy the State Government and oppose any efforts by the Legislature to alter the structure or autonomy of the University

[1] Feuer, *op. cit.*, p. 470.
[2] Kopkind, A., Crisis in the knowledge industry, *New Statesman*, 3 February 1967
[3] Cooke, A., *op. cit.*
[4] Kopkind, *op. cit.*

The Board also decided to postpone until July further discussions as to whether to impose student tuition fees. A pledge by the State Assembly speaker, Mr. Jesse Unruh, California's leading Democrat and an *ex-officio* member of the Board, to suspend his proposed legislative investigation of student unrest was matched by an earlier statement by the Republican Governor that he was willing to postpone a similar investigation led by the former Central Intelligence Agency head, Mr. John McCone. In June 1967 Mario Savio began his 4 month prison sentence.

The conscious interrelation of education and politics, unlike the implicit British link, may suggest many problems of control. These problems were raised during alarmed controversy again in February 1967 when the Central Intelligence Agency acknowledged that it had secretly financed a United States student organisation for the past 15 years to counter Communist activities at student meetings abroad. The disclosure was confirmed by the State Department. The subsidies to the National Student Association began at a time "when Communist agents were infiltrating international student festivals and conventions abroad", and the subsidies were admitted to amount to "possibly as much as £1,071,000 between 1952 and 1965". "In 1965 the association decided that its relationship with the CIA was intolerable and inconsistent with the ideal of an open democratic student organisation, and ended the links with it."[1]

Claims were made that the CIA had been subsidising other student organisations, including the International Student Conference, of which the British National Union of Students was a member. In the midst of rather cloak-and-dagger accusations about CIA agents (creating an atmosphere since recently repeated after the discovery that the magazine *Encounter* had been financed by the CIA), President Johnson named Mr. Nicholas Katzenbach Under-Secretary of State to deal with the controversy. A congressional investigation was also announced on 15 February. Accusations which were rumoured about included claims that members of NSA staff had received special call-up deferments and were used by the CIA as foreign agents. These agents, it was claimed, passed reports on foreign student leaders to the CIA to help it to judge the political tendencies of prospective political leaders in critical areas of the world. Members of the NSA counter-claimed that they had been intimidated by the CIA not to reveal the relationship between the association and the CIA.

[1] Students subsidised by CIA, Report from Washington, *The Guardian*, 14 February 1967.

The White House on 23 February[1] issued a statement to a press con
ference that President Johnson agreed with a report from Mr. Katzen
bach that the CIA subsidies had been paid in accordance with policie
established by the National Security Council, the country's leading
political security planning body. Indeed, there was some change of Whit
House reaction, and the President upheld the CIA's conduct.

At the same time Mr. Carl Rowan, a former director of the United
States Information Agency, raised the possibility that *Ramparts*, the
magazine which exposed the CIA's sponsorship of student groups, had
in turn been financed by the Communists. The whole debate thus took
on the air of a sophisticated "cops and robbers". The chase is, of course
still not finished yet.

Returning to the Berlin crisis we can observe the political ramification
in the internal struggles of students.

"From the outset both the academic staff and the students regarded
it as their duty to keep a critical eye on the development of democrac
in Germany."[2] However, it was only in the 1950's that doubts began to
grow among the students regarding the policies of the Federal Govern
ment when the question of nuclear arms was being quite openly debated
in Bonn.

> The political atmosphere in Berlin seeped into the university, hardening position
> all round. The building of the wall had thrown into relief the contrast between the
> seemingly frozen policies of the government and the harsh realities of the division
> in Germany. For tactical reasons the main political parties in the Federal Republi
> had tried to play down their differences. The University left—including liberal and
> protestant groups and a few left-wing catholics as well as socialists—saw the SPD's
> part in all this as a virtual renunciation of its role as the parliamentary opposition
> As a result they set about turning the University into a substitute opposition.
>
> The social philosophy of the left wing students led them to see this change of rol
> as a strengthening factor, although it meant that the way to University reform now
> lay through wholesale social reform.

In this situation it was protests about the Vietnam war which triggered
off the crisis. This protest was seen by officialdom as a sign of ingratitud
and communist subversion, since the Free University has been developed
by American endowment right up to the present time.

However, more positive aspects have emerged in the moves for univer
sity reform in which both sides of the dispute collaborated. In the com

[1] Report from Washington, *The Guardian*, 23 February 1967.
[2] Rexin, *op. cit.*, p. 697.

ission covered by the Berlin SPD to prepare new legislation on the univer-
ties, students and academic staff worked on it together.

Meanwhile everything was driven to extremes. Students mobilised
ehind "ASTA"—the student union which led the revolt.

These national controversies, of course, increase in students their
wareness of their own potential power and reinforce any aspirations
or changing the social order which they may have.[1] As has already been
aid, a number of European and Asian countries have a tradition of
tudent involvement in political affairs and consequently in social reform.
he recent political movements of Spanish students is a good case in
oint. It has been said that in Spain students are always being involved
i clashes with the police and authorities about something, but recent
iots seem to be more serious than a youthful letting-off of steam. Stu-
ents were involved in demonstrations of one kind or another through
966, and these were often quelled brutally by the police. The demonstra-
ions have centred on academic freedom and freedom of students to form
heir own organisation. In the University of Barcelona there was almost
ontinual turbulence throughout the year.

> However, the students won—more or less—their battle for a free students'
> union: a decree published during the summer vacation has satisfied most of their
> demands. But recently, in a manoeuvre that appears to have been extremely mala-
> droit, the Rector expelled nearly 70 lecturers and senior students who had signed
> telegrams to the Minister of Education protesting against his methods and policy.
> It is against these dismissals that the strikers will be protesting: and here it seems
> unlikely that the authorities, who have already given way on the question of the
> students union, will yield.[2]

In Spain as elsewhere there is conflict resulting from the breakdown
of traditional internal controls.

The interrelation of internal and external movements is exemplified
y the demonstrations in Madrid University in 1967 in sympathy with
vorkers striking for higher pay and the establishment of independent
rade unions. These demonstrations were denounced as "Communist"
y the police. The ensuing struggle became very violent, and on 31
anuary 1967 the Council of Governors closed the University for 3 days

[1] There was widespread sympathy for Mexican students after the Battle of Tlateloco,
Oct. 1968, "the massacre in which the Mexican army and police smashed the student
movement to ensure a dignified opening for the Olympic Games". Price, C., Death
on the Mexican campus, *New Statesman*, 26 Nov. 1969.

[2] Mockler, T., Barcelona students prepare to renew struggle for rights, *The Guardian*,
November 1967.

to avert more clashes. The Faculty of Political and Economic Sciences where riots began, was closed indefinitely.

At this time the trouble spread through Spain, and Madrid, Barcelona, Seville, Valencia, and Asturias all experienced outbreaks of rioting and strikes and was claimed to be organised largely by the Communists and the illegal workers organisations. Although the demonstrations began in sympathy with workers, students were soon staging strikes in most Spanish provincial universities against the arrest of delegates at an illegal national students' conference in Valencia. Staff became involved in the struggle after protesting at sanctions imposed on students and professors. In Barcelona thirty architecture lecturers were barred from the University. A number of other signatories to a protest letter were expected to lose their jobs. At the beginning of February strikes spread to Saragossa and Valladolid. "Neither workers nor students enjoy much freedom of manoeuvre in Spain; yet the Government has had to make concessions —some voluntarily and others under duress. There remains a great deal to concede—and this is what makes the situation explosive."[1]

The demonstrations continued well into May with student leaders being arrested—particularly in Madrid—and with students being tried by a military court for their part in clashes with the police. The universities were opened again, but only after severe penalties had been imposed on dissidents. On 18 May 1967, "as classes opened mounted police armed with pistols and truncheons patrolled the university while others waited in jeeps, supported by armoured water tankers with powerful hoses".[2] On 30 May, 11 of the 12 members of the ruling directorate of Barcelona's powerful but technically illegal Democratic Student Union went on trial on charges of illegal association. The twelfth member was in the Army and not allowed to attend. The prosecutor claimed that the only legal student organisation was the government-supported Professional Student Association. The accused claimed that their group had *de facto* recognition from the university authorities, and produced witnesses, including a well-known professor. The struggle goes on.

The University City in Madrid was still under police occupation in May 1969. The number of revolutionary students is growing despite the fact that only 1 per cent are workers' children. The declaration of a state of emergency is seen as a sign of failure of the government. "This does not mean that everyone subscribes to the strict Communist theory of a

[1] Tremors of change in Spain, Editorial, *The Guardian*, 8 February 1967.
[2] Report, *The Guardian*, 18 May 1967.

bourgeois revolution' as the first stage, but that they need some advance on the Thirty Year Silence. If there is any general agreement it is that only strikes can bring down the government."[1]

That student links can cross national boundaries and local disputes was demonstrated by the expression of solidarity for the Spanish students made by the French students through UNEF (National Union of French Students). Mass meetings and marches on the Spanish Embassy were organised when the President of UNEF was imprisoned in Madrid for 2 hours. The student President, Pierre Vandenburie, had responded to a request from Spanish students to recognise in person the outlawed Democratic Students' Union. The demonstrations which greeted Vandenburie's imprisonment and triumphal return seemed to indicate an impressive unity and organisation. However, splits had began to appear in the student body, and the Association of Strasbourg students in particular, representing a new extreme movement called the "situationists", was critical of Vandenburie as a "flunkey of the government". The aim of the situationists is to create a "situation from which there is no going back, and their global aim is to undermine the existing values of modern society". They have been described as the "Provos" or "California" action in France.

Further examples of revolt have been evident all over the world since 1967. In April and May 1968, Columbia University, USA, erupted into violence when students occupied and "liberated" buildings on the campus in protest against the building of a gymnasium on land taken over from the Harlem community in which the University is set. The confrontation with university officials was engineered mainly by the Students for a Democratic Society (SDS), active on so many other campuses, and brought in its wake a reassessment of many of the internal relationships within the institution. After 6 days of occupation the police were called in and much needless violence ensued. For the rest of the academic year education was at a standstill, and a strike committee claimed the allegiance of many members of the faculty as well as the students.

The fact-finding commission report suggests that

"Conditions common to a number of other campuses were among the underlying causes of the explosion, but that Columbia's special geographical situation tended to intensify many of the underlying factors. Other factors resulted from

---

[1] Adam, C., The Spanish underground, an end to Thirty Year Silence, *New Statesman*, 25 April 1969.

Columbia's own organisational structure, from the attitudes of the faculty, and from the Administration's and Trustees' prior handling of matters of intense student concern, including problems involving increasingly self-conscious black students.[1]

Again we see the importance of external issues, radical students groups, and the handling of the situation by those in authority.[2]

The Columbia revolt took place at approximately the same time and was partially inspired by the French students' revolts of May 1968, which became a matter of national and international interest and concern.[3]

The trouble began originally in the Sorbonne overflow annexe at Nanterre where the authorities antagonised the student body by closing the whole University to prevent demonstrations in support of a group of suspended students. Excessive violence by military security police roused widespread public sympathy. The student revolt spread, radical groups went out and enlisted the support of worker groups in local factories, then in time-honoured fashion students and workers took to the streets, erecting barricades, hurling paving stones at police, and themselves facing police violence.

> The street violence which has been raging in Paris is unlike anything seen in Western Europe since the end of the war. In a few days it has grown from a small demonstration in the forecourt of the Sorbonne to pitched battles across barricades throughout the Latin Quarter and to a nation-wide general strike. Each step in the process has had its own logic, but the combined effect is a bitter embarrassment to President de Gaulle on the eve of his tenth anniversary in power and with the eyes of the world on Paris. The Government's hasty concessions will probably lower the temperature again, although they only restore the position which existed two weeks ago and leave the students' original discontents unanswered.[4]

Universities in France have been characterised by rapidly expanding numbers, inadequate facilities, impersonal faculty and administrational feudal power structure, "authoritarian regulations in a stultifying political climate, hostile and oppressive police tactics".[4]

It is outside the scope of this chapter to discuss the reasons for and the ramifications of the French students revolt which threatened to bring the Government to its knees and which still simmers gently waiting for

[1] Cox Commission Report, *Crisis at Columbia*, Vintage Book, Random House, New York, 1968.

[2] Lusky, L. and Lusky, M. H., Columbia 1968: The wound unhealed, *Pol. Science Quart.*, June 1969, **34**, No. 2, pp. 169–289.

[3] Searle, P. and McConville, M., *French Revolution 1968*, Penguin, 1968.

[4] French students in revolt, *The Guardian*, 16 May 1968.

another spark. Suffice to mention it here as an example of the way in which student conflagrations can spread to the whole of society.[1]

> Modern student radicalism according to its own practitioners is genuinely international. It has succeeded, where the twentieth century's working class parties have failed, in creating a mood where boundaries are no more than an administrative inconvenience—at any rate to the mobile, uncommitted materially undemanding students who cross them so often and so easily.[2]
>
> It is traditional that the young should talk as if they had just discovered well established truths; it is relatively new to claim that they will be the first to do something about them.[3]

Of course Marxism is strong in the international student movement and in the European New Left.

> However, it is a new kind of Marxism distrustful of "existing Socialisms" reliant upon "struggle" rather than ideology to decide salient issues. Admiration for Debray, Guevara or Mao seems to be based not so much on Marxist theory as on the romantic appeal of toughness and idealism combined and the great desire to repudiate the "imperialism" imputed to one's own country.[4]

Despite common solidarity during "struggle", the international movement tends to break down in times of "peace", so that the institutionalisation of student solidarity is difficult. A conference called by American Students for a Democratic Society in September 1968—called International Assembly of Revolutionary Students—demonstrated both ideological and methodological differences between the participating groups.

Clearly one could go on indefinitely quoting instances of student "political" behaviour. However, it is not the aim to describe merely a series of historical happenings but to try to elucidate some underlying principles. Examples discussed have not included any of students involved in national revolutionary movements as the aim has been to show student rebellion rather than revolt where ultimate control as yet rests in the hands of the university authorities and the established government, but where change is effected by student intervention.

If we return finally to the British scene, we see a cutting of the ground from under the feet of student revolutionaries from the end of 1968 after the Committee of Vice-Chancellors of the British Universities had discus-

---

[1] "Teleguided from outside", and deliberately resorting "to violence and provocation". Crouzet, Francois, A university besieged: Nanterre 1967–69, *Pol. Science Quart.*, June 1969, **34**, No. 2, pp. 328–50.

[2] Their students and ours, Editorial, *New Statesman*, 19 April 1968.

[3] *Ibid.*

[4] Hanson, P., Ideology and the New Left. *New Society*, 26 December 1968.

sions with officials of the National Union of Students. An agreement was reached which provides for a degree of student participation in university management and decisions relating to curricula.[1] Discipline will be modified as a response to the students' demands that they be treated as persons of maturity.

Geoffrey Martin, then President of the NUS, declared the agreement to be the first of its type in Britain or any country. (A separate agreement is expected between students and the Scottish universities.) The joint statement issued lays down the principle that on curricula and management "the ultimate decision must be that of the statutorily responsible body", but it assumes that "the students' views should be properly taken into account". It suggests the establishment of new committees bringing together students and university staff members, and said that students should be represented on governing bodies, participating even in questions of examination methods.

The Committee of Vice-Chancellors represents the administrative heads of all the British universities. The Committee Chairman was Dr. D. G. Christopherson, Vice-Chancellor of the University of Durham (one of the universities here under survey).

> The agreement was negotiated during the summer recess and was made public on the eve of the fall university session:
>
> The negotiations stemmed from student demands, often backed by violent demonstrations, during the spring and early summer. Student groups had threatened militant action if they were ignored.
>
> In contrast to student militancy in Continental Europe, most of the demonstrations in Britain concentrated on educational complaints and had very little political content. One violent demonstration against the war in Vietnam that was staged outside the United States Embassy here last March was not organised by the National Union of Students, to which the vast majority of students belong.
>
> Mr. Martin said at a news conference that he doubted the agreement would be acceptable to "the revolutionary flank". But he said he thought the great majority of union presidents at individual universities would be able to start negotiations at their institutions within its framework.
>
> The agreement gives a great lift to the status of the student union. It is now negotiating an agreement with local education authorities to meet the complaints of students at technical colleges and art schools about the value of their courses.
>
> The fact that the university authorities accepted in principle most of the demands of the students indicates how deeply they were shaken by the demonstrations and rowdyism at some of the universities, especially newer ones.[2]

---

[1] *Student Relations*, Vol. 1, Report from the Select Committee on Education and Science, Session 1968-9, HMSO, London, 1969.

[2] British students to get more say, *New York Times*, 9 October 1968.

This development seems particularly enlightened and should bring about reforms in institutional controls *if it is acted upon.* By relieving the pressure of demands and frustration of students it does clear the way for further discussions and developments to take place by legitimate channels, officially sanctioned. In this move the NUS may be seen as taking the role of trade union as chief negotiating body meeting on responsible and respected footing with "the bosses". In a sense the methods of industrial democracy have begun to move into the academic world, but given the societal and academic changes outlined this seems no bad thing.

The radical militants will no doubt criticise the move, and will most certainly see it as a threat to their aims since it removes many of the more controversial issues on which they seek "confrontation". Now that the agreement of the liberals is drawn up it must push the militants into a position of increasing irrationality. While placating the majority of students, the new agreement and new climate of opinion may push militant students to further extremes of illegitimate action is seeking "confrontation". The militants in so doing would, however, find fewer fellow students willing to justify violence. In this situation we may begin to see British left-wing militants explicitly allying with radical societal and labour movements in attempts to gain support and also to espouse other ongoing causes. This is only speculation; we must wait for the outcome.

Certainly, however, the British student movement has taken a unique path and may well prove, as have other historical events, that the British have little taste for revolution.[1]

A variety of student revolts and rebellions have been discussed in some detail as they relate to changes which have taken place in society and in universities and in relation to changes which students with varying degrees of committedness demand to see. Some of the organisational features have been discussed in the course of the analysis, but clearly, if we are to try to draw together our findings, we should have some kind of framework within which to set historical events.

---

[1] At its annual conference in Nov. 1969 the National Union of Students, under its new president, Mr. Jack Straw, pledged its 400,000 members to a programme of political and community action in which students will work towards solution of social problems. At the same time it seems that demonstrations in Britain are decreasing. Twenty-three demonstrations were reported in *The Times* in 1969 compared with 48 in 1968 and these were mainly "small" incidents. The only universities with more than one incident were Essex and LSE. Devlin, T., Student fires begin to die down, *Times Ed. Supp.,* 26 Dec. 1969.

It would appear, indeed, from what has been said, that there are some broad general conclusions which we can draw which may be applicable whenever we find similarly structured situations and which may therefore have some predictive power. These will be presented rather briefly: it is beyond the scope of this chapter to elaborate very fully.

Firstly, we have seen that universities represent very special interstitial control zones in that a certain amount of criticism and dissension is encouraged within the situation, and that this is tolerated—even licensed—within the society at large. In this way more widespread damage of a militant younger generation is avoided. The *cyclone* zone of limited hurricanes was mentioned. In a sense the universities represent points by structural weakness within the fabric of social controls, thereby serving both as a weak spot and a focus of disorder. This serves a purpose because it keeps youthful protest concentrated and allows it to work itself out relatively harmlessly (for society though not for the institution). Destruction of university property, for instance, is destruction on a very limited scale. It is worth remembering that students represent the most able and intelligent members of the next generation and are those from whom succeeding élites will be recruited. They are valuable to society and at the same time a threat to society. Therefore containment of youthful high spirits and reformism helps to "neutralise" their effect and prepare the young for reintegration into the existing order. It is when dissension spreads outside the campus that society is threatened. This has always been so since universities have existed.

There are special factors in recruitment of authority figures within the institution. As has been remarked, "academics are the last people in the world equipped to cope with a revolution". The autonomy of the university in society affects both selection and self-selection of faculty and administrators. Scholars in the past have been typically withdrawn from the demands of social and political involvement by virtue of their intellectual concerns and lengthy training. The situation is changing in that junior faculty are increasingly recruited who are involved in social and political events and movements outside the university. However, one must take account of the time lag which it takes to replace faculty and administrators. The time lag of turnover for faculty overall is very much longer than that for students. Consequently the nature and demands of the students and the "character" of the institution change long before the faculty does; there is an even longer time lag involved in the turnover of principals, presidents, and administrators who have been recruited from faculty of a previous generation. There may at times be a three-generation institution gap between the highest authority and the students. Those junior faculty nearer the students in age and experience usually have no power in the institution and therefore are able to add little to the "climate" of authority.

This, then, is the general setting of the university into which is fed the human input but at different speeds and rates of change. These interlocking time variables are crucial to our understanding of the structure but have never been really accounted for or plotted.

The authority reaction to student unrest must be seen in relation to what we shall call the Boyle's law effect of universities. Boyle's law states that for gases, pressure times volume is always constant for the same temperature. If we take the volume to be the volume of students within the institution, which in most cases today is expanding at an ever-increasing rate, and take the pressure to be the strength of control of sanctions exercised by the authorities over the students, we begin to see the analogy. The container itself is the institutional structure—both socially and physically. The "temperature" is the social climate within which institutional changes are set, such that the external temperature clearly affects both the student masses and the administration. Thus we have the analogy of various organisational variables as they interact to product various effects. Explosion—or student revolt—will occur under various conditions relative to the build-up of pressure.

If the volume of students increases and the pressure of authority is not gradually released, the institution will be placed under strain. If, then, the external temperature rises, explosion may result. If the authority reaction to either internal unrest or external "hotting up" of tension is to increase pressure on students, explosion may similarly result. Sharing of power may be regarded as perforation of the pressure mechanism which allows gases to escape, releases the pressure, and cools the temperature.

What has not been recognised before is that a too rapid release of pressure of authority will result in an explosion inwards, with equally disastrous results. This may be equated with authority, and abrogation of responsibility and failure to give a clear sense of direction to those in the institution. That explosions have been created as often by undue weakness of authority as of repressive strength is clear from our examples. Similarly, if the authority lead given is inconsistent, that is a clamping down and letting up of pressure alternately, there is danger of internal friction which will increase temperatures and risk danger of explosion. The inconsistent reactions of faculty to Black demands at Cornell which went hand in hand with extremism of students, gun carrying, and violence, is an example.

Whatever happens, equal, steady pressure must be applied or released—anything else creates undue strain and tension.

It is at this point which the author will suggest that many of the reactions of older and more senior, rather than junior, faculty have been to react in panic or to give the students everything they demand as a gesture of appeasement. In the early days of revolt perhaps the junior faculty did align with students as symbols and champions of their own marginality and desire for change. This will be increasingly less true as the students' demands become more extreme, irrational, and hysterical. In time the student militants may alienate the support of the junior faculty, who were with them at the beginning when their demands seemed to promise benefits for all. At the same time, older and senior faculty will capitulate, often to outrageous demands, just for the sake of restoring some kind of order. More senior faculty who negotiate out of fear do so because they do not understand students;[1] junior faculty have recently been students themselves and are less likely to be intimidated. Also one must consider that senior faculty fear to be considered old fogeys—junior faculty are young enough not to be worried by such fears. Junior faculty speak the language of the young but have crossed the barrier to the "outside". As senior faculty appear to become more liberal, junior faculty will appear to become more conservative.

In effect, as we have seen, where senior faculty respond to students inconsistently or with obvious fear they repeat what students have learned to despise in their own parents and therefore invite symbolic "parricide". On the other hand, as we have also seen, a consistent authoritarian figure will be similarly despised—but for different reasons. Certainly we may relate these issues to middle-class family structures from which students come, but we cannot understand group reactions outside the organisational framework. A firm but flexible and truly democratic father figure will always invite respect. If the authorities are not sure of themselves and their policies, how can they expect either students or other faculty to do so? In the past persons have hidden behind status—there is nowhere to hide now. The students demand that they be able to respect their faculty and administrators as men and women—which really seems an advantage if true learning is to be developed.

---

[1] Students have been aggravated by the "theoretical liberals" of the classroom, who do not put ideals into practice.

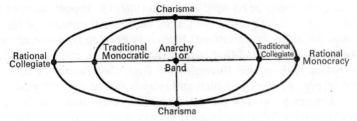

FIG. 15.1. Curvilinear model of organisational change in changing societies.

Junior faculty have less status to hide behind so that there are fewer protective shields between them and students—a better communication link from the first. In addition, whereas senior faculty are often near retirement, junior faculty who wish to remain in universities will have to live with whatever changes are brought about for the next 40 years. It is of more than hypothetical interest to them what will be established for years to come.

It would seem that in future the generation gap of misunderstanding between students and the authorities will widen, the groups polarise, and that any hope for rapprochement will lie with the 30-year-olds[1] (significantly late twenties are in their many "establishment" student leaders). Universities would do well to utilise junior faculty much more in negotiations, and to use them to build a bridge (ideologically, culturally and socially) over the gulf which threatens to swallow up the universities. (The Marxist analogy of the role of the *petit-bourgeoisie* is not without point.) It would be interesting to correlate existing status and demographic structures of institutions with amount of unrest.

Of course, we have seen that what goes on in the university cannot be abstracted from the changes going on in society. If we observe Fig. 15.1, which represents a curvilinear change model[2] of society, we may observe possible change paths in organisations and societies as a-historical

[1] The author was delighted (Dec. 1969) to see this prediction being fulfilled for instance by the election of a 30-year-old sociology assistant lecturer, Rolf Kriebich, as *Rektor*, or Vice-Chancellor of the Free University of Berlin. He was elected by a committee of faculty, students and employees. Conservative professors predict chaos. The author is more sanguine.

[2] Abbott and Oromaner, *op. cit.* Marion, J. Levy (Jr.), Professor of Sociology and International Affairs at Princeton University, has criticised this model and pointed out that it is geometrically incorrect. At the risk of exposure to further criticism while the model is being rethought the author hopes she will be forgiven for including it in this book as a starting point for discussion.

processes which may be equated to system time. The model suggests that
although society is at present typified by the rational monocratic form of
organisation, other organisational types may develop concurrently without being "deviant", and that bureaucracy is not an end state in itself.
Universities have moved through time from the traditional collegiate
model of organisation (in which authority is shared through traditional
personal means) towards the rational monocratic structure in which
authority is pyramidical and statuses are delegated according to rules. Student revolts represent an attempt on the part of the students to push the
institution towards a rational collegiate structure in which authority is
shared according to explicit rules. The model suggests that there is no
direct way to accomplish this without the institution moving through a
period of disruption, ambiguity, and emergence of charismatic leaders.
It is significant that all the charismatic leaders have been on the side of the
students so far. We must now await the emergence of charismatic leaders
who represent the older generation though not necessarily "established"
authority. Of course one structural reaction to anomie and charisma may
be for the authorities to attempt to reassert the monocratic bureaucracy,
which may bring its own threat of revolt against authoritarianism.

As one may see from the model, as the charismatic leaders appear there
is a threat of anarchy, but usually charisma is routinised and embedded in
a new organisational form. How long the charismatic period lasts may
relate to the pressure oscillations mentioned in relation to the Boyle's law
effect.

These, then, are some of the push–pull forces involved in student reaction and counteraction, and in their activities we see an attempt to move
to a form of organisation—even society—which many alienated students
regard as inherently more satisfying. They are fighting for something as
well as against it. This is developed in Chapter 16.

Against this background we should now consider the possible paths
which student disturbances may take in relation to these institutional
and societal forces. To this end the author has devised what she calls the
"Snakes and Ladders of Student Revolt". This chart of organisational
alternatives is presented as Fig. 15.2.

Disturbances may follow any of the paths indicated (following the
arrows) depending on the constraining actions of authority (which cool
temperature or reduce pressure or redirect gases) and on the explosive
actions of students. In a sense it represents a map of possible escalations
and de-escalations. A move to the left is a "win" for established authority

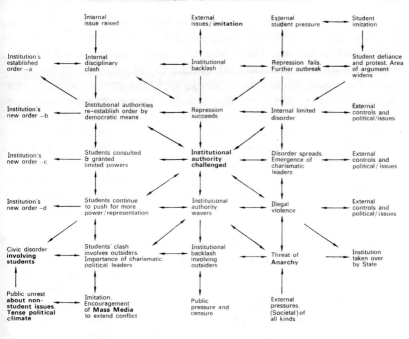

1. a,b,c,d - represent different kinds of Institutional Organisation which incorporate to a greater or lesser extent student participation in University government
a-d represents a progressive increase in student participation

2. "External controls" - may include societal legal sanctions and/or police intervention, and/or other uses of force

FIG. 15.2. Snakes and ladders of student revolt.

although the authority structure may change, as may the whole social order. The institutional orders are ranked in increasing liberality in the figure, (a)–(d). A move to the right is a "win" not for students *per se* but for militancy and disorder. External political issues may enter the institution from the right and spread the conflagration. Imitation may enter the process at any point but is more likely at certain points than at others.

The central point of the whole process is the challenge to authority—for that is what student unrest is all about. The particular course run by any disturbance and the particular outcomes will of course depend on the number and characteristics of contending groups, the strength of their convictions and the methods they use to further their ends. It will also depend, as we have seen, as much upon what they *think* they are doing, and what they *think* is being done to them, as upon what may be said to be actually happening. This is why information, or lack of information, about the motives and methods of the other groups taking part is so central an issue. We have seen how lack of "perceptual mesh" of what the struggle is all about can lead to a spiralling effect of situations, in which rebellion or repression is an often unintended or certainly un- planned consequence. Thus students are correct when they underline the problems created by non-communication or limited communication. Limited communication is almost more misleading than non-communi- cation and can lead to all kinds of differing definitions of the situation. As in the interpersonal *interstitial situation*, where ambiguity and ambiva- lence exist, stress, anger, embarrassment and avoidance can result—or even physical hostility.

Of course it cannot be denied that even when the contending parties are fully informed there is often a real divergence of interests which causes conflict. However, it is necessary to separate out those instances of con- flict which result from lack of clarity in the situation and those which result from direct opposition of recognised interests. Both these contin- gencies are comprehended by Fig. 15.2 since it is a progression of *actions* and not intentions. It is also worth noting that redefinition of the situation by the contending parties will take place at each stage and that therefore the possibility of misinterpretation is reintroduced at each stage. It seems fairly clear from a number of instances that the role of the *audience* either through the mass media to the general populace, or as played by decision makers of the mass media (e.g. editors, programme planners, producers), does affect both the performance and the definition of the situation by the participants and may increase misinterpretations. For all we know it may even affect the intentions. Students have been known to time disturbances for the six o'clock news. The researcher herself heard students in a New York College discussing revolt and its possibilities. The idea was dropped because the students said "we'd never make the newspapers, like Princeton and Harvard". This is not to say that all student activists consciously gear their activities to a particular audience —but clearly this must play a part in many cases. The techniques of revolution are so much more effective when played on the larger stage.

The author has noticed personally that the information and literature of militant groups are geared to particular audiences and with different aims. In a black student demonstration, for instance, certain general handouts directed against white faculty used emotive language—such as "vipers in the grass"—and contained dark threats against those who opposed the setting up of a Black Studies Department. On the other hand, memoranda and statements of intent issued to faculty a few days later at a faculty meeting called to debate the matter formally were very reasoned and restrained. The students won their department. It appeared that the first set of literature had been directed more towards the black students themselves to bolster their courage in the confrontation to enhance solidarity and to present a united front to outsiders. Hence the clarion call —an emotional response. In the later formally organised meeting Black students were able to present their real demands, and to offer them in a reasoned argument which would appeal to faculty. Had the faculty misread the black students' appeal for some kind of emotional as well as reasoned response the situation could have "broken" into open conflict. It is at just such *sensitive* points in the dialogue between groups that the audience of mass media can make or mar a developing situation. The need for news does sometimes override the needs of the newsworthy and where conflicts are magnified by publicity—in the nature of the self-fulfilling prophecy they do become magnified. This therefore is another variable in the situation.

The model in Fig. 15.2 incorporates some of the variables involved which push or pull the situation various ways. The existing structure of the university (order *a*) is the starting point so that different decisions will be made with that at *a* and may have different effects in different institutions. The characteristics of protagonists will clearly enter into the situation in relation to differing degrees of acceptance or rejection of solutions offered. The progressive series of orders (*b, c, d,* etc.) represent relative increases in student participation and thus a move from monocracy to collegiality as in Fig. 15.1. These moves may be achieved peaceably and legally, or violently and illegitimately. At each stage there is the possibility of outside intervention which, in terms of the Boyle's law effect, increases pressure and the danger of explosion. Physical violence resulting from police "busts" of student demonstrations are most likely to spread the conflagration to the rest of society. Other influences are outside political issues, imitation and student solidarity movements—which as it were *boost* any activity. Once again the mass media may contribute to the situation, providing sources of information about what is happening or what is intended by and to the contending parties. The opinions of power figures in mass media may therefore remould the perception of the situation, and thus its eventual consequences in particular ways.

Everything which has been discussed in terms of Boyle's law effect, organisational change and snakes and ladders of student revolt has been designed *not* to imply any judgements of right and wrong, of justified or unjustified actions on the part of any of the contending groups. Particular sequences of social action only have been suggested and in particular social situations the actors and audience must decide the morality themselves.

This lack of judgement upon generalised categories of actors applies also to their characteristics as conformers or nonconformers to particular social orders. It is not always right to conform, nor wrong to dissent—and this applies to *all* kinds of groups. Thus we might say that, in terms of student cultures, nonconformist culture is most likely to grow among middle-class members of a "working-class" university so perceived; among working-class members of a middle- and upper-class university particularly if collegiate; and among middle-class students in a middle-class university where those students represent a socioeconomic rather than educational or cultural middle class. This is not to make any value judgements, but to note certain structural propensities.

If as one activist notes "the objective of University life must remain the pursuit of academic excellence"[1] student militants would do well, as he and others have done, to turn their attention to some positive rethinking of the content of university courses, of curricula and of teaching methods —so that the academic experience may be made truly rewarding, for teachers and taught. In this the student leaders *must* give a lead, and it is to the credit of the National Union of Students that moderate leadership has seen great gains for students as a whole, and may successfully implement student action in community affairs with the approval of a "committee representing every sort of political opinion which unanimously declined to take an anti-student back lash line".[2] In the student snakes and ladders of revolt reason does sometimes prevail.

[1] Crouch, Colin, The role of student power, *New Statesman*, 31 Oct. 1969.
[2] M.P.s and the campus revolt, *New Statesman*, 17 Oct. 1969.

CHAPTER 16

CONCLUSIONS DRAWN
AND PROBLEMS UNSOLVED

THE book started with an examination of social class characteristics of
students in three particular British institutions, and we have moved
through various stages of analysis to show the part played by these
characteristics and student awareness of them in student interpersonal
relations. In order to understand those relations we have had to study
the intra-institutional constraints which operate to adjust the structural
distances involved between persons and groups. In turn we have been
compelled to take account of inter-institutional and extra-institutional
constraints in addition, and are eventually confronted with the need to
understand the social movements which are going on in contemporary
society. These social movements comprehend student political movements
within them, but student movements are only one small aspect of social
and educational changes with, which societies are currently trying to
cope. This takes us back to the begining of our argument—as put forward
in Chapter 1—that the social characteristics of the students, and their
attendant modes of behaviour, will change as the structure of society
changes. It is a circular process—reflecting the relation between thinking,
acting man, and the constraints of his social environment. The student is
restricted in his area of social choice by his past experience and present
social position—as we have constantly seen, but he is, as are all social
beings, an active element in the structure rather than a passive container
of outside influences. Individual interpretation and choice in turn affects
the pattern of future constraints by being a part of them. This is how
social change comes about—in education as in any sphere of life. Students
are a product of their social environment; they are also able, consciously
or unconsciously, to produce changes within the social environment.
Therefore, although in a class society we must understand the socioeconomic constraints upon student behaviour, we must also be aware of
the impact of constraints within the educational structure upon the socio-

economic structure of groups. Our studies of social mobility are particularly pertinent here.

It has been thought proper on a number of issues to move out from the study of constraints operating in three institutions to a more general view of student relations and student behaviour. This attempt to draw general conclusions on the basis of particular cases was seen to be justified, where evidence supported it, because it has been the aim to study principles of structure rather than unique historical, geographical, or temporal circumstances. Thus the last chapter on student rebellion is a departure from the techniques used elsewhere in the book because it deals with particular happenings of contemporary interest and importance in a rather more historical and descriptive manner than will be found in other chapters. This was undertaken not only in order to set the findings on student behaviour in a broad social context, but also in order to show, however vaguely, the relation between the structural constraints discussed within the institution and some of the social processes which are going on in society. The relation of the structural and dynamic processes is imperfectly made here for a number of reasons, although it is hoped that there is something of usefulness in it. Firstly, the events discussed are too recent for their significance to have been properly digested, and at this time the British movements are so far mainly documented in press reports and student handouts. This material is direct, but is naturally biased and may not bring out specific points in which the sociologist would be interested. Secondly, the author has not been able to make personal observation of any of the events outside the local manifestations of the student strike on overseas fees on 22 February 1967. To have observed and to investigate the viewpoints and characteristics of those involved would have necessitated a fresh piece of research and another book. The discussion is, therefore, to some extent impressionistic and unsystematic, with some huge gaps in the source data. Nevertheless, it was thought that it would be better to write a somewhat unfinished kind of chapter on student movements rather than to ignore them altogether. These dynamic aspects do, after all, add a new perspective to our picture of student behaviour.

Thirdly, in order to analyse in any scientific way the interrelation of internal structure and external social processes, the author would need to examine in detail the particular aspects of structure of the universities *involved* in order to see whether the general principles can be upheld. Some attempt at analysis has been made on the evidence at hand and a cross-comparison made between institutions, but clearly this is in many ways unsatisfactory. The author believes the conclusions to be valid but regrets being unable to prove them on this particular point. (Similarly, the model of institutional socialisation is somewhat tentative and needs further testing.) However, a number of points can be inferred from the evidence available, and it is interesting to note, for instance, that the Radical Students' Alliance caught hold in Newcastle but not in Durham or Edinburgh. Knowing what we know about the social composition of these institutions, we could assume that it is not just a matter of personnel but of structure. On the other hand, the fact that the new universities, as, for instance, York and Essex, are active members of the RSA shows that there may be other structural features at work which we could not properly account for in the three universities studied. Relative age or establishment of the institution may be a factor here since this may affect both selection and self-selection of personnel (staff as well as students).[1] The three universities studied are *all* comparatively old so that this factor would not emerge as relevant. Then there is the distribution and preponderance of faculties, particularly where there is a heavy weighting to social science. We have noticed the influence of faculty distribution and organisation of the three universities, but there are generally too many faculty divisions for any one to emerge as overridingly important. In the small new university, without its full complement of faculties, particular faculties may emerge as influential. This is especially true if staff are young and go-ahead. The order in which faculties were established also emerges as important, and this again introduces the time factor which is levelled out in old-established universities. If the life span of the university is only three or four years, then what happens from month to month will be crucial for future development. Therefore not only is the distance threshold lower, but the time and sequence threshold is also concomitantly lower. This has to be taken account in our weighting of the importance of various factors.

Thus in York, for instance, the importance of residential colleges in the transmission of a middle-class culture is overridden in some activities by the factors of youth and smallness and the preponderance in age and size of the social sciences. These factors bring to the fore certain radical tendencies and have brought the students into conflict on occasion with

[1] It is true, for instance, that average ages of academic staff in new universities is generally younger than in older universities. This immediately gives the institution a youthful radical climate.

the cohesive paternalism of the institution.[1] This kind of "rebellion" against pressures to conform was, however, found in Durham, with similar consequences, although not identical causes. On the other hand, the contact between groups encouraged by the institution in York, coupled with its size, does seem to produce rather more harmonious social class relations than is found elsewhere, and this supports the other university findings. However, there are departmental differences, and it would be necessary to investigate the nature of internal groups and divisions in order to show exactly why this is so. The lack of rigid hierarchy is another factor in internal social relations which minimises tensions in certain areas and creates them in others—and this would need to be accounted for.

In informal observation and comparison of other universities with the three surveyed in this book, it has become clear that while the general principles seem to hold in a variety of different cases, the specific social consequences cannot always be properly explained without viewing particular factors within the whole context and structure of factors. The weightings attributed to the factors have not been properly worked out because it appears that the relative weightings differ with context or the way in which factors are combined. Thus a comparison of social class relations in institutions of comparable age, or size, or class composition will tell us nothing where these factors are treated independently. It is clear that a sophisticated set of measurements must be worked out if the model is to be universally and precisely applicable. At the moment it presents only a crude approach to kinds of influences and consequences and not necessarily to their extent. This use of measurement can only come with further use and refinement of the model.

If we examine briefly what has happened to the universities studied since the survey we find a remarkable lack of violent change and revolution. On the other hand, the disturbances which have taken place do reflect what has been concluded about the structure of social relations and of institutional authority. Newcastle University has been active in the Radical Students' Alliance and in radical students' movements in general. Of the three universities, Newcastle University exhibits most involvement with external political movements and issues, and its left-wing students are most organised. This relates to what we have said of

[1] Where the two goal systems exist uncompromisingly side by side over time one might expect signs of anomic or disintegrative behaviour of those who ascribe to neither system.

the perceived "common-man" image of the University, its relation to external urban influences, and its strong Students' Union. It must also be remembered that material living conditions are worse for students in Newcastle than in the other two universities. The urban areas are often depressing and flats are quite often substandard. This state of affairs is by no means peculiar to Newcastle—all overcrowded university towns have this problem. At one point, for instance, Leeds University had to house new students temporarily in a sports pavilion.

For a variety of reasons, students are often treated in the same way as coloured immigrants by estate agents and landladies. This discrimination against students in "good" housing areas tends to lead to the formation of student ghettos in large towns with the same effect on material conditions and morale of students—Black and White—as for coloured minorities. The justification then of potential landlords and landladies in refusing to rent to students is that used against the coloureds—as "they live like pigs", etc. This assessment overlooks the conditions in which students were forced to live in the first place, which may not have encouraged cleanliness and tidiness. There is no doubt that some landlords make much money out of renting to students who, after all, are a captive minority during their course of study. In some areas students represent the new poor. This is true of students from all social backgrounds. It is no wonder that bad material conditions, coupled with overcrowded working conditions, produce a revolutionary fervour among the students on their own behalf: and in identification with the struggle of the Anciens Pauvres who, unlike the students, have no possibility of escape. Students then may identify with societal causes because of the conditions they find themselves in at university—if they are working class in frustration, and if middle class in idealistic experimentation. Although we have heard much of the "bourgeois students' revolution" (which, incidentally, as in Edinburgh is more thought of than performed, and tends to be linked with increasingly élitist rather than socialistic postures), it is evident that bourgeois students tend not to revolt while their lives are comfortable and their consciences unpricked. The new universities, as we have suggested, constitute a separate category since they have many bourgeois students, pleasant conditions, and yet revolutionary fervour. For reasons outlined, the new universities start by being radical and involved with societal causes. However, the student causes do not always capture the imagination of the workers. One student group in the University of Essex, for instance, trying to enlist the support of workers on a nearby building site, were fought off with snow balls and told to get back to work and stop wasting everyone's time, and the taxpayers' money.

Durham has remained largely quiescent despite the awakening of radical consciousness encouraged by the development of the social sciences, the establishment of an active Sociology Department (named very primly the Department of Social Theory and Institutions), the strengthening of the SRC, and the expansion in size. In a sense Durham is too far from the hub and mêlée of industrial life to borrow social motivation from its environment, and, as we have seen, its close-knit cohesion tends to prevent any but internal clashes. Internal issues may spread—as the snakes and ladders of student revolt (Fig. 15.2) clearly demonstrates—but external issues are less likely to inflame students. Also, as we have seen, the very complexity of organisation seems to provide its own checks and balances of control which delimit possible conflagration. Often students are too concerned with parochial matters of internal inequalities and power struggles to bother with external movements.

In terms of the earlier classification of British universities, students at Oxbridge and Oxbridge style universities seem to have to spend so much time putting their own house in order and in modernising organisation that they have less time to spend on revolutionary causes promoted by societal changes.

One factor which has been noted as influential in the promotion of student unrest and mobilisation is the development of a strong Students' Union with strong-minded student leaders. Where there is such a union, student power is centralised. It would seem that politicisation of the Union, as at the LSE, is an essential ingredient in rebellion or revolt. SRCs do not exist in all British universities but are, in general, the older institution and are found, for instance, in Scottish universities. The system of election of both representatives and leaders is different for the SRC and the Union—the Union often tending to be dominated by central interests because of election by direct vote and not by "constituency". When a ruling clique gets hold of union power it may monopolise the power machinery for some time; this is less possible in an SRC although it does sometimes happen. The analogy was made previously of the difference between the TUC and the House of Commons. The university authorities also differ in their attitudes to the two bodies, usually regarding the Students' Union Committee as less respectable or responsible and usually less representative of the student body as a whole than the SRC and its various sub-committees. Normally there are more constitutional links between the student government and university government where there is an SRC, than where there is a students' union; and where the two bodies exist side by side (as in Durham and Newcastle), the SRC is usually more highly regarded by the authorities (in other words it is itself more likely to be "establishment"). Sometimes unrest may be promoted by left-wing union leaders as a way of driving a wedge between the SRC and its electorate in the struggle for power.

It has been remarked that the Scottish universities have experienced far less student unrest than have universities south of the border, and this may be partly attributable to the structure of student government and representation which has been built in to the university statutes over a period of time. The relationship between student and university government is, as it were, established, though the nature of the mechanisms involved may have to be changed from time to time. The need for student consultation and representation was recognised by the Scottish universities long before the English universities, although it was brought about in a more gradual, evolving, and less heralded process, so that, despite the effects of expansion and the need constantly to revise the disciplinary proceedings (as seen in the Glasgow case discussed earlier), there really is less for the students to complain about in relation to their role in the university. Also it is quite obvious that the role of the student—and indeed of the scholar and academic—is more clearly defined in the Scottish universities than in the English, outside Oxbridge. As we have seen, revolt is often an attempt to restructure an ambiguous role or situation rather than to reject utterly a situation clearly defined. The constant need of left-wing students to force a confrontation shows there may not initially be one. In the Scottish universities there has always been a tradition of reverence for learning and scholarship—one shared by the Scottish populace. Learning rather than status must command its own respect.

It was thus possible for Professor Michael Swann, Vice-Chancellor and Principal of Edinburgh University, and himself a renowned and respected scholar, to say in his address to the General Council of the University on 27 June 1968 the following words:

> It is worth considering for a moment the philosophy that underlies the (current) thinking. There is a currently fashionable notion that everyone in a university, teachers and taught alike, are "students", from which it follows that all should join equally in decision making at every level. This sort of thinking you may say, can hardly weather the cooler intellectual climate north of the Border.

Nevertheless, there is a grain of truth in the contention. University teachers are students in that, like all good students, they spend much of their days and some of their nights, hacking away into the unknown. But there is one crucial difference, for whereas the teachers know a lot about their subjects, their students know rather little. This gap diminishes, of course, as the educational process advances, and may be said to close somewhere around the end of the postgraduate phase. But the plain fact of the matter is that, inadequate as we may be in other respects so far as our own subjects are concerned, we do know more, and we do know better than our students. And I believe we should have the courage to say so. . . .

Some people, particularly the intellectual left, see in the present student discontent the stirrings of a moral revolt against all the forms and consequences of advanced industrial society—capitalist and communist alike. And all of us, I suspect, if we examine our consciences, are dismayed at the misuses of science—the great force that promised so short a time ago to reform the world for us. We are dismayed at the vast impersonal management of our lives by government machines, even though the more mature of us recognise that the machine consists of myriads of people trying their best. And we are dismayed that so much goes wrong all over the world, despite so many good intentions.

The young are right to be concerned; but they are wrong to imagine that there is some short cut to a golden future. We have in the universities a compelling responsibility to bring home to our students the most painful lesson mankind has learnt throughout civilisation—that there is no short-cut.

It is only scientists, doctors, vets, and agriculturists—who have been trained with the full force of their very demanding disciplines—who can relieve suffering and help to end starvation. It is only men and women who have had the toughest education in the disciplines that impinge on man and on society in the Arts, the Social Sciences, in Law, and in Divinity—who can gain the knowledge and acquire the insight to make a fresh contribution to the appalling problems that beset us all over the world.

The best we can do therefore is to give our students the fullest, most rigorous education that lies in our power. The best they can do for the generations to come is to learn all they possibly can from us. As educators we must help them to stand at the level of our own eyes in the hope that they will then see further than we can and do better than we have done. But we help no one if we allow them to imagine for one moment that there is some quick way of doing better than all the great minds of the past. There is not.[1]

Professor Swann admitted that his views might appear reactionary, but argued that there was actually much tacit agreement among students with these views. He further argued for student criticism, while against student decision-making on academic matters. He favours student representation on non-academic committees (of which there already is a great deal) and consultation on academic committees, while recognising that in other universities demands for representation are as high as

[1] The Principal's address in the report of the meeting of the General Council of the University of Edinburgh, January 1969, pp. 10, 13, 14.

50 per cent on every university committee. Various groups, he says, have an interest in the running of the university.

> Some can criticise by virtue of paying the bills; others by virtue of particular knowledge, interests or experience. But we ought to remember that students do not pay the bills, that their knowledge though growing is limited, and their experience is slight. It is only their immediate interest and involvement that are great, and even these are transitory. On balance I think they have just as much but no more entitlement to attention on major issues than many other groups.

In addition Professor Swann argued that student representation for instance on the Senate should not be brought about; firstly, because it would be sham representation, and, secondly, because there ¦should be some decision-making body free from outside pressures of any kind student or otherwise, and that this is the essence of academic freedom.

As it happens, Edinburgh has only experienced one period so far of upheaval, and that was largely an internal issue. It did threaten to develop into something more but only because of the publicity accorded by the mass media. The measured and reasoned way in which the university authorities reacted to the situation, and the reform in internal organisational relationships which they instituted, helped to avert confrontation.

Mr. Malcolm Muggeridge, critic and television personality, elected by Edinburgh students as their Rector, resigned from his post of Rector of the University on 14 January 1968 amidst a blaze of publicity and public furore. Mr. Muggeridge argued that he could no longer represent the students since he disagreed with views expressed by student leaders on the SRC and in the student newspaper that the birth-control pill should be made available to all students free upon request. What started out as a youthful kite-flying and authority-testing enterprise became a *cause célèbre*; an opinion of a few made public was taken to represent the view of the majority. Somewhere the machinery of consultation and control had broken down. Public outcry stimulated by sensational reports did the rest. However, the authorities fortunately did not panic and used channels open to them to deal with problems of student government and journalism which had been raised. The University Court set up a committee under Mr. David West, one of the non-professorial Senate Assessors, to investigate the issues. The SRC was also asked to consult and debate.

> And at the end of the day, following the recommendation of the Committee, both the Court and the SRC have reaffirmed their faith in the rectorial system, and have agreed on a brief statement, to be given to future Rectors, which makes it clear that neither the Rector, nor the Rector's Assessor, are necessarily required to support student views, if they don't agree with them, but rather that they should

further student interests as they see them..... The Rectorship is an old, and pe
culiarly Scottish, institution. In spite of recent storms it has worked well and we-
intend to hold on to it.[1]

The election of a new Rector took place in November 1968.

As to the other issues involved—firstly, the fears of moral decay
were seen to be unfounded, and, secondly, the control of the student
newspaper was left in the hands of the SRC but under the supervision of
a small board with full powers to appoint and suspend. "And written
into the Constitution will be the National Union of Journalists' Code of
Ethics, slightly modified for the student context."

The outcome of this dispute and the way it was handled would seem
to suggest that Edinburgh University is by no means a likely seed bed for
violent unrest. However this may change in the future if, for instance, the
new student Amenities Centre being built becomes a centre for unioni-
sation.

After this brief survey of structure and trends one might say that it is
unlikely in the near future that the three universities studied will flair
into revolt on broad issues, but that if they do Newcastle is the most likely.
Unrest in Edinburgh would largely result from imitation or provocation
by small groups of the right or left. Edinburgh is most likely to experience
right backlash should left-wing agitation occur. The next General Election
in Britain could form a rallying point for action as did the last in 1966.
Of course, as in the Eugene McCarthy (1968) campaign in the United
States, most student activity was directed into established political channels
for change until it appeared this would not achieve its goal; then other
means of bringing about change were sought. This could happen again.[2]

It is clear that intra-institutional and extra-institutional pressures and
changes impinge on group structures and on decision-making machinery
constantly, but that the reactions to these differs with the institution.
The outcomes may be seen in the snakes and ladders of student revolt
(Fig. 15.2). As an example we may take the Edinburgh situation. The
position of the student newspaper has always been to some extent
ambiguous in relation to the parent body the SRC, and there have been
endless debates and disputes about editorial policy, often embarassing
to the SRC for years before the Muggeridge affair: that only crystallised

---

[1] Principal's address, *op. cit.*, p. 6.

[2] The low percentage of eighteen-year-olds registered to vote, as they are newly
qualified to do in Britain, could indicate that young people have lost faith in "establishment" radicals.

the issues. The student newspaper has always taken a radical position on everything, and in a sense represented a steam valve for dissidence in the student body. This was expected and accepted by the university authorities who have never tried to exercise direct control—and did not do so after the Muggeridge affair. Yet the freedoms of the press had been from time to time overstepped, and in November 1967, for instance, as Professor Swann points out: "the back page spread invited readers to try LSD and got the dosage 5 to 10 times too high." Naturally, hysterical national press reports followed on from the events outlined, and served to panic some members of the university and arouse public ire—particularly among local churchmen and civic leaders. Had constitutional supports been lacking, had the authorities wavered, or in terms of the Boyle's law effect had they taken repressive measures such as a takeover of the student newspaper, or had the students allied a free speech movement to some external political cause, we might have seen a Scottish Berkeley. But none of these things happened—reason prevailed and revolt was averted. Coupled with this, certain long-needed redefinitions of internal relationships were brought about and, if anything, the power of the SRC and of the Rectorship strengthened. The outcome of the Muggeridge affair was in reality a triumph for a certain kind of constitutional government. As in all university situations we should ask not why issues should from time to time flair up into prominence, but why the structure of some institutions allows possibility of conflagration to be averted.

On the other hand, we cannot analyse the situation completely without taking into account the nature of the human input in terms, for instance, of the social class of students (and, of course, of faculty and administrators). We have seen that Newcastle gains much of its industrial radicalism from assumed working-class bias which derives from distribution rather than proportions of social classes. Yet in that situation the working-class students are able to move into certain power positions. Not so in Edinburgh, where in general the working-class students are an anomic and alienated minority. Now should the situation in Edinburgh change in such a way that either the proportion of working-class students greatly increased, or should those already there seek actively to restructure their position, particularly in relation to the power structure of the university, we might well see the emergence of further student unrest. However, we have to account for the further factor in the Edinburgh situation that most working-class students live at home and that students living at home are less likely to participate in full scale rebellion. Indeed, in terms of the Trow students culture classification, most of the Scottish working-class students at Edinburgh would come into the consumer/vocational culture category. It is usually those in the nonconformist culture category who start revolutions.

On the other hand, as we have seen, a growing proportion of students from every social class wants to move away from the impersonality of the bureaucratic education machine towards meaningful and personally rewarding learning situations, and in this they are joined by an increasing number of disenchanted faculty. But change can be brought about without violence. If we look again at Fig. 15.1 (p. 527) we see that he only way for the university to pass gradually from an organisational form of rational monocracy to a rational collegiate organisation is through a period of charismatic leadership. However, this period may be so short that the impact is hardly noticed by the institution, and is accomplished without great upheaval. However, it does suggest that there must be persons in the institution who are willing to make a personal stand in order to restructure the power relations of the institution, and in this case who are willing to share power under stated rules. It is movement along the horizontal or vertical diameters which represents the rapid or revolutionary change. For instance, where students wish to move at once to a position of shared power in the institution—to the extent of 50 per cent representation on committees—they are trying to push the institution from rational monocracy to traditional collegiate structure without any intervening stages. This must lead to violence. In terms of the model any move of an organisation along an elliptical path in any direction represents developmental change which can be accompanied without violence; whereas movement along a linear vertical or horizontal path represents violent change—in fact change not possible without some violence. There is no backwards or forwards, no higher or lower order—only change. When these organisational changes are taken within the context of changing societies, which are complexes of organisations, we can begin to see some of the cross-pressures at work in student movements. Indeed, the principles at work in the model of change presented in Fig. 15.1. may be applied to changes in society as a whole—planned and unplanned.

It will have been seen in Fig.15.1 that various concepts have been utilised as developed by Max Weber[1], but they are related in a curvilinear

[1] Weber, Max, *The Theory of Social and Economic Organisations* (trans. A. M. Henderson and Talcott Parsons and ed. Talcott Parsons), Free Press, Glencoe, Illinois, 1947.

sequence which is a-historical and relates only to system time. It is impossible to discuss the change model presented at length, its conceptual bases, and antecedents. For further information see the paper already cited.[1]

Before we introduce the societal model of change in social class terms, let us discuss a few of the underlying principles in Fig. 15.1. This model of change has particular application for large-scale organisations. It is represented by twin interlocking ellipses. The left-hand ellipse represents the change path of organisations sharing the basic structural quality of shared power or authority; the right-hand ellipse represents the change path of organisations sharing the basic structural quality of centralised power or authority, often in the person of a supreme head. The left-hand ellipse, therefore, represents all structural variations of acephalous organisations with what Weber calls "collegiate" structure; the right-hand ellipse represents all structural variations of cephalous organisations with what Weber calls "monocratic" structure. The latter structure may or may not take the form of a pyramidical organisation—or may be a version of this form. It will be seen that in this twin typology, dimensions of authority and structure of positions are both included. This is further accentuated by the fact that the horizontal diameter of both ellipses represents respectively a developmental continuum from organisations in which positions of authority (or indeed all positions) are ascribed by "tradition" in terms of Weber's ideal type, to those in which positions are ordered by rational –legal means and are therefore achieved by possession of relevant criteria. In the left-hand ellipse, therefore, we have mapped an elliptical progression from Traditional Collegiate type organisations to Rational Collegiate type organisations. In the right-hand ellipse we have mapped a progression from Traditional Monocratic to Rational Monocratic although, since the process is curvilinear, the progression could be the other way.

It will be seen that the interlocking formation of these two change paths makes a central ellipse path which touches the outer ellipse in two parts. This central ellipse then represents that change path of all Traditional organisations between the types Monocratic and Collegiate or vice versa, while the outer ellipse represents the change path of all Rational organisations between the types Monocratic and Collegiate and vice versa. Any organisation will not only represent a point on one of these lines but will move continually between the "ideal type" points. (Of course different types of universities represent different points on

[1] Abbott, J. and Oromaner, M. J., A curvilinear model of organisational change in changing societies, unpublished manuscript.

the ellipses.) These "ideal types" stand in a linear *and* a curvilinear relationship to one another: Weber, as far as one can ascertain, posing only a linear relationship. The ideal types are points respectively furthest from the centre of each of the three ellipses, so that they represent the most extreme logical combination of structural dimensions. All other organisations will be scattered at different distances from the centre, mean, or focus as they move along the line. The direction of the movement can take place in any direction or any ellipse between the types. (Therefore no form of organisation can be regarded as a "deviation"—just a variation.)

It will be noted that it has not been necessary to speak of bureaucracy *per se*, this is because it becomes more precise to use bureaucracy to describe only a staff of paid professional officers or administrators who may be associated with any kind of organisation. Such a staff will most likely be associated with rational organisations, particularly monocratic, but it is possible, for instance, to speak of a rational collegiate organisation with a bureaucracy. This makes more clear, the authors suggest, Weber's own distinctions and clarifications in this area and leaves the way open for discussion of a variety of "monocratic" organisations and a variety of complex organisations utilising bureaucracies. Bureaucracy therefore is taken as a translation of officialdom *per se* (more in keeping with Weber's own usage we suggest).[1]

Although charismatic authority is of necessity a "transitional" type which will become routinised, nevertheless it does represent an organisational type at the central intersection of the two ellipses, and in a sense is a response to changeover of organisational type.

The centre of the larger ellipse may be seen as the centre of the whole organisational process—the centre from which the organisational ellipses ripple outwards. This may be characterised as a point of anarchy, or a point representing the unstructured band. The further out an organisation is from this centre the more is it formally and rationally structured.

Obviously, anarchy, or breakdown into bands, is always a threat in rapid or violent change, and will be a greater or lesser possibility depending on the starting point for change. For instance, the May 1968 uprising of French students was characterised by more violence, in terms of both revolution and repression, than was, for instance, the sit-in at the LSE. If we look at the model we can explain this in terms of the organisational change path chosen. The French universities were notoriously

---

[1] Weber, *op. cit.*, pp. 332–7.

ierarchically organised, outdated in discipline, and—in comparison to he British and United States systems—élitist. One might therefore suggest hat the French universities were nearer the Traditional Monocratic ype than the British or American, which are nearer the Rational Mono-ratic type. Thus in terms of the change model, if students wanted to nove to a position of community—or Traditional Collegiate organisa-ion—then the only direct path was through a period of anarchy. For the 3ritish students to move the organisation of the university to either Traditional Collegiate of Rational Collegiate it is not necessary to have anarchy, only a period of unrest and charisma. Despite the destruction, n a sense the French students did achieve their objectives.

> The mandarins wring their hands—but also fight back. The students now enjoy an almost total liberty—they can study what they like, as hard as they like, and conduct as much activity as they like on the premises. But the lecturers and assistant lecturers have yet to win the same liberty. The autocracy of the "Patrons" was broken last May, but the old guard, which won its way to the top in the old days by clearing a long series of scholastic and administrative hurdles, is clinging to as much of its former authority as it can. . . .
>
> At the moment the communists are making the running at Vincennes. Elections of student representatives have been held in all the other universities in France, and the communists emerged as the dominant force.[1]

This quotation draws attention to some of the points made earlier and particularly to the structure and bases of authority and the interstitial position of junior faculty. The move to community has only partially been achieved, and there may thus be further violence; but for the moment student militancy has died down. And now the Ministry of Education and the university authorities are aware of the ineptitudes which last year drove the bulk of non-revolutionary students to rally to the militants. (Consider the Boyle's law effect.)

As we have seen, there is always the possibility that groups outside the university will be brought into the struggle and that rebellion will spread to wider sectors of the populace. This, of course, is exactly what radical groups such as Students for a Democratic Society are working for in that the changes they wish to bring about are not just in organisations in society but in the structure of society itself. For SDS, therefore, as for others, certain consequences are consciously aimed at which may happen in certain other circumstances by accident. The occurrence of outright revolt and violence may be one such outcome. The SDS recognises the

[1] Brogan, P., Left confronts left in French university struggle; progress of student power: 2, *The Times*, 18 June 1969.

university as the weakest point in the system, and the attack on the German universities has rendered them so

> vulnerable that they are creaking as if on the verge of collapse.
> Large parts of the student body are to the left of the Establishment, yet the SDS can only rarely play a clear leading role (as it did in Berlin). It operates rather as a catalyst, starting the process of rebellion over and over again. Nowhere can it impose its tactics on the students, let alone its revolutionary theses.[1]

More hangs upon revolutionary tactics if the order of the society is being attacked than if the order of the university is being attacked, and consequently there is more likelihood of violence. The likelihood is increased both by apathy, indecision, and abasement of those with power and authority, and alternatively by reactionary backlash and oppression. Either way students can shake the foundations.

> The moral self-abasement of a large part of the French literary and academic intellectual class in the face of the student "revolution" in May and June 1968 expressed a disposition which is to be found in nearly every Western country. The students have for the time being replaced the "working classes" at the highest point of the pantheon of the "progressive" intelligentsia.[2]

The self-abasement of authority is a necessary component of both revolt and violence in revolt, since it leads the revolutionaries to mistrust and despise. "Split, disunited, temporising, half-hearted authority which repeats against itself the charges made by the student radicals serves only to encourage more hostility."[2]

The argument and the criticism and the struggle is of power and the distribution of power, of inequality in power, resources, and life chances and is an attempt to restructure the existing relationships in organisations and in society itself one way or another, and to maximise the benefits of particular groups as they see them and believe them to be meaningful.[3] Let us then apply what we have been discussing to our societal model of change as it relates to inequality and power. All that we are doing is translating the underlying principles of structure of organisation

---

[1] The cult of violence. A special report from Germany prepared by editors and correspondents of *Der Spiegel*, in *Encounter*, May 1969.

[2] Shils, E., Plenitude and scarcity: The anatomy of an international cultural crisis. *Encounter*, May 1969, p. 47.

[3] As for instance the Worker–Student Alliance (a group well to the left of SDS) whose aim is to "organise people around the issues that oppress them", especially in relation to the "military/industrial gorgon which threatens both". See Sayre, N., *Upheaval at Harvard*, 16 May 1969.

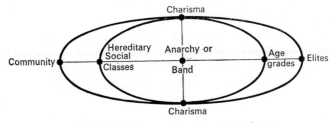

Fig. 16.1. Social class and organisational change

nto terms which are meaningful for our understanding of the prevailing order of society. Fig. 16.1 show social class and organisational change.

Figure 16.1 reveals the same organisational principles, in terms of power distribution, as we saw in Fig. 15.1. Traditional collegial structure is that in which power is shared on the basis of tradition and usually (as in preliterate societies) on the basis of age and sex. An age grade system usually therefore in the past has involved councils of elders, or gerontocracies. This is because to ageing are attributed certain desired qualities. However, in their attempts to return to an age grade system youth have sought to reverse the value placed on the qualities of youth and ageing—by asserting that power should be held by the juvenocracy and that "no one over 30 can be trusted." A structure of shared power in which positions are allotted by rational means is one of community—an ideal situation—and since it is rationally ordered, more akin to the voluntary association than to the community of birth and settlement.[1] This is the utopian kind of university and society for which students feel they are struggling, and they hopefully feel that one will follow from the other. The kind of society from which they want to move is that of hereditary social classes, the "traditional" form of inequality and monocracy, or from the more meritocratic but still unequal system of élites, which is encouraged by an élitist education system. It is readily apparent how organisational reform and societal reform are linked. Reference to the findings of the author's survey provide many examples. For instance, it is clear that working-class students would benefit from a more collegial structure of universities because they would then share not only in the power but in the institutional culture. This applies also and even more so to Black students.

[1] Hippie family "communes" represent an attempt to move to this kind of organisation—as groups in which everything is shared and held in common, but in which "family" members are chosen as well as born.

The spread of institutional influence would operate ultimately to the benefit of the universities as well as the society.

If the students appear unreasonable in their push to a juvenocracy the model would support this contention. It would be far quicker and less disruptive to push for community of benefit to all age groups. But because youth want to fight for their own kind of community they have chosen the harder road and may have to go through anarchy to get it, or, alternatively, may put the whole idea of community in jeopardy by their arrogance. But the young forget that although they may be fighting against the more traditional inequalities of social class and race, they may be seeking to set up a new system of inequalities based on age. Not only this, but since those involved are largely educated youth, they would perpetuate an élitist system different in kind from those which presently exist but in a sense more rigid because of the inevitability of ageing.

As the present survey shows, there are many deleterious effects of the class system in terms of individual life chances. However, the alternative with which we are confronted by student revolutionaries may not, in their present form, suggest that they have thoroughly formulated any workable solutions.

Let us now re-examine in conclusion, therefore the major findings about social class relations of students in the three universities studied and the structural model which was built up from these. (The structure however, cannot be reduced to a sum total of these relations.)

The author set out to prove that social class is a factor in social relations of students in the three universities studied, and indeed in social relations of students in similarly structured situations in other institutional contexts. The weight of the findings—both qualitative and quantitative—furnish ample proof that this is so. Not only this, but the material has suggested certain qualifications and conditions under which the findings are valid in a wider variety of contexts. Since the conclusions of any thesis are in a sense the beginning of the next—through problems raised and hypotheses suggested—implications of the findings for the study of social class will be discussed in conjunction with the conclusions drawn.

The first concern of the book—following on the findings of research into educational selection discussed in Chapter 1—was to discover whether social as well as academic selection is continuing at university entrance level despite overall increases in university places. Previous writers have come to the conclusion that social class differentials persist and that the working class is not taking its share of the expansion of educational opportunity. The "cultural" reasons for this have been discussed—reasons such as differential language use; role of gross material factors such as economic pressures, family size, and occupancy rate; differences in the social class value systems as expressed in the interest and encouragement of parents in their childrens' higher education. All these have their effect on academic achievement at each educational level.

What was found in the present survey was that far from the proportion of working-class students in the universities having increased in response to educational expansion, the proportion was slightly smaller than that previously estimated at 25–26 per cent by Glass and Kendall. The correspondence between these figures is interesting in that figures of Kendall and Glass refer to the proportion in the country as a whole, and the students studied are not necessarily a representative sample of it.

In addition a point not discussed before and which should be mentioned in this connection concerns the "unclassified" students of Durham and Newcastle. It may have been seen in many of the results that this category approximates most closely in many details and responses to the working-class sample, and it well may be that this particular category of those who would not or could not state father's occupation is comprised mainly of working-class students. If this were so, and because it is merely speculation, this has not been stated in the body of the thesis, then this would bring the percentage of working-class students up to the 25–26 per cent suggested previously.

Nevertheless, it is clear that there has been no vast expansion of working-class students on the scale which was hoped or feared at the end of the 1940's. The investigation of Durham University's register of admissions in fact revealed a declining proportion of working-class students since 1937—before the 1944 Act was passed. The greatest expansion there was experienced by the lower middle class who, since 1950, had comprised the majority of Durham students.

This finding is in accord with other and with those of earlier works on the subject, which show that it is the lower middle class which is taking advantage of the expansion in educational opportunity and which is growing in proportion to the other classes in the university. The author's theory of the cyclical expansion of social classes in the universities, on the basis of empirical evidence, outlines how this might take place.

The failure of the working class to take advantage of the expansion of educational opportunity and the reason for the corresponding expansion of lower middle-class students may be attributed to cultural factors at work at grammar school level, already discussed.

It is clear, therefore, that the working-class students who do succeed at university are to some extent atypical of the working class. How far they are atypical and how far they remain members of the working class while at university has previously been little discussed because the notion of atypicality seemed to preclude the idea of maintenance of social class traits. The thesis has attempted to discover what in fact the statistical social-class proportions within the student body mean (a) in terms of what they *are*, (b) in terms of what they *do*.

In fact, much has been assumed in the early stages of the argument of what the social classes *are* in order to discover what they *do*—or what part they play in students' social relations.

The problems of methodology involved in discovering the social class proportions—and what these proportions signify—will be discussed later in that these problems lead to a reappraisal of what we mean by social class in certain contexts.

However, within the limits which the researcher set herself—by taking as the primary index of social class of origin the occupational status of father—certain findings were made about the social classes as cultural groupings within the university. The fact that social class patterns emerged with regard to both characteristics of the students' family and of himself would seem to show that social classes as cultural collectivities do exist within the university framework despite the unconscious social biases of selection. These characteristics have regard to family size, education of siblings and of parents, and school education of the student himself—and these in turn are related to the socioeconomic position of the family and its life-style and value systems. These were discussed in Chapter 4.

The fact that cultural patterning is not always clear-cut along social class lines and that, for instance, sex differentials may at times predominate, shows that blurring of social class divisions may be dependent upon the presence of other variables in the situation. This has important implications for the study of students' social relations. The blurring is sometimes due to the predominance of dimensions of social class other than the socioeconomic—such as the educo-cultural—and this is touched upon in Chapter 5 in the discussion of students' motivation for coming to university and of their expectations of it in the light of their experience, information, and cultural background. The way in which the students react to university life is to some extent conditioned before they come, and this conditioning owes much to social class background.

The way in which students react to university life—to work and residence and to fellow students—is reflected in their participation within the student body in societies and organisations and in the degree in which they take responsibility for the running of student affairs. This affects the formal relationship which the social classes have with one another in the student body in terms of "interest" groupings particularly, and to some extent regulates the degree of contact by delimiting areas of cultural concentration. This was discussed in Chapter 6.

As we saw in Chapter 7, the effects of this "culture contact"—or lack of it—are acknowledged tacitly or explicitly by the students and expressed through daily contacts in social relations. Students have shown that they are influenced in choice of friends by considerations of social class, for instance, but this influence is defined by a complex set of dependent factors and upon the particular situation in which the students interact. In one situation the sex attribute may predominate in the definition of the situation; in another it may serve only to accentuate the relevance of social class. In yet another situation, geographical region of home residence may provide a bond and in another create a division reflecting social class differences. In all these situations a complex set of variables is at work in students' social relations which mask or accentuate the relevance of social class.

The brief theoretical discussion of the findings in Chapter 8 tended to underline the structural patterning of social class relations in terms of this complex configuration of variables revelant in differently defined social situations. The situation itself is a structure of relevant attributes, and what the author has called "situational space"—within which it is structured—is defined by the interaction of cultural and spatial factors which delimit the range of potential student contact. The situational space is that social area outlined by the relative spatial and cultural concentrations within a given context, and within the boundaries it sets the social situation is defined and enacted.

Degree of contact of the social classes has been seen to be one of the most important influences on their relations with one another and this has been analysed in the spheres of residence, work, and leisure. As has been discussed, the relative proportions of the social classes in terms of statistical size, the nature of overlapping social dimensions, and degree of contact of the social classes are those crucial conditions which regulate social relations and define situational space.

Chapters 9 and 10 have shown that the social classes are differentially distributed in faculties, i.e. in terms of work space—in residence—in terms of living space—and in societies and student organisation—or interest space. Indeed, it has been found that social and spatial distance are often closely allied, more working-class students living in digs rather than in halls; living out rather than in colleges; and living in spatially separate areas of the city—as in Newcastle. The spatial concentration leads to reduced contact of the social classes and accentuation of existing social class divisions and cultural differences. This has repercussions on the definition of situational space and on the relevance of social class as a factor in social relations.

Geographical attachments in terms of students' home residence express in turn both cultural and social class configurations and have especial relevance in certain situations. This is particularly true in a cosmopolitan university where local is equated with low status. In a local university the spatial dimension of local rather than the status dimension tends to be stressed.

This brings us to the discussion of the totemic features of the university which affects the perception of the total context within which social class relations are set. Factors of urban setting and locality ties are seen as part of the university "image". We have seen how this may lead to an erroneous assessment of social class proportions in the university—as in the case of Newcastle University—with its working-class ethos. The perceived situation which guides students' responses within the institutional context is seen also as a symptom of structural relationships which are defined by those very factors and conditions which we see at work in other contexts of student interaction. These are once more the comparative size, nature, and degree of contact of the composing groups. Where there is reduced contact this will lead to erroneous suppositions of the size and nature of the social class groups in the university. Erroneous perception of this kind, by guiding mores and attitudes of those interacting within the overall situational space, works in the nature of a self-fulfilling prophecy to bring about what is supposed.

The perception of situations at small group level is guided by the same factors and conditions and defined by spatial and social concentrations, so that within the limits of the perceptional region attributes are selected as relevant—among them social class. Where there is a multiplicity of factors which overlie the socioeconomic factors there may be blurring of social class divisions; where there are common boundaries this tends to accentuate the relevance of social class. Thus students' school background, where it coincides with social class, tends to emphasise external social class divisions; where it does not coincide it tends to create a new kind of cultural division based on a more personalised social class identity. This is true particularly since the student is abstracted from family background and most of the gross material class clues which act as indicators of social class. Indeed, in such a situation social class becomes largely attributional and as such is relevant only in defined social situations. There are times when students' social class is interactional, but this depends on spatial and cultural concentrations which allow for enduring contacts between members of the same social class within the institutional framework. Such is the organisation of the universities studied that this is by no means precluded by the conscious community orientation. Residential set-up particularly may make for the growth of social class identity among students at the expense of "student culture" by encouraging those spatial and cultural concentrations which define such situations.

There the student category is interactional rather than attributional; there is transmission of elements of social class culture and mutual adaptation of social classes in interaction, leading to what has been called bourgeoisification of the working class.[1] Where the necessary conditions do not obtain, there is no such transmission or adaptation and no automatic assimilation of the working-class students into the predominantly middle-class student body. Thus it is possible for the social classes to remain unchanged within the university and to exhibit those features which are exhibited by external social classes. This will to some extent depend on institutional organisation and the degree of separation of the institution from external influences. This was discussed in Chapter 11. Where the institution is able to separate itself from the external social environment—as in a collegiate university—it is able to substitute its own inequalities based on its own criteria. Since these inequalities may suppose equality within each particular stratum, this may act as a cohesive factor in student relations since students themselves form an equal stratum in the academic hierarchy. This is only one of the aspects of institutional socialisation discussed in Chapter 11 along with structural distances between groups and culture transmission within them.

[1] But also of course to conscious resistance to bourgeoisification.

Students' perception of social class within the university will in fact in part depend upon the degree of institutional separation and also upon the social class models to which they consciously or unconsciously refer in terms of past, actual, or vicarious experience, as discussed in Chapter 12. The degree of definition of internal and external reference groups will again be delimited by spatial and cultural factors. Students' definitions of social class tend to vary with their own social class position. Working-class students tend to stress the socioeconomic dimension of social class—the middle-class students tend to speak in terms of value systems. This kind of definition influences what the student perceives to be his own social mobility, i.e. different students may see themselves as moving along a different social continuum, so that movement means different things.

Indeed, since social relations of social classes within the university are ordered to some extent by conditions outlined, these also are necessary for the process of assimilation or bourgeoisification to take place. This is associated with social mobility, and implies that social mobility is by no means automatically accomplished by the student. It becomes imperative to define mobility as the students see it as well as in the objective terms of occupational status. Since in institutionalised terms all working-class students have undergone a certain amount of social mobility we have to differentiate between differential capacities for movement and between those who have experienced movement relative to others within the same status category. The concept of motility introduced by the author attempts to separate out one of the variables in the process of mobility, which in itself is a configuration of variables, in order to analyse its differential effect in different situations. This applies, for instance, to relations with parents and peers and to the relative significance of locality ties. Although conclusions are drawn, much of this evidence is qualitative so that what is suggested is a hypothesis which needs to be tested by objective data which may be measured.

Mobility rates are not discussed in this book since they are outside the cope of the institutional context. Nevertheless, it seems possible that these will probably be affected by the expansion of university places if higher education continues to become the primary avenue of mobility. Therefore, it was pertinent in Chapter 14 to complete the study of the whole process with some student attitudes to expansion in university places and to the prospect of a growing democratisation of higher education. The responses of present-day students would appear to be somewhat reactionary—and this may be seen as a feature of the sponsored system of mobility outlined by Turner. Students, in fact, seem to think that expansion and democratisation will lead rather to a lowering of standards and to the entry of a different kind of student.

However, in the light of what was discovered about the social class proportions within the universities, in fact expansion of places so far has not represented a wide democratisation of higher education, and it is probable that this will not change radically in the future. In a sense the system is self-maintaining and class differentials remain, so that social as well as academic selection continues to operate. However, one must not overlook the fact that there have been fairly radical changes in the very nature of the societal social classes which are represented in the university, so that what is meant by the social class proportions of students today is probably rather different from what it meant, say, 50 years ago. This is because the very nature of the social classes, as a configuration of variables, within the total population is changing, and, for instance, gross material inequalities are not as evident as they were. Nevertheless, social class differences may be maintained by stressing a different dimension.

It is true also that there is some change in the kind of students in the universities through the increasing numbers of students from the lower echelons of the lower middle class. These form the majority of the first-generation university students in whose families higher education was previously unknown. This represents a shift in social emphasis in the universities, which may affect their totem or image in the wider society, and may offer for some a threat to the élite values which in times past the universities ideally conveyed.

If, as we have seen, there persist large numbers of working-class students who remain culturally of the working class, one may argue as to what will be the effect of this growing (albeit slowly) number of proletarian intellectuals, influential in movements discussed in Chapter 15. One may question how far they will become an academic or how far a proletarian class when their numbers increase. Will they drop back into the existing social class structure or form what one student called a "floating population"? The implication for student protest and social movements of all kinds is great, and we may already be experiencing the outcome.

It is difficult to ignore the wider implications of the findings of this study. If, as we have seen, the social classes persist both as cultural collectivities and conscious groups within the student body, and if the nature of their social relations leads some social class features to be accentuated rather than lost, then we may assume that institutionalised mobility will only have a limited effect on the *value systems* of the social classes passing through the universities. Indeed, where social class sub-cultures predominate more than student sub-cultures, there will be a limited growth of the mores and values of an élite, except among those in whom they are already closely associated with social class background.

Thus if social class identities persist it is quite likely that institutionalised mobility through higher education may create a new kind of élite. This would represent an élite in socioeconomic terms and one harnessed to the societal means of production and power as bearers of knowledge useful to society, and one which retains original social class values, culture, and identity. This could lead to an increasing fragmentation of social class dimensions and indices in society, and to an increasing shatterbelt zone of situations in which social class is attributional and of delimited relevance. This by no means indicates a disappearance or shrinking of social classes. It would seem to point to changes in number and kind rather than in degree of existing social classes.

These are a few of the wider issues raised by the findings, but naturally there are questions raised at every level of investigation which cannot always be answered. For instance, we have seen how situational space is defined in cultural and spatial terms and have narrowed down the investigation to examine these components. Yet we cannot go beyond this on the basis of the present findings. It is as yet impossible to state which defined situations reveal the relevance of social class or how such situations are defined in terms of relevant attributes. It is possible only to infer what happens from the information to be had.

It is also not possible to observe role performance and role change at first hand, nor the operations of interpersonal physical and social space. This again must be inferred. Findings suggest that the same kind of cultural and spatial factors, though different in degree, are at work at the various contextual levels, so that there is a kind of continuum of spatial and cultural concentrations, whose effects may be plotted at different points in time and space. This has yet to be investigated. Another subject for further study is the theory that in the configuration of variables which make up social class, different weightings are accorded in different situations. This could only be examined at first hand, and unfortunately it would be almost impossible at this level to quantify and measure in a meaningful way.

It would be possible, however, to narrow down the area under investigation to a very small element of the contextual analysis as a whole. The present piece of research would thus act as a springboard to further investigations. Within the contextual framework outlined, what is required is an analysis of dynamic situations which make up and are made by structural contexts—rather like molecules which make up solid matter. It has been established that molecules of activity are there; what needs to be investigated is the individual nature of the atoms: protons and neutrons.

As molecules differ, so do social situations, and their particular structure is of vital interest.

This means of approach is different from that which isolates a particular social variable or attribute and finds the way in which these define a situation and are themselves clustered. One would attempt to isolate and define a meaningful social situation from the evidence available and examine it to see which attributes were present and which were perceived to be relevant. Thus one moves from the structure to its dynamic components rather than from dynamic components to a semblance of structure. And just as matter is made up of molecules, so are structural contexts and role-playing in terms of attributional selection.

Parsons has said

> that a bridge may with perfect truth be said to consist of atoms of iron, a small amount of carbon, etc., and their constituent electrons, protons, neutrons and the like. Must the student of action, then, become a physicist, chemist, biologist, in order to understand his subject? In a sense this is true, but for the purposes of the theory of action it is not necessary or desirable to carry such analyses as far as science in general is capable of doing. A limit is set by the frame of reference with which the student of action is working. That is, he is interested in phenomena with an aspect not reducible to action terms only in so far as they impinge on the scheme of action in a relevant way—in the role of conditions or means. So long as their properties, which are important in this context, can be accurately determined, these may be taken as data without further analysis. Above all, atoms, electrons or cells are not to be regarded as units for the purposes of the theory of action.[1]

Conditions rather than units of action have been studied in this book, and the pattern of those conditions constitutes, as it were, the situational space within which the actors interact. The molecule imagery is appropriate in that a molecule may be said to be a configuration rather than a system and the protons and neutrons within it have apparently random paths. It may be suggested that apparently random individual acts take

---

[1] Parsons, T., *The Structure of Social Action: A Study in Social Theory with Special Reference to a Group of Recent European Writers*, Free Press, Glencoe, Illinois, 1949, p. 47.

place within structured situational space which delimits but does not dictate those acts. Also operating in the situation are the multidimensional reference groups to which the actors refer in terms of past, actual, or vicarious experience, so that the structure is changing even while the social choice is made or the social dilemma (in terms of pattern variables) is solved. This may lead to a change in the actual fabric of social relations.

It will be seen that what the author means by "condition" differs to some extent from that indicated by Parsons, so it is pertinent to quote Parson's definition here:

> [An act] must be initiated in a "situation" of which the trends of development differ in one or more important respects from the state of affairs to which the action is orientated, the end. The situation is in turn analysable into two elements —those over which the actor has no control, that is which he cannot alter, or prevent from being altered, in conformity with his end, and those over which he has such control. The former may be termed the "conditions" of actions—the latter the "means".[1]

However, in the present analysis of conditions it is clear that the actor has some control in terms of future situations if not the present one, and this very selection of attributes, patterns relations in such a way that future roles are adjusted accordingly.[2] The spatial and cultural concentrations already discussed are in themselves conditions which delimit or define situational space, and yet they continually undergo modification through time and space. This results partly from the relation of the normative and non-normative aspects of the system through the definition of the situation by the persons in it in terms of past, actual, or vicarious experience. These are some of the considerations which the present analysis bring us to, which are not exclusively concerned with social class but rather with the social relations in which it is a factor.

On the other hand, the findings raise many questions about the nature of social class itself, especially within the university context. For example, points of methodology arise which are concerned to inquire, firstly, how one discovers social class and then how one analyses exactly what it is once it has been discovered.

The author did not initially discuss the definition of social class at great length because certain assumptions must be made about what social class is in order to discover what it does, i.e. what part it plays in the students'

---

[1] Parsons, *op. cit.*, p. 45.

[2] "Our world is definitely mapped out for us by the responses which are going to take place." Mead, G. H., *On Social Psychology*, Selected papers ed. by Anselm Strauss, Phoenix Books, University of Chicago, 1964, p. 190.

social relations. However, in a sense what has been demonstrated is that the nature of social class is in fact manifested by the part it plays in social relations. It is an operational concept.

By examining what part social class plays in social relations we may escape from the position outlined by Lipset and Bendix: "Having essentially no problems other than accurately describing the hierarchical structure, more and more of the literature in this field is becoming methodological."[1]

Although until now a certain starting point or base line has been assumed, one cannot escape the methodological implications of selecting such a base line for "stratification in any population exhibits various facets according to the contexts in which and the methods by which it is examined".[2]

In this particular case both subjective and objective indices of social class identity have been used—and both are seen to be relevant.

There are obvious dangers in analysing social class in terms of what people themselves think of their own social class and that of others. It is for this reason that the starting point for analysis was the attempt to establish by means of objective indices the social classes as statistical cultural collectivities. Lipset and Bendix discuss some of the weaknesses of using self-evaluations of social class in their critique of the Lloyd Warner school. They say that

> if class is what people say it is then a finding that people of the same class associate in voluntary ("subjective") organisations, seems merely to confirm that they act and think alike. Analysis should reveal more than this; it should enable us to predict the conduct of people in terms other than the way in which they rank their own prestige and that of others. That is to say, we should be able to infer from a people's conscious system of prestige ranks how they would behave and think in circumstances which are not themselves the result of these prestige ranks. Otherwise the theory of class is tautological.[3]

By taking student circumstances, i.e. those "which are not in themselves the result of these prestige ranks", and by testing in them both objective and subjective social class evaluations, the author hopes that she has broken out of "the circle" while not throwing away the valuable insights of what it means to "belong" to a social class. This feeling of "belonging" relates most closely to interactional rather than attributional social class situations, so that in itself it can tell us little of the varieties of meaning of

[1] Lipset, S. M., and Bendix, R., Social status and social structure: A re-examination of data and interpretations: II, *BJS*, 1951, **2**, 246.
[2] Littlejohn, J., *Westrigg*, 1963, p. 76.
[3] Lipset and Bendix, *op. cit.*, p. 152.

social class in different contexts and for different people. This can only be discovered by multivariate analysis of all available data both objective and subjective. For it would seem that there is indeed a statistical reality of cultural concentration or configuration within the university—how it is experienced depends on the other factors which enter into the situation and with which it is variously combined. Thus what people consciously know and what is statistically true may differ, but both are relevant and necessary to any analysis of social class as a feature or property of social structure.

Therefore in effect what Lipset and Bendix criticise in Lloyd Warner's work is incomplete rather than irrelevant information on social class.

> Rather he [Warner] seems to have concluded that if any resident or group of residents was aware of these distinctions then a systematic knowledge or these distinctions would contribute to social class analysis.
> This conclusion arises from a failure to emphasise that any theory of class is a conceptualisation which highlights some and ignores other facts. A study of class which is based exclusively upon people's awareness of class treats this awareness as a substitute for the concepts of the social scientist.[1]

It is indeed true that the awareness of social class is no substitute for the concepts of the social scientist, yet it may well—as we see in the evidence of the thesis—give certain structural insights which explain why the awareness does not convey what happens in statistical and structural terms.

Indeed, the fact that social class does not mean the same thing to different people, or is viewed differently from different points on the scale, should tell us much about the nature of the social classes. For it would seem to be true that social class represents a complex configuration of variables or a constellation. Although it may be mapped like a chart of the heavens, if viewed from inside the constellation not only is the aspect different but the whole appears to be completely fragmentary with its boundaries ill defined. And as planets and stars move relative to one another, so do the status dimensions within the total constellation. This points to a kind of social as well as spatial relativity within the structure of the status-set. Obviously the analogy cannot be taken too far, but the idea of composite positions changing relative to one another has heuristic value. In other words, we cannot expect to come up with the same answer each time, and our measurements of social class will have little meaning if they are not taken relative to some other measurement.

Therefore, although what is taken as an objective measurement is in

---

[1] Lipset and Bendix, *op. cit.*, p. 154.

itself a relative fact, when objective and subjective measurement are compared in relation to the part they play (i.e. what they do in a dynamic sense), they become a constant relative to one another in a manner which allows of some meaningful structural conclusions to be drawn.

"Thus it is hoped that in a limited way the dangers of a unidimensional point of view"[1] are avoided. From this point one may then "attempt to account for the behaviour of large numbers of people in terms of their common response to the shared experiences of their position in social and economic life".[2] In this book there has been an attempt to examine the nature of the positions occupied in terms of the variety of people's "common response to the shared experiences of their position" in terms of defined situations, and their "interlocking status evaluations"[3] are seen as a feature of their structural positions.

Naturally, however, "the 'facts' pertaining to social class (or to any other aspect of society) are infinite, and any investigation of social class must perforce select some and neglect other 'facts' ".[4] So it was that the initial starting point was an analysis of students' socioeconomic social class of origin as based on father's occupational status. This in itself represents only one dimension of social class, and to try to discover more about what social class is from this point may have led to arid speculation. However, more is revealed of what social class is by an analysis of social class as a factor in social relations than by an attempt merely to classify students upon a social status scale.

Obviously the socioeconomic dimension of social class is of prime importance and implies a whole configuration of variables. "By virtue of their common experience within the same exigencies of everyday living they probably think alike in many respects. But, as Marx saw, these factors only facilitate, they do not necessitate organisations and organised common action."[5] The same principle applies equally well to the concept of student behaviour.

However, since student is in Weber's sense a status group rather than a social class, there are limitations in the comparison.

Ossowski postulates that there are three assumptions which appear to be common to all conceptions of a "class" society:

> (i) The classes constitute a system of the most comprehensive groups in the social structure.

---

[1] *Ibid.*, p. 242. [2] *Ibid.*, p. 243. [3] *Ibid.*, p. 168.
[4] *Ibid.*, p. 233. [5] *Ibid.*, p. 248.

(ii) The class division concerns social statuses connected with a system of privileges and discriminations not determined by biological criteria.

(iii) The membership of individuals in a social class is relatively permanent.

In the first assumption two elements must be distinguished: (a) that classes are the most comprehensive groups; (b) that classes form a system of such groups. By the most comprehensive groups in the social structure I understand here a small number of groups—two or more—differentiated in consequence of the division of society according to criteria that are important in social life. The second element introduced by this assumption involves treating a class as a member of a certain system of relations. This means that the definition of any class must take into account the relation of this class to the other groups in the system.[1]

Ossowski considers three basic schemes of class structure.

Two of these schemes, the dichotomic and the functional, present the social structure as a system of dependence, the third as a system of gradation. In schemes based on relations of dependence the various terms in the system are characterised by different attributes; in a scheme of gradation they are characterised by a differing degree of the same characteristic.

It has already been pointed out that the social classes themselves within the university context have at times been spoken of as attributional, i.e. a certain class membership represents a quality or label with "an all or none existence". Yet this attribute in itself implies a whole configuration of variables which exists in varying degrees in different social classes. Thus in the university context social class may be "attributional", and in combination with other characteristics and in certain conditions it may become "interactional". Also, in any social situation an attribute of a person may be a variable in terms of the situation.

The attributional classes themselves refer to classes in the external structure outside the university which may be conceptualised in terms of the three basic schemes outlined. The infinite complexity of studying social class relations among students arises because both social classes and universities are "basic groups"[2] and ranked in a system of gradation upon different continua.[3] The fact of gradation itself introduces the complex question of degree as well as kind, which makes it well-nigh impossible to speak in terms of a simple typology which is meaningful in empirical terms. When complex theorisation does not advance the understanding of social phenomena, one must use the tools to hand and

[1] Ossowski, S., *Class Structure in the Social Consciousness*, 1963, p. 133.

[2] *Ibid.*, p. 141.

[3] In students' social class the dimension of power is missing—although the Student Power movement attempts by direct action to remedy the situation.

"leap into the dark". The findings which result may well show that the "various definitions of a class society may in reality differ less between themselves than one would believe in view of the different formulations".[1] For in fact what may seem in many cases to be contradictory evidence may be merely different aspects of the same social phenomenon—and one which it is well-nigh impossible to analyse in its entirety and in all its social ramifications. In such circumstances, a proliferation of models of social class can tell us much of the social phenomenon being studied. For Ossowski:

> The model of a social class is made up of several different characteristics admitting of gradation. Several criteria overlap in it, and the absence of one criterion may be offset by a higher degree of another characteristic, just as in the evaluation of a work of art a lower level of artistic technique may be offset, for instance, by originality of idea or power of expression. A work of art can be a work of art to a greater or lesser degree, just as a social class may be a class to a greater or lesser degree.[1]

This being true, in the empirical situation one is left without a much clearer idea than before of what is meant by "social class". Theory and method go hand in hand, and so until this question is more fully answered all empirical research will exhibit the inadequacies of the conceptual schemes. Ossowski admits this when he says that:

> As the criteria are not commensurable, the final decision as to what is and what is not a social class must ultimately be reached by intuitive judgments made in a given milieu about the importance of various criteria (compare the conceptions of American sociologists) or by considering practical consequences and the requirements of action (compare the Marxist theory of class).[1]

Naturally this gives rise to many incongruities and divergences of opinion.

> The common basic assumptions concerned with the concept of class sometimes make it difficult to see clearly whether, when faced by discrepant definitions, we are in fact dealing with differences of conceptual apparatus or with contradictory views regarding the scope of the phenomena which is established by these common assumptions.[2]

Of course it is not only the models of social class which may differ or change but the thing studied may differ and change from place to place and from time to time, so that additional variables are constantly being added to confuse the picture, and one is left ultimately with a question or series of questions.

[1] Ossowski, *op. cit.*, p. 138.
[2] *Ibid.*, p. 139.

As we have seen in this book, the expansion of educational opportunity which has been planned for and awaited has been and is at the present time a starting point for many speculations about the changes which the democratisation of higher education may bring about in the total social class structure and among those who are to fill some of the key positions in it. These must as yet remain only speculations, but the findings suggest that changes are taking place more slowly than has been anticipated and that the relations of the social classes in the university correspondingly fall into a more traditional pattern than may previously have been supposed.

The divisions and inequalities in higher education and the influence of social class in student social relations are, of course, only a reflection of the kind of divisions and inequalities which exist in society. This is why it is so difficult to establish equality of opportunity in education in a society whose structure is based on the principle of inequality; it is also why educational institutions in themselves are fighting an uphill battle to improve the life chances of the underprivileged child. There must be a continual dialogue between the home and the school if one environmental influence is not to work against the other.

By the time the young person reaches the university, many of the crucial decisions in his life have been made and the crucial stages passed; what happens at the university is only a final stage in an obstacle race in which not only the handicaps, but the hurdles, are different for each runner. We do not all run the same race and we do not all compete against the same runners. Inequalities are built into not only the runners but the structure of the race, and this is what makes it so difficult at any point in the educational process to say why one person succeeds and another fails. Of course, this is true not only of education but of any human activity or endeavour.

However, although this difficulty remains it is fairly clear that there are patterns of manifest inequality between groups which are reflected in their relative life chances or chance of improving their position. These patterns of difference or inequality may be distinguished in various significant areas of life, and it is these which in turn are reflected in the educational system. Firstly, of course, there are inequalities in wealth, income, capital, and material conditions. The effects of such inequality are immediate and obvious, and, as we have seen, the importance of housing and general living standards play a central part in the general development of the child and in educational achievement. It is in housing that not only material and cultural inequalities are expressed, but structural concentration and distance which accentuates social divisions. Where racial segregation enters into this structure the problems of inequality are accentuated.

> We are in danger (as the Plowden Report once again emphasised) of perpetuating a submerged class in our big cities where slum housing and slum schools breed poverty and ignorance. But, if it is difficult for a white child to escape from such conditions, it is infinitely more difficult for a coloured child.
> Yet equality of conditions of life and of education for the child of immigrants is not enough. As the PEP survey shows, they actually need far higher qualifications than their white competitors if they are to win good jobs. In effect a policy of *positive* discrimination in favour of the at present under-privileged is needed in both housing and education, if they are to gain equality.[1]

Not only are there inequalities in the conditions of life, but in access to the facilities societally provided for their improvement. It is notoriously true for instance that those most in need of the social benefits of the welfare state are those most likely to be woefully ignorant of the benefits there are. In a complex and impersonal society differential access to information and to sources of information reflects social inequality; poverty and ignorance are closely allied. Indeed, Marris and Rein[2] would suggest that as the agencies of welfare are usually middle-class institutions manned by middle-class staff, they are off-putting to potential users—and therefore help to keep the poor poor.[3]

The educational system itself is marked by complex differences and inequalities. Some parents can buy an education of their choosing—others must take what the State supplies. The tripartite system of secondary education, established by the 1944 Education Act, rigidifies a structure of inequalities, and the binary system in higher education imposes yet another set of status differences. Not only this, but there are regional differences in educational provisions; different local authorities vary in generosity of awarding grants; for structural financial and demographic reasons there are regional differences in chances of gaining grammar school and university places; and there are regional differences in public examinations as, for instance, the reputed ease or stiffness of the GCE papers of different university boards.

[1] Colour Editorial, *The Observer*, 23 April 1967.
[2] Marris, P. and Rein, M., *Dilemmas of Social Reform*, Routledge and Kegan Paul, 1967.
[3] See also Moynihan, D., *Maximum Feasible Misunderstanding*, Free Press, New York, 1969.

The interrelation of lateral and vertical inequalities, as expressed in regional differences, is of significance in the whole of social life. However, it is particularly influential in education since educational facilities are locally and regionally organised, and lateral or geographical and social inequality may coincide. Hence in areas where comprehensive education is introduced, if the school draws its children exclusively from the surrounding area, it may become socially homogeneous. Although internal differences may disappear there may appear social and material inequalities between schools w hich reflect differences in residential areas. Similarly, inequalities between urban and rural areas are reflected in the quality of educational and welfare provisions.

The operation of lateral with vertical inequalities is seen not only at local level but in the organisation of the affairs of the whole country. Area of home residence therefore affects differential life chances. Geographical groups as well as social groups are privileged or underprivileged.

> There *are* two nations, and the world looks a lot poorer when seen from hundreds of areas north of Potters Bar. One official report after another in recent years has stressed it isn't only the appearance and the crumbling environment of the industrial revolution: the north has poorer health and education, lower income, more unemployment, a higher rate of emigration, worse housing—the list is near endless.[1]

Of course it is not just a north–south dichotomy; there are differences within the north and south. National differences between England, Wales, Scotland, and Northern Ireland also represent the next stage in structural alignment of groups along with religious discrimination as in Northern Ireland.[2] Therefore we are faced with the structural context of social and geographical inequalities. If we look at the distribution of pretax personal incomes[3] in Britain we find a map of differences which is not dissimilar in shape from that of other inequalities.

> The southerly drift of incomes—which was apparent during the 1950's—seems to have eased between 1960 and 1965. The South-east is still the richest region in terms of pretax personal incomes and Northern Ireland is still much the poorest. The decline from the South-east outwards is clearly apparent, with the Northern region, Scotland and Wales the lowest in Great Britain and Northern Ireland even further behind in bottom place. The only regions with a mean above

[1] McGlashan, The nationalist revolt, *The Observer*, 12 March 1967.

[2] From a regional survey of incomes by Coates, B. E. and Rawstron, E. M., reported in *The Guardian*, 1967.

[3] The election of 21-year-old Bernadette Devlin as M.P. for Mid-Ulster was a triumph for youthful reform. Her subsequent conviction for riotous behaviour in the Ulster troubles should increase rather than decrease her youthful following.

that of the United Kingdom were South-eastern, Southern, Eastern and West Midlands.

These differences, along with others, are clearly important considerations in all social planning.

> Regional planning and national budgeting will remain arts rather than sciences for as long as there is no central agency with statutory powers to undertake the systematic collection and presentation of the differences in economic and social conditions within the United Kingdom. The systems used must be consistent from place to place, and from time to time. The Meteorological Office prepares its data in this way. Why do we lack a similar methodological approach to the more important aspects of our lives?[1]

The differences in economic and social conditions within the United Kingdom represent a set of structural constraints which pattern achievement in various ways. It is not surprising therefore that there are regional differences in educational attainment and qualifications.

For instance, 84·6 per cent of the entire Tyneside male population over 15 left school when they were 15 or younger. In London and the South-east the figure is 71·6 per cent. The national average of men who left at or before 15 is 78 per cent. The differences are more pronounced for those who left school between 16 and 19. One in five of the London population fell into this category; in the Northern region only 1 in 10 did so.[2]

In the South-east, 25·3 per cent of 1964 school leavers had at least five O-level passes and/or at least one A-level. Only 14·1 per cent had these qualifications in the Northern region and 15·3 per cent in the North-west. In the London Metropolitan area only 35·1 per cent of children left school at 15, the minimum leaving age, compared with 60·1 per cent in the Northern region. At the same time, qualifications and progress on to full-time further education did not coincide neatly and reflects differential provision of places for which even those qualified must compete. However, school leavers in the north who went on to higher education tended to go in disproportionate numbers to colleges of education and to technical colleges.[3]

Reasons put forward for these figures by local education authorities varied, but a spokesman for the Cumberland Education Authority, instead of blaming the parents, put the stress upon what we have discussed as the structure of inequalities.

[1] Arnold-Forster, M., report in *The Guardian* of the Coates–Rawstron survey.
[2] Education Tables from 1961 Census material, HMSO, 1966.
[3] *1964 Statistics of Education*, Part 3, HMSO, 1966.

Miss Gillian Sharp said that there were fewer University entrants from the North because there were fewer Grammar Schools with large sixth forms and with a tradition of sending their people on to University in the North than the South. Local industry was less interested in academic qualifications in the North and the whole system was more geared to craft apprenticeships.[1]

Clearly intelligence, motivation, values, and family culture have great influence on attainment, but if provisions are inadequate ability and willingness alone may be to no avail.

One of the chief aims of educational administration should be to ensure that wherever a child lives he or she should have the same amount of resources devoted to his or her education. Data about the expenditure of local authorities per head of the school population would have been helpful here.

Such data would have shown clearly that many local authorities in the North-east were spending much less than the national average for each child in primary and secondary school.[2]

These regional inequalities in resources, in income, public expenditure, and material provision cannot but have unequal results in terms of attainment of all kinds. What we have been looking at are traditional or temporal, spatial and social inequalities which affect favourably or adversely the life chances of the individual. It is clear that we cannot consider only the dimension of social inequality—temporal and spatial inequality or distance must come into our analysis. What we need is a status distance *contour map* instead of a one-dimensional scale.

The contour map of inequalities is reflected in distances between groups, as in the university; and the status-set of the person is structured in relation to the shape of the status contour map of the group or social class to which he belongs. This is what we have discovered and had to take account of in analysis of the many social factors which operate with social class in student social relations.

It well may be that the signs and symbols of an affluent society lead some to suppose that "we're all middle class now"—although even the evidence only of the most manifest inequalities would suggest that this simplistic view does not do justice to what we know of reality. As to the evidence of more subtle differences discussed in this book, we are led back to question what we mean by social class and what we experience of social class; and everything suggests that even within a privileged status group—as students are—social class differences are preserved.

[1] South beats north—disparities—results, *Times Educational Supplement*, 22 April 1966, p. 1218.
[2] Statistics Editorial, *ibid.*

APPENDICES

SELECTED TABLES ON BASIC COMPOSITION OF INTERVIEWEES

(a) *Edinburgh University* (numbers only)

1. *Nationality and Class*

	UC	UMC	LMC	WkC	Total
Scottish	—	9	1	4	14
English	—	9	5	3	17
Overseas	—	1	—	—	1
TOTAL	—	19	6	7	32

2. *Sex Composition*

Single men	18
Single women	11
Married men	2
Married women	1
TOTAL	32

3. *Faculty Composition*

	UMC	LMC	WkC	Total
Arts	9	4	3	16
Divinity	—	—	—	—
Law	2	—	—	2
Medicine	3	1	1	6
Dentistry	1	—	—	1
Veterinary science	—	—	—	—
Music	—	—	—	—
Science	4	1	2	7
TOTAL	19	6	7	32

4. Residence Composition

	UMC	LMC	WkC	Total
Lodgings	11	3	4	18
Hostel	2	2	1	5
Home	6	1	2	9
TOTAL	19	6	7	32

(b) *Newcastle University*

1. *Sex Composition* (per cent)

	Sgl. Male	Sgl. Female	Mrd. Male	Mrd. Female	Total
Willing but not interviewed	51·5	54·9	51·7	—	52·3
Interviewed	16·4	13·6	20·7	50·0	15·9
Not willing	32·1	31·5	27·6	50·0	31·8
TOTAL	100	100	100	100	100
No.	(414)	(184)	(29)	(2)	(629)

	Sgl. Male	Sgl. Female	Mrd. Male	Mrd. Female	Total	No.
Willing but not interviewed	64·7	30·7	4·6	—	100	(329)
Interviewed	68·0	25·0	6·0	1·0	100	(100)
Not willing	66·5	29·0	4·0	0·5	100	(200)
TOTAL	65·8	29·3	4·6	0·3	100	(629)
No.	(414)	(184)	(29)	(2)	(629)	

2. *Faculty and Social Class Composition*

	UMC	LMC	WkC	Unknown	Total
Arts	22·6	26·1	31·8	100·0	27·0
Law	6·4	—	—	—	2·0
Medicine	19·4	13·0	18·2	—	16·0
Dentistry	6·4	—	—	—	2·0
Agriculture	—	8·7	9·1	—	6·0
Applied science	19·4	17·4	13·6	—	17·0
Pure science	19·4	26·1	22·7	—	23·0
Education	3·2	—	4·6	—	2·0
Economics and social studies	3·2	6·5	—	—	4·0
Architecture	—	2·2	—	—	1·0
TOTAL	100	100	100	100	100
No.	(31)	(46)	(22)	(1)	(100)

	UMC	LMC	WkC	Unknown	Total	No.
Arts	25·9	44·5	25·9	3·7	100	(27)
Law	100·0	—	—	—	100	(2)
Medicine	37·5	37·5	25·0	—	100	(16)
Dentistry	100·0	—	—	—	100	(2)
Agriculture	—	66·7	33·3	—	100	(6)
Applied science	35·3	47·1	17·6	—	100	(17)
Pure science	26·1	52·2	21·7	—	100	(23)
Education	50·0	—	50·0	—	100	(2)
Economics and social studies	25·0	75·0	—	—	100	(4)
Architecture	—	100·0	—	—	100	(1)
TOTAL	31·0	46·0	22·0	1·0	100	(100)
No.	(31)	(46)	(22)	(1)	(100)	

(c) *Durham University*

1. *Sex Composition* (per cent)

	Males	Females	Total	Males	Females	Total	No.
Not inter-viewed but willing	54·4	52·0	53·7	72·5	27·5	100	(189)
Not willing	29·4	34·0	30·7	68·5	31·5	100	(108)
Interviewed	16·2	14·0	15·6	74·5	25·5	100	(55)
TOTAL	100	100	100	71·5	28·5	100	(352)
No.	(252)	(100)	(352)	(252)	(100)	(352)	

2. *College Composition* (numbers only)

Male	Total	Female	Total
1. Bede	2	1. St. Aidan's	4
2. St. Chad's	0	2. St. Hild's	3
3. St. Cuthbert's	6	3. St. Mary's	6
4. Grey	11	4. Neville's Cross	1
5. Hatfield	8		
6. St. John's	5	TOTAL	14
7. University	9		
TOTAL	41		

3. *Social Class Composition* (numbers only)

	UMC	LMC	WkC	Total
Male	15	20	6	41
Female	5	7	2	14
TOTAL	20	27	8	55

APPENDIX II

SAMPLE COVERING LETTERS

1. *Edinburgh Covering Letter*

Social Anthropology Department,
4 Buccleuch Place,
Edinburgh, 8

DEAR SIR/MADAM,

It is an acknowledged fact that social class is an important factor in almost all spheres of modern industrial society, not least of these being the field of education. The British system of education at present has been proved to have a certain class bias, but exactly how and why this is, is still being investigated and studied. You will agree that it is important for us to find out about such questions in view of the expanding opportunities for education in every class, and the attendant problems which changes in opportunity may bring, both within families and society at large. Social mobility is a vital topic of interest for our generation and one with which any society moving towards equality of opportunity should be concerned.

It is with this in mind that I ask you if you would be so kind as to complete the enclosed questionnaire. The questionnaire is being sent to 20 per cent of the students in this University as part of a survey on the composition and influence of social class in the student body, the results of which will be written up as an academic dissertation. Although I prefer to remain anonymous as I am a student in my final honours year and may be known to some of you I can tell you that this survey is being carried out with the approval of the Head of the Department of Social Anthropology, and after consultation with the Secretary to the University. The survey will be completely impersonal, and no names are asked for. Indeed the results will appear purely as statistics.

This survey has a very serious aim and may uncover facts of interest to students in general. You will realise that as many people as possible should answer and return this questionnaire if the survey is to be at all representative and worthwhile. I hope very much for your co-operation. When you have filled in the questionnaire, will you please return it as soon as possible and in no case later than ... to the above address under the heading "Dissertation Survey of University".

If you would be willing to take part in an interview—of course strictly confidential—at a time convenient to you, please indicate on the questionnaire. I hope as many of you as possible will find time to take part in this very valuable follow up.

Yours sincerely,
FINAL HONOURS STUDENT,
conducting survey

577

2. Durham Covering Letter

c/o Department of Geography,
Science Laboratories,
South Road,
Durham City

2 March 1964.

DEAR STUDENT,

You will have heard and read a great deal about the effect which the expansion in the number of University places will have upon individual Universities if the recommendations of the Robbins Report are implemented. There has, however, been a notable lack of literature on the effects of such expansion on the individual student. Yet the expansion of educational opportunity which this represents will affect the lives of an increasing number of students in future years and we can, for instance, expect to find in Universities an increasingly large proportion of students from families where Higher Education was previously unknown. If we are to plan for, and achieve, "the full community life traditionally associated with Universities" mentioned by the Vice-Chancellor of the new University of Essex in his third Reith Lecture, it is vital that we should try to find out more about those for whom the plans are made—their opinions and attitudes—particularly these "first generation University students", who, in the words of Dr. Halsey of Oxford, are the "pioneers of a new society".

It is with this end in view that a survey is being carried out in this University of certain aspects of the social structure and organisation of the student body. You have been selected completely at random from the University residence lists as one of a sample of 500 students chosen to take part in this survey. I should be most grateful if you would complete the enclosed questionnaire and return it as soon as possible.

The survey is being carried out as part of a comparative study of the student bodies of the Universities of Durham, Newcastle and Edinburgh (of which the Edinburgh survey is already completed) afterwards to be written up as a doctoral thesis in Social Anthropology. The Vice-Chancellor and Registrar of this University have been consulted and have given the project their full approval and support. The President of the SRC and the Senior Men and Women of all the Colleges have been informed of the purpose of the survey and of when it is taking place, and have also given their support.

The questionnaire is completely confidential and should not be discussed with your friends before you answer it—the answers should be spontaneous and completely your own—otherwise the results are invalidated. Those students who are upset or annoyed by the questions on family background and social class should remember the academic nature of the enquiry and the fact that their replies are anonymous. It is only by discussing such matters rationally that we shall rid ourselves of the unnecessary ill-feeling caused by such questions at the present time.

I am the only person in possession of the list of names which will in no case be used or attached to completed questionnaires. The names of those willing to be interviewed will be kept only so long as it is necessary for the students to be contacted, and will eventually be destroyed. All other names I have undertaken to destroy immediately replies are received.

Since it is not intended to draw hard and fast conclusions from the results of the questionnaires, interviews will be held in which students may discuss their views in greater detail. I very much hope that you will be willing to be interviewed.

Please return your completed questionnaire, sealed up in the envelope provided, to the Senior Man or Woman of your College, who has agreed to send on all completed questionnaires to me. You can, if you prefer, or if you find it more convenient, return it directly to me c/o the Registrar's Office, Old Shire Hall, or c/o the Geography Department, Science Laboratories, South Road. I should be grateful if you would return it as soon as possible, and in no case later than *Saturday March 14th*.

I shall welcome any comments, suggestions or criticisms—space is provided at the end of the questionnaire for this. If you are unwilling to fill in the questionnaire I should be glad to hear your reasons for this.

Yours sincerely,

JOAN ABBOTT

(Joan Abbott, M.A., *Research Student*)

3. Newcastle Covering Letter

Department of Social Anthropology
4, Buccleuch Place,
Edinburgh, 8

November 1964

DEAR STUDENT,

You may perhaps have heard and read a great deal recently about the effect which expansion in the number of University places will have upon individual Universities and upon the country at large if the recommendations of the Robbins Report are implemented. There has so far, however, been insufficient investigation of the effects such measures will have on the individual student—on his social and academic life, and on his attitude to the changing University environment. Yet the expansion of educational opportunity which these measures represent will affect the lives of an increasing number of students in future years, and, for instance, an increasingly large proportion of students from families where higher education was previously unknown will have the opportunity of a University education. It is vital therefore that we should try to find out about the attitudes and opinions of present day students, particularly these "first generation University students", if we are to plan for, and achieve, what the Vice-Chancellor of the New University of Essex has called "the full community life traditionally associated with Universities".

It is with this end in view that a survey is being carried out in this University as part of a doctoral thesis. You have been selected completely at random from their University residence lists as one of a sample of 800 students chosen to take part in the survey. I should be most grateful if you would complete the enclosed questionnaire and return it as soon as possible.

The survey is being carried out as part of a comparative study of the student bodies of the Universities of Newcastle, Durham and Edinburgh—of which the Durham and

Edinburgh surveys are completed. The Registrar of this University has been consulted and has given permission for the project. The Presidents of the Students' Representative Council and of the University Union have also been informed of the purpose of the survey and have given their support.

The questionnaire is completely confidential in that there are no names or numbers on the forms and the addresses of students in the selected sample are known only to the University Registrar. The questionnaire should not be discussed with your friends before you answer it, the answers should be spontaneous and completely your own—otherwise the results are invalidated. Those students who are upset or annoyed by the questions on family background and social class should remember the impartial and academic nature of the enquiry and the fact that their replies are completely anonymous.

Since it is not intended to draw hard and fast conclusions on the basis of statistical results gained from the questionnaires interviews will be held in which students may discuss their views in greater detail. Interviews will be held, at times convenient to those taking part, during the first three or four weeks of next term. I very much hope that you will be willing to be interviewed.

Please return your completed questionnaire sealed up in the stamped addressed envelope provided, as soon as possible, and in no case later than the end of term.

I shall welcome any comments, suggestions or criticisms—space is provided at the end of the questionnaire for this. If you are unwilling to fill in the questionnaire I should be glad to know of your reasons.

Yours sincerely,

JOAN ABBOTT

(Miss Joan Abbott, M.A., *Edinburgh University*)

SURVEY QUESTIONNAIRES

1. *Edinburgh Questionnaire*

Confidential and anonymous

for Office use only

QUESTIONNAIRE ON SOCIAL CLASS COMPOSITION AND INFLUENCE
IN THE STUDENT BODY OF EDINBURGH UNIVERSITY

Please tick where applicable

YOU	*Questions*	*Answers:*
	1. Male or female	1. ....
	2a. Course of study	2a. ....
	2b. Year of study	2b. ....
YOUR FAMILY	3. Please state your father's or guardian's (including stepfather's) occupation (Describe in full, e.g. if engineer, type of engineer)	3. ....
	4. In what social class would you say your parents are (or "were" if dead), i.e. upper class; upper middle class; lower middle class; working class?	4. UC UMC LMS ☐ ☐ ☐ WkC ☐
	5. To what level did your parents complete education? (If applicable, age of school leaving if known)	5. Mother .... Father ....
	6. How many brothers and sisters have you (including stepbrothers and sisters)? Please state number	6. Brothers .... Sisters ....
	7a. How many of these are of or over secondary school age? Please state number	7a. Brothers .... Sisters ....
	7b. How many have received or are receiving grammar school or public school education or equivalent (i.e. excluding secondary modern or	7b. Brothers .... Sisters ....

commercial course)? Please state number

8a. How many of them are over university or college entrance age? Please state number

    8a. Brothers ....
    Sisters   ....

8b. How many of these have received or are receiving college or university education? Please state number

    8b. Brothers ....
    Sisters   ....

9a. Since you came to university, do you consider your own class position to have changed from that of your parents?

    9a. Yes No Don't know
    □ □   □

9b. If answer *yes*—what class are you now?

    9b. UC UMC LMC
    □   □   □
    WkC Don't know
    □   □

THIS UNIVERSITY

10. Do you consider that awareness of social class in this university is:
(a) Maintained   (c) Diminished
(b) Fostered   (d) Irrelevant?

    10. a   b   c   d
    □   □   □   □

11. State specifically by what means (following on from question 10)
(a) Whole system of education
(b) Individual members of staff
(c) Students themselves

    11. a   b   c
    □   □   □

12. Do you consider this to be (a) consciously or (b) unconsciously done?

    12.
    a□□b a□□b a□□b

YOUR FRIENDS

13a. When you make close friends *of the same sex* is your choice influenced by consideration of family background and social class?

    13a. Yes   No
    □   □
    □ possibly unconsciously

13b. When you make close friends *of the opposite sex* is your choice influenced by considerations of family background and social class?

    13b. Yes   No
    □   □
    □ possibly unconsciously

SOCIETIES AND ORGANISATIONS

14a. Are you now or have you ever been a member of any student societies, organisations, SRC, etc.?

    14a. Yes   No
    □   □

14b. If answer *yes* state which society organisation, etc. Please abbreviate

    14b. ....
    ....

15a. Are you now or have you ever been an official in any of these? (Include also officials in halls of Residence)

    15a. Yes.   No.
    □   □

15b. If answer *yes* state what position   15b.   . . . .
in which society. Please abbreviate   . . . .
. . . .

16. In elections of officials in student   (a). Yes   No
organisations do considerations of   □   □
social class and background influ-   Possibly
ence: □ unconsciously
(a) You   (b) Yes   No
(b) Others (in your opinion)?   □   □
Possibly
□ unconsciously

SOCIAL
CLASS
CRITERIA

17. What do you think is the most   17.   a   b   c   d   e
important factor in determining   □   □   □   □
the social standing of a *student* in
this university?
(a) Family background   If e state what
(b) Wealth   . . . .
(c) Academic prowess   . . . .
(d) Other abilities and talents
(e) Other

18. What do you think is the most   18.   a   b   c   d   e
important factor in determing the   □   □   □   □   □
social standing and class position of
any *individual* in *society at large*?
(a) Family background   If e state what
(b) Income   . . . .
(c) Occupation   . . . .
(d) Education
(e) Other

19. Do you consider that the criteria   19.
you have indicated in questions   (a)   Yes   No
17 and 18 are useful in the case of: □   □
(a) Students in this university   (b)   Yes   No
(b) Individuals in society at large   □   □
20. Would you be willing to be inter-   10.   Yes   Nc
viewed?   □   □

Thank you very much for your co-operation

Student Life in a Class Society

2. *Durham Questionnaire*

Confidential

QUESTIONNAIRE ON SOME ASPECTS OF THE SOCIAL
STRUCTURE AND ORGANISATION OF THE STUDENT
BODY OF DURHAM UNIVERSITY

(Please tick where applicable)

	Questions		*Answers*
1.	Sex	1.	....
2.	Year of study	2.	....
3.	Course of study	3.	....
4.	Nationality	4.	....
5.	While at university do you live in lodgings (include flats); in college; or at home?	5.	Lodgings College ☐ ☐ Home ☐
6.	Please state your father's or guardian's (including stepfather's) occupation	6.	....
7a.	What age were each of your parents respectively when they completed their education?	7a.	Mother .... Father ....
7b.	What level of education did each parent reach? (e.g. primary or secondary or grammar school, college, university, etc.)	7b.	Mother .... Father ....
8.	If *neither* parent had a university education please answer:		
	(a) Do you feel that you experience or have experienced any special difficulties or disadvantages as a result of the fact that neither of your parents has had personal experience of university life?	8a.	Yes No ☐ ☐ Don't know ☐
	(b) If you answered *yes* please could you outline briefly what these difficulties are?	8b.	....
9a.	How many brothers and sisters have you? (Include stepbrothers and stepsisters)	9a.	Brothers .... Sisters ....
9b.	How many of these are of or over secondary school age?	9b.	Brothers .... Sisters ....
9c.	How many of these have received or are receiving a grammar school or public school education (exclud-	9c.	Brothers .... Sisters ....

ing secondary modern or commercial course)

9d. How many brothers and sisters have you who are of or over university or college entrance age?

9d. Brothers ....
Sisters ....

9e. How many of them have received or are receiving a university or college education? (including any who recently gained acceptance to these institutions)

9e. Brothers (College)..
Sisters (College) ...
Brothers (Univ.) ...
Sisters (Univ.) .....

10. What type of school did you yourself last attend before coming to university? (e.g. grammar, public, direct grant, etc.)

10. ....
....

11. To what social class would you say your parents belong? (i.e. upper class; lower middle class; or working class)

11. UC UMC LMC
☐   ☐   ☐
WkC
☐

12a. Since you came to university do you consider your social class to have changed from that of your parents?

12. Yes No Don't know
☐   ☐   ☐

12b. If you answered *yes*—what social class are you now?

12b. UC UMC LMC
☐   ☐   ☐
WkC Don't know
☐   ☐

13a. Do you consider that in this university class consciousness is
(a) Maintained
(b) Fostered
(c) Diminished
(d) Irrelevant
in social relationships

13a.

a   b   c   d
☐ ☐ ☐ ☐

13b. (Following on from this) please state specifically by what means:
(a) Students themselves
(b) Individual members of staff
(c) College system
(d) Whole system of education

13b.

a   b   c   d
☐ ☐ ☐ ☐

13c. Do you think that on the whole what you have described is consciously or unconsciously done?

13c. Conc. Unconc.
☐   ☐

14a. In making close friends of the *same sex* are you at all influenced by considerations of family background and social class?

14a. Yes No
☐ ☐
Possibly unconsciously
☐

14b. In making close friends of the *opposite sex* are you at all influenced by considerations of family background and social class?

14b. Yes No
   □   □
   Possibly
unconsciously
   □

14c. Are the majority of your friends of the same sex in your own college?

14c. Yes No
   □   □

14d. Are the majority of your friends of both sexes in the same faculty?

14d. Yes No
   □   □

15a. Do you think that students feel there is special social prestige attached to being a member of certain colleges?

15a. Yes No
   □   □
Don't know
   □

15b. If you answered *yes*—how would you personally rank the men's and women's colleges in terms of social prestige in the student body? (Please put No. 1 by the highest, 2 by 2nd highest, etc. They are named in alphabetical order)

15b.
Men's	*Women's*
Bede	St. Aidan's
St. Chad's	St. Hild's
St. Cuthbert's	St. Mary's
Grey	Neville's Cross
Hatfield	
St. John's	
University	

15c. What do you think is the most important factor determining whether a college has high social prestige or not?

15c.

(a) The academic achievement of its members

(b) The family background of its members

   a b c
   □ □ □

(c) The wealth of its members

(d) The abilities and talents of its members

   d e f
   □ □ □

(e) The social adaptability of its members

(f) The social conformity of its members

(g) The enthusiasm and drive of its members

   g
   □

(h) Other (please state)

(h) ....

16. What do you think is the most important factor determining the social standing and class position of an individual in society at large?

16.

		a	b	c	d
(a)	Family background	□	□	□	□
(b)	Income				
(c)	Occupation				
(d)	Education				
(e)	Other (please state)				

(e) ....

17a. Are you now or have you ever been a member of any student societies?

17a. Yes □ No □

17b. If you answered *yes*—please state the number of societies in each category provided

17b. Departmental......
Social and cultural .
Religious ....
Sport ....
Political ....
Other.............

17c. How many of these are *university* societies (i.e. drawing membership from all the colleges)?

17c. ....

17d. How many of them are *college* societies (i.e. drawing membership largely or exclusively from your own college)?

17d. ....

18a. Do you now hold or have you ever held any position of authority or responsibility in the study body?

18a. Yes □ No □

18b. If you answered *yes*—please state each position held, and n which society or organisation (include SRC, Union, NUS, and positions held in college)

18b. ....
....
....
....

19a. Did you have any particular reason for wanting to come to Durham University rather than any other university?

19a. Yes □ No □ Don't know □

19b. If you answered yes—would you please outline your reason very briefly

19b. ....
....
....
....

20a. Was Durham University your first choice on your university entrance application forms?

20a. Yes □ No □

20b. If you answered *no*—which university was first?

20b. ....

21a. In the light of what you now know about the collegiate system in Durham, do you think that before you came you had a reasonable idea of what it would be like?

21a. Yes □ No □

21b. If you answered *no*—would you say that your reactions to college life as you find it are favourable, unfavourable or neutral?

21b.   Fav.   Unfav.   Neut.
      □   □   □

21c. If there is such a thing as an ideal size for a college, what do you think it might be?

21c. ....

22a. Do you think that a vast expansion of places on the scale envisaged by Robbins will in any way affect the character of this university?

22a.   Yes   No   Don't
      □   □   know
                 □

22b. If you answered *yes*—which features do you think will undergo most change?

22b. ....
       ....

22c. Do you think that the changes you have outlined are desirable, undesirable, or do you not know?

22c.   Des.   Undes.   Don't
      □   □   know
                 □

23. Are you willing to be interviewed? The interviews will take place early next term, at a time convenient to you, to be arranged

23.   Yes   No
      □   □

Thank you for your co-operation

This space is provided so that you may make comments, suggestions or criticisms. Please use it.

3. Newcastle Questionnaire

Confidential Questionnaire

Questions	*Answers* (Please tick where applicable)
1. Sex	1. Male Female
2. Married or single	2. Married Single
3. Age (in years and months)	3 ....
4. Nationality	4 ....
5. If British please state county of residence	5 ....
6. Faculty	6 ....
7. Course of study	7 ....
8. Year of study	8 ....
9. Please state your father's or guardian's occupation	9 ....

10a. What age were each of your parents respectively when they completed their education?

10a. Mother ....
Father ....

10b. What level of education did each parent reach? (e.g. primary, secondary, grammar school, college, university, etc.)

10b. Mother ....
Father ....

11. If neither parent had a university education please answer:

11. ....

11a. Do you feel that you experience or have experienced any difficulties or disadvantages as a result of the fact that neither parent has had personal experience of university life?

11a. Yes No Don't
☐ ☐ know
☐

11b. If you answered *yes*—please would you briefly outline these difficulties

11b. ....
....

12a. How many brothers and sisters have you? (please include stepbrothers and stepsisters)

12a. Brothers ....
Sisters ....

12b. How many of these are of or over secondary school age?

12b. Brothers ....
Sisters ....

12c. How many of these have received, or are receiving a grammar school or public school education?

12c. Brothers ....
Sisters ....

12d. How many brothers and sisters have you who are of or over university and/or college entrance age?

12d. Brothers ....
Sisters ....

12e. How many of them have received or are receiving a university or college education? (including any who have recently gained acceptance to these institutions)

12e. Brothers (College)..
Sisters (College)....
Brothers (Univ.) ...
Sisters (Univ.) .....

13. What type of school did you yourself last attend before coming to university? (e.g. grammar, public, direct grant, technical, etc.)

13. ....
....

14a. Did you have any particular reason for wanting to come to university?

14a. Yes No Don't
☐ ☐ know ☐

14b. If you answered *yes*—would you please briefly outline your reason?

14b. ....

15a. Did you have any particular reason for wanting to come to Newcastle University rather than any other university?

15a. Yes No Don't
☐ ☐ know
☐

15b. If you answered *yes*—would you please briefly outline your reason?

15b. ....

16a. Was Newcastle your first choice on your university entrance application forms?

16a. Yes ☐ No ☐

16b. If you answered *no*—which university was first?

16b. . . . .

17a. In the light of what you now know about university life do you think that before you came you had a reasonable idea of what it would be like?

17a. Yes ☐ No ☐ Don't know ☐

17b. If you answered *no*—would you say that your reactions to university life as you find it are favourable, unfavourable or neutral?

17b. Fav. ☐ Unfav. ☐ Don't know ☐

18a. Do you think that the vast expansion of places on the scale envisaged by Robbins will in any way affect the character of this university?

18a. Yes ☐ No ☐ Don't know ☐

18b. If you answered *yes*—which features do you think will undergo most change? Please outline the changes envisaged

18b. . . . .
. . . .

18c. Do you think that the changes just outlined are desirable, undesirable, or do you not know?

18c. Des. ☐ Undes. ☐ Don't know ☐

19a. Has the changing of this university from a college of Durham University in its own right in any way affected the life or attitudes of the ordinary student?

19a. Yes ☐ No ☐ Don't know ☐

19b. If you answered *yes*—please state in what way the change has affected or will affect students.

19b. . . . .

20. During the university term do you live at home, in hall of residence, or in lodgings (including flats)?

20. Home ☐ Hall ☐ Lodgings ☐

21. Are you reasonably satisfied on the whole with your present accommodation?

21. Yes ☐ No ☐

22. Do you think that the proportion of residential places in this university should be increased, decreased, or maintained as now?

22. Inc. ☐ Dec. ☐ Same ☐

23. Do you feel that on the whole you are reading for the course most suited to your abilities and inclination?

23. Yes ☐ No ☐ Don't know ☐

24a.	Are you now or have you ever been a member of any student societies?	24a.	Yes No ☐ ☐

24b. If you answered *yes*—please state the number of societies of which you are a member in each category provided

24b. Departmental......
Social and cultural.
Religious ....
Sport ....
Political ....
Other............

25a. Do you hold or have you ever held any position of authority or responsibility in the study body?

25a. Yes No ☐ ☐

25b. If you answered *yes*—please state each position held, and in which society or organisation (include SRC, Union, NUS, etc.)

25b. ....

26. Are most of your friends members of the same faculty as yourself?

26. Yes No ☐ ☐

27a. In making close friends of the same sex are you at all influenced by considerations of family background and social class?

27a. Yes No Possibly ☐ ☐ unconsciously
☐

27b. In making close friends of the opposite sex are you at all influenced by considerations of family background and social class?

27b. Yes No Possibly ☐ ☐ unconsciously
☐

28. Do you think that within the wider community there is any prestige attached by others to being a student?

28. Yes No ☐ ☐

29. What do you think is the most important factor determining the social standing and class position of an individual in society at large?

29.

(a) Family background
(b) Income
(c) Occupation
(d) Education
(e) Other (please state)

a b c d
☐ ☐ ☐ ☐

(e) ....

30. To what social class would you say your parents belong? (i.e. upper class; upper middle class; lower middle class; or working class)

30. UC UMC LMC
☐ ☐ ☐
WkC
☐

31a. Since you came to university do you consider your social class to have changed from that of your parents?

31a. Yes No Don't ☐ ☐ know
☐

31b. If you answered *yes*—what social class are you now?

31b.   UC UMC LMC

□   □   □

WkC Don't know

□   □

32a. Do you consider that in this university class consciousness is

32a.

(a) Maintained
(b) Fostered
(c) Diminished
(d) Irrelevant

a   b   c   d

□   □   □   □

in social relationships?

32b. (Following on from last question) Please state specifically by what means:

32b.

(a) Students themselves
(b) Individual members of staff
(c) Whole system of education

a   b   c

□   □   □

33. Are you willing to be interviewed? The interviews will take place early next term, at a time convenient to you, to be arranged.
If you are willing to be interviewed please give name and address to which future communications should be sent.

33.   Yes No

□   □

. . . .

. . . .

. . . .

. . . .

Thank you for your co-operation

This space is provided so that you may make comments, suggestions or criticisms. Please use it.

BIBLIOGRAPHY

ABBOTT, JOAN, Students' social class in three northern universities, *BJS*, Sept. 1965, **16** (3).

ABBOTT, JOAN, *Residential Organisation and Students' Social Class*, Report of a Conference organised by Society for Research into Higher Education Ltd., Dec. 1965.

ABBOTT, JOAN, The concept of motility, *Soc. Rev.*, July 1966, **14** (4).

ABBOTT, JOAN, University environment and the socialisation of students—York University, *The Twentieth Century*, 1030, Summer 1966, **175** (1030).

ABBOTT, JOAN, The expansion of educational opportunity and the changing role of the student, *Soc. Econ. Admin.*, July 1967, **1** (3).

ABBOTT, JOAN, Social effects of University selection, *Journal of Careers Research & Advisory Centre*, Summer 1967.

ABBOTT, JOAN, *Career Patterns of British Sociology Graduates*, British Sociological Assn., S.T.S., 1969.

ABRAMS, M., Rewards of education, *New Society*, 9 July 1964, No. 93.

ABRAMS, P. and LITTLE, A., The young activist in British politics, *Brit. Journal of Sociol.*, **16** (4), 331.

ACLAND, H. and HATCH, S., *Three Aspects of Student Residence—Recruitment, Participation and Academic Performance*, London Inst. Educn., 1968.

ADAM, C., The Spanish underground—an end to thirty years' silence, *New Statesman*, 25 April 1969.

ADAMEK, R. J. and GOUDY, W. J., Identification, sex and change in college major, *Sociol. Educ.*, 1966, **39** (2), 183–99.

ADAMSON, J. W., *English Education: 1789–1902*, Cambridge, 1930.

ADLER, C., Some social mechanisms affecting high school drop out, Paper presented to the VIth World Congress of Sociology, 1966.

ALBROW, M. C., The influence of accommodation upon 64 Reading University students, *BJS* (4), Dec. 1966, **17** (4).

ALBROW, M. C., Ritual and reason in the selection of students, *Univs. Quart.*, **21** (2), March 1967.

ALLEN, PHYLLIS, Hostel planning: 1, The social unit as a basis of planning, *Architects' Journal*, 7 April 1965.

ALLEN, PHYLLIS, Hostel planning: 2, Social and other influences, *Architects Journal*, 14 April 1965.

ANDERSON, C., *et al.*, Intelligence and occupational mobility, *J. Pol. Econ.*, June 1952, **60**, 218–39.

ANDERSON, C. A., Common problems for universities, *Int. Rev. Educ.*, 1965, **11** (1), 3–19.

ARCHER, R. L., *Secondary Education in the Nineteenth Century*, Cambridge, 1921.

ARGYLE, M., *The Psychology of Interpersonal Relations*, Penguin, 1967.

ARON, R., Social structure and the ruling class, I, *BSS*, 1950, **1** (1).

ARON, R., Student rebellion—vision of the future or echo from the past? *Pol. Sci. Quart.*, June 1969.

ASCHERSON, N., Students declare war on professors, *The Observer*, March 1967.

ASHBY, SIR ERIC, *Technology and the Academics*, Macmillan, London; St. Martin's Press, New York, 1958.

ASHBY, SIR ERIC, *African Universities and Western Tradition*, OUP, 1964.

ASKHAM, J., *A Survey on the Application and Recruitment of Students to Degree Level Courses at Technical College*, Cambridge Advisory Centre for Education, 1967.

ASSOCIATION OF UNIVERSITY TEACHERS, Some problems of university development, AUT, May 1960.

ASSOCIATION OF UNIVERSITY TEACHERS, Report on university expansion, AUT, Sept. 1949.

ASTIN, A. W. Some characteristics of student bodies entering higher educational institutions, *J. Educ. Psych.*, 1964, **55**, 267–75.

BANKS, OLIVE, *Parity and Prestige in English Secondary Education*, Routledge and Kegan Paul, London, 1955.

BANTOCK, G. H., *Education and Values*, Faber, London, 1965.

BANTON, M. P., *White and Coloured: The Behaviour of British People towards Coloured Immigrants*, Jonathan Cape, London, 1959.

BANTON, M. P., Social alignment and identity in a West African city, paper prepared for symposium No. 26, "Cross-cultural Similarities in the Urbanisation Process", Burg Wartenstein Symposium, 1964 (Wenner-Gren Foundation for Anthropological Research Inc.).

BANTON, M. P., *Roles: An Introduction to the Study of Social Relations*, Tavistock Publications Ltd., London, 1965.

BANTON, M. P. (ed.), *The Social Anthropology of Complex Societies*, ASA Monograph No. 4, Tavistock Publications Ltd., 1966.

BANTON, M. P., *Race Relations*, Basic Books, New York, 1967.

BARBER, B., *Social Stratification: A Comparative Analysis of Structure and Process*, (gen. ed., Merton, R. K.), New York, 1954.

BARGER, B. and HALL, E., The interrelationships of family size and socioeconomic status for parents of college students, *J. Marr. Fam.*, 1966, **28** (2), 186–7.

BARKER, R. G. and WRIGHT, H. F., *Midwest and its Children: the Psychological Ecology of an American Town*, Harper and Row, 1954.

BAYER, A. E., Birth order and college attendance, *J. Marr. Fam.*, 1966, **28** (4), 480–4.

BEALE, R. J., The organisational structure of large colleges of technology, *Techn. Educ.*, 1966, **8** (7), 310–12.

BECKER, H. S., Schools and systems of social status, *Phylon*, 1955, **16** (2).

BECKER, H. S., and GEER, B., Latent culture: A note on the theory of latent-social roles, *Admin. Sci. Quart.*, 1960, **5**.

BEGGS, D. W. and ALEXANDER, S. K., *Integration and Education*, Rand McNally & Co., 1969.

BELOFF, M., The LSE Story, *Encounter*, May 1969.

BEN-DAVID, J., Professions in the class system of present-day societies, *Current Sociol.*, 1963–4, **12**, 3.

BENDIX, R. and LIPSET, S. M. (ed.), *Class, Status, and Power, a Reader in Social Stratification*, Free Press, Glencoe, Ill., 1953.

BENDIX, R. and LIPSET, S. M., *Social Mobility in Industrial Society*, Heinemann, London, 1959.

BERDIE, R. F., *After High School—What?*, University of Minnesota Press, Minneapolis, 1954.

BERDIE, R. F., LAYTON, W. C., HAGENIAH, T. and SWANSON, E. D., *Who Goes to College*, Minnesota Studies in Student Personnel Work, No. 12, Univ. of Minnesota Press, 1962.

BERNSTEIN, B., Some sociological determinants of perception, *BJS*, June 1958, 159–74.

BERNSTEIN, B., Language and social class, *BJS*, 1960, **11**, 271–6.

BERNSTEIN, B. and HENDERSON, D., Social class differences in the relevance of language to socialisation, *Sociology*, 1969, 3 (1), 1–20.

BIDDLE, B. J. and THOMAS, E. J., *Role Theory: Concepts and Research*, Wiley, New York, 1966.

BIE, P. DE, Aspects socio-culturels des classes sociales ascendantes in Belgique (Sociocultural aspects of social mobility in Belgium), *Cahiers Int. de Sociol.*, 1965, **39**, 19–109.

BLACKBURN, R., Inequality an exploitation, *New Left Review*, **42**, March/April 1967.

BLALOCK, H. M., The identification problem and theory building: the case of status inconsistency, *ASR*, Feb. 1966, **31**, 52–61.

BLAU, P. M., The flow of occupational supply and recruitment, *ASR*, Aug. 1965, 30 (4).

BLAUG, M., Loans for students?, *New Society*, 1966, **210**, 538–40.

BLOOM, R., WHITEMAN, M., and DEUTSCH, M., Race and social class as separate factors related to social environment, *Am. J. Sociol.*, 1965, **70** (4), 471–6.

BOARD OF EDUCATION, *Report of the Consultative Committee on Secondary Education* (Spens Committee), London, 1938, pp. 81–92.

BOARD OF EDUCATION, *Educational Construction*, Cmd 6458, London, 1943.

BORGATTA, E. F. (ed.), *Social Psychology: Readings and Perspectives*, Rand McNally, New York, 1969.

BORGATTA, E. F. and CROWTHER, B., *A Workbook for the Study of Social Interaction*, Rand McNally, Chicago, 1965.

BOTTOMORE, T., *Elites and Society*, Pelican Books, 1966.

BOTTOMORE, T. and RUBEL, M. (eds.), *Karl Marx: Selected Writings in Sociology and Social Philosophy*, Pelican, 1963.

BOURDIEU, P., La transmission a l'héritage culture, in DARRAS, *Le Partage des Benefices*, Editions de Minuit, Paris, 1966, pp. 383–420.

BOURDIEU, P., L'Ecole conservatrice. Les légalités devant l'école et devant la culture, in *Rev. Française Sociol.*, 1966, 7, 325–47.

BOURDIEU, P., Differences et distinctions, in DARRAS, *Le Partage des Bénéfices*, Editions de Minuit, Paris, 1966.

BOURDIEU, P. and PASSERON, J. C., *Les Héritiers, les Étudiants et la Culture*, Editions de Minuit, Paris, 1964 (Centre de Sociologie Europeenne).

BOURDIEU, P., and PASSERON, J. C. in collaboration with MICHEL, E., *Les Etudiants et leurs Études*, La Haye, Paris (ed. Moulton), 1964.

BOWLES, F. (ed.), *Access to Higher Education*, Vol. 1. UNESCO and the International Assoc. of Univs., Columbia Univ. Press, 1963.

BOX, S. and FORD, J., Commitment to Science: a solution to student marginality? *Sociology*, 3 (1), 1967.

BOYLE, SIR E., Parliament and University policy, *Minerva*, 1966, **6**, 3–19.

BREDEMEIR, H. C. and STEPHENSON, R. M., *The Analysis of Social Systems*, Holt, Rinehart and Winston, 1965.

BREWSTER, B. and COCKBURN, A., Revolt at the LSE, *New Left Review*, May–June 1967 (Issue on Student Power).

BRIM, O. G. (Jr.), *Sociology and the Field of Education*, Russell Sage Foundation, New York, 1958.

BRIM, O. G. (Jr.) and WHEELER, *Socialisation after Childhood*, Wiley, New York, 1966.

BROTHERS, J., *Church and School*, Liverpool Univ. Press, 1964.

BROTHERS, J., *Going up to University*, Dorton, Longman & Todd, London, 1967.

BRUNNER, E. DE S. and WAYLAND, S., Occupation, labour force status and education, *J. Educ. Sociol.*, 1958, **32** (1).

BUGLER, J., The Glasgow Student affair, *New Society*, 10 Feb. 1966.

BURNS, T., *Revolt of the Privileged*, SSSRC Newsletter 4, November 1968.

BURTON, D., Birth order and intelligence, *Journal of Soc. Psychol.*, 1968, **76**, 199–206.

BUTCHER, H. J., The attitudes of student teachers to education: a comparison with the attitudes of experienced teachers and a study of changes during the training course, *Brit. J. Soc. Clin. Psychol.*, 1965, **4** (1), 17–24.

BUTTERFIELD, H., *The Universities and Education Today*, Routledge and Kegan Paul, London, 1962. (The Lindsay Memorial Lectures given at the University College of N. Staffs., 1961.)

CAMPBELL, D. T., KRUSKAL, W. H., and WALLACE, W. P., Seating aggregation as an index of attitude, *Sociometry*, 1966, (1), 1–15.

CANTOR, L. M. and ROBERTS, F. I., *Further Education in England and Wales*, Routledge & Kegan Paul, 1969.

CAPLOW, T. and McGEE, R., *The Academic Marketplace*, Basic Books, New York, 1958.

CARLSSON, G., *Social Mobility and Class Structure*, C.W.K. Gleerup Lund, 1958.

CARO, F. G., Deferred gratification, time conflict and college attendance, *Sociol. Educ.*, 1965, **38** (4), 332–40.

CARO, F. G., Social class and attitudes of youth relevant for realisation of adult goals, *Soc. Forces*, 1966, **44** (4), 492–8.

CARTER, C. F., Do MPs threaten academic freedom? *The Observer*, 29 Jan. 1967.

CARTER, C. F., The Franks Report from the outside, *Univs. Quart.*, **20** (4), Sept. 1966.

CASTLE, E. B., *Ancient Education and Today*, Penguin Books Ltd., London, 1961.

CENTERS, R., *Psychology of the Social Classes: A Study of Class Consciousness*, Princeton, NJ, 1949.

CENTERS, R., Education and occupational mobility, *ASR*, 1949, **14²**, 143–4.

CENTRAL ADVISORY COUNCIL FOR EDUCATION, *15–18*, 1959.

CENTRAL ADVISORY COUNCIL FOR EDUCATION, *Early Leaving*, HMSO, Dec. 1954.

CERVANTES, L. F., The isolated nuclear family and the drop out, *Sociol. Quart.*, 1965, **6** (2), 103, 118.

CERVANTES, L. F., Family background, primary relationships and the high school drop out, *J. Marr. Fam.*, 1965, **27** (2), 218–23.

CHAPARRO, A., Social structure and agricultural education, paper prepared for the Round Table on the Sociology of Education and Development, VIth World Congress of Sociology, 1966.

CHILMAN, C. S. and MEYER, D. L., Single and married undergraduates' measured personality needs and self-rated happiness, *J. Marr. Fam.*, 1966, **28** (1), 67–76.

CHOPRA, S. L., Family size and sibling position as related to measured intelligence and academic achievement, *J. Soc. Psychiat.*, 1966, **70**, 133–7.

CICOUREL, A. V. and KITSUSE, J. I., *The Educational Decision Makers*, Bobbs Merrill, Indianapolis, Ind., 1963.

CLARK, B. R., *The Open Door College*, McGraw-Hill, New York, 1960.

CLARK, B. R., The "cooling out" function in higher education, *Am. J. Sociol.*, May 1960, **65**, 569–76.

CLARK, B. R., The coming shape of higher education in the United States, *Int. J. Comp. Sociol.*, Sept. 1961, **2**.

CLARK, B. R., *Educating the Expert Society*, Chandler Press, San Francisco, 1962.

CLARK, B. R., Inter-organisational patterns in education, *Admin. Sci. Quart.*, 1965, **10** (2), 224–37.

CLARK, B. R., College image and student selection, in *Selection and Educational Differentiation*, Centre for the Study of Higher Education, Berkeley, Calif., 1959.

CLARK, B. R. and TROW, M., Determinants of college student subcultures, in NEWCOMBE, T. M. and WILSON, E. K. (eds.), *College Peer Groups*, Aldine, Chicago, 1966, pp. 17–70.

CLARK, K., *Dark Ghetto: Dilemmas of Social Power*, Harper Torch Books, 1965.

CLARKE, F., *The Study of Education in England*, London, 1942.

COHEN, P., *Modern Social Theory*, Basic Books, N.Y., 1968.

COLE, G. D. H., *Studies in Class Structure* (Int. Lib. of Sociol. and Soc. Reconstr.), London, 1955.

COLEMAN, A. B., Parents help their children succeed, *High School Journal*, 1969, **52** (6), 298–305.

COLEMAN, J. S., Academic achievement and the structure of competition, *Harvard Educ. Rev.*, 1959, **29**, 330–57.

COLEMAN, J. S., The adolescent sub-culture and academic achievement, *Am. J. Sociol.*, 1960, **65**, 337–47.

COLEMAN, J. S., *The Adolescent Society*, Free Press, Glencoe, Ill., 1961.

COLLIER, K. G., *The Social Purposes of Education* (Int. Lib. of Sociol. and Soc. Reconstr.), Routledge and Kegan Paul, 1959.

COMMITTEE OF VICE CHANCELLORS AND PRINCIPALS OF THE UNITED KINGDOM, *Memorandum of evidence to the Committee on Higher Education*, Committee of Vice-Chancellors, London, 1961.

CONANT, J. B., *Education and Liberty*, Harvard Univ. Press, Cambridge, Mass., 1953.

COSER, A., America's intellectuals—the twin temptations, *New Society*, **120**, 10–13.

COUPER, M., Why some prefer CATs, *New Society*, **123**, 12–13.

COWLEY, W. H., The American Higher Education Labyrinth, *From High School to College: Readings for Counsellors*, New York College Exam. Entrance Board, 1965.

COX COMMISSION REPORT, *Crisis at Columbia*, Vintage Books, Random House, New York, 1968.

COX, R., *Examinations and Higher Education—A Survey of the Literature*, Society for Research into Higher Education, 1966.

CRAMPIN, A., Forecasting student numbers in higher education. Paper delivered to the Society for Research into Higher Education, Annual Conference, Dec. 1969.

CRICK, B., Student politics and violence, *The Observer*, 5 Feb. 1967.

CROUZET, F., A university besieged: Nanterre 1967–69, *Pol. Sc. Quart.*, June 1969, **34** (2), 328–50.

CURTIS, S. J., *A History of Education in Great Britain* (foreword by W. R. Niblett), London, 1948.

DAHRENDORF, R., *Class and Class Conflict in Industrial Society*, London, 1959.

DAHRENDORF, R., The present position of the theory of social stratification, Paper presented to the VIth World Congress of Sociology, held at Evian, 3–10 Sept. 1966.

DALE, R. R., *From School to University*, Int. Lib. of Sociol. and Soc. Reconstr.), Routledge and Kegan Paul, 1954.

DALE, R. R. and GRIFFITH, S., Selected findings from a five year study of academic deteriorators in a grammar school, *Educ. Res.*, 1966, **8** (2), 146–54.

DAVIES, H., The social effects of the 1944 Act on the grammar school, *Bull. of Educ.*, Nov. 1950, no. 23.

DAVIES, J. G. W., Graduates and industry, *New Society*, **143**, 12–15.

DAVIS, A., *Social Class Influences upon Learning*, Cambridge, Mass., Harvard Univ. Press, 1952.

DAVIS, F., Professional socialization; a subjective experience: the case of student nurses (San Francisco Medical Center, Univ. of Calif.), paper presented to VIth World Congress of Sociology, 1966.

DAVIS, F. and OLESEN, VIRGINIA, Baccalaureate students' images in nursing, *Nursing Res.*, Winter 1964, **13**, 8–15.

DAVIS, F. and OLESEN, VIRGINIA, The career outlook of professionally educated women, *Psychiatry*, 1965, **28**, Initiation into a women's profession, *Sociometry*, March 1963, **26**, 89–101.

DAVIS, K., Conceptual analysis of stratification, *Am. Sociol. Rev.*, 1942, **7**, 309–21.

DELSANT, YVETTE, *L'Idéologie comme Moyen d'Intégration chez les Étudiants des Facultés de Letters*, CSE, 1966, VIth World Congress Communication.

DENT, H. C., *Secondary Education for All*, London, 1949.

DENT, H. C., *Universities in Transition*, Cohen and West, 1961.

DEUTSCH, M., The role of social class in language development and cognition, *Am. J. Orthopsychiatry*, 1965, **35** (1), 78–88.

DEUTSCH, M., KATZ, I., and JENSEN, A. R. (eds.), *Social Class, Race and Psychological Development*, Holt, Rinehart & Winston, 1968.

DEVLIN, T., Student fires begin to die down, *The Times Ed. Supp.*, 26 Dec. 1969.

DOCKRELL, W. B., Secondary education, social class and the development of abilities, *Brit. J. Educ. Psychiat.*, 1966, **36** (1), 8–14.

DONOVAN, P., Rebellion at the school for rebels, *The Observer*, 19 March 1967.

DOUGLAS, J. W. B., *The Home and the School*, MacGibbon and Kee, London, 1964.

DRAPER, H., *Berkeley: The New Student Revolt*, N.Y., Grove Press, 1965.

DUCRET, and RAFE-UZ-ZAMAN, *The University Today: Its Role and Place in Society*, WUS, Geneva, 1960.

DUMONT, L., Caste, racism and stratification—reflections of a social anthropologist, contributions to *Indian Sociol.*, Oct. 1961, no. 5 (Moulton and Co.).

DURHAM UNIVERSITY, *Durham University Calendar*, 1963–5.

DURKHEIM, E., *Suicide*, Routledge and Kegan Paul (Lib. of Soc. and Soc. Reconstr.), 1952.

DURKHEIM, E., *Education and Sociology* (trans. S. D. Fox), Free Press, Glencoe, Ill., 1956.

DURKHEIM, E., *Elementary Forms of the Religious Life*, 5th impression, George Allen and Unwin Ltd., London, 1964.

DURKHEIM, E., *The Division of Labour in Society* (trans. George Simpson), Collier–Macmillan, London, 1964.

ECKLAND, B. K., Social class and college graduation: some misconceptions corrected, *Am. J. Sociol.*, July 1964, **70**, 36–50.

ECKLAND, B. K., Academic ability, higher education and occupational mobility, *ASR*, 1965, **30** (5), 735–46.

EDEN, A., Social life in a provincial university, *BJS*, Dec. 1959, **10** (4), 291–310.

EDINBURGH UNIVERSITY SRC, *Constitution and Standing Orders*, 1963.

EDUCATION ACT, 1944, Published in *Chitty's Annual Statutes*, J. Burke, 38, 7 & 8 George VI, Pt. I, No. 8.

EELLS, K. W., *et al.*, *Intelligence and Cultural Differences*, Univ. of Chicago Press, 1951.

EGGLESTON, S. J., Going comprehensive, *New Society*, 1966, **221**, 855–6.

ELDER, G. H. (Jr.), Family structure and educational achievement: A cross national analysis, *ASR*, 1965, **30** (1), 81–96.

ELDER, G. H. (Jr.), Role relations, sociocultural environments, and autocrative family ideology, *Sociometry*, 1965, **28**, 173–96.

ELDER, G. H. (Jr.), *Life Opportunity and Personality: Some Consequences of Stratified Secondary Education in Great Britain*, Institute of Internat. Studies, University of California, Reprint No. 170. (Reprinted from *Sociol. of Educ.*, **38** (3), Spring 1965).

ELLIOT, D. S., VOSS, H. V., and WENDLING, A., Dropout and the social milieu of the High School: A preliminary analysis, *Amer. J. Orthopsychiatry*, 1965, **35** (2), 390.

ENGELSTADTER, H. and HEINZE, H., Social progress and higher education under socialist conditions, paper presented to VIth World Congress of Sociology, 1966.

ERBE, W., Accessibility and informal social relationships among American graduate students, *Sociometry*, 1966, **29** (3), 250–64.

ERIKSON, E. H. (ed.), *The Challenge of Youth*, Basic Books, New York, 1963.

ERON, L. D. and REDMOUNT, R. S., Effect of legal education on attitudes, *J. Legal Educ.*, 1957, **9** (4).

EVANS-PRITCHARD, E. E., *The Nuer. A Description of the Livelihood and Political Institutions of a Nilotic People*, Clarendon Press, Oxford, 1940.

FALK, L. L., Occupational satisfaction of female college graduates, *J. Marr. Jam.*, 1966, **28** (2), 177–85.

FARBER, B., Social class and intelligence, *Social Forces*, 1965, **44** (2), 215–25.

FESTINGER, L. A., *A Theory of Cognitive Dissonance*, Row, Peterson, New York, 1957.

FESTINGER, L. A., and KATZ, D. (eds.), *Research Methods in the Behavioral Sciences*, New York, 1953.

FEUER, L. S., *The Conflict of Generations: the Character and Significance of Student Movements*, Basic Books, 1969.

FINGER, J. A. and SCHLESSER, G. E., Non-intellective predictors of academic success in school and college, *School Rev.*, 1965, **173** (1), 14–29.

FLEMING COMMITTEE (BOARD OF EDUCATION), *The Public Schools and the General Education System*, London, 1944.

FLEXNER, A., *Universities American, English and German*, DUP, New York, 1930.

FLOUD, J. and HALSEY, A. H., Intelligence tests, social class and selection for secondary schools, *BJS*, 8 March 1957, 33–39.

FLOUD, J. and HALSEY, A. H., The sociology of education: a trend report and bibliography, *Current Sociol.*, 1958, **7** (3).

FLOUD, J., HALSEY, A. H., and MARTIN, F. N., *Social Class and Educational Opportunity*, Heinemann, 1956.

FORD, J., YOUNG, D., and BOX, S., Functional autonomy, role distance and social class, *BJS*, **18** (4), Dec. 1967, 370–81.

FORD, J., *Social Class and the Comprehensive School*, Routledge and Kegan Paul, 1969.

FRANKS COMMISSION, *Report of Commission of Inquiry*, Vol. I, OUP, 1966.

FRESHERS CONFERENCE, University of Newcastle upon Tyne SRC, 1964.

FRESHERS CONFERENCE, University of Durham Pamphlet, 4–7 Oct. 1963, University of Durham SRC.

FRIEDENBERG, E. Z., New value conflicts in American education, *School Rev.*, 1966, **74** (1), 66–94.

FRIEDENBERG, E. Z., *The Vanishing Adolescent*, Delta, 1968.

FURNEAUX, W. D., *The Chosen Few: An Examination of Some Aspects of University Selection in Britain*, OUP, 1961.

GALES, K. E., A campus revolution, *BJS*, 1966, **17** (1), 1–19.

GAMSON, Z. F., Utilitarian and normative orientations towards education, *Sociol. Educ.*, Winter 1966.

GARFINKEL, H., Trust and stable actions, in HARVEY, O. J., *Motivation and Social Interaction*, Ronald, New York, 1963.

General Information on the University of Newcastle upon Tyne—*Academic Year Book*, 1963–4.

GENNEP, A. VAN, *The Rites of Passage* (trans. Vizedom, Monika B., and Caffee, Gabrielle L.), Routledge and Kegan Paul, London, 1960.

GERSTL, J. and PERRUCCI, R., Educational channels and elite mobility: a comparative analysis, *Sociol. Educ.*, 1965, **38** (3), 224–32.

GERTH, H. and WRIGHT MILLS, C., *From Max Weber*, Kegan Paul, London, 5th edit., 1964.

GIDDENS, A., Aspects of the social structure of a university hall of residence, *Sociol. Rev.*, July 1960, **8** (1).

GINSBERG, M., *Sociology*, Butterworth, London, 1934.

GINSBERG, M. (ed.), *Law and Opinion in England in the 20th Century*, Stevens & Sons Ltd., London, 1959.

GINZBERG, E., Education and national efficiency: The United States, *The Yearbook of Education*, Evans Bros., London, 1956; World Books Co., Tarrytown, 1956.

GIRARD, A., Enquête nationale sur l'orientation et la selection des enfants d'âge scolaire, *Population*, Oct.–Dec. 1954, pp. 597–634.

GANDHI, M. K., *Indian Home Rule*, Navijivan Trust, Ahmedabad, 1946.

GLASS, D. V. (ed.), *Social Mobility in Britain*, Kegan Paul, 1954.

GLAZER, N., The multiversity goes to war, *New Society*, **133**, 26–27.

GLICK, P. C., Educational attainment and occupational advancement, in *Transactions of the 2nd World Congress of Sociology*, Internat. Sociol. Assoc., London, 1954, vol. 2, pp. 183–94.

GLISCINSKA, Z. and KAMINSKI, A., Budzet czasu studentek uniwersystetumeszkanek domn studenckieg (The budgeting of time by girl undergraduates living in a university hostel), *Przeglad. Socjol.* 1966, **19** (2), 45–64.

GLUCKMAN, M., *Custom of Conflict in Africa*, Blackwell, 1955.

GOFFMAN, E., Cooling the mark out: some aspects of adaptation to failure, *Psychiatry*, Nov. 1952, **15**, 457–63.

GOFFMAN, E., *The Presentation of Self in Everyday Life*, University of Edinburgh Social Sciences Research Centre Monograph, No. 2, 1958.

GOFFMAN, E., *Asylums*, Anchor Books, New York, 1961.

GOLDSEN, ROSENBERG, WILLIAMS and SUCHMAN, *What College Students Think*, Van Nostrand, 1960.

GOLDTHORPE, J. H. and LOCKWOOD, D., Affluence and the British class structure, *Sociol. Rev.*, 1963, **11**, 133.

GOLDTHORPE, J. H., Social stratification in industrial society, *Soc. Rev.*, Monograph 8, Keele, 1964.

GOLDTHORPE, J. H., LOCKWOOD, D., BECHHOFER, F. and PLATT, J., The affluent worker and the thesis of embourgeoisement: some preliminary research findings, *Sociology*, **1** (1), 1967.

GOODE, W. J. and HATT, P. K., *Methods in Social Research*, Series in Sociol. and Anthrop., McGraw-Hill, New York, 1952.

GORDON, M. M., *Social Class in American Sociology*, McGraw-Hill, 1963.

GOSLIN, D. A. (ed.), *Handbook of Socialisation Theory and Research*, Rand McNally, 1969.

GOTTLIEB, D., Processes of socialisation in graduate schools, *Social Forces*, Dec. 1961, **40**.

GOULDNER, A. W., Cosmopolitans and locals, *Admin. Sci. Quart.*, 1957–8.

GOULDNER, A. W., Organisational analysis, in MERTON, R. K., BROOM, L. B. and COTTRELL, L. S. Jr. (eds.), *Sociology Today*, Harper and Row, New York, 1965.

GOURLAY, D., University teachers call for talks on redundancy, *The Guardian*, 22 May 1967.

GOUVEIA, A. J., Preference for different types of secondary school among various ethnic groups in São Paulo, Brazil, *Sociol. Educ.*, 1966, **39** (2), 155–66.

GRIGNON, C., Centre d'apprentissage ou collèges d'enseignment technique?, in *Les Temps Modernes*, Sept. 1965, No. 232, pp. 467–85.

GRINDER, R. E., Relations of social dating attractions to academic orientation and peer relations, *J. Educ. Psychol.*, 1966, **57** (1), 27–34.

GROSS, N., MASON, N. S., and McEACHERN, A. W., *Explorations in Role Analysis*, John Wiley, 1958.

GULBENKIAN EDUCATIONAL DISCUSSION (1962), Research into higher education, *Universities Quart.*, March 1963, **17** (2), 111–81.

GUSFIELD, J. and RISEMAN, D., Academic standards and "The Two Cultures" in the context of a new state college, *School Rev.*, 1966, **74** (1), 95–116.

HABER, A., Cognitive lag, *Soc. Res.*, Spring 1965, **2**, 42–70.

HALBWACHS, M., *The Psychology of Social Class*, Heinemann, London, 1958.

HALL, E. T., *The Silent Language*, Fawcett Publications Inc., USA, 1961.

HALL, V. C., Former students' evaluation as a criterion for teaching success, *J. Exp. Educ.*, 1965, **34** (1), 1–19.

HALLS, S., Leisure, entertainment, and mass communications, paper to BSA Conference, April 1967.

HALMOS, P. (ed.), *Sociological Studies in British University Education*, Sociological Review Monograph No. 7, University of Keele, 1963.

HALSEY, A. H., British universities and intellectual life, *Univ. Quart.*, Feb. 1958, **12**.

HALSEY, A. H., The changing functions of universities in advanced industrial societies, *Harvard Educ. Rev.*, Spring 1960, **30**, 119–27.

HALSEY, A. H., University expansion and the collegiate ideal, *Univ. Quart.*, Dec. 1961, **16** (1), 55–58.

HALSEY, A. H. (ed.), *Ability and Educational Opportunity*, Paris, 1961.

HALSEY, A. H., Education and mobility, talk on Third Programme, 10 April 1963.

HALSEY, A. H., Education and equality, *New Society*, 17 June 1965, No. 142.

HALSEY, A. H. and MARKS, S., British student politics, *Daedalus* (Special Issue on Students and Politics), Winter 1968.

HALSEY, A. H., FLOUD, J., and ANDERSON, C. A. (eds.) *Education, Economy and Society*, Free Press, Glencoe, Ill., 1961.

HANSON, P., Ideology and the New left, *New Society*, 26 Dec. 1968.

HARP, J. and TARETZ, P., Academic integrity and social structure: a study of cheating among college students, *Soc. Prob.*, 1966, **13** (4), 365–73.

HARRINGTON, M., *The Other America*, Macmillan, New York, 1962.

HARRIS, S. E., *The Market for College Graduates*, Harvard Univ. Press, Cambridge, Mass., 1949.

HATCH, S. *Student Residence: A Discussion of the Literature*, Soc. Res. Higher Ed., 1968.

HAVEMANN, E. and WEST, P. S., *They Went to College*, Harcourt Brace and Co. New, York, 1952.

HAVIGHURST, R. J., Education, social mobility and social change in four societies, *Int. Rev. Educ.*, 1958, **4** (2).

HAVIGHURST, R. J. and NEUGARTEN, B. L., *Society and Education*, Allyn and Bacon, Boston, 1967.

HAWLEY, A. H., BOLAND, W., and BOLAND, M., Population size and administration in institutes of higher education, *ASR*, 1965, **30** (2), 252–5.

HEILBRONNER, R. L. *The Great Ascent: The Struggle for Economic Development in Our Time*, Harper Torchbooks, 1963.

HERBST, P. G., The demand for engineers: a critical reappraisal, *Technologist, 1965–6*, **2** (4), 369–64.

HERKOVITS, M., *Aculturation*, Peter Saite, New York, 1958.

HICKS, J. R., *The Social Framework: An Introduction to Economics*, Oxford, 1942.

HILIARD, T. and ROTH, R. M., Maternal attitudes and the non achievement syndrome, *Personnel and Guidance Journal*, 1969, **47** (5), 424–8.

HIMMELWEIT, H. T., HALSEY, A. H., and OPPENHEIM, R. N., The views of adolescents on some aspect of social class structure, *BJS*, June 1952.

HODGE, R.W. and TREIMAN, D. J., Occupational mobility and attitudes toward Negroes, *ASR*. 1966, **31** (1), 93-102.

HODGE, R. W., SIEGEL, P. M., and ROSSI, P. H., Occupational prestige in the United States, 1925–63, *Am. J. Sociol*, 1964, **70**, 286–302.

HOGGART, R., *The Uses of Literacy*, Chatto & Windus, London, 1957.

HOLLINSHEAD, B. S., *Who Should Go to College*? Columbia Univ. Press, 1952.

HOLMES, B., *Problems in Education: A Comparative Approach*, Routledge & Kegan Paul, 1965.

HOMANS, G. C., *Human Groups* (Int. Lib. of Sociol. and Soc. Reconstr.), Routledge & Kegan Paul, London, 1951.

HOMANS, G. C., *Social Behaviour: Its Elementary Forms* (Int. Lib. of Sociol. and Soc. Reconstr.), Routledge and Kegan Paul, 1961.

HOROWITZ, M., Learning styles and learning outcomes in medical students, *School Rev.*, 1966, **74** (1), 48–65.

HUFFINE, C. L., Inter-socio-economic class language differences: a research report, *Sociol. Soc. Res.*, 1966, **50** (3), 351–7.

HUGHES, E., *Men and their Work*, Free Press, Glencoe, Ill., 1958.

HUGHES, E., and STRAUSS, A. L., *Boys in White*, University of Chicago Press, Chicago, 1961.

HUTCHINS, D., *The Science Undergraduate*, Univ. of Oxford Department of Education, 1967.

HUTCHINSON, H. and YOUNG, C., *Educating the Intelligent*, Penguin Books Ltd., London, 1962.

ILERSIC, A. R., *Statistics*, HFL (Publishers) Ltd., London, 1959.

JACKSON, B., The great social bargain, *New Statesman*, 28 April 1961, p. 665.

JACKSON, B., *Streaming: An Educational System in Miniature* (Institute of Community Studies), Routledge & Kegan Paul, 1964.

JACKSON, B. and MARSDEN, D., *Education and the Working Class* (Institute of Community Studies), Routledge and Kegan Paul, 1962.

JAHODA, C., Job attitude and job choice among secondary modern school leavers, *Occupational Psychol.*, April and October, 1952.

JAHODA, MARIE, *The Education of Technologists: An Exploratory Case Study at Brunel College*, Tavistock Publications, 1963.

JENCKS, C. and REISMAN, D., *The Academic Revolution*, Doubleday, New York, 1968.

JONES, M., What's worrying the students?, *New Statesman*, 17 Feb. 1967.

KAHL, J. A., Educational and occupational aspirations of 'Common Man' boys, *Harvard Educ. Rev.* Summer 1953, 23.

KAHL, J. A., *The American Class Structure*, Holt, Rinehart, 1962.

KALDEGG, A., Heroin addiction, *New Society*, 2 Feb. 1967.

KALTON, G., *The Public Schools: A Factual Survey*, Longmans, London, 1966.

KELSALL, R. K., *Report on an Enquiry into Applications for Admission to Universities*, Association of Universities of the British Commonwealth, London, 1957.

KELSALL, R. K., University Commentary, *Univ. Quart.*, Aug. 1957, pp. 331–4.

KELVIN, R. P., LUCAS, C. J., and OJHA, A. B., The relation between personality, mental health and academic performance in university students, *Brit. J. Soc. Clin. Psych.*, 1965, **4** (4), 244–53.

KEMPER, T., Reference groups socialisation and achievement, *ASR*, **33** (1), Feb. 1968, 32.

KENDALL, P. L., Attitudinal studies among medical students in the United States (Bureau of Applied Soc. Res., Columbia Univ.), paper presented to VIth World Congress of Sociology, 1966.

KENNISTON, K., *The Uncommitted*, Harcourt, Brace and World, New York, 1965.

KENNISTON, K., *Young Radicals*, Harcourt, Brace and World, 1968.

KERR, C., *The Uses of the University*, Harvard University Press, Cambridge, Mass., 1963.

KLINGENDER, F. D., Students in a changing world: I and II, *Yorkshire Bull. Econ. Soc. Res.*, 1954, **6** (2) and (2).

KNAPP, R. H. and GREENBAUM, J. J., *The Young American Scholar: His Collegiate Origins*, University of Chicago Press, Chicago, 1953.

KNOX, H. M., *Two Hundred and Fifty Years of Scottish Education*, Oliver and Boyd, Edinburgh, 1963.

KOHN, M. L. and WILLIAMS, R., Situational patterning in intergroup relations, *ASR*, **21**, 164.

KOILE, E. A., HARREN, V. A. and DRAEGER, C., Higher education programmes, *Rev. Ed. Res.*, **34**, 2, April 1966.

KOMAROVSKY, M., Cultural contradictions and sex roles, *Am. J. Sociol.*, 1946, **52**, 184–9.

KOMAROVSKY, M., *Women in the Modern World, their Education and their Dilemmas*, Little, Brown, 1953.

KOPKIND, A., Crisis in the knowledge industry—the Berkeley sacking, *New Statesman*, 3 Feb. 1967.

KOPKIND, A., The military connection: The Pentagon shadow over U.S. universities, *New Statesman*, 12 Sept. 1969.

KOWALEWSKA, S., Higher education and the preparation for industrial work in Poland (Polish Academy of Sciences), paper presented to the VIth World Congress of Sociology, 1966.

KUNODA, Y., Agencies of political socialisation and political change: political orientation of Japanese law students, *Hum. Org.*, 1965, **24** (4), 328–31.

KUNZ, G. and LUSCHEM, G., Leisure and social stratification, communication presented to the VIth World Congress of Sociology, 1966.

LACEY, C., Some sociological concomitants of academic streaming in a grammar school, *BJS*, Sept. 1966, 17 (3).

LAUWERYS, J. A., United Kingdom, England and Wales, in *Access to Higher Education*, Vol. 2, UNESCO and Int. Assoc. of Univs. 1965.

LAZARSFELD, P. F. and ROSENBERG, M., *The Language of Social Research*, Free Press, Glencoe, Ill., 1957.

LAZARSFELD, P. F., and THIELANS, W., *The Academic Mind*, Free Press, Glencoe, Ill., 1958.

LEEDS UNIVERSITY, *Report of a Committee on Student Accommodation*, Feb. 1962.

LEHMANN, I. J., SINHA, B. K. and HARTNETT, R. T., Changes in attitudes and values associated with college attendance, *J. Educ. Psychol.*, 1966, **57** (2), 89–98.

LESTER SMITH, W. O., *Education: An Introductory Survey*, Penguin, London, 1957.

LEVENSON, W. B., *The Spiral Pendulum: The Urban School in Transition*, Rand McNally, Chicago, 1968.

LEVY-STRAUSS, C., Social structure, *Anthropology Today, An Encyclopedic Inventory* (ed. Kroeber), University of Chicago Press, Chicago, 1953.

LEWIS, L. S., Faculty support of academic freedom and selfgovernment, *Soc. Prob.*, 1966, 13 (4), 450–61.

LIGHT, D. W., JR., Social participation in public and catholic schools (University of Chicago), paper presented to the VIth World Congress of Sociology, 1966.

LINTON, R., *The Study of Man*, Appleton Century, 1936.

LIPSET, S. M., Special issue on student politics, *Comp. Educ. Rev.*, 1966, 10 (2), 129–31.

LIPSET, S. M. and ALTBACH, P., Social mobility and occupational career patterns, *AJS*, Jan. & March 1952, 57, 366–74, 494–504.

LIPSET, S. M. and ALTBACH, P., American student protest, *New Society*, 1966, 105, 328–32.

LIPSET, S. M. and ALTBACH, P., U.S. campus alienation, *New Society*, 1966, 206, 361–4.

LIPSET, S. M. and BENDIX, R., Social status and social structure: A re-examination of data and interpretations: III, *BJS*, 1951, 2, 150–68 and 230–54.

LIPSET, S. M. and WOLIN, S. S., *The Berkeley Student Revolt*, Doubleday Anchor Books, 1965.

LIPSITZ, L., Working class authoritarianism: a revaluation, *ASR*, 1965, 30 (1), 103–9.

LITTLE, A. N., Will more mean worse?, *BJS*, 1961, 12 (4).

LITTLE, A. N., and WESTERGAARD, J., The trend of class differentials in educational opportunity in England and Wales, *BJS*, Dec. 1964, 15 (4).

LITTLE, J. K., *A State-wide Inquiry into Decisions of Youth about Education beyond High School*, School of Education, University of Wisconsin, Madison, 1958.

LITTLE, K., *Negroes in Britain: A Study of Race Relations in English Society*, Kegan Paul, Trench, Trubner Co. Ltd., London, 1948.

LITTLE, K., *Social Anthropology in Modern Life*, Inaugural Lecture delivered before the University of Edinburgh, 18 Jan. 1965, University of Edinburgh Press.

LITTLE, K., Academic protest in the United States, *The Listener*, 12 Aug. 1965.

LITTLEJOHN, J., *Westrigg: The Sociology of a Cheviot Parish*, Internat. Lib. of Sociol. and Soc. Reconstr., Routledge and Kegan Paul, 1963.

LOCKWOOD, D., Can we cope with social change?, *New Society*, 28 Nov. 1963, No. 61.

LOCKWOOD, D., Social mobility, in WELFORD, A. T., *et al.*, *Society: Problems and Methods of Study*, Routledge, 1962.

LOCKWOOD, D., The new working class, *Eur. J. Sociol.*, *Archives Européennes de Sociologie*, 1 (2) 1960, 248–59.

LOCKWOOD, D., Sources of variation in working class images of society, *Sociol. Rev.*, Nov. 1966, 14 (3).

LOCKWOOD, D., and GOLDTHORPE, J. H., Affluence and the British class structure, *Sociol. Rev.*, 1963, 11, 133.

LOCKWOOD, D., GOLDTHORPE, J. H., BECHHOFER, D., and PLATT, J., The affluent worker and the thesis of embourgeoisement: some preliminary research findings, *Sociology*, 1967, 1 (1).

LOWNDES, G. Y. N., *The Silent Social Revolution*, Oxford, 1937.

LUSKY, L. and LUSKY, M. H., Columbia 1968: The wound unhealed, *Pol. Sci. Quart.* June 1969, 34 (2), 169–289.

LYNN, K. S., *et al.* (ed.), *The Professions in America*, Houghton-Mifflin C., Boston, 1965.

MACK, E. C., *Public Schools and British Public Opinion, 1780–1860*, London, 1938.

MACPHERSON, J. S., *Eleven Year Olds Grow Up*, Scottish Council for Research in Education, London, 1958, pp. 64–77, and 126–9. Reprinted in Floud *et al.*, 1961, *Selection in Scottish Secondary Schools.*

McCLELLAND, D. C., *et al.*, *The Achievement Motive*, Appleton-Century Crofts Inc., New York, 1953.

McCLELLAND, D. C., *et al.*, *Talent and Society*, Van Nostrand, New York, 1958.

McDILL, E. L. and COLEMAN, J., Family and peer influences in colleges plans of high school students, *Sociol. Educ.*, 1965, **38** (2), 112–16.

McDONALD, I. J., Educational opportunity at university level in Scotland assessed in the light of a comparison of the social origins of a sample of students in the University of Glasgow in the years 1910, 1934 and 1960. Unpublished B. Ed. thesis, Glasgow University, 1964.

McKINLEY, D. G., *Social Class and Family Life*, Free Press, Glencoe, Ill., 1964.

MALCOLM, X., *Autobiography*, Grove Press, N.Y., 1966.

MALLESON, N., Student performance at University College, London, 1948–57, *Univ. Quart.*, May 1958, **12**.

MALLESON, N., Operational research in the university, *Brit. Med. J.*, 18 April 1959, pp. 1031–5.

MALLESON, N., The study of students, *J. Med. Educ.*, Dec. 1959, **34** (12), 1147–1153.

MALLESON, N., Must students be wasted?, *New Society*, 2 May 1963.

MANGALAM, J. J., Rural-urban differences in academic performance of Pakistani college students, and their implications for change, Paper prepared for Research Group in Sociology of Education, VIth World Congress of Sociology, 1966.

MANN, P. H. and MILLS, G., Living and learning at redbrick: a sample survey at Sheffield University, *Univ. Quart.*, Dec. 1961, **16**, 19–35.

MANNHEIM, K., *Man in Society in an Age of Reconstruction*, Kegan Paul, 1940.

MARRIOTT, M. Interactional and attributional theories of caste ranking, *Man in India*, 1959, **39** (2), 92–107.

MARRIS, P., *The Experience of Higher Education*, Routledge and Kegan Paul, 1964.

MARRIS, P. and REIN, M., *Dilemmas of Social Reform*, Routledge and Kegan Paul, 1967.

MARSHALL, T. H., Social class—a preliminary analysis, Originally in *Sociol. Rev.*, 1933, **26**, reprinted in *Citizenship and Social Class*, Cambridge University Press, 1950, pp. 86–113.

MARSHALL, T. H., *Citizenship and Social Class and Other Essays*, Cambridge University Press, 1950.

MARSHALL, T. H., Social selection in the welfare state, *Eugenics Rev.*, 1953, **45** (2).

MATZA, D., Subterranean traditions of youth, *Ann. Am. Acad. Polit. Soc. Sci.*, 1961, **338**, 102–18.

MAYNTZ, R., *Soziale Schichtung und sozialer Wandel in einer Industriegemeinde*, Stuttgart, 1958.

MEAD, G. H., *Mind, Self and Society*, University of Chicago Press, Chicago, 1934.

MEAD, G. H., *On Social Psychology*, Selected papers (ed.) Strauss, A., Phoenix Books, University of Chicago, 1964.

MEAD, M., *The School in American Culture*, Harvard University Press, Cambridge, Mass., 1957.

MEADE, J. E. and PARKES, A. S. (eds.), *Genetic and Environmental Factors in Human Ability*, Oliver & Boyd, 1966.

MERTON, R. K., *Social Theory and Social Structure*, rev. edn., Free Press, Glencoe, Ill., 1967.

MERTON, R. K., BROOM, L., and COTTRELL, L. S. (eds.), *Sociology Today*, Basic Books, New York, 1959.

MERTON, R. K., READER, G. C., and KENDALL, P. L. (eds.), *The Student Physician*, Harvard University Press, Cambridge, 1957.

METZER, W. P., SANFORD, H. K., DE BARDELEBEN, A., and BLOUSTEIN, E. J., *Dimensions of Academic Freedom*, Univ. of Illinois Press, 1969.

MILLER, M. V. and GILMORE, S. (eds.), *Revolution at Berkeley*, Dell, New York, 1965.

MILLER, S. M., Comparative social mobility, *Current Sociol.*, 1960, **9** (1).

MILLER, W., Concerning student government, M.A. dissertation presented Edinburgh Dept. Soc. Anth., June 1965.

MINISTRY OF EDUCATION, *Education in 1956*, Cmd. 223, London, 1957, pp. 56, 94–95, 111, 119.

MINISTRY OF EDUCATION, *Statistics of Education*, Vols. 1–6, HMSO, 1966.

MOORE, W. E., *The Impact of Industry*, Prentice Hall, 1965.

MORONEY, M. J., *Fact from Figures*, Penguin Books Ltd., London, 1951.

MORRIS, D., *The Naked Ape*, Corgi Books, 1968.

MORRISON, A. and McINTYRE, D., The attitudes of students towards international affairs, *Brit. J. Soc. Clin. Psych.*, 1966, **5** (1), 17–23.

MORRISON, D. E. and HENKEL, R. E., Significance tests reconsidered, *Am. Sociol.*, May 1969, **4** (2), 131–40.

MOSER, C. A., *Survey Methods in Social Investigation*, Heinemann, 1958.

MOSER, C. A. and LAYARD, P. R. G., La Planification du développement de l'enseignement supérieur en Grand Bretagne: Quelques problèmes de statistique, *Paedogogica Europaea*, 1965, **1** (1), 153–208.

MOYNIHAN, D. P., *Maximum Feasible Misunderstanding*, Free Press, N.Y., 1969.

MUSGROVE, S., *The Migratory Elite*, Heinemann, 1963.

NADEL, S. F., *The Theory of Social Structure*, Cohen and West Ltd., 1957.

NASATIIR, D., Education and social change: the Argentine case, *Sociol. Educ.*, 1966, **39** (2), 167–82.

NATIONAL UNION OF STUDENTS, *Case against Loans: N.U.S. Policy on Student Support*, N.U.S., London, 1966.

NETTL, J. P. and ROBERTSON, R., *International Systems and the Modernisation of Societies: the Formulation of National Goals and Attitudes*, Basic Books, 1968.

NEUBECK, G. and HEWER, V., Time of marriage and college attendance, *J. Marr. Fam.*, 1965, **27** (4), 522–4.

NEVIN, M., A study of the background of students in University College, Dublin, *J. Statist. Social Inquiry Soc. Ireland*, 1967.

NEWCASTLE UNIVERSITY, Calendar, 1963–4.

NEWCOMBE, T. M. and WILSON, E. K., *Personality and Social Change: Attitude Formation in a student community*, Holt, Rinehart & Winston, 1943.

NEWCOMB, T. M. and WILSON, E. K. (eds.), *College Peer Groups*, Aldine Publishing Co., Chicago, 1966.

NEWSOM REPORT, *Half Our Future*, Ministry of Education, A Report of the Central Council for Education (England), HMSO, 1963.

NEWFIELD, J. G. H., The academic performance of British university students, *Sociol. Rev.*, Special Monograph No. 7, Oct. 1963.

NIGHTINGALE, B., The student schism, *New Society*, 16 Feb. 1967.

NISBET, J. D., Family environment and intelligence, *Eugenics Rev.*, 1963, **45**, 31–42.

NISBET, J. D. and GRANT, W., Vocational intentions and decisions of Aberdeen arts graduates, *Occup. Psychol.*, 1965, **39** (3), 215–19.

NORWOOD, C., *The English Tradition of Education*, London, 1929.

OELTING, E. R., Dogmatism in college students, *Alberta J. Educ. Res.*, 1966, **21** (1), 37–39.

OLDMAN, D. and ILLSLEY, R., Measuring the status of occupations, *Sociol. Rev.*, 1966, **14** (1), 53–72.

OLESEN, VIRGINIA L. and WHITTAKER, ELVI W., Some thoughts on images of man implicit in sociological students of professional education, paper prepared for VIth World Congress of Sociology, 1966.

OLESEN, VIRGINIA L. and WHITTAKER, ELVI W., Open Committee L.S.E. Socialist Society, *L.S.E.*, *What it is and how we fought it*. Agitator Publication, Pirate Press, London, 1967.

OLESEN, VIRGINIA L. and WHITTAKER, ELVI W., *The Silent Dialogue*, Jossey-Bass Inc., California, 1968.

OPPENHEIM, A. N., Social status and clique formation among grammar school boys, *BJS*, 1955, **61**, 288–45.

ORLEANS, L. A., *Professional Manpower and Education in Communist China*, The National Science Foundation, Washington D.C., 1961.

OSSOWSKI, S., *Class Structure in the Social Consciousness* (Internat. Lib. of Sociol. and Soc. Reconstr.), Routledge and Kegan Paul, 1963 (trans. from the Polish by Sheila Patterson).

OTTAWAY, A. K. C., *Education and Society: An Introduction to the Sociology of Education* (Internat. Lib. of Sociol. and Soc. Reconstr.), Routledge & Kegan Paul, 1953.

PACE, C. R., *College and University Environment Scales: Preliminary Technical Manual*, Princeton, E.T.S., 1963.

PARETO, V., *Sociological Writings*, Selected and Introduced by FINER, S. E. (trans. by Mirfin Derick), Pall Mall Press, 1966.

PARETO, V., *The Mind and Society*, III (trans. Livingstone and Bongiorno), New York and London, 1935.

PARSONS, T., *The Structure of Social Action: A Study in Social Theory with Special Reference to a Group of Recent European writers*, Free Press, Glencoe, Ill., 1949.

PARSONS, T., *The Social System*, Routledge and Kegan Paul, 1956.

PARSONS, T., The school class as a social system: some of its functions in American society, *Harvard Educ. Rev.*, Fall 1959, **29**, 297–318.

PARSONS, T., Unity and diversity in the modern intellectual disciplines: the roles of the social sciences, *Daedalus*, 1965, **94** (1), 39–65.

PARSONS, T. and BALES, R. F., *et al.*, *Family Socialization and Internation Process*, Free Press, Glencoe, Ill., 1955.

PASSERON, J. C., QUEYSANNE, B., and SAINT-MARTIN, M., *Les Etudiants en Médecine*, Centre du Sociologie Européenne, Paris, 1966.

PATRIDGE, P. H., Universities in Australia, *Comp. Educ.*, 1965, **2** (1), 19–30.

PAVALKO, R. M. and BISHOP, D. R., Socio-economic status and college plans: a study of Canadian high school students, *Sociol. Educ.*, 1966, **39** (3), 288–98.

PEDLEY, R., *The Comprehensive School*, Penguin, revised edition, 1969.

PETERSON, A. D. C., *A Hundred Years of Education*, Gerald Duckworth & Co. Ltd., London, 1952.

PHILLIPS, E. G., More and more students, *Univ. Quart.*, Feb. 1958, **12**, 126.

PILKINGTON, G. W., POPPLETON, P. K., and ROBERTSHAW, G., Changes in religious attitude and practices among students during university degree courses, *Brit. J. Educ. Psych.*, 1965, **35** (2), 150–7.

PLOWDEN REPORT, *Children and their Primary Schools*, Department of Education and Science, a report of the CACE (England), HMSO, 1967.

PLOWMAN, D. E. G., MINCHINTON, W. E., and STACEY, MARGARET, Local status in England and Wales, *Sociol. Rev.*, July 1962, **10**, 161–262.

PORTER, J., *The Vertical Mosaic*, University of Toronto Press, 1965.

PRESIDENT'S COMMISSION ON HIGHER EDUCATION, *Higher Education for American Democracy*, Government Printing Press Office, Washington, 1947.

PRICE, C., Death on the Mexican campus, *New Statesman*, 26 Nov. 1969.

QUARANTELLI, E., The career choice patterns of dental students of health, *Human Behav.*, Summer 1961, **2**.

QUARANTELLI, E., HELFRICH, M., and YUTZY, D., Faculty and student perceptions in a professional school, *Sociol. Soc. Res.*, Oct. 1964, **49**.

RAMSAY, N. R., College recruitment and high school curricula, *Sociol. Educ.*, 1965, **38** (4), 297–309.

RASHDALL, H., *The Universities of Europe in the Middle Ages*, Clarendon Press, Oxford, 1936.

RAYNAUD, J.-D., and TOURAINE, AL., Deux notes à propos d'une enquête sur les étudiants en médecine, *Cahiers Int. de Sociol.*, nouvelle série, troisième année, 1956, **20**.

REGISTRAR-GENERAL, *Classification of Occupations*, 1951 Census, and 1961 Census, HMSO.

REIL, MARGARET, Ghanaian university students: the broadening base, *BJS*, 1965, **16** (1), 19–27.

REISS, A. J., JR., OCCUPATIONS AND SOCIAL STATUS, Free Press, Glencoe, Ill., 1961.

REISSMAN, L., Levels of aspiration and social class, *ASR*, 1953, **18**, 233–42.

REPORT OF ROYAL COMMISSION ON THE UNIVERSITY OF DURHAM, Cmd. 4815, HMSO, 1935.

REX, J., and MOORE, R., *Race Community and Conflict*, OUP (for Instit. of Race Relations). 1967.

REXIN, M., The Berlin university crisis, *New Soc.*, 11 May 1967.

RIESMAN, D., *Constraint and Variety in American Education*, Doubleday Anchor Books, New York, 1958.

RIESMAN, D., *The Lonely Crowd* (with Denney, R. and Gleizer, N.), Yale UP, 1950.

ROBBINS REPORT, *Higher Education*, HMSO, Cmd. 2154, London, 1963, and Appendix I, Cmd. 2154–I, 1963.

ROBERTSON, SIR C., *The British Universities*, London, 1944.

ROBINSON, J. B. and BELLOWS, R. M., Characteristics of successful dental students, *J. Am. Ass. Coll. Regents*, Jan. 1951.

RODGER, A., Capacity and inclination for university courses, *Occup. Psychol.*, 1965, **39** (1), 37–43.

ROETHLISBERGER, F. J. and DICKSON, W. J., *Management and the Worker*, Harvard University Press, Cambridge, Mass., 1939.

ROGERS, E. M. (In assoc. with SVENNING, L.), *Modernisation among Peasants: the Impact of Communication*, Holt, Rinehart & Winston, 1969.

ROGOFF, N., American public schools and equality of opportunity, *Journal of Educn. Sociol.*, Feb. 1960, pp. 252–9.

ROGOFF, N., Local social structure and educational selection, Chapter 20 in HALSEY *et al.*, *Education Economy and Society*, Free Press, Glencoe, Ill., 1961.

ROMAN, F. W., *New Education in Europe: An Account of the Recent Fundamental Changes in the Educational Philosophy of Great Britain, France and Germany*, London, 1924.

ROSE, E. J. B. and Associates, *Colour and Citizenship: A Report on British Race Relations*, Oxford Univ. Press, 1969.

ROSS, J. M. and CASE, P., Who goes to Oxbridge?, *New Society*, 1966, **190**, 11–13.

ROSTOW, W. W., *The Stages of Economic Growth*, Cambridge University Press, N.Y., 1960.

ROSZAK, T. (ed.), *The Dissenting Academy*, Chatto & Windus, 1969.

RUDD, E., What students spend, *Univ. Quart.*, Sept. 1962, **16** (4), 379–92 (published DSIR).

RUDD, E., The Student Conflict, *New Society*, **285**, 14 March 1968.

RUDMAN, H. C. and FEATHERSTONE, R. L. (eds.), *Urban Schooling*, Harcourt, Brace & World, 1968.

RUNCIMAN, W. G., Embourgeoisement self-rated class and party preferences, *Sociol. Review*, new series, July 1964, **12**, 137–54.

SAINT-MARTIN, MONIQUE, *L'Engrénage: les Étudiants en Sciences Originaires des Classes Populaires*, Centre de Sociologie Européenne, 1966, communication to VIth World Congress of Sociology, 1966.

SAINT-MARTIN, M., BOLTANSKI, L., CASTEL, R. and LEMAIRE, M., *Les Étudiants en Sciences du Premier Cycle*, Centre de Sociologie Européenne, Paris, 1966.

SANDFORD, C. T., COUPER, M. E., and GRIFFIN, S., Class influences in higher education, *Brit. J. Educ. Psychol.*, June 1965, **35** (2).

SANDFORD, N., (ed.), *The American College*, John Wiley, New York, 1962.

SAYRE, N. The Black Panthers are coming: America on the eve of Race Revolution, *New Statesman*, 2 May 1969.

SAYRE, N., Upheaval at Harvard, *New Statesman*, 16 May 1969.

SCHACHNER, N., *The Medieval Universities*, Allen & Unwin Ltd., London, 1938, and Barnes and Noble, New York, 1962.

SCHAEFER, H., Études médicales et reforme de l'enseignement en Allemagne, *Rev. Enseignement Supérieur*, 1957, **3**, July–Sept.

SCHWARZWELLER, H. K., Educational aspirations and life chances of German young people, paper prepared for Research Group on Sociology of Education at the VIth World Congress of Sociology, 1966.

SCOTT, J. F., The American college sorority: its role in class and ethnic endogamy, *ASR*, 1965, **30**, 514–27.

SCOTT, J. W. and EL-ASSAL, M., Multiversity, university size, university quality and student protest—an empirical study, *ASR*, Oct. 1969, **34** (5), 702–23.

SEALE, P. and McCONVILLE, M., *French Revolution 1968*, Penguin, 1968.

SEARLS, LAURA G., Leisure role emphasis of college graduate homemakers, *J. Marr. Fam.*, 1966, **28** (1), 77–82.

SEGAL, B. E., Fraternities, social distance, and anti-semitism among Jewish and non-Jewish undergraduates, *Sociol. Educ.*, 1965, **38** (3), 251–64.

SELBY, H. A. and WOODS, C. M., Foreign students at a high pressure university, *Sociol. Educ.*, 1966, **39** (2), 138–54.

SEWELL, W. H., Community of residence and college plans, *ASR*, 29 Feb. 1964, pp. 24–38.

SEWELL, W. H. and ARMER, J. M., Neighbourhood context and college plans, *ASR*, 31 April 1966, pp. 159–68.

SEWELL, W. H. and ORENSTEIN, A. H., Community of residence and occupational choice, *Am. J. Sociol.*, 1965, **70** (5), 551–63.

SEWELL, W. H. and SHAH VIMAL, P., Socio-economic status, intelligence and the attainment of higher education, paper for the Research Group on the Sociology of Education of the VIth World Congress of Sociology, 1966.

SEWELL, W. H., HALLER, A. O., and STRAUSS, M. A., Social status and educational and occupational aspiration, *ASR*, 22 Feb. 1957, pp. 67–73.

SHATZMANN, L. and STRAUSS, A., Social class and modes of communication, *Am. J. Sociol.*, Jan. 1955, **60**, 329–38.

SHILS, E. A., The intellectuals, Great Britain, *Encounter*, April 1955, **6**.

SHILS, E. A., The study of universities: the need for disciplined enquiry, *Univ. Quart.*, Dec. 1961, **16** (1), 14–18.

SHILS, E. A., Plenitude and scarcity: the anatomy of international cultural crisis, *Encounter*, May 1969.

SHUTZ, A., On multiple realities, in NATANSON, MAURICE (ed.), *Collected Papers: I, The Problem of Social Reality*, Martinus Nijhoff, The Hague, 1962.

SILVER, E. and SHEARER, L., LSE runs to California pattern, *The Guardian*, 15 March 1967.

SILVER, H., Salaries for students?, *Univ. Quart.*, Sept. 1965, **19** (4).

SILVER, H., Education and the working of democracy, *Techn. Educ.*, 1966, **8** (5), 204–5.

SIMEY, T. S., *The Sociology of Higher Education: A Note on Research Priorities*, Sociological Review Monograph No. 7 (ed. P. Halmos), pp. 199–204.

SLOMAN, A., *A University in the Making*, BBC, 1964, Reith Lectures 1963 (Plans for the University of Essex).

SMITH, D. M., The changing university: a report on Cambridge today, *Encounter*, May 1956.

SOMMER, R., Further studies of small group ecology, *Sociometry*, 1965, **28** (4), 337–48.

STACEY, B. G., Some psychological aspects of intergeneration occupational mobility, *Brit. J. Soc. Clin. Psych.*, 1965, **4** (4), 275–86.

STATISTICS OF EDUCATION, U. K., Vols. 1–6, 1967. HMSO, 1969.

STEDMAN JONES, G., BARNETT, A., and WENGRAF, T., Student power: what is to be done? *New Left Review*, May–June 1967, No. 43.

STIVERS, E. H., Motivation for college in high school boys, *School Rev.*, 1958, **66**, 341–56.

STIVERS, E. H., Motivation for college in high school girls, *School Rev.*, 1959, **67**, 320–34.

STONE, R., A model of the educational system, *Minerva*, 1965, **111** (2), 172–86.

STONQUIST, E. V., *The Marginal Man*, Scribner, New York, 1937.

STRAUSS, A., *Mirrors and Masks*, Free Press, Glencoe, Ill., 1959.

STREZIKOZIN, V., Certain questions concerning the further perfection of the educational process, *Soviet Educ.*, 1966, **8** (3), 38–50.

STRONG, J., *History of Secondary Education in Scotland—from Early Times to the Education Act of 1908*, Oxford, 1909.

STUDENT RELATIONS, Vol. I. *Report from the Select Committee on Education and Science, Session 1968–69*. HMSO, London, 1969.

SUMPF, J., Aperçu la sociologie de l'éducation aux États-Unis, l'étude des effets, *Rev. Française Sociol.*, April–June 1965, **6**, 203–14.

SURFT, D. F., Social class and achievement motivation, *Educ. Res.*, 1966, **8** (2), 83–95.

SVALASTOGA, K., *Prestige, Class and Mobility*, Scandinavian University Books, London, 1959.

TAYLOR, W., The University teacher of education in England, *Comp. Educ.*, 1965, **1** (3), 193–202.

TAYLOR, W., Higher education in Britain, *Nature*, 31 July 1965, 207 (4996).

TAYLOR, W., Student culture and residence, *Univ. Quart.*, Sept. 1965.

TAYLOR, W., Regional origins of students in colleges of education, *Educn. for Teaching*, **74**, Autumn 1967.

THODAY, D., Halls of residence, *Univ. Quart.*, 1957, **12**, (1).

THODAY, D., Residence and education in civic universities, *Int. Soc. Psychiat.*, 1958, 4 (3).

THODAY, D., University expansion and student life, *Univ. Quart.*, June 1960, **14** (3), 272–7.

THOMAS, W. I., *Social Behaviour and Personality*, Soc. Sc. Res. Council, New York, 1951.

TOMASSON, R. F., From elitism to egalitarianism in Swedish education, *Sociol. Educ.*, 1965, **38** (3), 203–23.

TREANTON, J. R., Le concept de Carrière, *Rev. Française Sociol.*, Jan.–March 1960, **1**.

TROPP, A. and LITTLE, A., Blueprint for a university, *New Society*, 6 June 1963, No. 36.

TROW, M. The undergraduate dilemma in the large state universities, *Univ. Quart.*, 21 (1), Dec. 1966.

TROW, M. and HALSEY, A. H., British academics and the professorship, *Sociology*, **3** (3), Sept. 1969, 321–41.

TURNER, G., *The North Country*, Eyre & Spottiswoode, 1967.

TURNER, R. H., Sponsored and contest mobility and the school system, *ASR*, 1960, **25** (5) (reprinted in Halsey, Floud and Anderson).

TYMIENICKA, ANNA-TERESA, *Phenomenology and Science in Contemporary European Thought*, Farra, Strauss and Cudaly, New York, 1962.

UNION OF LOUGHBOROUGH COLLEGES, *Student Survey*, Union of Loughborough Colleges, 1964.

UNITED STATES GOVERNMENT, *Conditions of Negroes in the United States*, Washington, D.C., 1967.

UNIVERSITY CENTRAL COUNCIL FOR ADMISSIONS. *First Report 1962–63*, London, 1964.

UNIVERSITY CENTRAL COUNCIL FOR ADMISSIONS. *Second Report 1963–64*, London, 1965.

UNIVERSITY CENTRAL COUNCIL FOR ADMISSIONS. *Third Report 1964–65*, London, 1966.

UNIVERSITY GRANTS COMMITTEE, *University Development 1952–57*, Cmd. 534, HMSO, London, 1958.

UNIVERSITY GRANTS COMMITTEE, *University Development—Interim Report on the Years 1952–56*, Cmd. 79, London, March 1957.

UNIVERSITY GRANTS COMMITTEE, *Report of the Sub-committee on Halls of Residence*, HMSO, London, 1957.

UNIVERSITY OF NEWCASTLE UPON TYNE, *Students' Representative Council: Articles of Constitution Laws and Bye-Laws*, first edition, 1963.

UNIVERSITY OF NEWCASTLE UPON TYNE, *Students' Handbook, 1963–4, 1964–5*, SRC.

VAIZEY, J., *The Costs of Education*, London, 1957.

VAIZEY, J., Patterns of higher education, *Education*, 6, 13, 20, 27 Jan. 1961.

VEBLEN, T., *The Higher Learning in America*, B. W. Huebsch, New York, 1918.

VEBLEN, T., *The Theory of the Leisure Class*, Allen and Unwin, London, 1924.

VENABLES, E. C., Success in technical college courses according to size of firm, *Occup. Psychol.*, 1965, **39** (2), 123–34.

VERNON, P. E., *Secondary School Selection: A British Psychological Inquiry*, Methuen Co. Ltd., London, 1957.

VERNON, P. E. (ed.), *Ability and Attainment Testing*, London, 1960.

VREELAND, R. S. and BIDWELL, C., Classifying university departments: an approach to the analysis of their effects upon undergraduates' values and attitudes, *Sociol. Educ.*, 1966, **39** (3), 237–54.

WALLACE, W. L., *Student Culture*, Norc. Monograph No. 9, Aldine, 1965.

WALLER, W., The rating and dating complex, *ASR*, 1937, **2**, 727–34.

WARNER, R., *English Public Schools*, London, 1945.

WARNER, W. L., *et al.*, *Social Class in America: A Manual of Procedure for the Measurement of Social Status*, Harper, Torch Books, New York, 1960.

WARNER, W. L. and ABEGGLIN, J. C., *Big Business Leaders in America*, Harper, New York, 1955.

WARNER, W. L., HAVIGHURST, R. J., and LOEB, M. B., *Who Shall Be Educated?*, New York, 1944.

WATSON, W., *The Managerial Spiralist in the Twentieth Century*, London, 1960. Also Social mobility and social class—industrial communities, in *Closed Systems and Open Minds* (eds. Devons, E. and Gluckman, M.), Oliver and Boyd, Edinburgh, 1964.

WEBER, MAX, *The Theory of Social and Economic Organisations* (trans. A. M. Henderson and Talcott Parsons), Free Press, Glencoe, Illinois, 1947.

WEINBERG, C., Institutional differences in factors associated with student leadership, *Sociol. Soc. Res.*, 1965, **49** (4), 425–36.

614 *Bibliography*

WEINBERG, C., The price of competition, *Teach. Coll. Record*, 1965, **67** (2), 106–14.
WEINSTEIN, E., The development of interpersonal competence, in GOSLIN, D. A., *Handbook of Socialisation Theory and Research*, Rand McNally, 1969.
WELFORD, A. T., *et al.*, *Society: Problems and Methods of Study*, Routledge, 1962.
WERTS, C. E., Social class and initial career choice of college freshmen, *Sociol. Educ.*, 1966, **39** (1), 74–85.
WESTBY, D. L. and BRAUNGART, R. G., Class and politics in the family backgrounds of student political activists, *ASR*, 1966, **31** (5), 690–2.
WESTERN, S. C., Community college and school, *Adult. Educ.*, 1965, **38** (4), 191–7.
WESTLEY, W. A. and EPSTEIN, N. B., *Silent Majority*, Jossey-Bass Inc., California, 1969.
WHILLIE, R. W., Ghanaian university students—a research note, *BJS*, 1966, **17** (3), 306–11.
WHITE, E. C., *These will go to College*, The Press of Western Reserve University, Cleveland, 1952.
WHYTE, W. F., *Street Corner Society*, Chicago University Press, Chicago, 1943.
WHYTE, W. F. (ed.), *Industry and Society*, New York, 1946.
WHYTE, W. H., *The Organisation Man*, Cape Ltd., London, 1957.
WILLIAMS, R., *Whose Public Schools?*, London, 1957.
WILLIAMS, R. M. (Jr.), Individual and group values, *Annals of the Am. Assoc. of Pol. & Soc. Sc.*, May 1967, **371**, 20–37.
WILSON, B., Threats to university values, *New Society*, 22 April 1965, No. 134.
WINCH, R. F., *Identification and its Familial Determinants*, Indianapolis, Ind., Bobbs Merrill, 1963.
WINCH, R. F. and CAMPBELL, D. T., Proof? No. Evidence? Yes. The significance of tests of significance, *Am. Sociol.*, May 1969, **4** (2), 140–3.
WING, C. W., JR., Student selection, the educational environment and the cultivation of talent, *Daedalus*, 1965, **94** (3), 632–41.
WOLFLE, D. (ed.), *America's Resources of Specialized Talent*, Harper, New York, 1954.
WOOD, S. M., Uniform—its significance as a factor in role relationships, *Sociol. Rev.*, July 1961, **14** (1).
WOODHALL, M. and BLAUG, M., Productivity trends in British university education, *Minerva*, 1965, **3** (4), 483–98.
WORSLEY, P. M., Authority and the young, *New Society*, **147**, 10–13.
WORSLEY, P. M., The distribution of power in industrial society, *Sociological Review* Monograph 8, Keele, 1964.
WRIGHT, H. and BARKER, R. G., *Methods in Psychological Ecology*, Ray's Printing Service, Topeka, Kansas, 1950.
WROCZYNSKI, R., Srodki masowej Komunikacji i wychowanie (The mass media and education), *Kwartalnik Pedag.*, 1966, **11** (2), 59–73.
WRONG, D., The oversocialised conception of man, *ASR*, April 1961, **26** (2), 183–93.

YATES, A. and PIDGEON, D. A., *Admission to Grammar Schools*, Newnes Educational Publishing Co., London, 1957.
YEARBOOK OF EDUCATION, 1950, Evans, London, pp. 639–44.
YOUNG, M., *The Rise of the Meritocracy, 1870–2033*, Thames and Hudson, 1958.

ZWEIG, F., *The Student in the Age of Anxiety: A Survey of Oxford and Manchester Students*, Heinemann, 1963.

NAME INDEX

SUBJECT INDEX

Aberdeen University 24, 178, 201
Ability 8, 28, 29, 32, 33, 38, 39, 45, 48,
 49–51, 54, 57, 62, 65, 73, 78, 169,
 170, 263, 267, 402, 403, 404
Academic class of students 418, 419,
 548
Academic concentration 70, 298, 299
Academic divisions 371
Academic freedom 25, 477, 486, 496, 541
Academic gowns 379, 382
Academic hurdles 15, 42, 307–8
Academic interest 189, 191
Academic market place 18
Academic record 49, 266, 402
Academic standards 59, 60, 186, 187,
 342, 530
Academic subculture 43, 44, 71, 266 n.,
 344, 356, 373, 381, 386
Accents (status of) 202, 223, 231, 261,
 269, 272, 278, 279, 280, 310, 340,
 341, 347, 348–9, 399, 401, 411
Accentuation of class divisions 434
Acceptance patterns 210, 222, 224,
 272–4, 337, 348, 354
Accidental drop-ins to courses 177
Accommodation 70, 96–104, 128, 129,
 161, 170, 313–35, 354, 355, 438,
 443, 537
Accommodation changes 315
Accountability of universities 477, 478
Achieved status 337
Achievement (in education) 3, 4, 6, 8,
 15, 18, 34, 36, 49, 52, 54, 55, 56, 57,
 58, 59, 63, 70, 78, 147, 158, 177, 551
Achievement motive 78 n., 79, 177, 309,
 429 n.
Act of Confirmation 1621, Edinburgh
 University 86
Action model 176, 257, 258, 275–93,
 353, 533, 559–60

Activists 16, 464, 466, 489, 506
ADAMS, DR. WALTER (Director, LSE)
 490, 491, 492, 494, 499, 501, 502
Adaption to university (problems of)
 159
ADELSTEIN, DAVID (President, LSE Stu-
 dents' Union) 492, 496, 497, 498–
 500, 501, 509
Administration (college and university)
 6, 23, 42, 73, 87, 360, 375, 441, 444,
 493, 519, 520, 524, 546
Administration (national) 9, 21
Admissions policies 25, 39, 40, 41, 42,
 49, 140, 177–82
Adolescence 469 n.
Advisory system 165, 166, 179, 205,
 314
Affluence 26, 36, 59, 77, 428, 464, 570
Affluent families of student activists
 15, 464
Age grades 14, 464, 504, 527, 550
Age set 14
Age of students 18, 29, 216
Agitator conflicts, LSE 490, 492, 493,
 500–3
Alienation 60, 69, 78, 129, 207, 469 n.
Allocation 6, 21, 22, 23, 53, 66, 67, 78,
 388, 414
Ambitious students 138, 154, 302
American student movements 9, 18,
 377, 438, 441, 475, 493, 511–16
American students in English revolts
 493, 497, 503
Amnesty 492, 476–7, 500
Anarchy (threat of) 527, 546, 547
Anderson Committee 31
Anomie 80, 377, 439, 441, 528, 536 n.
Anticipatory socialisation 72, 361,
 362
Anti-semitism 71 n., 251

621